The History of Guernsey and Its Bailiwick

THE

HISTORY OF GUERNSEY

AND ITS BAILIWICK;

WITH OCCASIONAL NOTICES OF JERSEY.

BY

FERDINAND BROCK TUPPER, Esq.

AUTHOR OF

"THE LIFE AND CORRESPONDENCE OF MAJOR-GENERAL SIR ISAAC BROCK, K.B."
AND "THE CHRONICLES OF CASTLE CORNET."

"Autrefois on écrivait l'histoire à l'usage du dauphin; aujourd'hui c'est à l'usage du peuple qu'il faut l'écrire."—*Félix Bodin*.

GUERNSEY:

PRINTED BY STEPHEN BARBET, NEW STREET.

1854.

PREFACE.

In the Introduction to the second edition of his History of Jersey, (1734,) the Rev. Philip Falle, alluding to a brief description of Guernsey in Camden's Britannia, said : "They who are not satisfied with those sketches, must have patience till some gentleman of Guernezey (which cannot want able hands for such service) shall take upon him to illustrate his native country, as I have done mine ; including in his Account Alderney, Sark, &c., which depend on that greater island, as members of the government and jurisdiction of it." Exactly one hundred and twenty years have elapsed since Mr. Falle thus expressed himself; and as his suggestion has hitherto been unheeded, I have been induced to illustrate the annals of my "native country." Mr. Falle's memory is highly reverenced in Jersey, and there it will doubtless be objected to me that I have not treated him with the respect he deserves. I have indeed animadverted on some passages in his history, because he himself did not hesitate to speak disparagingly of men, to whom posterity has since done justice, and especially because, according to his own biographer and countryman, he passed through life " in strict conformity with the opinions and the prejudices of his age." That spirit of subservience extended to his work, which has otherwise many merits, and betrayed him into a feeling of hostility against all who differed from him in political opinion, or who were not members of the Church of England, in which he himself had risen, from humble beginnings, to dignity and

emolument. Nor is it easy to account for his studied omission of every incident in these islands during the Great Rebellion; as, in his first edition, (1694,) he observes, that "he
well remembers to have heard certain events, connected
with the civil wars, spoken of among his people, when the
past evil times were fresh in men's memories."

The following work is a sequel of the "Chronicles of Castle
Cornet," of which it is both an amplification and an abridgment—an amplification as regards the general history of the
island, and an abridgment as relates to the Osborne correspondence and Chevalier's Diary. Of that correspondence it
is necessary that I should repeat here, somewhat in brief,
the account which I have given in the Chronicles, of its accidental discovery, and of the means by which I obtained it.
Having learnt that the lineal descendant of Sir Peter Osborne,
of whom repeated mention is made in the text, was the
present Sir George Osborn, Bart., of Chicksands Priory,
Bedfordshire, I applied to him for such documents relative
to the siege of Castle Cornet, during the civil war, as I hoped
were in his possession. In reply, soon after his father's
death, he informed me that he had as yet met with no papers
relative to Sir Peter Osborne and the gallant defence he
made; but when he could put his library and MSS. in order,
he thought it probable that he might light on some matter
which would elucidate the subject. His letter was dated
February 17, 1849, and great was my delight when, on the
5th of April following, I received a large packet of papers,
with another letter from Sir George, who wrote: "Your
very interesting letter of the 20th ultimo should have met
with earlier attention, but that chance led me to an old bureau
in quest of some letters relating to Dorothy Osborn,[1] (afterwards Lady Temple,) and embracing some matter mentioned
in Macaulay's Historical Essays, when, to my great gratification, I found a large number of papers relating to Castle
Cornet and its defence by my ancestor, Sir Peter Osborne.

(1) A daughter of Sir Peter Osborne, and wife of Sir William Temple, the celebrated
diplomatist and statesman.

I have collected those that are most likely to be acceptable to you, and which contain the most matter."

But I begged of Sir George Osborn to send me the remainder of these papers, which he very kindly did, the whole exceeding one hundred; and, at my subsequent request, he further allowed me to make any use of them that I thought proper.

The receipt of the Osborne Correspondence made me anxious to peruse Chevalier's Diary, or Chronicle, mentioned also in the text; having become aware of its existence through the Rev. E. Durell's Notes on Falle's History of Jersey; and, after much delay and difficulty, I happily succeeded in procuring the loan of it. This Chronicle is written in French, and is extremely rare, never having been printed; and, notwithstanding the prolixity and tautology of the narration, it is now invaluable: indeed, I cannot but express my surprise that the States of Jersey have not caused a digest of it to be published; because it contains a faithful record of a period of which the natives of that island have ever been, and still are, justly proud.

I have not hesitated to reproduce from Mr. Duncan's History of Guernsey such passages as I supplied to him, and which he so handsomely acknowledged in his preface. But at the time that work was published, (1841,) I knew very little of the early records of the bailiwick, having previously resided both in North and South America for many years, and consequently had no opportunity of consulting documentary materials on the subject.

It has been my object not only to narrate the political, commercial, and religious annals of the bailiwick, but also to pourtray the great changes effected within two or three generations, in the houses, furniture, hours, modes of communication, public and private entertainments, &c., of the islanders. In doing so, I may possibly give offence to some, who, in their present affluence, are ashamed to look back on the more primitive and lowly condition of their ancestors, and who will perhaps consider such details as beneath the dignity of history. But I should indeed be unworthy of the task I have undertaken, if, regardless of the truth, I had stooped to minister to the vanity or the weaknesses of any class or family, and if I had not attempted to shew the wonderful progress which all these islands, equally with England and France, have made in wealth and civilization since the commencement of the last century. Guernsey especially rose and flourished with the funded system, and is now mainly dependant on its continuance.

It will be seen by the Biographical Notices at the close of this volume, that Guernsey, considering its very limited extent and population, produced, in the course of about a century, an unusual number of individuals distinguished in science, literature, and arms. I have given these Memoirs because Biography is not only the handmaid of History, but portrait painting for posterity.

F. B. T.

St. Peter-Port, Guernsey,
    August 15, 1854.

N.B.—All letters, &c., with [o] prefixed, were found among Sir Peter Osborne's papers.

QUEEN VICTORIA'S VISIT TO ALDERNEY.

On Tuesday evening, August 8, 1854, between five and six o'clock, the Queen, with the Prince Consort, the young Prince of Wales, Prince Alfred, Prince Arthur, and the Princess · Helena, and their suite, arrived within the new breakwater of Alderney, in the royal yacht Victoria and Albert, which was followed by three other steamers, viz. the Dasher, Captain Lefebvre, (of Guernsey,) Black Eagle, and Fairy; the squadron having left Osborne at eleven o'clock the same day. Colonel Le Mesurier, town major and commanding officer, immediately repaired on board the royal yacht, and was honored with a command to dine with her Majesty the same evening. Prince Albert, accompanied by the Prince of Wales and Prince Alfred, and attended by Major-General the Honorable C. Grey and Colonel the Honorable C. B. Phipps, soon after landed, and the party was received by Colonel Le Mesurier, Judge Gaudion, the jurats, Captain Jervois, R.E., &c. After inspecting the new fortifications and the breakwater, the royal visitors returned to the yacht.

On Wednesday morning, August 10, at nine o'clock, Judge Gaudion, accompanied by five of the jurats, the officers of the court, &c., proceeded on board the yacht to present a loyal address·from the States of Alderney to the Queen, who, on receiving it, graciously stated that she felt great pleasure in visiting their island.—A company of the royal artillery, and the militia under Major Barbenson, were drawn up on the breakwater; and at half-past nine o'clock her majesty, with Prince Albert, the Prince of Wales, Prince Alfred, and the Princess Helena, as also their attendants, landed under the usual salute, and amid the enthusiastic cheers of the inhabitants. The royal party, of whom the two young princes were dressed like sailor boys, walked from the barge to a railway car, in waiting at the top of the slip; and, on entering it, the car was drawn slowly by two horses along the railway as far as Corblets barracks, where her Majesty alighted and repaired, in another carriage, to Château l'Etoc, and thence drove to the Grandes Folies, at Mannez, returning to the said railway, on which she proceeded, as far as the entrance of Braye, where the Queen, Prince Albert, and the three children entered a phæton, and drove to the town of St. Anne, going as far as the church recently erected at the sole cost of the Rev. John Le Mesurier, only surviving son of Lieut.-General Le Mesurier, the last hereditary governor of Alderney.[1] Her Majesty entered the said church by the southern gate, and remained there several minutes, expressing her satisfaction of the edifice.   On returning to Braye, the royal party again got into the railway car, and, alighting at the upper extremity of the slip, they walked down to the barges in waiting.   The embarkation took place at a quarter to twelve, under a salute and the hearty cheers of the population.   At noon, the royal squadron was under weigh : the Fairy went direct to Cowes, while the three other steamers, passing through the Swinge, coasted the south and east sides of the island, and then proceeded through the Race for the Isle of Wight.—Queen Victoria is not only the first sovereign, but probably the first royal personage, who ever landed in Alderney, and her visit will form a memorable epoch in the history of that island, which, until the commencement of the breakwater in 1847, was almost separated from the rest of the world.   Her Majesty and Prince Albert particularly noticed several Alderney women, attired in the ancient costume of the island—the well known bonnet and bedgown ; and they commended the small Alderney cows, some of which were purposely placed within their view.

---

(1) This church, having been designed by his parents, was erected by Mr. Le Mesurier, in fulfilment of their purpose : it was commenced in 1847, and consecrated August 21, 1850. The Queen made some inquiries relative to the Rev. J. Le Mesurier : she was told that he did not reside in Alderney, but in England ; and, on being informed of his motive for building the church, her Majesty said : "A very noble act on his part."

THE HISTORY OF GUERNSEY

AND ITS BAILIWICK.

---◆---

CHAPTER I.

THIS work will probably appear, at first sight, one of supere-
rogation, because Dicey, Berry, Jacob, and Duncan, have
in turn published a History of Guernsey; although the first
and third were under other titles; and of an island so limited
in extent and population, it will be thought that nothing
more remains to be written.[1] But our researches have
supplied us with many materials, with which these authors
were evidently unacquainted or had overlooked; and, in
point of size, Guernsey exceeds the celebrated island of
Ithaca, which, lying on the western coast of Greece, is very
rocky and mountainous, and only twenty-five miles in circumference. And yet Ithaca was part of the kingdom, and
long the residence, of Ulysses, whose adventures on his return
to it from the Trojan war form the subject of Homer's
Odyssey. Small as Guernsey is, she is not barren in interesting historical incidents; and both Jersey and herself have
records peculiarly their own, as well as a language, laws,
and institutions; because they were in a manner isolated from
the rest of the world until towards the close of the last
century, or rather, until the extension to them of steam
navigation, in 1824, removed the barrier which had so long
checked the intercourse with England and other countries.
Notwithstanding the removal of this barrier, the natives,
especially in the country parishes, yet retain a distinct national
character; and as the continental Normans were incorporated with France 650 years since, the islanders may be

[1] "Though Hollingshead, and Speed, and especially Mr. Camden, in his *Britannia*,
have each attempted a description of all these islands, they have done it so briefly, and
from such imperfect memoirs, that they can give but little satisfaction to an inquisitive
reader. Doctor Heylin is he who has wrote the fullest concerning them." — *Falle's Preface*, 1694.

B

said to be the last remnant of that warlike people. There exists in all civilized communities, even the smallest, a natural desire to be fully acquainted with not only their own annals and statistics, but those of their immediate neighbours; and we believe it to be the general opinion in the island that another History of Guernsey is wanting.

The bailiwick of Guernsey consists of eight islands, of which all, with the exception of the rocky islet of Burhou, are inhabited; viz. Guernsey, Alderney, Sark,[1] Herm, Jethou, Lihou, and Brechou, or *Isle des Marchands*, near Sark. Castle Cornet and the Casket rocks are also peopled. By the last census, taken in 1851, the population of the bailiwick was 33,646 souls; viz. Guernsey, 29,732 souls,[2] or 1,238 per square mile; Alderney,[3] 3,333 souls; and Sark, 581 souls. Burhou, which is separated from Alderney by the impetuous Swinge, is interesting to the naturalist, as it is the haunt of the stormy petrel, the bird better known to British seamen as "Mother Carey's Chicken"—the only other spots in the British Isles where it is said to be found being the Scilly Isles and the Calf of Man. Burhou, Brechou, Jethou, Lihou, Brehon, and other similar names, are of Celtic origin.

Guernsey is one of the Anglo-Norman or Channel Isles, which are all situate in the bay of *Mont St. Michel*, and on the coast, and in sight, of the "Cotentin,"[4] a district of Lower Normandy, deriving its name from the city of Coutances,—the *Constantia* of the Romans. Guernsey is the second of these islands in extent and importance, Jersey being the first, and is about thirty miles in circumference, including the windings of the coast; nine miles in length; and five miles in breadth, with an area of a little above 24 square miles, or 15,560 English acres. The land is elevated to the South, and shelves to the North, and some of the bays and sea views are of great beauty. In old charts, Guernsey appears as two islands, the northern, or smaller, with the Close of the Vale,

(1) Captain Carteret, in his voyage round the world, (1766-9,) discovered a cluster of islands in the South Seas, to which he gave the general name of Queen Charlotte's Islands, distinguishing four of them by the names of New Jersey, New Guernsey, New Alderney, and New Sark: they are situated in lat. 11° 10′ S., long. 164° 43′ E. Captain, afterwards Admiral, Carteret, was a native of Jersey, and a scientific officer.

(2) In the town of St. Peter-Port 17,047, and in the nine country parishes 12,685 souls, exclusive of the garrison at Fort George, not enumerated.

(3) Previous to the commencement, in February, 1847, of the naval harbour of observation in Alderney, its population was scarcely 1,000 souls: by the census of 1841, it was 1,038 souls.

(4) The Cotentin forms a peninsula in the North of Dép. de la Manche, its northern extremity being Cape La Hague, and its southern near *Mont St. Michel*.

(*Clos du Valle,*) being separated from the main land at high water by a narrow channel, which was closed in 1803,[1] and of which the eastern end was in St. Sampson's harbour, and the western in *Grand Havre*, near the Vale church. The island is divided into ten parishes, which, with Alderney and Sark, constitute the twelve parishes of the deanery of Guernsey, in the diocese of Winchester. The nearest part of England is the Start Point, distant 57 nautic, or 66 statute, miles; and of France, Cape Flamanville, distant 24 nautic, or 28 statute, miles. From St. Peter-Port, the only town, which is in latitude 49° 33′ N., and in longitude 2° 40′ W. of Greenwich, the islands and sea ports named bear and are distant in English statute miles as follows, viz. Jersey, the nearest point, S.E. 19½ miles, and the pier of St. Hélier, 29 miles; Alderney, N.E. 21 miles, and the Caskets, N.N.E. 20 miles; Sark, E. 7½ miles, and Herm, E.N.E. 3¾ miles; Weymouth, N. ½ E. 75 miles; the Needles, N.N.E. ½ E. 90 miles; Southampton, N.N.E. ⅝ E. 113 miles; Plymouth, N.W. ¼ W. 92 miles; and Falmouth, W.N.W. 120 miles; Cherbourg, E. by N. 42 miles; St. Malo, S.S.E. 61 miles; and Granville, S.E. 62 miles. The average depth of water in the neighbourhood of the islands is 35, and seldom exceeds 40, fathoms. The tide in Guernsey rises about 32 feet.

Alderney is in circumference nearly twelve miles, being in length from East to West scarcely four miles, and in breadth about 1½ mile. It is distant from the Casket rocks nearly seven miles, and from Cape La Hague, in Normandy, ten miles, all statute. The strait which divides Alderney from Cape La Hague is called by the French, *Le Ras de Blanchard,* and by the English, the Race of Alderney, the tide running through at the rate of six knots an hour. The harbour of the Braye, where a naval station is now in progress, is on the North side of the island; and the old pier there, which was built in 1736, was but a rude structure, with one projecting arm. The only town, called St. Anne's, is placed on a hill, about half a mile from Braye harbour: in 1830, it consisted of 255 houses, and contained 973 inhabitants, the trade of Alderney being at that time, and up to 1846, in a state of utter prostration; but, since the commencement of the naval station already mentioned, St. Anne's has risen like a Phœnix from its ashes, and the population has more than trebled. The island shelves to the N.E., and is intersected by deep

(1) The policy of closing the passage may well be questioned, as it appears to us that it might easily have been deepened and converted into one long wet dock, with quays, by means of a gate at each end.

valleys, with a plain or table land ; but it is almost destitute
of trees, shrubs, and hedges. The rock scenery is, however,
very fine, and the air is remarkably bracing and salubrious.
When we visited Alderney in 1846, it struck us that the
lower classes not only spoke English with more fluency, and
with a better accent, but that in appearance they were more
English, than the peasantry of the other Anglo-Norman
islands—a peculiarity probably arising from the former living
chiefly in the town, and from the comparatively large English
garrison during the last war.

Sark is rather more than three miles in length, with an
average breadth of about one mile, and is about nine miles
in circumference. It is divided into two unequal portions,
called Great and Little Sark, which are connected by the
Coupée, a very singular and lofty narrow ridge, or natural
bridge, of about 300 feet long. Sark is a table land with a
few valleys, and has no declivity towards the sea, excepting a
trifling one at the northern extremity. Although there are
five landing places, there is no harbour where ships can lie,
and only one beach where boats and other small vessels can
be wintered. Altogether, Sark is a very remarkable spot,
and, with its caverns, its steep and variegated rocks, its picturesque valleys and dells, its *creux terrible*, and its beautiful
cliff and distant island scenery, it is perhaps the most romantic
and interesting island of the group, although its geometrical
area is only about three square miles. There is a border
village in Scotland called Sark, near a river of the same name.

Herm.—The name of this islet, which contains about 400
English acres, denotes, in old French, land deserted or uncultivated, and from the same root is evidently derived the
French word *ermite*, and the English hermit.[1] In the sixth
century, during the time of St. Magloire, a small chapel was
erected in Herm, which Camden states belonged to the Fran-
ciscan order of monks, and part of the walls are still standing.
Brother Claude Panton, hermit in the island of Herm, and
his brother saints, are said, in the "*Dédicace des Eglises*,"
to have been present at the consecration of St. Sampson's
church, Guernsey, in 1111. Herm and Jethou, together with
Sark, not only shelter the roadstead of St. Peter-Port from
about N.N.E. to E.S.E., but add considerably to the beauty of
the sea view as seen from Guernsey.

(1) " Herm, Hermes, ou Ermes. La coutume du Bourbonnais, Art. 331, dit que les
terres *hermes* et vacans sont au seigneur justicier. Ell entend par là les terres en friche,
que ne sont occupées par personne. On trouve le mot Herma employé de la même
manière dans la loi 4, C, de censibus, et dans une foule de chartes. V. le Glossaire du
droit Français, au mot Ermes (G.D.C)."—*Répertoire Universel et Raisonné de Jurisprudence,
par M. Merlin.*

The other three islands need not detain us, as they are too small to require further notice here.

Of the history of Guernsey, which, unlike that of the sister island of Jersey, has never yet appeared from the pen of a native, nothing authentic or documentary, with perhaps two or three exceptions, can be found anterior to the eleventh century; and its meagre annals previous to that period are based chiefly on conjecture, with scarcely a ray of tradition. If there ever were any early written chronicles, they were probably lost or destroyed during the incursions, ravages, and massacres, of the North-men. The Rev. Doctor Ubele, vicar of Alderney, now deceased, sought to establish, by a learned disquisition in Berry's History, that these islands were visited by the Phœnicians[1] in the course of their traffic with Britain; but is it not quite as likely that such traffic has been mistaken, from a similarity of names, for that of the Veneti, or Venetians, a people inhabiting part of modern Britany, and mentioned by Cæsar as trading with Britain? The existence of cromlechs,[2] (commonly known as Druid's Altars,) of *Maenhirs*, or detached upright stones, and of other Celtic remains, proves that Guernsey was inhabited long before the Christian era, having doubtless been first peopled from the adjacent continent of Gaul, when it was yet immersed in the grossest superstition and barbarism; and celts,[3] &c., continue to be occasionally discovered to this day.[4] Cromlechs, &c., have also been found in Herm, but none in Jethou. The remains of a stone circle at Little Sark — the quantity of fragments of

(1) The Phœnicians planted several colonies in the Mediterranean, particularly Carthage, and possessed a powerful fleet; their capital cities were Sidon and Tyre; ["Tyre, the crowning city, whose merchants are princes, whose traffickers are the honourable of the earth."—Isaiah xxiii. 8.] and, being subdued by Alexander, 332 years B.C., they remained tributary to his successors and to the Romans. Ezekiel xxvii. contains a very interesting record of the commerce and navigation of the Tyrians, but we much doubt the latter having ever extended to Britain. In her tempestuous seas, sails of "fine linen, with broidered work from Egypt," would have been of little service.

(2) "The true form of a cromlech, or chamber of long triangular area with the only entrance at the apex, is seen in the magnificent examples of Gavr' Innis, in the Morbihan, those on the coast of Normandy, and in the Channel Islands."—*Dr. Lukis.*

(3) By "celt" is meant a wedge-shaped instrument, formed of various kinds of hard stone. It has a cutting edge, regularly sharpened on both sides, and it is rounded and pointed at the opposite end. About one hundred of these are yet preserved in Guernsey, found in different localities, but chiefly in or near places once occupied by the Celtic tribes. The above are made of quartz, chert, flint, or agate, serpentine, greenstone, porphyry, jasper, granular-porphyry, and granite. Those of indurated steatite and actinoliteschist often resemble the Indian jade hatchets. They vary in size from one inch to twelve or thirteen in length. As this instrument, which is found in every country, differs so little in shape, its general adoption bespeaks a similar design and origin. Antiquaries are not agreed as to its original use, or the manner of its being made serviceable.

(4) Frederick C. Lukis, Esq., Grange Road, has with great industry and research made a collection of these Celtic remains, which does him the highest credit as an antiquarian and a geologist, and to which every Guernseyman, who has it in his power, should contribute, in the hope that the collection will long be preserved entire.

pottery—several stone celts, known, as in Guernsey, by the name of *coins de foudre*—the stone disc, or amulet, called *rouette des fétaux* — all attest that Sark was occupied in very early times, although it has no cromlechs. The primeval or Pagan ages are divided by antiquarians into three periods, viz. first, the stone ; secondly, the bronze ; and, thirdly, the iron ; each betokening a different degree of civilization :[1] and Guernsey has many remnants of the first period, which belongs to a time before all authentic history, to a people who lived precariously by fishing and hunting upon the sea coasts, or along the large rivers of Europe. Alderney, considering its extent, was particularly rich in remains of both the stone and bronze periods, as several cromlechs, cists (pronounced kists) or stone graves, celts, querns, and many fragments of pottery ; as also a great variety of bronze instruments, including celts or ferules, a kind of modern reap-hook, and spear heads, have been discovered there.[2]   But since the commencement of the sea and land works, now in progress in Alderney, several cists have been removed.   Cromlechs were sepulchral, or tombs containing skeletons, implements of stone or bone, vases of clay, and rude ornaments of amber or bone. There are various opinions relative to the origin of the bronze implements and weapons : some assert that they are all of Phœnician[3] or Roman workmanship, and others contend that they belonged to an early European Celtic population ; but the fact seems to be that they were used, only in slightly varying forms, by the different people of Europe in about the same state of civilization, and that they were partly replaced by iron, before the Romans had commenced their conquests. Cæsar tells us that, in his time, the Gauls made use of iron chains and nails, and that the Britons armed their chariots with iron scythes.   Although Hesiod, who flourished about 900 years B.C., expressly states that brass, or bronze, was in general use before iron was known ; and most of the arms and implements found in Herculaneum, Pompeii, &c., were of bronze, while those of iron were comparatively very few ; yet the sole use of bronze could not long have preceded the

(1) The author feels the greater interest in the subject from having, in 1838, visited the celebrated museum at Copenhagen, which contains innumerable specimens of the three periods.

(2) "Portions of daggers and swords were likewise found, and castings of copper, such as spikes or nails, lumps of bronze metal in its raw state, and a large cake or ingot of copper, weighing about twelve pounds, which, on being assayed, gave the following proportions: twelve ounces of pure copper to the pound, three grains of gold, and four of silver."—*Alderney Guide.*

(3) If the bronze instruments found in Alderney be of Phœnician manufacture, it is, we think, far more probable that they were brought thither from Marseilles through Gaul, than by sea through the Straits of Gibraltar. Marseilles was a colony of the Phœnicians.

discovery of iron, as frequent mention is made both of brass and iron in the Old Testament.[1] Doubtless iron was used in Asia before it was known in Europe, and Mr. Layard, in his recent excavations at Nineveh, exhumed remains of iron armour, which had been worn by Assyrian warriors. While on this subject, we may also add, that Layard found among the ruins of Nimroud a bas relief, one of the figures on which was a warrior clothed in a complete suit of mail of metal scales, and whose head dress he thus describes: "On his head was a pointed helmet, from which fell lappets, covered with scales, protecting the ears, lower part of the face and neck, the whole head dress resembling that of the early Normans." Nations in all ages have been copyists of each other, and it is no proof that the North-men were descended from the Assyrians, whose empire terminated about 820 years B.C., because the early Norman helmet was but a copy of one which was in use nearly 2,000 years before the times of Rollo, who founded the dukedom of Normandy.

We have said that Guernsey and Alderney were rich in Celtic remains and we may add, that Jersey was once equally so, as will be seen by a list of them in Falle's History, with Durell's Notes, page 176. A very fine cromlech, better known in Jersey as a *Pouquelaye*, was discovered in 1785 on the commanding height near St. Hélier—on which height Fort Regent now stands—and most unpardonably presented, by the unanimous vote of the States of Jersey, to Marshal Conway, the governor of that island. By him it was removed with similar bad taste to his seat near Henley, in Berkshire, and there re-erected; but while displacing the stones in Jersey, several were broken! Thus, by a wanton act of desecration, was the sister island deprived of a precious relic of antiquity, which also lost a great part of its value by the removal from its original position. We fear that the States of Guernsey would have been quite as complaisant, as even now they appear utterly indifferent as to the fate of many of the Celtic antiquities in the island.[2] A sketch and ground plan of this splendid cromlech, which was removed from Jersey, are given in Baker's CÆSAREA, with a copious description. It was 64 feet in circumference, composed of 45

(1) "Iron is taken out of the earth, and brass is molten *out of* the stone." (Job xxviii. 2.) The history of the Old Testament commenced about 1450 years B.C., and finished about the year 430 B.C.

(2) Are we not justified in saying this from the fact, that as late as June, 1853, we found the cromlech at Le Rée—"the far-famed" *Creux des Fées*—in use as a cow stable ? The States of Guernsey ought long since to have purchased all the cromlechs in the island, with a view to their preservation.

large stones, measuring 7 feet in height, 6 in breadth, 4 in thickness, containing four perfect lodges, (or cells,) besides one destroyed : the supposed entrance to it was apparently a subterraneous passage, facing the East, and measuring 15 feet in length by 4½ in breadth, from the inside of the two outward pillars, or stones. Baker describes also other Druidical remains in Jersey, not sufficiently noticed by Falle ; and he states that some years since a considerable number of Celtic coins were discovered in that island in a bank, the falling of which disclosed them. "All have a head on one side, and generally a horse on the reverse. Some of them are composed of an impure silver amalgam, but the greater part of copper blended with some other metal." Relative to Celtic remains, Dr. Lukis, of Guernsey, observes, in his Memoir on the Cromlechs of the Channel Islands, as read in London before the Society of Antiquaries, in June, 1853 : "It is a generally received opinion that the Celtæ were the authors and architects of these megaliths ; these are, however, found universally distributed from Scandinavia to India ; and in America, especially in the North. It must further be observed, that the same types of construction and use are equally universal, and that they are usually situated near the sea or the vicinity of some extent of water. It is evident from the universal distribution, likewise, of identical forms of the stone implements accompanying them, that the cromlech-building races sprang early from one central typical stock. Central Asia and the site of Nineveh produce *genuine Celtic relics*."

The worship of stones, whether memorial or sacrificial, lingered so long among the Gauls, that, even after the introduction of Christianity, it was slowly and with difficulty abolished in remote and isolated spots. Thus the second Council of Arles, held A.D. 452, put forth the following canon :

"Si dans le territoire d'un Evêque des infidèles allument des flambeaux, ou vénèrent les arbres, les fontaines, ou les *pierres*, et qu'ils négligent d'abolir cet usage, ils doivent savoir qu'ils sont coupables de sacrilège."—Canon XXIII.

A Council of Tours thus expressed itself in the year 567 :

"Nous conjurons les Pasteurs de chasser de l'Eglise tous ceux qu'ils verront faire, devant certaines *pierres*, des choses qui n'ont pas de rapport avec les cérémonies de l'Eglise." — Canon XXII.

And even as late as the reign of Canute of England, in the eleventh century, the following command was put forth :

● "We forbid idolatry—the worship of stones and of woods. Gentilis est adoratis sine quis *saxa*, arboris, lignare coluerit."

That Guernsey was known to the Romans, while they were masters of Gaul, appears from the Itinerary,[1] commonly, but it seems erroneously, thought to be that of the emperor Antoninus; and it is the very generally received belief in the island, that his testimony is confirmed by the traces of a Roman encampment or fortification on the promontory of Jerbourg, where three distinct entrenchments, one behind the other, are supposed by many to be still visible. In the opinion of others, there never was any such Roman triple line of defence; but in place thereof, one commanding embankment, stretching quite across the isthmus, which is flanked by nature with almost inaccessible cliffs. If the latter supposition be correct, as we believe it is, this single earthern rampart was raised either by the North-men, or more probably by the natives, as a place of security from piratical invasion. Of the Romans, the only memorials found in the island consist of a little pottery and several coins. On the promontory of Jerbourg, sixteen Roman brass coins, some of Antoninus Pius, A.D. 137, and others of Commodus, A.D. 180, were exhumed as late as in the year 1848. But as Roman coins passed current in Gaul, even after the Romans had left it, those found in Guernsey may well have been brought over by the islanders, and buried to secure them from the North-men. The same remark applies to the pottery, and thus these memorials afford no proof that the Romans formed settlements in the island, although they very probably visited it. In Jersey and Alderney, doubtless on account of their greater proximity to Gaul, there are many more evidences of their occupation by the Romans, such as arms, coins, and pottery. In Jersey, the great earthen ramparts that existed not many years since—one called *La Petite Cæsarée*, or Cæsar's Wall, near *Havre de Rozel*, and another at *Dielament*—are supposed to have been the works of that people. The former, which was once of considerable length, and about 24 feet in height, inclining to four feet at the top, with twelve feet at the base, was doubtless a fortification, and probably the work of the Romans: its name is not only a strong evidence of this, but Roman bricks and tiles were found in demolishing this immense rampart. Although *Mont Orgueil*

(1) This Itinerary is more probably the abstract of a journal kept by some officer, who visited different parts of the Roman empire.

Castle is of the Norman style of architecture, yet as there is a part of it still called *Le Fort de César*, it may be that a Roman castle once stood on the present site. *Grosnez* castle is also supposed by some to be a Roman work; but so little remains of it that no decisive opinion can be formed on the point. In February, 1848, a jar of coarse earthenware, which contained 400 brass coins of different Roman emperors, in an excellent state of preservation, was dug out from the substratum, where it may have been lodged during the period of the Roman settlement in that island. In Alderney, Roman coins, tiles, pottery, &c., have been discovered, and its occupation by the Romans is easily accounted for from its vicinity to the promontory of La Hague, which still retains their earth works. In that promontory, Roman coins, arms, &c., have been frequently turned up by the plough; and in the neighbourhood of Jobourg, according to that indefatigable antiquary of the " Cotentin," Monsieur de Gerville, the traces of a Roman camp may yet be seen.

Having observed that cromlechs, &c., are still existing in Guernsey, it may be well to add, that Druidism was peculiar to the Celts, and that nothing resembling it was to be found among the Gothic or Teutonic tribes. The Druids are said to have consisted of three orders : the first were the Druids, emphatically so called, who were the chief men, and consulted by the kings in all important concerns; the next were the Bards, who were also prophets; and the third were the Philosophers, who studied the phenomena of nature, according to some — according to others, they were the sacred musicians and poets. The origin of Druid worship may be traced to the East, afterwards diversified to suit the more northern habits of the Celts. The Druids did not admit of idols, and they believed in the immortality of the soul. The earliest notice of the Celts places them, about the year 500 B.C., in the neighbourhood of the Pyrenees, whence they were driven by the Goths, or Germans, on the East, and the Aquitani on the South, into that part of Gaul, where they were found in the time of Cæsar. The Celts were a people of an inferior stature, swarthy in their complexion, with dark eyes; and hair short, coarse, and black. This description applies to many of the peasantry in the most remote or southern parishes of Guernsey, in whom Celtic blood is very manifest. History records but little of the victories and conquests of the early Celts, and they appear to have been unusually incapable of

instruction or advancement.[1] In the introduction to the first
book of Cæsar's Commentaries, Gaul is represented as divided
into three parts, and that part, which lies between the rivers
Marne and Garonne, was called Celtic Gaul; that to the eastward of the Seine and Marne, as far as the Rhine, Belgic
Gaul; and all the territory to the South of the Garonne was
inhabited by the Aquitani.

Cæsar states, in his Commentaries, that that portion of
Celtic Gaul which lay between the rivers Loire and Seine,
and the country a little to the North of the latter, was called
by the inhabitants Armorica;[2] it comprehended the western
parts of the present provinces of Normandy and Britany, the
name being derived from its situation on the coast, ar signifying upon, or near, and mare, the ocean. The Armorici,
who consisted of at least eight distinct states, or tribes, under
different names, were a warlike, resolute, and intractable race;
and the Romans experienced great difficulty in subjugating
them, which they finally did about fifty years B.C. Among
these tribes were the Unelli and Veneti. The Unelli inhabited the adjacent coast of Normandy, or the modern "Cotentin," (Constantinus,) their district being nearly bounded on
three sides by the sea, and they doubtless possessed these
islands. The Veneti dwelt in Britany, in the neighbourhood
of the present Vannes. (Venetia.) Cæsar, in Book III.,
gives a graphic description of the battles by sea and land with
the Armorici, and he thus speaks of the Veneti:

"This last state is by far the most powerful and considerable
of all the nations inhabiting along the sea coast, and that not only
on account of their vast shipping, wherewith they drive a mighty
traffic with Britain, and their skill and experience in naval
affairs, in which they greatly surpass the other maritime states;
but because, lying on a large and open coast, against which the
sea rages with great violence, and where the havens, being few
in number, are all subject to their jurisdiction, they have most of
the nations that trade in those seas tributaries to their state."....
"For the ships of the Veneti were built and fitted out in this
manner: their bottoms were somewhat flatter than ours, the
better to adapt themselves to the shallows, and sustain without
danger the regress of the tides. Their prows were very high and
erect, as likewise their sterns, to bear the hugeness of the billows
and violence of tempests. The body of the vessel was entirely of

(1) The Highlanders of Scotland, the Welsh, and part of the Irish, are the only remains
now existing of the ancient Celts in the British dominions.

(2) "Universis civitatibus, quæ Oceanum attingunt, quæque eorum consuetudine
Armoricæ appellantur, (quo sunt in numero Curiosolites, Rhedones, Ambibari, Caletes,
Osismii, Lemovices, Veneti, Unelli."—De Bello Gallico, Lib. VII. 75.

oak, to stand the shocks and assaults of that tempestuous ocean. The benches of the rowers were made of strong beams of about a foot in breadth, and fastened with iron nails an inch thick. Instead of cables, they secured their anchors with chains of iron,[1] and made use of skins, and a sort of thin pliant leather, by way of sails, either because they wanted canvass, and were ignorant of the art of making sail cloth, or, which is more probable, because they imagined that canvass sails were not so proper to bear the violence of tempests, the rage and fury of the winds, and to govern ships of that bulk and burden. Between our fleet and vessels of such a construction, the nature of the encounter was this, that in agility and a ready command of oars, we had indeed the advantage, but in other respects, regarding the situation of the coast, and the assault of storms, all things ran very much in their favour; for neither could our ships injure them with their beaks, so great was their strength and firmness, nor could we easily throw in our darts, because of their height above us; which was also the reason that we found it extremely difficult to grapple the enemy, and bring them to close fight. Add to all this, that when the sea began to rage, and they were forced to submit to the pleasure of the winds, they could both weather the storm better, and more securely trust themselves among the shallows, as fearing nothing from the rocks and cliffs on the recess of the tide. The Romans, on the other hand, had reason to be under a continued dread of these and such like accidents.

"Cæsar having taken many of their towns, and finding that he only fatigued his army to no purpose, because he could neither prevent the retreat of the enemy, nor force their garrisons[2] to a surrender, resolved to await the arrival of his fleet,[3] which, being accordingly come up, was no sooner descried by the Veneti than about 220 of their best ships,[4] well equipped for service, and furnished with all kind of weapons, stood out to sea, and drew up in order of battle against us. Neither Brutus,[5] who commanded the fleet, nor the centurions and military tribunes who had the charge of particular vessels, knew what course to

(1) Chain cables are an invention of the present century, but it would appear that they were used nearly 2,000 years ago, of course for small vessels only.

(2) Cæsar previously relates that the besieged, when reduced to extremity, brought up their ships, of which they had always a great number in readiness, and, easily carrying off their effects, withdrew into the nearest towns, where they again defended themselves by the same advantages of situation as before.

(3) Cæsar being informed by Crassus of the revolt of the Veneti and other states in alliance with them, "and being then at a great distance from Gaul, ordered in the meantime that a number of galleys should be built on the Loire, a river which runs into the ocean; and that mariners, rowers, and pilots, should be drawn together from the province. These orders being executed with great dispatch, he himself, as soon as the season of the year permitted, came to the army."—*Commentaries.*

(4) These appear to have belonged not only to the Veneti, but to their Armorican and British allies; and among them may have been some from these islands, Guernsey having in very early times possessed an extensive fishery, especially of congers.

(5) This was Decimus Brutus, and not the same—"*Tu, quoque, Brute!*"—who stabbed Cæsar in the Senate House at Rome,-44 years B.C.

take, or in what manner to conduct the fight; for they were no strangers to the strength and firmness of the Venetian shipping, which rendered them proof against our beaks; and when they had even raised turrets on the decks, yet, being still overtopped by the lofty sterns of the enemy, the Romans could not with any advantage throw in their darts; whereas those sent by the Gauls, coming from above, descended with greater violence on our men. In this exigence, a particular kind of instrument, used by the mariners, proved of signal service in giving a favorable issue to the combat. They had provided themselves with long poles, armed at one end with long scythes, not unlike those made use of in attacking the walls of towns. With these they laid hold of the enemy's tackle, and, drawing off the galley by the extreme force of oars, cut asunder the ropes that fastened the sail yards to the mast. These giving way, the sail yards necessarily came down; insomuch, that as all the hopes and expectations of the Gauls depended entirely on their sails and rigging, by depriving them of this resource, we at the same time rendered their vessels wholly unserviceable. The rest depended altogether on the valour of the troops, in which the Romans had greatly the advantage; and the rather, because they fought within view of Cæsar and the whole army, so that not a single act of bravery could pass unobserved, for all the adjoining hills and eminences, which afforded a near prospect of the sea, were covered with our men.[1]

"The enemy's sail yards being, as we have said, cut down, and many of their ships singly surrounded by two or three of ours at a time, the Romans used their utmost endeavours to board them; which the Veneti observing, and that we had already made ourselves masters of a considerable part of their fleet, as they could fall on no expedient to prevent so great a misfortune, they began to think of providing for their safety by flight. Accordingly, they tacked about, in order to have the advantage of the wind, when all of a sudden so dead a calm ensued, that not a vessel could stir out of its place: nor could any thing have fallen out more opportunely towards putting at once a final period to the war; for the Romans attacking their ships one after another, took them with ease; insomuch, that of all that vast number that came out against us, but a very few, under favor of the night, escaped to land, after a conflict that continued from nine in the morning until sunset.

"This battle put an end to the war with the Veneti, and all the nations on the sea coast; for as the entire body of their youth,

(1) This description reminds us vividly of the naval battle of Algesiras, July 6, 1801, in which the English squadron under a Guernseyman, Sir James Saumarez, whose flag ship was the CÆSAR! fought within sight of the garrison of Gibraltar. Six days later, when the same British admiral left Gibraltar to encounter, with a very inferior force, the combined French and Spanish squadrons, the whole population of the Rock crowded the walls, batteries, and mole-head, to witness the scene, the band of the CÆSAR! playing "Come, cheer up, my lads, 'tis to glory we steer!" and the band of the garrison responding with "Britons, strike home!" What Briton could hang back under such inspiring influences?

and all those also of more advanced age, who were capable of serving their country by their credit and counsels, were present in the action, and as they had likewise drawn together their whole naval strength; such as survived this defeat, having neither any place of refuge whereunto to retire, nor means left of defending their towns, surrendered themselves and their all to Cæsar's mercy. But he thought it necessary to proceed against them with the greatest severity, that he might impress on the minds of the Gauls for the future a more inviolable regard to the sacred character of ambassadors.[1] Having, therefore, caused all their senators to be put to death, he ordered the rest to be sold for slaves."

It will be seen by the preceding extracts that anterior to the subjugation of the adjacent continent of Gaul by the Romans, the people there, and the inhabitants of these islands, must have possessed many more facilities in holding intercourse with each other, and in passing to and fro in larger vessels and in greater safety, than is now generally supposed. After that subjection, the Romans could avail themselves of the same facilities; but we repeat, that there is no satisfactory proof that they ever formed a permanent settlement in Guernsey. It must be remembered, however, that Cæsar wrote according to the conceptions of his time, as the navy of the Veneti and their allies evidently consisted of what would now be termed galleys or large row-boats, with masts and sails, probably not exceeding some thirty tons; and we know that the harbour of Vannes is at present only capable of accommodating small vessels.

After describing the subjugation of the Veneti, &c., Cæsar proceeds to narrate the campaign of his lieutenant, Sabinus, against Viridovix, the chief of the Unelli, whose territory, as we have just said, was the modern "Cotentin." We give Cæsar's description at length, because it relates to the conquests of the Romans in the neighbourhood of these islands:

"During these transactions against the Veneti, Q. Titurius Sabinus entered the territories of the Unelli, at the head of the troops put under his command by Cæsar. Viridovix was invested with the supreme authority in these parts, and had been appointed general-in-chief by all the states concerned in the revolt: out of which he had drawn together a very numerous and powerful army. Nay, but a very few days before, the Aulerci, Eburovices, and Lexovii,[2] having massacred their senate, because

---

(1) The Veneti and their allies had detained, and loaded with irons, the ambassadors, or military officers, sent to them by Crassus, to solicit a supply of corn. This was Publius Crassus, apparently a son of the rich Crassus.

(2) The Eburovices dwelt on the left bank of the Seine, and the Lexovii were between them and the sea. The chief city of the Eburovices was the modern Evreaux, in Upper Normandy.

they refused to engage in the war, had shut their gates against the
Romans, and joined themselves to Viridovix. Besides all this,
he had very much strengthened his army by the great numbers
that flocked to him from all parts of Gaul; men of desperate
fortunes, or accustomed to live by robbery, whom the hopes of
plunder and love of war had drawn off from the daily labours of
their calling and the cares of agriculture.

"Sabinus kept close within his camp, which was situated in a
manner every way advantageous; while Viridovix, who had
posted himself at the distance of about two miles, daily drew out
his men, and offered him battle. This behaviour of the Roman
general not only drew on him the contempt of the enemy, but
occasioned also some' murmuring among his own troops, and
filled the Gauls with so high a conceit of his fear, that they even
adventured to come up to his very trenches. The reason of his
acting in this manner was, that he thought it not justifiable in a
lieutenant, in the absence of the commander-in-chief, to hazard a
battle with so superior an army, unless on terms of evident
advantage.

"Having confirmed them in this belief, that his reserve was
the effect of fear, he made choice of a certain Gaul, from among
the auxiliaries, a man of address, and every way qualified for
carrying on his design. Him he persuaded, by great rewards,
and still greater promises, to go over to the enemy, instructing
him at the same time in the part he was to act. This Gaul,
coming to their camp as a deserter, laid before them the fear of
the Romans, and the extremities to which Cæsar was reduced in
the war against the Veneti: nor did he fail to insinuate that there
was great reason to believe Sabinus intended the next night privately to draw off his army, and march to Cæsar's assistance.
No sooner was this heard by the Gauls than they all cried out
with one voice that they ought not to lose so fair an occasion of
success, but go and attack the Roman camp. Many reasons
concurred to fix them in this resolution. The reserve of Sabinus
for some days past; the intelligence from the deserter, confirming
their belief of his fear; the want of provisions, of which they had
taken no great care to lay in a sufficient stock; the hopes conceived from the Venetian war; and, in fine, that readiness with
which men are apt to believe what falls in with their expectations
and wishes. Urged by these considerations, they would not suffer Viridovix and the rest of the general officers to dismiss the
council before they had obtained their consent for the taking up
of arms and falling on the Roman camp. The proposal being at
last agreed to, they provided themselves with fascines and hurdles
to fill up the ditch, and joyfully began their march, as to a certain
victory.

"The Roman camp stood on an eminence, which rose with a

gentle ascent for the space of about a mile. Hither the Gauls
advanced with so much haste, in order to come on our troops
unprepared, that by the time they were arrived they had run
themselves quite out of breath. Sabinus having encouraged his
men, whom he saw eager to engage, gave the word of onset.[1] As
the enemy were very much encumbered with the loads of fascines
they had brought to fill the ditch, he ordered a sudden sally
from the two several gates of the camp; and so well did it succeed, by reason of the advantage of the ground, the inexperience
and weariness of the Gauls, the bravery of the Roman troops,
and their ability acquired in former battles, that the enemy could
not sustain the very first charge of our men, but immediately
betook themselves to flight. The Romans, who were fresh and
vigorous, pursuing them under all these disadvantages, put great
numbers to the sword, and the rest being followed by the cavalry,
very few escaped the slaughter. Thus, at one and the same time,
Sabinus had an account of the defeat of the Veneti by sea, and
Cæsar of the victory obtained by Sabinus on land. All the several
states in those parts readily submitted to Titurius; for, as the
Gauls are very prompt and forward to undertake a war, so are
they of a disposition that easily relents, and gives way to the
strokes of adversity."

The Armorici remained for a long time in quiet subjection
to the Romans; but when the Roman power began to yield
to the ravages of the barbarians, they revolted against Constantine, and regained their independence. Mezeray, in his
history of France, mentions a division of Gaul into provinces,
under Octavius Cæsar, and a sub-division of modern Normandy into presidencies. "These ten nations," says another
French historian, "together with the inhabitants of the islands
lying near them, were known in Celtic Gaul by the name of
'The League of the Eleven Cities,'" and this appears to have
been in the time of the Romans. About the end of the fifth
century, however, in consequence of the turbulence and rest-
lessness of their dispositions, the Armorici submitted to Clovis,
whose reign commenced in the year 485, and their country
became a part of the new kingdom of France, dating from
Merovée, A.D. 451. It must be remembered that the
French were not the same people whom the Romans subdued
—they were of German extraction from the other side of the
Rhine, and it was they who drove the Romans out of Gaul.
When the Britons were subjugated by the Saxons, many of

(1) In a previous passage, Cæsar says: "Q. Titurius Sabinus, at the head of three
legions, entered the country of the Unelli, Curiosolitæ, and Lexovii, to find employment
for the troops that had been drawn together in those parts."—A Roman legion, if complete,
consisted of about 4,000 men, including cavalry.

them, and particularly a colony of the Welsh, settled in the southern part of Armorica, and formed a powerful state : hence the name of Lesser Britain, or Britany.[1] On the other hand, the Saxon Chronicle tells us that Wales was peopled by men from Armorica ; but certain it is that there is so great a similarity between the language of the Welsh and Bas-Bretons, that the natives of either country understand each other. The northern part of Armorica, after belonging to the Franks, or German conquerors of Gaul, above 400 years, was disjoined from the French kingdom by conquest, and became Normandy, as will appear shortly. The Franks were so called from their having formed, about the year 240, a confederacy to fight for freedom ; and modern France finally took its name from them. On the subject of Britany, Thierry, in his *Histoire de la Conquéte de l'Angleterre par les Normands*, (Paris, 1835,) says :

" De nombreux vaisseaux de fugitifs Bretons abordèrent successivement à la pointe la plus occidentale de l'Armorique, dans les cantons qui, sous les Romains et même avant eux, avaient été appelés territoires des Osismiens et des Vénètes. D'accord avec les anciens habitants, qui reconnaissaient en eux des frères d'origine, les nouveaux venus se répandirent sur toute la côte septentrionale jusqu'à la petite rivière qu'on nomme Coësnon, et vers le sud, jusqu'au territoire de la cité des Vénètes, aujourd'hui Vannes. Ils fondèrent sur cette étendue de pays une sorte d'état séparé, qui embrassa tous les petits lieux voisins des côtes, mais hors duquel restèrent les grandes villes de Vannes, de Nantes, et de Rennes. L'accroissement de population de ce coin de terre occidental, le grand nombre d'hommes de race et de langue celtiques[2] qui s'y trouvèrent ainsi rassemblés sur peu d'espace, le préservèrent de l'irruption du langage romain qui, sous des formes plus ou moins corrompues, gagnait peu à peu toute la Gaule. Le nom de Bretagne fut attaché à ces côtes, et en fit disparaître les noms divers des populations indigènes, pendant que l'île qui, depuis tant de siècles, avait porté ce nom, le perdait elle-même, et, prenant le nom de ses conquérants, commençait à être appelée terre des Saxons et des Angles, ou, en un seul mot, Angleterre."[3]

Cæsar mentions in his Commentaries, Book VI., that Ambiorix — a powerful and determined enemy of the Romans in Gaul — being defeated and driven to extremity, counselled his followers to provide for their own safety, " on which some

---

(1) Edinburgh Encyclopædia, 1830.

(2) Celti, Kelti, Galati, nom que les Romains et les Grecs donnaient aux populations gauloises.

(3) Engel-seaxna-land, Engla-land, prononcez Engle-land ; par corruption, England.

C

took refuge in the forest of Arduenna, and some in the adjoining morasses. Those who lived on the sea coast hid themselves in the islands formed by the tide at high water; and many, abandoning their country altogether, trusted themselves and their all to the faith of foreigners." Berry, page 41, after saying that he had "examined more accurately into the Roman history than Mr. Falle or Mr. Dicey seem to have done"! comments on the passage just quoted, which, however, he does not give, and observes: "The islands here meant by Julius Cæsar, as I have hinted in the Introduction, were most probably those of Jersey and Guernsey; their proximity to the coast of France, and there not being any other islands in the British Channel, confirm me in this opinion . . . . I will therefore venture to call this the most early mention made in history of the islands of Jersey and Guernsey." [1]   A more reckless venture was never made by any historian; as Ambiorix was joint king with Cativolcus of the Eburones, a people of Belgic Gaul, inhabiting what is now the country about Liege, on the West bank of the Meuse; and Cæsar evidently refers to localities near the Rhine, from which river the forest of Arduenna (now *Ardennes*) mentioned by him, extended about fifty miles. Moreover, Jersey and Guernsey must have wonderfully changed in their relative positions to the adjoining continent to make them islands "formed by the tide at high water:"—the isles of Chausey, or Le Bœuf, the latter now a mere group of rocks, would have been a much more probable supposition, if Ambiorix had commanded and fought among the Armorici, or in the *West* instead of the *East* of Gaul. Speaking of a long chain of rocks extending from Alderney to the Caskets, Berry says (p. 295): "It was on this dangerous part of the coast where the young prince, the son of Henry I., was shipwrecked and lost." This sad disaster occurred near Barfleur, in Normandy, as an historian of Guernsey ought surely to have known. With similar unpardonable inaccuracy, Berry states, (p. 106,) that during the civil war Guernsey held for the king, which it never did, and, "after a vigorous defence, was at last forced to submit to the usurper"—meaning the parliament, with which the island sided from the first! [2] And yet he had the modesty to palm on a goodly list of subscribers a quarto termed by him "The History of Guern-

(1) Baker, in his Cæsarea, copying Berry, has repeated this ridiculous supposition.
(2) We have only noticed Mr. Berry's most glaring errors: others are, that Celtic Gaul was separated from Aquitaine by the Loire, instead of by the Garonne, page x.; that Edward III. was justly called the English Justinian, instead of Edward I., page 231, &c.

sey, containing an Interesting Account of the Island," and this at the moderate price of three guineas, although the work is any thing but what it professed to be, the only valuable parts being supplied by Mr. Henry Budd, and the late Bailiff, Mr. Brock. Berry, moreover, contemplated (at page 298) compiling a History of Jersey, but that island was happily spared the infliction. It may appear ungenerous to speak thus of a preceding historian; but when we contrast his description of the people of Guernsey with that of Mr. Chenevix, an accomplished scholar and gentleman, who resided here at the same time, it becomes our duty to expose the secret of the defamatory tone[1] of his "General Observations," (page 298 *et seq.*) viz. his effects being arrested in June, 1813, for house rent due to an Englishman, and his being imprisoned, for two days, in September following, in the public gaol of St. Peter-Port, for refusing to return an unpublished map of Guernsey, which had been lent to him by a surveyor.

Du Moulin,[2] whose history of Normandy was published in 1631, thus described the Cotentin:

"Le Costentin, comme ie croy, est vne des Prouinces de Normandie la plus considerable; car si vous regardez le terroir qu'on y appelle le Closet et le voisinage de Montebourg, vous verrez que c'est vn des meilleurs de France, foisonnant en bleds & autres grains, & tellement gras, qu'il est impossible d'en sortir lors que la pluye a esté grande. Les herbages, ou (comme l'on dit) l'herbe croist du soir au matin, sont si chargez de bœufs, qu'on ne les peut voir sans admiration; aussi on en tire toutes les sepmaines vne grande quantité pour distribuer à la haute Normandie & à la France: Les sidres y abondent & sont fort excellens, principalement l'escarlatin qui ressemble en couleur au vin paillé, & l'égalle presque en bonté. Le gibier s'y trouue en plus grande quantité qu'en autres lieux, & par toute la coste on pesche tant de poissons & de toutes sortes, que l'on les vend quasi pour rien; il est vray que celui des costes de Barfleur & Cherbourg est plus gras & meilleur que celuy de la Hogue & de l'Occident, & la viande est à si bas prix à Montebourg & par tout ce pays, lequel est bas de soy & arrosé de la riuiere Douue, qu'on est fort bien traité en vne hostellerie pour demy quart d'escu à chaque repas. Le peuple y est assez delié, & neantmoins vers la Hague fort

(1) Harris, in his "System of British Geography," was misled by Berry; and Mr. Duncan, in reviewing Harris' work in the Guernsey and Jersey Magazine, vol. ii., page 125, says: "The first paragraph in this libel, to which we shall advert, seems from the mode of expression to have been borrowed by Mr. Harris from that scamp, Berry, who had the impudence to put forth a large quarto of twaddle and personal spleen as a History of Guernsey."

(2) Du Moulin's history is a folio, commencing with the first irruptions of the Northmen, and terminating with the expulsion of king John from Normandy.

rude, & d'vn langage assez difficile; il aime bien à boire, fait
marchandise par terre et sur mer, a de bons pilotes qui font de
grands voyages, de bonnes laines & de bons draps, & pour places
d'asseurance, Constances, Carentan, Cherbourg, Vallongnes, &
Barfleur."

CHAPTER II.

THE island of Guernsey is of triangular form, whence it
perhaps derives its name, which is said to be a corruption of
Kerniow-è, the Celto-Breton word for an island of angles.[1]
In the Itinerary attributed to Antoninus, who governed the
whole of Gaul, Guernsey is called *Sarnia*,[2] and, in some copies
of that work, *Sernia;* Alderney is mentioned by the name of
Arica or *Aurica*,[3] and Jersey by that of *Cæsarea*. According to Cellarius,[4] the Latin name of Alderney was *Riduna;*
but Mr. George Métivier, of Guernsey, a profound etymologist,
thinks that it was *Arinia*, signifying the island of the Cape or
Point. The learned Mr. Poingdestre,[5] of Jersey, who made
great researches into the antiquities of these islands, contends
that Guernsey was anciently called in Latin *Vesargia, Veser-*

(1) " *Guernesey*, une des îles anglaises, dont la forme est celle d'une harpe, a également
emprunté son nom du celto-breton *Kerniow-è*; et par corruption, *Guernesey;* en français,
formé d'angles ou de cornes."—*Origines Gauloises, celles des plus anciens peuples de l'Europe, par La Tour-D'Auvergne Corret, premier grenadier de la république française.
Troisième Edition. A Hambourg,* 1801.—The final é signifies, in celto-breton, island.

(2) Camden's Britannia, page 825. " Quæ Antonio Sarnia, hodie Garnsey appellata."

(3) Holland's Translation of Camden's Britannia, page 224. " Alderney may seeme to be
that Arica which, in Antonine, according to the king of Spaine's copie, is reckoned among
the Isles of the British Sea."

(4) Christoph. Cellarii Notitia Orbis Antiqui. Insulæ circa Galliam CXLVI., p. 263.
Edit. L. I. C. Schwarz, Lips. 1731. " Inter Galliam et Britanniam plures sunt, nec verò
nominatæ à veteribus, quæ Lugdunensi parti objacent, nisi quod auctor Itinerarii Mari-
timi, quod cum Antoniniano conjunctum est, plures Oceani Britanniam et Galliam inter-
fluentis, unà serie, sed indistinctè, nominat, ut nemo facilè ex illius narratione discreuerit,
quod huic nomen, quod illi conueniat. Has autem post Vectam, quæ Britanniæ proxima
est, enumerat: *Riduna, Sarnia, Cæsarea, Barsa, Lisia, Andium, Sicdelis, Uxantisina,
Vindilis, Siata, Arica.* E quibus plerique putant, nominis inducti similitudine, quæ nunc
Garsey sive Jersey est, veterem Cæsaream esse: quæ verò Gransey, major altera, esse
Sarnicam sive *Sarmiam*, quæ Aldinâ Editione est *Arnia*. Cæteras inuestigare, et prisca
nomina componere recentioribus, supra notitiam nostram est, et ab aliis expectandum,
qui mare illud navigarunt, et obscuriorum insularum nomina, et situm, singulari curâ
et industriâ examinauerunt."

(5) Mr. Poingdestre held a fellowship of Exeter College, Oxford, and was ejected from it
for his loyalty by the parliamentary visitors. His skill in languages, his acquaintance
with the civil and Roman laws, and his other acquirements, introduced him into the
Secretary of State's Office, under Lord Digby, where he continued until the affairs of
Charles I. had grown desperate. He afterwards assisted in the defence of Jersey and
Elizabeth Castle against the " Rebels," as Falle calls the parliamentary forces. After the
restoration, he was made lieutenant-bailly of Jersey, and died in that island at the great
age of 83, in 1691.

gia, and *Vesorgia*, all written with a B instead of a V, as *Besargia*, &c.; and his authority is a donation of Childebert, king of France, to Samson, bishop of Dol, in Britany, of four islands, named *Vesargia, Augia, Sargia*, and *Rima*, which he takes to be Guernsey, Jersey, Sark, and Herm; *Augia* being the name of Jersey before the Romans gave it that of Cæsarea. Alderney was not included in the grant, probably on account of its being more distant from Dol. The oldest French historians speak of these islands under the general title of *Les Isles de Coutances*,[1] either because they belonged to that diocese, or from their proximity to that city, whose cathedral, which is considered one of the finest Gothic structures in Europe, commands from its lofty towers a view of Jersey. In the royal mandates of the thirteenth and fourteenth centuries, which are chiefly in Latin, Guernsey is spelt Gernesey, Gerneseye, Gernesie, Gernezeye, and Jerneseye; and, by the old Norman historians, Grenezay and Grenezey. Heylin calls it Garnzey and Guernzey; and Camden, Garnzey or Garnsey.[2] According to the *Dédicace des Eglises*, Guernsey was known as "*la bienheureuse isle sainte*," the very happy holy island, at the consecration of the Vale church, A.D. 1117. Warburton, the antiquary, says that it derived this name from the monks, who settled in the island towards the close of the tenth century. Alderney was anciently known as *Aurigny, Origny*, and *Auréné;* and Sark as *Sercq*, and *Cercq*.

That Guernsey was visited by the fleets of the Danes and Norwegians, whose first descent on the western coast of France is stated to have been early in the ninth century, is certain. According to some modern Danish authors, whose testimony, however, must be received with caution, the Northmen were the chief, if not the only, navigators of their time; and as they were possessed of handsome ornaments and well made swords, inlaid with gold and silver—moreover, as they built vessels in which, so early as the ninth and tenth centuries, they sailed across the Atlantic, and colonized Iceland

---

[1] Constantia Castra, now Coutances, appears to have been a great Roman station. It possessed, in Falle's time, Roman remains, such as aqueducts, &c.

"Les empereurs entretenaient à Bayeux, comme à Coutances, une garnison sédentaire de Bataves et de Suèves, enrôlés au service de l'empire."—*Goubé, Histoire de Normandie*.

The chief town of the Unelli at the Roman conquest, was Crociatonum: on its site the modern Valognes is erected.

[2] Camden says, "Garnzey, or Garnsey, formerly gave a title of Baron Guernsey, in the second year of Her Majesty Queen Anne, to Heneage Finch, second son of Heneage, late Earl of Nottingham, and Lord Chancellor of England." p. 1514. It is now the second title of the Earl of Aylesford, as Baron Guernsey.

and Greenland—in other words, visited America several
centuries before Columbus; (?) it would-seem that the much-
dreaded North-men, although Pagans and addicted to rapine
and cruelty, were not so uncivilized as is generally supposed.
In that age, Christians were often equally rapacious and
cruel. We learn from Wace, the Jersey poet, that the celebrated Danish chieftain, Hasting, landed on, and pillaged,
all the islands, in the year 838 according to one authority,
and 856 according to another :

> En Auremen, en Guernesi,
> En Sairc, en Erm, en Gersi.[1]
> *Roman de Rou.*

As Hasting next invaded Touraine, where he put every
thing to fire and sword, it is probable that these islands were
subjected by him to the same barbarous treatment.

Vaice,[2] or Wace, i.e. Eustace,[3] was a native of Jersey; he
was born at the commencement of the twelfth century, was
partly educated at Caen, and died in England about the year
1180. He was the author of several poems, but his most
celebrated production is the " Roman de Rou," which contains
an account of the first incursions of the North-men into England and France, and the history of Rollo and his successors,
down to A.D. 1106, being the sixth year of the reign of
Henry I. This poem contains 16,547 verses, partly in octo-
syllabic, partly in Alexandrine metre, and it is the most curious
literary monument that remains of the history and language
of ducal Normandy. A beautiful edition of " *Le Roman de
Rou, et les Ducs de Normandie,*" was published in two volumes
octavo, at Rouen, in 1827.

According to tradition, the northern freebooters, who were
termed, by the old French historians, Sarrazins, *anglicé*
Saracens,[4] by way of reproach, established themselves in
Guernsey, where they erected a strong-hold, which was named,
probably after their leader, *Le Chastel du Grand Jeffroi,* or,

(1) Alderney, Guernsey, Sark, Herm, Jersey. In the Rouen edition. Erm is printed Erin,
with a foot note, " lieu inconnu." Erin is clearly a miscopy.

(2) " Ie di et diray que ie suis,
    Vaice de l'isle de Gersui."

(3) The prefix of Robert to Wace is an unwarranted and modern addition ; he called
himself simply Mestre Wace, and in his time family surnames appear to have been chiefly
taken from localities, and usually confined to the landed proprietors.

(4) The Saracens were Moslems from Arabia, who, after conquering Spain, entered
France early in the eighth century, and extended their ravages with fire and sword as far
as Tours, which city they reduced to ashes. Charles Martel, the general of the Franks,
at length defeated them with great slaughter, A.D. 732, and compelled them to return
into Spain. Their name was subsequently transferred by the Crusaders to the Mahometan
occupiers of the Holy Land.

The Castle of the Great Geoffrey; and it appears to have also borne the name of the Chastel of the Grand Sarrazin. This castle was situated on an eminence nearly in the centre of the island, and commanded an extensive view of the ocean and of many of the landing places, as well as of the coast of Normandy: it subsequently gave the present name to the parish, Câtel, a corruption of "Chastel," pronounced vernacularly K-à-té. On its site now stands the church of Sainte Marie de Castro—St. Mary of the Castle—consecrated in the year 1203; but it is an error to suppose that the north wall of the chancel and the transept are a remnant of the old castle walls, as they certainly show no evidence of such antiquity, although the masonry is very rude, being composed of large and small stones put together without any order. In the angle made by the chancel and transept, a projecting perforated stone about the middle, and a bracket near the bottom of the wall, are pointed out as the spot where the castle standard was planted !! Two artificial earthen mounds still exist in Guernsey, which are generally supposed to have been watch stations, one in the parish of St. Andrew, called "La Hougue Fouque," and the other in the parish of St. Martin, on the road to the Forest, called "La Hogue Hatenai." Fouque is probably derived from PHUKA, or spirit. Hougue, s. f., a hillock or barrow. O. F. Hogue, s. f., elevation, colline. *Roquefort.*—Base Latin Hoga, probably deducible from a verb which signifies *to throw up,* whence the old Norman French Hague, French Hague, and Flemish Hagen.— *G. Métivier.*—Mr. Poingdestre, of Jersey, already mentioned, wrote—in a MS. now in the British Museum—relative to the *Hogues* in that island, as follows:

"The second kind of monument, and which I take to be next to the Poquelayes in antiquity, are by ye Islanders called *Hogues,* which are nothing else but round hillocks or eminences, raised up with men's hands: the most part of them not much higher than those which are to be seene in many parts of England, thought to be sepulchers of eminent men slayne in battaille: those in Jersey seeme to have beene made for a farre different use, that is for *speculæ,* or hills to espye a farre off, from the land into the sea, which necessity brought the Islanders to provide for theire security at the time, when the Danes, Vandalls, and other Northerne people, invested the coast of France, and other southerly parts of Europe, not long after the time of Charles the Great, to the end that the inhabitants, discovering theire shipps a farre off, might have time to hide such things as they desired to preserve. It may be objected that the sea is not seene from some of them, which is against my conjecture, but the cause is the improvement made since those times of the ground, by the planting of trees and enclosing of ground, which have quite changed the surface of the island, where as in antient times it was all champain and open ground. Of these Hogues there are two of more especiall notice,"—viz. the *Hougue-bye* and the *Castell de Lecq.*

Samson

Among the refugees from Britain who sought safety from the ravages of the Saxons was Samson, bishop of St. David, in Wales. Vertot fixes the date of his arrival in Britany in the year 520, during the reign of Childebert,[1] son of Clovis. Both these princes had embraced Christianity, and Childebert established Samson at Dol, where he could only have been a nominal prelate, as Mabillon expressly states that there were no bishops in Britany, the bishop of Laon excepted, before the ninth century.[2] However, it is certain that St. Samson, who was canonized, exercised full spiritual jurisdiction in Dol and its neighbourhood, and that he established Christianity in these islands, in which it appears to have been introduced by his master and preceptor, Pyro, if we can credit a passage from the Life of St. Samson, cited by Vertot.[3] Other accounts state that St. Samson obtained an interview with king Childebert at Paris, in 557, in which year his signature of " Samson, a sinner," is recorded at a synod held in that city ;[4] and that Childebert added Jersey, Guernsey, and the isles contiguous,[5] to the diocese of Dol, of which St. Samson was bishop. Childebert, however, was dead, or at least had ceased to reign, in the year 557.

(1) Childebert reigned from the year 511 to 549.

(2) " L'on appelait évêques régionnaires des missionnaires revêtus du caractère épiscopal, qui avaient droit de prêcher et de conférer les sacrements dans une étendue de pays déterminée, mais qui n'avaient point de siège. Ainsi, quoiqu'il y eût des évêques à Saint Brieux, Dol, et Saint Malo, ou plutôt Aleth, dès le sixième siècle, ces évêques habitaient dans des monastères, et n'étaient point évêques de Saint Brieux, Dol, et Aleth. Ces villes n'ont été érigées en évêchés que long-temps après ; ce qui est certain au moins pour la ville de Dol."—*Histoire des Evêques de Coutances, par M. Lecanu, Curé de Bolleville, à Coutances, 1839.*

(3) " Erit autem non longè ab hoc monasterio insulâ quædam nuper fundata à quodam egregio viro ac sancto presbytero, Pyro nomine, in quâ insulâ et ego fui, apud quam, inquam, Samson cohabitare volebat."—*Etablissement des Bretons dans les Gaules, t. 2,* p. 348.
" These islands were then under the kings of *France,* who had lately embraced Christianity ; and *Childebert,* son of *Clovis,* made a gift of them to St. *Samson,* for an augmentation to his small diocese ; as we learn from *D'Argentré,* who affirms that he himself had perused the writings of that donation. '*A cest archevesque* Childebert *donna quelques isles et terres en* Normandie; Rimoul, Augie, Sargie, *et* Vesargie, *qui estoint isles en la coste; car je trouve cela aux vieilles lettres,*' i.e. 'To this archbishop, *Childebert* gave some islands and lands in *Normandy; Rimoul, Augie, Sargie,* and *Vesargie,* which were islands on the coast; for so I find in old instruments and records.'"—*Falle.*

(4) Magdeburg Centurists.

(5) Life of St. Samson, by Baldric, bishop of Dol; MS.—Mémoire sur l'Origine des Bretons, par l'Abbé Gallet.

Accompanied by his kinsman, Judual, duke of the northern Gallican Bretons, and a selection of monks from the community of Pentale, in the future Normandy,[1] St. Samson is said to have landed in Guernsey at the only harbour then used, as it was formed by nature ; and on the south side of it he caused a chapel to be erected, which, being enlarged or rebuilt in the year 1111, and raised to the rank of a parochial church, was dedicated to his memory, and called St. Samson's, a name which it still retains, and which is also that of the harbour and parish. He was considered in earlier days as the patron saint of Guernsey, and numerous miracles are ascribed to him by his biographer; but they are of too puerile a character to require further notice.

St. Samson was succeeded in the abbey of Dol by his kinsman, Maglorius, who was the companion of his exile from Wales, and was also canonized. The name of this celebrated saint seems derived to be from Mac Glor, or Mac Gloir, " a son of glory." He had distinguished himself, in what was afterwards Glamorganshire, as a disciple of the famous Hiltutus, and he possessed that touching eloquence which penetrates and subdues the most obdurate hearts. Magloire appears to have also visited these islands, and is said to have been very successful in converting to Christianity Count Lojesco and the insular Pagan garrisons in the French king's pay. About the year 565, he founded a monastery in Jersey and another in Sark, the latter being abandoned after his death, in consequence of the ravages of the North-men. But a convent or chapel bearing his name existed 800 years after his time, as in the reign of Edward III. a pension was allowed to it by the crown—" Conventui Sancti Maglorii in insulâ Sargiensi " —to the convent of St. Magloire in the island of Sark.[2] There was formerly a tenement in that island called " *La Moinerie*," or house of monks, which is supposed to have been the site of the ancient monastery, and it is now that of the seigneurie house. St. Magloire, who died at his monastery in Sark,[3] about the year 587, also built a chapel at the

---

(1) Ancient Acts of St. Samson.—Mémoires pour servir de preuves à l'Histoire de Bretagne, tome i., col. 196.

(2) " Serck formait une paroisse avec Herms. Saint Magloire fonda dans l'île de Serck un monastère, qui subsistait encore huit cents ans après lui, c'est-à-dire, du temps d'Édouard III.; car à cette époque la couronne d'Angleterre lui payait une rente : *Conventui Sancti Magiorii in insulâ Sargiensi.* L'évêque de Coutances était patron de cette paroisse."—*Histoire des Évêques de Coutances.*

(3) " I have since received a very circumstantial life of St. Magloire, composed about the year 1319, in French rhymes, by a canon of the convent of St. Magloire, in Paris, from a Latin original of the twelfth century. Both documents throw great light on the conversion of the Channel Islands, and on the death of St. Magloire in the island of Sark, and the preservation of his body in that island until it was removed to the priory of Lehon, near Dinan, under the reign of the Carlovingians, and thence carried to Paris, for fear of his being desecrated by the northern pirates."—*Monsieur De Gerville, Valognes,* 1848.

Vale, which has long since gone to decay;[1] but its site retains
the name of St. Mallière, or Maglère, not a corruption, be it
remembered, of the modern French, which the vernacular
language of Guernsey preceded by several centuries. When
Magloire established himself in Sark, he appears to have
been accompanied by 62 priests. That island was, we learn,
the property of Nivo, a nobleman, who chose it for his burial
place, and who at this time seems to have held hereditary
possession of Viss-Sargia,[2] or West Sark, now Guernsey.
It is stated in the Latin Acts that when Magloire arrived at
Viss-Sargia, or Ghernereia, (Guernsey,) there were ploughs
at work, ships in the haven; that it was fruitful in corn,
(*dives frugum*,) and that during the great famine of its mother-
land, Armorica, in the memorable year of distress and pestilence, 586, many of the continental relatives of the islanders
were glad to avail themselves of the abundance in West Sark.
Of Magloire it is related on this occasion: "Une cruelle
famine réduisit les plus riches de la Bretagne Armoricaine à
la dernière misère, et plusieurs personnes, même de qualité,
vinrent dans l'île de Magloire chercher les aliments dont ils
avaient besoin."—The good prelate's supply must have come
chiefly either from his Jersey estate, (the seventh part of that
island,) or from the territory in Guernsey of his wealthy
friend, Nivo.

While on the subject of Magloire, it may be well to add
here that a chapel in Sark, bearing his name, was granted by
William de Vernon at the close of the twelfth century, with
the land which had been occupied by Magloire, to the abbey
of Montebourg, built towards the year 1090 by his ancestor,
Richard de Reviers. Richard de Vernon confirmed, A.D.
1190, his father's donation and augmented it; the original
charter bearing his seal being still extant.

In a learned work, entitled "De l'Etat Ancien et de l'Etat
Actuel de la baie du Mont-Saint-Michel et de Cancale, par
M. Manet, à Saint-Malo, 1829," the author seeks to prove that
the Channel Isles were once joined to "Cotentin," ou Pays
de Coutances; in other words, to Normandy; and he says:

"Ainsi est-il au-jourd'hui à peu près démontré qu'il fut un
temps où la Grande-Bretagne tenait à la Gaule, l'Espagne à
l'Afrique, l'Italie à la Sicile, et peut-être le Nouveau-Monde à

(1) This chapel was situated near the sea side, upon a point of land, on the N.E. corner
of the *Clos du Valle.*
(2) With slight variations of form, VISS, in all the Teutonic dialects, denotes fair, calm,
serene, eventide, the west, *vesper, hesper.*

l'Asie.—Ainsi est-il encore mieux constaté que, par l'effet
d'autres envahissements lents ou subits, mais beaucoup moins
considérables que les précédens, Jersey, Guernesey, Aurigny,
Batz, Ouëssant, le Texel, Yerland, et une multitude d'autres
lieux dans l'Angleterre, la Bretagne, l'Aunis, la Saintonge, la
Flandre, la Zélande, la Frise, la Poméranie, etc., ont subi
d'étrangers métamorphoses." (pp. 1, 2.)

"On tient, disent les savans auteurs du *Dictionnaire de
Trévoux*, article Jersey, que cette île a fait autrefois partie du
continent du Cotentin."—"Les îles de Serck, de Guernesey et
d'Aurigny, ajoute M. Deric (*Hist. Eccl. de Bret.*, t. 1, p. 104,
et t. 11, p. 130,) appartenaient alors également à la terre ferme,
comme en font foi nos meilleurs géographes, et les Titres de
l'église de Coutances." (p. 30.)

"*Ancienne jonction présumée de tout l'archipel Anglo-Normand au Cotentin.*—D'abord, c'est une présomption fondée sur
les autorités les plus respectables, que, bien antérieurement a
l'envahissement de l'océan sur nos côtes, au mois de Mars, 709,
détaillé ci-dessus, Jersey, Guernesey, et en général tout le reste
de cet archipel Anglo-Normand, appartenaient à la terre ferme.—
C'est même une tradition dans la première de ces îles (tradition
appuyée sur des très-anciens manuscrits que nous avons lus,)
qu'encore au temps de Saint-Lo, mort le 21 Septembre, 565,
Jersey n'était séparé du territoire de Coutances, dont il dépen-
dait pour le spirituel, que par un simple ruisseau, sur lequel
les habitants étaient tenus de fournir une planche à l'archi-
diacre de l'église-mère, lorsqu'il allait faire chez eux sa visite."
(pp. 123, 4.)

This convulsion of nature appears to have occurred in
March, 709 ; and although we do not believe its having
caused the disruption of these islands from Normandy, yet it
was probably at this period that Vazon bay was submerged,
and that the Hanois rocks were dissevered from the main
land of Guernsey. Geologists account for the upheaval and
subsidence of land by the increase or reduction of igneous
agency or subterranean fire ; and instances of the partial operation of the internal heat of the globe are not wanting.
Moreover, it is known that the bed of the sea is liable to
subsidence, and that the land and ocean have occasionally
exchanged places. Beneath the fine sand of Vazon bay,
which tradition states was once a forest, are found the *débris*
of the oak, the larch, the willow, and other trees, which had
remained unknown for ages, and were first discovered about
the year 1750. The deposit being found excellent fuel, the
peasantry regarded it as a God-send, and called it *corban*,

or a gift, whence the present appellation of *gorban*. Birds'
nests, nuts with the kernel, and a few earthen vessels, pieces
of copper, and celtic stone instruments, have also been found
among the vegetable remains, and occasionally trees so hard
that they could not be extracted.   The Hanois rocks—a
dangerous ridge extending nearly two miles to the S.W. of
Guernsey—there can be little doubt once joined the land,
near which the traces of a road leading seaward are said to
be still visible ; and it is also stated that the hinges of a gate
could be seen not many years since on one of the rocks !
The existence of both these indications has more probably
been handed down by tradition.   Certain it is, however, that
in the year 709, *Mont St. Michel*, in Normandy, which stood
in the midst of the marshy forest of *Sesciacum*, in French
Scissy, (signifying a *barren, moorish* wilderness, according to
its Gaelic interpretation,) six miles from the sea, became what
it is now : the woods were swallowed up, so that their site has
ever since been the dominion of waves and quicksands.   The
disjunction at high water of the " Clos du Valle" from the
rest of Guernsey, as already mentioned, probably occurred at
this period, and not in 1204, as stated by Berry and Duncan,
if indeed it were ever fully connected with the main land.
The year 811 was the period of fresh and considerable en-
croachments.

The Chronicler of the Abbey of Fontenelle, who was witness
of the effects, relates that from the 22d to the 29th of October,
842, the islands were visited by a violent earthquake, accompanied by subterranean rumblings, which threw down the
monument and houses, and also engulphed the sea shore of
the neighbouring continent of " Cotentin."

A memorable epoch is now before us, the foundation by
Rollo of the duchy of Normandy, which, although small in
extent, was great in renown, as it became celebrated not only
for its conquest of England, but for the exploits of the Tancreds of Hauteville[1] and other Normans in Italy, Sicily, and
Apulia.   In these countries, the Tancreds[2] sprang from a
small village in the Cotentin : with no other auxiliaries than
courage and genius, gained battles, overturned thrones, mas-

(1) Hauteville is a village near the sea coast, and about five miles S.W. of Coutances.

(2) " Cette année (1032) fut fertile en événemens honorables pour la Normandie. Tancrède
de Hauteville, vassal du duc Robert, au Cotentin, envoya trois de ses fils, Guillaume-Fier-
à-Bras, Drogues ou Drogon, et Humfroi, rejoindre les Normands établis à Averse, dans la
Pouille.   On cite, entre les gentilshommes qui les suivirent, Tristan-Citeau, Ranulfe et
Richard-de-Cariel ; Robert-de-Grosmesnil, et Guillanme-de-Groult."—*Goube, Histoire de
Normandie.*

tered the pontiffs of Rome, conquered with one hand the
Cæsars of Constantinople, and with the other smote the
emperors of Germany, while they made even the sultans of
Babylon tremble on their thrones. This line of heroes was
extinguished, after a duration of above two centuries, in the
year 1260, by the beheading of Conradin, at Naples, a youth
of only sixteen years of age. With one common origin and
language, it is very probable that some of the natives of these
islands were among the Norman adventurers, who followed
the fortunes of the Tancreds.

The Channel Islands having formed part of the dukedom
of Normandy, and now being the last remnant of the Anglo-
Norman possessions, it may not be out of place to relate here
briefly how the duchy was severed from the kingdom of
France. In the early ages, Denmark and Norway are said
to have been densely populated, and to have furnished what
is termed by modern writers, " the Northern Hive," swarms
from which established themselves in Britain, Gaul, and other
parts of Europe. Towards the close of the ninth century,
Rollo, a Norwegian chieftain, who had been condemned to
perpetual banishment by the king of Denmark, sailed up the
river Seine at the head of a large body of his countrymen,
and obtained possession of the city of Rouen, where, induced
by the beauty and fertility of the surrounding country, they
resolved on settling. Some authors date this event in the
year 876, others in 887; but certain it is that Rollo continued
de facto master of the capital and the neighbouring country
until the year 912, when Charles the Simple, king of France,
who was deposed in 922, unable to expel the invaders, demanded a conference with their chiefs. Accordingly, the
principal Norwegian adventurers met Charles, attended by
many of his barons, at *St. Clair sur Epte,* a town three
leagues from Gisors, where a treaty was concluded, by which
Charles ceded to the invaders all the country, with the towns
and strong places, between the river Epte and the sea: this
country they called Normandy, after their own name of
North-men, or Normans.[2] The French king had a daughter,
named Gisele, whom he offered as wife to Rollo; and the
latter, says an old historian, finding her of sufficient height,
married her: she died the same year without issue. Rollo
was forthwith invested with the ducal authority, and baptized
in the Christian faith, observes Thierry, in order that he might

---

(2) "Quam Northmanniam Nothmanni vocaverunt, eò quòd de Norwegiâ egressi
essent." (Script. rer. Northmannicar. Page 7.)

be recognized by the other sovereigns. "Of all the northern hosts who established themselves in other countries by conquest, those who gave their name to Normandy are they who most rapidly advanced in civilization. They seem immediately to have grafted themselves upon the old Romano-Gallic stock, and, adopting the language of the people whom they subdued, thus to have qualified their children, in the first generation, for receiving the religion, manners, and arts of Christendom. They seem also, like the Jutes, Saxons, and Angles, who fixed themselves in Britain, to have disregarded maritime concerns when they had won a country for themselves.—When William resolved upon claiming the English crown, by virtue of Edward the Confessor's testament, the ships for transporting his army were to be built." [1] The Normans, adds Thierry, were not slow in extending their territory on all sides : they invaded and conquered the country about Bayeux, which was still inhabited by an ancient Saxon people, who preserved their German idiom amidst the "Romanesque," or French Latin. This conquest was followed by that of the peninsula of Coutances as far as *Mont St. Michel*, now the "Cotentin;" and thus the borders of Normandy were extended to Britany. The Bretons, who had preserved their national independence of the Franks, whom they hated, now became exposed to a double peril ; for the Normans, after invading and devastating their country, sowed divisions among them by their intrigues, and from that time commenced the progressive decline of the liberties of Britany. Some Norman historians, however, state that Charles at once ceded the whole of Neustria, or the modern province of Normandy,[2] as an hereditary duchy to Rollo, on condition of his renouncing Paganism, and, with his followers, being baptized in the Christian faith ; and they add that Rollo insisted on having Britany also, as he alleged that Normandy alone was incapable of subsisting his followers, it having been reduced to sterility by his own ravages and those of his predecessors ; although it is now one of the most fertile provinces of France. Rollo's demand was conceded, and the Count of Rennes, which city is the capital of Britany, was compelled

(1) Southey's Naval History of England.

(2) William of Jumièges fixes the limits of the cession from the river Epte to the borders of Britany. "Mandans si Christianus efficeretur, terram maritimam ab Eptæ flumine usque ad Britannicos limites, cum suâ filiâ nomine Gislâ, se ei daturum fore."

The little river Coësnon separates Normandy from Britany, emptying itself into the sea at Mount Saint Michael, which it leaves in Normandy, by the sinuosities of its stream ; a circumstance which has given rise to the distich,

"Coësnon par sa folie
A mis le mont en Normandie."

to do him homage, as was the Count of Dol. These statements in some measure confute themselves, because it is clear that if Charles were powerful enough to impose conditions in favor of Christianity, Rollo could not have insisted on adding Britany to Normandy, even if Charles were master of the former province, which it does not appear he was. It was only in 933 that Raoul, king of the French, by the terms of a treaty still extant, surrendered the "Cotentin" to Duke William, son of Rollo.[1] The rule of Rollo was so much more mild and equitable than that of the Franks had been, that many artisans and labourers came from France to become his subjects : he established a rigorous police throughout the duchy, enacted salutary and equitable laws, protected the rights of person and property, and displayed the virtues of a legislator as ably as he had those of a warrior. He was a contemporary of Alfred, of England, to whom he was in no way inferior, as he is described both by the French and Norman historians as possessing great wisdom and energy of character, with a noble mien and majestic stature. Such were the fruits of his wise and vigorous government, that Normandy soon became one of the most flourishing little states of Europe; and was thereby enabled in the following century to achieve the conquest of England, which kingdom thus became possessed of the Channel Islands. Rollo died in the year 917, according to some historians; in 931, according to others ; and from him sprang a line of six ducal sovereigns singularly remarkable, without an exception, for their capacity and prowess.[2] The dukes of Normandy, to the Conquest, were as follow :

Dukes.	Surnamed.	Years of Accession.
1. Rollo	——	912
2. William I	Longsword	926
3. Richard I	Sans Peur.	943
4. Richard II.	The Good	996
5. Richard III.	——	1026
6. Robert I.	The Magnificent	1028
7. William	The Conqueror.	1035

And from William the Conqueror to John, the twelfth and last duke of Normandy, who inherited no territory, and there-

(1) Chronicle of Frodoard, anno 931, 933.

(2) "Nous devons cette remarque glorieuse à la mémoire de nos ducs de Normandie, que depuis Raoul—il ne s'en est pas rencontré un seul foible, lasche, ou meschant, non pas seulement médiocre; mais tous ont esté excellens en toutes, ou en la pluspart des qualitez requises en des Princes, capables de commander aux plus grands Estats de la Terre."—Abrégé de l'Hist. de Norm. Liv. iv. p. 129.

fore received the surname of Lack-land, (in French, "Sans Terre,") as follow:

Dukes.	Surnamed.	Years of Accession.
8. Robert II	Courte-Heuze	1087
9. Henry I[1]	Béauclerc	1106
[2]Stephen[1]	—————	1135
10. Henry II[1]	————	1154
11. Richard I[1]	Cœur de Lion	1189
12. John[1]	Lack-land	1199

Haro

The *clameur de haro*,[3] in matters of trespass, derived from the Normans, exists to this day in the Channel Islands, and is stated by many writers to have been originally an appeal to Rollo, the first and great duke of Normandy, celebrated for his strict and impartial justice: they add, that Haro is derived from Aa! or Ha! an exclamation of suffering, and Ro, the duke's name abbreviated; the cry of Haro, à l'aide, mon Prince! signifying O Rollo, my prince, succour me! Mr. George Métivier considers this derivation a vulgar error, and asserts that "centuries before Rollo's arrival, Hara, a cry, Haro, Harou, Hareu, and if there be any other derivations from the Frankish verb Haran, to cry, or call, or hoot, or summon, formed part of the vernacular tongue of all the northern provinces of Gaul." The *clameur de haro* is tantamount to a summary injunction to stay proceedings, and is exercised by the person who conceives that his land is infringed upon by another; the party so infringing is bound to respect the *clameur*, at his peril, and to desist until the matter in dispute has been judicially decided. Historians mention a remarkable instance of the efficacy of the *clameur* at the interment of William the Conqueror in the great abbey of St. Stephen, at Caen. When William built that abbey, he pulled down several houses, and did not compensate all the

(1) King of England.

(2) Or the interregnum during the usurpation of the crown of England by Stephen, count of Bologne, nephew of Henry I., and grandson of William the Conqueror.

(3) "Clameur de Haro, citation devant le juge."—*French Dictionary.*
"Pour la bonne paix et justice qu'il maintînt en sa Duché, ses subjects prindrent une coustume, tant de son vivant comme apréz sa mort, quand on leur faisoit force ou violence, ils crioyent Aa-Rou, &c."—Chron. de Normand. ch. xxvi.
"Et en l'année 1418, la ville de Roüen étant assiegée par Henri, roi d'Angleterre, un prêtre fut deputé pour lui faire cette harangue, et au duc de Bourgogne: *Tres excellent prince, et seigneur, il m'es enjoint de crier contre vous le grand Haro, qui signifie l'oppression qu'ils ont des Anglois;* comme raporte Monstrelet."—*Coutumes de Normandie, par Basnage.*
" Et quód illi qui clamant Harou, vel clamari faciunt, debent illud Jüdicibus domini Regis nunciare, et etiam apportare, et ipsi Judices secundum conquestum vel clamorem debent procedere, et non ultra, nisi sit in casu criminali. Et si illi, qui audiunt dictum clamorem de Harou, ad dictos Judices non apportaverint, propter hoc in aliquo gravamine non debent permanere, quomodocunque aliquo tempore usum fuerit."—*Placita coram Henrico Spigurnel, &c.* Gernereye, A.D. 1324.

owners. Ascelin, one of these, as the corpse was about to be deposited in the vault, stepped forward and exercised the *clameur*, saying : " I appeal to Rollo, the father and founder of our nation, who, though dead, *lives in his laws*." His claim was immediately investigated and allowed, none offering him any violence for interrupting the ceremony ; but, on the contrary, all respected the Haro.

These islands were doubtless quickly annexed by the Normans after their conquest of the "Cotentin," of which they naturally formed a part ; and thus they were greatly benefitted, as thenceforth there was a stop put to the further incursions of the North-men, so much dreaded in that age. Had these sea-rovers been disposed to invade and plunder their own countrymen in Normandy, its dukes were powerful enough to repel them. Moreover, the conversion of the Normans to Christianity was attended with the happiest results, for as soon as they yielded to the influence of its precepts, they relinquished their lawless habits, and advanced rapidly in civilization. The monasteries and churches, which had been ruined by their incursions, were quickly re-edified, and these islands were certainly not neglected in the general restoration. Long before the conquest of England, A.D. 1066, there existed not only the present parochial divisions in Guernsey, but churches on their present sites; as is proved by William the Bastard's charter, which granted to the abbey of " Marmoutier," near Tours, about the year 1055, six churches, viz. "ecclesia Sancti Petri de Portu ;" ecclesia Sancti Andree de Patenti Pomerio ; ecclesia Sancti Martini de la Berlosa ; ecclesia Sancti Marie de Tortavalle ; ecclesia Sancti Samsonis Episcopi ; et ecclesia Sancti Trinitatis de Foresta. All these churches have since been rebuilt ; as St. Sampson's, the oldest now existing, is of the year 1111. The charter of Henry I., son of the Conqueror, confirms his father's donations, and it mentions the six churches by name, with the following addition relative to St. Peter-Port : " et quoddam molendinum in cimiterio ejusdem ecclesie ;" that is, the water mill still existing at the bottom of the market. If we can credit Berry, a copy of a mandate is still preserved in the abbey of Fontenelle, in Normandy, by which Charlemagne, who was king of France from the year 768 to 814, commanded the abbot to visit Jersey and Guernsey in the character of imperial legate, so that Christianity must have gained ground among the islanders. They had been under the see of Dol since

. D

about the year 550, but were transferred by one of Rollo's immediate successors, apparently duke Richard II. or III., to the diocese of Coutances.   When these islands became under the latter diocese, they were included in the archdeaconry of Beauteis, (from the small parish of Beauté on the opposite coast,) the said archdeaconry consisting of the deaneries of Carentan, Beuteis, la Haye du Puits, St. Sauveur le Vicomte, Barneville, Jersey, and Guernsey.   The islands were very early the favorite retreat of monks of several religious orders, probably on account of their seclusion.   The order of the Cordeliers appears to have been firmly established in Alderney, Herm, and Guernsey.   A seal was found in the convent of the Cordeliers at Valognes, (*Crociatonum*) deposited there when the order was abolished.   A fac-simile of it may be seen in the "Journal of the British Archæological Association," for April, 1847, in a very interesting article on the Antiquities of Alderney, by Mr. F. C. Lukis, already mentioned.   The legend is :

" Sigillum custodis insularum inferioris Normaniæ,"

and the appropriate symbols are in accordance with the work of sending the Gospel tidings to pagan lands—the cross carried in a frail bark beyond the sea.

A fleet of North-men from Armorica, not of the Celtic or Christian inhabitants of that country, and apparently from Britany, in the year 918, went round the Land's End, entered the Bristol channel, wasted the Welsh coast, and, landing high up the Severn, entered Herefordshire in force.   Here the natives gave them battle, and they were so beset that they engaged to depart from the realm ; nevertheless, in going down the Bristol channel, they landed twice with the intent of revenging themselves for their defeat.   In both descents they were defeated with great slaughter, and the survivors took refuge in one of the islands near, probably Lundy, where many died from starvation.   At length they escaped to the Welsh coast, and in the autumn made their way to Ireland.

In the year 965, the Benedictine monks were put in possession of the monastery of *Mont St. Michel*, in Normandy, by duke Richard I., who about the same time expelled its previous tenants, the secular clergy, on account, it would seem, of their dissolute conduct.   The exiled clergy are stated to have established themselves in the Vale parish, and to

have built there a monastery or priory, which, in memory of
their late residence, they named St. Michael of the Vale.
About the same time, the inhabitants are said to have fortified
an eminence near St. Sampson's harbour, on which now
stands Vale Castle, as a security against pirates, who however
could not have been the North-men; as the latter, being
sprung from the same ancestors, were the unfailing allies of
the Normans. It will be seen in the sequel that the priory
of the Vale, then so called, was in ruins in the year 1406;[1]
but we have some doubt as to the period of its erection, because every Guernsey historian has erroneously stated that
the exiled clergy possessed themselves of lands in "the
Close" of the Vale, whereas it appears that anterior to the
charter of duke Robert, father of William the Conqueror,
about the year 1030, the monks had no possessions whatever
in Guernsey. This fact, moreover, goes far to disprove the
statement that the clergy exiled from *Mont St. Michel* settled
in the island, whose earliest annals are in truth shrouded in
much doubt and obscurity. Some portion of Vale Castle is
thought to be the work of the Normans, although certainly
not so ancient as the tenth century. The original structure
was named the Castle of St. Michael the Archangel.

DUKE ROBERT I.—1028 to 1035.

This prince, who succeeded his brother Richard III., was
brave, liberal, and just. Having espoused the cause of his
two cousins, Alfred and Edward, against Canute of England,
who withheld that kingdom from them, Robert embarked at
Fescamp with his "noblesse and gendarmerie," intending to
land on the coast of Sussex; but the day after sailing, a tempest drove the fleet down the channel as far as Guernsey.
Robert was detained fifteen days on the island by the winds,
and as they were quite contrary for him to proceed to England, he relinquished his intended descent, and commanded
the Count de Longueville,[2] a brave man and great captain, to
range along the coast of Britany and pillage all he could
find, while he himself landed at *Mont St. Michel*, to con-
strain Alain to render him the homage which he owed.[3]

(1) Speaking of this priory, Dicey says : " Some small part of the ruins whereof are at
this time to be seen !" (1751)

(2) According to Du Moulin, who, however, appears to have been in error, as, in Robert's
time, there were no counts in Normandy out of the ducal family. The person named is
simply called RAVEL by the old historians, and he is supposed to have been an ancestor of
the chamberlains de Tancarville.

(3) Histoire Générale de Normandie, par Gabriel du Moulin, curé de Maneual, à
Rouen, 1631.

As the Guernsey fishermen had put out to the rescue of the fleet, and piloted it into a bay, which has in consequence ever since borne the name of *l'Ancresse*, or the place of anchorage, Robert, in recompense to the inhabitants for this service, is said to have left two engineers to finish the castle in the Vale, and to erect such other defences as might be found necessary to protect the islanders from the incursions of pirates. According to Berry, these officers executed their task so well that two other very strong castles were built in the course of a few years, one at Jerbourg, which has long since disappeared, and the other, which still partly exists, is now known as Ivy Castle, its original name being *Le Château des Marais*, from its situation in marshy land. It was doubly walled, having a deep moat round the inner wall; and the original structure, with its angle towers, is still easily traced. In the Inquest of Henry III., A.D. 1248, the marsh, on which the castle stands, is named the Marsh d'Orgueil,[1] possibly from the castle standing in its midst, as the castle itself is not mentioned. It was probably built on the rocky eminence in the centre of the marsh from the facility of filling the moat with water, as an additional means of defence against pirates. There was, however, no castle erected at Jerbourg at the same time, as the Fœdera contains a mandate in Latin to "Johanni de Roches," keeper of the isles of Guernsey, Jersey, Sark, and Alderney, headed *De castro vocato Girburgh, in insulâ de Gerneseye, perficiendo,* and dated A.D. 1328, An. 2, Edw. III., or about three centuries after duke Robert's visit to Guernsey. By this mandate,[2] it would seem that the castle of Jerbourg had only recently been begun to be built, (nuper inchoatum fuit ad construendum,) and was not yet finished, although Edward the Second had ordered that it should be completed out of the revenues of the aforesaid isles. Des Roches was therefore commanded to carry this order into execution; but we think that the castle was never worthy of the name, and that its chief defences consisted of outer earthen embankments. The name of Jerbourg is derived by some from that of the engineer left in Guernsey by duke Robert, and who is said to have built the castle there; by others, from Cherbourg, which is supposed to be a corruption of "Cæsaris-Burgus;"[3] but may it not be far more correctly traced to the promontory of Jobourg

(1) At the Christmas Chief Pleas of 1566-7, the marsh and tunnel of *Mont Orgueil* are named. In the castle was the chapel of "Notre Dame des Marais."

(2) This mandate is given in Duncan's History, p. 579.

(3) Burgus; a castle, fort, or redoubt.

in the Cotentin, opposite to Alderney, to which, in name and locality, it bears a singular resemblance? The following description of that promontory by M. de Gerville appears almost to have been written for the Jerbourg of Guernsey. " Dans la partie N. O. du promontoire près du nez de Jobourg, j'ai reconnu les traces d'un petit camp romain, connu sous le nom de *Castel de Jobourg;* c'est un de ces camps-vigies (*exploratoria,*) qui bordent nos côtes et semblent avoir été destinés à surveiller les descentes des pirates saxons." [1] In the same manner the island of Lihou probably takes its name from cape Lihou, near Granville, as both are head-lands.

As we shall have to revert again to duke Robert's sojourn in Guernsey, we give the following extract from Du Moulin (p. 115) in proof of it:

" Pendant que Robert auoit encor les armes en main, il pense à remettre ses cousins Alfred & Edward en possession de l'Angleterre, iniustement occupée par Kanut: mais auant qu'y apporter de la violence, il tente par vn Ambassade si la douceur y pouuoit rien; Kanut ne veut ouyr parler de restitution: Parquoy suiuy de sa noblesse et gendarmerie il s'embarque à Fescan; sa flotte couloit assez heureusement, quand vne tempeste s'efleua & la porta en l'isle de Grenezay, où les vents les arresterent quinze iours: voyant le temps totalement contraire pour voguer en Angleterre, il commanda de relascher, & à Rabel ou Tanel Comte de Longueuille & Chambellan de Normandie, homme valeureux & grand capitaine, de courir la coste de Bretagne & piller tout ce qu'il trouueroit, pendant que luy descendu au mont de S. Michel, feroit vn gros de caualerie pour contraindre Alain à luy rendre l'hommage qu'il estoit obligé."

In the middle ages, the feudal system was at its height, and, in the tenth and eleventh centuries, these islands appear to have been reserved by the Norman dukes to be bestowed as benefices on favoured subjects. Benefices were at first usually granted for life only, but afterwards became hereditary. A natural result of hereditary benefices was that their possessors carved out portions to others to be held of themselves by a similar tenure, probably with additional servitudes. The ceremonies used in conferring a fief were chiefly three — homage, fealty, and investiture. Upon investiture commenced the duties which the vassal had agreed to perform; but the services of military tenure were in their nature so

(1) Recherches sur le Hague-dike et les premiers établissements militaires des Normands sur nos côtes; par M. de Gerville. The Hague-dike is an entrenchment, which enclosed the nine parishes adjoining Cape La Hague, and formed a vast citadel and defence against the North-men.

uncertain, that it is difficult to define or enumerate them.
Whoever held a benefice was bound to serve his sovereign in
the field. It is not within the province of this work to pursue
the subject further; but he who wishes to study the baneful
effects of feudalism on a small scale, may do so with advantage in the bailiwick of Guernsey, in which this remnant of a
barbarous age still exists, although necessarily with many
modifications, in the second half of the nineteenth century!

At the accession of duke[1] Robert I., in 1028, Guernsey
was divided into two great fiefs, on which the *seigneurs* had
to pay the *chefrente*, called *meslage*. The fief of Niel,
vicomte de St. Sauveur, comprised the parishes of St. Samson,
St. Peter-Port, St. Andrew, St. Martin, the Forest, and
Torteval. The parishes of the Vale, Câtel, St. Saviour, and
St. Peter-in-the-Wood, formed the fief of Ansquetil, vicomte
du Bessin, (or Bayeux,) part of which is now known as the
fief du Comte. This name is derived from its having belonged to the earls of Chester, into whose possession it came
through Renoulf, vicomte du Bessin, who obtained the earl-
dom of Chester from Henry I., when Richard, the second
earl, kinsman of Renoulf, perished A.D. 1120, in the wreck
of *La Blanche Nef*, (*Candida Navis*, the white ship,) with
prince William, near Barfleur, leaving no issue.

Robert, soon after his departure from Guernsey, as related
above, compelled Alain, duke of Britany, to sue for peace,
which he obtained through the mediation of the archbishop of
Rouen, uncle of the two dukes or counts. The treaty was
signed in the abbey of *Mont St. Michel;* and, in honor of the
occasion, both dukes evinced their liberality to that abbey.
Robert gave the half of Guernsey, which had been held *en fief*
by the vicomte du Bessin, who for some transgression appears to have forfeited it. But duke William, on attaining his
majority, restored the said fief to the vicomte du Bessin, son
and heir of the preceding; although, notwithstanding this
restitution, the abbey retained possession of the four churches
before named, with their tithes.

Nigel, or Niel, sieur de St. Sauveur, succeeded to the title
of vicomte du Cotentin, hereditary in his family since the
time of duke Richard, and continued to exercise it under
his successors, dukes Richard II. and III., and Robert. His
name figures frequently, and with honor, in the chronicles of
Normandy. Besides holding *in beneficio* a moiety of Guern-

(1) Before the Conquest, the Norman sovereigns styled themselves counts, thus:
COMES GRA: DEI DUX ET PRINCEPS NORMANNORUM; but, after the Conquest, they relinquished the title of count, because it was then common among their Norman subjects.

sey, he had in charge the castle in the Cotentin, *quod dicitur
Hulmé.*[1] This beneficiary or feudal fief in Guernsey appears
to have belonged to the title of vicomte du Cotentin, as
both reverted together to the ducal crown on the death of
the last *seigneur de St. Sauveur,* without heirs male. Nigel,
son and successor of the preceding, was one of the chiefs who
conspired against William; and it was during the vicomte's
exile in Britany that William gave to the abbey of Marmoutier the six churches in Guernsey, in the fief of Niel, as
already narrated. The expression twice repeated in William's charter, in reference to Niel's possessions in the island,
"videor habere in meo dominio," is remarkable, inasmuch as
it demonstrates that the estates of the refugee, although sequestered, were not forfeited—a fact proved by the charter
of Niel himself, by which he confirmed the donation of the
duke. Du Moulin speaks of him as "Neel, de St. Sauveur,
le viconte," and as "Neel, le viconte de Costentin," in his
catalogue of "*seigneurs*" who accompanied William at the
Conquest: he is best known by the former title.

We have said that parish churches existed in Guernsey
anterior to the conquest, and it is well to add that the chapel
of St. Apolline, in the parish of St. Saviour, is the only one
standing entire of the ecclesiastical structures in the island
prior to that period. This chapel consists of a chamber about
27 feet long by nearly 14 feet wide, having a narrow square-
headed opening or loop-hole at the east end, a rude round-
arched or segmental doorway, and a narrow window on the
south side, besides a smaller segmental doorway and window
on the north side. The whole is covered in by a thick and
ponderous vaulted roof. Of the date of the erection of this
chapel, which was only capable of admitting thirty or forty
persons, nothing is known, but it is evidently of great antiquity, and is considered the oldest building in Guernsey.

The islet of Lihou was in early times occupied by monks,
who were attracted thither by its lonely situation, and it soon
acquired an air of sanctity which rendered it a safe and quiet
spot for the residence of a prior, or, as has been erroneously
said, of an abbess and her nuns. The period of the erection
of the priory and chapel is unknown, but it could not be
later than the eleventh century, although the *Dédicace des
Eglises* fixes the consecration of the chapel in 1114. Towards
the close of the last or eighteenth century this chapel was

[1] Stapleton's Norman Exchequer.

entire, as regarded the walls and roof, the ornamental parts, which were of Caen stone, alone being mutilated. But soon after, during the revolutionary war with France, the lieutenant-governor, fearing that the building might be turned into some use by the enemy, ordered its complete demolition, which was effected by means of gunpowder. Sufficient ruins, however, are left to indicate the chapel, which was vaulted with stone, and consisted of a chancel and nave, with a square tower on the north-east side of the nave.

CHAPTER III.

WILLIAM THE CONQUEROR.

WILLIAM was only eight years of age when his father, duke Robert, died in his pilgrimage to Jerusalem, A.D. 1035; and he did not succeed him without much opposition, on account of his illegitimacy; but the sinister bar in that age was not insuperable in the succession to a throne. Mabillon cites a charter in which William himself took the title of Bastard: *Ego Guillelmus cognomento batardus, rex Angliæ.* This is the more surprising, as he would admit of no raillery on his birth. One of his most powerful opponents was finally his uncle, Mauger, archbishop of Rouen, son of duke Richard II. by a noble Danish lady; the Norman dukes long retaining an utter insensibility to the influence of *French* female charms. After William was quietly settled in his duchy, Mauger excommunicated him on pretence that his wife Mathilda was too nearly related to her husband. This indignity from a subject exasperated William much more than Mauger's pretensions to the dukedom; and in the year 1055 the primate was deposed and banished for life to the island of Guernsey, where he is said by the Norman historians to have cohabited with a young female of the name of Guille, by whom he had several children. Insular tradition has fixed his residence at "Saint," near Saint's Bay, in the parish of St. Martin. Du Moulin narrates that "Mauger, thus justly deposed, was banished to the island of Guernsey, near Coutances, where, says Walsingham, he fell into a state of madness, and had a miserable end. Others affirm that during his exile he gave his mind to the black arts, (*sciences noires*,) and that he had a familiar spirit, which warned him of his death while he was taking recreation in a boat; on which he said to the boatman: 'Let us land, for a certainty one of us two will be drowned to-day,' which happened, for, as they embarked at the port of Winchaut, he fell into the sea, and was drowned. His body, being found a few days afterwards, was interred in the church of Cherbourg."

When William was twenty years of age, Guy, count of Burgundy, claimed the duchy in right of his mother, Alice, daughter of duke Richard II., and was supported by many of the Norman barons; among them Niel, de St. Sauveur,[1] vicomte de Cotentin, and Renoulf, vicomte du Bessin, both just named as possessing large fiefs in Guernsey.

In the emergency, William consulted Mauger, archbishop of Rouen, before mentioned, who recommended him to apply to Henry, king of France, for assistance; and accordingly the duke repaired to Poissy, where the king was then residing. Henry not only promised aid, but engaged to lead his troops in person; and William was, soon after his return, joined by the French auxiliaries.

The combined forces advanced on Caen, where they learnt that the malcontents were encamped at *Val-des-Dunes*. The French under Henry, and the Normans under William, hastened forward in two divisions, and gained a complete victory, A.D. 1047. The battle of *Val-des-Dunes* is memorable in Norman history. Guy fled with the remnant of his cavalry to his strong fortress of Briosne, where he was soon compelled to surrender. William spared his life, but deprived him of Vernon and Briosne, and thenceforward refused to acknowledge him as one of his vassals: he also confiscated the estates of the rebel barons. Niel, de St. Sauveur, escaped into Britany; and, three years later, having rendered William a valuable service, he was reinstated in all his possessions; as appears to have been also the vicomte du Bessin, at least as regards his feudal property in Guernsey.

In the year 1061, Guernsey is stated to have been attacked by a new race of pirates, who, according to Berry, issued from the southern parts of France bordering the Bay of Biscay, and committed great ravages on the neighbouring coasts of Britany. Duke William was at Valognes when he received information of this attack, and he immediately dispatched troops under the command of his esquire, Sampson

(1) There are two St. Sauveurs on the opposite coast of Normandy; one eight miles S.S.W. of Valognes, population 2,774, and the other six miles N. of Coutances, population 1,950 souls.

d'Anneville, who landed at the harbour of St. Sampson. Being joined by the inhabitants, who had sought refuge in the castle of the Vale and other places of retreat, he defeated the invaders with much slaughter. Duke William is also said to have made large concessions of land in Guernsey to d'Anneville, as a reward for his valour; and in the thirty-ninth year of queen Elizabeth, (1597,) six royal commissioners[1] were appointed to examine the feudal tenures or manors existing in the island, when Thomas Fachion, laid claim to the *fief d'Anneville*, producing an extract from the Rolls of the Exchequer of Rouen, dated in 1061, which certified that duke William had granted, in fee farm, to the abbot of *Mont St. Michel*, in Normandy, and to Sampson d'Anneville, one half of the island of Guernsey, to be taken out of the western side of the said island, and to be equally divided among them. That such an extract was produced is certain; but it is utterly irreconcileable with the fact, as we have shown, that, during the dukedoms of Robert and his son William, Guernsey was divided (*à titre de fief*) between the powerful vicomtes of St. Sauveur and Bessin, (the latter better known as vicomte de Bayeux,) who would not quietly have submitted to this spoliation of their manorial rights.

The present fief of *d'Anneville* was doubtless named after Sampson, and may have been conferred upon him: it is situate in the parish of St. Sampson, and is the noblest tenure in Guernsey. The *seigneur* ranks after the clergy, and is bound, when the king visits the island, to attend him as his esquire. After various changes, the fief appears to have been sold by king Henry III. to William de Cheney, and was inherited by his descendant, Edmond de Cheney, warden of these islands in 1366: it afterwards descended by marriage into the family of Willoughby, and continued in their possession until 1509, in which year it was sold to Nicholas Fachion, gentleman usher to Henry VIII. The fief continued some years in the family of Fachion, long extinct in Guernsey, and then passed into that of Andros, in whose possession it now is.

The fief *le Comte* also belonged to the Fachions, and in 1630 was sold to Peter Priaulx by George Fachion. It subsequently was long the property of the Le Marchants, and now appertains to Mrs. Hutchesson, in right of her father, Charles Le Marchant. A great part of this fief lies in the

(1) The commissioners were Sir Thomas Leighton, knight, governor of Guernsey; George Paulet, bailiff of Jersey; Louis de Vic, bailiff of Guernsey; Henry Smith, of Guernsey; Amias de Carteret, of Jersey; and John de Vic, queen's procureur in Guernsey.

Câtel parish, and the *seigneur* is entitled to use a seal, which has the appearance of great antiquity. It represents a knight in armour, on foot, drawing a sword; his head is surrounded by a glory, and above his shoulders are the letters S. G. It was probably intended to represent St. George, as it is near the ruined chapel of that name that the court of the fief is held. On a scroll surrounding the figure is the following legend: SIGILL **** CURIE COMIT. The second word is so obliterated, that it cannot be deciphered.

The only other feudal court entitled to a seal is the court of the fief St. Michel. The seal represents the archangel vanquishing the devil, with the legend LANEL. S. SENESCHAL. DU. VALLE.

In an old MS. said to be a copy of an inquest drawn up by Fressingfield and Ditton, who in 1309, during the reign of Edward II., were sent over to the island to hold assizes, it is asserted that in addition to the grants made to the abbot of *Mont St. Michel* and Sampson d'Anneville, duke William I. also bestowed a tenement in fee farm on John de Jerbourg, who was appointed ducal cupbearer whenever the duke visited Guernsey, and also *châtelain*, or keeper of Jerbourg. This assertion is, however, disproved not only by Jerbourg forming part of the fief of the vicomte de St. Sauveur, as already mentioned, but by numerous writs to be found among the records of the fourteenth century. The fief of Jerbourg appears to have been conferred upon a remote ancestor of the present family of De Sausmarez by Henry, tenth duke of Normandy, afterwards Henry II. of England. In the twenty-seventh year of Edward I., at a court of chief pleas held in Guernsey, in the presence of the judges of assize, Matthew de Sausmarez did homage for this fief. When the promontory was fortified in the reigns of Edward II. and III., it belonged to the said Matthew de Sausmarez,[1] or to his successor of the same name, who was appointed hereditary captain, or *châtelain* of the place. The fief of Jerbourg was subsequently incorporated with, or took the title of, that of Sausmarez, by which latter name it is now known. Among the privileges attached to the fief of Sausmarez, there was one which deserves mention. Whenever the *seigneur* wished to cross over to Jersey, his tenants were obliged to convey him thither once a year, on receiving three sols in money

---

(1) A.D. 1325, Ann. 18, Edw. II. Gernesey.—"Plitum de quo waranto cora Hen. Spigurnill & Willo de Demr justic. itinantibus ibidem tangen, libtates clam. p Matheum de Saumaryse p totam. terram suam in Gerburgh plene plitatur hic cui adjudicatur dicte libtates."—*Abbreviatio Placitorum.*

and their dinner; but it does not appear that they were bound to bring him back. The fief of Sausmarez remained in the family down to the year 1553, when it came into the possession of John Andros, in right of Judith de Sausmarez, his mother; but in 1748 it reverted, by purchase, to the descendants of the original proprietors, whose property it is at this day. The above John Andros was the ancestor of Sir Edmund Andros, who held the fief, as did his father Amias, and both will be noticed in the sequel.

In the year 1051, duke William passed over from Normandy to England on a visit to Edward the Confessor, and returned after a short sojourn. In 1065, Harold, son of earl Godwin, proceeded to Normandy, but with what object is doubtful: the Norman chroniclers affirm that he was ordered by Edward to inform William that he had named him, the duke, as his successor to the throne of England. However improbable this may be, Harold was wrecked on the coast of Ponthieu, and seized by Guy, count of that province, who incarcerated him in a fortress. When William heard of his detention, he ordered Guy, who was his vassal, to release Harold, which he did, and delivered him to the duke. At this time William was engaged in a war with Britany, to serve in which Harold cheerfully volunteered, in the chivalrous spirit of that age: in command of a detachment of Normans, the English prince attacked the besiegers of Dol, and compelled them to retire. He then laid siege to Dinan, which soon surrendered. For these services, William conferred the honor of knighthood on Harold.

In January, 1066, Edward the Confessor died, and Harold lost not a moment in seizing on the throne, notwithstanding his promise to do all in his power to secure the sceptre for William, after the demise of the king. When the duke heard of the accession of Harold, he dispatched a messenger to him to require the observance of the promise he had made while in Normandy; but Harold not only refused to do so, but forthwith expelled from England all the Normans who had enjoyed the protection of Edward. He further desired the messenger to tell William that he acknowledged having sworn to deliver up the English throne to him at the death of Edward, but that such oath was not binding, having been extorted by compulsion; and moreover, that having been chosen by the people, he could not transfer the sceptre to a foreigner, without treason to his country.

William now undertook the memorable invasion, to which his barons were at first greatly opposed, as they disliked crossing the sea, of which element they appear to have been much afraid ; but they were won over, and, with the clergy, contributed largely to the outfit. By a papal bull, the duke was invested with the title of king of England ! It was read in all the churches throughout the duchy, and the enthusiasm of the Normans was soon raised to the highest pitch. William published his declaration of war in all the neighbouring countries, and offered pay and pillage to every man who would serve him with lance, sword, or cross bow. Numbers flocked to his standard from near and far, from Maine and Anjou, from Poitou and Britany,[1] from France and Flanders, from Aquitaine and Burgundy, from Piedmont and the banks of the Rhine ; so that, in fact, the invading army was composed of many nations. The rendezvous of the fleet and the troops was at the mouth of the Dive, whence, after a detention of a month, a southerly breeze carried the Norman navy to St. Valery, near Dieppe. The number of vessels composing this armament is variously stated, some writers declaring that there were 3,000, while the Chronicle of Normandy gives 907 large vessels, besides small craft. Thierry says that there were 400 large vessels and above 1,000 boats of transport. Wace, on the authority of his father, who served in the expedition, reduces the number to 609 ; but this is evidently too low, as the detailed list of the vessels, furnished by the different barons, gives 781. Supposing each vessel to carry fifty men, and this is a high estimate, there must have been at least 1,000 vessels. That the ships were of no great burthen may be inferred from the Bayeux tapestry, on which the process of ship building is represented ; the vessels all appear very low in the hull, and the men are seen drawing them to the sea by ropes. This very curious relic of that age, which is still preserved at Bayeux, is supposed to have been the work of William's queen, Mathilda, and her female attendants. The fleet put to sea on the 29th of September, 1066, the day of the festival of St. Michael. The vessel of William took the lead, the white consecrated banner, given him by the pope, at its mast-head, and bearing a cross on its ensign : she outsailed all the others, and on the following morning dropped anchor off the coast of Sussex, to await the arrival of her consorts. This vessel had been presented to William by his queen ; its vanes were gilded — on its

(1) De Moulin states that there were above 5,060 Bretons in the expedition.

crimson sails were painted three lions,[1] says Thierry, the arms of the Normans—and at its head was the figure of a child, armed with a bow and arrow, and ready to let fly. In the day it was distinguished by its splendid decorations, and in the night by the light at its topmast. The debarkation was effected at Pevensey, near to Hastings, without any opposition. The archers landed first—then the knights, with their horses—and, lastly, the mechanics and other followers of the army, which consisted of 60,000 (?) combatants. A camp was immediately formed and fortified with timber. Before the battle, William exhorted his men to take vengeance for the massacre in England of the Danes, their kinsmen, which had occurred more than three score years before, and for which other Danes had speedily and signally revenged themselves. The Danes, moreover, had subsequently become one people with the Anglo-Saxons, by compact, or intermarriage and language, whereas the Normans had abandoned the speech of their ancestors, the North-men. But pretexts never fail those whose end is conquest. The result of this invasion is so well known, that it will suffice to add that Harold and his two brothers nobly fell on the battle field; and at nine o'clock on the evening of the 14th of October, 1066, the victory of Hastings was achieved. "The Normans," says Raleigh, "grew better shipwrights than either the Danes or Saxons, and made the last conquest of this land—a land which can never be conquered whilst the kings thereof keep the dominion of the seas."

Of the vast Norman fleet, only two vessels were lost, in one of which was the astrologer; *(astrologue;)* and in consequence, says Du Moulin, the duke took occasion to blame the men of that profession, as predicting the good fortune of others, and not foreseeing the evil which pursues themselves. The carnage at the battle of Hastings has been variously estimated. The MS. chronicle of De Thou states that 67,654 of the English were slain; but this is a miscopy or a wilful untruth, as it appears that their numbers in the field did not exceed 25,000 combatants. According to De Thou, of the invaders 6,013 men were killed, while Ordericus Vitalis raises the number to 15,000 men. Du Moulin gives the loss as mentioned by these two authorities, but, evidently unable to account for their manifest improbability as regards the English, offers no computation of his own. Another Norman

---

(1) We rather think that the armorial bearings of Normandy at that time were *two* lions, or leopards, *passant, guardant.*

historian, Goube, boldly says, " that 67,000 English and 6,000 Normans perished in this memorable combat, which lasted above twelve hours"! Thierry, more discreet, is silent on the subject of the losses of either army.

William introduced the Norman feudal tenure into England, and divided such part of it as did not belong to the church, and was not reserved for himself, into 700 baronies or great fiefs, which he bestowed on his friends and those who had distinguished themselves in his service : these baronies were sub-divided into 60,215 knights' fees, or smaller fiefs. No Englishmen had any of the first, and few only were fortunate enough to receive any of the second.

Du Moulin gives a " Catalogue des Grands Seigneurs Normands" and " Seigneurs Normands," who accompanied William ; and in these lists there occur the names of :

de Bailleul, de Beauchamp, de Carterays, de Cary,
du Chesne,[1] Corbet, de la Lande,[2] de Lisle,
de La Mare, de Marey, des Moulins, des Ports,
des Preaux,[3] le Sauvage, de Somery, and de Tracy.

Families bearing similar surnames, or nearly so, have long been seated in Guernsey, or were anciently so ; but we question de Somery being the same as de Sausmarez, which signifies a salt marsh. There is, however, no documentary evidence of these islands having furnished either men or shipping for the conquest ; that they did so is very probable, because it may be presumed that Niel, viscount of Cotentin, one of the most powerful barons in the Conqueror's train, induced, if he did not command, some of his numerous tenants and vassals in Guernsey to follow him ; and, moreover, the Guernsey fishermen were as good sailors as existed in that age ; but the point cannot now be decided, and must ever remain a matter of uncertainty. By the Domesday Book,[4] it appears that the bishop of Coutances was endowed by the Conqueror with no less than 280 manors in England ! Among the commissioners appointed to compile Domesday Book, there are the names of Anquetil, Bouteiller, Le Clerc,

(1) Edmund de Cheneye, or Chesne, was bailiff of Guernsey from 1409 to 1412.

(2) John de la Lande was bailiff of Guernsey in 1350.

(3) Preaux is in the arrondissement of Rouen. In the Monasticon Anglicanum, vol. ii. p. 889, there is an account of an embassy to Edward the Confessor, by the then possessors of the castle and estate of Preaux.

(4) The Domesday Book contained a survey of all the lands in England, (excepting Northumberland, the greater part of Cumberland, the northern part of Westmoreland, and Durham,) made by the order of William the Conqueror. It consists of two volumes, written in Latin, on parchment, commenced some time prior to its completion in 1086, and now in excellent preservation at the Chapter House of Westminster Abbey.

Giffard, Gille, De la Mare, Dumont, Normand, and De Simon, which are still borne by native families of the Anglo-Norman Isles.

From the catalogue in Du Moulin, just cited, we extract the names of such of the chiefs who accompanied William in the invasion, and whose names have since become English:

Mallet,[1] de Basquerville,[2] de Tancarville, du Puys,[3] Desbiars,[4] d'Aubigny,[5] de Lacy, de Montfort, de St. Jean,[6] du Bois, de Roumilly,[7] de Bernieres,[8] du Tourneur,[9] de la Haye,[10] de Monbray,[11] de Mortemer, de St. Clair, de Harcourt, d'Evreux,[12] de Montgommery, de Courtenay, de Vernon, Cardon,[13] d'Anvers, de Hasting, de Camois,[14] de Hautains,[15] de St. Aubin, de Fienes, de Turbeville, Gorges, de Spenser, de Brus,[16] Bouteiller, St. Quentin, de St. Mor,[17] de St. Leger, de St. Vigour,[18] de Rivers, de Ros, de Burnel, Biset, Basset, de Musgrave, de Mautravers, du Chesne,[19] du Vesey, Bertran, Pigot, de Foliot, Talbot, de Sanford, de Vaux, Besil, de la Rocheford,[20] de Neville, de Percy, de Greville, de Mandeville, de Bohon, de Rodes,[21] Bourdon, Hansard, Montaigu, de Grez,[22] de Pomeray, de Ferriere, de Quincy, de Courcy, and de Lestrange. Wake, who also accompanied William, was a Fleming, and a family of that name was subsequently possessed of immense landed property in England.

The conquest of England, perhaps the most momentous event in the middle ages, caused no change in the constitution and government of these islands. William, who preferred his title of duke of Normandy to that of king of England, died at Rouen, September, 1087, in his sixty-third year: he was buried in the abbey, named St. Stephen, built by himself, at Caen; and the following simple inscription is placed there on his tomb, which we have at two distant intervals visited with the greatest interest: HIC SEPULTUS EST, INVICTISSIMUS GULLIELMUS, CONQUESTOR, NORMANIÆ DUX, ET ANGLIÆ REX, HUJUSCE DOMUS CONDITOR, QUI OBIIT ANNO MLXXXVII.

It is difficult to estimate truly the character of the Conqueror, because it has been so oppositely drawn by the Norman and English historians; and yet this was to be expected. It is certain, however, that William greatly surpassed all contemporary sovereigns in capacity for command,—in war unquestionably, and probably in peace. None can deny his courage, his sagacity, his vigour, and his vigilance; and that he overcame difficulties which long appeared insuperable. He was in short the hero of his age. On the other hand, he

---

(1) ? Malet. (2) Baskerville. (3) Dupuis. (4) Desbarres. (5) Daubeney. (6) St. John. (7) Romilly. (8) Berners. (9) Turner. (10) Hay. (11) ? Mowbray. (12) Devereux. (13) ? Carden. (14) Camoys. (15) Hawtayne. (16) Bruce. (17) St. Maur, or Seymour. (18) Vigors. (19) Chesney. (20) Rochfort. (21) Rhodes. (22) ? Grey.

was cruel and perfidious, and the excesses which he committed at Mantes and York cannot be extenuated; but the foulest blot on his memory is the execution of the English nobleman, Waltheof. Under his tyrannic rule, lands, honors, and power, were exclusively bestowed on the Normans, in whose favor justice was usually outraged; and the English bore indeed a heavy yoke of bondage. William ordered that all law pleadings and statutes should be in the Norman language; and, to prevent nightly meetings and conspiracies, he instituted the *curfew*, or "cover fire bell," at the sound of which, every night at eight o'clock, all fires and lights were to be extinguished. In 1078, he finished the tower of London, for the purpose of overawing the people. According to the spirit of his time, he was considered truly religious, because he founded abbeys, and patronized the monks.[1] William was of tall stature, but very stout—the face full and red—of an expression of countenance sufficiently disagreeable, and which shewed without disguise the violence of his passions. His personal strength was so great, that while on horseback he easily strang his bow, which even the strongest man could with difficulty bend. On his death-bed, he repented of some of his atrocities, and ordered all the reparation in his power. It is perhaps some excuse for him that, according to Ordericus Vitalis,[2] the English were rude and almost illiterate, and we know that severity often followed insurrection. A beautiful equestrian statue has recently been erected to his memory at Falaise, in Normandy, his birth-place.

William gave to the abbey of *Mont St. Michel*, in the bishoprick of Coutances, the church of Alderney,[3] with the tithe and terrâ quatuor boum, or as much land as four oxen could plough in one day; and the church of Sark, with the tithe, all the other revenues, and eighteen acres of land. This grant is stated to have been in compensation for the fief, comprising the four western parishes of Guernsey, restored to the vicomte du Bessin, as already narrated.

(1) "Il estoit grandement pieux, faisoit de grandes aumosnes, cherissoit les religieux ; il donna presque à toutes les abbayes de Normandie quelques revenus de la mer."—*Du Moulin.*

(2) Ordericus was an Englishman, who, when ten years old, passed into Normandy, A.D. 1084, where he became professed in the monastery of Eu.

(3) "Aurigny, l'Arica de Ptolémée, ne forme qu'une paroisse. On croit qu'il y a eu un couvent de filles au lieu nommé *Nunnery*, c'est-à-dire, la Nonnerie, et l'on y montre des ruines qui ont dû lui appartenir. Il y a eu une chapelle dédiée à Saint Michel, auprès du cimetière, ou dans le cimetière de ce nom.

"Le chapitre de Coutances avait une partie des produits de l'île d'Aurigny, et l'on possède encore l'acte d'une convention relative à leur partage, passée entre les officiers du dit chapitre et ceux de Henri II., roi d'Angleterre, vers l'an 1240."—*Histoire des Evêques de Coutances, par Lecanu,* p. 227.

E

The Conqueror left three sons, Robert, William, and Henry: to Robert, the eldest, he bequeathed Normandy; to William, England; and to Henry, 5,000 marks of silver. When Henry enquired what service the money could be to him without an inch of land, his father replied prophetically: "The day will come when you will unite the two portions of your elder brothers, and when you will reign alone over the states which I leave them,"—a prediction which was fully verified.

ROBERT II.—1087 to 1106.

Robert possessed all the courage and daring of his ancestors; but he was prodigal, thoughtless, and vacillating. Requiring money to satisfy his wants, he applied to his brother Henry for a loan, which was refused without some security, upon which Robert proposed to sell the "Cotentin," containing about one-third of Normandy, for 3,000 *livres* of silver. Henry accepted this offer, and thus the Cotentin, with doubtless these islands, was transferred to him: he governed it with wisdom and moderation, maintained order and peace, and established public gratuitous schools, in which the young men learnt the exercise of arms.

Henry, now styled Comte du Cotentin, passed over to England in the summer of 1088 to claim of his brother William, surnamed Rufus, the property of their mother, Mathilda. Having obtained a portion of it, he returned to the "Cotentin;" but it being intimated to his brother Robert, that his only object in visiting England was to induce William to invade the duchy of Normandy, Robert sent troops to all the ports of the "Cotentin," when Henry was arrested, and imprisoned at Bayeux: he was set at liberty after some time.

The intrigues of Rufus, who aspired to Normandy, and the misgovernment of Robert, reduced the duchy to a state of lawless insubordination. The "Cotentin" alone was quiet under the wise administration of Henry, who now meditated avenging himself both on Robert, for his detention at Bayeux, and on Rufus, for withholding some portion of his mother's property. Henry fortified the towns of Cherbourg, Avranches, Coutances, and Gavré: he exercised his troops, and the malcontent Norman barons came to increase his ranks and his court. But soon after, to thwart the views of William, Henry found it expedient to assist Robert, and with that purpose reached Rouen, the capital, on the 3d of November, 1090, the very day that the malcontents within had agreed to give up that city to the adherents of William.

The plans of William were thus disconcerted; but Normandy continued to be the scene of domestic troubles. The year following, an English army landed at Eu, and Robert, unable to face it, obtained peace by giving up to William Cherbourg, *Mont St. Michel*, and many other strong fortresses. William, on his part, agreed to restore their English estates to all those barons who had been faithful to Robert. The two brothers also reciprocally covenanted that in case either should die without issue, the survivor should inherit his territorial possessions.

This treaty was necessarily displeasing to Henry, for Cherbourg and *Mont St. Michel* belonged to him. Knowing how little justice he could expect at the hands of his brothers, he strongly garrisoned the Mount, and fortified his other castles. The combined forces of Robert and William entered the "Cotentin," and compelled Henry to seek shelter in *Mont St. Michel.*[1] Henry made a gallant defence, and killed many of the besiegers in his sallies; but, at the end of fifteen days, want of water compelled him to surrender. He retired into Britany, and thence into the French Vexin, where he remained two years in exile and poverty. William, having possessed himself of *Mont St. Michel*, returned to England.

HENRY I.—1106 to 1185.

In August, 1100, William was killed, whether accidentally is doubtful, while hunting in the New Forest. Henry, happening to be of the party, immediately seized the crown of England; and thus was Robert a second time deprived of it by a younger brother, who is known in English history as Henry I., or Beauclerc. Robert soon after arrived from the Holy Land in Normandy, where, after a few years, his government became so distasteful, that his own subjects appealed to Henry for redress. Accordingly, in 1106, Henry entered the duchy with a numerous army, and completed its conquest. Robert and his son William were made prisoners — the latter escaped from confinement, and was subsequently killed in warfare at Alost; but the former, after being imprisoned in several fortresses for twenty-seven years, died in Cardiff castle, in his eightieth year. Robert was at first permitted to walk in the neighbourhood, attended by guards; but, having one day seized a horse and attempted to escape, he was conducted

(1) Le Mont Saint Michel est assis sur un rocher dans la mer qui baigne les côtes de la Normandie, à quatre lieues d'Avranches. Il y avait une célèbre abbaye, qui, sous le règne de Louis XI., donna lieu à l'institution de l'ordre militaire de Saint Michel.—*Goube.*

back to his prison, and, by the order of his own brother, Henry, deprived of sight! He endured his long and tedious captivity with a dignity and resignation worthy of a better fate.

We have stated that, by the bequest of the Conqueror, Normandy was severed from the sovereignty of England, and it so continued for nineteen years, until both countries were reunited by Henry I., in 1106. It was prince William, the only legitimate son of Henry I., who was shipwrecked and drowned in the year 1120, while on his passage, in the *Blanche Nef*, from Normandy to England; and thus all the good fortune of the father was blasted in a moment. Truly may it be said of this disaster: *Nullam potentiam esse potentem,* —" that no power is powerful enough to preserve itself." Henry never smiled again, and his own conscience must have reproached him acutely for his cruelty to his brother Robert; for there are times when coward conscience will resume her authority. The English historians, however, viewed the death of prince William not only as a visitation of Providence for the crimes of the father, but for the personal vices of the son. The prince had openly manifested his dislike to the English, and was wont to say that if ever he became king, he would make the wretched Anglo-Saxons draw ploughs like oxen. But the Caskets rocks, near Alderney, were not the scene of the calamity, as is often supposed. It is the more singular that this historical error[1] should have arisen, because William of Malmesbury correctly wrote: "The king's son set sail from Barfleur just before twilight, and the carelessness of the intoxicated crew drove the ship on a rock, which rose above the waves *not far from shore.*" The *Blanche Nef* struck on a rock called the "Catte-raze," near Barfleur, which uncovered only at low water.

Henry I. may be said to have been emphatically the sovereign of the Anglo-Norman Isles, because he ruled them (probably) first as comte du Cotentin, next as king of England, and, lastly, as duke of Normandy; and it was perhaps owing to his favor and protection that the three oldest churches existing in Guernsey were built during his reign, viz. St. Sampson's, 1111; the Vale, 1117; and Torteval, 1130.[2] Although nothing can excuse Henry for his treatment of his brother Robert, yet he was eminent for his great learning, his personal bravery, and the vigilance of his government. He abolished the *curfew* bell, established a standard for

(1) Falle, in his first edition, fell into the same error, but corrected it in the second.
(2) Rebuilt in 1816.

weights and measures, and signed the charter which proved the origin of the English liberties; but, like his father, William the Conqueror, his character has been very differently estimated. English historians assert that Henry set at nought his charters, and violated his promises to his people without shame. "The Norman clergy in that reign," says the contemporary Eadmer, "were more wolves than shepherds. No virtue nor merit could advance an Englishman." Matthew Paris adds that to be called an Englishman was an insult. Allowance, however, must be made for the outraged feelings of the Anglo-Saxon or conquered race.

HENRY II.—1144 to 1189.

Henry I. died in 1135 without surviving male issue, but leaving a daughter, Mathilda or Maud, wife of Geoffrey Plantagenet, count of Anjou.[1] During the usurpation of the throne of England by Stephen, count of Bologne, the Normans were for several years distracted by the claims of the various competitors for their duchy; but in 1144, Rouen, which was held for Stephen, capitulated to the count of Anjou, when Normandy submitted to Mathilda, and their eldest son Henry was acknowledged duke, the count reserving to himself the regency during Henry's minority. In September, 1151, the count of Anjou died; and Henry, then nineteen years of age, received the ducal sword, mantle, and tiara, in presence of the barons of Normandy. During the contest between Henry, who was the first of the Plantagenets of England, and Stephen, the islanders, as Normans, adhered faithfully to the former; but from the period of his accession to the English throne, in 1154, they have continued for seven centuries sincerely attached to the British crown. This connection has accordingly produced rights, immunities, and privileges, of two distinct characters: first, those which belonged to the islanders, as Normans, before the conquest; and, secondly, those subsequently conceded to them by the sovereigns of England, and ratified by parliament. The former regard the islanders as ancient subjects of Normandy, the latter as British subjects.

Among the privileges enjoyed by the islanders, one of the most important is their not being subject to the acts of the British parliament, unless they are specially named therein.

[1] "Surnommé *Plante-Genest*, à cause de l'habitude qu'il avait de mettre en guise de plume une branche de genêt fleuri à son chaperon." *Thierry.*—Surnamed Plantagenet, in consequence of a custom which he had of wearing on his cap a sprig of broom in blossom, instead of a feather.

Moreover, to give any act of parliament validity in these bailiwicks, it must be transmitted to the Royal Courts of Jersey and Guernsey, with an order from the sovereign in council, when the bailiff and jurats examine it, to ascertain if it trenches on their ancient privileges; and if it do, they forward a remonstrance to the throne; but in no case does the act acquire the force of law before it is registered on the insular records, and thus time is obtained for the reconsideration of any objectionable clauses. In this manner the Royal Courts have a co-ordinate jurisdiction with the British legislature in framing laws for the islands, and this privilege they derive from their Norman origin. A similar rule obtained before the revolution in the French provinces, whose local parliaments possessed the right of verifying and registering the royal edicts, and also of suspending them, if they militated against their privileges.

Henry II., king of England, and tenth duke of Normandy, was possessed, in right of his father, of the provinces of Anjou and Touraine; in that of his mother, of Normandy and Maine; and in that of his wife, of Guienne, Poictou, Xaintonge, Auvergne, Perigord, Angoumois, and the Limousin. On the death of his brother Geoffrey, who had been elected count of Britany, Henry declared himself his heir, and, enforcing his claim by the sword, a majority, if not the whole, of the Bretons were compelled to submit to his usurpation. When they revolted some years afterwards, he defeated them in a pitched battle, and captured Dol after a short siege. Thus, with these many provinces, Henry was possessed of about one-third of modern France, or a territory extending from the Seine to the Garonne.—Guernsey does not appear to have been affected by his domestic troubles, or his consequent wars with France, as during his reign no less than three churches were built in the island, viz. St. Saviour's, the Forest, and St. Peter's-in-the-Wood.

According to an extract from an old register in the abbey of Cherbourg, duke Henry II., before his accession to the throne of England, made a grant of the island of Herm to certain religious persons, with the privilege of fishing, &c.; and in this document, which was without date, and in other respects imperfect, he was styled, Dux Normaniæ et Comes Andegarviæ. (Anjou.)

It may be here cursorily mentioned, that in the year 1091 an earthquake in the "Cotentin," and which extended to these islands, threw down the copper cock of the cathedral of Coutances, that cathedral having been built in 1056; and that there was another earthquake more disastrous in 1161. In 1095 commenced a famine of several years duration, which terminated in 1104 by a frightful plague in the islands. In 1149 the famine was so great, that even the "seigneurs" could with difficulty procure a few oats to make bread, while the count of Anjou, regent for his son, duke Henry, caused a butcher at Coutances to be hanged for selling human flesh, that of one of his parents, who had died of hunger.

A manuscript of the abbey of *Mont St. Michel* makes mention, about the year 1150, of the chapel of St. Gregory in the island of Guernsey. This chapel was evidently the same existing at St. George, in the Câtel parish, in the middle of the last century, and in which the court of the fief le Comte was held. In 1157, a clerk was instituted by the abbot to the said chapel of St. Gregoire. In the twelfth century the names of St. Gregoire and St. George were often confounded.

CASTLE CORNET.

With the exception possibly of Gouray, now Mont Orgueil, castle, in Jersey, no fortress in the Anglo-Norman islands possesses a greater historical interest than Castle Cornet; and this interest is heightened by its picturesque appearance, standing as it does in the sea, almost half a mile from the pier and town of St. Peter-Port, and in bold relief of the clear waters which encompass it. The tiny islet on which this ancient castle is built is scarcely three quarters of a mile in circumference; and small and insignificant as this spot is, nevertheless, for about five centuries, it served to protect the only roadstead and town of the island from pirates and other enemies; as the erection of Fort George, which completely commands Castle Cornet, was only begun in the year 1780. The exact period of the commencement of the castle, which in the lapse of ages has received very considerable additions, is not known; and we consider that every account, which dates its origin anterior to the year 1204, when Normandy was wrested from John, is apocryphal. While Guernsey was annexed to that duchy, there was no necessity for such a fortress, as, although the Normans had frequent contests with the Bretons, the scenes of those wars were chiefly in Upper Normandy, of which Rouen is the capital, as Caen is of Lower Normandy. The Rev. J. C. C. Ubele, D.D., of Alderney, "in a very ingenious and learned *Inquiry into the*

Ancient Names of the Islands enumerated in the Itinerarium Maritimum Antoninianum," as given by Berry, says: "From Jethou the boat went to the fortress or Castle Cornet of Guernsey." "That the fortress, now called Cornet, was originally constructed by the Romans, is not denied"!! Now, there is not the slightest proof that the Romans ever formed a settlement in Guernsey, and much less that they erected a castle in any part of it. The islet is said by some to have been fortified about the year 1145, by Rodolphe de Valmont, who was sent from Normandy by the count of Anjou, regent for his son, duke Henry, afterwards Henry II. of England, during Stephen's usurpation of the English crown, to place Guernsey in a state of defence; but de Valmont visited the island as a justiciary to hold assizes, and was not a military personage. The earliest mention in ancient records that we can discover of the castle, under the name of Cornet, is in the reign of Edward III.; but the islet was undoubtedly fortified above fifty years before his accession to the throne, in 1327. The castle is mentioned, but not named, in an order of Edward I., dated Windsor, March 2, 1275, authorising the levy of certain dues on shipping, if a quay or pier were constructed, "inter castrum nostrum ibidem et villum nostram de portu Sancti Petri," between our castle there and our town of the port of Saint Peter."[1] Many conjectures have been hazarded by speculative or ingenious men, as to the true etymology of its name of Cornet: by some, it is derived from that of a guard-house existing in the twelfth century, near to Rozel, in Normandy, called Cor Nez; by others, from the fanciful resemblance of the original construction to a horn; (in French, "cornet;") but we conceive these derivations to be utterly hypothetical. According to the "*Glossaire de la Langue Romane,*" (Paris, 1808,) the word Cornet, from the eleventh to the sixteenth centuries, signified *lieu retiré, caché*—a retired place, secluded, or which may also bear the interpretation of a place of refuge; and we think it far more probable that the castle took its name from that of the islet, which is said to have been called Cornet before it was fortified. There formerly existed some manuscript accounts, in French, of the dedication of the various parish churches in the island, entitled "*La Dédicace des Eglises,*"[2] by which it appears that Sir Peter Cornet was governor of Guernsey in the year 1312; and if these accounts

(1) The order is given in Berry's History, p. 162.
(2) These manuscripts were printed and published in Guernsey, in 1850.

were not now believed to be of very doubtful authority, we should rather derive the name of the castle from this functionary. It is related in the *Dédicace*, that at the consecration of the church of St. Peter-Port, there were present sixteen brothers of the name of Cornet, the sons of the same father and mother. Probably this is also fabulous, and certain it is that the surname of Cornet, if it ever existed in Guernsey, has long been extinct there. There was anciently a family of the name of Cornet in the bailiwick and town of Falaise, in Normandy;[1] and in the Exchequer Rolls of that province, for the year 1198, membr. 9 recto & verso, the names of Gervais, Luke, and Matthew Cornet occur.—Among the charters belonging to the bishoprick and chapter of Bayeux is found the sale of a house at Bayeux by William Cornet and Cecilia his wife, in 1288.—Among the charters deposited in the Archives du Calvados, occur the names of Gervais, Gerard, Matthew, and Robert Cornet.—Hays Cornet was a nun in the priory of Villers Canivet, founded in 1140 by Roger de Moubray.[2]

The tower of Beauregard, which stood on an eminence near the top of the steep street of Cornet, and commanded the town of St. Peter-Port, is also said to have been raised by the same Rodolphe de Valmont; but it was apparently built about the year 1350, after the strong hold of Jerbourg had been captured, and when Edward III. ordered the town to be walled in. In a warrant or commission issued by that monarch, in 1376, Thomas de Beauchamp, "chivaler," was appointed "custodem castri nostri de Cornet, ac turris nostri de Beauregard in insulâ de Gerneseye;" and this is the first mention we find of the tower. No remains of it exist at this day; but that it was maintained as late as the year 1460, appears by a commission addressed by Richard Nevil, the renowned earl of Warwick, lord of these islands, to John Le Marchant, as captain of the tower, the locality of which still bears the name of *La Tour de Beauregard*.

(1) We have searched in vain in the Fœdera and other volumes of English printed old records for the surname of Cornet, and doubt if it ever existed in England—certainly not of any note. From the reign of Edward III. inclusive, there exists no trace of any family of the name of Cornet being seated in Guernsey, so that, in the short period of fifteen years, the sixteen brothers said to have been present at the consecration of the church of St. Peter-Port, in 1312, must have disappeared from the island.

(2) We are indebted to John Métivier, Esq., for this summary: having sojourned in Normandy for the purpose, he has formed a very valuable collection of documents relative to the early history of Guernsey.

CHAPTER IV.

JOHN.—1199 to 1216.

WE devote a separate chapter to the reign of this detestable monarch, and to that of his worthless son and successor Henry III.; because we conceive it is not fitting that the annals of two such bad sovereigns should be intermingled with the memorials of better men. Indeed, had history from the earliest times been written more in the spirit of truth and less in that of adulation, in reference to princes, their evil passions might have been restrained, and their deeds would be now less open to censure and reproach. . It is, however, perhaps some slight palliation for the wretched John, that he lived in a barbarous age, in which kings seldom bore a rival near the throne.

John was in Normandy when he heard of the death of his brother Richard, Cœur de Lion, who was mortally wounded at the siege of a castle in Guienne, and whose rightful heir was their nephew, Arthur, son of their deceased brother Geoffrey, born prior to John. The young Arthur was duke of Britany, in right of his mother, heiress of that duchy. But Richard, when dying, declared John successor to all his dominions. John hurried to Rouen, and, having secured Normandy, passed into England, and without opposition possessed himself of the throne. Arthur, when only in his sixteenth year, after marching into Poitou, laid siege to Mirebeau, which town he captured; but the castle defied his attacks, until it was relieved by John in person. A peace ensued, but John basely violated it by imprisoning his nephew Arthur, first in the castle of Falaise, and afterwards in the tower of Rouen. Here he is said to have been stabbed to the heart by John, April 3, 1203, while on his knees imploring mercy; and when the Bretons heard of the murder of their duke, they united in one generous burst of indignation. Constance, the mother of the young prince, and the barons invoked the aid of Philip, king of France, who cited John to answer for his crime; but the vile culprit, refusing to appear, was found guilty by the French peers, and declared to have forfeited not only Normandy, but all the other provinces which he held from the crown of France.

Philip now quickly invaded Normandy at the head of a powerful army, and, being supported by the Bretons, who had already taken *Mont St. Michel*, Avranches, and the country as far as Caen, the two armies formed a junction in the neighbourhood of the last named city. The French proceeded from victory to victory, while John passed his time in pleasure, until at last the only two places of note which remained to the English were *Château Gaillard* and Rouen. The former stood on an eminence overhanging the Seine, whose waters flowed at its base, and it was considered the rampart of Normandy. The defence was entrusted to the earl of Leicester; and so well did he resist every attack, that the siege was finally converted into a blockade. At length, Leicester was reduced to the greatest extremities from the scantiness of provision; and he applied to John for assistance. The king in reply thanked the earl and the garrison for their courage, and earnestly entreated them not to capitulate; adding, however, that if food failed them, then Leicester was to follow the orders of Peter de Preaux and two others. After a desperate resistance of six months, the earl was compelled to surrender the castle, and the victors now marched boldly to Rouen. The capital held out for a whole year, during which the attacks were incessant and furious, when a want of food drove the besieged to request a truce, which Philip granted on condition that the city should surrender, if not relieved within thirty days. The Rouennais sent deputies to England to inform John of their very desperate condition: they found him playing at chess; and such was his unconcern, that he dismissed them until he had finished the game! Then his only answer was that he could not relieve the city within the time specified, and therefore he advised the besieged to make the best terms they could, which they did. Thus the duchy of Normandy, ceded by Charles the Simple in 912, was reunited to the crown of France by Philip Augustus, in 1204, after a separation of two hundred and ninety-two years.

The provinces of Touraine, Maine, and Anjou, had the year previously been annexed to France, and the loss of Poitou followed that of Normandy. Guienne alone remained to England. Eleanor, the sister of Arthur, and a princess of great beauty, became heiress to the duchy of Britany after the murder of her brother. But her brutal uncle had carried her a prisoner to England, and the ducal crown devolved on her half-sister, the daughter of Constance by her third husband. The unfortunate Eleanor was kept immured for forty years in a convent at Bristol, first by John, and next by Henry.

The loss of Normandy Proper effected a very great change in the political condition of these islands, as, although geographically appertaining to that province, the natives preferred the English connection, and thenceforth transferred their hearty allegiance to the sovereigns of England. In ecclesiastical matters, however, the islanders remained attached to the diocese of Coutances, and thus their ancient connection with the Cotentin was not entirely severed.—Falle[1] states that the French, after getting possession of Normandy, attacked the islands twice, and says: "But sure it is, that the ports and landing places had been left too much exposed to descents, which gave opportunity to the *French* to gain entrance into the islands. Nevertheless, though they so far prevailed at that time, they could not keep their ground. They were beaten out again, and forced to retire with loss. They came a second time, yet neither then could they maintain themselves against a people resolved to perish rather than fall under their power. At the Pleas holden before the itinerant judges sent to JERSEY in *Edward the Second's* reign, it was set forth by *William Demareys*, the king's advocate, *that a certain king of* France (*meaning* Philip Augustus) *had disinherited* John, *king of* England, *of the dutchy of* Normandy, *and had also twice ejected him out of these islands,* &c. *But that the said king* John *had twice reconquered the said islands,* &c." Falle next mentions that John, on hearing of the brave stand made by the islanders, and fearing that they might be overpowered if the French returned in greater force, not only sent over the necessary succours, but hastened over in person that he might animate the people, and keep up their courage. He was "very liberal of his favors to them, visited the islands with great care, viewed those weaker places which had let in the French, and caused the same to be fortified. He gave us a body of constitutions, which have been the foundation of all our franchises and immunities to this day, and may not improperly be called our **Magna Charta.** But I find him again in Jersey in the fifteenth year of his reign, i.e. three years only before his death, which I take for a further proof of his care of us, continued to the last."—Thus wrote Falle on very insufficient authority, and,

(1) "An Account of the Island of Jersey," by the Rev. Philip Falle.—Falle observes, page 37, that if these islands had been annexed with Normandy to France in the reign of John, all the inheritance of the inhabitants would have been "*popery and wooden shoes*, the wretched lot of our *neighbour Normans* in their present state under the *French.*" ! !

unable to account for John's energetic conduct relative to these islands, he ascribes it to an interposition of Providence in their favor, and not to his own willing credulity, as he should have done. That the islands were attacked during the reign of John there is evidence, not however to the extent of their double conquest and reconquest; but that he ever visited them is very doubtful. The Rev. Edward Durell, in his notes on Falle, (No. 29,) candidly observes: "What were the fortifications which king John raised in Jersey, I know not;" and certain it is that he erected none in Guernsey, or in the smaller islands. Falle gives Matthew Paris as his authority for stating that John visited Jersey only three years before his death; but Paris was the copyist of Wendover, author of "The Flowers of History"—a work said to be replete with exaggeration—and substituted Jersey for Guernsey. Roger of Wendover, whose work terminated in 1235, the year of his death, mentions "that John had some disagreement at Portsmouth with an immense number of his knights, who complained that they had spent their money, and asked for more from the treasury. This the king refused; but, flying into a rage, he embarked with his private attendants, and after three days landed at Guernsey, whilst his nobles returned home; and the king, seeing himself thus abandoned, was compelled to return to England himself." [1] But even Wendover, if he could be trusted generally, may have been mistaken, as Southey, writing on the same subject, says that John, after sailing from Portsmouth, kept hovering off for two days, in the vain hope that the troops would follow him. Had the king crossed over to these islands, which could well dispense with his odious presence, surely Southey would have mentioned his doing so. The troubles in which John was continually involved reduced him, in his later years, to such extremities, that he was fain to conceal himself in the Isle of Wight; and it is incredible that he, who displayed such utter indifference at the loss of Normandy should so exert himself to preserve these islands, which were a very small and insignificant part of that duchy. It is, however, due to him to add, that amid his many disputes with the people and with his barons, he never neglected his navy; and, unpopular as he was generally, he preserved the good will of the seamen, of whom as many as 14,000 are said to have been on board the fleet which was collected at Portsmouth in 1205, for the projected recovery of Normandy.

(1) Roger of Wendover's Flowers of History, from the Descent of the Saxons to A.D. 1235, vol. ii., p. 274.—London, 1849.

During the reign of John, the islands appear to have occasionally possessed small stranger garrisons, as, when struggling for Normandy in 1203, he wrote to the bailiffs of Peter de Pratel, the warden, from near Alençon, on the 24th July, to require the lords of fiefs, &c., to raise sufficient sums of money to be deposited with Regnault de Carteret, for the maintenance of soldiers and others required for their defence. And on the 13th of the following month, he issued another mandate to the said bailiffs, headed : " De auxilio in insulis Gernesey & Jersey levando, ad sustendand' milites qui prædictas insulas ab extraneis defendent," in which he fixed the amount to be levied at one-fifth part of the revenues of the islands.[1]

We have said that these islands were attacked during this reign, as we now proceed to show.—Among the many foreigners in the king's service was a notorious Boulognese or Flemish adventurer, by name Eustache le Moine, (Eustace the Monk,) whom the romancers of the time delight in describing as a nautical Robin Hood or Red Rover, and withal an adept in sorcery.   When he first entered John's service does not appear, but by a writ tested at Gillingham, November 13, 1205, he seems to have then sent a prize into Sandwich. He remained in the king's service until the year 1212, and soon after withdrew from it, siding probably with the confederate barons.   In October, 1214, he made an unsuccessful attack on these islands, and fifty-four of his men, among them his brother and his uncle, were made prisoners in Sark. It is, however, not quite clear that Sark escaped capture—if not, it was quickly regained. Of the prisoners fourteen men at arms (servientes) were confined in Winchester, and placed in the lowest dungeon, (in fundo carceris,) while six knights were in the custody of the constable of Porchester castle. On the repulse of Le Moine, the king wrote to the islanders, (militibus et probis hominibus insularum,) thanking them warmly for their good service, and telling them that he had released the hostages he had taken from them, as he was fully assured of their fidelity. These hostages were seventeen in number—among them John Le Petit, William Malet, John Normand, and Richard Turgis—and writs for their release were issued on the same day to no less than seven parties in whose custody they were, viz. the

(1) A.D. 1203, Ann. 5. John.—Quòd omnes Religiosi et Laici infra Insul' de Gernesey &c. dent quintam partem reddituum suorum unius Anni sive feodorum ad sustendand' Milites et al' qui eos defend' contra extraneos, apud Alenc' 13 Aug.—Calendarium Rotulorum Patentium.

prior of Winton, (Winchester,) the sheriff of Northampton, the sheriff of Nottingham, the abbot of Gloucester, the mayor of Winton, the prior of St. Alban's, and the abbot of Romsey. This release occurred scarcely two years before the king's death at Newark; and that hostages should have been required by him disproves, we conceive, several of the preceding statements of Falle.

The king's letter in Latin, just mentioned, is to the following effect:

"At HAVERING, 2d November, 1214.

"The king to the knights and good men of the islands, &c. We return you many thanks for the good and faithful service you have so readily performed in furtherance of our honor and service. We also return you your hostages, that they may remain with you. Because we place entire confidence in your fidelity. Testo, &c."

After this attack on the islands, Eustache le Moine appears to have been included in the treaty with the insurgent barons; but soon after, when Louis, son of the king of France, was invited by them to assume the English sceptre, Le Moine entered into that prince's service, and was actively engaged in the naval operations which ensued. In the emergency, king John committed the defence of the southern coast of England to the warden of these islands, Philip d'Aubigny, one of the ablest and most faithful of his adherents; and in the midst of more important cares, it is not surprising that the islands were neglected. Of this neglect Le Moine seems to have taken advantage by seizing and retaining them shortly before the death of John, in October, 1216, as in the treaty of peace between Henry III. and Louis, which followed the naval victory off Sandwich, August 24, 1217, the latter engaged to send orders to the brothers of Eustace (fratribus Eustachii Monachi) to restore the islands to Henry, king of England; or otherwise the said brothers to be subject to certain heavy penalties named, such as the forfeiture of their fiefs, lands, and moveables. See Fœdera, vol. i., pars 1, page 148. Londini, 1818.

Falle was not happy in his narration of the reign of John, whom he eulogizes for conferring "a body of constitutions" on these islands, and which he gives in the Appendix of his History under eighteen distinct clauses or heads, with the following foot note: "The original of these constitutions of king John is lost, but they are extant in an Inquest of his son Henry III., which recites and confirms them." In disproof of this assertion, we must observe that the said Inquest of 32 Henry III. still exists among the records in the Tower of London, but only contains, with slight variations, the first, second, and eighteenth clauses of Falle, not so numbered, the remaining fifteen being wanting. The Inquest is written on one skin of parchment; and it is supposed by Mr. Hardy, the learned antiquary, in whose immediate custody it is, that another membrane, long since lost, may have been at one time attached to it.[1] Even admitting this to be the case, the circumstance of the eighteenth clause following the second is not accounted for, and leads one to suspect that the missing fifteen clauses are interpolations. It is true that in the *Placita coram Henrico Spigurnel*, &c., 17 Edw. II. (A.D. 1324) the purport of most, if not all, of these missing clauses is expressed *in other words*, with additional provisions, the inhabitants of Guernsey having then urged that their laws and privileges, as set forth in the said *Placita*, had existed from time immemorial.[2] Had they dated from John, it would surely have been known, as he died only 108 years before. But setting the preceding discrepancies aside, there is great doubt whether the document in Latin, given by Falle as "the constitutions of king John," ever emanated from that monarch, and at most they appear to have been only a declaratory enactment of a pre-existing system. Constitutionally, the point is immaterial, the purport being the same; but historically there is this distinction, that if the "constitutions," so yclept, be anterior to John, as we doubt not they are, they date probably from the early part of the eleventh century; if otherwise, from the commencement of the thirteenth century, a difference in antiquity of about 200 years. Twelve jurats or jurymen are very ancient, as, although Polydore Virgil asserts that William the Conqueror first brought the jury of twelve into England, it is clear from Ethelred's laws that the institution existed there many years before the conquest. Falle's document is a mere list of promiscuous articles of polity and regulation, and bears on the face of it no formality or style usually characterizing charters or statutes. It is headed, or rather superscribed: "*Constitutiones*

---

(1) See Report of the Guernsey Royal Commissioners of 1846, p. 293.

(2) "Et ipsi per quosdam servientes dicunt quod ipsi et omnes antecessores eorum, Insulani insulæ prædictæ, de lege et eorum consuetudine à tempore quo non extat memoria usitatis, habere consueverunt duodecim Juratos de se ipsis, qui eligi debent per ministros domini Regis et optimates patriæ, cum opus fuerit, scilicet, post mortem unius eorum, alter fidedignus loco ejus eligi debet."—*Pleas before H. Spigurnel*, &c.

et provisiones constitutæ per dominum Johannem regem, post-quam Normannia alienata fuit,"—" Constitutions and provisions by the lord John, the king, after Normandy was alienated ;" but the people for whom they were intended are not named ; the place of emanation and the date are not given ; and no seal is affixed. The original is not extant, and is not known to have been ever in existence ; and Falle's copy, which is not addressed to any authorities in or out of the islands, bears the appearance of a compilation at an epoch *certainly posterior* to king John's death. That he should voluntarily grant free constitutions to these islands—he from whom the celebrated Magna Charta was afterwards extorted by the English barons—is somewhat incredible. Had he done so, he would doubtless have referred to some pre-existent jurisdiction to be superseded, and would probably have assigned some reason for the change; but he did neither, and we cannot but think that the greater part of Falle's document is apocryphal, at least as relates to king John.

Duncan says, that " when Guernsey was a dependency of Normandy, each fief had its court ; and once a year a general court appears to have been held by the bailiff and four knights, two of whom, with the bailiff, resided in the island, the others coming from Normandy. The place of meeting was in the Vale parish, at a place then, and still, called ' *Les Landes du Marché*,' where the public market was held; and afterwards at St. Anne's, near the King's Mills, in the parish of St. Mary de Castro. At these assizes, the ancient laws were proclaimed, and new regulations made in presence, and by the advice, of the military and other tenants. These regulations had force of law as soon as enacted, but political ordinances of importance were regarded only as provisional until they had received the assent of the duke.

" After the separation of the islands from the duchy of Normandy, king John is said to have appointed twelve jurats to replace the knights.[1] They, with the bailiff, the tenants *in capite*, and other principal inhabitants representing the community, continued to hold pleas and pass provisional ordinances three times a year."

The church of St. Martin was built in the reign of Richard, Cœur de Lion, and that of the Catel in the reign of John. These churches were respectable edifices for the age, and did

(1) So said from the Constitutions of king John, at the *Précepte d'Assise*, 5 Edw. III.

F

credit to the islanders.—" Several copies exist of an act of chief
pleas concerning the reparation, or rather the erection, of a
bridge, now called *Le Grand Pont*, for the convenience of
the inhabitants of the parishes of the Vale and St. Sampson,
who complained ' that they had been greatly impeded and
damnified by the incursions of the sea, which had swept away
and destroyed the convenient passage which existed between
the said parishes, so that it was impossible to continue
religious processions or traffic one with the other, and impracticable to go to the parish of the Grand Sarrassin,' now
St. Mary de Castro.   This act was passed by Nicholas De
Beauvoir, bailiff, John Le Gros, James Le Marchant, Peter
De La Lande, Robert De La Salle, Colin Henri, Rauf Meril,
Gautier Blondel, and Guilet Lefebvre, jurats, dated the 4th
of October, 1204, the very year in which Normandy was
united to the crown of France."—*Duncan.*

In the middle ages, the condition of the unprivileged classes
in Europe was one of great and general misery, and the
social state of the islanders must have been sufficiently wretched if it bore any analogy to that of the French at the same
period ; although, as it appears that the lower ranks in Normandy were among the first who enjoyed the least glimpse
of real liberty, the concession of it to them must have quickly
extended to the same classes in these islands.

It has been shewn that, in the eleventh century, Guernsey
was divided into two beneficiary fiefs ; and it is evident that
the possessors, both wealthy and powerful Norman barons,
never resided in the island.   Next in rank to the barons—
and all who held lands immediately from the crown were
comprised in the order—were their higher tenants or vassals,
usually termed *vavasseurs*, and the châtelains, who held only
arrière fiefs with fortified places.   Of the vavasseurs and
châtelains, all of whom were either knights or esquires, or
the gentry in the modern acceptation of the term, there were
doubtless several resident in the islands, which have from
very remote times been considered frontier garrisons.   The
classes, below those of gentle blood, were three, viz. the freemen, the villeins, and the serfs.   Even the first, being considered of ignoble birth, were held in little estimation, and by
the ancient laws of France were obliged to live under the
protection of some *seigneur*, who subjected them to many
tributes and to much oppression : a plebeian could not possess a fief.   During seasons of famine, which were not unfre-

quent, many freemen were compelled to exchange their liberty for food, and to sell themselves and their families into a species of slavery. The villein was obliged to remain upon his lord's estate, and could not dispose of the land upon which he dwelt; nay more, the *seigneur* could reclaim him if he strayed; but he was only bound to fixed duties and payments The serf felled the timber, carried the manure, and performed other menial employments for his lord. The *seigneur* might take all belonging to his serf, alive or dead, and imprison him at his pleasure, " being accountable," says Beaumanoir, " to none but God." In France, the children followed their mother's condition; and the clergy inveighed against the sinfulness of keeping Christians in bondage, although they preached what they themselves did not practise, the villeins upon church lands being the last who were emancipated![1] But as civilization advanced in Europe, the manumission of slaves became more frequent; and it finally grew into a custom that villeins might not only possess property, but purchase their own redemption. As these islands were anciently held by the feudal tenure, Guernsey being finally divided into sixteen fiefs, of which six belonged to ecclesiastics and ten to laymen, there can be little doubt, we think, that a vast majority of the inhabitants were included in the three degraded classes we have named; although from their isolation, their general occupation of fishing, and their Norman origin, they were probably kept in a less grievous state of vassalage than the same classes in France. In any case, the present generation should rejoice that they live in happier and better times. As in Normandy there were *francs tenants*, or holders of *terres libres*, so there were in these islands; and in a mandate of Edward III., dated 1337, the *libere-tenentibus* are named between the *militibus* and *ballivis*. Felix Bodin, who has justly been styled the French Sallust, in his RÉSUMÉ DE L'HISTOIRE DE FRANCE, thus speaks of the social being of that country from the eleventh to the fourteenth centuries:

- (1) "Il restait encore de nos jours des serfs de *main-morte*, à Saint Claude en Franche-Comté. Louis XVI. les a affranchis. Ils appartenaient à des moines!"—*Bodin.*

The acute Hallam, in his "Middle Ages," very truly observes that the sole hope for classical literature depended on the Latin language, which would probably have been lost if three circumstances had not combined to maintain it, viz. the papal supremacy, the monastic institutions, and the use of a Latin Liturgy. Through the first, a continued intercourse was maintained between Rome and the several nations of Europe, so that a common language became necessary. The parochial clergy were very ignorant, and the little learning which existed was among the monks, whose monasteries served as secure repositories for books and manuscripts, which could scarcely have descended to us by any other channel. Thus papacy and its concomitants, which Protestants are properly accustomed to condemn, were eventually of the utmost advantage to learning and to the establishment of a purer (and, we will add, of a more liberal) Christianity.

"Arrêtons-nous ici : c'est l'époque moyenne de la féodalité pure, de ce régime odieux qui pesa sur la France pendant près de trois siècles, et qui réduisit l'espèce européenne au dernier degré de misère. Tout le peuple était devenu *serf* ou esclave. Sa condition était peu différente de celle du bétail. Chacun pouvait frapper, mutiler, ou même tuer son *serf* impunément, sauf intercession du clergé. Presque tous les hommes libres avaient renoncé d'eux-mêmes à leur liberté, afin d'être moins vexés par les seigneurs. Mais ceux-ci jugèrent, pillèrent, rançonnèrent cruellement leurs vassaux. L'axiome féodal, *Nulle terre sans seigneur*, s'établissait : il n'existait donc aucun asile contre ces hommes, qui sans doute n'étaient pas nés plus méchants que d'autres, mais qui, dans ce désordre, étaient brigands par état : il fallait être oppresseur ou opprimé. Les gens d'église et les seigneurs se pillaient tour à tour, et ruinaient le peuple. La force physique ou l'autorité religieuse pouvait seule prévaloir. La justice devait être méconnue là où tous les différends se jugeaient et tous les torts se redressaient à main armée. La cavalerie, dont les Francs avaient presque ignoré l'usage, était devenue, ainsi que le port d'armes, le privilége exclusif des seigneurs. Un noble et son cheval, couverts d'une armure de fer, faisaient trembler tout un canton. Les serfs, qu'on menait de force à la guerre, combattaient à pied. Accablés de corvées, de tailles, de péages, de taxes de toute espèce imposées par des hommes de guerre ou d'église, humiliés par des droits seigneuriaux qui révoltent la pudeur et la nature, ils ne savaient auquel obéir, et ne se battaient que pour river leurs fers. On appelait *villains* ceux de la campagne, *bourgeois* ceux des villes et bourgs. Ni les uns ni les autres ne pouvaient produire qu'au profit de leurs seigneurs, qui venaient souvent vivre chez eux à discrétion, avec leurs *hommes, sergens* et *varlets ;* ceux-ci étaient des aspirans à la profession de chevalier ou homme d'armes. Les valets ont, comme on le voit, une origine assez noble.

" De leur côté, les seigneurs se battaient entre eux à outrance ; les déclarations de guerre atteignaient les parens, les alliés. Une querelle de famille pouvait ensanglanter un pays pendant trente ans. L'état de guerre était l'état habituel ; tous les châteaux, toutes les abbayes étaient des forteresses, ou plutôt des repaires où cent mille tyrans se renfermaient avec leur butin : la France était un vaste champ de bataille. Enfin, ce carnage en permanence finit par lasser la férocité elle-même. On imagina, dans un concile, d'imposer à ces furieux ce qu'on appela la *paix de Dieu*, puisqu'on ne pouvait l'obtenir des hommes. Les évêques ordonnèrent des jeûnes et des pénitences pendant lesquelles l'humanité respira. Mais cette paix, ainsi que la *trève de Dieu*, qui défendit seulement de combattre du Samedi soir au Lundi matin, tomba bientôt en désuétude. C'eût été beaucoup qu'un

tel relâche au brigandage.   On voit quel était cet odieux régime
féodal, véritable anarchie tempérée par l'anatbème."

The following abstracts from the records in the time of
king John relate to these islands, and as such are interesting :

E Rotulis Chartarum.

1 JOHN.—September 6, 1199.— Exchange effected between the
    king and Vitalis de Villa of a rent of £50, granted him
    by king Richard on the fisheries (esperquerie) of Guern-
    sey, for a like rent to be taken in the port of Beiarid.(?)

  ,,   May 5, 1200.—Grant of the islands to Peter de
    Preaus, dated at Caen.

  ,,   Grant made to the abbey of Blanchelande of the pre-
    bend of Cherbourg, in the island of Guernsey.

E Rotulis Litt. Patentium.

3 JOHN.—At Morlaix, November 12, 1201.—That a reasonable
    aid be sent to the king from the islands of Guernsey
    and Jersey ; directed to Peter de Preaus, or his bailiffs
    in those islands.

17 JOHN.—Runemede, June 21, 1215.—The abbess of Wilton
    . is ordered to surrender to Eustace Le Moine his daugh-
    ter, whom she has in her custody as his hostage.

E Rotulis Litt. Clausarum.

8 JOHN.—Beaulieu, May 19, 1206-7.— The king orders G. de
    Lucy and his other *fideles* in the islands immediately to
    send out the two galleys, having one knight and one
    clerk, both discreet and well spoken men on board, to
    meet the fleet, (navagium,) now coming from La
    Rochelle, and to prevail if possible on the masters and
    mariners to enter the king's service.

8 JOHN.—Woodstock, May 13, 1206-7.—The bailiffs of Ports-
    mouth are ordered to provide a smack (sernecum) for
    the passage, by the king's orders, of brother Robert de
    Hambeie and his attendants to the island of Gernes.

9 JOHN.—Rokingham, August 12, 1207.—The custody of the
    islands of G'ner, &c., which G. de Lucy held, is granted
    to Philip d'Aubigny, during the king's pleasure.

  ,,   Guildford, April 6, 1208.—Safe conduct granted to
    Eust. Le Moine, until the feast of Pentecost, to come,
    dwell, and return to and from England.

10 JOHN.—1208.—The wardens of the islands of Guernsey,
    &c., are ordered to receive and protect Guy de Guivilt
    and his men, whilst cruizing against the king's enemies.

15 JOHN.—Winton, July 20, 1213.—Philip d'Aubigny is or-
    dered, out of the lands which belonged to Baldwin

Wake, in Guernsey, to assign 20 librates (And.) to
Thomas Daniis, bequeathed to him for his services by
the said Baldwin.

16 JOHN.—Gillingham, December 8, 1214.—The king orders
P. Bishop of Winchester, to deliver the island of Sark
to Philip d'Aubigny, to whom the king has committed
its custody.

16 JOHN.—Westminster, November 3, 1214.—Philip d'Aubigny is informed that the king sends him three galleys,
to be kept in his parts, according to his request. And
W. Archdeacon of Taunton, is ordered to deliver the
said galleys to the men of the said Philip, by whom
they are to be taken to the island of Guernsey.

HENRY III.—1216 to 1272.

Henry, the eldest son of John, succeeded his father when
only in his tenth year; and as in England his long and confused reign was singularly barren in interesting events, so
there is little to relate of these islands in his time. Duncan
states that in this reign Castle Cornet fell into the hands of
the French, through the negligence of the captain, " who had
failed to supply it with ammunition," (? arms and provisions,
as gunpowder was then unknown in Europe,) but that it was
soon recovered by the courage of the inhabitants. We believe, however, that this capture occurred in the following
reign, that of Edward I. Duncan also says that in the latter
end of king John's reign, Guernsey was afflicted with a great
mortality, when the Normans attempted to surprise it, but
were repulsed.

Having already made mention of the naval battle off
Sandwich, in the year 1217, we must add here that the English commander on that occasion was Philip d'Aubigny, the
lord or warden of these islands. Falle, ever anxious to introduce the loyalty and prowess of the natives, says that " the
fleet consisted of the shipping of the Cinque Ports, with such
additional strength as the islands could bring." But, as we
have shewn, the islands appear at this time to have been in
possession of Eustache le Moine, and, if so, could not have
sent any assistance to their warden. Eustache was found,
after a long search, concealed in the hold of one of the captured ships: he offered a large sum for his ransom, so that
his life might be spared, and likewise to enter the service of
Henry; but, as he had rendered himself singularly odious,
Richard, an illegitimate son of king John, killed him, and
sent his head to the young monarch as a brotherly offering,

and as a proof of this important victory. Eustache had left his monastery — hence his name of le Moine, or the Monk — and, having dissipated his patrimony, afterwards " he became a notable pirate, and had done in his days much mischief to the Englishmen."

Henry, in the thirty-second year of his reign, A.D. 1248, ordered an extent or inquisition to be instituted in these islands, when Drogo de Barentin[1] was warden thereof : the result was drawn up in Latin, and furnishes a good idea of the state of Guernsey in the thirteenth century. By this inquest, it appears " that one half of the island belongs to the lord the king, and to lords and others who hold of him in chief; and that the other half is divided between the abbot of *Mont St. Michel*, in peril of the sea,[2] and Robert de Vere ; and that the quarter which Robert de Vere holds is called *La Terre du Comte*. Also that those who held *terres villaines* paid camparts ; that two hens were due on each house, as also *pesnage* for hogs ; and if such *pesnage*, after being declared and cried in the market place, should not be paid before sunset, the owner forfeited the hog and five sols tournois.—" If the lord the king should desire to send his corn to Normandy, viz. between *Mont St. Michel* and Cherbourg, he shall in peace time find a vessel and a master, and the said men shall find, at their own cost, the rest of the crew for a fortnight ; but if delayed longer than a fortnight, they shall then be kept at the lord the king's own cost ; and the said mariners are to have the wastage of the corn in the vessel."—The inquisitioners further add that the inhabitants were accustomed, in time of peace, to take to Normandy or elsewhere, at their pleasure, all their goods, live or dead stock, as well the produce of the sea as of the land, for sale, (except only the congers, during the *esperkerie*,[3]) and to pay no duty on them. The season of the *esperkerie* continued from Easter to the feast of St. Michael; and " when the merchants, who arm the *esperkeries*, and the fishermen, disagreed" as to the price of the fish, two fishermen were chosen on either side as appraisers.

We have said that after the loss of Normandy, these islands

(1) Probably the founder of an eminent Jersey family, long since extinct. Another Drogo de Barentin was one of the Justices Itinerant in 1308 ; and a third, seigneur of Rosel, was slain in the defence of Mont Orgueil, about 1340.

(2) This refers to the monastery of *Mont St. Michel*, in Normandy, known as that " in periculo maris," evidently from the year 709, when it was nearly swallowed up by the sea.

(3) " *Esperkerie* was the drying season for conger and mackerel, derived from *perques*, the perches or poles on which the fish was placed to dry."—*Lieut.-Colonel de Havilland.*

remained attached to the diocese of Coutances, although its
suffragan was thenceforth an alien to the crown of England.
Thus the abbeys of *Mont St. Michel*, St. Sauveur Lesset,
and Cherbourg, continued to enjoy the revenues they possessed in this bailiwick, which however appear to have been
sequestered in time of war.   It is a great proof of the power
of the papacy in that age that a foreign, and probably hostile,
priesthood was thus allowed not only to administer to the
spiritual wants of the natives, but that the abbeys in Normandy were so long permitted to draw their insular revenues.
But it was a happy circumstance for the islanders that their
ancient dependence on the see of Coutances was not suddenly
severed, as it was evidently owing to the influence of the
bishop that the pope issued a bull enforcing the privilege of
neutrality granted to the islands by Edward IV.   And this
dependence, doubtless, caused a more amicable and frequent
intercourse with the inhabitants of the Cotentin, at a time
when the communication with England was very limited.
From documents which have recently been collected in Normandy for the States of Guernsey, we are enabled to illustrate the ecclesiastical connection of the island with Normandy.

A.D. 121⅚. 3 Henry III. — Philip d'Aubigny, bailiff
(warden) of the isles, by order of the king, restores in full
the rights and possessions of the abbey of *Mont St. Michel*
in the island of Guernsey, and in addition grants to the said
abbey divers immunities and privileges.

A.D. 1238.   22 Henry III. — Henry de Trubleville, warden of the isles, replaces the abbey of *Mont St. Michel* in
possession of the priory of the Vale and of all other rights,
&c., in the isle of Guernsey, by letter dated at the castle
du Homet, in the said island.

Letter of Richard, bishop of Avranches, to Edward, eldest
son of Henry III., containing " vidimus" of an inquest held
at Guernsey, 125¾, before Sire John de Gray, son and deputy
of Sire Henry de Gray, warden of the isles, which inquest
recognizes the right of the abbey of *Mont St. Michel* to the
varech and " adventures of the sea," viz. to the whole of the
varech of the isle of Lihou and at " Keuhou," and to a quarter
part of the said *varech* on the remainder of the island.

A.D. 126⅔.   March 24. — Letter of Edward, eldest son of
Henry III., orders his bailiffs in the isles to be obedient to
Sire Rauf d'Aubigné and Sire William de Saumareis, his
justices, in the cause of the abbot and convent of *Mont St.
Michel* against William de Cheyne, knight, for the land
which the said William has acquired of Bauldoin de Vere.

A.D. 1270.—Agreement between the abbot of *Mont St. Michel* on the one part, and Hugues de Turbeville, knight, bailiff (warden) of the isles, on the other part, witnesseth that, in consideration of the good services of the said Hugues, the abbot engages, if he gain his cause against the lady de Cheney, to cede to him the moiety of the *Terre du Comte.*[1]

A.D. 1270. London, May 23.—A letter of Edward, eldest son of Henry III., declares that the abbot of *Mont St. Michel*, having at his request given his fisheries to farm to the merchant of the said Edward, this concession was not to prejudice the abbot's rights in times to come.

A.D. 1270.—"*Bail*" to William *dit* Estur of the land which belonged to Hamelin Estur in Guernsey, for twelve quarters of wheat, *grande mesure*, four loaves, and four capons, annually.

A.D. 128‡.—Letter of king Edward I., commanding the royal justices going to the isles, to investigate, and do justice to, the plaints of the abbot and convent of *Mont St. Michel*, that their men of the isles refuse to render them *campart*[2] accustomed of ancient times, viz. of parsnips, onions, and leeks.

A.D. 1289.—Letter of Edward I., transmitting to his bailiff of Guernsey the complaint of the abbot and convent of *Mont St. Michel*, that the king's people in the said isle levy a custom on the mackerel caught by the men of the said abbot, contrary to his right, and to his great damage and prejudice.

A.D. 1307.—Letter of John de Newent, lieutenant of Sir Otho de Grandison, warden of the isles, dated St. Peter-Port, March 26, an. 30 Edw. I, restoring to the abbey and convent of *St. Sauveur Lesset* the lands and possessions in the said isles, which had been sequestered in consequence of the war.

A.D. 1347.—Letter of Rauf de Hermesthorp, lieutenant of the isles, declaring that the annual pension of fifteen liv. tournez, paid by the prior of the Vale to the prior of Lihou, is in his opinion too small, as times have been and are.

A.D. 1364.—The abbot of *Mont St. Michel* appears before

(1) In other words, the priest, having a bad cause, bribed the judge to cheat the widow.

(2) "The champart is derived from *campi pars*, a part of the profit of the land reserved for ever, to be paid by the under-tenants to him who was the last owner of the fief, and let it out to tenants, with the reservation of this duty upon it. The first dukes of Normandy granted several parcels of land in the island to such as had served them in their wars, and granted likewise a very considerable part to some religious houses. These, whether churchmen or soldiers, not being themselves skilled in agriculture, let out these lands to tenants under them, reserving such rents and services as they thought most convenient. Such was this champart, which is undoubtedly the most ancient duty ; and such were the *chefrentes*, or rents reserved to the chief lord, which are the most ancient rents, and these have been in use, at the least ever since Richard the First, duke of Normandy, who sent monks from St. Michael *de monte tumbâ*, and placed them in the island, which was about A.D. 966, and possibly they may yet be of more ancient date."— *Warburton.*

l'abbé de la Luzerne, special commissioner of Edward III., and names Denys Le Marchant, with several others, his attorneys in England and the islands.

A.D. 1480.   February 27.—Letter of Geoffrey, bishop of Coutances, instituting brother William Guyffart *religieux de l'abbaye de notre dame du Voeu*, near Cherbourg, in the cure of the *prieure*, or parish church, of Saint Tugual of Herm, in the isles of Guernsey, dependent of the said abbey.

Henry, towards the close of his reign, although reduced to the necessity of relinquishing his pretensions to Normandy, which duchy had been lost by his father, yet in his treaty with Louis, king of France, he took especial care that these islands, which were the appanage[1] of his son, prince Edward, should be reserved to him, with the province of Gascony. It appears by an inspeximus of the reign of king Henry IV. that this prince Edward granted to William de Chesneye the right of keeping a warren both in Jersey and Guernsey, by a charter dated 9th of June, in the forty-fifth year of his father's reign ; so that he held these islands by an independent authority before he became Edward I., as we have already shewn.

The extent of Henry III. says : " Sed tempore illo non fuerunt castella in insulis ;" but in that time there were no castles in the islands." It is not quite clear to what period this passage refers, but certainly not earlier than the commencement of the eleventh century.   In the preceding reign there were such castles ; as John, by an order dated the 14th of November, 1212, directed Asculf de Suligny to deliver the isle of Jersey and CASTLE to Philip d'Aubigny.   There is likewise, in 1223, a writ of Henry III., addressed to Philip d'Aubigny, requiring him to deliver the islands of Jersey and Guernsey, with THE CASTLES, to Geoffrey de Lucy.

When prince Edward was about to proceed to the Holy Land, in the year 1270, he appointed his uncle guardian of his children and estates, by an indenture, of which we extract the heading and the first clause, as a specimen of Norman French in the thirteenth century.

" *Edwardus primogenitus concessit custodiam filiorum suorum domino Ricardo Regi Romanorum avunculo suo, dum fuerit in Terra Sancta.*

" Edward, fiz esne a l' noble Rey de Engletere, a tuz ke ceste lettre orrunt ou verrunt, saluz.

(1) The term *apanage* signified the provision made for the younger children of the kings of France.

"Siche ke, par le otri e le assentement de l'avant dit Rey nostre pere, avum ordine e establi de la garde de nos enfans, e de nos chasteaus, e de nos terres, e de nos seignuries en Engletere, en Gales, en Irlonde, en Gayscoyne, e des isles de Gernesie e de Geresie, oue tute les apurtenances, ensement oue les issues des terres, e de choses avaunt dites, en la forme desut escrite, ceo est assaver."—*Fœdera.*

Of the seven witnesses to this indenture one is Rog' de Someri, proving pretty clearly that the de Somery, who accompanied William at the conquest, bore a different surname to that of de Sausmarez.

CHAPTER V.

EDWARD I.—1272 to 1307.

At Henry's death, the sceptre passed from a feeble to a vigorous hand, ·Edward having during his father's life displayed that great ability and courage which he afterwards evinced in the conquest of Wales—a conquest, however, more politic than just. As these islands had been the appanage of Edward before he came to the throne, he probably felt an additional interest in their welfare.

In the seventh year of his reign, Edward gave a public seal to Jersey and Guernsey, the grant of which was addressed in Latin to the bailiff of each, and thus prefaced : "Whereas our subjects (literally our men, homines nostri) of the aforesaid islands have hitherto frequently sustained divers losses and no small dangers, sometimes at sea by shipwreck, sometimes on land by depredations and other risks of travelling, ·for this reason especially that in these islands we have had up to this time no seal, with which writs (or briefs—brevia) of the men from those parts might be certified, or their own transactions on the spot be facilitated," (expediri,) &c.—The original seal of Edward I. is now in the official possession of Peter Stafford Carey, esq., the talented and respected bailiff of Guernsey, and it corresponds exactly with an impression in wax affixed to a document bearing date in 1315. The seal is of metal, and the arms on it are three

leopards or lions, *passant guardant*, badly executed: the
shield is surmounted by a sprig of laurel, but whether intended for a crest or not it is difficult to determine: there is
no wreath under the sprig.[1] It is clear, however, that the
laurel, if a crest, was not granted as a crest of honor for the
relief of Mont Orgueil Castle by the Guernseymen, in 1467,
as is often supposed. Round the shield are the words, "S
Ballivie Insule de Gernereye." The public seal of Jersey
has, we believe, nothing resembling a crest.

In this reign, according to Dicey,[2] the French attempted
to take Guernsey, but were repulsed: they, however, captured Castle Cornet, which was obliged to surrender for want
of arms and provisions, and it was soon after retaken by the
valour of the inhabitants. Edward issued an order to reward
such inhabitants of Jersey and Guernsey as had signalised
themselves in repelling their French invaders, and to provide
for the widows and orphans of those who had fallen.[3] To
effect these objects, the lands, rents, &c., which belonged to
fugitives and deserters, were escheated. "These fugitives
and deserters, as it appears from Riley, were persons who
held lands, both in the island and France; and whenever
war broke out, they were in the habit of retiring to the continent and giving information as to the weakest points of the
coasts; but when peace was restored, they used to return and
claim their rents, and the enjoyment of all such franchises
and liberties as belonged to permanently resident Guernseymen." Duncan adds "that all Edward's orders are replete
with royal justice, and prove the devoted loyalty of the inhabitants and the gratitude of the sovereign." There exists
indeed ample evidence of the sore evils and trials to which
the islanders were subjected for at least two centuries, in
consequence of their unswerving adherence to the British
crown after the loss of Normandy, and when England was
unable to afford them much protection.

The Rev. Edward Durell, in his notes on Falle, page 428,

(1) Little seems to be known at the Herald's College of the armorial bearings of the
English monarchs anterior to Richard I.; (1189-1199) but it is said there that William the
Conqueror and his three sons bore the arms of Normandy, "gules, two leopards *passant*,
or;" and that Eleanor of Aquitaine brought to Henry II. the arms of that province,
"gules, a lion *passant guardant*, or," which he added to his two leopards, converting
them then into lions, like that of Aquitaine, for uniformity's sake. But the abbé de la
Rue, an eminent Norman antiquarian, was clearly of opinion that the ancient arms of
Normandy were neither lions nor leopards, but a composite imaginary animal, with the
head and mane of the lion, and the body spotted like the leopard, in French heraldic
language styled *lions léopardés*. In either case, the arms of Normandy, up to Henry II.,
were, we believe, composed of *two* animals only.

(2) Dicey's Historical Account of Guernsey. London, 1751.

(3) " Brevia facta de petitionibus hominum Geres, et Gernes, retornatis in Concilio in
autumpno an. "regni regis Ed. xxiii."—Ryley's Placita Parliamentaria, in Appendice.

says, most unaccountably : " The Fœdera, vol. i., part 2, page
928, A.D. 1301, contains a list of the several English ports,
which were ordered to send their contingents to the fleet of
Edward, at Berwick, for the invasion of Scotland. It is
gratifying that our islands were in that list, and that they
were ordered to furnish ten vessels." [1] We have consulted
this list, and cannot discover in it any mention of these islands.
Mr. Durell can scarcely have mistaken Jern' (in other pages
Magna Jernemuth) or Great Yarmouth for Jersey, as that
port was ordered to send *six* vessels. Moreover, as only two
other ports, Lenn' (the modern Lynn) and Youghal, were
required to furnish three ships each ; London, Bristol, &c.,
only two ships each ; and many other ports only one ship
each, these islands could never have been ordered to send
ten vessels, especially to so great a distance. Indeed, we
much doubt if they then possessed *one* fit for the purpose.
All England was only required to supply fifty-eight, and
Ireland ten ships ; together sixty-eight ships.

Soon after Edward's accession, commotions arose in some,
if not in all, of these islands, whereupon John Wigger and
Rodolph de Brochton were, by a royal commission, dated
the 11th of October, 1274, empowered to inquire into the
conduct of the jurats and inhabitants ; and in case it should
appear that any of the said jurats had committed acts prejudicial to the royal prerogative, the commissioners were authorized to eject and punish them, subject, however, to the king's
revision and pardon. The cause of these commotions is not
mentioned, but they appear to have been connected with the
royal prerogative, and to have arisen from the imperfect state
of the extents, or surveys, at that time, for, within a month
after the date of the commission, separate extents were drawn
up for Guernsey, Alderney, and Sark. It would seem that
the people of Guernsey justified themselves from every imputation of disloyalty, because the commissioners, observing
that the harbour of St. Peter-Port was insecure, so represented that insecurity to the king that, by an order already
mentioned, and addressed to the bailiff [2] and the principal
inhabitants, (Ballivo et probis hominibus,) he authorized the
levy, for a limited term of three years, of a duty of twelve
tournois on all ships laden, and of six tournois on all boats,
(duodecem et sex turonenses,) for the erection of a stone wall

(1) Mr. Durell's annotations are written with so much candour, liberality, and truth,
that this is evidently an unintentional error on his part.

(2) In the concluding passage, the order speaks of "Ballivus Insularum," so that he
was clearly the warden, or captain, and not holding the present office of bailiff.

or pier between the castle and the town of St. Peter-Port.
Duncan, page 20, supplies the omission of the coin or money
with sols, and adds : " If these twelve sous tournois were of
the same value as those mentioned in the extent of Sark,
under the name of sols tournois, it must have been a heavy
duty, since a quarter of wheat was therein estimated to be
only worth six of them."   In this case, each boat paid fully
sixteen shillings of the present money, an evident impossibility,
and the duty was clearly twelve and six denarios, or deniers,
of which twelve were one sol ; in other words, one sol, and
half a sol, respectively.

Nor was this regard for the harbour the only act by which
Edward, who has been deservedly termed the English Justinian, testified his good feelings towards Guernsey.   He cited
Otho de Grandison [1] to appear before parliament to answer
for his unjust proceedings against the inhabitants, upon whom
he had imposed many additional burdens.[2]   The office of
lieutenant to the warden, and bailiff, appears to have been
held at this time by the same individual, as an order of
Edward was addressed to Peter Le Marchant, holding the
office of Lord Otho de Grandison in the island of Guernsey,
(Petro Le Marchant, tenenti locum Domini Ottonis de Grandison in insula Gernesey,) and two months later the said
Peter Le Marchant was styled bailiff.   These two offices,
however, have since been usually separated, as being incompatible with each other ; although, in the reign of James I.,
Lord Carew, the governor, appointed the bailiff, Amias de
Carteret, as his lieutenant during his absence ; and in the
reign of queen Anne, Sir Edmund Andros, a native of
Guernsey, was invested with the joint commissions of lieutenant-governor and bailiff, as will appear in the sequel.[3]

By an extent of the royal revenues in the bailiwick of
Guernsey, drawn up in the second year of this reign, the
annual income amounted to 900 livres tournois, Guernsey

(1) O. de Grandison accompanied Edward I., when heir apparent to the throne, to the
Holy Land, and was rewarded, soon after the king's accession, by large grants of land in
England and Ireland, and the lordship of these islands.   In the 17th Edward I. he was
sent as ambassador to Rome, and he was subsequently employed to negociate a treaty
with France.   He died about 12th Edward II., leaving his brother his heir.—*Dugdale's
Baronage.*

(2) " Otho de Grandison, lord or governor of these islands in the reigns of Edward the
First and Edward the Second, forced an impost on congers salted for exportation, and it
amounted to four hundred livres tournois (fourteen of which specie made a pound sterling)
by the year, at only one penny tournois for every conger above ten pounds weight so
salted and transported.   This was, however, an illegal act of an arbitrary governor, for
which his widow suffered severely in Edward the Third's time."   (Dicey, page 172.)

(3) " The civil and military authority, according to the best information we can procure,
seems to have been first separated in the reign of Edward I., who issued his order, in the
year 1314, commanding the jurats to obey the bailiffs appointed in each island by Otho de
Grandison."—*Berry,* page 189.   This passage must refer to Edward II.

being rated at 765, Sark at 80, and Alderney at 55. It is singular that Alderney was rated at less than Sark.

The seas were very insecure during the reign of Edward, France having now raised a naval force. Six ships of war were fitted out by England, and sent to Bordeaux for the defence of the coast of Gascony. Two of these, as they sailed along the coast of Normandy, before war had been declared, were captured by the Norman navy, and several of the crews hanged; upon which the commander of the English fleet sailed with the intention of revenging himself upon any Norman ships he might fall in with. Meeting with none, he entered the mouth of the Seine, and there captured six vessels, many of whose men were slain. While he lay at anchor not far from the land, a strong fleet of Normans came that way, freighted with wine from Gascony, and the whole were captured with the loss of a third of their crews, and taken to England. Thus reprisals were provoked by wrongs, and, frequently falling upon the innocent, such reprisals were avenged by fresh acts of violence. Piracies were general, and often most audacious: a piratical squadron from Biscay and Asturias carried off three ships from Southampton, and there plundered the house of a brave man, who scarcely escaped with life. And as these islands lay in the neighbourhood of these excesses, the inhabitants must have been in constant dread of attack, and sorely exposed to invasion and pillage. With England they could have had little or no intercourse, and their trade must have been chiefly confined to the neighbouring coasts of Normandy and Britany.

" It was a very ancient prerogative claimed by the bishops of Coutances, that if the king, or guardian of the islands, delayed six months in filling up a vacant benefice, the bishop, in that case, had a right of appointing a curate, though king Edward the First paid but little attention to it. In the twenty-sixth year of his reign, having nominated Robert Lyset to the rectory of St. Peter, the bishop of Coutances refused to give him induction, on pretext that, by the lapse of six months, the right of nomination had devolved upon him; on which the king sent him a mandate, commanding him to induct his nominee, under the penalty of forfeiting all he held within the royal dominions. There are some instances of the rectors having been appointed by the pope, of which we give the following example. His holiness having appointed Peter Le Valleys to the rectory of St. Peter, and put him into possession, one Guillevin ousted him by force, by pleading that he had authority from the patron so to do ; but this intrusion was cancelled by an order from king Edward the Second to Otho de Grandison, guardian of the islands, to reinstate the papal nominee.

" While the Channel Islands remained under the episcopal jurisdiction of Coutances, the bishop of that diocese appointed a surrogate or substitute in Guernsey, who held the office of dean, and united in his own person the offices of chancellor and archdeacon, having power to give institution and induction, to pronounce sentence in cases appertaining to ecclesiastical cognizance, to certify wills, and to hold visitations. He held the principal benefice of the island, and had a proportion of tithes collected from the different parishes. He took the fees of the ecclesiastical court, and the rents due to the island of Lihou. When the religious houses were suppressed, he received an allowance of 100 quarters of wheat, paid him by the king's receiver, for his tithes. Those religious houses enjoyed all the predial tithes, for which some of their members performed the cure of souls ; but the bulk of the revenues belonging to them were paid to certain monasteries and abbeys in France, on which they were dependent, and of which they were branches. " [1]

The church of St. Andrew was built in this reign, A.D. 1284, being the ninth which had been completed in 173 years, during a period when the population of Guernsey was comparatively limited, and when the principal wealth of the island was derived from its fisheries.

This chapter would by many be thought incomplete without some mention of the legend of the Bailiff's Cross ; and, as the tale is very firmly and generally believed, we shall relate it ; although it belongs rather to romance than to history.

Gaultier (*Anglicè* Walter) De La Salle, who is said to have been the bailiff of the island in 1284, resided on his estate then called " La Petite Ville," and now bordering the high road from Mount Row to St. Martin's. A peasant, Massy by name, was proprietor of a cottage with a little land near the bailiff's house, and possessed the right of drawing water from a well on the bailiff's premises. The exercise of this right annoyed the bailiff, who sought in consequence to purchase Massy's land ; but, not succeeding, he determined on revenging himself. With this design, he concealed two silver

(1) Duncan's History of Guernsey, p. 324, 325.

cups in one of his corn ricks, and accused Massy of stealing them. The peasant was tried and convicted of the theft. On the day appointed for the condemnation or execution, the bailiff ordered his men to remove into a barn the rick which he pointed out to them, and then left home for the court-house. Happily, the men mistook their master's orders, and commenced removing the wrong rick, in which they soon found the missing plate. One of them ran instantly to the court-house, in which the bailiff was sitting with the jurats, and, rushing in breathless, he exclaimed : "The cups are found ! the cups are found ! " The wicked bailiff, taken by surprise, betrayed his guilt by replying : "That was not the rick I ordered you to remove." Accordingly, he was tried and sentenced to that death which his victim had so narrowly escaped. On his way to the place of execution, he stopped to receive the Sacrament on the summit of the hill leading from the Vauquiédor to St. Andrew's church, and where two roads now intersect each other at right angles. The name of the *Croix-au-Baillif*, or Bailiff's Cross, is supposed to be derived from this circumstance, and is corroborated by a cross rudely cut upon a large stone of granite close by, and at present nearly embedded in the earth. But, on examining the cross, we found it to resemble far more the capital letter T, the upper arm being entirely wanting,—a fact not confirmatory of the legend.[1] Certain it is, however, that the supposed cross has been there from time immemorial ; but whether it is as old as the thirteenth century, or whether it was cut to commemorate the bailiff's presence, are questions purely conjectural. The bailiff's estate being forfeited to the crown, was thenceforward called " La Ville-au-Roi," a name it bears to this day, and it is still liable to a feudal servitude. Whenever the Cour St. Michel holds a *chevauchée*, the proprietor is bound to furnish the *peons*, or esquires, with sweet milk. In 1825, when the procession took place, the members halted opposite the estate, and milk was abundantly served to them in a large silver cup. The estate, which now belongs to Mr. Thomas Le Retilley, a much esteemed jurat, offers at present few traces of its former note ; its extent has been greatly diminished, having in ancient times joined *Les Granges*, on the Câtel road, for many years in the possession of the De Beauvoir family. To the casual observer, the house of the *Ville-au-Roi* presents nothing remarkable ;. but,

(1) It has been suggested to us that the T may have been intended to represent a gibbet—if so, it must have been to hang two persons.

G

on a closer inspection, the sculptured granite door-way, the granite spiral staircase, and other parts of the building, which have escaped the ravages of time, amply repay the observer. Tradition has done a cruel and irreparable wrong to the memory of a chief magistrate, if the legend be not true, and, if fictitious, we trust that his manes will not rise up in judgment against us for recording it.[1]   While on the subject of bailiffs, we may add that, in the thirteenth century, the same individual was appointed by the warden to be not only his deputy but the bailiff and receiver, which three offices were held during pleasure, and seldom for any length of time. Occasionally the same person filled these offices at one period in Jersey, and at another in Guernsey.

EDWARD II. — 1307 to 1327.

Edward was so nearly allied to France by his marriage with Isabel, daughter of one, and sister of three, of the sovereigns of that kingdom, that, during the greater part of his reign, peace was maintained between the two countries, and these islands happily ceased to be molested, unless by piratical incursions.   But, according to Falle and our later historians, his copyists, they could scarcely have suffered more from a French invasion than they did by the arbitrary and illegal proceedings of the English justices itinerant, who occasionally visited them.   In consequence, so great was the violation of the privileges of the inhabitants that no one was sure of his property, and no prescription availed against the unjust claims of the crown.   If the proprietor established his right, he was yet liable to be annoyed by a ruinous and vexatious appeal to the courts of Westminster, which issued highly unconstitutional *Quo Warrantos*, compelling attendance ; but this last named grievance, although often resisted, was at length finally abolished by an order in council of June 22, 1565.   Falle observes that this attendance on the English courts was directly contrary to the fundamental constitution of the islanders, which exempted them from the power and jurisdiction of those courts.   He might have added that in that age such attendance was a grievous wrong, considering the many dangers and delays attendant on all intercourse with England.   But we suspect that the islanders, generally, suffered quite as much from the despotic rule of the warden, Otho de Grandison, and the exactions of the *seigneurs*, as from either " Quo Warantos " or English justices itinerant.

(1) A ballad of this legend is given at great length in Dickens' Household Words, vol. ii., pp. 85, 86.—1850.

In those days the *seigneurs* enforced their rights with vexatious pertinacity — rights which were as inconsistent with justice and humanity as with individual liberty, and which bore great resemblance to the more modern ones of the slaveholder. During the long and imbecile reign of Henry III., the royal revenues in England, as well as in these islands, appear to have been greatly diminished by tenants *in capite* alienating without licence, and by ecclesiastics as well as laymen withholding from the crown its just rights. The same parties moreover claimed the privilege of holding courts and other *Jura Regalia*, and greatly oppressed the people by enforcing the laws of free chase, free warren, &c. These feudal lords were very clamorous about their rights, utterly regardless of those of the people, who could not make themselves heard as well as their oppressors, and whose only reliance was on the impartiality and benevolence of the sovereign.

One of the first acts of Edward I., on his return from the Holy Land, in the second year of his reign, was to correct these abuses, and not (as erroneously asserted by Lord Coke, 2 Inst. 280 and 295,) to fill his exchequer with money by unfairly depriving his subjects of their just rights. Before, however, any specific remedy could be provided for the correction of these abuses, evidence was required of their nature and extent; and for this purpose Edward I., on the 11th October, An. 2 of his reign, appointed special commissioners through whom the crown was furnished, by the means of a jury upon oath, with the necessary information relating to the alienated demesne lands of the crown and manors; tenants *in capite*, and tenants in ancient demesne; courts, wrecks of the sea, free chase, &c. A few of these inquisitions were not completed until the reign of Edward III.: those relating to these islands were held in the reign of Edward II., and the following is the heading of a patent or commission issued for Guernsey by the latter monarch, in 1324, to Henry Spigurnel and other justices itinerant, who were empowered to enquire into the alienation of the insular crown dues.

Edwardus, Dei gratia, Rex Angliæ, Dominus Hiberniæ et Dux Aquitaniæ, dilectis et fidelibus suis Henrico Spigurnel, Magistro Henrico de Clif, Johanne de Ifeld, et Willielmo de Denum, salutem. Sciatis quod cum nuper, dato nobis intelligi quod diversæ terræ et tenementa, cum homagiis et servitiis, advocationibus ecclesiarum et cappellarum, eschaetis, wreccis maris, warrennis, chaciis, custumis makerellorum, esparkeriarum, coungrorum, et aliis libertatibus diversis, quæ ad nos pertinent, et de jure pertinere debent, in insulis nostris de Gernereye, Jereseye, Serk, et Aureneye, per quosdam homines et habitatores insularum prædictarum, religiosos, et alios, tam tempore domini Regis Henrici avi Regis nostri, quam tempore domini Edwardi Regis patris nostri, et nostro, usurpata fuerunt indebitè et detenta, et aliæ diversæ subtractiones libertatum et jurium nostrorum in partibus illis, ac purpresturæ similiter factæ fuerunt ibidem, in nostrum præjudicium et exhæredationem nostram manifestam.

In the " Placita de Quo Warranto, Temp. Ed. I. II. III.," will be found the reports of causes tried in Guernsey and Jersey by English justices, in the reign of Edward II. They contain some curious matter, but are much too long for insertion or even analysis here, the report for Guernsey alone consisting of nine pages and a half folio, closely printed. These placita, or pleas, were held at the close of the second year of Edward II., (1308,) viz. first, before John de Fresingfeld and William Russel, to hear complaints of divers persons against the officers of the king and Otho de Grandison ; and secondly, before the said John de Fresingfeld, Drogo de Barentyn, and John de Dittone, when the several *seigneurs*, ecclesiastical and lay, were summoned to establish their feudal tenures and rights, and among them was Matthew de Sausmareys[1] for his fief of " Gerebourg." A general default was taken against the abbot of *Mont St. Michel*, in periculo maris. In the proceedings, which are drawn up in Latin as usual, the following names occur, viz. Robert Le Marchaunt, and Cecilia his wife, and Nicholas de Cheney, as also Abbia de Blancalanda ; Abbas and Prior de Wale ; (Vale) Insula and Insuletta de Geyteho ; Prioratus de Lyho ; and Russemare.

The parishes of Guernsey are named as follows in the said pleas of Quo Warranto ; William Des Mareys, on behalf of the crown, having then laid claim to certain lands and rents, " in parochiis Sci Petri in Portu, Sce Marie de Castro, Sci Salvatoris, Sci Andr', Sci Martini de Bellosa, Sci Samps', Sci Petri de Bosco, de Wale,[2] Fortenal,[3] et Foresta."

The present church of St. Peter-Port was consecrated in this reign, (1312,) and as it was the last of the ten parish churches, so it was by far the largest and handsomest. It is built in the form of a cross, and consists of a chancel, nave, north and south aisles, and north and south transepts, with a square tower at their intersection. This cathedral-like

(1) In the assizes of 1331, spelt Saltmares.   (2) The Vale.   (3) Torteval.

edifice, which is well worth the attention of the antiquary and stranger, is of the style of the later gothic of France termed the flamboyant, and it is richly decorated in some parts. "The mouldings and the canopies," says the Rev. W. C. Lukis, "of the north porch and west door, which are crocketed, finialed, and pinnacled, deserve especial notice. The pillars of the south transept are octagonal, without capitals, and the mouldings of the archivolt die away into them. In the east wall of the transept is a granite piscina, ogee-headed and trefoiled, with a shelf across it.[1] In the east walls of the north and south aisles are most elegant piscinæ, the canopies of which are crocketed, finialed, and pinnacled, and the interior moulding of the arch and sides formed of crumpled leaves and creeping animals. The shelves consist of brackets of leaves, above which are two niches, square-headed and trefoiled. In the south-east pier of the north aisle, there is also a piscina. Against the south pier of the chancel arch there was a stone pulpit, which was removed during the repairs, in 1824, in consequence of its extremely mutilated state."

In the year, 1308, Edward II. ordered, by mandate to the guardian, Otho de Grandison, "that the men of the islands of Guernsey, Jersey, Sark, and Alderney, shall not be cited to appear before the bishop of Coutances, in causes of which the cognizance appertains to the king."

Edward, towards the close of his reign, found it necessary to engage in a war with France, and in a short time 120 Norman vessels were brought into England as lawful prizes.

CHÁPTER VI.

EDWARD III.—1327 to 1377.

THIS warlike prince was only fifteen when, through the crimes of his mother and the successful efforts of her partisans, he succeeded to his unhappy father's throne. Powerful, however, as Edward became, in no preceding or succeeding reign did probably the inhabitants of all the islands fare so ill

(1) At the period when the repairs were made, (1824,) a piece of carved oak was found in the same wall, with the following inscription: "an: mill: cccc. xlvi. fut faite," which probably refers to the date when this transept was erected.

and suffer so much as in this; for not only were they occasionally ravaged, but Guernsey and Castle Cornet were at least each once for a short time in possession of the enemy. Edward found England at war with France, but it was quickly terminated after his accession.

On the death of Charles IV., king of France, Edward III. considered himself entitled to the crown of that country, in right of his mother Isabel, sister to the three last kings; but he delayed preferring his claim for several years, while he was young, and his attention was occupied with the affairs of Scotland. The events of his wars with France are too well known to require more than a notice of those which relate to this history, or to the adjacent provinces of Normandy and Britany, especially the former; and suffice it to add here, that in the course of about twenty years Edward reduced that previously powerful kingdom to an utter state of exhaustion.

In *Le Précepte d'Assize*[1] of 5 Edward III., A.D. 1331, it was ordered, among other regulations, that as it had been customary from ancient time for the bailiff and jurats to visit and inspect the insular castles and other fortresses, they should continue to do so; the reason given being that Castle Cornet is the protection (garde) and fortress of the isle of Guernsey, and is detached from it, beset and surrounded on all sides by the sea; that, in consequence, it could not be succoured by the men of the said isle, owing to which "the said castle of Cornet, by the fault of the captain who commanded it, and the insufficiency of the munitions therein, by a force and in truth was taken by the enemy," and soon after was recaptured "through the prowess (prouesse) and diligence of the lieges and inhabitants of Guernsey." This capture evidently refers to that in the reign of Henry III., as stated by Duncan, or to that in the time of Edward I., mentioned by Dicey.

About the year 1336, the French, although bound by treaty towards England, covertly afforded assistance to the Scotch; and Philip, king of France, aided David Bruce, the exiled king of Scotland, with a well appointed fleet, in which David embarked, and with which he inflicted much evil, not only upon the Anglo-Norman islands, where he burnt, slew, and

---

(1) This term signifies or embraces a declaration of the insular rights and privileges made before, and approved by, the justices of assize. The Précepte d'Assize is given in Berry, p. 317, translated from French into English.

committed other enormities, but upon the Hampshire coast.[1]
Edward III., in a long manifesto against Philip, dated 1340,
thus speaks of Bruce's atrocities in Guernsey, where he
spared neither age nor sex : " Et insulam nostram de Gernesey invadentes hostiliter, ecclesias, et ædificia singula redi-
gerunt in miserabilem cibum ignis, interficientes quos illuc
invenerant, ætati, sexui, vel ordini non parcendo." We
learn, moreover, from the continuator of Nangis, a French
annalist, that in 1338 certain "galleys ravaged Guernsey,
and set fire to the principal town, except a castle." This
exception must apply to some other castle than Cornet, probably the Vale, or that now known as Ivy Castle, as in the
same year a French admiral, Bahuchet by name, took Castle
Cornet and the islands of Guernsey, Sark, and Alderney, as
appears upon record in the Exchequer, thus : "Anno XII.
(1338,) Edw. III., Mémorandum, quod in festo nativitatis
Beatæ Mariæ, captum fuit Castrum Cornet cum insulâ
Geners, Serk et Aulnerey, per Gallos, et in potestate Regis
Franciæ." In consequence, the inspection of Castle Cornet
by the bailiff and jurats, as ordered by Edward, had not the
desired effect. Falle,—who in the first edition of his History
of Jersey, published in 1694, erroneously fixed the loss of
Guernsey in 1339, which date he found it convenient to omit
in the second edition, published in 1734,—says, that until
this time Castle Cornet was thought impregnable, and he
adds that the French retained their conquest "three whole
years ;" but the following extract relative to the castle proves
the island to have been in possession of England in 1339 :
" Anno XIII. Edw. III. m. 32. (1339.)—Item, fait à remem-
bre que Monsieur Thomas de Ferrars ad empris d'envoyer
saunz delay un homme suffisant au chastel de Gerneseye,

---

(1) *Mandatum de intendendo commissariis antedictis*; *in quo Res iterum vendicat sibi
dominium maris Anglicani.*

[Extract.]

A.D. 1336.   Rex, universis et singulis comitibus, baronibus, &c., salutem.
An. 10 Edw. III.   Nuper, ut pro certo intelleximus, David de Bruys & nonnulli alii
          de Scotiâ, hostes nostri, & sibi adhærentes, copiosam navium &
, Rot. Scot.   galearum multitudinem, in diversis locis supra mare, & etiam in aliis
10 Edw. III. m. 3.   locis & portubus exteris, congregari fecerunt, & mercatores & alios
in Turr. Lond.   regni nostri per mare transeuntes hostiliter agredientes, tam naves ac
           bona & res ipsorum subditorum nostrorum quam quasdam alias naves,
propè litora Insulæ Vectæ jacentes ancoratas, mercatoribus & marinariis, in dictis
navibus existentibus, nequiter interfectis, pluries ceperunt, & secum abduxerunt, insulas-
que nostras de Gernereye & Jereseye hostiliter etiam sunt ingressi, incendia, homicidia,
& alia mala & facinora, tam ibidem quam supra mare, diversimodè & inhumaniter
perpetrantes.—*Rymer's Fœdera.*
" Rex Edwardus mandat quod homines eligantur, armentur, et in insulas Gernereye,
Jereseye, &c., mittantur, ad eas defendendum ab invasione sociorum Scotiæ." (10 Ed.
III. A.D. 1336.) *Rotuli Scotiæ*, vol. i. p. 455. David II., son of Robert Bruce, returned to
Scotland from France, after an absence of nine years, and assumed the government,
Balliol having been expelled by the nobles.

pour sursur les défautes et l'état de meisme le chastel ; pur
pleinement **certifier** ent **au conseil, et en moen temps** de
trover gages à ceux qui y demeureront en garnisons illecques,
tant que la some de cent livres ; et le dit Monsieur Thomas
ferroit pourvoir tote mancre de morte garnisture pur le dit
chastel, disore selon ce qui est requis par les messages du dit
chastel.   Et l'Ercevesque Canterburie et le Trésorier sont
accordez, coment que serra fait à dit Monsieur Thomas trente
tonneaulx de pomadre,[1] cinquante quintals de fer, deux quintals d'acier, pur le meisme garniture ; et pur ceo que Guillaum
Pein,[2] un des juretz de l'isle de Gerneseye, est alors contre
defens à les enemys ; soit brief mande au bailiff et jurez de
meisme l'isle de eslire un antre suffisant en son lieu, et de
seiser ses terres, biens, et châteaux en la main le roi à res-
pondre ent les issues.—*Harl. MSS. No.* 14, *p.* 58.[3]

Falle adds also on the same subject, and on the sole authority of a very questionable manuscript : " The deliverance of
Guernsey was too great an enterprise for those of Jersey to
go upon, on their own strength alone.   But, hearing of a
fleet ready to sail from England with recruits for the king,
and of orders given to the commanders Regnault de Cobham
and Geoffrey de Harcourt to attempt in their way the recovery of the captive island, they raised a contribution of 6,400
marks for that service, went out and joined the fleet, and
assisted in retaking both the island and the castle ; many
Jerseymen of note losing honourably their lives on that occasion, as the Sieurs de Vinchelez, de Matravers, des Augrez,
de Garis, de la Hougue, Lempriere, and other leaders specially named, besides private adventurers."   On this extract
we shall briefly observe ; first, that the attack of Cobham and
Harcourt occurred in 1344, or five years after the date originally assigned by Falle for the capture of Guernsey, and
that this attack seems to have failed ; and, secondly, that the
sum of 6,400 marks was equivalent to fully £16,000[4] of the

(1) Pomadre (correctly pomade) is the old French word for cider.   Mr. Bree supposed
pomadre, from the context, to mean gunpowder, and observes that he had found the word
no where else, except in a MS. record, " reciting letters of pardon to several persons for
arrearages of debt due to the king, where, in one granted to Thomas de Brockhall, pur
trente et deux tonneaulx de pomadre, des queux il est charge de son account, di tems
que il estoit assigne de faire divers purveyances ad opus le roi, en conté de Kent."—
Southey adds to this note, that "the signification of the word is altogether doubtful."
(2) This William Pein had probably lands in both Normandy and Guernsey, and if so,
he preferred his Norman possessions, as more secure and valuable.
(3) Bree's Sketch of this Kingdom, (England,) during the fourteenth century, printed
in 1791.
(4) This is the very lowest computation.   Falle states that the livre tournois (libra
turonensis) was worth as much then as an English pound sterling was in his time, and,
allowing for the change in the value of money from Falle's time to this, the mark, which
appears to have passed in Jersey for at least one livre five sols, would now represent fully
£2. 10s. sterling.   But Mably (*Observations sur l'Histoire de France*, tome iii.) says :
" Sous Philippe le Bel, les monnaies varioent continuellement, et en 1305, le marc d'argent valoit huit livres dix sols."

present money, a sum so improbable[1] as to throw discredit on
the entire statement, which is somewhat confusedly disproved by Duncan in his History of Guernsey.[2] In 1379,
or forty years after the Jersey contribution, Bristol, a very
rich commercial city, gave 1,000 marks to Richard II., which
appears to have been thought a large donation, and we doubt
if Jersey then possessed a tithe of the wealth of Bristol,
that island having at that time no harbour, and probably no
shipping and no trade. But, above all, as Edward was rising
into the zenith of his fame, having in 1340 gained a complete
naval victory near Sluys, he never would have allowed the
French to retain their conquest of Guernsey "three whole
years," viz., from 1338 or 1339 to 1341 or 1342. We doubt,
moreover, the Sieur de Garis being a Jerseyman, that name
being then one of note in Guernsey.

We have dwelt the longer on the preceding statements of
the Jersey historian, because Inglis, in his "Channel Islands,"
(London, 1834,) after saying that "the authority of Falle in
this matter is not recognised in Guernsey," observes that
"the general authenticity of Falle is an important corrobo-
ration of the truth of his assertion, although his authority is
neither Froissart, nor Sir Robert Cotton, nor Walsingham,
but is simply stated to be Ex. MMS." Now, in answer, we
prove in this chapter, from the Harleian MSS., that although
Guernsey and Castle Cornet were taken in 1338, they could
not have been long occupied by their captors, as both were
in the possession of England in 1339 and 1340 ; while the
Fœdera further shews that such possession was retained in
July, 1341, and June, 1342. If further evidence were wanting, it is furnished by the truce which Edward entered into
for nine months with Philip of France, on the 25th of September, 1340, and which truce, by the intervention of the
pope, was continued for two years longer. Its purport was
to this effect : "It is agreed, that if any of the confederates
or generals of the two kings shall lay siege to any towns in
Gascony or Aquitaine, or in Guernsey or Jersey, such sieges
shall be instantly raised after this truce shall have come to
their knowledge."[3] The castle must have been again sub-

(1) The Rev. E. Durell says, that, about 1750, in Jersey, "payments to a considerable
amount were often made in *liards* or small French copper. This must have been owing
to the poverty of the country."

(2) Duncan, at page 31, by an evident error in his own calculation, wherein he reckons
pence as shillings, makes 6,400 marks as equal to £95,040 sterling.

(3) "VII. Item, Est accordé que, si par ascun des ditz Rois, par lour gentz, ou lour
alliés, & coadjutours, ascun siege soit mys en Gascoigne, ou ep le duché d'Aquitaine, ou
en altres isles de mier, en Gerneseye, ou Jerseye, ou aillours, les seiges se leveront si .
tost com les trewes vendront à lour conissaunce."—*Fœdera.*

sequently captured, as it was regained by the vessels from
Bayonne, in 1345 ; and it is also very possible that Guernsey
was held by the enemy at the same time, as the Fœdera
makes no mention of any of these islands from the 8th of
June, 1342, to the 28th of August, 1345.   But, after diligent
research, we feel convinced that the " Memoir," relating
to the 6,400 marks, any effectual assistance afforded by the
Jerseymen, and the death of their leaders, was a pure fabri-
cation too willingly adopted by Falle, who, as he admitted
that the sum, said to have been raised, " must seem exor-
bitant," ought not to have given credence to the MS. account
without some authentic confirmation of its truth.

We have shewn that Guernsey was captured by the French
in 1338, and it is said, on private authority, that several of
the parishioners of St. Martin's, to the number of 87, conspired
to expel the enemy, whom they fought at " Mare-Madoc,"
in the district of the " Hubits."   The Guernseymen, being
defeated, embarked in the steep and sandy bay called " La
Petite Porte," near Jerbourg, and sailed for Jersey, where
they found refuge in the parish of St. Ouen.   Among them
are mentioned John de la Marche, who was captain of the
parish, Peter de Sausmarez, James Guille, Peter Bonamy,
John de Blanchelande, and Thomas de Vauriouf ; but it is
strange that the inhabitants of the other parishes did not
unite with those of St. Martin's to expel the invaders, who
must have been so small in numbers for 87 men to attempt it
that the islanders collectively would have succeeded in doing
so.   Philip, king of France, appears to have considered this
conquest of Guernsey as finally accomplished, as, in the
month of October, 1338, by a charter, he bestowed the island
on his eldest son John, " *chier aisné fils Jehan, duc de Normandie, conte d'Anjou et du Meynne.*"   The said John ceded
also by charter " *la seigneurie et baronnie de l'ille de Guer-
nerrieu à son aimé et féal chevalier Robert Bertram, sire de
Briquebec, mareschal de France,*" one of the most distinguished commanders in that age of heroes and adventurers.

In March, 1338, Bahuchet, with his French galleys, also
landed a large force near Portsmouth, which town was almost
entirely burnt, after many of its inhabitants had been killed ;
but, having been captured with his fleet in the great naval
victory off Sluys, by Edward, in June, 1340, Bahuchet was
hanged at the main-yard, on account of the enormities which,

"to say no more," he had permitted at Southampton. In the battle off Sluys, piles of stones on deck formed a part of the missiles. The archers of both nations used their cross bows, as if they had been on land. Grappling irons for boarding were employed, and the crews came to such close quarters as to exhibit a succession of single combats. In the Harleian MSS. there exists a proclamation, dated at Berkhampstead, August 3, 1340, to the sheriffs, mayors, bailiffs, &c., to arrest, man, and victual ships in Portsmouth harbour, and all the other ports and towns westward, to transport Thomas Ferrars, knight, with his armed force, going to the relief of Gerneseye, Gerseye, and Dureney, at that time in danger from the enemy's fleet of galleys and ships of war; and in 1344, according to Sauvage's Chronicles of Flanders, another French naval commander, Marans, (who was also subsequently hanged, as a punishment for his numerous cruelties,) captured five English vessels near the island of Guernsey, and put to death all the English on board.—When Edward was informed of the circumstance, he sent Geoffrey d'Harcourt and Regnault de Cobham with 10,000 men to attack the castle, which must have been again in the enemy's possession; they went and made many fierce assaults, the garrison, consisting of 500 men, long defended themselves: their "chastelain" was a stout knight and brave man, named Nicholas Aliart. The number of the assailants, if not of the defenders, is doubtless much exaggerated, especially as the attack appears to have failed; for in the following year, 1345, the castle was regained by the "masters and admirals of the galleys," (magistris & admirallis galearum,) last from Bayonne, which town was then under the sovereignty of Edward, and evidently of some importance, the said officers being assisted by others of his faithful subjects ("per vos & quosdam alios fideles nostros de guerrâ captum, & in custodiâ vestrâ jam existens.") By the king's order or warrant,[1] dated 5th of August, 1345, we learn the names of five of these commanders, viz. Peter Bernard, of Toulouse, (Tholosa,) of the ship called the Katherine; Peter de Benessa, of the ship called La Dieu le Garde; Raymond de Vallibus, of the ship called La Navedieu; Arnaldus de Caressa, of the ship called the St. Mary, and Peter Darbins, (elsewhere Darby,) of the ship called the St. Peter, pilots or masters (rectores seu magistri) of Bayonne, with their ships, galleys, and other vessels. The warrant adds that as these individuals had come to Edward's

(1) Fœdera, vol. iii., pars 1, p. 56. Londini, 1825.

succour, to expel the French (ad expugnationem Gallicorum) and other of his enemies, he took them under his special protection and defence. (defensionem.) The king soon after issued a command in Latin to these officers to deliver the castle to Sir Thomas Ferrars, warden of the Anglo-Norman Isles, and to return to Bayonne, or elsewhere. A copy of this order, dated 28th of August, 1345, is preserved in the rolls of the tower of London, headed, " De Castro de Cornet, in insula de Gereseye nuper capto, Thomæ de Ferrariis liberando." [1]   It contains an assurance of indemnity for the capture or retention of the castle, as well as a safe conduct to Bayonne, the reasons for which we do not well comprehend, as the captors were unquestionably either Edward's subjects or his foreign auxiliaries. The necessity of an indemnity is the more incomprehensiblè, because, only fifteen years previously, the chief of the captors, Peter Bernard, was a joint warden of the isles, with Laurence de Gaillard, as will be seen by the following entries in the "Abbreviatio Rotulorum Originalium," temp. Edw. III., vol. ii., pp. 37, 50 :

(Ann. 4, Edw. III. A.D. 1330.) — " R. commisit Petro Bernard de Pynsole, & Laurencio de Galars de Baiona, custodiam Insula. R. de Gerneseye, Jereseye, Serk, & Aureneye, & alia. insula. adjacencium hend' & regend' cum omnib. pficuis, &c., qmdiu, &c., reddo inde p ann' quingentas libr'. Ita qd, &c."

(Ann. 5, Edw. III. A.D. 1331.)—" Mand' est Petro Bernard de Pynsole, & Laurencio du Gaillard, custodib.   Insula. de Gernereye, Jereseye, Serk, & Aureneye, qd molendinum R. de Beauveir in dca Insula de Jereseye ad tram pstratum est & consumptum p qd, &c., de firma insula. pdca. reparari seu de novo construi fac'. Ita qd de decem marcis respondeat annuatim.   Et de custub., &c." [2]

Guienne and Gascony, of which Bordeaux and Bayonne were the principal sea-ports, were then subject to Edward ; and as Bernard and Gaillard were evidently master mariners, either cruising in the channel or engaged in the conger fishery of Guernsey, it would now seem that the king found it convenient, in 1330, to entrust the keeping of these islands to them : they were doubtless dispossessed of their government during the invasions of Guernsey, a few years afterwards, and they appear to have returned in 1345 with a sufficient force to recapture Castle Cornet   Although Laurence de Gaillard

(1) The whole is given in Duncan, p. 583, and in the Chronicles of Castle Cornet, p. 317. It is taken from the Fœdera, vol. iii., pars 1, p. 57.

(2) See also Report of the Royal Commissioners in 1846, p. 303 and 324.

was a native or inhabitant of Bayonne, there was unquestionably a family of his name seated in Guernsey in the fourteenth century;[1] it was apparently of Gascon origin, as is that of de Garis,[2] and we translate from the French the following notices[3] relative to them :

" A.D. 1313.—The fisheries of Saint Michel at Guernsey are let for a term of five years to Michael de Gaillart and to Peter de Garris, at the price of 15 sols tournois per hundred of congers."—*Bible d'Avranches MSS. St. Michel.*

" A.D. 1319.—The said fisheries are let for another term of five years, and at the same price, to Peter de Gaillart and Peter de Garris."—*Ibid.*

"`A.D. 1336.—Thomas de Ferrars, warden of the isles, presents William de Gaillart, ' clerc,' to the bishop of Coutances, to be instituted to the parochial cure of Notre Dame du Castel, then vacant."

" A.D. 1342.—The bishop of Coutances—in contempt (au mépris) of the presentation made to him, on the part of the king, of the person of William de Gaillart—having instituted a stranger, residing in the enemy's country, to the cure of the ' Castel,' king Edward III. commands the warden of the isles to sequester the revenues of the said cure."

The conger and mackerel fisheries[4] of Guernsey, in the fourteenth century, were very extensive; and the Gascony merchants appear to have resorted to the island to purchase conger, &c., in the same manner as, two centuries later, the English and other merchants resorted, and still resort, to Newfoundland for codfish. In the document in Latin, styled The Constitutions of king John, the twentieth article is as follows : " At the same time, the salting of congers was appointed to be between the festival of Michaelmas and Easter, which the bailiffs of our lord the king farmed out, as being a fishery. And this regulation for the salting of congers was first made on account of the fishermen, who carried fish to the enemies of our lord the king." The duty paid to the crown on salt congers and mackerel was called *esperkeria,* and by the extent or king's rent roll of 1331, for Guernsey,

(1) The *Dédicaces des Eglises* states that there were persons of the name of du Gaillard at the consecration of the following churches : the Vale, in 1117; St. Pierre-du-Bois, in 1167; St. Martin, in 1199; and the Câtel, in 1203. According to the same authority, the name of de Garis appears also to have been common in Guernsey in the twelfth century.

(2) Garris, a town six and a half leagues S.E. of Bayonne. Peter de Garis was bailiff of Guernsey in 1325, and the name still exists in the island.

(3) We are indebted to Mr. John Métivier for these notices.

(4) A.D. 1325. An. 18 Edw. II.—Gernesey : " Similiter libtates clam. p abbem de Monte Sci Michis in piclo maris p piscacione congro. & mackrello. dicto abbi allocantur."—*Abbreviatio Placitorum.*

this duty appears to have been farmed out for 266 livres, 13 sous, and 4 deniers. Mackerel was caught between Easter and Michaelmas.—Durell thinks it not improbable that the conger fishery lasted until it was replaced by that of Newfoundland, early in the seventeenth century. The English justices itinerant sent over to these islands, 5 Edward III., A.D. 1331, were furnished with no less than 64 items of enquiry, among which are the following :

Item, de vendentibus pisces alibi quam loco statuto.

Item, de alienantibus, elongantibus, vel concedentibus pisces regales, per quod domino Regi non respondeatur de parte sua.

Item, de salientibus congros contra statutum, vel alios vendentibus contra statutum est, vel alibi ducentibus quam ad esperkariam domini Regis.

Duncan, (p. 26,) on the sole and unsupported authority of Mr. Thomas Le Marchant, who, during the middle of the last century, wrote a Commentary on Falle's History, which was never published, and which Duncan too implicitly followed, dwells at some length on "a certificate signed by the Royal Court of Jersey, under the seal of that island, and addressed, in December, 1340, to John Le Marchant, wherein the bailiff and jurats acknowledge his great services in defending their island and castles against the enemy, who had made several attempts upon them ; and they further admit that, without his assistance, they would most probably have been subdued." Having just accused Falle of blindly following a very questionable MS., it behoves us the more to add, in justice to Jersey, that until the certificate under seal, mentioned by Mr. Le Marchant, or a well authenticated copy thereof, be produced, it will remain a matter of great doubt that it ever existed. The services said to be therein recorded are of themselves very improbable ; and it is natural to suppose that the Le Marchant family, which has maintained its rank and consideration since that time, would carefully have preserved a document so honorable to one of its ancestors. Falle, who very seldom gives dates, after speaking of the capture by the French of Guernsey and Castle Cornet, in 1338, says : "They fared not so well in JERSEY, being repulsed before *Mont Orgueil* Castle, yet did a great deal of damage to the open country. In one of the attacks upon the castle, the brave governor, *Droûet* (or *Drogo*) *de Barentin, seigneur de Rosel*, was killed ; but his place was supplied by *Renaud de Carteret*, a gentleman of

equal courage and valour." Here is no mention of Le
Marchant, whose services would have been required in Guernsey, his native island. We have shewn from the Harleian
MSS. that all the islands were threatened with an attack in
August, 1340; but there is no proof that any one island was
invaded, and here again Le Marchant's services and "great
military genius" were equally wanted at home.

During the long and somewhat chequered reign of Edward
III., the Anglo-Norman Islands were exposed to constant
invasions,[1] as we have already observed, and their insecurity
at that period may be easily conceived when the character of
England suffered by the impunity with which its coasts were
insulted and ravaged by French, Genoese, and other adventurers. The Fœdera gives many examples of that insecurity,
viz. 1335, order to fortify the islands, which are endangered
by the appearance of a large hostile fleet—1337, a commission to levy and train the inhabitants of Guernsey, Jersey,
Sark, and Alderney, to the use of arms, and to array them
in thousands, hundreds, and twenties; (in millenis, centenis,
& vintenis, ponendum;) so that there was already a militia: in
this commission the burnings and slayings by the Scots in Sark
are particularly mentioned[2]—1338, ravages of the French
in the islands—1342, Thomas de Hampton, warden of the
isles, unable to make a remittance to the exchequer, in consequence of their having been ravaged. And if the islanders
fared thus sadly while their gallant sovereign was attaining
the noon-tide of his manhood and the meridian of his prosperity, it is not surprising that Guernsey should, thirty years
later, be subjected to other invasions and their attendant

(1) "The old Chronicle of Flanders speaks of hostilities against the same island of
Guernsey, by the admirals of France and Castille, the year before king Edward died;
but these came only as pirates and robbers, for the sake of plunder."—*Falle.*

(2) [Extract.]

De arraiando homines insularum Gernereye, Jereseye, Serk, & Aureneye.

A.D. 1337.
An. 11. Edw. III.
Pat. 11. Edw. III.
p. 1. m. 5. d.
in Turr. Lond.

Rex, universis & singulis, archiepiscopis, episcopis, abbatibus, pri-
oribus, comitibus, baronibus, militibus, libere-tenentibus, ballivis,
ministris, & omnibus aliis fidelibus suis insularum suarum de Gerne-
reye, Jereseye, Serk, & Aureneye, salutem. Quia datum est nobis intelligi quod quidam, Scotis, inimicis nostris
adhærentes, dictam insulam de Serk, & quasdam alias partes earum-
dem insularum, nuper hostiliter invaserunt, & incendia, homicidia, &
alia facinora diversa, ibidem inhumaniter perpetrarunt, & proponunt iterùm ibidem mala
consimilia perpetrare, nisi ipsorum militiæ viriliùs obvietur;
Nos, de fidelitate & circumspectione dilecti & fidelis nostri, Thomæ de Ferariis, quem
custodem insularum nostrarum prædictarum jam constituimus, confidentes;
Assignavimus ipsum Thomam, adlevandum & arraiandum omnes homines insularum
prædictarum defensabiles, & in millenis, centenis, & vintenis, ponendum, & ad eos, benè
arraiatos, & armis competentibus sufficienter munitos, ducendum, pro salvatione & defen-
sione insularum prædictarum, contra hujusmodi hostium incursis, si qui dictas insulas,
vel aliquam earumdem, invadere, vel gravare, præsumpserint, clam vel palam; &c.—
Rymer's Fœdera.

calamities, when, as if to wean him from the world, his evening was overcast, and his star of victory was dimmed.

In July, 1341, Edward III. issued a declaration in Latin to the islanders, which was prefaced thus : "The king to all to whom, &c., health — Know ye that we, considering with thankful remembrance how constantly and nobly our beloved and faithful subjects of our islands of Jersey, Guernsey, Sark, and Alderney have ever heretofore continued in their allegiance to us and to our forefathers, kings of England, and what they have endured for the preservation of the said islands, and the maintenance of our rights and honour therein, as well at the risk of their lives as by the expenditure of their resources ; and desiring, in consequence, to distinguish them by our gracious favor, we have granted," &c. — This grant was a full confirmation for himself, his heirs and successors, of all the immunities and privileges which the islands enjoyed, and it must have been rendered doubly valuable to the inhabitants, by the testimony of this martial sovereign to their loyalty and sufferings,—a testimony which forcibly reminds us of that of queen Victoria, in 1848, or five centuries later, when she commanded Sir George Grey "to express her Majesty's deep sense of this new proof[1] of the loyalty and attachment of her faithful and excellent people of Guernsey."

In the disputed succession to the dukedom of Britany, in which Edward III. supported the count de Montfort, a fleet of forty-six sail, few or none of burden, was collected at Southampton, in 1342 or 1343,[2] to convey succours to the adherents of the count in that province. Charles de Blois, his brother and rival, aware of this armament, stationed Don Luis of Spain,[3] a naval officer in his service, with thirty-two large vessels,[4] having on board 1,000 men at arms, and 3,000 Genoese cross bowmen, off Guernsey, to intercept it. The English were long on the passage, because of contrary winds ; but upon approaching the island, they descried the enemy, when the seamen pronounced them to be Genoese and Spaniards, and called upon the soldiers to arm quickly. The

(1) The erection of a tower, in the parish of St. Peter-Port, to commemorate the queen's visit to Guernsey, on the 24th of August, 1846.

(2) "1342, Don Luis, Sir Char. Grimaldi, and Sir Otho Doria, off Guernsey, to intercept Sir Rob. of Artois and the Countess of Montfort—Encounter—no advantage gained on either side."—*Knyghton.* Southey gives the year 1343.

(3) His real name was don Luis de la Cerda.

(4) Barnes, in his History of Edward III., calls them "Spanish carricks, high built, and greater than any one of the English."

Genoese, in that age, were as celebrated for the use of the cross bow as the English were for the long ;[1] and the Genoese and Spanish seamen were alike remarkable for their skill and courage, in which qualities they were held by the English to be superior to either the French or Scotch mariners. The battle began towards evening, and raged fiercely; but as the night was dark and dismal, the combatants separated and cast anchor, "remaining in their harness," and thinking to renew the fight on the following morning. But about midnight there arose such a storm, "as though all the world should have ended, the elements contending with as great animosity as lately the two fleets had joined." The English weighed their anchors, and, "bearing but quarter sail," got safely into a little harbour, not far from the city of Vannes, so that the wind was evidently from the north-east, while the Genoese and Spaniards reached Rochelle, after losing two of their ships with all on board. The circumstance of the two fleets casting anchor, is a proof that they must have engaged each other very near the shore.[2]—We have introduced this event here, because it accounts partly, we conceive, for Castle Cornet being in possession of the enemy, as before related, in 1344 and 1345, as it is very improbable that Don Luis would continue under sail about the rocky and dangerous coasts of Guernsey, when, with so imposing a force, he could easily capture the castle, and remain securely at anchor in the roadstead to await the long expected appearance of the fleet from England, which a scout or two, cruising outside, would enable him to do. The war of succession in Britany[3] endured for some years; and the castle, if taken by Don Luis of Spain in 1342 or 1343, could have been garrisoned and provisioned from that province, until Charles de Blois and his Bretons were dispossessed of it, two or three years afterwards, by the vessels from Bayonne. After the naval fight off Guernsey, Don Luis soon refitted his fleet, with which he did much damage upon the coasts of England, and intercepted the communication between that kingdom and Britany. As Guernsey is about midway between them, the advantage of possessing its castle and roadstead for the latter purpose could

(1) "Les Anglais qui sont la fleur des archiers du monde."—*Comines*.

(2) For a detailed account of this naval fight near Guernsey, see Southey's Lives of the British Admirals, vol. i. p. 278.

(3) The illustrious warrior, du Guesclin, constable of France, and a native of Britany, distinguished himself in this war, and was long a victorious opponent of the English. He was, however, foiled in his attack, in 1374, on Mont Orgueil, or Gouray castle, in Jersey.

H

not fail to strike that inhuman[1] but indefatigable commander, who died during the siege of Calais, in 1347, and who, while he lived, was renowned for his courage, his enterprise, and his bitter animosity towards the English.

In 1341, a force, consisting of 6,000 archers and 620 men at arms, under Sir Walter Manny, was dispatched from England in all haste for the relief of the countess de Montfort, then besieged in Hennebon, on the river Blavet, at that time the strongest castle in all Britany, "standing," says Froissart, "on a port of the sea, and the sea running about it in great dykes." This English force on its way could easily have recaptured Guernsey, had it been in possession of the French, as stated by Falle—another proof that it was not. When Charles of Blois had taken Rennes, he proceeded to Hennebon, seeing that, if he could get the countess and her son into his hands, the war would terminate. Accordingly, he besieged both the town and the castle on all sides, except where the castle was open to the sea, for he had no ships. The place was well stored and well manned, but, after a gallant defence, it was reduced to the last extremity, and the garrison was on the point of surrendering when the English succours, which had been delayed above forty days by contrary winds, arrived just in time to save the countess and the town. The English and the Bretons sallied out, and destroyed the largest engine of the besiegers, who on the following day joined Charles of Blois before Auray; but as he had with him a sufficient force for that service, he sent Don Luis of Spain (de la Cerda) to besiege Dinan. On his way thither, Don Luis attacked a castle called Comper, which he took after a gallant defence, and put the garrison to the sword. He next laid siege to Dinan, a place not otherwise fortified than by a palisade, by its lofty position on the river Rance, and by a marsh. Having failed in the first attack, he got together some small vessels, which enabled him to threaten it both by land and water. The craven-hearted townsmen then called upon their young commander to surrender; but, on his refusal, they butchered him in the market place, and admitted the besiegers—thus showing that cruelty is often allied to cowardice. Hostilities were continued in Britany, with varying fortune, until the year 1345, when the count of Montfort sailed from England with a considerable force, and, after winning and sacking Dinan, laid siege to

(1) On his way to Rochelle, as just related, he captured four ships of Bayonne, homeward bound from Flanders, and in the brutal spirit by which his exploits were generally sullied, he put all on board to death.—*Froissart* and *Barnes.*

Quimperlé; but, being seized with a burning fever, he died soon afterwards, "leaving the management of his pretensions to the conduct of his virago lady and his young son John." On his death, most of the English force passed into Gascony, where their presence was then more needed. In this war many of the transports from England probably put into Guernsey on their way, either wind-bound or for pilots, as even now vessels bound to Britany from the North frequently come in wind-bound, or call off the island for pilots.

In the year 1346, Edward, the most popular king that England had had since the conquest, prepared a naval armament consisting of about 700 sail, of which fifty only were large vessels; and in this fleet were embarked 4,000 men at arms, 10,000 archers, 12,000 footmen of Wales, and 6,000 Irish; together, 32,000 men. It was now the end of June, and the fleet sailed from Southampton, making down the channel, as if its course was designed for Bayonne or Bourdeaux, to relieve Aiguillon, then closely besieged. On the third day, when far on their way, the whole fleet was driven back upon the coast of Cornwall by a contrary wind. Six days they lay there, and, on the wind becoming fair, set forward again, only to be again driven back. The wind continuing adverse, Geoffrey d'Harcourt, already named, who had been banished from France, took occasion to divert the king from Gascony to Normandy, a province which had not been the scene of war for nearly 150 years. "Sir," said he, "the country of Normandy is one of the plentiful countries of the world, and if ye will make thither, on jeopardy of my head, there is none that shall resist you. The people of Normandy have not been used to war; and all the lords, knights, and esquires of the country, are now with the duke at the siege before Aiguillon. And here, sir, you shall meet with great towns that are not walled, whereby your men shall have such winning, that they shall be the better for it twenty years hence; and thus you may proceed, without any hinderance, till you come to the great city of Caen. I beseech you, sir, put some confidence in me in this matter, for I know that country well." Edward,—whose plans were not maturely fixed, and who looked on Harcourt as his friend, calling him cousin—readily inclined to this counsel, and bade the pilots steer for Normandy. On the 11th July, the whole fleet arrived safely at the roadstead of La Hogue St. Vast,[1]

(4) In this roadstead or bay, which lies a few miles S.E. of Cherbourg, Sir George Rooke burnt thirteen French ships of war, which had escaped thither after the battle of La Hague, (Cape,) in 1692.

near Barfleur, within a few leagues of St. Sauveur le Vicomte, Harcourt's rightful heritage, of which he had been unjustly deprived.   Edward's determination of carrying the war into the enemy's country, instead of waiting for it on his own shores, was bold and politic, because the French king had formed a like design ; and, besides his own ships, was daily expecting a powerful squadron from Genoa. The English speedily reduced Caen and Lower Normandy on the south of the Seine, and then marched on the left bank of that river towards Paris, burning St. Germain and St. Cloud.   Next came the famous victory of Cressy, one of the most signal that has ever been achieved.   From the time of his landing in Normandy, Edward had determined upon laying siege to Calais, then a place of great strength ; and on the last day of August he pitched his camp before it, wel l knowing that the French could not relieve it after the defeat they had just sustained.   Calais was defended with the same gallantry and perseverance with which it was attacked, but was at length compelled to surrender.

The two following letters,[1] which were written in French, relate to the campaign of the English in Normandy.   The first is taken from a copy of the " Chronicle of Lanercost," in the British Museum, and is singularly corroborated by the second, which moreover describes other circumstances omitted by Edward, and is curious from the comparison drawn between the size of the different Norman towns mentioned and those in England.

King Edward III. to William le Zouch, archbishop of York.

"Edward, by the grace of God, king of England and of France, and lord of Ireland, to the honourable father in God, W. by the same grace, archbishop of York, primate of England, health. As we know well that you are desirous to hear good news of us, we inform you, that we arrived at the Hogue, near Barfleur, the 12th day of July last past, with all our forces well and safe, praise be to God ; and remained there to disembark our forces and horses, and the provisions of our forces, until the Tuesday next following, on which day we removed with our host towards Valognes, and took the castle and town; and then on our route we rebuilt the bridge of Ove, which was broken by our enemies, and passed it, and took the castle and town of Carentan : and from thence we kept the direct route towards the town of Saint Lo, and found the bridge Herbert, near that town, broken to prevent our passage, and we caused it to be rebuilt, and the next

(1) From Jones' " Recollections of Royalty." London, 1828.

morning took the town; and we proceeded direct to Caen without stopping one day from the time of our departure from the Hogue until our arrival there; and then on our taking up our quarters at Caen, our people began to besiege the town, which was strongly garrisoned, and filled with about one thousand six hundred men at arms, and more than thirty thousand armed commoners, who defended it very well and ably; so that the fight was very severe, and continued long; but, thanks be to God, the town was at last taken by assault, without loss of our people. There were taken the count of Eu, constable of France; the chamberlain Tankerville, who was for the time styled marshal of France; and about one hundred and forty other bannerets and knights, and a great number of esquires and rich burgesses; and several nobles, knights, and gentlemen, and a great number of the commons, were slain. And our fleet, which remained near us, to burn and destroy all the sea coast from Barfleur to the "fosse" of Colleville,[1] near Caen, have also burnt the town of Cherbourg and the ships in the harbour; and of the enemy's large ships and other vessels above one hundred or more have been burnt either by us or by our people. Therefore, we pray you devoutly to render thanks to God, for the success which he has thus granted us, and earnestly entreat him to give us a good continuance of it; and that you write to the prelates and clergy of your province, that they do the same, and that you signify this circumstance to our people in your neighbourhood to their comfort; and that you laboriously exert yourself to oppose our enemies, the Scots, for the security of our people in your vicinity, by all the means in your power, so that we rely entirely on you: for, with the consent of all our nobles, who evinced a great and unanimous desire that we should do so, we have already resolved to hasten towards our adversary, wherever he may be, from one day to another as well as we can; and we trust firmly in God that he will protect us well and honourably in our undertaking, and that in a short time you will hear good and agreeable news of us.[2] Given under our privy seal, at Caen, the xxxth day of July, in the twentieth year of our reign in England. [1346."]

From Robert de Avesbury's Historia de Mirabilibus Gestis Edwardi III.

" Be it remembered, that our lord the king and his host landed at Hogue de St. Vast the xiith day of July, and remained there until the Tuesday next following, (July 18th,) to disembark his horses, to rest himself and his men, and to provide provisions. (et fourner payn.) He found at the Hogue eleven ships, of which eight had castles before and behind, the which were burnt. And

(1) Colleville is a small port near the entrance of the river Orne.
(2) On the 26th of August following, Edward gained the battle of Cressy.

on the Friday, whilst the king remained there, some troops went to Barfleur, and expected to have found many people, (gentz,) but they saw none; and they found there nine ships with castles before and behind,[1] ij good craiers,[2] and other smaller vessels; the which were also burnt: and the town was as good and as large a town as the town of Sandwich; and after the said troops were gone, the sailors burnt the town, and many good towns and houses (manoirs) in the neighbourhood were burnt. And the Tuesday (July 18th) that the king left he went to Valognes, and remained there the whole night, and found sufficient provisions. The next day he proceeded a long journey as far as the bridge of Ove, which those of the town of Carentan had broken down, and the king caused it to be rebuilt the same night, and passed it the next day, and proceeded as far as the said town of Carentan, which is not more than about an English league from the said bridge: the which town is as large as Leicester; where he found an abundance of wines and provisions; and much of the town was burnt, notwithstanding all the king could do.[3] And on Friday the king came to and slept in a village (villes campestres) on a river, which it was difficult to cross; (mal à passer;) and those of the town of St. Lo broke the bridge, and the king rebuilt it and passed the next day, he and his host, and took up his quarters adjoining the town; and all belonging to the town began to fortify it, and collected many armed men (gentz d'armes) to defend it, who waited for the arrival of the king; and they found in the said town full one thousand tuns of wine and an abundance of other goods; and the town is larger than Lincoln. The next day (Sunday, July 23d,) the king proceeded on his march, and slept at an abbey, and his host in the villages around him; and the soldiers of the host committed inroads (et chivacherent les gentz del ost) all the day, robbing and destroying within about v or vj leagues, and burnt many places. And the Monday the king removed, and took up his quarters in villages; and the Tuesday also: and on Wednesday (July 26th) at the hour of nones,[4] he came before the town of Caen, and was informed that a great number of armed men were in the town; and the king arrayed his fine and numerous battles,[5] and sent some persons to the town to examine it,[6] and they found the castle

(1) " Ove chastiels devant et derere."—It is scarcely necessary to state, that the ships of war in the fourteenth century had elevated places in the bow and stern, called castles, which contained the fighting men. " Fore-castle " is still used to describe the fore part of a ship.

(2) A "craier," or "crayer," was a small vessel, but whether for war or merchandize does not exactly appear,—most probably the latter. See *Ducange*. " Volumus quod centum naves vocatæ Pessoneræ et *Creyeris* et aliæ minutiæ naves," &c.

(3) Et fust mult de la ville ars p'r rien qe le roy purroit faire.

(4) A houre de none. Roquefort explains " none" to be the ninth hour of the day, i.e. three after noon; and which agrees with the meaning of the English word "nones."

(5) Et le roy fist arraier ses batailles beals et grosses.

(6) "A la ville des veer," in Johnes's copy, but "à la ville de les veer," in the Harleian MS. 200, f. 99b.

fine and strong, in which were the bishop of Baions, (Bayeux)
knights, and troops, (gentz,) who defended it.   And towards the
river the town is very fine and very large; and at one end of the
town is an abbey, as noble as possible, where William the Conqueror lies buried; and it is surrounded by walls and embattled
towers, (tours battaillis,) large and strong, in which abbey there
was no one.   And at the other end of the town, another noble
abbey of ladies; and no one remained in the said abbeys, nor in
the part of the town towards the river as far as the castle; and
the inhabitants were in the town on the other side of the river,
where were the constable of France and the chamberlain de Tankerville, who was a very great lord, and many troops, to the
amount of five or six hundred, and the commons of the town.
And our people of the host, without permission or order,
attacked the bridge, which was well fortified with bretages and
walls, and they had much to do, as the French defended the said
bridge bravely and behaved very well until they were taken; [1]
and then were taken the said constable and chamberlain, and to
the amount of one hundred knights, and one hundred and
twenty, or one hundred and forty esquires, ; and a great many
knights, esquires, and other people of the town were killed in
the streets, houses, and gardens; but no one could ascertain
how many were persons of consequence, (gentz de bien,) because
they were so stripped that it was impossible to recognise them;
and no gentleman of ours was slain, excepting an esquire who
was wounded, and died two days afterwards.[2]   And there were
found in the town, wines, provisions, and other goods and chattels
innumerable; and the town is larger than any town in England,
excepting London.   And when the king quitted La Hogue,
he left about two hundred ships which went to Rothemasse,
(Rouen) and proceeded and burnt the country two or three
leagues in land, and took many goods and brought them to their
ships; and then they went to Cherbourg, where was a good
town and a strong castle, and a fine and noble abbey, and they
burnt the said town and abbey;[3] and all on the sea coast was
burnt from Rothemasse as far as Hostrem (?) on the haven of Caen,
extending to twenty-six English leagues, and the number of ships
which were burnt is sixty-one of war, with castles before and

(1) Saunz assent & sannz arrale assaillerent le pount que fust mult bien afforce des
bretages, et barrer, et avoient mult affeare, et les Fraunceys defenderent le dit pount
fortment, et a eaux porteront mult bien devant qil poel estre pris sour eaux. Roquefort
explains "bretages" to be fortresses, citadels, parapets, strong places, moveable towers
of wood to attack and defend places, &c.

(2) Froissart, in his description of the taking of Caen, mentions that the inhabitants,
who had taken refuge in the garrets, flung stones, benches, and other missiles, upon the
English, by which they killed and wounded, he says, upwards of 500 of the besiegers,
which so enraged Edward that he commanded the inhabitants to be put to the sword
and the town burnt; but on the remonstrance of Geoffrey d'Harcourt, he revoked his orders.

(3) This was doubtless the abbey which enjoyed certain revenues in the bailiwick of
Guernsey, as already mentioned.

behind, and twenty three craiers, besides other smaller vessels, many laden with from twenty-one to thirty tuns of wine. And the Thursday after the king arrived before Caen, those of the city of Baions (Bayeux) offered our lord the king that they would render to him themselves and their town, and perform homage to him; but he would not receive them upon any terms whilst it was in their power to do him harm." [1]

St. Peter-Port.—The first mention that we find of the town of St. Peter-Port [2] is in the middle of the eleventh century, when duke William, afterwards the Conqueror, granted the church to the abbey of Marmoutier, as already narrated; so that the church, if not the town, existed anterior to that time. As a protection against pirates and other hostile invaders, the town appears to have been walled in in the latter half of the fourteenth century, Edward III. having, in 1350, issued an order to John Mautravers, warden of the isles, sanctioning the levy of a duty on merchandize of four deniers in the livre, towards the payment of a strong wall, with which St. Peter-Port was to be enclosed, to serve as a place of refuge to the people, instead of the fortification of Jerbourg, which had been stormed and ruined by the enemy. This accounts partly for the extreme narrowness of the old streets in the lower town.

It appears by Buchon's Froissart, I. 304, 5, (Paris, 1836,) that in 1355 or 1356, Edward III. with 200 men at arms and 4,000 archers, embarked at Southampton for Normandy, intending to go to Cherbourg, where the king of Navarre was awaiting him. Having been driven into the Isle of Wight by stress of weather, the day after his departure, he remained there fifteen days, and when he sailed again he was unable to reach Cherbourg, so contrary was the wind; but he landed on the island of Guernsey, on the coast of Normandy. When he had been on the island fully seven weeks, he heard that the king of Navarre had agreed with the king of France, and that peace was sworn to between them. Edward, in consequence, returned with all his navy to Southampton.— So relates Froissart, and we wish that we could establish the noblest of the Plantagenets as a temporary resident in the island, notwithstanding the total silence of our insular histo-

(1) ¹ The original is, " meas il ne lez voleit resceure pour ascuns enchesouns, et tanq' les purreit salver de damage."

(2) St. Peter-Port is mentioned in a patent, An. 33, Edward I. (A. D. 1305,) in the " Calendarium Rotulorum Patentium," thus: " Kaiagium pro villa de Sancto Petro portu in insula de Gernesey." Kaiagium signifies quay dues.

rians on the subject; but, had Edward come to Guernsey[1] and remained seven weeks, tradition would doubtless have recorded the royal visit, while, moreover, the wind that would have brought the king from the Isle of Wight to Guernsey would have taken him to Cherbourg. In the king's speech to Parliament, in November, it is said: "The king went in the fleet from the Thames towards Guernsey and Jersey," and this appears to be the only foundation for the statement of Froissart, as we find that Edward was forced by contrary winds into Portsmouth, whence he went to Calais.—Falle, without giving his authority, and in contradiction to that we have cited, says that Edward, on this occasion, "put to sea from the Thames, with a royal navy, steering directly for Jersey." With its safer roadstead, it is more probable that the king, having due regard to the security of his navy, would rather have come to Guernsey. In the same manner Falle lays claim to duke Robert, whose visit to Guernsey has already been described, and who, he says, "in his passage met with such tempestuous contrary winds, as forced him with his fleet into Jersey, as *Gulielmus Gemmeticensis*, or as Walsingham and others have it, into Guernezey; tho' I rather think into the former, because 'tis added that from thence he afterwards sailed to *Mont-Sainct-Michel*, to which Jersey is much nearer than Guernezey."[2] But Fescamp, in Normandy, where Robert embarked, is "much nearer" to Guernsey than to Jersey, and persons at sea do not usually go out of their way to seek shelter from a storm; besides, the testimony of Du Moulin, whom we have quoted at length in a preceding chapter, and of other Norman historians, confirmed by insular tradition, is decisive on the subject.[4] We should have stated also that Robert gave the islet of Jethou to his Guernsey pilot, as a reward for his services.

(1) A.D. 1313, 1314. By an account roll, headed "Valor prioratûs de Vallia de Anno Domini m.ccc.xiiij," it appears from the following entry, "Item pro expensis familie regis, xx. lib," that the family of Edward II. had been entertained by the prior of the Valle, or Vale.

(2) We quite concur in the following remark of the Rev. E. Durell: "What was formerly observed of Poggio, a Florentine, who was remarkable for the praises of his countrymen and the vituperations of their enemies, that he was a good patriot, but a bad historian, may be strictly applied to Mr. Falle. It is unpleasant to speak thus of an author so highly respected by his countrymen, and whose veracity and honesty are in most instances unquestionable."—Ahier, a Jerseyman, if we understand him correctly, accuses Falle of bad faith in interpolating the words, "et est adjacens Pago Constantino," after Augia, to prove his argument. (See Falle, p. 3.)

(3) "Il" [Robert] "fist vne puissante armée qu'il embarqua à Fescamp. Mais le destin, qui reseruoit cette conqueste à son successeur, s'opposa à sa route. Les vents contraires le ietterent à l'Isle de Grenezey, & s'opiniastrerent de sorte à le combattre, qu'apres vne attente de plusieurs mois, il fut contraint de relacher."—*Inventaire de l'Histoire de Normandie. A Rouen*, 1646.

(4) Had Mr. Durell consulted Du Moulin, or any other ancient Norman historian, he might have spared himself a long and somewhat inaccurate Note, No. 23, on this point, in Falle's History of Jersey.

In 1372, five years before the death of Edward III., Sir Owen of Wales, with 4,000 men from Normandy, according to Froissart, and only 3,000 men, according to Buchon, invaded Guernsey, and popular tradition has named this invasion "La Descente des Aragousais," or people of Arragon,[1] who appear to have constituted a large portion of the invading force. The enemy are supposed to have landed during the night opposite the pond of the *Grande Mare*, and, finding water in their front, to have remained stationary until daylight, which delay saved the island. The first encounter with the Welsh commander took place near the *Houguette*, in the Câtel parish, when the islanders were defeated with a very severe loss, and retreated in the direction of Castle Cornet. Froissart states that the governor, Rose, "assembled with his own and them of the isle, a body of 800 men," and fought a severe battle, "which endured for a long time; howbeit, finally the English were defeated, and more than 400 slain on the field of battle." This loss refers to the action in or near Vazon Bay, and even if the killed include both sides, the number seems much exaggerated, although, as the combatants then fought hand to hand, many more fell than in modern warfare. A subsequent battle appears to have been fought on some high ground, which now forms part of the upper town, and which maintains to this day the name of "La Bataille;"[2] this stand being probably necessary to gain time until the recession of the tide enabled the governor, Rose or Rous, and his men, to reach the castle. The "Rouge Rue," (red road) on the hill leading west of St. John's church, is also said to derive its name from the blood spilt there during a second or third engagement on this occasion. Speaking of Castle Cornet, Froissart relates that Evan "laid siege thereto, and made several assaults; but the castle was strong, and well provided with good artillery, so that it was not easy to be won. Then the French king sent his letters to the said Evan, who lay at siege before the castle of Cornet, of which siege the king was well informed, and also that the castle appeared to be impregnable; therefore, the king commanded him, after the sight of his letters, to raise his siege and depart, and enter into a ship which the king had sent him for that purpose, and so to sail into Spain, to king Henry, to get of

(1) "The Arragon, a little stream which falls from the Pyrenees into the Ebro, first gave its name to a country, and gradually to a kingdom."—*Gibbon·*

(2) Between St. John and Havilland streets, New Town, is a lane called "Battle Lane," and it was about or near this spot that the subsequent encounter is said by tradition to have occurred.

him barks and gallies, and his admiral and men-of-war, to come and lay siege by the sea to the town of Rochelle. When the said Evan saw the king's message and commandment, he obeyed thereto, and broke up the siege, and gave leave to his company to depart, and delivered them ships to bring them to Harfleur, and he himself entered into a great ship, and took his course towards Spain. Such was the termination of the siege of Cornet, in the isle of Guernsey." [1]

This extract from Froissart leaves the reader in doubt as to the exact duration of the siege, and the description of the artillery with which the castle was provided. The siege probably continued several weeks, as the intercourse between Guernsey and France, and England, must have been very tedious and uncertain in those days, even far more so than history tells us it was three centuries later. But the mention of the word "artillery" suggests a brief critical inquiry into its interpretation. When we remember that gunpowder[2] was first employed in war in the fourteenth century, about the year 1330, and that cannon is said to have been first used by the English at the battle of Cressy; in 1346, the natural inference is, that Castle Cornet must have been a fortress of great consequence to have been so soon afterwards furnished with artillery, if written in its modern sense.[3] That it was not so, however, we incline to believe, and think that Froissart's *artillerie* meant *arrows*, not cannon, as, when he speaks of cannon and mortars, he describes them as " cannons," " espingalles," " grand engins." In another passage, he writes : " Then the king made all his navy to draw along by the coast of the Downs, every ship well garnished with bombards, cross-bowers, archers, springalles, and other artillery, whereby the French host might not pass that way." In his account of the siege of Ypres, eleven years after the attack on Castle Cornet, he mentions *deux tonneaux pleins d'artillerie*, which can only mean two casks full of missile weapons, and there is little doubt that he used the term

(1) Speaking of this attack, Berry says, p. 84 : "The Guernsey breed of horses, (which certainly differ much in form from most others,) it is imagined, was derived from those left behind by the enemy." (!) This extract is a worthy *pendant* to Jersey and Guernsey, being islands formed by the tide, as mentioned by Cæsar : it is not likely, and it certainly does not appear, that Sir Owen had any cavalry. The Guernsey horses owed their peculiarity to coarse food, exposure to weather, and, above all, to constant "breeding in."

(2) The antiquity of gunpowder is unknown. We are taught to believe it an invention of the fourteenth century, when it was perhaps introduced into Europe from the East; but there are good grounds for ascribing the discovery to a period much more remote.

(3) "Nor was the legion" (Roman) "destitute of what, in modern language, would be styled a train of artillery. It consisted in ten military engines of the largest, and fifty-five of a smaller size; but all which, either in an oblique or horizontal manner, discharged stones and darts with irresistible violence."—*Gibbon*.

artillerie, not in its present acceptance, but as the translators of the Bible used it : " And Jonathan's lad gathered up the arrows, and came to his master." " And Jonathan gave his artillery unto his lad, and said unto him, Go, carry *them* to the city." (1 Sam. xx. 38, 40.) Southey, in his Naval History, observes that " it is remarkable there should be any doubt concerning the first use of cannon, and that the introduction of such deadly instruments should not be distinctly specified by the writers of that age." [1] He adds, that " Froissart's use of the word bombard is not sufficient proof" of such introduction. As regards artillery in Castle Cornet, it appears by the *Précepte d'Assize* of 5 Edward III., A.D. 1331, already quoted, that the bailiff and jurats of Guernsey were required to see that the castles and fortresses of the island were properly repaired, "and provided and furnished with soldiers, cannon, (canons,) gunpowder, (pouldres de calnon,) and other harnesses and habiliments of war." Thus cannon and gunpowder are distinctly specified about the period they are known to have been first used in war ; but it is evident that the terms were substituted for arms, when the *Précepte d'Assize* was recited and verified in the year 1441 ; or, they may have been substituted later in the French copy of 1693, neither the original nor the recital, both of which were doubtless in Latin, being in existence. When Edward III., in 1328, ordered the castles in these islands to be supplied with victuals, arms, and other necessaries, for their security, the royal mandate concluded thus : " Mandavimus enim vicecomitibus nostris London', quod centum & viginti targeas, centum arcus balistos ad pedem, & viginti arcus balistos ad troll' ; necnon vicecomiti nostro Sutht', quod ipse centum milia de parvo Talshid & duo milia carbonum buscæ, in eorum ballivis emi & provideri, & usque Portesmuth' cariari faciant, pro municione castrorum predictorum, & vobis, vel attornato vestro in hâc parte, liberari.

Holingshed's account of Evan's invasion is as follows : " Edward III. 47, A.D. 1373. [apparently a misdate.] About the same time, the French king sent 4,000 men to the sea, under the guiding of one Yvans, a banished Welsh gentleman, the which, landing in the isle of Guernsey, was encountered by the captain of that isle, called Sir Edmund Rous, who had gathered 800 men of his own soldiers, together with them of the isle, and boldlie gave battell to the Frenchmen ; but in the end the Englishmen were discomfitted, and 400 of them

(1) Barbour, a Scottish historian, states that cannon were used by Edward III. in his expedition against Scotland, A.D. 1328.

slaine, so that Sir Edmund Rous fled in the castell of Cornett, and was there besieged by the said Yvans, till the French king sent to him to come backe from thence, and so he did, leaving the castell of Cornett and Sir Edmund Rous within it as he found him."—*Holingshed's Chronicles*, first published in 1575, and from the reprint of 1809.

Of this Owen of Wales we learn that a year after his invasion of Guernsey, it was reported in England that he was about to infest the English coast with a powerful squadron, and to burn and lay waste the country. In consequence, the earl of Salisbury was appointed to guard the Channel, and with a strong fleet he sailed from Cornwall directly for St. Malo, where finding in the haven seven large Spanish carracks, he burnt them all. Probably the strength of the intended invasion consisted in these carracks, for it was not heard of afterwards. A few days after Edward's death, the crews of a combined French and Spanish squadron, in which was "the brave Welsh adventurer," Sir Owen, made a descent on the coast of Sussex, and burnt the town of Rye, where they slew men, women, and all they found. They afterwards landed in the Isle of Wight, and burned several towns there. They burned Portsmouth also, and next Dartmouth and Plymouth. Coasting back again, they made an attempt upon Southampton, but were repulsed and chased to their ships. After burning Hastings, and making a vain attempt on Winchelsea and Rottingdean, they returned to France, satisfied with the booty they had acquired, and the devastation they had committed. So that other places besides Guernsey had sad cause to remember "Sir Owen of Wales," and England herself in that age appears to have been scarcely less defenceless. "In the moneth of Septembre, [1368] king Charlys mannyd and vittailyd certeyne gallies and other shippes, and sent them into Wayls, & so to have entryd into Englonde; but they retourned with lytle worship, notwithstandynge that he had ïi noblemen of Walys, named Owan & James Wynne, whiche made to hym fast promesse of great thynges, by reason that they were enemyes unto the kynge of Englonde." —(*Fabyan in Carol. v.*) Froissart narrates that while Evan was blockading Mortain, in Poitou, there came to him John Lambe, a Welsh squire, "who was scarcely a gentleman," and who, on his departure from England, was instigated by some English knights to murder Evan. Lambe had landed in Britany, and continued his journey thence to Poitou. On approaching Evan, he fell on his knees, and said

in Welsh, that he had left Wales to see and serve him. Evan,
not harbouring the least suspicion, received Lambe kindly,
and made him his chamberlain. Evan " was a valiant
knight, a good man, and the son of a prince of Wales, whom
king Edward had caused to be beheaded." In his infancy
he served as page to Philip, king of France : he bore arms
under king John, and was at the battle of Poitiers, but fortunately escaped, " otherwise death would have soon followed
his captivity." While Evan was dressing one morning,
Lambe plunged a short Spanish dagger into him, on which
Evan, who was nearly naked, fell down dead, and the assassin
escaped into the castle of Mortain. Thus two of the invaders
of Guernsey, Eustache le Moine and Evan of Wales, came
to violent ends. Lambe was subsequently recompensed for
this treacherous murder, as appears by the Fœdera, under the
head of payments made in 1381 for the war in Aquitaine, as
follows : "Item, paie le xviii jour de Septembre à Johan
Lambe & à ses deux compagnions, en recompensacion &
regarde, si bien de les bons & agréables services qu' il a fait à
monsieur le prince, que Dieu assoile, & fera au roi q'ore est,
come de la mourt de You de Galles—C francs."

The first mention that we have discovered of these islands
being possessed of shipping of any burden, is in the reign of
Edward III., who, in a mandate headed " *De Navibus ares-
tandis,*" and dated " A.D. 1370," in the forty-fourth year of
his reign, commanded ships in the several ports named to be
impressed for his service, and in which mandate the islands
are included thus ; " *Johannes Cok et Bernardus Seint Johan
in singulis portubus et locis maritimis in insulis de Gernesey,
Jereseye, Sark, et Aureneye jam existentes, &c., et usque
portum de Suthampton, &c.*"—The next mention is in the
time of Henry V., the hero of Azincourt, when the *Mary,* of
Guernsey, Geoffry Capelle, master, was included in the enumeration of a fleet of two hundred and thirty-eight sail,
employed by that monarch to transport himself and his army
from England to France, The enumeration is given in the
" Rotuli Normaniæ," vol. i, which work also contains a
certificate of Henry, dated September 1, 1417, at the royal
abbey [1] of St. Stephen, in Caen, granting certain privileges
to the commander of a Dutch vessel, which had formed one
of the fleet, and it appears that a similar certificate was
given to the said Capelle. The surname is now extinct in

(1) This was the abbey founded in Caen by William the Conqueror, in the church of
which he was buried, and where his tomb may be seen.

Guernsey, but from it was evidently derived "Les Grandes Capelles" and "Les Petites Capelles," two estates so called to this day in St. Sampson's parish.

As after the loss of Normandy, in 1204, the islands continued under the laws and customs of that province, so considerable confusion and vexation arose, chiefly owing to the justices itinerant from England being strangers to the insular institutions. In consequence, commissions of inquiry were issued to investigate the complaints and the privileges of the islanders, and the most remarkable of these commissions were those of 32 Hen. III., of 17 Edw. II., and 5 Edw. III., the first and last especially. Had John really given a body of Constitutions to the islands, the English justices would have known better how to proceed; and it was only the *Précepte d'Assize* which is said to have produced order and consistency in the administration of justice.

Having quoted the *Précepte d'Assize* of 5 Edward III., A.D. 1331—in which year, as we have shewn, two Gascon naval commanders were joint wardens of the isles,—it may be well to explain here, as its history is not generally known, that the earliest authenticated copy of this document is in French, and dated in September, 1693; all the records of the Royal Court anterior to 1527[1] having been lost or destroyed, or, as some suppose, carried off by the monks, which is very improbable. The *Précepte d'Assize*, or declaration of rights, according to the copy, is a recital, as collated by the Royal Court on the 30th of September, 1441, of the usages, liberties, and ancient customs of the isle of Guernsey, " of all the time whereof memory of man is not to the contrary," approved of by the justices errant in the said island, in the fifth year of Edward III., and set forth in an instrument called the Extent. The Extent, or l'Estente, of Edward III., said also to have been compiled in the year 1331, is a survey and valuation of the island, and refers chiefly to the revenues and property of the crown. Certain dues on foreign vessels casting anchor are therein mentioned as producing, with some trifling others in the same article, 160 livres in time of war, and nothing in peace. These dues imply a privilege of neutrality, which certainly did not exist in 1331. There is no copy of the Extent in Latin; and that in French, at the greffe, was collated in 1818 with the most ancient copies, by two of the jurats, the

(1) The oldest document existing in the "greffe," or registry office, is dated January 20, 1527.

said jurats believing it to be authentic. The two royal commissioners, Ellis and Bros, who visited Guernsey in 1846, to inquire into the state of its criminal law, observe in their Report, that " a document was produced to us, regarded as of very high authority in Guernsey, styled the *Précepte d'Assize* . . . . . We thought it necessary, from the importance attached to this document by the Royal Court, on our return to England, to search among the records in the custody of the Master of the Rolls for the documents referred to. The record of the pleas before Sir Henry Spigurnell and William Denon, in the seventeenth year of Edward II., still exists among the records of the public record office ; but we have not been able to trace the connection between those proceedings and the *Précepte d'Assize* . . . . . We also caused search to be made for the document referred to in the *Précepte d'Assize*, and there called the Extente of the King ; but the record is missing." The royal commissioners further add : " The Extente and *Précepte d'Assize* are, however, recognized in the Approbation des Lois, (to be presently mentioned,) and there directed to be kept and inviolably observed, ' *tant pour l'élection, estat, et direction des justiciers et autres officiers de sa majesté, que aussi pour les droits, rentes, revenus, services, hommages et suittes de Court, apartenants et dues à sa majesté en cette dite isle de Guernezey.*' And the *Précepte d'Assize*, whatever its origin, has always been regarded as authority in questions touching the jurisdiction of the Royal Court and the limits of the power of the bailiff and the governor, as representing the crown."

In the early times, and up to Henry VII., (1485 to 1509,) it was usual to appoint only one " custos," or warden, for all the isles, and when the government of Jersey and Guernsey was separated, the warden of each was styled captain, and finally, governor, which last title was fixed by an order in council, June 15, 1618. Occasionally, however, " custodes," or wardens, appear to have been appointed to each of the two bailiwicks, as in a commission from Edward III., A.D. 1373, William de Asthorpe was appointed " custos " of Guernsey, Sark, Alderney, Herm, Castle Cornet, and the tower of Beauregard, Jersey not being included ; and the same omission occured in the following year, when Thomas de Beauchamp was named as custos. The term " custos " is used in the most ancient documents, and it is written thus : " Dominus rex habere consuevit unum custodem insularum," but in the

thirteenth century the warden was occasionally styled "ballivus." In several mandates of Edward I. and II., the words
are "Edwardus rex, &c., dilecto et fidelissimo custodi insularum;" and in a commission of Edward III., A.D. 1374,
Thomas de Beauchamp is constituted "capitaneum et custodem insularum," &c. The title captain is mentioned by
Cowel in his dictionary, thus: "We have captains in Gearsey,
Guernsey, the Isle of Wight, &c." The first wardens appear
to have enjoyed the whole of the revenues, without deduction; but in the reign of Edward III. John des Roches,
about A.D. 1328, had a fixed allowance of only £40 a year.[1]
(quadraginta libras per annum.) Subsequently, in the same
reign, the "custos" received the whole revenue, and paid a
certain amount of it into the king's exchequer, besides maintaining the royal castles, &c.; (castra R. &c. sustentent;) thus
we find four wardens successively bound to pay fifty marks
a year each.[2] Soon after, William Stury, by indenture dated
in 1354, agreed to pay 200 livres a year; (c.c. li. p. an.) and
his successor, Edmund de Cheney, had to pay first, 300 livres,
(libras,) and next, 230 marks. The revenue was then comparatively large, much having been alienated by succeeding
sovereigns, especially in Jersey, by Charles II. during his
necessities, while in exile. After the separation of the two
governments, the garrison was maintained in each island by
the captain or governor, who usually enjoyed the whole
revenue; but in the reign of Charles II. the castles were
placed under the Board of Ordnance, and the governors were
exempted from maintaining the garrisons. Lord Hatton
was the last governor of Guernsey who appears to have
appointed the officers, and paid them and the troops; and he
was also the last who resided in Castle Cornet. The powers
of the wardens were once very great, and often arbitrary, as
is proved by the complaints made against Sir Thomas Leighton, in the reign of James I. The governor, from the time
of James II., was a mere sinecurist, who enjoyed the insular
crown revenues without any equivalent; and the office was
very properly abolished in 1835, General Sir William Keppel
being the last who held it. The emoluments, then worth
from £1,500 to £1,800 a year, have since been given in part
to the parochial rectors, to schools, increase of salary to the
crown law officers, &c.

(1) We are not quite certain whether these were livres tournois; although, from the
smallness of the sum, we suppose that they were not.
(2) "*Abbreviatio Rotulorum Originalium.*" (1810.) Falle is again at fault in saying of
two of these wardens, Thomas de Ferrars and Thomas de Hampton, that they "were
charged each with 500 marks."

I

Edward III., in the fiftieth year of his reign, (A.D. 1376,).
granted Alderney once as a separate government, thus : " R.
commisit Thome Porteman de Salesbury mercatori custodiam
Insule de Aurenaye juxta Insulam de Gerseye hend' usq, ad
term' trium anno. reddo inde R. p ann' viginti libras tam
tempore pacis qm guerre salvis R. feodis militum, &c. Ro. 8.—
Abbreviatio Rotulorum Originalium.

In the year 1352, an. 26 of Edward III., John Maltravers,
or de Mautravers[1] (misspelt Mantaners by Berry) "was
constituted governor of the isles of Guernsey, Jersey, Alderney, and Sark," and nine years afterwards " he founded the
hospital of Bowes, in the island of Guernsey, and shortly
after died, viz. the 38 of Edward III." (Bank's Dormant
and Extinct Baronage of England. London, 1808.) Bowes,
evidently so spelt for Bosq, was probably the hospital of St.
Julien, which anciently existed near the Tourgand, or Truchot.

It was in this reign, after a lapse of nearly three centuries,
that it was ordained, at the suit of the commons, " that men
of law should plead their causes and write their actions and
plaints in the English tongue, and not in the French, as they
had been accustomed to do ever since the Conquest ; and
that schoolmasters should teach their scholars to construe
their lessons in English, and not in French."—*Holingshed.*
This enactment extended only to England, but certainly the
time has arrived that such inhabitants of Guernsey as cannot
express themselves freely in French—and fully two-thirds of
the natives cannot—should be permitted to speak in English,
in the States or insular parliament. It is surely a gross act
of injustice and oppression to compel a parishioner to serve
as a constable or douzenier, and deprive him of the highest
privilege of either office, that of being sent as a deputy to the
States, because he cannot address that body in French. It
is a mockery to call an assembly deliberative, in which all
the members cannot deliberate, and in which a vast majority
think in one language and speak badly in another. Sir
Charles Lyell, referring in his North American travels to the
legislature of Louisiana, says : " In the House of Representatives, English is spoken exclusively ; but in the Senate many
were addressing the house in French, and, when they sat
down, an interpreter rose and repeated the whole speech over
again in English." That the Anglo-Saxon or dominant race
should submit to such an inconvenience proves their respect

---

[1] Pardon of John de Mautravers of all offences against the peace of the late king.
(1329.)—*Rymer,* ii. 760.

for the freedom of debate and the rights of the members, and contrasts very favorably with the exclusiveness and illiberality of the States of Guernsey, the more so as nine-tenths of the members perfectly understand English. Again, in the parliament of Canada both English and French are indiscriminately spoken ; and as a jurat, recently deceased, addressed both the Royal Court and the States in English for several years, it is insulting, as well as unjust, to deny the same privilege to the constables and douzeniers, many of whom in birth, education, and fortune, are fully equal to the jurats. The difficulty of finding competent jurats increases every day, and assuredly some are now chosen, not for their intelligence or capacity, but because they profess to speak French ; while a gentleman, who may have been educated in an English public school and university, and have attained the degree of M.A., is ineligible because he will not stultify himself by voting in monosyllables, or speaking in broken French ! The question is, however, but one of time ; and the insular authorities might as well endeavour to stay the spread of the English language in North America and Australia as to prevent its ultimate admission into the States and Royal Court of Guernsey.

We give the following digest of three mandates issued in Latin during this reign, as they faithfully illustrate the ecclesiastical government, and the mode of providing for the defence, of these islands during the fourteenth century.

In a mandate from Edward III., dated York, June 3, 1327, the king informed Otto de Grandison, guardian of the islands of Guernsey, Jersey, Sark, and Alderney, that, "having received fealty from Nichola, abbess of the Holy Trinity of Caen, (Cadomo,) in Normandy, for the lands and tenements which she holds of us in the aforesaid islands, and which at the death of the last abbess we took into our hands, and have (now) restored them to her. We therefore command you to deliver to the said abbess, or to her proctor or attorney, the aforesaid lands and tenements, with all their appurtenances, saving every one's just claims."

By another mandate, dated at Clipston, August 30, 1328, directed to John de Roches, guardian of Guernsey, &c., the king, having "heard that the bishops, abbots, priors, and other men of Normandy, who hold (lands) of us by homage, fealty, and other services, assert that they owe no (such) homage and fealty to us, except where their predecessors paid them to our ancestors at the time the aforesaid islands were parts of Normandy,"—his majesty ordered that the said homage, &c., should be paid without delay, and continue to be exacted as long as it was his royal pleasure.

By another mandate, dated Westminster, April 22, 1373, addressed "To all and singular the viscounts, mayors, bailiffs, ministers, and other lieges, in whatever towns and ports between Southampton and Plymouth;" the king having "appointed William de Asthorpe, knight, (chivaler,) governor of the islands of Guernsey, Jersey, &c., and John Coke, esquire, (armigerum,) to go to the aforesaid islands with as much speed as possible, for their preservation and defence," most strictly enjoins and commands the said viscounts, &c., "to supply the same William and John with the utmost celerity, and at their own cost, with such barges (bargeas) or other vessels beneath the burden of twenty casks,[1] or tons, (infra portagium viginti doliorum,) as may be sufficient and necessary for the passage of themselves, their men and horses, their victuals and harness, (hernesiorum,) and to be ready to answer their requirements. Provided always that no barges, or vessels, or other ships appointed for the conveyance of John, king of Castile and Leon,[2] (Johannis Regis Castellæ et Legionis,) or any other lords, shall be taken away under colour of these presents" for the purpose aforesaid.

In the "Placita Coronæ," or pleas of the crown, held before the justices itinerant in St. Peter-Port, 5 Edward III., A.D. 1331, are given "Nomina Ballivorum, Præpositorum, Bedellorum, Juratorum, et Sectatorum curiæ Insulæ de Gernereye," viz. the names of the bailiffs, provosts, beadles, jurors, and followers of the court.[3] (literally.)

The bailiff was Thomas de Esterfeld; the provost, Nicholas Bernard, and the beadle, (sergeant,) Nicholas Collochit. There had been six bailiffs since the last assizes, among them Peter le (de) Garrys. Among the twelve jurats were John Nichol, (Nicolle,) R. de Wike, (de Vic,) Matthew de Saltmares, (Sausmarez,) and R. de Bello Campo. (de Beauchamp.) Among the four wardens since the last assizes were Petrus Bernard de Pynsole and Laurentius Gaylard. (Gaillard.) Among the provosts, since the last assizes, were Dionisius (Denis) Marchaunt, John de la Marche, Matthew de la Rue, and Radulphus le Provost.

The "Sectatores Curiæ" were Episcopus Custanciensis,[4] Abbas de Monte Sancti Michaelis, Abbas de Mermoustre, (Marmoutier,) Willielmus de Cheyny, Abbas de Blancâ Landâ, Abbas de Cruce Sancti Leufridi, (St. Leufroy,) Abbas de Longnes, Abbatissa de Cadamo, (Caen,) and Matheus de Saumareys.

The two first jurors in each parish were styled "Electores

(1) It is difficult to understand the motive for this limitation.

(2) This appears to have been John of Gaunt, duke of Lancaster, "time-honoured Lancaster," who assumed the title of king of Castile, in right of his wife.

(3) The ecclesiastical and lay seigneurs, owing suit to the king's court.

(4) The bishop of Winchester is now evoked at the court of chief pleas in the place of the bishop of Coutances.

Juratorum," by which it would appear that they only were members of the states of election, and not the whole of the jurors or douzainiers, as now. Among these parochial jurors were: in St. Sampson's: W. de la Capelle, M. Blondel, P. Maugyt,[1] and M. de Port; the Forest: P. Poitevin, J. Le Mesurier, and R. Tourgys; St. Peter-in-the-Wood: R. Corbyn, J. de Lisle, R. Falle, (? Falla,) and G. Rougier; St. Martin: J. Corbyn and W. le Carpentier; Câtel: R. de la Court and J. Blondel; Torteval: R. Brouard, J. le Clerc, and R. Simon; St. Saviour: R. Henry, N. Nicolle, P. David, and G. Alexandre; St. Andrew: R. Corbyn; Vale: T. Hamelyn, R. Mainguy, and M. Gosselyn; St. Peter-Port: J. de la Cour, and R. Tourgys.

Many of the family names mentioned in the Extent or Survey of Edward III., (1331,) already noticed, are extinct in Guernsey, and those which remain, or existed recently, are as follow:

Alexandre, Anquetil, Allye, (? Allez,) Bailleul, Blondel, Brehaut, Brouard, de Beauchamp, Carée, (Carey,) Corbin, David, De Garis, De Lisle, De Beauvoir, De Havilland, de la Mare, de la Court, de la Rue, de Moulpied, du Moulin, (? Moullin,) du Mont, Fallaize, Guilbert, Gosselin, Hamelin, Hallouvris, Le Roy, Le Marchant, Lucas, Le Messurier, Le Hardy, (Hardy,) Le Lacheur, Le Prevost, Le Huray, Le Roux, Le Clerc, Mainguy, Marquis, Martin, Nicolle, Ollivier, Poitevin, Rose, Renouf, and Vidamour.

Edward III., in order to cancel a royal debt to one of his subjects, granted him the wardenship of these islands on certain conditions, as will appear by the following indenture:

Indentura de custodia insularum de Gernereye, Gereseye, Serk, & Aureneye.

A.D. 1354.
An. 28 Edw. III.
———
Claus. 28 Edw. III.
m. 27. d.
in Turr. Lond.

Ceste endenture faite entre nostre seignur le Roi d'une part, et monsieur William Stury d'autre part, tesmoigne:

Que le dit William ad empris la gard des isles de Gernereye, Gereseye, Serk & Aureneye, pur terme de trois annz, commenceant le second jour d'Averill preschein avenir, à ses propres custages es totes choses, & receivera à son oeps toutz les profitz, issues, & revenues des dites isles, durant le terme susdit, rendant à nostre dit seignur le Roi CCli. par an à son escheqer:

Et outre nostre seignur le Roi ad grante de sa grace especiale, que la dite ferme lui soit allowe d'an en an au dit escheqer, en

(1) Originally Mainguy, but long spelt Maingy. In 1840, one branch of this family, by the queen's royal license, changed their names to Maingay.

partie de satisfaction des dettes, queles il saura monstrer par cleres evidences, que nostre seignur le Roi lui doit, jus à la summe de CCCClxvi. li. xiii s. iv d.

En tesmoignance de quele chose, à l'une partie de ceste endenture demorante devers le dit monsieur William, nostre seignur le Roi ad fait mettre son grant seal, & a l'autre partie de meisme l'endenture devers nostre dit seignur le Roi, le dit monsieur William ad mis son seal.

Don' a Westmonster le xx. jours de Marz, l'an du regne nostre dit seignur le Roi, c'estassavoir, d'Engleterre vyntoytisme, & de France quinzisme.

Per ipsum Regem & concilium.

CHAPTER VII.

RICHARD II.—1379 to 1399.

RICHARD, who was the son of the Black Prince, was but eleven years of age when he succeeded to the throne of his grandfather, Edward III.   His reign was one continued scene of discontent and trouble; because, like Edward II., he was entirely influenced by worthless favorites.   In the first year of this reign, says Duncan, the kings of France and Castile entered into a confederacy, the object of which was to devastate these islands, as well as the Isle of Wight, by every possible act of destruction.   To carry this barbarous design into effect, the king of Castile bound himself to furnish 20 galleys, each of them to have on board 10 men at arms, 30 cross-bowmen, and 180 mariners, exclusive of officers, to be maintained at the joint expense of the allied kings, who were to share the plunder equally.   But it does not appear that the design was ever carried into execution.   "Richard granted a charter to these islands in 1394, as a reward to the inhabitants for their good behaviour and fidelity, that they should be for ever freed, in all parts within the kingdom of England, from all sorts of tolls, exactions, and customs, in the same manner as his majesty's liege subjects of the said kingdom, provided the islanders should continue to well and faithfully behave themselves for ever."—*Berry*, p. 89.

In this reign, A.D. 1386, the young king of France determined on the invasion of England, so as to obtain vengeance for all the calamities which the English had brought upon his kingdom. He was encouraged thereto by the absence of John of Gaunt, who, with a strong body, was engaged in an expedition against Castile, and, above all, by the dissensions which prevailed in England. Accordingly, preparations were made upon the most extensive scale, and the invading force was appointed to rendezvous at Sluys, in early times the most flourishing port upon the Flemish coast. Here 60,000 men were to be embarked; and the constable of France sailed from Tréguier, in Britany, to join the armament with a fleet of 72 ships, but, being dispersed in a gale near the river Thames, several of them were captured by the English cruisers, and the constable was glad to reach Sluys with the remainder. And as the winter was approaching, the French embarkation was deferred until the spring, when the expedition at Sluys was abandoned. Another was, however, projected; and this time the principal preparations were made at Tréguier, near Morlaix, where the constable assembled 4,000 men at arms and 2,000 arbalisters, while an equal force was got ready at Harfleur, in Normandy. The day of departure was fixed and close at hand, when the whole scheme was suddenly frustrated by the duke of Britany. We have introduced these projected invasions to shew how very insecure these islands must have been at that period, and to express our surprise that the constable did not possess himself of Guernsey on his voyage from Tréguier to Sluys, as it lay in his direct track, and could not have offered him any effectual resistance. These islands have indeed, on more than one occasion, owed their safety rather to the negligence or supineness of the French than to their own strength, or to the protection of England.

"*Anno* 14, *Ri.* 2, *m.* 30. (1392.)—The king hath granted to the men of the isles of Guernsey, Jersey, Sarcke and Aureney, that they, for the space of eight years, shall be free of all manner of tolls, exactions, and customs within the realm, as his liege people and denisons are."—*Harl. Manus. No.* 21, *p.* 179.

HENRY IV.—1399 to 1413.

Sir John de Lisle, knight, was appointed warden of Guernsey in 1405, during the reign of Henry IV., as appears by Nicholas' "Acts of the Privy Council," published in 1834; and there is a letter from him, dated at Castle Cornet, July 30, (apparently,) 1406, to the council, in which he repeats that the castle is on the point of falling, and ruinous through default of the timber, as he had previously certified. He asks permission to take the timber from a house called the Priory of the Vale,[1] which was in a state of ruin, to assist in repairing the castle, as he could procure no kind of timber either from Normandy or Britany, or any other part, on account of the war. This letter is written in old French, and is, we believe, the most ancient extant, dated from the castle, "escrit au dit chastel Cornet," &c. It is singular that in no history or account of Guernsey is the name of Sir John de Lisle[2] included among the governors, and we have discovered many other omissions.

Falle states, without, as usual, giving any date, that in the reign of Henry IV. a bloody battle was fought between an English and French fleet, in which the former lost forty ships and above 2,000 men in killed and prisoners. And he adds: " When by that victory the enemy had cleared the sea of the English, they fell upon the islands ; and though, for want of being provided with things necessary for a siege, they could do nothing against the castles, they wrought all the mischief and damage they were able to the inhabitants. And this is all I find in this reign that particularly concerns us." This naval battle, which occurred in 1403, and after which the greater part of the prisoners were thrown overboard, did not permanently clear the sea of the English, as, in 1405, the French applied to the king of Castile for naval aid, which he granted by ordering forty ships and three galleys to be sent with all speed. Pero Niño, afterwards Conde de Buelna, a man of high birth, and who had previously distinguished himself in the Mediterranean, was appointed to the command of the galleys, then lying in Santander ; and happily his share in this expedition has been preserved by his standard bearer, who accompanied him, and wrote the history of his master, one of the most curious chronicles of its kind.[3] It mentions that, in 1405,[4] the French and Spanish squadrons made descents on the coast of Cornwall and Portland, cap-

(1) " A small portion of the monastery of St. Michael, at the Vale, is still standing, and is converted into a farm house. There are buttresses of two stages supporting the south wall, and segmental arches in other parts of the house."—*Rev. W. C. Lukis.* (1841.)

(2) A very respectable family of this name has been, for several centuries, resident in Guernsey. The mothers of two distinguished Guernseymen, — Major-General Sir Isaac Brock, K.B., " the Hero of Upper Canada," and Dr. MacCulloch, the celebrated geologist, —were de Lisles of this family. Sir John de Lisle was from Hampshire.

(3) Cronica del Conde D. Pero Niño. Only one edition of this work was ever published.

(4) In this year, the Anglo-Norman Islands were seized into the king's hands, upon the arrest of Edward, duke of York, to whom they belonged.—*Rymer.*

tured, Poole, &c., and afterwards wintered in the Seine. The year following, Niño, who had reaped little profit from his adventures, and had learnt that galleys were not suited to the tidal harbours and rough seas of the British Channel, easily persuaded the Breton lords to join him in an expedition against Jersey — a rich island, says his chronicler — where he might gain much honour, and moreover levy a large contribution. In two days, a force, well equipped for such service, was embarked ; in a few hours it reached the island, and of Spaniards, Normans, and Bretons, there were not less than 1,000 men at arms, exclusive, it appears, of ill-armed men. They landed that evening on a small islet, which had a chapel on it dedicated to the Virgin Mary, and the space which separated it from the land was left dry at low water.[1]   At daybreak the next morning, when the tide was falling, the trumpets sounded, and the invaders crossed the sands. The Jerseymen, who, by the Spaniard's account, were about 3,000, besides 200 horse, came on bravely ; the struggle was fierce and bloody ; so much so, that in the opinion of the chronicler, who was an eye witness, few on either side would have been left alive, if the " receiver-general,"[2] a brave man, who defended a white banner with the cross of St. George, had not been mortally wounded. He could not be borne from the field, and many of the Jerseymen fell around him ; but the banner was at length beaten down ; and having, it seems, lost their commander in the " receiver," the islanders took to flight, when the invaders were in no condition to pursue them, so many were hurt, and so wearied were they all. The battle was fought upon a fine sand about half a league in length, doubtless the bay of St. Aubin, while the islet[3] was apparently that on which Elizabeth Castle now stands, and on a rock near which St. Hélier resided in a solitary cell.[4]   The invaders being informed that there were

(1) " In this reign " [Henry II., 1154 to 1189, king of England and eleventh duke of Normandy] " began the declension of the abbey of St. Hélier, in Jersey, once the glory of this island. I mentioned before how it was founded by a Norman nobleman, in honour of the martyr of that name. It stood on the same plot where now is the lower ward of Elizabeth Castle, and was, if not a magnificent, yet a handsome fabric, as one might judge from part of the church yet in being within my remembrance ; and if there be truth in the tradition, that all betwixt the castle and the town, which the sea now overflows, was then rich meadow land, the situation must needs be very delightful."—*Falle.*

(2) " Llamabule el *Receveur;* é yo le vi yacer entre mis pies, é finabaso yā, y non podian con el andar adelante ; tanto era el apretamiento de la gente."—*Cronica,* p. 156.

(3) In digging for the foundations of the vast pier lately built at St. Hélier, earth was discovered under the sand, and it was evident that the whole space between the town and Elizabeth Castle had been once under cultivation ; many stumps and branches of trees, and even filberts, being found embedded in the earth, which was carted by individuals for gardening purposes, or for laying over the soil.

(4) Mr. J. P. Ahier, of Jersey, thinks that the islet, with the chapel, was that on which the present tower of St. Aubin is built.

five strong castles in the island well garrisoned, finally agreed
to accept a ransom of 10,000 crowns of gold and depart, so
states the chronicler : as much of the ransom as could be
immediately raised was paid, and four hostages were given as
security for the rest, which was afterwards paid by the Breton
merchants.   Both Falle and his annotator Durell were manifestly ignorant of the existence of the Spanish chronicle, and
of the details it contains relative to this invasion : we feel,
therefore, the greater pleasure in narrating, although briefly,
the gallantry and devotion of the Jerseymen on that occasion ;
and as many in these islands will naturally wish to peruse a
fuller account than our limits admit of, we refer them to
Southey's Naval History, London, 1833, vol. ii., pp. 38-45,
where the subject is narrated at length.   Some allowance,
however, must be made for the evident quixotism of the
chronicler, who wrote in the spirit of exaggeration so common
in that age, when, in dealing with numbers, romance appears
to have been the rule, and truth the exception.   Indeed, in
all times men have been prone to magnify the numbers of
their opponents so as to enhance their own gallantry.   As
the French in this reign were occasionally masters of the
channel, it is probable that they made descents also on
Guernsey, although we have seen no other evidence than
Falle's to that effect.   Dicey, probably on the authority of
Falle, says : " In Henry the Fourth's reign, these islands
were pillaged in a most inhuman manner by the French."

HENRY V.—1413 to 1422.

Of the short reign of Henry V., beyond the mere fact of
his employment of a Guernsey vessel, as already narrated,
we find little relating to these islands.   When the religious
houses were suppressed, and the priors aliens banished from
these islands by Henry, who was at this time engaged in war
with France, the property of the latter fell into the hands of
the king, and became part and parcel of the *demesnes* of the
crown.   A composition was then entered into between the
governors and the rectors, by which the latter obtained certain small proportions of the tithes confiscated.

It was during this reign—when Henry, profiting by the
discord which prevailed among the French nobles, had obtained possession of Coutances, Avranches, and other places
on the adjacent coast, with the exception of Cherbourg and
Mont Martin—that James Mauger, of Somerhuse, (?) now
Sommeilleuse, in the parish of the Forest, arrived with his

people from Guernsey at the little port of Agon, and captured by escalade the castle of Mont Martin, near Coutances, on the 24th of June, 1419. The seigniory of Bosques, in Normandy, was in consequence conferred by the king on Mauger, who established himself there; and, as an additional recompense for his exploit, the following grant of arms was made to him and his heirs, viz. argent, the cross of St. George, gules, quartering in the first and fourth his paternal arms; that is to say, argent, two chevrons sable; and in the second and third, the arms of Bosques, argent, a lion sable. These particulars are derived from a MS. belonging to the cathedral of Coutances; but in the first place, we incline to think that this Mauger was a refugee Norman, and not a native of Guernsey; and in the second, according to Goube's *Histoire du Duché de Normandie*, the English, in 1417, were masters of all Lower Normandy, with the exception of Cherbourg, which surrendered after a siege of three months, in 1418, through the treachery of its governor, who might have held out above a year. In July, 1418, the English laid siege to Rouen, which surrendered by a treaty signed on the 18th of January, 1419; and the following year, 1420, a solemn embassy reached that city to offer the throne of France to Henry of England. Unless, therefore, the year given as that of the exploit of Mauger be a miscopy for 1417, which is very possible, the entire incident is open to much doubt. Evreux has now a clock tower, built during the domination of the English, about 1419, so completely were they at that time masters of all Normandy. As early as 1415, they had taken Harfleur, after a memorable siege of forty days.

HENRY VI.—1422 to 1461.

With Henry VI., who was an only son, and not nine months old when his gallant father died, commenced the civil war in England, known by the name of the War of the Roses. The merchants of Guernsey during his reign, "being much obstructed in their trade by the officers of the customs in England, in violation of their privileges, a complaint was forwarded to his majesty, on which, in the year 1443, he sent express and peremptory orders to the collectors and comptrollers of the ports of Plymouth, Poole, and Southampton, and of all creeks and rivers appurtenant to the same, forbidding them to exact from the inhabitants of the island any other toll or custom than was paid by those of other free ports, in conformity with their ancient privileges and liberties.

The reasons assigned by the king are sufficiently curious to warrant the insertion of the following paragraph :

"We have been informed by the humble representations of our beloved inhabitants of the island of Guernsey, which island is one of the free ports of this our realm, that, whereas all the inhabitants of our said free port are bound to serve us, as well on the day of our coronation, as also to accompany us and conduct us whenever it is expedient for us to cross the sea, and go into foreign parts, with all the power and forces they can raise, and also attend us at such times as may be required for the space of six weeks at their own expense, in consideration of which our royal progenitors (whom God absolve) anciently granted and confirmed to the inhabitants of the said island," &c. &c.

During the reign of Elizabeth, this charter was entered on the records of Dover Castle. It is evident from the obligatory duties described, which compelled the inhabitants to carry the king over the sea, and assist at his coronation, that these were all the services required from them out of the island, which exactly accords with the spirit of the earl of Anjou's grant, by which they are exempted from serving abroad, unless to follow the duke of Normandy to recover the English crown. It is not improbable that the cause of their being obliged to attend at the coronation, after the loss of Normandy, was to keep up the king's claim on that duchy, for lord Coke says, that a seizin of the Anglo-Norman Islands is a good seizin in law of the whole province.

The first thirty years of this reign were marked by the languid progress and final ignominious failure of the second war for the re-establishment of the Plantagenets in France, conducted by Henry V. with so much success as to conceal its impolicy and iniquity. Generally, however, the countries between the Loire and the Seine were the theatre of active warfare. "France, to the north of the Loire, had become one vast solitude ; the country was deserted, and there were no men but in forests or fortresses ; even the cities were rather quarters for soldiers than dwelling places of the inhabitants. The cultivation of the soil was abandoned, except around the walls, under the ramparts, and within sight of the sentinel in his tower. As soon as an enemy was discovered, the alarm bells were rung, the labourers flew into the town ; the very cattle had learnt a sort of instinct which taught them to take to flight. Theft and robbery were of necessity the only occupations of houseless wretches."—*Barante*. Du Moulin gives the names of 119 *gentilshommes*, who in the year 1423[1] defended *Mont St. Michel* so well that the English could not take it. Among these names we find le Sieur R. Roussel, le Sieur R. de Beauvoir, le Sieur François Hamon, le Sieur G. Le Vicomte, le Sieur T. Benoist, le Sieur P. du Moulin, le Sieur R. de Bailleul, le Sieur J. Thomas Guerin, le Sieur G. de la Mare, le Sieur Guillaume Artur, le Sieur J. le Carpentier, and le Sieur Jean le Brun; all names now existing in the Anglo-Norman islands. In the years 1448-9, Normandy, which the Plantagenets had never ceased to look upon as their inheritance, was wrested from them, as was Gascony in 1451. The people of Guienne, which province had belonged to England for three centuries, shewed a desire of obtaining English succour; and Talbot, a renowned captain, who had fought at Azincourt, was sent to Bordeaux to their aid, in the eightieth year of his age. He died at the battle of Chatillon, like a brave soldier, and the surrender of Bayonne, in 1453, completed, with the exception of Calais, the expulsion of the English from France; thus closing a contest which had, in some degree, been waged for a century.

During the fatal struggle between the houses of York and Lancaster, which for thirty years deluged the kingdom in blood, and nearly annihilated the ancient nobility of England, the earl of Warwick, who was governor of Calais and high admiral, espoused the cause of the former. When the civil war had broken out, and the duke of York had taken the field, Warwick came from Calais to his aid, bringing with him a body of old soldiers accustomed to the wars of Guienne and Normandy; but, on the eve of a battle, in Shropshire, October, 1459, the greater part of these men deserted the Yorkite camp during the night, and went over to the king. In consequence, the duke fled to Ireland; and Warwick,[2] says Holingshed, with the earl of March (afterwards Edward IV.) and a select company, could find no safer course than to escape into Devonshire, and embark at Exmouth for Guernsey, in a ship which a certain squire, by the name of John Dynham, purchased for them at the price of 110 marks. At Guernsey they recruited themselves, and sailing from thence to Calais, were there joyfully received at a postern by their friends.[3] This visit of the earl of March is confirmed

(1) According to Girard's *Histoire du Mont St. Michel*, (Avranches, 1843,) this defence occurred in 1434.

(2) Richard Nevil, earl of Warwick, the most conspicuous personage of that turbulent age, and who bore the name of "*king maker*," quarrelled with Edward IV. after his elevation to the throne, and was killed at the battle of Barnet, in 1471. Warwick was lord of these islands, his "receiver" in Guernsey being Thomas Guille, a copy of whose accounts may yet be seen.

(3) Southey's Naval History of England, vol. ii., p. 104.

by a report of Sir Thomas Leighton, knight, and other commissioners of queen Elizabeth, dated November 21, 1597,
which report states that in the parish of St. Sampson, Guernsey, there are certain lands called the "Franc Fieu Gallicien,"
on which the tenants pay "nothing besides," the said lands,
by common report, having been exempted (affranchies) by
king Edward IV., in acknowledgment of the services which
the possessors, being seafaring persons, had rendered him in
transporting him to the said island. As this visit accounts in
a great measure for the interest taken by the latter sovereign
in these islands, it seems strange that no Jersey or Guernsey
historian, excepting Warburton, has mentioned it.

It was near the close of this unfortunate reign that the
French, in 1461, obtained possession, through treachery, of
the castle of Mont Orgueil, in Jersey; which, with the six
adjoining parishes, remained in their power during six years,
until the accession of Edward IV. The other six parishes
were bravely maintained by the Jerseymen, headed by Philip
de Carteret, *seigneur of St. Ouen*, who secured the castle of
Grosnez, situated to the west, as Mont Orgueil is to the east,
of the island ; and frequent skirmishes occurred between the
contending parties. The manor house of St. Ouen was
doubtless another means of defence, as it appears that a moat
of considerable width can still be traced round the house, with
other indications of a fortification.

The oldest charter under the great seal, which Guernsey
holds from the English crown, preserved entire in its records,
is that of Henry VI.,[1] and contains an inspeximus of the
charters of Edward III., Richard II., and Henry IV. and
V., and it begins thus : " Henry, by the grace of God, king
of England and France, and lord of Ireland : To all those to
whom these presents shall come, greeting. We have seen
the letters patent of the lord Richard, late king of England,
the second *after the conquest*, made in these words :

" Richard, by the grace of God, king of England and
France, and lord of Ireland, to all those to whom these
letters patent shall come, greeting :

" Know ye, that we, considering the *good behaviour*, and
good fidelity, which we have found from day to day in our
liege and faithful nations, and communities of our islands of
Guernsey, Jersey, Serk, and Alderney, have, of our special
grace, granted for ourselves and heirs, (as far as in us lies,)

---

(1) According to Duncan, in the Guernsey and Jersey Magazine, I., 363 ; but the charter
is not preserved at the *Greffe*, or Registry Office, of Guernsey. This charter doubtless
once existed, or may still exist.

to the said nations and communities, that they, and their heirs and successors, shall for ever *be free and acquitted* in all our cities, boroughs, markets, and trading towns, fairs, mart towns, and other places, and harbours, *within our kingdom of England*, from all sorts of tolls, exactions, and customs, in the same manner as our faithful and liege subjects are in our kingdom aforesaid; provided, however, that our said nations and communities, and their heirs aforesaid, shall well and faithfully behave themselves towards us, and our heirs aforesaid, *for ever.*"

This charter of Henry VI. was confirmed by the Parliament of England in the following words: "Cum assensu Dominorum Spiritualium et Temporalium in parliamento nostro apud Westmons, anno regni nostri primo: With the assent of the Lords Spiritual and Temporal in our parliament held at Westminster in the first year of our reign." And it may be well to observe, as the distinction is important and worthy of notice to all who study legal and political antiquities, that the islanders were, anterior to the year 1394, considered as Norman subjects, enjoying as such, previously to the charter of Richard II., independent rights, liberties, and privileges; and that the charter of Richard admitted them to participate in the immunities of English subjects, which they of course could not claim *de jure* by virtue of the institutions of Normandy.

EDWARD IV.—1461 to 1483.

The singular privilege of neutrality possessed by these islands in time of war, for at least two centuries, cannot be traced higher than the reign of this monarch, although it is believed by some historians to have existed before his time; certainly not, however, in the fourteenth century, as we have shewn. Moved by the calamities to which the islanders were subjected from their proximity to France, and which he had probably witnessed while in Guernsey, that monarch conceded this neutrality to them, and solicited of the Pope to enforce it with the anathemas of the church. Accordingly, Pius IV., by a bull dated March 1, 1483-4, or a year after Edward's death, confirmed the privilege, and threatened to excommunicate all persons who should molest the islanders in any way. The insular clergy were also instrumental, through their suffragan at Coutances, in procuring this confirmation, which enabled them to maintain a more easy intercourse with that see. To give it every possible effect, the bull was published at Coutances in the usual form.[1] This bull[2] made especial mention of the church of St. Peter-Port,[3] thus proving its consideration at that early period, as it was the only church in the islands so named. Indeed, it is evident that Guernsey, owing to its fisheries, especially the conger, to its greater commerce, and to its better roadstead, was long deemed the most important of these islands,[4] although she is now indisputably second to Jersey, which has about double her trade and population. This privilege of neutrality comprehended not only the harbours but the seas, within sight of the islands, "as far as the eye of man can reach," and it appears to have been generally respected, as several instances can be adduced of the restitution of vessels captured from the islanders, and even from strangers in their havens, as also of French vessels being protected, while in the islands, from English cruisers. On the other hand, there are occasional proofs, up to the year 1689, when the neutrality ceased, of its being disregarded ; and although the original privilege was confirmed by subsequent British sovereigns, we incline to think that it was continued more as a truce between the Normans and Bretons and the islanders, for their mutual advantage and convenience, than as a tacit compact between England and France, especially after the separation of the islands from the bishopric of Coutances, in the year 1568.

Camden mentions the privilege, though by a mistake he applies it to Guernsey only : he says, *Veteri Regum* Angliæ *privilegio, perpetuæ hic sunt quasi induciæ ; et* Gallis, *aliisque, quamvis bellum exardescat, ultro citroque huc sine periculo venire, et commercia securè exercere, licet ;* i.e. " By an ancient privilege of the kings of *England*, there is here a kind of perpetual truce ; and how hot soever the war be, the *French*, and others, have free liberty to come hither to trade, and to depart again in safety." [5]

Mr. Selden introduces the privilege as an argument in support of his hypothesis of the dominion of the sovereign of England over the narrow seas, thus : *Neque enim facilè conjectandum est, undenam originem habuerit Jus illud induciarum*

(1, Lecanu's Histoire des Evêques de Coutances. À Coutances, 1839.

(2) This bull is given in the Appendix, No. viii., of Falle's History of Jersey.

(3) Tradition states that this church was originally designed as the cathedral of these islands.

(4) The harbour of St Sampson, the only natural one in these islands, doubtless contributed also to that importance.

" Guernsey was reckoned, though the most distant from France, the most considerable of all the islands, on account of the safety and convenience of its harbours, and the quantity of fish on its coast."—*Cæsarea, or the Island of Jersey.* London, 1840.

(5) De Insul. Britan. p. 855.

singulare ac perpetuum, quo CÆSAREÆ, Sarniæ, *cæterarumque Insularum* Normannico *Littori præjacentium incolæ, etiam in ipso mari fruuntur, flagrante utcunque inter circumvicinas gentes bello, nisi ab* Angliæ *Regum dominio hoc Marino derivetur :* i.e. " It is not easy to conjecture whence first sprung that singular right (or privilege) of perpetual truce, which the inhabitants of JERSEY, GUERNEZEY, and the other islands adjacent to the coast of NORMANDY, enjoy in the midst of the sea, notwithstanding any war betwixt the neighbouring nations round about them, unless it be derived from this maritime dominion of the kings of ENGLAND." [1]

Falle says : " Even strangers have acknowledged this privilege, and entered it into their books of navigation and commerce. Thus the anonymous author of *Les Us et Coutumes de la Mer*, printed at Rouen, 1671, speaking of prizes taken at sea, says that a prize is not good, *si elle a esté faite en lieu d'asyle ou de refuge, comme sont les isles et mers de* GERZAY *et* Grenezay, *en la coste de* Normandie ; *ausquelles les* François *et* Anglois, *pour quelque guerre qu'il y ait entre les deux couronnes, ne doivent insulter ou courre l'un sur l'autre, tant et si loin que s'estend l'aspect ou la veúe des dites isles*, i.e. 'if the prize be made in places of security and refuge (places exempted and privileged) as are the isles and seas of JERSEY and GUERNEZEY, on the coast of NORMANDY ; where the *French* and *English*, whatever war there be betwixt the two crowns, ought not to insult, or in a hostile manner pursue, each other, so long and so far as they have the said islands in prospect and in view.'" (Part III. Art. XXI. § 6.)

The bull of Pius IV., already mentioned, speaks of the advantage which these islands afforded as places of shelter for vessels in distress, and of their conveniences for the prosecution of trade ; but the Rev. E. Durell thinks that the strongest reason for the concession of this state of neutrality was the very limited commerce of those times, and in consequence that the privilege excited little jealousy among the contending powers. In the year 1523, temp. Henry VIII., during the war between England and France, a Guernsey vessel, taken in the Channel by a privateer of Morlaix, was, by order of count de Laval, governor of Britany, released in consequence of this privilege. The order provided for the release only of the islanders, and the restitution of their effects ; while the English who were on board, and their merchandize, were declared good and lawful prize. The

---

(1) Mare Clausum, Lib. II. Cap. XIX. et iterum Cap. XXII.

K

motive of William III. for not continuing the privilege to
the islands appears to have been his apprehension that it
would open a channel of communication between James II.
and the Jacobites in Britain and Ireland.

Sir Richard Harliston, vice-admiral of England, coming to
Guernsey, in the year 1467, with a squadron of the king's
ships, Philip de Carteret sent to inform him of the great
difficulty he experienced in preventing the French from sub-
duing the whole of Jersey; whereupon, according to Falle,
the admiral left his ships in Guernsey roads, and hastened
privately to de Carteret, who was at his manor of St. Ouen.
It seems strange that the admiral should thus leave his squadron, and run the risk of being captured on the passage;
but Falle adds, that after a consultation with de Carteret as
to the best means of recovering Mont Orgueil Castle, he
returned to Guernsey.   Soon after, he sailed over with his
ships to Jersey and blockaded the French by sea, while the
islanders invested the castle by land.   After a defence of
nineteen weeks, the garrison, unable to obtain any relief from
the opposite coast of Normandy, and being in a state of
famine, surrendered; and Harliston was rewarded with the
governorship of Jersey.   The only Jerseyman of note who
seems to have fallen, was Reginald Lemprière, seigneur of
Rosel, and he was slain in a sally of the besieged.   If the
Jerseymen assisted at the recovery of Castle Cornet, temp.
Edward III., as Falle pretends, the Guernseymen appear,
with far more certainty, to have returned the favor at the
reduction of the castle of Mont Orgueil, although that histo-
torian has failed to notice their assistance, both in men and
money.   On the other hand, Duncan has erroneously cited
a patent, as extant under the great seal of England, in proof
of this assistance; for the document in question does not at
all bear the interpretation given by him to it, as in a spirit of
fairness and truth we proceed to shew.

Speaking of the reduction of this castle from the French,
Duncan says, at page 37, that the Guernseymen "had a
considerable share in the honour of its recapture," and that
Edward IV., in the first [ninth] year of his reign, "not only
confirmed the patent of king Richard II. in favor of the
inhabitants of Guernsey, but greatly enlarged its provisions,
in consideration of the great dangers they had encountered,
and the heavy losses they had sustained at the reduction of
Mont Orgueil Castle, which charter was afterwards confirmed

by those of queen Elizabeth and king Charles II." And to these remarks he appends a foot note, as follows : " Henry VII., when earl of Richmond, visited Jersey, and he mentions the courage and zeal of the Guernseymen in his charter ; and a patent under the great seal of England is extant which names ten Guernseymen and five Jerseymen, who most distinguished themselves at the recapture of Mont Orgueil Castle : John Perrin, John Fyot, William Duport, J. Rougier, Thomas De Havilland, Lawrence Carey, William Maingy, Reynold Agenor, Richard Cosins, and Nicholas De Lisle, of Guernsey ; Peter Le Serkais, Peter Tehy, John De Soulsmont, Nicholas Le Petit, and John Le Moigne, of Jersey."

Happily, in the month of April, 1851, the ORIGINAL patent of Edward IV., and evidently that alluded to by Duncan as above, was accidentally discovered among some other documents in the possession of Mrs. Hutchesson, eldest daughter of the late Charles Le Marchant, Esq. This very valuable insular record came to light through the indefatigable historical researches of Mr. Edgar MacCulloch, jurat, and is in an excellent state of preservation, the seal being as perfect as if affixed yesterday. The patent is in Latin, and the following is a correct summary of its contents.

Edward, having learned from the information of the inhabitants of Guernsey and Jersey, that they had expended the sum of 2833 libras, 6 solidos, and 8 denarios[1] (livres, sols, and deniers,) in the recovery of Jersey and Mont Orgueil Castle from the enemy, to their great impoverishment, grants to ten Guernseymen, viz. John Peryn,[2] John Tyaut, William Duport, Jordan Rogier, Thomas de Haveillant, (Havilland,) Lawrence Carée, (Carey,) William Mangy, (Maingy or Mainguy,) Renovet Agenor, Ralph Cousin, and Nicholas De Lisle ; and to five Jerseymen, viz. Peter Le Serkees, Peter Tehy, John de Souslemont, Nicholas Le Petit, and John Le Moigne ; the privilege of exporting from England to Guernsey and Jersey, in vessels subject to his majesty, goods and merchandize of the staple of Calais, the duties on which would, in any one year, amount to £150 ; or of importing into England goods subject to duties to the same amount.

(1) These Latin denominations apply equally to pounds, shillings and pence ; but as the sum advanced was so great, and as accounts were then kept in the islands in French money, we feel convinced that livres, and not pounds sterling, were meant. A livre in that age would represent at least a pound sterling now.

(2) " Et viron ce temps-là [A.D. 1533] mourut Jean Lemprière, seigneur de Rozel, la succession duquel parvint à Edouard Perrin, fils de Dominique Perrin, de l'île de Guernesey, à cause de sa femme, sœur et prochaine héritière du dit Jean Lemprière, en son vivant seigneur de Rozel, comme devant est dit."—*Chroniques de Jersey*. Guernsey, 1832.

These goods were to be exported from, or imported into, the ports of Poole, Exeter, and Dartmouth ; and the privilege was to last for six years, reckoning from the 20th of January preceding the date of the grant, and to continue after the six years, if it should please the king, until the sum of £2,000 was remitted.   The duties thus remitted were to be retained by the patentees before named, for the use of all the inha-bitants of the said islands ; and if the duties so remitted did not amount, in any one year, to the full sum of £150, they might in that case make up the balance in another year. There is also a proviso, that the goods exported from the islands shall be the property of the patentees, or other inha-bitants of the said islands.   The grant is by authority of parliament, and dated in Michaelmas term, in the ninth year of the reign of Edward IV. (A.D. 1470.)

Thus the patent makes no mention whatever of the great dangers encountered by the Guernseymen, or of the ten Guernseymen and the five Jerseymen who most distinguished themselves at the siege : it is therefore quite evident that Duncan was misled by those who formerly had access to the document, and who so singularly misconstrued, or wilfully misrepresented, its purport. There is, however, very little, if any, doubt that the Guernseymen, perhaps in no great numbers, joined Sir Richard Harliston's squadron, when he sailed from Guernsey to co-operate in the reduction of Mont Orgueil Castle, although the evidence to that effect is rather corroborative than conclusive ; their descendants claimed, in a petition to Lord Carew, about 1610, to have "helped" the people of Jersey in the recovery, and that claim is mentioned in some of the royal charters ; while Durell, in his Notes on Falle, (No. 41, p. 296,) candidly acknowledges that at least one Guernseyman was engaged in the siege, thus : " It ap-pears from an original grant of Sir Richard Harliston, dated September 15, 1479, now in the possession of Mrs. Symonds, of Trinity Manor, that he gave corn and money rents, the former to the amount of 8 qrs. 7 cab. 2s., and the latter to 12 groats, 13 sous, 6 deniers, to Perrotine Famget, relict of Philip Johan,[1] of Guernsey, for the services he had rendered during the siege for the recovery of Mont Orgueil Castle from the count de Maulevrier. This fact, so honourable to the island [? Jersey or Guernsey] and to Harliston, is not mentioned by any of our historians, or rather chroniclers."

We have said that the garrison of the castle was starved

(1) Probably Jehan, which surname is still existing in Guernsey.

into a surrender, and therefore we cannot discover that any great credit was due to the besiegers, whether aided by the Guernseymen or not. He who was entitled to the most merit was unquestionably Philip de Carteret, because he prevented the French from obtaining possession of half the island for about six years; and notwithstanding it is very uncertain whether he ever obtained any reward from the crown for so acceptable a service. His son married the only daughter and heiress of Harliston, who is said to have borne her husband twenty sons.[1] This lady and her husband suffered much persecution from the governor and bailly of Jersey; and Durell observes that "the history of Margaret de Harliston," the wife of Philip de Carteret, "as detailed in the Chronicles of Jersey, wants only the pen of some Walter Scott to give it all the interest of one of the tales of olden times." Harliston, who was a Yorkite, was also unfortunate in his later years, for, being induced to believe that the person known in the annals of England by the name of Perkin Warbeck was really the duke of York, younger son of Edward IV., he went over to the duchess of Burgundy, who was in Flanders; but on the failure of Warbeck's enterprise, Harliston remained at the court of that princess, having a few years previously lost his government of Jersey. A tower built by him in Mont Orgueil Castle long bore his name.

EDWARD V. to HENRY VIII. — 1483 to 1547.

The fate of the two sons of Edward IV., whose sins were visited upon his children, is one of those disputed points of history which will never be cleared up, although the probability is that they were put to death in the tower by order of Richard III., the last of the Plantagenets, whose usurpation endured only from 1483 to 1485. He granted a charter to Guernsey, in which were confirmed all the concessions of preceding monarchs, and he would have been most worthy of the crown, says Southey, had it rightfully devolved to him. Indeed, his character and person are so differently described by different writers, that it is very difficult to form a correct judgment of either the one or the other.

The earl of Richmond, (afterwards Henry VII.) on his flight to Britany, landed in Jersey, whether designedly, or

(1) It is generally said that when Charles II. visited Jersey in his exile, a lady, of the name of De Carteret, presented to him her twenty sons, as ready to engage in his service; and it is added that each of these sons had a sister, so as to make the bearer believe that there were twenty sisters also, whereas there was only one. This anecdote, which evidently relates to Margaret de Harliston, is however an anachronism, as all the sons were probably dead at least a century before Charles went to Jersey.

driven in by contrary wind, is uncertain. From Britany, Richmond embarked, in 1483, with a fleet of forty sail in his first attempt against the usurper; but the ships were dispersed by a terrible tempest, some being driven into Normandy, and others compelled to return to Britany. The earl himself, with only one other bark, arrived off the entrance of Poole, and, finding no support there, he proceeded to Normandy. The tempest had been his preservation, for if he had effected a landing after the failure of his confederate the duke of Buckingham, whose head was struck off in the market place of Salisbury, it is probable that he would also have lost his life. Early in August, 1485, Richmond embarked again at Harfleur, and in a few days landed at Milford Haven with about 5,000 men; when the victory of Bosworth, and the death of Richard, placed him on the throne, which he filled from 1485 to 1509. Soon after his accession, he granted to Jersey thirty-three articles for the better administration of the existing laws; and he likewise conferred a charter on Guernsey, in the preamble of which are recorded the services of its inhabitants, some twenty years antecedently, in the expedition to Jersey under Sir Richard Harliston. During his reign, and that of his son and successor, Henry VIII., (1509 to 1547,) the islands remained unmolested. When the latter sovereign introduced the reformed religion into Guernsey,[1] he completed the work commenced by Henry V., and vested in the crown all the tithes of foreign priors and abbots not yet so appropriated. In the fourth year of Henry VIII., (1513,) the parochial school of St. Peter-Port was founded by the free gift of Thomas Le Marquant (doubtless Le Marquand) and Janette Thelry, his wife, who conveyed "a certain house and garden, being and lying within the said parish, to the northward of, and near to, the chapel of St. Julien, therein to keep and hold a school for the time to come." And they endowed the school with two quarters of wheat rent for the maintenance of a master, who was to teach each scholar, every evening before going home, an anthem of our lady the virgin, the *De Profundis*, and an *Ave Maria*, for the repose of the souls of the donors.

(1) L'hérésie faisait de grands progrès dans les îles de Jersey, Guernesey, Serck, Herma et Aurigny, qui devaient bientôt faire schisme avec leur antique église. Le diocèse de Dol s'attribue, mais à tort, la possession primitive de ces îles, sous le prétexte qu'elles furent converties par Saint Magloire, évêque de Dol. Quelques historiens de Jersey sont dans le même sentiment, et ajoutent qu'elles ne furent adjointes au diocèse de Coutances que par les ducs de Normandie; mais outre qu'il ne reste aucun souvenir de cette prétendue adjonction, il est vrai que Guillaume le Conquérant, ni aucun de ses prédécesseurs, n'avaient le droit de ravir à un diocèse une portion de son territoire, pour la donner à un autre: l'église seule peut faire de tels changements.—*Histoire des Evêques de Coutances.*

EDWARD VI.—1547 to 1553.

In 1549, two years after the accession of Edward VI., the French, with a squadron of eleven galleys containing troops, seized on the little island of Sark, at that time nearly deserted, as the monks and friars, who had been its principal occupants, had retired to France about the year 1349. Having garrisoned the island with nearly 400 men under Captain Bruel, they sailed over to Guernsey in the night, hoping to surprise it; but Captain Winter's ships, then lying in the roadstead, fired into the enemy, as did the artillery at Castle Cornet. The roaring of the cannon roused the townspeople, and news of the attempted invasion was hastily spread through the country. The whole population was quickly under arms, and a division of the enemy, which had landed under cover of the darkness, was bravely repulsed and driven to their boats. This ill success, however, did not deter them from trying their fortune in Jersey, where they met with a similar reception, being obliged to retire, and having sustained a heavy loss in the two actions. The English government, having notice of the intended attack, had sent over Captain Winter with 800 men to reinforce the islanders. The capture of Sark was probably the cause why Sir Leonard Chamberlayne, governor of Guernsey, caused some additional works to be raised on Castle Cornet. In the *Chroniques de Jersey*,[1]. it is stated that the French garrison of Sark, getting tired of its seclusion, nearly all left the island in the course of five or six years, although they had erected two fortresses, one at the north, near the *Éperquerie*, in Great Sark, and the other near the *Coupée*, in Little Sark, the site and form of the latter being still very distinct. Heylin and Southey observe that when Sark was taken, it had only a poor hermitage, with a little chapel appertaining to it, the isle itself serving as a common to the people of Guernsey for breeding their cattle.

In this reign, differences arose among the English Protestants, because the Lutherans continued crucifixes and images with tapers and priestly vestments, while the Calvinists sought to eradicate them as the remains of popery; and the death of Edward probably prevented a nearer approach in the Anglican church to that of Geneva, both in ceremonial and discipline. During the persecutions of Mary, the Protestant clergy took refuge in Germany and Switzerland, and were kindly received by the Calvinists; but the Lutheran divines

(1' "Chroniques de Jersey," par George S. Syvret. Guernesey, 1832.

both neglected and insulted them. When the accession of Elizabeth recalled the exiles, the Calvinists were mortified to find that the queen was not their friend, and that the Lutherans were to be in the ascendant.

MARY.— 1553 to 1558.

Sark was recovered in this reign by a singular stratagem, of which there are some variations in the relation; but that of Sir Walter Raleigh best accords with popular tradition. Sir Walter states that Sark could never have been recovered by strong hand, having cattle and corn sufficient for as many men as were requisite for its defence, and being so inaccessible that it might be held against the Grand Turk; yet, by the ingenuity of a gentleman of the Netherlands, it was regained. Anchoring off the island with one ship, he pretended that the merchant, who had freighted it, had died on board; and he besought permission of the French to bury him in consecrated ground, in the chapel, offering them in return a present of such commodities as he had with him. This request was granted, on condition of the Flemings not landing armed with any weapon, not so much even as a knife; which being assented to, a coffin, containing, not a corpse, but swords, targets, and arquebusses, was put into the boat. The French, who, says Southey,[1] were some thirty in number, received the mourners on their landing, and searched every one of them so narrowly, that they could not have concealed a penknife. The coffin was drawn up the rocks with some difficulty. Part of the French, meanwhile, took the boat of the Flemings, and rowed to their ship to receive the promised commodities; but, as soon as they got on board, they were seized and bound. The Flemings on shore, after having carried the coffin into the chapel, shut the door, and, taking out the weapons, fell upon the French, who ran down to the beach, and called to their companions on board the vessel to return to their assistance; but when the boat landed, it was filled with Flemings, who, uniting with their countrymen, recaptured the island. It is proper however to add, that according to the *Chroniques de Jersey* just cited, Sark was retaken,

(1) "Raleigh's Hist. of the World, book iv. ch. 2, s. 18. Hakewell's Apology, 258. Heylin's Survey, 296. 'Thus,' says Sir Walter, 'a fox-tail doth sometimes help well to piece out the lion's skin, that else would be too short.' The archdeacon calls it a stratagem, 'in his judgment matchable to any that ever yet he heard of.' And Peter Heylin says it is 'to be compared, if not preferred, unto any of the ancients, did not that fatal folly reprehended once by Tacitus still reign amongst us, *quod vetera extollimus, recentium incuriosi.*' It was, however, no new stratagem; nor ought any stratagem ever to be recorded with approbation, in which the generosity or the humanity of an enemy has been abused."—*Southey.*

not by stratagem, but by some Dutch ships, which came to Guernsey to make war on the French; and sending their boats in the night with a few Guernseymen, as guides, the crews landed on Little Sark, and surprised the Frenchmen asleep in their beds.—This second account is more probable.

Shortly afterwards, Sir Hugh Paulet, governor of Jersey, in order that the French might not return to Sark, caused the fortresses to be razed to the ground, and again was the island left uninhabited. In spite of this, however, the French thought it worth making one more attempt to regain an island which might prove of future advantage to them in the Channel. The *seigneur* of Glatney, in Normandy, seeing how it had been lost by Captain Bruel without any defence, and that the island was without inhabitants, preferred a petition to the king of France, that, if it were granted to him and to his heirs, he would colonize it at his own expense. The grant was made, and a number of persons were sent by the *seigneur* of Glatney to the isle of Sark to inhabit it; but his scheme was defeated; for, not long after, war broke out between the queen of England and the king of France, in consequence of which the new settlers returned to their country, leaving the island as they found it.

The commencement of Mary's reign was advantageous to Guernsey, for she had not been six months on the throne when, on the inhabitants representing the scarcity of provisions and other necessaries, a royal patent, dated 18th of December, 1553, was issued, permitting them to import a sufficient quantity from England, as well for the island as for Castle Cornet, without payment of any export duty. The queen also confirmed the privilege of neutrality by an *inspeximus* of the bull of pope Pius IV. During the short reign of Edward VI., the English Protestant Liturgy, translated into French, was used in the churches, and the mass abolished in the islands; but the former was suspended, and the latter revived, under Mary, by whom the re-establishment of popery in England was unquestionably acceptable to great numbers, if not to a majority, of the people, who had been so averse to the reformation that German troops are said to have been sent from Calais to impose protestantism upon them. We cannot discover in what spirit the reformed religion was at first received in the bailiwick of Guernsey; but this much we know, that the dean and parochial clergy, and the Royal Court, appear to have been the too submissive instruments of Mary; and it is probable that, as in England, the change was far more acceptable to the lower than to the higher classes, the latter of whom have in all times, and in all countries, ever looked upon their consequence as bound up with the ancient state church establishment.

It was in this reign, on the 18th of July, 1556, that a mother and her two daughters were burnt for heresy in St. Peter-Port, Guernsey, and their cruel fate, with that of an infant martyr, has obtained a melancholy historical celebrity. One of the daughters was married to a minister, named Massy, who had fled the island in these dangerous times, and at her execution she was in the last stage of pregnancy. In the anguish of her torments, she is said to have brought forth a living male child, who was instantly snatched from the flames by one of the by-standers, and, on the command of the bailiff, cast into them again; " so that pretty babe," remarks Heylin, " was born a martyr, and added to the number of the holy innocents."—The women were condemned by the ecclesiastical court, the sentences of which the civil court was bound to execute. As the whole of this atrocious proceeding has been denied by some Roman Catholics, while others have urged " that the mother, by concealing her pregnancy, was the real cause of her child's death, which, however, happened previously to the burning of its body by the executioner," it is necessary to add, that the judicial sentence still exists in the archives of the Royal Court of Guernsey; but, if one act of brutality can justify another, it is some slight extenuation that, scarcely three years before, the great Protestant reformer, Calvin, was the cause of Michael Servetus being burnt alive for Arianism,[1] and that this was the age of religious persecution, which ever engenders cruelty. Suffice it to add, that Sir Isaac Newton was an Arian, and that Constantine the Great—who is said to have seen a cross in the sky, with an inscription in Greek, signifying *" By this conquer"* (?) —first persecuted the Arians, and afterwards inclined to their opinions. There must have been sufficient evidence of the pregnancy, and certain it is that no woman would conceal it in such an extremity. Foxe, in his " Ecclesiasticall Historie," London, 1641, gives many interesting documents relative to this " tragicall, lamentable, and pitifull historie," and thus describes the execution: " The time then being come when these three good servants and holy saints of God, the innocent mother with her two daughters, should suffer; in

---

(1) "Thus the death of Servetus has weighed down the name and memory of Calvin."— *Hallam.*

the place, where they should consummate their martyrdom, were three stakes set up. At the middle post was the mother, the eldest daughter on the right hand, the youngest on the other. They were first strangled, but the rope brake before they were dead, and so the poor women fell in the fire." He next relates that " Perotine," (Massy,) who was then great with child, "did fall on her side, where happened a ruefull sight," the birth of the infant, who was quickly snatched from the flames, and " laid upon the grasse. Then was the childe had to the prevost, and from him to the bayliffe, who gave censure that it should be carried back againe, and cast into the fire." Foxe distinctly mentions that the poor women were confined in Castle Cornet, " commandment being given to the king's officers to go to the castle to fetch the said women, to hear the sentence against them." After the death of Mary, in 1558, the inhuman dean, James Amy, was committed to prison, and dispossessed of his living, while the bailiff and jurats sued for and obtained the pardon of queen Elizabeth. The ecclesiastical sentence is in Latin, the judicial one in French ; and the latter states that the poor women " sont condampnées et adjugies de estre bruslées et arses au jour d'huy, jusques à consumation de cendre, au lyeu accoustumey, avvecqz conffiscation de tous leurs biens-meubles et héritages à la main de notre sire le roy et la roigne, accordant et selon l'effect de une sentence delyvrée en justice de p. monssieur le doyen et les curés, le xiiije. jour du moes de Juillet, en l'an susdit, en laquelle ils ont estey aprouvées hérétiques." Doctor Heylin says, in reference to this frightful tragedy : " Katharine Gowches, a poor woman of St. Peter-Port, in Guernsey, was noted to be much absent from the church, and her two daughters guilty of the same neglect. Upon this they were presented before James Amy, then dean of the island, who, finding in them that they held opinions contrary to those then allowed, about the sacrament of the altar, pronounced them heretics, and condemned them to the fire. The poor women, on the other side, pleaded for themselves, that that doctrine had been taught them in the time of king Edward ; but if the queen was otherwise disposed, they were content to be of her religion. This was fair, but it would not serve ; for by the dean they were delivered unto Hélier Gosselin, then bailiff, and by him unto the fire," &c. It has been doubted whether an infant could be born alive under such circumstances, but we are assured by competent medical authority that the case is very possible.

In July, 1558, during Mary's life, lord Clinton put to sea with a stout fleet, and, landing 7,000 men in Lower Britany, took the town of Conquet, near Brest, but soon after re-embarked. On the return of the fleet to England, it was joined by a squadron of thirty Spanish ships, when the admiral was induced to attempt the taking of Brest; but arriving on the coast of Britany a second time, he found the whole of the country in arms, and was constrained to abandon the enterprize. On his passage from England to Britany, lord Clinton came by Guernsey, and there took on board many of the inhabitants as pilots, mariners, and others, of whom he afterwards made a favorable report.

Heylin, speaking of Alderney, says: "The chief house herein belongeth unto the Chamberlains, as also the dominion or the farm of all the island, it being granted by queen Elizabeth unto George, the son of Sir Leonard Chamberlain, then governor of Guernsey, by whose valour it was recovered from the French, who in queen Mary's days had seized upon it." We have been unable to ascertain any particulars of this capture beyond the fact, that about the year 1610 the inhabitants of Guernsey, in their petition to lord Carew, claimed to have assisted in driving the French from Alderney, whence they brought some hundred prisoners to Guernsey, where they were kept for a long time in prison.

CHAPTER VIII.

ELIZABETH.—1558 to 1603.

Elizabeth received the tidings of her accession to the throne at Hatfield, where she had resided for several years in mild custody, but under the watchful eye of a guard. Having thus been schooled in adversity, nothing can excuse her after her unwomanly treatment of Mary. Her long and otherwise glorious rule was, however, very beneficial to these islands, and the more so as she had scarcely any war with France. In the first year of her reign, she confirmed the ancient privileges of Guernsey in an *inspeximus* of several charters granted by her royal predecessors; and soon afterwards she issued a patent to the same effect, the most ample that had yet been conceded, wherein the privilege of neutrality is distinctly expressed to extend as far as the eye can reach from any of the islands. Elizabeth's charter was also confirmed by parliament in the following words, which conclude it: "Per ipsam reginam, et de datâ prœdictâ, auctoritate parliamenti: By the queen herself with the sanction of parliament at the above-mentioned date."

Many of the Protestant ministers in France, flying from the cruel persecutions of the civil wars in that country, during the reign of Elizabeth, took sanctuary in these islands; and their education and preaching being very superior to those of the officiating clergy, the new discipline, which was similar to that of Calvin, at Geneva, and which they practised, was quickly introduced by them into St. Peter-Port, in Guernsey, and St. Hélier, in Jersey, whence it soon extended into the rural parishes of both islands. Queen Elizabeth, by an order, in the year 1565, sanctioned the innovation in the two town parishes only, " provided always that the residue of the parishes in the said isles shall diligently put apart all superstitions used in the said diocese, (Coutances,) and so continue there the order of services ordained and set forth within this realm." This permission was the more extraordinary because the queen was personally averse to the simple worship of the Presbyterians, and retained in her own chapel not only images, but the crucifix with lighted tapers before it, although the ecclesiastical visitors of 1559 were ordered to have all these symbols removed from the churches.[1] To the marriage of the clergy, Elizabeth manifested so decided a repugnance, that she never would repeal the statute of her sister Mary against it, and it was only in the first year of James that it was rescinded. In consequence, the Protestant bishops and clergy, who married by connivance or by an ungracious permission, were justly irritated at seeing their children treated by the law as illegitimate. Elizabeth, after being sumptuously entertained by archbishop Parker at Lambeth, thus took leave of his wife: " *Madam* (the style of a married lady) I may not call you ; *Mistress* (that of a single woman) I am loath to call you ; but, however, I thank you for your good cheer."—A dislike to innovation and dissent is perhaps natural to an established clergy ; and Falle, who from the

---

(1) "Those who have visited some catholic temples, and attended to the current language of devotion, must have perceived, what the writings of apologists or decrees of councils will never enable them to discover, that the saints, but more especially the Virgin, are almost exclusively the *popular* deities of that religion."—*Hallam.*

poor rector of St. Saviour, Jersey, became a prebendary of
Durham, and incumbent of the richly endowed living of
Shenley, near St. Alban's,[1] thus states the result in Jersey of
Elizabeth's permission : but great allowance must be made
for his high church bias :

"I am ashamed to say how the queen's gracious concession
was abused. The establishment in the other churches, so expressly fenced and guarded by her royal command, was daily
undermined. The people were taught to dislike in it, now one
thing, and then another. By degrees the very native clergy
suffered themselves to be led away with prejudices against it, or
perhaps to comply with what they could not help. So that in
few years all church order appointed by authority was subverted
throughout the island. The like was done in Guernezey, whither
a duplicate of the same letter as above, *mutatis mutandis*, had
been sent to as little purpose. They who had it in their power,
and whose duty it was, to have checked these novelties, to wit,
the governor in each island, Sir Amias Paulet, in Jersey, and
Sir Thomas Leighton in Guernezey, were the most forward to
encourage them ; whether out of principle, or affectation of
popularity, or a mean view of self-interest in the suppression
of the deaneries,[2] which of course must fall with the establishment, I will not determine. Perhaps all these might concur
together. And now every thing being ripe for a thorough change,
and new laws for an ecclesiastical regimen, excluding episcopacy
and liturgy, ready concerted and prepared, a synod of the
ministers and elders of all the islands was called to meet at the
town of St. Peter-Port, in Guernezey ; where, in presence of
both governors, those laws received the sanction which such an
assembly could give, and were set forth under this title : *Police
et discipline ecclésiastique des églises reformées ès isles de Jersey
et de Guernezey, Serk, et Oriny, arrestées et conclues d'un
commun accord par messieurs les gouverneurs des dites isles, et
les ministres et anciens, assemblés au synode tenu   Guernezey,
au nom de toutes les dites églises, le 28e jour du mois de Juin,
l'an* 1576: i. e. 'The ecclesiastical polity and discipline of the
reformed churches in the islands of Jersey and Guernezey,
Serk, and Oriny, unanimously concluded and agreed upon by
the governors of the said islands, and the ministers and elders,

---

(1) The fulsome dedication of his History of Jersey to William III. gives rise to the
suspicion that Mr. Falle owed his English preferment to fawning and flattery.

(2) "*The deans had an allowance out of the tithes, which was a drawback upon the revenue·
So much saving, therefore, there would be to the governors by the suppression of the deaneries.*"
To this remark of Mr. Falle, Mr. Durell adds : "John Pawlet, a brother of Sir Hugh
Pawlet, was the last catholic dean, and died in 1565 ; so that from his death to the esta-
blishment of Mr. Bandinel into that office, there had elapsed a space of almost sixty years.
Dr. Shebbeare has adopted the same opinion, that it was from a motive of economy that
the governors encouraged the suppression of the deaneries. There are, however, no
good reasons nor any documents remaining to warrant such a supposition."

assembled at the synod held at Guernezey, in the name of all the said churches, on the 28th day of the month of June, in the year 1576.'

"Thus were we drawn to depart from that union with the Church of England, which was our happiness and our glory, to let in presbytery ; of which after a time we grew no less weary than we were fond of it before, as will be shewn by and by."

In 1563, two years before the date of Elizabeth's permission just mentioned, Sir Francis Chamberlayne, governor of Guernsey, had allowed the clergy to appoint elders and deacons, and form themselves into a consistory, which met every Thursday, the governor, bailiff, and some of the jurats, being members of it. Warburton says:

"An alliance was made between them and the consistory of Jersey, of which Mr. Amias Paulett, then governor of Jersey, was a member ; and it was agreed between them, that a synod should be held, at least once every year, in each island alternately, for the regulation of the affairs of the churches in both islands. The first of these synods was held in Guernsey, on the 28th of June, 1564, of which John After, who had the title of dean of Guernsey, was a member, but did not preside, nor had he any other power or authority than the rest of the synod ; nor does it appear that he performed any sort of ecclesiastical function in the island as a minister. The probate of wills he retained, and there are yet some to be seen under the seal of his office ; and the same course was continued till Mr. John De Vic's time, who was the king's procureur, about the year 1607. On the 1st of September, 1564, by the desire of the governor of Jersey, and others of that island, Nicholas Baudouin [who came from Normandy, and was one of the first, and for some time the only presbyterian minister] was, by the consent of the consistory of Guernsey, permitted to go for two months to officiate in Jersey, where it seems at that time they had never a minister; and Adrian Saravia, a Fleming, settled as an assistant to Baudouin, in the parish of St. Peter-Port, Guernsey. The revenues of the church of that parish were taken into the hands of the consistory, to be by them distributed for the use of the church. A synod held in Guernsey, on the 22d of September, 1567, did depute some of their members to attend the bishop of Winchester, and so did a synod, held on the 1st of June, 1568, at which time they call him their bishop, although the order for uniting the island to the see of Winchester bears date the March after. In their synod, held in 1567, they took upon themselves to impose, not only pecuniary mulcts and fines, but corporal punishment upon such as should be found guilty of several crimes there mentioned ; but being better advised, in the synod held on the 12th of September, 1569, they ordered that all crimes should be first punished by the civil magistrate, and then the church shall take order; and that no pecuniary fines should be imposed by the consistory. In the same synod they ordered, that the articles of that and former synods, concerning church government, should be drawn up in form and presented to the bishop of Winchester, by the dean of Guernsey, in the name of all the islands, and, together with these articles, those of the government of the French reformed churches in London. At a synod held in Sark, in 1570, they again made an order, that although the civil magistrate should neglect the due punishment of offenders, yet the church shall proceed against them. Whereupon Nicholas Carey, the younger, a member of the consistory of Guernsey, absented himself from their meetings; and being summoned to show his reasons, gave this for the cause: that they trenched upon the civil jurisdiction; in which he persisting, was discharged from being a member of their consistory. At a synod held on the 14th and 15th of September, 1575, they made an order that a minister, not having a sufficient maintenance for himself and family from one parish, may receive a pension from another; that, in the country parishes, children may be baptised on the week days, provided there be first a sermon, according to the appointment of Jesus Christ. Matthew xxviii. In the consistory of St. Peter-Port, November 13, 1578, they order that there shall not, at any time, be an assembly of the people for prayers only; but whensoever they assemble there shall always be a sermon. In the synod held in Guernsey, June 20, 1576, a complete form of ecclesiastical discipline was agreed upon, to be observed in all the islands, perfectly agreeable to the presbyterian way. And the same discipline was again reviewed and confirmed in another synod, in October, 1579."

The queen—well knowing that the islanders had incurred the enmity of the French court by the retreat which they afforded to great numbers of Protestants from France, including some of the highest rank — strengthened both Jersey and Guernsey by additional fortifications. In the former island, an upper ward and other works were added to the unfinished castle, which took, and still bears, her name; and in the latter, a new battery was ordered to be erected on the north-east part of Castle Cornet. Her majesty exhorted her faithful subjects in Guernsey to continue, according to custom, their labour in the carriage of stone, sand, and other necessaries, at convenient days and times, to strengthen the fortifications of the castle. This important work was not completed until the 12th of August, 1594, when an early day was appointed for its consecration; and Sir Thomas Leighton,

governor, the bailiff and jurats, the clergy, and other principal
inhabitants, were present. The company being assembled,
they commenced the ceremonial with prayer, and specially
implored God's protection for the safety of the castle; after
which the governor named the new works, the "Royal Battery," which name was followed by a general discharge of
cannon.   Other works were also erected by the preceding
governor, Chamberlain, or Chamberlayne; and it is evident
that anterior to Elizabeth, the castle was a fortress of comparatively little strength.   "In her time," according to Heylin, "such improvements were made to Castle Cornet, that
for strength and beauty it yielded to none throughout the
queen's dominions."

Nor was the vigilance of Elizabeth limited to Guernsey
only, whose security depended upon that of the adjacent
islands; therefore, in order to prevent Sark from being again
surprised by the enemy, as it had before been from want of
inhabitants, she granted it, in 1564, to Hélier de Carteret,
seigneur of St. Ouen, in Jersey, to be held by him and his
heirs in perpetuity, at a yearly rent of 50 *sols tournois*, on
condition that he let it out in forty different tenements, that
there might be at least as many men to repel any sudden
attack.   Accompanied by his wife, who appears to have been
a woman of great courage and capacity, the *seigneur* removed
to Sark; and as there was no house to receive them, they
contented themselves with the ruins of a little chapel, until
one, covered with fern, was constructed.   Their suite, consisting chiefly of husbandmen and servants, proceeded to clear
and cultivate the ground, which was overspread with thorns
and brambles.   Every thing required was brought from
Jersey with infinite toil and trouble, there being no harbour
in Sark.   The original grantee — who was probably thus rewarded for the services of his ancestor in defence of Jersey,
exactly a century before—sold, in 1567, for a trifling rent, to
his "very dear friend," so termed in the deed of sale, Nicholas
Gosselin,[1] of Guernsey, the lands of Beauregard in Sark,
with the right of sporting, on condition that he caused four
men to reside on the said lands as long as he, the said Gosselin,
and his heirs remained on the island.   For several generations,
the de Carterets held the seigneury; and the capitulation
made by the royalists of Jersey, in 1651, expressed "that it
shall be left to the parliament's good pleasure to allow the

(1) The said Nicholas Gosselin was one of the clerks of the council to queen Elizabeth,
and sworn, in 1565, a jurat of the Royal Court of Guernsey.   He married Peronelle,
daughter of Louis Lemprière, bailiff of Jersey.

L

seigneur of St. Ouen to compound for the island of Sark."
In the beginning of the eighteenth century, Sark passed into
the family of Milner, bishop of Gloucester, from whom it was
purchased, in 1730, by Mrs. Susanna Le Gros, through whom
by marriage it vested, in 1738, in the Guernsey family of
Le Pelley. Peter Le Pelley, the *seigneur*, and late jurat of
the Royal Court of Guernsey, was drowned with the boat's
crew, in sight of the people of Sark, just after he had imprudently embarked for Guernsey in a gale, on the 1st of March,
1839. In 1852, the seigneury was transferred by purchase
to Mrs. T. G. Collings, of Guernsey, and is now the property
of her only son, the Rev. W. T. Collings, M.A. Sir Philip
de Carteret — appointed bailiff of Jersey in 1626, which office
he held at the commencement of the civil war — was born at
his father's residence, in Sark, in February, 1583-4 : he was
educated at Oxford, and, in point of family and fortune, was
the first personage in Jersey. He died while besieged in
Elizabeth Castle, in August, 1643, aged fifty-nine, and his
wife expired at Mont Orgueil Castle, in January following.

In 1563, Elizabeth founded a school in St. Peter-Port, out
of which has grown Elizabeth College. In the year 1826, the
present huge structure bearing that name, so disproportionate
to the limited extent and requirements of the island, was
commenced ; and in very bad taste, as, in place of the building being covered over with cement, it should have been
made smaller, and faced with the fine blue granite of the
island, cut for the purpose. The style should, moreover,
have been Elizabethean, in compliment to the founder. The
property with which the original school was endowed belonged
to a fraternity of Cordeliers ;[1] but the period at which that
religious institution was abandoned is doubtful, for it is not
clear whether it escheated to the crown, when the priors
aliens were banished by Henry V., or by virtue of the acts
of parliament passed during the reigns of Henry VIII. and
Edward VI., by which the Roman Catholic establishments
and lands were forfeited to the crown. The church of the
Cordeliers, or grey, or mendicant friars, stood opposite the
entrance of the *Cimetière des Frères*, on the ground now
occupied by stables, and seems to have been used for a few
years as the school-room of Elizabeth, as well as the residence

[1] " Richard II. y fonda un couvent de Cordeliers, là où est maintenant le Collège
Elisabeth ; c'est l'église de ces religieux qui sert d'église paroissiale à la ville. L'évêque
de Porphyre, Guillaume Chévron, y conféra les ordres en 1497." — *Histoire des Evêques de
Coutances.* This extract is incorrect.

of the master.   Besides the temple or church, and a grant of
land which was anciently "encompassed by a cloister," eighty
quarters of wheat rent belonging to the crown were assigned
to the school.   The college has at present (1853) annual
prizes to the amount of £114. 12s., and two exhibitions, viz.
the Queen's of £30, and lord de Saumarez's of £15—together
nearly £160 a year ; and yet, notwithstanding these advantages, the number of scholars has of late years averaged only
about 100, and is now rather less.   This is the more singular,
because Inglis wrote, in 1834 : " Elizabeth College, under its
present management, offers advantages for the instruction of
youth, not perhaps to be found in any public seminary elsewhere."   There has been no essential change in the system of
education since that time, and the college stands high, we
believe, both at Oxford and Cambridge ; but there are now
far fewer strangers in the island, and the natives, whose children are not intended for the university, complain that classics
are too much the rule, and other acquirements the exception.
—It is indeed to be regretted that living languages and the
physical sciences are not more taught in every seminary.   .

The following is a summary of the regulations, passed
September 27, 1563, for the establishment of the school :

"1. The school to be called the School of Queen Elizabeth.
"2. The church and cemetery of the Cordeliers, with twenty-
six perches of ground on the north side, and thirty perches on the
south side, given for the building of the school.
"3. To the westward of the church, it is ordered that there
be a playground for the pupils, and to the eastward, a garden
for the master.
"4. A marble statue of the queen, with the arms of England,
to be placed over the gate.[1]
"5. The free use of the public wells and pumps guaranteed to
the school.
"6. Eighty quarters of wheat rent assigned to the master.
"7. Defines the duty of the master, and enumerates his qua-
lifications.
"8. The school is open at seven in the morning during summer, and at eight in winter ; to close at eleven.
"9. Afternoon school from one to five.
"10. If the master neglect his duties, after having been three
times warned by the dean, or if he be guilty of crime or immo-
rality, he is to be dismissed by the governor or his lieutenant,
and another master appointed in his stead.

(1) The arms only appear to have been placed over the gate.

" 11. Pupils inadmissible, unless they can read perfectly and repeat the catechism.

" 12. When a pupil is presented for admission, the master is to exhort him and his parents to pray for queen Elizabeth.

" 13. The pupil shall be warned before his friends of his duty towards the master, and to avoid idleness, negligence, and too great an indulgence to play.

" 14. If the scholar be incorrigible, the master, having called together his relations, is to bring him before the dean, who is ordered to reprimand him severely; and if, after having been three times reprimanded, he does not amend his conduct, then he is to be expelled from the school."

The first master of Elizabeth school was Dr. Adrian Saravia, a native of Artois, and of Spanish extraction : having embraced the Protestant faith, he was driven from his country, and sought refuge in Guernsey.   He afterwards settled in England, where he obtained a canonry of Canterbury, as well as the friendship of the judicious Hooker, whom he attended on his death-bed.   In consequence of his superior attainments, Dr. Saravia was among those to whom, in the reign of James I., was entrusted the task of preparing what is to this day the authorized translation of the Bible.   He died in 1611.—Another eminent master of Elizabeth school was Dr. Isaac Basire, said to have been born in Jersey in 1607; but the place of his nativity is doubtful, as is that of his early education.   His first public employment was in the office just mentioned, in Guernsey; subsequently to which he became officiating chaplain to the bishop of Durham, who gave him the rectory of Stanhope and the vicarage of Egglescliff, both in the county of Durham.   He obtained other high preferments, and was made chaplain to Charles I., with whom he was shut up in the castle of Carlisle during the siege of that city, and suffered confinement for some time in Stockton. In 1646, he travelled through Syria and Palestine; and, on his return to Europe, was made professor of divinity in Transylvania, where he remained seven years.   During his stay of several months at Aleppo, he had frequent conferences with the patriarch of Antioch, and there he translated the Church Catechism into Arabic.   In 1652, he was at Jerusalem; and in Palestine he preached the doctrine of the Cross, and proclaimed the Gospel to the benighted Jews.   On his arrival at Constantinople, he was invited by the French Protestants to become their minister, with a liberal stipend; but, as they were Calvinists, and he a zealous Anglican, he appears to have declined the charge. After the restoration, he was recalled by Charles II., who made him his chaplain, and reinstated him in the preferments he had lost, of which the prebend of Durham was the principal. He wrote some religious pieces and an account of his travels; and, dying in 1676, was buried in the yard of the cathedral of Durham, where a tomb was erected over his grave, with a Latin epitaph.

Duncan, on very insufficient authority, observes, "that private affection, as well as public policy, might have induced Elizabeth to exercise so much kindness to Guernsey, she being very closely connected with the ancestors of the present Carey family, so numerous and respectable in the island," because her mother's sister, Mary Boleyn, was married to a Carey, who "was raised to the honor of knighthood; but, after Anne Boleyn was beheaded, Carey lost his title and perquisites, and became a poor man." Duncan adds, that "when Elizabeth came to the throne, she did not forget her cousins," one of whom, "Nicholas Carey, was appointed receiver of her majesty's rents in Guernsey, and one of the commissioners for the erection of the grammar school which she endowed."—"This fact," says Duncan, "is worthy of being recorded, as the Careys are the only family in the island which can connect themselves with the blood royal of England; nor can there be any doubt on the point, as the arms of the Careys are quartered with those of Elizabeth in Westminster Abbey." Now, as the author of this work is nearly related to one branch of the Careys of Guernsey, he feels the more called upon to state, with a due regard to historical truth, that they never had the most distant connection with the blood royal of England—not more so, in fact, than any Irish cottier of the same name. The similarity of the arms, if true, proves nothing, as every one knows how easily these are assumed; and probably every Howard in the world considers himself entitled to bear the same coat as the duke of Norfolk. We have shewn in the third chapter that a de Cary was one of the Norman *seigneurs* who accompanied William at the Conquest; and we have little doubt that the ancestor of the Careys of Guernsey came over to the island direct from Normandy. There was a Caree in Guernsey in the year 1331, or above two centuries anterior to Elizabeth; and thus .the name was usually spelt until the reign of Henry VII. Indeed, there were Carees, or Careyes, or Careys, in the island much earlier, if we can credit the

Dédicace des Eglises, already quoted, it being therein mentioned that a Careye, captain of the parish, was present at the consecration of the church of Torteval,[1] in the year 1130! But as no two old copies of the *Dédicace* agree, there were probably many interpolations of names by persons wishing to establish the antiquity of their families in Guernsey. Falle says that the queen, well knowing the temper of the French, "resolved to enlarge her royal care" of these islands, and he extols her concern for the security and tranquillity of Jersey; so that her "kindness" was not confined to Guernsey. The two appointments which Nicholas Carey held were doubtless made by the governor, without the slightest suggestion of, or reference to, his royal mistress. So far from any Guernsey family being connected with royalty, or even with nobility, until the recent creation of the barony of "De Saumarez," the naked truth is, that the upper classes belong to what in England would be termed the middle orders of society, because fortunately the equal division of property prevents that marked difference of rank which exists in Great Britain and Ireland. The Anglo-Normans should be proud of this comparative equality, as surely that state of life is most favorable to virtue and happiness which is not exposed to the temptations either of great wealth or of extreme poverty. The poet, Cowley, who was secretary to lord Jermyn, governor of Jersey, and who visited that island during the civil war, is said to have intended the following lines for the small landed proprietors of these islands:

> " Fœlix, quem misera procul ambitione remotum,
> Parvus *Ager* placidè, parvus et *Hortus* alit.
> Præbet *Ager* quicquid frugi Natura requirit,
> *Hortus* habet quicquid luxuriosa petit ;
> Cætera sollicitæ speciosa incommoda vitæ,
> Permittit *Stultis* quærere, habere malis."

In April, 1565, the bishop of Coutances obtained an order from the lords of the council, addressed to the governor, bailiff, and jurats of Guernsey, requiring in the queen's name payment of all such dues and sums of money as ought heretofore to have been paid to him. This prelate, who claimed these payments, as well in right of his abbey of Lessey (? St. Leufroy) as of his bishopric, sent an agent with instructions

(1) According to the *Dédicace*, this church was erected by Philip de Carteret, a noble gentleman of Jersey, in consequence of a vow made by him at sea in a storm, that if his life were spared, he would build a church wherever he landed. Having safely reached Rocquaine Bay, in the present parish of Torteval, at midnight, September 13, 1129, he fulfilled his vow, and the church was consecrated November 1, 1130. There was, however, a church at Torteval about the year 1055, as we have shewn in Chapter II.

to apply to the governor for their recovery, and the governor referred him to the bailiff and jurats. They summoned John After, the dean, to appear and answer to the bishop's claims. When the dean appeared, the agent protested against him, as having no right to the deanery or to the rectories of St. Martin and St. Peter-in-the-Wood, both of which he held by the queen's appointment, without the necessary authority from the bishop of Coutances. The dean replied that he had sworn obedience to the queen of England, and her laws in matters ecclesiastical—that he had renounced the pope and all foreign jurisdiction—and that he held the deanery and the two rectories by episcopal authority through the bishop of Winchester, who appears at that time to have possessed some power over the spiritual affairs of the island, although the order for annexing it to that see is of later date. The dean then declared that if the agent of the bishop of Coutances would, in his master's name, take the oath of fidelity to the queen, promise to obey her in matters ecclesiastical, and renounce the pope and his adherents, he would acknowledge the authority of the said bishop in the island; and he added, that he was ready to give any further answer that might be required of him. Thus the matter ended, and the bishop lost his dues. That he should have obtained such an order is the less surprising, because, as Hallam truly states, "as for the higher classes, they partook far less than their inferiors in the religious zeal of that age. Henry, Edward, Mary, Elizabeth, found an almost equal compliance with their varying schemes of faith. Yet the larger proportion of the nobility and gentry appear to have preferred the catholic religion."

About the year 1567, disputes arose between the captain, Francis Chamberlayne, and the Royal Court, which were submitted to the queen in council, and by that board referred to the bishop of London and Richard Onslow, the solicitor-general, who "harde what eche partie coulde alleadge for themselves." On receiving a report of the hearing, their Lordships ordered:

"Firste, it is by their lordshippes thoughte necessarye that, before all other thinges, the said capitayne, baylief, and juratts, forgettinge all pryvate or publick querrells, shall reconcile themselves, and joyne together in all good fryndshipp and concorde, whereby they maye with the more commoditie eche of them attende their sevrall chardgs. In which case also speciall respecte is to be had that the said capitayne, as the quenes majesties principall officer there, be cheefely regarded, obeyed and estemed, in suche degree as to the place he holdeth doth belonge, and enjoye suche rights, priviledges, and other duties, as other capitaynes holdinge his place have heretofore lawfully had and enjoyed . . . . It is also further ordered that the baylief and juratts of the said isle maye lawfully at all tymes when neede shall require visitte the state of the castels and fortificacions there, in suche forme and for suche purposes and intents as be comprised and declared in their libertres and priviledges, having in the doinge thereof good regarde by all gentill meanes to exhorte, advise, and perswade the quenes majesties lovinge and obedyent subjects there to contynue their endevour and good wills for the transportinge and careadge of stone, sande, and other necessaries, at convenyent dayes and tymes, as heretofore of late they have done, to the furtheraunce of the fortificacion of the said castell and good suretie of those isles."

The other points of dispute, which are too numerous to be mentioned here, were disposed of *seriatim*, some it appears by as pecies of compromise.

An order in council, dated Richmond, October 9, 1580, disposes of several complaints preferred by part of the inhabitants ; one of which was that the governor, Sir Thomas Leighton, exacted more "custome" on the wares and merchandize of strangers than authorized by the "petite coutume." In the succeeding year, Sir Thomas Leighton was the complainant, as will be seen by the following extracts from the order in council of July 30, 1581 :

" Whereas heretofore, uppon complainte exhibited unto their lordships by Sir Thomas Leyghton, knight, capten of her majesties isle of Gernezey, concerning sondrie disorders committed and maintained by the baillife & certaine of the jurates of the sayd isle to the greate prejudice of her majesties right and service, it pleased their lordships to sende for Wm. Beauvoyr, baillife ; Nicholas Martin and Henrie Beauvoyr, jurates ; their sayd lordships, havinge att severall times heard what both parties could alledge, uppon good deliberacion for the endinge of all matters in variance and establishing of good peace and unitie in the said isle, have thought meet to take suche order in certaine points which were in controversie between them, as followeth :

" Ffirst, whereas, about a year sithe, uppon the repaire hither of certaine inhabitants of the said isle, as populer procurers, to complaine against the sayd Sir Thomas Leyghton, (allbeit the same were without cause, as it then appeared, in that they were punished for the same,) it pleased their lordships to sett down certaine orders meete to be observed in that isle," &c.

" And finallie, forasmuch as Wm. Beauvoyr, now late baillife, Nicholas Martin & Henrie Beauvoyr, jurates, have, bothe in their owne name and in the name of the rest of the sayd isle, against whom Sir Thomas Leyghton exhibited his complainte, declared before their lordships that they are sorie to have geven anie cause of displeasure unto their sayd capten against them, and that they all meane to doe better hereafter, and so to behave themselves as they trust to geve him no just cause of offence : hereuppon their lordships have earnestlie required the said capten to remitte that which is past, and to staye his further proceeding in the proofe and triall of any faultes wherewith he hath chardged them or may chardge them, and to receave them to his former favour ; whereto, att their lordships' requeste, he hath yelded : there-uppon, with some good admonitions so to demeane themselves hereafter as that there may be no just cause by them offred of anie further complainte, the above named baillife and jurates were dismissed, and licenced to depart and retorne home.

" And, last of all, whereas the sayd William Beauvoyr, late baillife, Nicholas Martin and Henry Beauvoyr, jurates, have of their owne free will & accorde made suite unto their lordships that they might be discharged of their sayd offices of baillife & jurates, and that by their lordships' appointment some others might be chosen to supplie their places ; their lordships' pleasure hereuppon was that, by letters from hence, so much sholde be signified unto the inhabitants of the sayd isle, requiring them to proceade to the election of others in their roomes, according to the custome and manner of the sayd isle."

At this distance of time, it is difficult to ascertain which party was in the right; but it is evident that Sir Thomas Leighton possessed more influence with the privy council than his opponents in Guernsey, and in England the claims of justice are too often subservient to those of interest. It is singular that the inhabitants were required to elect not only two other jurats, but also to appoint a new bailiff.[1] Sir Thomas Leighton is said, however, to have been guilty of many exactions on the natives, and to have so grossly imposed upon strangers as to drive them from the island. As an instance of his general conduct, it may be stated that several French vessels, belonging to Havre-de-Grace and St. Brieux, and of the burden of from 20 to 150 tons, laden with corn, salt, wine, &c., were, in violation of the queen's charter granted but a few years before, seized by him in the road-stead, and detained for a long time, under the pretext that the cargoes were Spanish property. This infraction of the

(1) Thomas Wigmore, an Englishman, succeeded William de Beauvoir in 1588, and was probably appointed bailiff by Sir T. Leighton, or through his influence.

privilege of neutrality might have been attended with serious consequences, if the Royal Court had not taken the matter in hand ; for although the repeated remonstrances of that body did not induce the governor to release these and other ships, he was subsequently compelled to do so by different orders in council, dated in April, May, June, and July, 1587.

In 1568, the Anglo-Norman islands were finally separated from the bishopric of Coutances, and transferred to that of Winchester ; but they appear to have been previously attached not only to the diocese of Exeter, but to that of Salisbury, as Warburton says that " when king John was dispossessed of Normandy, he brought them under the bishop of Exeter's jurisdiction for a short time ; but they were soon restored to the bishopric of Coutances, and so continued until the reign of Henry VII., when, by a bull of pope Alexander VI., of the 5th of November, 1496, they were again separated from Coutances, and annexed unto the diocese of Salisbury, but afterwards re-attached to Coutances, and so remained till queen Elizabeth transferred them to the see of Winchester, about the year 1568."

It was after the events we have just narrated that the Roman Catholics in Guernsey, in turn, became the victims of Protestant persecution, as if cruelty in any shape could ever be acceptable to the Creator, or advance the cause of genuine Christianity.   The Royal Court, on the 1st of October, 1571, issued an ordinance, commanding the delivery of all popish idols and books, under heavy penalties ; and on the 25th of April, 1573, one Richard Girard was flogged through the town for upholding mass ; while by an ordinance, dated the 22d of January, 1593, all strangers were ordered to profess the established religion within a given period, or quit the island.   In England, there were numerous executions of the Roman Catholics ; and, what was worse, the common law was set aside by the privy council for the infliction of torture, so that the rack was constantly used in the Tower towards the close of Elizabeth's reign.

It is a proof of the scrupulous regard paid by the sovereigns of England to the privileges of Guernsey, that when the island books of law, compiled by the governor and the Royal Court, were presented for her majesty's approbation, the lords of the privy council expressed themselves in the following terms : " The lords of the queen's most honorable privy council, after having seen, heard, and considered the contents of this book, signed by Sir Thomas Leighton, captain and governor of the island of Guernsey, and by the bailiff and jurats of the said isle, have ratified and approved, and do ratify and approve, the laws and customs therein contained, to be practised and observed in the said isle of Guernsey, saving always to her majesty, and her heirs and successors, the power to add thereto, and correct the same, according to her pleasure : and also all prerogatives, profits, rights, and pre-eminence, belonging to her said majesty, her heirs and successors, *without prejudice nevertheless to the ancient and just privileges* granted heretofore to the inhabitants of the said isle. Done in her majesty's privy council, the 27th day of October, 1583."

Notwithstanding the efficient government and great power of Elizabeth, piracy was openly carried on in the British Channel, at least for some years after her accession ; so that at that time there could have been very little intercourse between England and these islands. An instance of this piracy exists in the seizure of part of the crew of the John, of Sandwich, wrecked on the coast of Guernsey in 1565. The men confessed their guilt, and were lodged in the prison of Castle Cornet till her majesty's pleasure was known. On the 25th of September, 1566, Elizabeth sent her orders, which were, after noticing that the commander and principal officers of the pirate had escaped in a pinnace, and that the prisoners were deceived by representations made to them that the voyage was purely commercial, as also that they had been some time in custody : " You shall cause *two or three* of them, such as you shall think most culpable and fittest for example, to be *executed out of hand*,"—while the remainder were directed to proceed to England, and sue for their pardon. The authorities in Guernsey appear, however, to have been more merciful than their royal mistress, and to have been satisfied with the execution of one of the prisoners, as on the 23d of November they pronounced the following sentence : " Forasmuch as it appeareth by the circumstances of the process maintained against thee, Richard Higgins, that you have, among others your consorts, pirates, confessed divers and sundry piracies, namely, upon Flemish fishers and other merchants, as well upon the coast of England as upon the coast of Spain, and minding to persevere in that most horrible and detestable life, have resisted to the uttermost of your power the queen's majesty's ships sent to call back and impeach you and your consorts' most wicked enterprises against the glory of God, the queen's majesty's honour, and the public peace between her majesty and her highness' most dear friends and allies : we, Francis Chamberlain, esq., captain and governor of this island of Guernsey, with the advice of, &c., ordain that you, Richard Higgins, shall be pinioned by the officer of justice, and by him be led from this place to St. Martin's Point, near the full sea-mark, and there, by the same officer, be hanged and strangled till thou be dead."

In 1560, the queen granted the island of Alderney in fee farm to George, son of Sir Leonard Chamberlain, and brother to Francis Chamberlain, then governor of Guernsey; but her rights in the former island were then so little known, that commissioners were appointed by her majesty to inquire into their extent.   This inquiry not having been made, Sir Thomas Leighton, governor, and Thomas Wigmore, bailiff of Guernsey, were named in 1585 as commissioners to hear and determine causes between John Chamberlain, holding in fee farm from the crown, and the inhabitants of Alderney.   In 1590, the said John Chamberlain disposed of all his right and title to that island to Robert, earl of Essex, his heirs, &c., for the term of one thousand years; and, by an act of the Royal Court of Guernsey, dated 1st of April, 1601, and granted on the representation of the queen's procureur, that Robert Devereux, earl of Essex, had been executed for high treason, (*leze majesté,*) and thereby forfeited all his estates, goods, and revenues, the prevost, or sheriff, was ordered to proceed with the said procureur to the island of Alderney, there to seize the property belonging to that unfortunate nobleman. This property had, however, probably never come fully into his possession, for in 1607 William Chamberlain was again the occupant, either in right of the old grant or of a new one.   That right seems to have expired with this person, as, after his death, the name of Chamberlain is no more mentioned in the records of Alderney.

The Spanish armada, consisting of 130 large ships, with 19,295 soldiers, 8,450 mariners, 2,088 galley slaves, and 2,630 great pieces of brass, having completely refitted, after being damaged in a storm, sailed from Corunna on the 12th of July, 1588, with orders to keep along the coasts of Britany and Normandy ; but the admiral, who was instructed to repair to Calais, and there wait for the prince of Parma, steered direct for England, in the hope of surprising and destroying the English fleet in Plymouth. The first land which the Spaniards made was the Lizard ; and, mistaking it for the Ram's Head, they stood out to sea for the night, by which means the fleet in Plymouth, which was quite unprepared, was saved. On Tuesday, the 23d July, the Spaniards were abreast of Portland, with the wind at north, the ships, says Camden, having "lofty turrets like castles ;" and many of them were doubtless seen from Alderney, as the armada, with wings spread about seven miles, sailed slowly along up the Channel, closely followed by the English, who attacked and captured the stragglers. In the English fleet, the largest ship (the Triumph) was of 1,100 tons ; in the Spanish, there were only three larger than the Triumph ; but, although the former outnumbered the latter by nearly sixty sail, its tonnage amounted to not one half of that of the enemy.

It now appears strange that so small a supply of artillery for the additional defence of Castle Cornet as one demi-cannon and two demi-culverins could not be furnished without a royal warrant, which is still extant; but Elizabeth's exchequer was small, and in her time cannon were costly, being chiefly of brass. "Very many pieces of great ordnance of brass and iron she cast," says Camden, "and God," (?) "as if he favored what she undertook, discovered a most rich vein of pure and native brass, which had been long time neglected, near Keswick, in Cumberland, which abundantly sufficed for that use, and afforded brass to other countries also." The queen likewise presented to Hélier de Carteret, for the defence of Sark, two demi-culverins, weighing 29 cwt. each ; two sakers, weighing 16 cwt. each ; and two falcons, weighing 9 cwt. each, all new and complete, with 50 iron balls, and 200 lb. of powder.

On Thursday, the 18th of August, 1597, two of the residents in that sea-girt fortress, Castle Cornet — Mr. Isaac Daubeney and Master Walter St. John — were drowned at the little island of Herm under very melancholy circumstances, as appears by the evidence, in French, given on oath at the inquest before the Royal Court in Guernsey; but as no less than twenty-nine witnesses were examined on the occasion, we must greatly condense the details. Herm was at that time kept as a preserve for the governors, and was stocked with deer, pheasants, and partridges.

Mr. Peter Carey, jurat, and subsequently lieut.-governor for a short period, deposed that on the invitation of the governor, Sir Thomas Leighton, he went with him to Herm to hunt (*chasser*) the deer; Masters Thomas Leighton, son of the governor, Walter St. John,[1] Peter Carey,[2] son of the deponent, and Samuel Cartwright,[3] accompanying them, as did Mr. Daubeney and others, with several of the governor's servants. On their arrival, Sir Thomas Leighton, the deponent, and some of the servants, proceeded to hunt the deer, leaving the four young gentlemen, just named, with their tutor, (*pédagogue*,) Mr. Daubeney, who remained with them all the morning, and made them do their lessons until nine o'clock, after which Mr. Blake, the music master, made them sing (*chanter*) until ten o'clock. The governor then caused Mr. Daubeney to say prayers, and soon after they all sat down to dinner! Having dined, and while still at table, the youths asked permission to bathe, but Sir Thomas refused them twice or thrice: however, on their continuing their importunities, he at last consented, on condition that some grown-up persons went with them. Upon this the four lads, accompanied by Mr. Daubeney and two attendants, proceeded to the beach on the eastern side of Herm, young St. John outstripping his companions, and entering first into the water. About an hour afterwards, one of the servants came to inform Mr. Carey that Mr. Daubeney was drowned; and upon Mr. Carey going to tell the governor, he found him fast asleep in his tent, as he had arisen at one o'clock, a.m. Mr. Carey pulled the governor by his cloak two or three times before he awoke, and then begged his excellency's pardon for disturbing him, as he did so to inform him that Mr. Daubeney was drowned! In that age the *grand gouverneur* was looked upon in Guernsey with as much awe and reverence as is now the emperor of Russia or the sultan of Turkey, each in his respective dominions. "Drowned," said the governor, "alas!" (*noyé, deist-il, hélas!*) and, beginning to rise, they heard that St. John was drowned also; upon which the governor was seized with such grief, that he became quite astounded and lost. (*étonné et esperdu.*) Mr. Carey inquired where the bodies were, and, being told that the tide had carried them off, he ran to the beach with four of the governor's

---

(1) Doubtless a brother-in-law of lady St. John, who was a daughter of Sir Thomas Leighton, and a brother of Lucy St. John, who married Sir Allan Ap-ley.

(2) Father of Peter Carey, who, being a parliamentarian, was confined in, and escaped from, Castle Cornet with Messrs. De Beauvoir and De Havilland, in 1643.

(3) Doubtless the son of the celebrated presbyterian chaplain of Castle Cornet.

servants, and calling to the crew of a boat which was near—
the governor's shallop being at Jethou—they picked up the
bodies and took them to Castle Cornet, the governor accompanying them in his shallop.

By the evidence of Mr. William Taylor, gentleman, (*gen-
tilhôme,*) porter of the castle, it appears that having called the
governor two or three hours before daylight, according to his
orders, he asked him if the young gentlemen were to go to
Herm, and was answered in the negative; but, on passing
their door, while on his way to send the boat to the town for
Mr. Carey and some boatmen, he saw Master St. John, who
was at the door in his shirt, and who asked him if it were not
time to go to Herm. On the porter telling him that he was
not to go, he said that the governor had given him leave the
evening before, and the youths began to dress themselves.
Upon this, the porter informed the governor of their wish to
go with him; and Mr. Daubeney, who was near, promising to
take their books and make them do their lessons, if they
went, the governor consented.

One of the attendants deposed that when young St. John
began to swim, he was quickly carried away by the tide,
upon which Mr. Daubeney, who was an excellent swimmer,
undressed himself and swam to the youth, whom he requested
to get on his back: this St. John did, but suddenly Mr.
Daubeney rolled over and disappeared. St. John then called
the attendant to come to his aid, which he attempted to
do, (?) and was nearly drowned himself in endeavouring to
save him. (?)

Thus the boating party, which had left the castle early in
the morning with all the joyous anticipation of coming pleasure and delight, returned in the afternoon in grief and anguish with the corpses of two of their companions, who had
been so suddenly, and now so unaccountably, deprived of life;
for it is difficult to comprehend how Mr. Daubeney perished,
unless possibly from cramp, if he were the excellent swimmer
he is described. Judging from the governor's retinue of
chaplain, tutors, porter, visitors, servants, &c., his household
at the castle seems to have been one of baronial hospitality
and extent, although the hours kept would be considered
unreasonably early by any labouring peasant of the present day.

The following act of the Royal Court of Guernsey, translated from the French, is curious:

" The 27th day of the month of August, 1597, before Louis
De Vic, bailiff; present, Nicholas Martin, sen., William Beau-
voir, Andrew Henry, John Andros, John de Sausmarez, Peter
Beauvoir, Peter Careye, John Effart, Nicholas Martin, Jun.,
George Guille, and Leonard Blondel, jurats.

" Seeing that Mr. the Governor,[1] the viii day of the present
month, had informed the court (*la justice*) that he had heard of
Mr. Henry Smyth that Eleazar Le Marchant, some time previously, (*a jours passés*) had told him that he had heard of
James Beauvoir that Nicholas Careye had said to the said Beauvoir, about two years previously, that on the approaching death
of her majesty he would be one of the first to pull the said Mr.
Governor by the ears out of his castle.   Information and due
examination by every means, (to search and ascertain the truth
of this,) made at the instance of the officers of her majesty, and
the whole duly and maturely considered, it is the opinion of the
said jurats that the said Nicholas Careye is not found convicted
of the information (*délation*) given against him."

The Royal Court had previously, on the 8th and 9th of the
same month, sat twice to examine witnesses on this subject;
and by the testimony of these witnesses it appears that Mr.
Carey had been a prisoner in Castle Cornet, and that he was
excited with wine when he made use of the dreadful threat
imputed to him by the governor, who had heard it fourth
hand two years after!   Verily, the Royal Court was most
complaisant and obedient to sit thrice on such an accusation;
but that body had previously felt the governor's power, and
the law of evidence in England at that time was equally faulty.

The ordinances of the Royal Court of Guernsey—the oldest commencing in 1527, and of which a selection[2] was published in 1851-2—present very curious illustrations of the
arbitrary and multifarious powers exercised by that body at
the periods of enactment, and prove that in the sixteenth and
seventeenth centuries the inhabitants generally possessed very
limited conceptions of political economy and freedom; otherwise, enjoying as they did the happy privilege of electing
their own magistrates, they never would have submitted to
such despotic legislation.   The court defined the hours for
selling meat, fish, &c.; it affixed the prices of corn, beer,
cider, wine, oil, candles, &c., and even the wages of mechanics; and it appears to have viewed strangers with a most

---

(1) Sir Thomas Leighton.   (2) Edited by Robert MacCulloch, Esq., advocate.

jealous eye. The following examples, translated from the French, will be confined to the sixteenth century only:

"October, 1534.—That no one shall engross any merchandize or victuals coming to the island, until they have been three days on the beach, (*galley*,) and that those who have bought the merchandize shall deliver it to each person who may wish to have some at the price affixed during the discharge, under a penalty of 10 livres.

"That no one shall keep more than one dog in his house, under a penalty of 5 sols, excepting those who have a right to do so.

"That no one shall lodge any stranger to live in the island, under a penalty of lx sols, unless as a servant.

"October, 1535.—The exportation of corn from the island prohibited, under a penalty of 10 livres; and of fat cattle, under penalty of forfeiture.

"April, 1537.—It is ordered by justice that no servants, as well those of the magistrates as of the gentlemen and incumbents, (curés,) shall go sporting, (chasse,) unless in the presence of their masters, under a penalty of 10 livres, and excepting the children of the jurats and gentlemen.

"October, 1537.—The prevost to have the superintendence of all boats arriving in the island, as well from Jersey as Normandy and other ports, and he shall visit the said boats, and write down the names of all on board: he shall keep the rudder until their departure, and see that each passenger returns from whence he came, nor shall they go without his leave.

"May, 1546.—It is ordered by justice that no vessels or mariners shall go out of the island until the vessels, which are away, return, which vessels are in England.

"October, 1546.—All those who have had the plague, or who have any one ill in their house, shall not frequent public places, such as the church, &c., unless after the parishioners have been, under a penalty of lx sols.

"September, 1566.—Each in his parish shall assist on Sundays at the sermons and prayers, as well in the morning as in the evening, under penalty of being punished at the discretion of justice.

"October, 1575.—Divine service shall be performed in each country parish on Wednesdays, where there is a minister; and one person at least from each house, capable of hearing and comprehending, shall assist at such service, if there be no reasonable excuse: the same in the town on Wednesdays and Fridays, under a penalty of 5 sols fine, half to the queen and the other half to the poor; and the shops in the town shall be closed during the said service on Wednesdays, under the like penalty.

"St. Michael, 1581.—All adulterers shall be imprisoned three weeks, and on each Saturday during the three weeks shall be put

M

in the cage, from nine o'clock, a.m., until dark, and on the last Saturday shall receive, in the "quarre-fours" of the town, twenty-four lashes, until blood be drawn; and those convicted of fornication shall receive the same punishment, excepting that they shall have only twelve lashes before the cage. (Women convicted of the same offences received the same punishment, the whipping being inflicted on the first Saturday.)

" No one shall drive a cart through the streets of the town on a Saturday, from nine o'clock, a.m., to three o'clock, p.m., under a penalty of 5 sols fine for each offence.

" No one to take strangers as servants, to employ them at sea, under a penalty of xx écus soll. to her majesty. *Item*, no one in future to take any stranger to live with him, without first receiving the permission of the queen's receiver, under a penalty of x livres; and such strangers shall profess the religion (Protestant) in half a year after their arrival at latest.   .

Synopsis in English of a few of the acts of the colloquy, (*colloque*,) or conference, of the ministers (Calvinist) and elders of the churches of the island and bailiwick of Guernsey, held with the authority of the governor, commencing August 2, 1585, and ending September 24, 1619.   The synopsis is taken from a complete and very able digest of the said acts, made by the late James de Sausmarez, Esq., of the Inner Temple, barrister at law.   The arbitrary nature of many of these acts should be a lesson to those who may feel inclined to entrust secular power to the clergy, as all past experience has proved that

" Ill fares the land, to hastening ills a prey,"

where the laity is under priestly domination.

" At a ' colloquy ' held before the governor, the bailiff and jurats, the minister of the town, and the elders of the other parishes, six French ministers, who had taken refuge in the island from the disturbances in France, are received and assigned to the different churches. (August 31, 1585.)

" Interments in the town church forbidden, with exception in favor of the governor and his family.   Governor, bailiff, and jurats, to confer with *chefs de familles* for converting into a cemetery the ground formerly known as the *Cimetière des Frères*. (1586.)

" Resolved by colloquy, (at which were present the governor, bailiff, and four jurats, and twenty ' des plus notables chefs de familles de la paroisse,') that there should be morning and evening prayers in the town church. (1586.)

"St. Martin's stated to be the richest parish in the island.
(1586.) [*Probably as regarded its ecclesiastical revenue.*]

"Governor issues 'une billette,' requiring inhabitants to be
present at church at the commencement of the sermon, and to
be regular in communicating. (1586.)

"Proposal made by Mr. Thomas Dickenson that service should
be performed in English at Castle Cornet. (1586.)

"Prayers for the dead, and praying in churches, apart from
the congregation, forbidden. (1587.)

"Sir Thomas Leighton's letter, complaining of charges preferred against him to council, (November 10, 1587,) and resolution of colloquy thereupon.

"Offer of Adrian de Saravia, S. T. P., of Leyden, to serve the
ministry, accepted. (1587.)

"Colloquy submit to the court eight ordinances to be enforced.
Governor recommends that the same should be submitted to the
next Chief Pleas, and that the fines levied should be applied, half
to the poor and half to the pier. (1587.)

"St. Saviour's church to be closed, on account of 'la superstition qui s'y commet.' (June, 1589.)

"'Billettes' to be obtained from the governor and published
in the parishes, for banishing from the island such as refuse to
hear the Word of God and neglect communicating! (December,
1589.)

"Letter from M. Cosmo Brevin, minister of Serk, 'pleine
d'injures et de rébellion.' Consistory of Serk ordered to make
reparation. (1590.)

"Touching the baptism of a six months' child. (1590.)

"Marriages between cousins german pronounced unchristian,
&c.[1] Cases of incestuous marriages considered. (1591.)

"Cartwright (minister of Castle Cornet) and Snape (minister
of the castle of Jersey) sent to effect a reconciliation between the
churches of both islands. (September, 1595.)

"Upon opposition made to a marriage proposed to be celebrated, parties referred to the douzaine to decide whether the
marriage be expedient to the parish. (1596.)

"Governor proposes that the synod of the two islands should
not be held at Serk, but that the ministers of Guernsey should
sail for Jersey on the 4th of September; (1695;) the expenses of
the voyage to be borne by all the parishes.

"Proceedings at synod read at colloquy. Each parish to
reimburse its deputy x sterling for his expenses. (1596.)

"Cartwright[2] submits three propositions to the colloque, viz.

"1. Touching the education of two youths for the ministry.

---

(1) It is much to be regretted that the colloquy did not possess the power of pronouncing
such marriages illegal, as they are productive of both mental and corporeal disease, and
their deteriorating effects are very visible in these islands.

(2) The last colloque at which Cartwright's name appears was in September, 1601.

" 2. For a fast, in consequence of the disturbances in Ireland.

" 3. The admissibility to the Sacrament of an Englishman charged with incontinence; resolutions thereon. Snape to be written to. (1599.)

" Appeal to the colloquy of Jersey to send over ministers to Guernsey, where there were too few to perform the duty. Mr. Milet thereupon lent for three months, and is appointed to St. Saviour's. (1602.)

" Elders of parishes enjoined to seize dangerous books : " Vita Christi" and others, which have been sold by pedlars from Normandy. (1602.)

" No stranger to be received in any parish without a certificate of good conduct from his last place of residence. (1602.)

" Ministers to keep a list of persons neglecting to communicate. (1602.)

" Commissioner from Geneva presents his credentials. A collection ordered to be made in aid of the town and church of Geneva. (1603.)

" Voyage to Jersey to attend synod resolved upon. The governor, being prevented by illness from attending, appoints Amias de Carteret,[1] seigneur of Trinity, his substitute. (1605.)

" Deputies appointed to attend Chief Pleas, to request that no court be held on days appointed for colloquy, and to request attendance of bailiff and governor. Claim of jurats, as such, to be exempted from attending colloquy, rejected. (1604.)

" Collection ordered for relief of Southampton, visited with plague. (September, 1604.)

" Mr. Leighton, in the name of the governor, presents Mr. Bradley to the church of the Castle, (Câtel,) who promises faithfully to discharge the duties thereof, and to elect elders and deacons to serve the said church. (1605.)

" Monsieur Peter Painsec appointed to preach at St. Andrew and the Castel, and to enjoy the revenues of both parishes as paid. He refuses to officiate in the town parish until his salary has been paid—is informed that there has been ' taxe faicte' for payment thereof, and is exhorted to comply—persists in refusing. The colloquy remonstrate with him, and threaten suspension; governor quits the assembly. Painsec persists in his refusal, and cites as an authority the police of the French church, which the colloquy rejects; and he finally acknowledges his error. Text of scripture assigned him whereon to preach on Sunday following, and to express his penitence. (1605, 9.)

" Mr. Simon Herne (having been found competent in the English language) appointed to the Castle (Câtel) in the absence of Mr. Bradley; but to receive only £13 sterling yearly, until he is qualified to perform duty in the French language. (1606.)

(1) Amias de Carteret was bailiff of Guernsey.

" The town parish without a minister; ministers to preach there in turn. Mr. Herne to preach in English on Sunday evenings. (1606.)

" Litigants not to receive Sacrament until their differences are settled. (1606.)

" Notice sent from Jersey, of a synod to be held in May following. (1606.) Governor to be informed thereof, in case he should have any subject to propose. (1606.)

" Expediency of receiving a dean referred to the synod, as a question affecting the interests of both islands. (1606.)

" Complaint from Alderney that the people there are without a pastor—exhorted to patience—' nous ne sommes pas dieux,' &c. (1607.)

" In the general dearth of ministers, resolved that the Vale and St. Sampson's, ' pour leur grande importance,' shall be first provided. (1607.)

" Simon Masons sent to serve the island of Alderney, being invited thither, his life and doctrine being approved of by H. M. commissioners. (November, 1607.)

" Mr. Thomas Milet, lent by Jersey, appointed to parishes of St. Martin's and St. Saviour's; parishes to furnish him with a horse on Sundays. (1608.)

" Mr. Milet, (or Millet,) seeking to return to Jersey, is arrested by order of the governor. (1609.)

" On refusal of parishioners of St. Martin's to receive Mr. Herne (or Hearne) as their minister, alleging their inability to understand him, colloquy overrule their objection, whereupon they appeal to the synod. (1609.)

" A person convicted of having been present at a mass whilst abroad, to make acknowledgment of his error. (1610.)

" Letters addressed to colloquy to be opened only in presence of two ministers or three elders. (1610.)

" A general fast ordered with the consent of the magistrates, in consequence of the great drought, and as an act of humiliation for the sins of the people. (May 24, 1611.)

" A fast ordered in consideration of the bloody flux, the long drought, &c. (June, 1612.)

" Monsieur le lieutenant proposes a fast, but the colloquy think right to postpone it, the people being ' si mal disposé.' (1614.)

" A fast ordered, in consequence of the mortal diseases which prevail; ' messieurs de justice' requested to give public notice thereof. (September, 1615.)

" The custom of having the head covered during divine service, and particularly during the administration of the Sacrament, reprobated. (1618.)

" Upon information received that a dean had been appointed to Jersey, colloque to devise means to prevent a similar appointment in Guernsey. (October, 1618.)

"Upon request from Jersey that Guernsey would unite in petitioning the crown against appointment of the dean, it is determined to communicate with 'messieurs de justice,' and to pray the interference of the States. (December, 1618.)

"Peter Le Marchant charged with absenting himself from church and the communion, and living 'en payen et épicure,' deemed worthy of excommunication; but inasmuch as he had never communicated, the case is referred 'au magistrat.' (1619.)

"·Hilary Gosselin cited before colloquy for not having received the Sacrament for three years. (1619.)

"A fast to be proclaimed, in consequence of the wars and rumours of war. (March, 1619.")

[NOTE.—The last colloquy mentioned was held on the 24th of September, 1619. —A tract, entitled "Police et Discipline Ecclésiastique pour le Réglement des Eglises de Guernsé, Gersé, Sark, et Origni, comme elle a été faite au synode tenu à Guernsé, le 18e Juin, 1576."—Cottonian MSS. Caligula E vi. 106, 324.]

PIER OF St. PETER-PORT.

The present pier having been virtually commenced in this reign,—although there appears to have been previously a short slip or jetty,—a narrative of its origin, progress, and completion, will be best given here under one head, commencing however with a brief notice of the insular havens in the thirteenth century.

In the so-called Constitutions of king John are these words in Latin: "Item, it is ordered for the preservation and security of the islands and castles, and principally as the islands are near and in the neighbourhood of the dominion of the king of France and of other enemies, that all the havens of the islands be well guarded; and our lord the king orders that guardians of the havens (*custodes portuum*) be appointed, to the end that no damage may come, either to him or to his subjects."

In the Inquest of Henry III., (A.D. 1248,) already cited, it is said also in Latin: "Moreover, the said jurors declare by their faith, and on their oath, that if the fishermen of this island (Guernsey) be permitted to go and come with their fish and other products from and to whatever harbour they choose, and without license and inspection, our lord the king and his subjects will incur every year great losses; the islands will be almost lost; the havens will be worth nothing; the king's dues on the fishery will be entirely lost; the prerogatives of the king will be diminished; and the possessions of his enemies will be benefitted and subsisted by the products

of the island : and thus the isles and dominions of the king
will be deprived of their products, and will remain uninhabited. (*et vacuæ remanebunt.*) It is difficult to comprehend
at this time the object of this declaration, because, although
the king might be deprived of his dues on fish, a very unfair
source of revenue, the fishermen, who in those days formed a
large majority of the inhabitants, would thereby be benefitted.
The jurors, however, were probably not fishermen, and they
evidently knew nothing of the advantages of free trade, which
is the less surprising, seeing that even now it is occasionally
maintained that the market people should be prevented from
selling their fish for exportation until the inhabitants have
been supplied !

From the reign of Edward I., whose grant of certain
dues for the erection of a sea wall has been previously mentioned, to that of Elizabeth, there appears to be nothing
relating to the pier, with the exception of the Extent of
Edward III., which makes mention of dues on shipping and
merchandize.   But in the year 1563, Elizabeth authorized
the bailiff and jurats of Guernsey to levy a reasonable toll, or
petite coutume, on the goods of strangers brought to the island,
for the erection and maintenance of a pier, the repair of bulwarks, the supply of ammunition, &c., and exclusive of the
rates levied among the inhabitants for these purposes.   The
ordinances passed at the Court of Chief Pleas exist only from
1533, and the earliest mention therein of a pier (*chaussée*) is
in 1566-7, which was probably the old slip or jetty.   The
petite coutume was accordingly raised ; but, being either mis-
appropriated, or applied to other objects, the queen, seventeen
years later, in 1580, reproved the bailiff and jurats in the following severe terms :

" Whereas there has been heretofore a certain petty custom
given by her majesty, to be levied upon strangers, to the inhabitants of the island, towards making a certain pier, or chaussée,
before the town of St. Peter's-Port, which was begun ten years
ago, and has ever since been left off and not gone further ; which
the bailiff and jurats, having notwithstanding ever since, for the
most part of the ten years, intermeddled with the said custom so
appointed to be levied as aforesaid, for which they have given no
accounts to the parishioners of the said town : the bailiff and
jurats shall be called before the captain for an account of the said
receipt, and so much as shall be found remaining in their hands
not employed for the uses aforesaid shall be converted to the
advancement of the said work ; and the said custom shall be

continued, and other contributions levied by the consent of the generality of the richest sort of the inhabitants, and a further charge for that purpose laid upon strangers, in such convenient and moderate sort, as they may not alienate their minds from resorting thither, as they have accustomed, with their merchandize, until the work be ended."

The following year, the Royal Court not only raised the new duties, but appointed the constables of St. Peter-Port to receive them, and obliged these officers to render an account before they were discharged from their office.

In his Britannia, (London, 1590,) Camden gives the preference to Jersey, on account of its extent and fertility; but to Guernsey, in regard to the security of its haven, and the assemblage of merchants who frequent it. He says: "This haven is situated nearly at the eastern extremity of the island: there is an arm erected towards the south, representing a half-moon. The little town of St. Peter-Port, which is long and narrow, is seated and borders on this haven, which is well provided with fortifications, and the merchants abound as soon as there is war." [1]

When the States of Guernsey sent deputies to congratulate James I. on his accession, and to solicit a confirmation of their privileges, the twelfth article of their requests was as follows:

"They humbly crave allowance of the petit custom by his majesty and your lordships, which they have enjoyed heretofore for the reparation of the pier and other public works."

These requests were referred to the procureur du roi and other personages, with orders to report thereon, and they returned the following answer to the twelfth article:

"It is true that we find the pier a matter of great use, and commodious to the merchants that trade thither, but withal of so great charge and burthen to the isle as of necessity craves help for maintenance; wherefore, though the work is almost accomplished, that which is already done cannot be kept up, nor that added which as yet remaineth to be done, without some such petit custom, or imposition, upon such merchandizes as are brought into the isles, for the ease of the country. We think it therefore reasonable that in this point they be eased by the allowance of these customs, according to the same rate they have been formerly used and levied."

(1) In extremâ ferè ad ortum parte, sed australi latere, lunato sinu portus admittitur: cui assidet oppidulum Sancti Petri, longâ plateâ, sed angustâ, productum; bellico apparatu plenum, & mercatoribus cum bellum ingruit frequentissimum

And the lords of council, in their report to the king, admitted the twelfth article, in the following terms :

" Their lordships do yield their consent to this demand for so necessary a work, that they shall be eased therein by the allowance of those customs, at the same rates as they have been formerly used and levied."

In 1684, Mr. James de Beauvoir, *des Granges*, one of the jurats, and *superviseur* of the pier for that year, represented to the Royal Court "that it was necessary for the good of the island and the commodiousness (*commodité*) of the pier, to build the north arm ; which he was authorized to do. But the troubles in the reign of James II., and the wars of William III. and Anne, caused the arm only to be commenced, i.e. heaps of large stones being deposited eastward. After the peace in Anne's reign, the merchants, who suffered considerable losses by tempests, either when their vessels were in the pier, or when they were at anchor outside, for want of a northern arm, made voluntary contributions for its erection ; and at length, at different periods, with the assistance of part of the proceeds of the *petite coutume, la neuve chaussée*, so called long afterwards, was completed. Mr. William Le Marchant, of l'Hyvreuse, a jurat, who, in 1750, published a history of the pier, from which we have condensed the preceding details, says, that it was then one of the safest and most commodious in Europe ; and he adds, that Sir Thomas Leighton[1] took great interest in its erection—hence doubtless the order of Elizabeth in 1580, just cited. Mr. Le Marchant states also : " If tradition can be relied upon, Mr. Amias de Carteret, lieut.-governor and bailiff of Guernsey at the commencement of the century 1600, ruined himself by his generosity in advancing this good work." In January, 1632, the Royal Court ordered that " sieur Jean Fautrat" should cause to be removed from the harbour " Le Rondin," sunk therein, in default of which she was to be sold to the highest bidder to be taken to pieces : this was many years anterior to the erection of the north arm.

Like Cæsar, whom we quoted in Chapter I., Mr. Le Marchant wrote according to the conceptions of his time, the present pier being only adapted to the small vessels which then frequented it. It has only ONE quay birth suitable for a ship of 300 or 400 tons, and that ONE, from the unevenness of the ground and exposure to S.E. gales, any thing but desirable.

(1) In 1750, one of the steps of the pier bore the initials of Sir Thomas Leighton, " T. L., 1589."

Such ships require a wet dock, which should be undertaken as soon as the first section of the new works,[1] commenced August 24, 1853, is completed, and the several piers named the "Harbour of the three Queens."

The present pier, a tidal one, is situated in front of the town; and the entrance of it, which is 565 yards to the north-west of Castle Cornet, is 68 feet wide at bottom, by 80 feet at top; the length of the harbour is 520 feet, and the width 320 feet, being an area of 3¾ acres. The depth at the entrance is 15 to 16 feet average neap, and 23 to 24 feet strong spring tides — at the western quays, 8 feet less. In low or dead neaps there are only 12 feet at the entrance, and 4 feet only at the quays. The harbour is fully sheltered from twenty-two points of the compass; partly, but not dangerously, open on four points; and completely open from the remaining six points, between S. and E. S. E.

An ordinance passed at the Chief Pleas of April, 1624, enacts " that the small house at the end of the pier shall be rendered secure at the public expense," so that the prevost might confine therein criminals whom, through the approach of night or bad weather, he was prevented from conducting to Castle Cornet. Thus there must previously have been such a building on the south arm.

From 1740 to 1755, about 5,000 livres tournois, equal to £3,571. 8s. 6d. sterling, are said to have been expended on the north pier, and on the repairs of the south pier.

The western quays were built from 1775 to 1779, and seven persons, whose tenements bordered on them, refused to pay their proportion of the cost: they were only brought to the exercise of reason by being prohibited any access to the quays through their own doors, and after the lapse of some years they understood their true interests, when they paid their quota,—it is to be hoped, with compound interest.

The arch over Cow Lane (*la Rue des Vaches*) was built in 1783, and the western quays were thus connected with the south pier.

The slips of the south pier were constructed in 1819, and the light-house erected on the south pier was first lighted on the 28th of February, 1832.

(1) Guernsey is greatly indebted to the present lieutenant-governor—lieutenant-general Sir John Bell, K.C.B.—than whom the island never had a more able or popular one; and to Peter Stafford Carey, esq., bailiff, for the effectual exercise of their official influence in furtherance of these new works, which have been so long and so ardently desired by the commercial classes.

CHAPTER IX.

JAMES.—1603 to 1625.

No sooner had Elizabeth expired, March 24, 1603, than there were courtiers riding furiously to convey the first intelligence to the new king; and the race was won by Sir Robert Carey, afterwards created Earl of Monmouth, and the son of lord Hunsdon, the queen's first cousin, whose fortune she had made! Carey reached Edinburgh on the 26th of March, with wonderful expedition in those days, forgetting the obligations of his family to the queen, in his anxiety to announce her death to her contemptible successor.—How many peerages have been earned by similar truckling and discreditable influences!

"The reign now commencing," says Sir James Mackintosh, "is the basest and most barren in English history. Peace abroad was but national ignominy." And yet that clerical courtier, Falle, thus speaks of the king: "King James I. was a most pacific prince, who, having little left him to do for us in the way of military defence, turned his thoughts to the better settling of religion in these islands, and bringing them to a conformity to the Church of England, which he happily effected in Jersey—a work doubtless more acceptable to God, and which will perpetuate his name among us no less than if he had environed this island with a wall of brass—a work of all others the most congruous to his peaceful reign."

Having described the introduction of Presbyterianism into Jersey and Guernsey, we shall here briefly narrate, according to Dr. Heylin,[1] the causes of its downfal in the former island. The rector of St. John's parish being dead, the colloquy appointed "one Brevin"[2] (so called by Heylin) to succeed him, and carried their point, although the governor, Sir John Peyton, who by his patent held the presentation of all the livings in Jersey, the deanery excepted, protested against the nomination. Soon afterwards, the governor, and Marret, the procureur du roi, forwarded several complaints to council

---

(1) Some allowance must be made for his religious opinions, as Hallam says: "Heylin, a bigotted enemy of every thing puritanical, and not scrupulous as to veracity."

(2) M. Cosmo Brevin, we believe, a Frenchman, previously minister of Sark, and father of Dr. Daniel Brevin, dean of Lincoln.—See digest of colloquy, *ante*.

against the colloquy, declaring that that body had usurped the patronage of all the benefices in the island, and praying the king to grant them such a form of discipline and church government as would prevent the repetition of similar abuses. In consequence, Sir Robert Gardiner and Dr. James Hussey were sent over to Jersey as commissioners, in 1607, when the clergy contended that their right of appointments to the ministry, and their exercise of ecclesiastical jurisdiction, had been confirmed to them by his majesty. While the questions at issue were pending, disputes occurred between the clergy and the laity; and the Royal Court annulled the sentences pronounced by the consistory, which was moreover accused of holding secret and treasonable meetings. About the year 1612, the parish of St. Peter becoming void, Sir John Peyton presented it to a clergyman named Messervy, who had resided some time at Oxford, and was patronized by Dr. Bridges, bishop of that city. The colloquy refused his admission, chiefly on account of his having been ordained by that prelate, as to accept Messervy seemed to them almost an acknowledgment of episcopacy. The new incumbent, however, notwithstanding the warmest opposition, enjoyed the emoluments of the living. In another complaint to the king in council, it was stated that the inhabitants generally were discontented with the Presbyterian discipline, and that they preferred the Anglican form, whereupon both parties were commanded to appear at court. Marret, the procureur, and Messervy, the rector of St. Peter, were furnished with a petition in favor of episcopacy; and on behalf of the Presbyterians were deputed Bandinel, (afterwards dean,) De la Place, rector of St. Mary, and two other ministers, who were instructed not to assent to any change.

On their arrival in London, the king referred both parties to the council, which ordered the case to be heard before the archbishop of Canterbury, lord Zouche, and Sir John Herbert, then principal secretary of state. The cause was privately argued before them by the deputies, who so contradicted each other that it became impossible for the judges to ascertain the real facts. At length, De la Place was given to understand that if episcopacy were revived, he would certainly be the new dean, and "being fashioned into this hope," (says Heylin,) "he speedily betrayed the counsels of his fellowes, and furnished their opponents at all their enterviews with such intelligence as might make most for their advantage." The Presbyterian deputies now disagreeing among themselves, the disputants were finally informed that the office of dean in Jersey would be revived; that the book of Common Prayer in French would be again used in the churches, with some discretion in particular passages; "that Messervy should be admitted to his benefice; and that so they might return unto their charges."

But the ministers "being somewhat backward in obeying this decree," the council intimated to them, through Sir Philip de Carteret, that they should make choice of three among themselves, and return their names to the board, when his majesty would select one as dean. This intimation caused great perplexity, not so much from dislike to the office, but because those who aspired to it would not name another, and thereby prejudice their own chance. But David Bandinel, rector of St. Mary, either having, or pretending to have, some business in London, was recommended by the governor; and by letters patent, dated March 8, 1619, was invested with the office of dean. The ministers, who had six months allowed them to deliberate, generally submitted to the new discipline; but De la Place, disappointed in not receiving the promised deanery, retired in disgust to Guernsey, where he obtained a benefice. The canons, &c., of James I. were definitively established in Jersey by royal letters patent, dated June 30, 1623. "Thus did the Church of England," says Falle complacently, "like an indulgent mother, take us again into her bosom, after we had for half a century estranged ourselves from her, and been under a presbytery."

Although Jersey was thus brought under the polity and ritual of the Church of England, Guernsey maintained the Presbyterian form and discipline for about forty years longer. Heylin assigns a plausible reason why the king did not attempt a conformity of both islands at the same time, which is, that had he done so, the ministers of both united would have formed a most formidable opposition; whereas one island, being brought to conformity, might induce the other to follow the example. But the reason rather seems to be that the people of Guernsey, being more unanimous in favor of Calvinism, gave James no opportunity for intermeddling with their ecclesiastical affairs. It is alleged by Berry as another reason that Sir Thomas Leighton, who had been instrumental in the introduction of Presbyterianism, was opposed to any change; but as he died about fifteen years before James, and moreover as he was very unpopular, his influence must have ceased with his life.

The States of Guernsey, ignorant, we trust, of James' despicable character, sent a deputation to congratulate him on his accession, and to solicit a confirmation of the insular privileges, which the king ordered to be examined, and ratified by his royal charter, dated the 15th of June, 1606. In the following year, the last Extent or estimate of the revenue of the crown in Guernsey and its dependant islands was made by the royal commissioners, whose decisions still form part of the laws of the bailiwick.

Sir Walter Raleigh, who was governor of Jersey from the year 1600 to 1603, on condition of supporting the insular establishment and remitting £300 a year to the Exchequer, is said to have introduced the Newfoundland cod fishery into that island.[1] In the report of the royal commissioners, Conway and Bird, in 1617, Raleigh was charged with having embezzled "130 pounds of the king's munition of powder at two several times, for the use of a ship in which he adventured to Newfoundland." He resided in Jersey in 1602, and kept the inhabitants on the alert with the fear of a Spanish invasion, possibly from the Netherlands. It was during his government that a public register was established for real property in Jersey, where his greatness of mind was very perceptible. Raleigh was beheaded in 1617, during this reign; and whatever doubts may be entertained of his guilt or innocence, there can be none of the wickedness of his conviction, as indeed of almost every conviction at that time. His son, Carew Raleigh, who was born in the Tower, became governor of Jersey in 1659, during the protectorate, and died in 1666.

In consequence of certain representations made to king in council by deputies from Guernsey, relative to the government of the isle, that body issued an order, dated Greenwich, June 9, 1605, of which we give the first article at length, as shewing how completely the inhabitants were placed at the mercy of Sir Thomas Leighton, who was governor of the island for the long period of nearly forty years—1570 to 1609—and who had long been most distasteful to them :

" Ffirst, for answere to their proposicion touchinge the authoritie of the governor for committing of men to prison in that isle : it is thought meete the governor shall not be restrayned to com-

(1) Sir Walter Raleigh is also said to have introduced tobacco into Jersey, and to have enjoyed his pipe while the "States" were sitting, when he was generally present.

mitt any islander to prison upon such cause as he shall thincke to have justlie deserved imprisonment: but, forasmuch as everie particular or private offence which deserveth restraint doth not admitt the laying on of irons, putting into the dungeon, or longe imprisonment, it is therefore thought fitt that no person shall be restrayned or kept in prison by the committment of the governor longer tyme than the space of ffower and twentie howres; nor be laied in irons, nor put into the dungeon, unlesse the partie stand charged with some such matter as is of higher nature than a private offence, and may concerne him in his loyaltie to the king's majestie's person, or to the state; in which case the bailiffe and jurates (if the matter be such as may without daunger be imparted to so many) are to be made acquainted with the cause of his committment; but, if the governor shale finde it daungerous or inconvenient so farr foorth to reveale it as to acquaint them or any of them with it, it ought to be left to his discrecion how to proceede both for the tyme and manner of imprisonment and for reteyning the cause private to himself: alwaies to be regarded that the governor committ not to prison the bailiffe, or any of the jurates, unlesse it be for some such great cause concerning the king's majestie or the state, as is before mentioned."

It was further ordered, that although the "captaine may, for the better guard of the isle, make from tyme to tyme provision of armour, weapon, and such like furniture," yet he shall not "impose any assessment or tax thereby to charge the inhabitants for the said provision, without conference had with the bailiffe and jurates, and by their consent and agreement."—The captaine (i.e. governor) was to have the nomination of the gunners, whose payment by the islanders was not to be greater than anciently accustomed.—The islanders seeking not to be burthened as heretofore with the maintenance of the fortifications of Castle Cornet, they were not relieved therefrom, but told to complain " of further burthen than is convenient and necessary should be exacted of them therein ;" and as to the retynue (garrison) of the said castle, it was "left to the discretion of the governor to make choise of such able persons of the islanders as shall be thought fitt from tyme to tyme to be in readynes for the better defence of the same," but such service was to "be equallie apportioned in the generalitie."—The islanders requesting to be authorized and allowed to visit the castle as they have done in times past, were answered that "if they shall make request to the governor to see the state of the castle, it is not to be doubted but in friendlie manner the governor will admitt them to vew the same in such sorte as hetherto alwaies

hath ben accustomed."—A " demand for encrease of wages
to the bailiffes" was referred to commissioners to be sent to
the island, provided "the same may be donne without encrease of charge to his majestie, or taking the same out of
the governor's entertainment and allowance."—"And to their
demand that the bailiffe may be nominated by the king himself, and not by the governor, it is answered, that in regard
alwaies heretofore the bailiffe hath been nominated by the
captaine," their lordships saw no reason for any change.[1]—
" To the request that the governor may not take from the
inhabitants muttons or any victuale," otherwise than such as is
due, it was answered, " that the governor shall content himself
with 100 muttons by the yeare," to be paid for at the market
value ; and that he should continue to receive " such a quantity of butter to be served by the countrey as heretofore hath
usuallie bin yealded."—"Concerning the provisions brought
into the isle," it was ordered, " because it is meete that the
castle be alwaies sufficientlie furnished of all such commodities as the governor shall finde needefull, therefore the pre-
emption of any of the said commodities ought to be yealded
unto him ; but not any advantage of taking at a lower rate
against the will of the seller."—" To their demand, that the
sallerie of congers may be duly practized according to the
first institution thereof, it is answered, that the resolucion
hereof is to be referred to the book of Extent made anno
quinto. Edward 3, whereupon the lordships of the counsell
did determine this question in the year 1583."—It was further ordered, that if any person, residing within the castle
(Cornet) and under charge of the governor, offended "against
the course of justice of the isle, either civile or criminall,"
the Royal Court " was to demand the offender at his handes
upon the laying open and unfolding of the cause ; and if the
governor refused to deliver him up, the court was to apply
to the counsell board for remedie," although forty days were
required to elapse, in hope of amicable adjustment.

To examine further into the preceding and other complaints,
not only against Sir Thomas Leighton, but also against the
bailiff and jurats of Guernsey, two royal commissioners, Sir
Robert Gardner, knight, and James Hussey, doctors of the
civil law, were sent over in 1607, to inquire into and finally
determine all disputes between the authorities and the inhabitants, both in Guernsey and Jersey.   Most of the com-

(1) The prerogative of appointing the bailiff was reserved to the crown by an order in
council of May 27, 1674.

plaints made from Guernsey appear by the report of the said commissioners to have been well founded, and among them we find the following. The inhabitants complained that the governor,[1] " of his own authority, erected a martial jurisdiction, to the prejudice of the ordinary jurisdiction granted by royal charter to the bailiff and jurats," and that he " hath constrained, these late years, a great many of the best inhabitants of this isle, under the degree of justices, to keep watch at the castle, sometimes in their own persons, being not able to procure any other to do it for them, howbeit the said parties were of weak disposition, and not used to such discommodities and travels ; at least wise, to hire others at great price, almost every one refusing to do that service, except only the soldiers of the garrison, because of the hard and dangerous course held by the governor and his officers, in the performance of the said watch ; which service hath been raised upon the people beyond all reason, being not bound to the same by any extent of the king's rights and duties that can be shewed." The complainants prayed to be exempted from this burdensome service ; and as the governor reaped all the profit of the government, which profit was very great in so little a country, that he should stand to all that was requisite for the safe keeping of Castle Cornet. The commissioners decided, that as " the governor hath a sufficient number of soldiers in the castle, or allowance for the maintenance of them, to watch and ward in the castle in time of peace," he should not compel the inhabitants to do that service, "except it be in time of war, or in time of foreign preparations for war against his majesty, or any of his subjects," and then not without consulting the bailiff and jurats as to the men fitted by their valour and discretion for such service, from which the jurats and gentlemen were to be exempted, unless they refused to find a substitute. The inhabitants further complained that they were constrained to carry the corn due to the king over to the castle, whereas, ever before, they delivered it into the king's granary in the town ; and the commissioners ordered that only 200 quarters of corn be yearly delivered into the castle, for a certain provision, and 400 quarters in the time of necessity, and the rest to be delivered in St. Peter-Port. They complained also that Sir Thomas Leighton compelled them to ship themselves to make war against pirates, although some were altogether unmeet

(1) It is due to Sir T. Leighton to observe, that he was absent during the visit of the royal commissioners : he was represented by Peter Carey, esq., jurat, and his lieutenant.

N

for such actions, and none bound to such service. Moreover, that the governor commanded many chargeable and useless fortifications in the isle; and their prayer, that they might not be forced to serve out of the isle, or castle, or to erect such fortifications, was deemed reasonable by the commissioners. Other complaints were that the governor constrained the people to carry to the castle, in boats and carts, stones, wood, fuel, earth, &c., without any payment, imprisoning those that refused; and further, "to provide him at the castle with beds and sheets, together with coverletts," the same being an innovation. These arbitrary exercises of power were ordered to be greatly modified. The inhabitants further complained "that the governor taketh, as well from the inhabitants as strangers coming into the isle, beer and wood, almost at such price as pleaseth him," &c.; and it was ordered that, as Castle Cornet required to be always furnished with such commodities as the governor deemed needful, among which were beer and wood, he should have a pre-emption or preference of them at such price as the seller might agree upon. "They complain that the said governor will not suffer the men of the isle to marry any other wives than such as are born subjects of our sovereign, without his leave, for which the husband must pay a fine, and sometimes a yearly tribute and rent;" and, in depriving the governor of this exaction, the commissioners remarked, "that both in time of peace and war, the inhabitants may lawfully and freely have trade, traffic, and commerce, with strangers, and strangers with them, and also that they are more nearly situated to Normandy and France (with whom they have especial and daily intercourse) than they are with his majesty's dominions."—"They complain that the governor hath removed and turned out of their benefices sundry ministers of the Word of God; some of them born in the isle, and brought up at the charges of the inhabitants, without any lawful cause proved against them; leaving the parishes destitute of ministers, whereof some remain at this day unprovided." This gross act of injustice and tyranny being fully proved, the commissioners "do therefore think meet that the governor should forbear to do the like hereafter"!

The inhabitants of Alderney having also sundry complaints to make, sent over two deputies, who appeared before the royal commissioners, at St. Peter-Port, November 30, 1607, and alleged "that their island hath been destitute of a minister these sixteen years past, by reason there is no maintenance allowed for one, the lord or fee farmer" [Mr. Chamberlain] "of the said isle taking and enjoying all the tithes, with the house and ground belonging to the parsonage," and that the people were obliged to repair to Guernsey to have their marriages celebrated and their children christened. In consequence, they had lately, " at their extreme charges,—(considering their miserable and poor estate,)" maintained a young man, with his wife and children, a whole year in Guernsey, to prepare himself for the ministry, and they prayed that he might have either a part of the said tithes, or "a certain pension" therefrom, and that the parsonage and grounds might be restored. The commissioners ordered that Simon Masons, a native of Southampton, and probably the young man just mentioned, should repair to Alderney as a minister, with a salary of £20 sterling, English payment, yearly, and the enjoyment of the parsonage house, with the garden ground appertaining. The people, moreover, complained that they were ordered " to furnish unto John Chamberlain and his heirs, for the provision of his house, yearly, three score muttons or lambs, paying for every mutton two shillings, and for every lamb thirteen pence ;" which order the commissioners confirmed, adding, however, " but because the inhabitants are very poor, and their deputies say that they were drawn to this agreement against their will, we promise to deal with Mr. Chamberlain, in England, for the alteration of the same, or else to acquaint the lords of his majesty's privy council therewith."—The inhabitants also complained that "a certain isle, called Burhou, which they were wont to enjoy time out of mind," was withholden from them ; but the commissioners ruled that the said isle belonged to those who held Alderney in fee farm. They further complained that they were compelled to furnish, twice a year, "a boat, and therein to carry whatsoever it shall please the said Chamberlain or his farmers to appoint, from Alderney to Guernsey ;" and the commissioners decided that this exaction was illegal.

The garrison of Castle Cornet must at this period have been very small, as Dicey says : " There formerly used always to be in Castle Cornet fourteen soldiers in time of peace, besides the lieutenant, the marshall, the porter, the sutler, the master gunner, the smith, the carpenter, the boatmen, and the watchman. And in time of war, twenty-eight. Besides, the governor may command out of the island such number of the ablest and most expert soldiers he shall think to make choice of, who are to have a soldier's coat given them every year, and are to serve whenever they shall be required.

"These soldiers were called the castle retinue, and were bound to repair thither whenever called upon; especially upon any alarm. But for many years past, by omissions or otherwise, that retinue of soldiers, and coats allowed them, are out of practice; and the castle is principally garrisoned and defended by soldiers sent over from England."

And Dicey adds: "For services to be done, it was likewise the custom for all such as had carts or boats, two days in the year, to carry stone, sand, or other materials, for the building or repairs wanting to the castle, whenever they should be required.

"Such as were able to keep carts and did not so attend, were obliged to find others; and such as were not able to keep any, were obliged to work themselves.—All strangers were likewise obliged, on proper notice, to work four days."

George Lord Carew, of Clopton, to Amias de Carteret, bailiff of Guernsey.

"Forasmuch as it hath pleased God to take your late governor, Sir Thomas Leighton, from this world into a better; and his majesty having been pleased to bestow upon me the government he had in Guernsey, I have been moved to desire you (in respect of certain rents are paid weekly for mills and other tenements, let out by the said Sir Thomas during his life) that you will give notice to all the parishes of the said isle, that all such rents, from the day of his death, may be reserved to the king's use; and if in any other thing, you can shew me a favor, in the preservation of things may be prejudicial to his majesty,[1] I will be ready to requite it with thanks, and remain, &c.

"Court Whitehall, 5th of February, 1609.

[Endorsed.]

"Letter rec. 1609, March 23, from my L. Carew, governor."

From the same to the same.

[Extracts.]—"Touching the minerals of Serke, it shall suffice if a trial be made any time before midsummer. I will hereafter consider of the boorer (boorier) you speak of; but let not that hinder your proceeding .... Divers of the jurats and others of his majesty's officers having recommended Peter Gosselin unto me, I have, upon your certificate, chosen him to be greffier. I pray you, and such of the jurats as you shall think meet, to take view of the late ruins about the castle, and under your hands to certify what reparations are fit to be done, with an estimate what

(1) The crown revenues in Guernsey were enjoyed, not by the king, but by the governor, who at this time appears to have maintained the insular establishments, and was perhaps bound to pay a certain sum into the exchequer.

the charges thereof, and the scarping of rocks, (by which there is danger of a surprise,) will amount unto, wherein I desire that expedition may be used, to the end I may inform the lords of the council with the same, and get it repaired this summer.

"You have my leave for to come to England, and I am content that seigneur Sausmarez[1] supplies your place during your absence.

"From Court, this 12th of February, 1610."

[o]

"George Lord Carew, of Clopton, master of the ordnance within the realm of England, vice-chamberlain to her majesty, governor and captain-general of the isles of Guernsey, Alderney, Sark, &c.," being called upon "to give my personal attendance as well upon the queen's majesty as upon the office of the ordnance in England, and for some other important causes of mine own, my purpose is, with the first conveniency I may, (by God's permission,) to pass into that realm." His lordship accordingly left Amias de Carteret,[2] esquire, bailiff of Guernsey, his lieutenant-governor, with numerous conditions, reservations, and instructions, dated at Castle Cornet, the 9th day of August, 1610, from which we extract the following:

"Moreover, I do in like manner reserve unto myself the placing and displacing of all the officers and soldiers of the garrison in Castle Cornet, the list of whose names and number, in a particular muster roll delivered unto you under my hand, is specified. Nevertheless, over all the soldiers, 'drome,' bellman, bellwatch, and boatmen, you shall have full power (if any of them shall carry themselves undutifully towards you, or neglect their duties in their particular places,) to discharge or punish the offenders, and to place some other sufficient man to serve in his room that is discharged, until I shall provide another of mine own election to supply his place. (But, concerning the porter and gunner, I do only give you power to suspend them if they offend, until I be certified of their offences, the determining whereof I reserve unto myself.)

"Albeit, for the increase of tillage, which will advance the common good of this isle of Guernsey, a further liberty for transportation of corn, than hath been accustomed, is meet to be granted : nevertheless, I do require you to foresee that no immoderate carrying away of corn may be admitted, but licensed in such a temper as the greedy desires of particular men, for their private gains, may not leave the isle destitute. And that provisionally you be thus far 'respective' of my particular, that when it shall appear unto you that corn, without detriment, may be

_____

(1) Thomas Andros, seigneur of Sausmarez, St. Martin's, son-in-law of Amias de Carteret, and father of Amias Andros, afterwards bailiff.

(2) Amias de Carteret was seigneur of Trinity manor, in Jersey, and we believe a native of that island. As the emoluments were trifling, it is strange that he was bailiff of Guernsey.

spared, then such corn as shall remain in my garner[1] may be first vented, which is a right belonging to the governor.

"Further, I do require you, that the orders made by my predecessor, Sir Thomas Leighton, and subscribed with his hand, now remaining in Castle Cornet, may be duly observed by those that are of the garrison, until such time as you shall receive others under mine own hand. And especially, I pray you be careful that no soldier be suffered to go into the island, otherwise than upon his day of liberty. And that none be permitted to lie out of the castle any night, except it be by your license.

"That you have a regard of the safe keeping of all his majesty's munitions, and especially to be careful of the powder, that none immoderate waste be made of it. And when it lightens, that you command the gunner, or some other of the soldiers, to hang either some old sails or blankets before the windows and doors of the powder room, that the store may be secured.[2] And to command the gunner to make a journal of expense of the powder, and at no time, but upon occasions, (for the which good reasons may be given,) that he do presume to make a shot but by your direction.

"Upon any intelligence of danger, or attempt to be made upon the island, you are to lodge within the Castle Cornet, and to send for such supplies out of the country as in such causes is accustomed. And also to command the inhabitants of the same, under their several captains, (according to the accustomed directions in former times,) to repair with their arms to the several rendezvous, and to be vigilant that the enemy take no land, inasmuch as in you lieth.

"More, for that of late times the exercise of arms is much decayed in these islands, I do pray you to take (as often as in your discretion it shall be thought meet) general musters of all the able men, as also of their weapons; and that their captains do train them as heretofore hath been accustomed. And whereas also every several parish hath been accustomed to maintain gunners and ordnance upon landing places, I do require you to see that their duties herein be not neglected; and likewise that due watches be kept, and beacons erected, when time of danger require it.

"I do pray you to oversee the keeper of the isle of Erme, (Herm,) that no wilful or negligent waste be made of the deer, pheasants, or conies there. And of the deer and pheasants, in your discretion, kill what you please; being confident that you will endeavour their preservation and increase as much as myself.

"For the provision of your table, I do give you out of Erme

---

(1) The governor received the great tithes as part of his perquisites.

(2) Had a similar precaution been taken in 1672, when the castle was much injured by the explosion of the powder magazine, the accident might have been prevented.

(for so long as you are my lieutenant) after the rate of two hundred couple of conies per annum.

" I do likewise give you, for the provision of your own table, carps without any certain limitation, praying you so to favor the pond, as that the increase may not be decayed.

" I do also desire you to be careful that the breed of swans, brought into the island by Sir Thomas Leighton, and cherished by him, may not be destroyed. Of them yearly you may take for your own use as many as you please, and unto John de Quetteville,[1] what you may spare, I pray you to bestow upon him : your moderation in both I am sure will be such as the game will be maintained.

" My predecessors, the governors, have ever accustomed to be careful that none in the country should keep greyhounds to destroy the hares, nor shoot at fowl, without their license, which laudable custom I pray you observe, wherein I do not wish you to restrain any man of quality, but the baser people, whose time spent in labour is proper to their calling. And, in like manner, not to permit any man to take partridges, of which game this island is almost destitute.[2]

" Finally, for so much as this isle of Guernsey is a frontier upon a potent monarch, and that the preservation of the said island from incursions and hostile invasion chiefly consisteth in order and discipline, I do require you to cause the inhabitants of the island to keep and observe the military orders which my predecessor, Sir Thomas Leighton, established since the happy entrance of his majesty that now is to the imperial crown of England, the copy whereof I received from yourself, until you shall receive new orders subscribed with my own hand.''

Lord Carew to Amias de Carteret, bailiff of Guernsey.

[Extract.]—" The mineral earths which I brought from Sark, Guernsey, and Jersey, upon trial ' flied' to smoke : the lead ore of Sark holds only lead, but in small assayes so uncertainly as no judgment certain can be made of it ; wherefore, I have written to John de Quetteville to send me a hogshead of the same ore,[3] and I pray you to speak to your nephew to permit him to dig for it, unto whom and to yourself I recommend my best affections.

" Savoy, this 20th day of May, 1612."

From the same to the same.

[Extracts.]—" Whereas I ' writt' to you by my servant Leche

---

(1) The governor's receiver.

(2) Deer, pheasants, swans, and partridges, have long since disappeared from Guernsey and Herm. Hares have been occasionally re-introduced into Guernsey within a few years, but they are soon destroyed.

(3) In 1835, a company was formed to work the mineral lodes of Sark, which exhibited traces of silver, lead, and copper. A quantity of silver lead ore was raised, but not sufficient to pay the cost ; and, after a loss of about £40,000, the works were abandoned in 1848. At Herm, also, a copper lode was worked, and abandoned after a small outlay.

that I intended to be with you in Guernsey this spring. I do still
continue in the same mind, but cannot set down any certain time,
by reason of my lord Lisle his sickness, who is at this present not
able to wait upon her majesty : as soon as he shall be recovered,
I am resolved to come thither.   In the mean season, I will take
order that Castle Cornet may be supplied with those things which
for the present are most chiefly to be desired . . . .   Lastly, the
project which Leche hath acquainted me withal, to wit, a suit
which you and the jurats (having first obtained the consent of
the inhabitants there) intend to make to his majesty for a license
to raise a certain small imposition upon such wines as shall be
spent in the island, to endure for a few years only, till such time
as the island, which (as I understand) is very poor, may be furnished with some public treasure, to be employed in the provision of things needful for the defence of the same.   I do hereby
certify you that I do very well like thereof, and will (when I
shall be more particularly informed therein, which you may do
by setting down the nature of the project in writing to be sent
unto me) be ready to yield you my best furtherance. for the obtaining of that which doth so much [tend] to the public good of
the island.

    " From the Court at Greenwich, 17th April, 1616."

From the same to the same.

    "My heart is at ease when I hear of no discord in the isle of
Guernsey, and I thank you that all is in the good temper as now
it stands, wherein I may not forget to commend your discreet
carriage and moderation, otherwise it would not be as it is at
present, and for the same I render you many thanks.   Although
I need not put a spur to your foresight and diligence, yet it is
my part not to be void of care, and especially in these troublesome times, when our neighbours in France are in combustion ;
wherefore, I pray you to be vigilant in the place you hold, and,
if any fears or dangers represent themselves unto you, that you
would give me timely notice of it to prevent the same, and also
that you would from time to time advertize me of news of France,
which many times comes to you before we can receive it here.
I am sorry that the heat between the governor of Jersey and the
bailiff[1] there is grown to so great a flame : it will in the end prove
ill for both parts, and in the present a general disquietness to the
whole island.   When Philip Carteret took his leave of me, I said
some things unto him concerning you which I leave to his report :
what I said I then thought, and do now think, and will evermore
remain towards you as I then professed, which shall in actions be

---

(1) Sir John Peyton and John Herault, bailly. The latter died in 1626 ; and the Rev. E.
Durell, in speaking of him, says : " He died poor, and no monument was erected to perpetuate his name ; but his memory has survived as that of one of the ablest and most
public spirited magistrates, whose virtues ever reflected honour on the high office of bailly
of Jersey."—See Durell's Notes on Falle, p. 409.

made manifest when you shall have occasion to make use of my friendship. Touching the ecclesiastical government in the islands, I can say nothing more than you have heard, until his majesty's return, at which time I conceive his intention for the church government there will be renewed. I could be glad to be furnished from you what your opinion is in the same. I moved his majesty (for the ease of the island) that some of the inhabitants' children might be brought up at school, in some of his colleges, whereby they might be freed for charges, whereunto he graciously assented; wherefore, if there be any that you desire should be preferred to be the king's scholars, such as you shall recommend unto me I will do my endeavour to get them placed. And so with my best affections unto yourself, I rest your constant friend.

" Savoy, the 9th of April, 1617.

[Endorsed.]

" Letter rec. 1617, May 6, from the L. Carew, my governor."

[George Carew, earl of Totness, whose patent was in reversion, 1 Jacob. I., 1603 ; he lived till 8. Carol. I. Warburton, 41.

Totness, in king Charles I.'s time, gave the title of earl to George Lord Carew, of Clopton, son of Dr. George Carew, dean of Windsor.—*Gibson's Camden.*

" The inheritance of the Cloptons descended in our time to two sisters, coheirs, one of whom married to Sir George Carew, a famous knight, (vice-chamberlain to her most serene majesty queen Anne,) whom king James created baron Carew, of Clopton, and whom, if for no other reason, I cannot omit for the great respect he paid to venerable antiquity."—*Gibson's Camden* in Warwickshire, 503.

Lord Carew appears to have resigned his government of Guernsey in 1620.]

Habitual intemperance, gout,- and vexation, produced in James what was called a tertian fever, of which he died in March, 1625, in the sixtieth year of his age, and the twenty-third of his reign in England.

Michael Drayton, the poet, published, in 1613, his " Poly-Albion," or a description of England. In the opening of the first canto, it contains the following :

> " The sprightly muse her wing displays,
> And the French islands first surveys.
>
> *　*　*　*　*　*　*　*
>
> Thus scarcely said the muse, but hovering while she hung
> Upon the Celtic wastes, the sea-nymphs loudly sung :
> O, ever happy isles, your heads so high that rear,
> By Nature strongly fenced, which never need to fear ;
> On Neptune's watery realms, when Æolus raiseth wars,
> And every billow bounds, as though to quench the stars.
> Fair *Jersey*, first of these, here scattered in the deep,
> Peculiarly that boasts thy double-horned sheep ;
> Inferior not to thee, thou *Guernsey !* bravely crowned
> With rough embattled rocks, whose venom-hating ground

The hardened emeril[1] hath, which thou abroad dost send;
Thou *Ligon*,[2] her beloved, and *Sark*, that doth attend
Her pleasure every hour, as *Jethou*, them at need,
With pheasants, fallow deer, and conies thou dost feed!
Ye seven small sister isles and sorlings, which to see
The half-sunk seaman joys : or whatsoe'er you be!
From fruitful *Aureny*,[3] near the ancient Celtic shore,
To Ushant and the Seams,[4] whereas those nuns of yore
Gave answers from their caves, and took what shapes they please,
Ye happy islands set within the British seas."

Ancient hours of the Royal Court.—"At the Chief Pleas
held on the 4th of October, 1624, it was ordered that, for the
future, the court should assemble at half-past nine on every Monday, and the advocates are directed to deliver their causes to the
bailiff or his lieutenant on the previous Saturday before sunset,
otherwise their causes will not be heard ; and it is further ordered
that the Saturday's court shall rise at one o'clock after mid-day,
without being obliged to sit later, however important the case
may be."

CHARLES I.—1625 to 1649.

Although the reign of Edward III. was very eventful to
these islands, that of Charles I. is the most interesting in their
annals, and the more so as Jersey and Guernsey espoused
different sides during the great rebellion.   Happily, we have
obtained materials in exemplification of that stirring period,
which were unknown to any previous Guernsey historian :
we allude to the recently discovered correspondence of Sir
Peter Osborne, who was resident lieutenant-governor and
governor of Guernsey for twenty-five years—1621 to 1646—
as well as to the MS. chronicle of John Chevalier, who was
an inhabitant of St. Hélier, Jersey, of which parish he was
vingtenier, or tithing man, and who kept a diary from the
years 1643 to 1650, in which he described many of the incidents of the civil war relating to both islands.

Charles, who was second son of James I., by Anne,
daughter of the king of Denmark, and grandson of the
equally unfortunate Mary, the Scottish queen, was born in
Scotland, in 1600, and, on the death of his elder brother
Henry, he became Prince of Wales.   In 1625, he succeeded
his father, and soon after commenced hostilities against Spain,
although his kingdom was filled with dissensions, owing in
a great measure to the mal-administration of Buckingham,
and the discontents of the puritans.   These dissensions were

(1) Emery.   (2) Probably Lihou.   (3) Alderney.

(4) Isle of Semo or Sein, where the nine priestesses, so much feared by the Gauls, were
said to reside.

moreover increased by his marriage with Henrietta Maria, a Roman Catholic, and daughter of the renowned Henry IV. of France. Her brother, Louis XIII., having renewed the persecution against his Protestant subjects and laid siege to Rochelle, their strongest hold, a war ensued between the two nations. Two parliaments were called, but as the members murmured about grievances, and would grant no supplies, they were quickly dissolved. In consequence, Charles commenced raising funds by means of loans, benevolences, and ship money, which increased the hostility against him; and the puritans, in attacking the hierarchy and form of worship, made the people believe that popery and arbitrary power were to be introduced by the king and the bishops. But the grievance which was perhaps the most felt was the revival of monopolies, which were granted to an extent truly appalling. An unsuccessful expedition under Buckingham, to relieve the Protestants at La Rochelle, when the duke was disgracefully repulsed in his descent upon the isle of Rhé, in 1627, embarrassed the king's affairs still more; and he was compelled to call another parliament, which, after voting the supplies, passed a bill, in which the rights of the subject were defined: this act, after some demur, was confirmed by Charles.

In consequence of Buckingham's descent upon the isle of Rhé, the French threatened to retaliate upon these islands; and in a recent work—" *The Court and Times of Charles I.*, London, 1848,"—we find among the correspondence the following extracts relating to their intended invasion:

" London, 6th June, 1627.—The next following upon advertisement sent hither from Guernsey that there are 4,000 men at the town of Coutance, which is near unto Jersey, and 7,000 at Newhaven,[1] ready with boats and arms to set upon those islands; which they had by several advertisements from that coast of Normandy, and out of confession of three spies which they apprehended, there was present order taken for the sending of four ships of war for the guarding of the said islands.

" London, 27th June, 1627.—My lord of Derby (Danby) or Sir Peter Osborne, his lieutenant of the castle of Guernsey, is shortly to be sent with ten ships for the guard of those islands, which are much threatened, and in danger of their neighbours.

" London, 6th February, 1627-8.—The isles of Jersey and Guernsey are in some fear and danger.

" London, December 5, 1628.—The earl of Danby is with all expedition to hie himself to his charge at Guernsey; for news is come to the court that the French king intends, ere long, to

(1) We believe Newhaven to have been the present Hâvre-de-Grace.

invade it and Jersey; for which he prepares some flat-bottomed boats.

"London, December 10, 1628.—Since my writing of my last letter the last week, there are come advertisements hither from both the islands of Jersey and Guernsey that there are great numbers of ships and shallops newly come to Newhaven and other parts of Normandy, with an intent, as they are informed, to invade them; and that, to the same end, great numbers of soldiers also are flocking to those parts. Whereupon the council is taking order to provide, as speedily as they can, for the safety of those islands, which it was ever suspected that the French would cast their design upon, to be revenged of the attempt made upon the Isle of Rhé, whensoever opportunity should be offered, both in regard of the facility of that enterprise (those islands lying so near that province) and of their old pretences upon them, as being members of Normandy.

"London, December 12, 1628.—It hath been misdoubted by his preparation of shipping and flat-bottomed boats, that the French king will have somewhat to say to Guernsey and Jersey; but some think he hath a greater design.

"London, December 17, 1628.—To prevent the danger threatened to the islands of Jersey and Guernsey, whereof I informed you by my last, my lord of Danby is appointed to repair thither —I mean to his government of Guernsey—with four good ships which shall serve for the guard of both the islands, and is within a few days to take his journey thither; although, for my part, I am persuaded that he might well spare that labour for any danger that is really intended to those places, because I do not conceive that the king of France hath in himself any desire to exasperate matters any farther with this state; and though he had, yet that he could not do it at this time, when, as by our last advertisement, we are informed he is farther off an accomodation with the Spaniards about the matters of Italy than he was before."

The earl of Danby, at that time governor of Guernsey, represented to the king the necessity of sending a naval squadron not only for the protection of these islands, but also to annoy the French traffic by sea between Britany and Normandy. In this necessity Charles concurred, and an order was issued accordingly. The secretary of state, lord Conway, also wrote to the bailiff and jurats of Guernsey on the 12th of August, 1627, to assure them, in the king's name, that his majesty would ever continue his gracious protection, as his predecessors had done, " as he greatly esteemed that portion of his inheritance, and the unspotted faith and duty of his subjects in the islands."

But, as we have just said, Charles' pecuniary difficulties

and troubles with his English subjects had already begun, and
this misguided monarch was unable to afford immediate assistance. It happened fortunately, in the meanwhile, that the
French, "pleased that the jealousies and quarrels between
king and parliament had disarmed so formidable a power,
carefully avoided any enterprise which might rouse either the
terror or anger of the English, and dispose them to domestic
union and submission." [1] At length, however, "it was
thought good to send the earl of Danby with a considerable
supply of men and arms, and ammunition, to make good
those islands, by testifying and assuring them against all invasions. This order, signified to his lordship about the beginning of December, anno 1628, he cheerfully embraced the
service, and prepared accordingly. But neither the ships,
money, nor other necessaries, being at that time brought
together" [2] the squadron only sailed from Portsmouth in
March following. His lordship, "being deserted by his own
chaplaines in regard of the extremity of the season, and the
visible danger of the enterprise," [2] Doctor Heylin engaged
to accompany him in that capacity; and the happy result of
his visit was a publication in 1656, entitled, "A survey of the
two islands, Guernzey and Jarsey, with the isles appending,
according to their politie and formes of government, both
ecclesiasticall and civill." Now that steamers easily perform
the passage between Portsmouth and Guernsey in nine hours,
and that, in moderate weather, with almost as much certainty
as a journey of the same distance by land, a smile cannot fail
of being excited at the fears of the poor chaplains, who
shrank from accompanying the earl in his perilous undertaking! The survey has become so extremely rare, that
copious extracts from it relative to the passage across and to
all the islands, in the author's own orthography and quaint
language, cannot but prove interesting, the more so as the
description of the passage from England is the earliest extant.
Witchcraft or sorcery, of which mention is made by Heylin
in the succeeding extracts, appears to have been a very dangerous vocation, as in the year 1563 three persons were
burnt for the offence; in 1570, two; and from that period
to 1605, *eight* more on similar accusations. Berry says, that
between the years 1598 and 1634 no less than nine women
and two men were burnt in Guernsey for sorcery! The
Rev. Thomas Le Marchant, minister of the Established Presbyterian Church of Guernsey, who, in 1662, was deprived of

(1) Hume.   (2) Heylin.

his livings of the Vale and St. Sampson, because, from con-
scientious motives, he refused to sign the act of uniformity,
compiled an able work on the laws and customs of Normandy,
as used in the Royal Court, which was first printed in 1826 :
in it he wrote with a forethought and benevolence which do
credit to his memory, that former bailiffs and jurats, most of
them illiterate men, had established " a new species of inquisition against poor simple persons, whom the credulity and
superstition of the ignorant regarded as sorcerers, instituting
against them proceedings as strange as they were rigorous ;
and often attributing the effects of nature, whose causes they
were incapable of fathoming, to witchcraft or satanic agency,
they have condemned them by dozens to be hanged and
burnt.   And, forasmuch as these poor creatures persisted in
maintaining their innocence, they have, from a dread lest the
people should believe their words and entertain a sinister
opinion of their judges, invented a species of cruelty which
not even barbarians practise, which is, that after sentence of
death has been pronounced on these pretended sorcerers, the
said judges, in order to justify their own proceedings and to
compel these poor wretches to confess their guilt, have immediately, before the execution of the sentence, caused them to
be put to the torture in a manner so cruel, that to some they
have torn off limbs, and to others they have lighted fires on
their living bodies."— Humanity now shudders at the thought
of such wanton barbarity as this ; and as a cell or a dungeon
in Castle Cornet then formed the only prison of the island,
how many an innocent creature must have passed its portals
to the torture and the faggot, which were both applied at the
south-western foot of the hill on which formerly stood the
" Tower of Beauregard," and very near the present pump
at the Bordage, in the town of St. Peter-Port.[1]

(1) Sir Matthew Hale, while presiding as lord chief baron at the trial of two unhappy
women, who were indicted at the assizes at Bury St. Edmunds, in the year 1665, for the
crime of witchcraft, is reported to have told the jury, "that he made no doubt at all
that there were such creatures as witches," and the women were found guilty and executed.   The conduct of Hale, on this occasion, has very justly been the subject of much
sarcastic animadversion, although not to profess a belief in sorcery and witchcraft, was
in those days considered, if not irreligious, as bordering on infidelity.

CHAPTER X.

EXTRACTS FROM HEYLIN'S SURVEY.

THE extracts from Heylin, already alluded to, will form the subject of a separate chapter : he sailed from Portsmouth.

" On Tuesday, March 3. [1629.] about ten in the morning, we went aboard his majesties ship called the Assurance, being a ship of 800 tun, furnished with 42 pieces of ordinance, and very well manned with valiant and expert sailors ; welcomed aboard (after the fashion of the sea) with all the thunder and lightning which the whole navy could afford from their severall ships. Our whole navy consisted of five vessels, that is to say, the Assurance, spoken of before ; two of his majesties pinnaces, called the Whelps ; a catch of his majesties, called the Minikin ; and a merchant's ship, called the Charles, which carryed the armes and ammunition for the use of the islands. Aboard the ships were stowed about 400 foot with their severall officers, two companies whereof, under the command of collonell Pipernell (if I remember his name aright) and lieutenant-collonell Francis Connisby, were intended for the isle of Guernzey ; the other two, under the command of lieutenant-collonell Francis Rainford and captain William Kil-legre, for the isle of Jarsey. The admirall of our navy (but in subordination to his lordship when he was at sea) was Sir Henry Palmer, one of the admirals of the narrow seas ; all of them men of note in their severall wayes, and most of them of as much gallantry and ingenuity as either their own birth or education in the school of war could invest them with. The sea was very calme and quiet, and the little breath of winde we had made us move so slowly, that the afternoon was almost spent before we had passed through the Needles, a dangerous passage at all times, except to such only who, being well skilled in these sharpe points and those dreadfull fragments of the rocks which so intituled them, could stear a steady course between them : Scylla and Charybdis in old times, nothing more terrible to the unskilled mariners of those dayes then those rocks to ours. Being got beyond them at the last, though we had got more sea roome, we had little more winde, which made us move as slowly as before we did, so that we spent the greatest part of the night with no swifter motion then what was given us by the tide. About three of the clock in the morning we had winde enough, but we had it directly in our teeth, which would have quickly brought us to the place we had parted from if a great miste, arising together with the sun, had not induced our mariners to keep themselves aloofe in the open sea for fear of falling on those rocks wherewith the south side of the Wight is made unaccessable.   About two of the clock in the afternoon, the winds turning somewhat eastward, we made on again, but with so little speed and to so little purpose, that all that night we were fain to lie at hull (as the mariners phrase it) without any sensible moving either backward or forward, but so uneasily withall, that it must be a very great tempest indeed which gives a passenger a more sickly and unpleasing motion.   For my part, I had found myself good seaproof in my voyage to France, and was not much troubled with those disturbances to which the greatest part of our landmen were so sensibly subject.   On Thursday morning, about daybreak, being within sight of Portland, and the winde serving very fitly, we made again for the islands.   At eleven of the clock we discovered the main land of Normandy, called by the mariners Le Hagge.   About two in the afternoon, we fell even with Aldernie or Aurnie; and about three discerned the isle of Jarzey, to which we were bound, at which we aimed, and to which we might have come much sooner then we did had we not found a speciall entertainment by the way to retard our haste ; for we were hardly got within sight of Jarsey but we descried a sail of French, consisting of ten barks laden with very good Gascoyene wines and good choyce of linen, (as they told us afterwards,) bound from St. Malloes to New-Haven for the trade of Paris, and convoyed by a Holland man of war for their safer passage.   These being looked on as good prize, our two whelpes and the catch gave chace unto them, a great shot being first made from our admiral's ship to call them in.   The second shot brought in the Holland man of war, who very sordidly and basely betrayed his charge before he came within reach of danger ; the rest, for the greatest part of the afternoon, spun before the winde, sometimes so neer to their pursuers that we thought them ours, but presently tacking about when our whelpes were ready to seaze on them, and the catch to lay fast hold upon them, they gained more way then our light vessels could recover in a long time after.   Never did duck by frequent diving so escape the spaniell, or hare by often turning so avoid the hounds, as these poor barks did quit themselves by their dexterity in sailing from the present danger.   For my part, I may justly say that I never spent an afternoon with greater pleasure, the greater in regard that I knew his lordship's resolution to deal favourably with those poor men if they chanced to fall into his power.   But at the last, a little before the close of the evening, three of them being borded and brought under lee of our admirall, the rest were put to a necessity of yeelding, or venturing themselves between our two great ships and the shoar

of Jarsey, to which we were now come as near as we could with
safety. Resolved upon the last course, and favoured with a strong
leading gale, they passed by us with such speed and so good
successe, (the duskinesse of the evening contributing not a little
to a fair escape,) that though we gave them thirty shot; yet we
were not able to affirme that they received any hurt or dammage
by that encounter, with as much joy unto myself (I dare boldly
say) as to any of those poor men who were so much interested in
it. This chase being over, and our whole fleet come together,
we anchored that night in the port of St. Oen, one of the principall ports of that island, the inhabitants whereof (but those
especially which dwelled in the inland parts) standing all night
upon their guard, conceiving by the thunder of so many great
shot that the whole powers of France, and the devill to boot, were
now falling upon them, not fully satisfied in their fears till by the
next rising of the sun they descried our colours.

"On Friday, March the 6, about nine in the morning, (having
first landed our foot in the long boats,) we went aboard his
majesties catch called the Minikin, and, doubling the points of
La Corbière and of Noirmont, we went on shoar in the bay of
St. Hélier's, neer unto Mount St. Aubin, in the parish of St.
Peter; the greatest part of which day we spent in accommodations and refreshments, and receiving the visits of the gentry,
which came in very frequently to attend his lordship. You need
not think but that sleep and a good bed were welcome to us, after
so long and ill a passage; so that it was very near high noon
before his lordship was capable to receive our services, or we to
give him our attendance. After dinner, his lordship went to
view the fort Elizabeth, (the chief strength of the island,) and to
take order for the fortifying and repair thereof; which having
done, he first secured the man of war and the three French barks,
under the command of that castle, and then gave leave to Sir
Henry Palmer and the rest of the sea captains to take their pleasures in forraging and scowring all the coasts of France which
lay near the islands, commanding them to attend him on the
Saturday following. Next he gave liberty to all the French
which he had taken the day before, whom he caused to be landed
in their own countrie, to their great rejoycing, as appeared by
the great shout they made when they were put into some long
boats at their own disposing, the three barks still remaining un-
touched in the state they were, save that some wines were taken
out of them for his lordship's spending. On Sunday, March 8,
it was ordered that the people of the town of St. Hélier's should
have their divine offices in that church performed so early, that
it might be left wholly for the use of the English by nine of the
clock, about which time his lordship, attended by the officers and
souldiers, in a solemn military pompe, (accompanied with the

o

governours of the town and chief men of the island) went toward the church, where I officiated divine service according to the prescript form of the Church of England, and after preached on those words of David, (Psalm xxxi. 51,) viz. " Offer unto God thanksgiving," &c., with reference to the good successe of our voyage past, and hopes of the like mercies for the time to come. The next day we made a journey to Mount Orgueil, where we were entertained by the Lady Carteret; (a daughter of Sir Francis Douse, of Hampshire;) and after dinner his lordship went to take a view of the regiment of Mr. Josuah de Carteret, seignieur de la Trinity, mustering upon the green upon Havre de Bowle, in the parish of St. Trinitie.   On Tuesday, March the 10, his lordship took a view of the regiment of Mr. Aron Misservie, colonel; and on Wednesday, March the 11, went unto St. Oen, where we were feasted by Sir Philip de Carteret, whose regiment we likewise viewed in the afternoon.   The souldiers of each regiment very well arrayed, and not unpractised in their armes; but such as never saw more danger then a training came to.   On Thursday, his lordship went into the cohu, or town hall, attended by Sir John Palmer, the deputy-governour, Sir Philip de Carteret, the justices, clergy, and jurors of the island, with other the subordinate officers thereunto belonging; where being set, as in a parliament or sessions, and having given order for redresse of some grievances by them presented to him in the name of that people, he declared to them in a grave and eloquent speach the great care which his majesty had of their preservation in sending men, money, armes, and ammunition, to defend them against the common enemies of their peace and consciences, assuring them that if the noise of those preparations did not keep the French from looking towards them, his majesty would not fail to send them such a strength of shipping as should make that island more impregnable then a wall of brasse; in which regard he thought it was not necessary for him to advise them to continue fathfull to his majesties service, or to behave themselves with respect and love towards those gentlemen, officers, and common souldiers, who were resolved to expose themselves (for defence of them, their wives and children,) to the utmost dangers; and, finally, advising the common souldiers to carry themselves with such sobriety and moderation towards the natives of the countrey, (for as for their valour towards the enemies he would make no question,) as to give no offence or scandall by their conversation. This said, the assembly was dissolved, to the great satisfaction of all parties present; the night ensuing and the day following being spent for the most part in the entertainments of rest and pleasures.

" The only businesse of that day was the disposing of the three barks which we took in our journey, the goods whereof having before been inventoried and apprized by some commissioners of

the town, and now exposed to open sale, were for the most part
bought, together with the barks themselves, by that very Holland
man of warre whom they had hired to be their convoy, which
gave me such a character of the mercenary and sordid nature of
that people, that of all men living I should never desire to have
any thing to do with them, unlesse they might be made use of
(as the Gibeonites were) in hewing wood and drawing water for
the use of the tabernacle ; I mean, in doing servile offices to some
mightier state, which would be sure to keep them under.

"On Saturday, March the 14, having spent the greatest part
of the morning in expectation of the rest of our fleet, which found
better imployment in the seas then they could in the haven, we
went aboard the merchant's ship, which before I spake of, not
made much lighter by the unlading of the one halfe of the ammunition which was left at Jarsey, in regard that the two hundred
foot, which should have been distributed in the rest of the ships,
were all stowed in her. Before night, being met by the rest of
our fleet, we came to anchor neer St. Pier-Port, or St. Peter's-
Port, within the bay of Castle Cornet, where we presently landed ;
the castle divided from the town and haven by the inter-currency
of the sea, in which respect we were fain to make use of the castle
hall instead of a chappell, the way to the town church being too
troublesome and uncertain to give us the constant use of that, and
the castle yeelding no place else of a fit capacity for the receiving
of so many as gave their diligent attendance at religious exercises.

"On Monday, March the 16, our fleet went out to sea againe,
taking the Charles with them for their greater strength, which to
that end was speedily unladen of such ammunition as was designed
for the use of that island. [Guernsey.]

"The whole time of our stay here was spent in visiting the
forts and ports, and other places of importance, taking a view of
the severall musters of the naturall islanders, distributing the new
come souldiers in their severall quarters, receiving the services of
the gentry, clergy, and principall citizens; and, finally, in a like
meeting of the States of the island, as had before been held in
Jarsey.

"Nothing considerable else in the time of our stay but that
our fleet came back on Wednesday, March 25, which hapned
very fitly to compleat the triumph of the Friday following, being
the day of his majesties most happy inauguration, celebrated in
the castle by the divine service for that day, and after by a noble
feast made by him [Lord Danby] for the chief men of the island,
and solemnized without the castle by 150 great shot, made from
the castle, the fleet, the town of St. Peter's-Port, and the severall
islands, all following one another in so good an order, that never
bels were rung more closely, nor with lesse confusion.

"Thus having given your lordship a brief view of the course

of our voyage, I shall next present you with the sight of such observations as I have made upon those islands at my times of leasure; and that being done, hoise sail for England.

*   *   *   *   *   *

" And, certainly, it could not be but an eyesore to the French to have these isles within their sight, and not within their power; to see them at the least in possession of their ancient enemy, the English; a nation strong in shipping, and likely, by the opportunity of these places, to annoy their trade; for if we look upon them in their situation, we shall find them seated purposely for the command and empire of the ocean, the islands lying in the chief trade of all shipping from the eastern parts unto the west, and in the middle way between St. Malos and the river Seine, the only trafick of the Normans and Parisians.   At this St. Malos, as at a common empory, do the merchants of Spain and Paris barter their commodities, the Parisians making both their passage and return by these isles, which, if wel aided by a smal power from the king's navy, would quickly bring that entercourse to nothing,—an opportunity neglected by our former kings in their attempts upon that nation, as not being then so powerfull on the seas as now they are, but likely for the future to be husbanded to the best advantage, if the French hereafter stir against us.   Sure I am, that my lord of Danby conceived this course of all others to be the fittest for the impoverishing, if not undoing, of the French, and accordingly made proposition by his letters to the councell that a squadron of eight ships (viz. five of the whelpes, the Assurance, the Adventure, and the Catch,) might be employed about these islands for that purpose—an advice which had this summer took effect, had not the peace between both realms been so suddenly concluded.

" Of these, four only are inhabited, and those reduced only unto two governments; Jarsey an entire province, as it were, within itself, but that of Guernzey having the other two of Alderney and Serke dependant on it.   Hence it is that in our histories, and in our acts of parliament, we have mention only of Jarsey and of Guernzey, this last comprehending under it the two others. The people of them all live as it were in *libera custodia*, in a kind of free subjection, not any way acquainted with taxes, or with any levies either of men or money; in so much that when the parliaments of England contribute towards the occasion of their princes, there is alwayes a proviso in the act, 'That this grant of subsidies, or any thing therein contained, extend not to charge the inhabitants of Guernzey and Jarsey, or any of them, of, for, or concerning any mannors, lands, and tenements, or other possessions, goods, chattels, or other moveable substance, which they the said inhabitants, or any other to their uses, have within Jarsey and Guernzey, or in any of them,' &c.   These priviledges and immunites, (together with divers others,) seconded of late dayes with the more powerfull band of religion, have been a principall occasion of that constancy, wherewith they have persisted faithfully in their allegiance, and disclaimed even the very name and thought of France; for howsoever the language which they speak is French, and that in their originall, they either were of Normandy or Britagne, yet can they with no patience endure to be accounted French, but call themselves by the names of English Normans; so much doth liberty, or at the worst a gentle yoak, prevail upon the mind and fancy of the people.

"To proceed unto particulars, we will take them as they lie in order, beginning first with that of Alderney, an island called by Antonine Arica, but by the French and in our old records known by the name of Aurigny and Aurney. It is situate in the 49 degree between forty-eight and fifty-two minutes of that degree, just over against the cape or promontory of the Lexobii, called at this time by the mariners the Hague, distant from this cape or promontory three leagues only, but thirty at the least from the nearest part of England.[1] The aire healthy, though sometimes thickned with the vapours arising from the sea: the soil indifferently rich, both for husbandry and grasing. A town it hath of well near an hundred families, and not far off an haven made in the manner of a semi-circle, which they call Crabbie. The principall strength of it are the high rocks with which it is on every side environed, but especially upon the south; and on the east side an old block-house, which time hath made almost unserviceable. The chief house herein belongeth unto the Chamberlains, as also the dominion or fee farme of all the island, it being granted by queen Elizabeth unto George, the son of Sir Leonard Chamberlain, then governour of Guernzey, by whose valour it was recovered from the French, who in queen Maries dayes had seized upon it. Neer unto the fort or block-house afore mentioned, a great quantity of this little island is overlaid with sand, driven thither by the fury of the north-west winde. If we believe their legends, it proceeded from the just judgement of God upon the owner of those grounds, who once (but when I know not) had made booty and put unto the sword some certain Spaniards, there shipwracked.

"Four leagues from hence, and to the south-west and by west, lyeth another of the smaller islands, called Serke, six miles in circuit at the least, which yet is two miles lesser in the whole compasse then that of Alderney; an isle not known at all by any name amongst the antients, and no marvail, for till the fifth of queen Elizabeth, or thereabouts, it was not peopled. But, then, it pleased her majesty to grant it for ever in fee farme to Hélier de Carteret, vulgarly called seigneur de St. Oen, a principall

<hr />

(1) Alderney is only sixteen leagues, S. by E., from Portland.

gentleman of the isle of Jarsey, and grandfather to Sir Philip de
Carteret, now living. By him it was divided into severall estates,
and leased out unto divers tenants, collected from the neighbour
islands; so that at this day it may contain some forty housholds,
whereas before it contained only a poor hermitage, together with
a little chappell appertaining to it, the rest of the ground serving
as a common unto those of Guernzey for the breeding of their
cattell. For strength it is beholding most to nature, who hath
walled it in a manner round with mighty rocks, there being but
one way or ascent unto it, and that with small forces easie to be
defended against the strongest power in Christendome—a passage
lately fortified by the farmers here, with a new platforme on the
top of it, and thereupon some four pieces of ordinance continually
mounted. In this island, as also in the other, there is a bailiff
and a minister, but both of them subordinate in matter of appeal
unto the courts and colloquies of Guernzey.

"Two leagues from Serke, directly westward, lyeth the chief
island of this government, by Antonine called Sarnia; by us and
the French known now by the name of Garnzey, or of Guernzey,
situate in the 49 degree of latitude, between the thirty-nine and
forty-six minutes of that degree, eight leagues or thereabouts from
the coast of Normandy, and well neer in an equall distance from
Alderney and Jarsey. The forme of it is much after the fashion
of the isle of Sicily, every side of the triangle being about nine
miles in length and twenty-eight in the whole compasse. In this
circuit are comprehended ten parishes, whereof the principall is
that of St. Peter's on the sea, as having a fair and safe peer[1] adjoyning to it for the benefit of their merchants, and being honoured
also with a market, and the Plaidery,[2] or court of justice. The
number of the inhabitants is reckoned neer about twenty thousand,[3]
out of which there may be raised some two thousand able men;
although their trained band consists only of twelve hundred, and
those, God knows, but poorly weaponed. The aire hereof is very
healthfull, as may be well seen in the long lives both of men and
women; and the earth said to be of the same nature with Crete
and Ireland, not apt to foster any venemous creature in it; out
of which general affirmation we may do well to except witches,
of whom the people here have strange reports; and if an ox or
horse perhaps miscarry, they presently impute it to witchcraft,
and the next old woman shall straight be hal'd to prison. The
ground itself, in the opinion of the natives, more rich and battle
then that of Jarsey; yet not so fruitfull in the harvest, because
the people addict themselves to merchandise especially, leaving

(1) The pier cannot have been safe, as the present north arm was not built until nearly
a century later.

(2) Although the seat of justice has been removed upwards of fifty years, the neighbourhood of the old court house is still called the Plaiderie, or Place of Pleading.

(3) Guernsey did not then contain half that number.

the care of husbandry unto their hindes. Yet bread they have sufficient for their use; enough of cattell both for themselves and for their ships; plenty of fish continually brought in from the neighbour seas; and a lake on the north-west part of it, neer unto the sea, of about a mile or more in compasse, exceeding well stored with carpes, the best that ever mortall eye beheld for tast and bignesse.

"Some other isles yet there be pertaining unto this government of Guernzey, but not many nor much famous. Two of them lie along betwixt it and Serke, viz. Arme and Jethow, whereof this last serveth only as a parke unto the governour, and hath in it a few fallow deer, and good plenty of conies. The other of them is well neer three miles in circuit, a solitary dwelling once of canons regular, and afterwards of some fryers of the order of St. Francis, but now only inhabited by pheasants, of which amongst the shrubs and bushes there is said to be no scarcity. The least of them, but yet of most note, is the little islet called Lehu, situate on the north side of the eastern corner,[1] and neer unto those scattered rockes, which are called Les Hanwaux, appertaining once unto the dean, but now unto the governour. Famous for a little oratory or chantery, there once erected and dedicated to the honour of the Virgin Mary, who by the people in those times was much sued to by the name of our lady of Lehu. A place long since demolished in the ruine of it, *sed jam periere ruinæ,* but now the ruines of it are scarce visible, there being almost nothing left of it but the steeple, which serveth only as a sea marke, and to which as any of that party sail along they strike their top-sail. *Tantum religio potuit suadere,* such a religious opinion have they harboured of the place, that though the saint be gone, the wals yet shall still be honoured.

"But, indeed, the principall honour and glory of this island, I mean of Guernzey, is the large capaciousnesse of the harbour,[2] and the flourishing beauty of the castle; I say the castle, as it may so be called by way of eminency, that in the Vale, and those poorer trifles all along the coasts, not any way deserving to be spoken of. Situate it is upon a little islet just opposite unto Pierport, or the town of St. Peter on the sea, to which and to the peere there it is a good assurance, and takes up the whole circuit of that islet whereupon it standeth. At the first, it was built upon the higher part of the ground only, broad at the one end and at the other, and bending in the fashion of an horne, whence it had the name of Cornet. By Sir Leonard Chamberlane, governor here in the time of queen Mary, and by Sir Thomas Leighton, his successour, in the reign of queen Elizabeth, it was improved to that majesty and beauty that now it hath, excellently

(1) The islet of Lihou is situate due west of Guernsey.

(2) The roadstead is evidently here meant.

fortified according to the moderne art of war, and furnished with almost an hundred piece of ordinance, whereof about sixty are of brasse. Add to this, that it is continually environed with the sea, unlesse sometimes at a dead low water, whereby there is so little possibility of making any approaches neer unto it, that one might justly think him mad that would attempt it. And certainly it is more then necessary that this place should be thus fortified, if not for the safety of the island, yet at the least for the assurance of the harbour,—an harbour able to contain the greatest navy that ever sailed upon the ocean, fenced from the fury of the winds by the isles of Guernzey, Jethow, Serke, and Arme, by which it is almost encompassed; and of so sure an anchorage, that though our ships lay there in the blustering end of March, yet it was noted that never any of them slipped an anchour. Other havens they have about the island, viz. Vazon, l'Ancresse, Fermines, and others; but these rather landing places to let in the enemy, then any way advantageous to the trade and riches of the people. A place not to be neglected in the defence of it, and full of danger to the English state and trafick, were it in the hands of any enemy.

" Upon the notable advantage of this harbour and the conveniency of the peer so neer unto it, which is also warranted with six peece of good canon from the town, it is no marvell if the people betake themselves so much unto the trade of merchandise. Nor do they trafick only in small boats between St. Malos and the islands, as those of Jarsey; but are masters of good stout barks, and venture unto all these neerer ports of Christendom. The principall commodity which they use to send abroad are the works and labours of the poorer sort, as wastcotes, stockins, and other manufactures made of wooll, wherein they are exceeding cunning; of which wooll to be transported to their island in a certain proportion they lately have obtained a licence of our princes. But there accreweth a further benefit unto this people from their harbour then their own trafick, which is the continuall concourse and resort of merchants thither, especially upon the noise or being of a war . . . . .

" And now at last, after a long passage and through many difficulties, we are anchored in the isle of Jarsey, known in the former ages and to Antonine the emperor by the name of Cesarea; an island situate in the 49 degree of latitude, between the eighteen and twenty-four minutes of that degree; distant five leagues only from the coast of Normandy, forty or thereabouts from the neerest parts of England, and six or seven to the south-east from that of Guernzey. The figure of it will hold proportion with that long kind of square which the geometricians call *oblongum*: the length of it from west to east, eleven miles; the breadth, six and upwards; the whole circuit, about thirty-three. The aire very healthy and little disposed unto diseases, unlesse it be unto a kinde of ague in the end of harvest, which they call *les settembers*. The soil sufficiently fertile in itself, but most curiously manured, and of a plentifull increase unto the barn; not only yeelding corne enough for the people of the island, but sometimes also an ample surplusage, which they barter at St. Malos with the Spanish merchants; the countrey generally swelling up in pretty hillocks, under which lie pleasant vallies, and those plentifully watered with dainty rils or riverets, in which watery commodity it hath questionlesse the precedency of Guernzey.

"Both islands consist very much of small inclosure, every man in each of them having somewhat to live on of his own; only the difference is, that here the mounds are made with ditches and banks of earth cast up, well fenced and planted with several sorts of apples, out of which they make a pleasing kinde of sider, which is their ordinary drink; whereas in Guernzey they are for the most part made of stones, about the height and fashion of a parapet, a matter of no small advantage in both places against the fury of an enemy, who in his marches cannot but be much annoyed with these incombrances, and shall be forced to pay deerly for every foot of ground which there he purchaseth.

"For other strengths, this island is in part beholding unto nature, and somewhat also unto art: to nature, which hath guarded it with rocks and shelves, and other shallow places very dangerous; but neither these nor those of art so serviceable and full of safety as they be in Guernzey. Besides the landing places, here are more and more accessible, as namely, the bay of St. Owen and the havens of St. Burlade, Boule, St. Katharines, with divers others. There is indeed one of them, and that the principall, sufficiently assured on the one side by a little block-house, which they call Mount St. Aubin, and on the other by a fair castle, called the fort Elizabeth. The harbour itself is of a good capacity, in figure like a semi-circle or a crescent, and by reason of the town adjoyning known by the name of the haven of St. Hilaries. On that side of it next the town, and in a little islet of itself, is situate the castle, environed with the sea at high water, but at an ebb easily accessible by land; but yet so naturally defended with sharpe rocks and craggy cliftes, that though the accesse unto it may be easie, yet the surprizall would be difficult. It was built not long since by our late queen of famous memory, at such times as the civill warres were hot in France about religion, and the king's forces drawn downwards towards Normandy: furnished with thirty pieces of ordinance and upwards, and now, upon the preparations of the French, there are some new works begun about it for the assurance of that well. On the east side, just opposite and in the view of the city of

Constantia, there is seated on an high and craggy rock a most strong castle, and called by an haughty name Mount Orgueil, of whose founder I could learn nothing, nor any other thing which might concern it in matter of antiquity, save that it was repaired and beautified by Henry V. It is for the most part the inhabitation of the governour, who is captain of it; stored with about some forty pieces of ordinance, and guarded by some five and twenty wardours: a place of good service for the safety of the island, if perhaps it may not be commanded or annoied by an hill adjoyning, which doth equall if not overtop it.

"This island, as before we noted, is some thirty-three miles in compasse, comprehending in it twelve parishes, whereof the principall is that of St. Hilaries, a town so called from an antient father of that name, and bishop of Poyctiers, in France, whose body they suppose to be interred in a little chappell neer unto the fort Elizabeth, and consecrated to his memory; but of his buriall here they have nothing further then tradition, and that unjustifiable, for St. Jerome telleth us that after his return from Phrygia, whereunto he had been confined, he dyed in his own city; and we learn in the Roman martyrologie, that his obit is there celebrated on the 13th of January. The chief name the which this town now hath is for the conveniency of the haven, the market there every Saturday, and that it is honoured with the cohu or sessions house for the whole island. The other villages lie scattered up and down, like those of Guernzey, and give habitation to a people very painfull and laborious; but, by reason of their continuall toyle and labour, not a little affected to a kinde of melancholy surlinesse incident to ploughmen: those of Guernzey, on the other side, by continuall converse with strangers in their own haven, and by travailing abroad, being much more sociable and generous. Add to this, that the people here are more poor, and therefore more destitute of humanity; the children here continually craving almes of every stranger, whereas in all Guernzey I did not see one begger.

"A principall reason of which poverty I suppose to be their exceeding populousnesse, there being reckoned in so small a quantity of ground neer upon thirty thousand living souls, a matter which gave us no small cause of admiration; and when my lord of Danby seemed to wonder how such a span of earth could contain such multitudes of people, I remember that Sir John Payton, the lieutenant-governor, made him this answer, viz. 'That the people married within themselves like conies in a burrow; and further, that for more then thirty years they never had been molested either with sword, pestilence, or famine.'

"A second reason of their poverty (add also of their numbers) may be the little liking they have to trafick,[1] whereby as they

(1) The Jerseymen have now a much greater "liking to traffic," and are a much more commercial people, than the Guernseymen.

might have advantage to improve themselves and employ their poor, so also might that service casually diminish their huge multitudes by the losse of some men, and diverting others from the thought of marriage.

"But the main cause, as I conceive it, is the tenure of their lands, which are equally to be divided amongst all the sons of every father, and those parcels also to be subdivided even *ad infinitum*. Hence is it, that in all the countries you shall hardly finde a field of corne of larger compasse then an ordinary garden, every one now having a little to himself, and that little made lesse to his posterity. This tenure our lawyers call by the name of *Gavel-kinde;* that is, as some of them expound it, *Give all-kinne,* because it is amongst them all to be divided, for thus the law speaking of the customes of Kent, in the 16 chap. *De prœrogativa Regis. Ibidem omnes hœredes masculi participabant hœreditatem eorum, & similiter fœminœ; sed fœminœ non participabunt cum viris:* a tenure which on the one side hath many priviledges, and on the other side as many inconveniences.

"For first, they which hold in this tenure are free from all customary services, exempt from wardship, at full age when they come to fifteen years, and, if they please, they may alienate their estates either by gift or sale, without the assent or knowledge of the lord; but which is most of all, in case the father be attaint of felony or murder, there is no escheat of it to the lord, the whole estate, after the king hath had *diem annum & vastum,* descending on the heires. *Et post annum & diem terrœ & tenementa reddentur, & revertentur proximo hœredi cui debuerant descendisse, si felonia facta non fuisset;* so the lawyers.

"On the other side, by this means their estates are infinitely distracted, their houses impoverished, the king's profits in his subsidies diminished, and no little disadvantage to the publick service in the finding of armours for the wars; whereupon as many gentlemen of Kent have altered, by especiall acts of parliament, the antient tenure of their lands, and reduced it unto knight's service, so is it wished by the better sort of this people, and intended by some of them, that their tenure may be also altered and brought into the same condition, a matter of no little profit and advantage to the king, and therefore without difficulty to be compassed.

"By this tenure are their estates all holden in every of the islands, except six only, which are held in capite, whereof four in Jarsey and two in Guernzey, and those called by the names of signeuries. The signeuries in Jarsey are, first, that of St. Oen, anciently belonging to the Carterets, and that of Rozel, bought lately of Mr. Dominick Perin by Sir Philip de Carteret, now living; thirdly, that of Trinity, descended upon Mr. Joshua de Carteret in the right of his mother, the heir generall of the

L'Emprieres; and, fourthly, that of St. Marie, vulgarly called Sammarez, descended from the Paines unto the family of the Du Maresque, who now enjoy it. Those of Guernzey, as before I said, are two only, viz. that of Anneville and that of De Sammarez, both which have passed by way of sale through divers hands, and now at last are even worne out almost to nothing: the present owners, Fashion and Androes, [Andros] both of them English in their parentage." [1]

CHAPTER XI.

CHARLES I.— 1625 to 1649. (Continued.)

In the year 1627, the insular charters were again confirmed, and a large quantity of provisions of different kinds was permitted to be imported from England, probably for the use of Castle Cornet, as Guernsey, with its population of about 8,000 souls, could not then require them, at least to any extent. A treaty of peace between France and England having been signed on the 14th of April, 1629, the islanders were relieved from all fear of invasion.

The following " reasons," which have no date or signature, were probably written in England, about the year 1630, after the earl of Danby's visit to the Anglo-Norman Islands. The Anglican discipline had been, we repeat, re-introduced into Jersey a few years before; the first Protestant dean, Bandinel, being sworn into office in April, 1620, when the presbytery, which had existed in that island for half a century, was abolished. But the Calvinistic form of worship, as used in the French church in London, was retained in Guernsey. These " reasons" are given, because, in the next chapter, it will be seen that Presbyterianism was one of the influences which prompted the people of Guernsey to side with the parliament during the civil war. They may, moreover, strike the reader as containing indubitable evidence that the French Protestants unwisely abused the toleration granted to them in the year 1590 by Henry IV., in the celebrated edict of Nantes;

(1) Doctor Heylin's Survey was addressed and dedicated to the Lord Marquesse of Dorchester. Heylin was eight days in Jersey, and nearly three weeks in Guernsey, viz. from March 14 to April 2, 1629.

and as affording some slight palliation to Louis XIV. for the revocation of that edict in 1685, the more so as only twenty years before, (1665,) when a war had broken out between England and France, and the latter power designed to get possession of these islands by surprise,[1] the lady of Marshal Turenne, a Protestant zealously attached to her religion, gave information of the project to the Rev. Daniel Brevint, of Jersey, who was afterwards prebendary of Durham and dean of Lincoln. In consequence of this private intelligence, Sir Thomas Morgan, a brave and experienced commander, was sent from England with the necessary force to counteract the design, which was abandoned as soon as the French court was aware that its intentions were no longer secret.

[o]

" Reasons given by my Lord of Danby against the alteration of the discipline of the Church, now settled in the isle of Guernsey.

" The uniformity of the islanders with those of the French church keeps such a correspondency and association between them, that those of the religion[2] esteem them a part of themselves.

" Whereupon they have continued intercourse and intelligence, giving the islanders notice of all practices and designs against them.

" And out of the same respect, they make alliances and marry their children with the islanders, sending into those islands great part of their stocks, joining in commerce and trade with the merchants there, and out of their mutual interest are much the more careful of their safety and welfare, even to enrich the place.

" In time of any general or particular danger of those of the religion in France, they fly over thither and live there secure till they may return, as lately many were received there with all manner of good usage, both by his majesty's special command unto me, and several letters from the lords of the council to the same effect.

" Besides, in former times, persons of great quality have retired themselves and families into that island, as the Prince of Condé[3] and his lady, who lived there more than a year; and divers of the chiefest and most famous ministers of the religion, who placed themselves there and followed their functions, which they would not have done, but that the discipline agreed with theirs practised in France. And it was always thought greater

(1) See Notice of General Lambert, in a subsequent chapter.

(2) Protestants appear thus to denominate the reformed religion in that age, as Lord Clarendon, alluding to it, says: "In the city of Nismes, which is one of the fairest in the province of Languedoc, and where those of the religion do most abound," &c.—*History of the Rebellion.*

(3) The leader of the Huguenots in France, born in 1530, and slain in 1569, at the battle of Jarnac. His memoirs of his own times were printed after his death.

wisdom rather to entertain in those islands French fugitives of quality and reputation, than to admit of them hither.

"Their strictness is such that no papists of any nation will dwell, or is permitted to inhabit, there, which the better secures them to the crown of England.

"Moreover, it may well be thought dangerous to give a general discontent unto the inhabitants, who are by ancient institution obliged, and particularly assigned, to guard the castle [Cornet] that commands the only harbour to succour and secure all those Norman islands, which must else necessarily be well manned with English soldiers, to his majesty's great charge; because it is not possible to send any seasonable aid out of England in defence of the place, upon all appearance of danger, standing so near to sudden attempts from France. And to trust the natives after we have given them this discontent, by altering the form of their discipline so affected by them, and long enjoyed, were not consonant to that rule of state whereby this crown hath held those islands these many years.

"These considerations, with divers others, were thought of such consequence in queen Elizabeth's days, that there being deans in both the islands, it was held fit to lay down that form of church government, and to suffer them to live under the same discipline with those of the religion of their neighbours.

"In the days of king James, of happy memory, when secretary Calvert much pressed to have had a dean in Guernsey, his majesty was then satisfied with these reasons, and would not suffer any alteration to be made.

"There can no prejudice come thereby to the present government of our church, against which no man is suffered to speak; and all the English come to the castle, [Cornet,] where service and sacraments are celebrated after the manner here.

"To these reasons I presume to add, that the time itself is no way meet for this alteration, in the respect of the troubles in Jersey, under the now dean, which will make those of Guernsey the more averse.

"Lastly, there being many old ministers in Guernsey, if they die, we shall not know from whence to supply them with others, for out of France they will not come to us, and here we can find few or none."

After the reformation, and during the time that the islands were under a presbytery, as well as subsequently, the natives who were designed for the ministry were sent to study among the Protestants in France, and particularly at the college of Saumur, a town situate on the Loire, between Tours and Nantes. But the advantage which the young students derived from being accustomed to preach fluently in French was thought to be counteracted by their acquiring opinions and principles not in accordance with those of the Church of England, and it became therefore desirable to provide other means of instruction. But the change was more easily proposed than executed, and the matter remained in abeyance until archbishop Laud came into power, when it so happened that an estate, comprising two gardens and seven houses in London, together with 123 acres of meadow and pasture land, and 205 acres of wood, in the county of Buckingham, escheated to the crown. The primate, who was beheaded on Tower Hill in 1644, anticipating the courtiers, prevailed on Charles I. to endow, out of this property, three fellowships at Oxford, one in each of the three colleges of Exeter, Jesus, and Pembroke, for the benefit of students from Jersey and Guernsey, born in the said islands, to be held by them alternately. In June, 1635, the endowment was carried into effect, the king reserving to himself the first presentation, and the alternation to proceed in this order, viz. that to whichsoever of the two islands the first presentation should fall, the other island should come in for the next two turns, and so on, in continued rotation for ever. After a suitable residence in the university, the fellows were required to return to their respective islands to serve God in the church, if becoming situations offered. But these fellowships have occasionally been enjoyed by laymen, although, as Falle very justly observes : "None, therefore, but they who, from the beginning, design to enter into holy orders, are regularly eligible into those places. 'Tis an abuse, and a contradiction to the will of the royal founder that any should enjoy them, who have in view and are in pursuit of other professions." Another abuse has arisen from the mode of nomination, which is vested in the dean and jurats — the former naming separately and the latter conjointly, thus forming as it were two distinct nominations. When the dean and jurats differ, which is often the case, a contest ensues, which generally ends by a compromise ; and although the clashing is of constant recurrence, the legal question has never yet been decided whether the dean possesses an equal vote with all the jurats. The natural presumption is that he does not, while, on the other hand, it is a matter of great indifference to the islanders generally, as the jurats usually combine to nominate the son or near relative of a jurat. It is singular that the bailiff has no vote. Notwithstanding that the three fellowships now produce nearly £500 a year — viz. Jesus, about £230 ; Exeter,

about £150; and Pembroke, above £100, all yielding more
during the high rents of the war—it is very doubtful whether
they have really benefitted these islands, as from their commencement they have been a source of intrigue, partiality,
and litigation, the deans being equally open to the charge of
favoring their own relations. How much to be regretted is
it that, where private interests are concerned, public men
should so often throw aside all the obligations of conscience
and duty.

While on this subject, we shall add that in the year 1678,
Dr. George Morley, bishop of Winchester, founded five
scholarships in Pembroke College, Oxford, three for natives
of Jersey and two for natives of Guernsey, under the title of
"Bishop Morley's Scholars." These scholarships are now
very trifling endowments, because the original grant of £10
a year each has remained stationary, notwithstanding the
decrease in the value of money. They are nominated in the
same manner as the fellowships, with the addition of the
bailiff's vote, and cannot be held longer than ten years. The
college deducts eighteen pence for each week of non-residence, which reduces the value to about £7 a year, with a set
of rooms worth £5 or £6 more. Bishop Morley was a
munificent prelate, and a great benefactor to his see of
Winchester: he died in 1684.

Having dissolved his third refractory parliament, as stated
in chapter IX., and, being now externally at peace, Charles
adopted strong measures to raise supplies, the most offensive
of which was the tax called ship-money, for the ostensible
purpose of providing a navy, which was indeed required, as
Algerine pirates had become bold enough to infest the Channel, and the Dutch were rapidly acquiring a maritime pre-
ponderance. He did not, however, act thus without legal
advice and precedent; but the times were altered, and expe-
dients, which had been complied with in the reign of Elizabeth, were now thought tyrannous. Hampden earned an
imperishable name by his resistance to this tax; and another
storm gathered when the king attempted to force upon the
Scotch the English Liturgy and Church Ceremonies, which
they abhorred. This occasioned the solemn league and covenant; and the covenanters, as they were called, took up
arms. Charles marched against them with an army, but
found it necessary to enter into a negociation, and the troops
were disbanded. In the spring of 1640, his affairs were so

disturbed that he called a parliament, which, taking into consideration the public grievances, was also hastily dissolved. The bearing of the covenanters compelled him to raise another army, which, meeting with a check near the Tyne, retreated into Yorkshire; and the king, with the advice of his council, summoned another parliament. This assembly, known by the name of "the long parliament," from its enduring thirteen years, met in November, 1640, and proved the ruin of the king, but the safeguard of the liberties of the people. It declared ship money illegal, abolished the arbitrary star chamber, and retrenched the royal prerogative. In the meantime, the Irish Roman Catholics, taking advantage of the confusion in England, committed dreadful outrages and massacres in Ireland,[1] which were afterwards frightfully revenged by Cromwell. They pretended to act under the king's authority, and to that effect shewed a commission with his name and seal, which was a forgery; but, nevertheless, it had a fatal effect in prejudicing the minds of the people against him. The public ferment continued, and was heightened by the king, who went to the House of Commons, where he took possession of the speaker's chair, and demanded the persons of five members whom he had accused of high treason. The house broke up in indignation at this breach of its privileges; the city militia was mustered for its protection; and the king retired to Hampton Court, whence he went northwards, and on the 22d of August,[2] 1642, erected the royal standard at Nottingham. The first battle was fought on the 23d of October following, at Edge Hill, in Warwickshire; but it was a drawn one. So ignorant were both armies of the art of war, that they were within six miles of each other before they were aware of their mutual approach, and, what is now scarcely credible, they had been ten days within twenty miles of each other without knowing it. Charles marched towards the capital; but, instead of entering it as he might have done, he proceeded to Oxford, where he established his head quarters, and thus enabled the parliament to recover from its alarm, and to concentrate its forces.

Sir Peter Osborne to Amias Andros, Seigneur of Sausmarez.

[Extract.]—" Instead of a courtesy I have done you an ill turn, for I see that I have put you into a troublesome office.

(1) From October, 1641, to September, 1643, lord Clarendon says that 40,000 Protestants perished in Ireland: other authors estimate the deaths much higher.

(2) It is singular that various authors assign different dates, from the 22d to the 25th of August, inclusive, to this memorable transaction; but Warburton proves the event to have occurred on the 22d.

P

But I meant you well, and in time we shall do well enough, and overcome all. If the times were settled that we might know whither to go for redress, these insolencies would be soon repressed. For the law is so clear that no colour of defence is left for them. I have asked advice. Mr. Bailiff can inform you what the lawyers' opinions are. It will not be long before I return, and I thought to have been in Guernsey by this. But some particular occasions stay me awhile.

" June 17, 1642."

We append the following curious narration of the form of homage done in person by one of the *seigneurs* of the island to the king, as extracted from the journal of Sir John Finett, when he was master of the royal ceremonies :

" One Monsieur de Sammares (father to Amias Andros, marshall of the ceremonies,) dying in Garnezey, where he had beene, by ancient descent, one of the seingneurs (as they are there styled) of that island. His sonne was to doe his homage for his teneure there, to the king, as duke of Normandy, and by the procurement of the earle marshall and lord chamberlaine earle of Pembroke, obtained the discharging of that duty to his majesty in person, which had beene done by his father before him to the governor in the island, though of ancient times wont to be done by his ancestors to the king himselfe (as it was now heere in England.)

" The manner of it being thus :

" His majesty, the 6th of June, 1637, (being a sermon day,) as he passed to chappell, tooke his seat in his chayre under the state in the presence chamber, the sword borne before him by the earle of Northumberland, and the great lords and officers of state attending; when the gentleman mentioned (wayting at the presence doore) was fetched thence, by and between the earle of Arundell, earle marshall of England, and the earle of Pembroke and Montgomery, lord chamberlaine of his majesties household, through a guard of the band of gentlemen pentioners; and after three reverences, laying downe his sword and cloake, all in forme, (as had beene before prescribed by garter king of arms, Sir John Burrowes,) he kneeled downe at the foot of his majesty, and with hands closed betweene his majesties hands, pronounced these words in French :

" ' Sire,—Je demeure vostre homme à vous porter foy et hommage contre tous.'

" To which the king read this answer, sett downe also in French :

" ' Nous vous acceptons, advouant tous vos legitimes droits et possessions, relevant en cette teneure de nous ; sauf pareillement à nous nos droits et régalitez.'

" This said, the seigneur de Sammares, (by which name he was thenceforth to be called,) quitting his ordinary appellation of Andros, receiving the honor of a kisse from his majesty, rose up, and, with most humble reverence reassuming his cloake and sword, departed."

The following document is given in the original orthography : it is without date, but it appears to be in the handwriting of Sir Peter Osborne, and was probably written about 1630, the account being brought down to that year :

The Annual Charge of the Government of Guernsey. [o]

	£	s.	d.
To the garrison, for a whole yeare	188	00	00
To the officers	017	06	08
For keeping of the chiefe pleas of the royall court and of the inferior courts	004	04	10
The ministers' wages	030	00	00
	£239	**11**	**06**

The annuall charge in execution of justice, for the diet of the prisoners that are criminalls, and execution of them when any are condemned, is uncertayne, coming sometime to more, sometime to less, but one yeare with an other may be valewed about................ 010 00 00

And for this last particular the governour hath the forfaicture of theyre land and goods, if they have any.

The revenue as it hath beene accounted for these severall yeare :

Anno.	£	s.	d.
1622	1204	10	05
1623	1218	05	11
1624	1162	06	05
1625	1239	01	10
1628	1160	15	02
1629	1187	08	10
1630	1189	19	05
	£8362	**08**	**00**

The medium thereof, one yeare with another	1194	12	06
Out of which deduct the annuall charge	0239	00	00
Remaynes for the medium	**£0955**	**12**	**06**

Particulars not reckoned :

The isle of Arme.—The isle of Gethow.—Duties upon salt.—Wardships.— Releifes.—Wracks.—The greate pond full of fayre carpes.

CHAPTER XII.

CHARLES I.—1625 to 1649. (Continued.)

THE commencement of the civil war, that deadly struggle between kingly despotism and limited monarchy, and the battle of Edge Hill, in October, 1642, in which Englishmen fought against Englishmen, were succinctly described in the last chapter; and we now proceed to narrate the events which occurred in Guernsey during that long and stirring epoch. It is not generally understood that Guernsey, and, through her example, Alderney and Sark, from the first espoused the cause of the parliament; while, astonishing as it must now seem, Castle Cornet was held for the king during the entire contest of nine years! Lord Clarendon, who ought to have known better, because he resided in Jersey above two years during this troublesome period, and there wrote some portion of his celebrated "History of the Rebellion," speaks of Guernsey in the following singularly confused and ungrammatical sentence: "The isles of Guernsey and Jersey, and Scilly,[1] were reduced; the former [first] presently after the battle of Worcester; and the other" (we suppose that he is alluding to Jersey) "after the king's return to Paris."[2] Moreover, as Charles II. did not reach the French capital until fully two months *after* the battle of Worcester, lord Clarendon is also at fault in stating that Guernsey, meaning Castle Cornet, surrendered before Jersey, as Elizabeth Castle, the last possession of the royalists in that island, was evacuated by them four days *before* the evacuation of Castle Cornet. In these erroneous relations, he has been followed by Hume[3] and other English historians, who have equally failed to mention the resolute and protracted defence of the castle; and therefore it shall be our endeavour

(1) The isles of Scilly surrendered to the parliament in June, 1651 — Jersey and Castle Cornet in December following.

(2) Oxford edition, A.D. 1707.

(3) "With equal ease were Jersey, Guernsey, Scilly, and the Isle of Man, brought under subjection to the republic; and the sea, which had been much infested by privateers from these islands, was rendered safe to English commerce. The countess of Derby defended the Isle of Man, and with great reluctance yielded to the necessity of surrendering to the enemy. This lady, a daughter of the illustrious house of Trimouille, in France, had, during the civil war, displayed a manly courage by her obstinate defence of Latham-House against the parliamentary forces; and she retained the glory of being the last person in the three kingdoms, and in all their dependent dominions, who submitted to the victorious Commonwealth."—*Hume.*

to repair this cruel injustice to Sir Peter Osborne and his successors, as their chivalrous fidelity to their sovereign, with that of their little garrison, deserves indeed to be recorded. Happily we can do so without any blush of humiliation for our parliamentarian ancestors, because the time has arrived when it is generally admitted that the people were fully justified in their resistance to the king; and when, after the lapse of above two centuries, the nation renders due homage to the patriotism and courage of Eliot, Pym, Hampden, and the other leaders who secured to it its present constitutional liberties.

As the sister island of Jersey was maintained for the king, by Sir George Carteret, during the whole war, with the exception of only eight months in 1643, when it was subject to republican rule, it may appear strange that Guernsey should have sided with the parliament. In Jersey, however, there was a strong party adverse to Charles, a party which numbered nearly one third of the native inhabitants, and was headed by Michael Lemprière, of Maufant, a jurat, of an ancient and affluent family, who was bailiff during the Commonwealth; the dean Bandinel, and his son, also a clergyman, and other gentlemen of note. The estates and seigneuries are much larger in that island than in Guernsey; and as the Carterets not only possessed many of them, but had long enjoyed the principal offices of dignity and emolument, their influence was all-powerful. Sir George Carteret undoubtedly deserves great credit for the able and effectual exercise of that influence in support of the king; but it is now a question whether he did not espouse the royal cause as much with a view to preserve the boundless and unconstitutional authority of the Carterets, as from a feeling of loyalty. He well knew that they would be shorne of that authority by the parliament. In Guernsey, no family possessed any thing like their influence, because in a small island, with almost equal laws of inheritance, a powerful family cannot long exist; and although there was also a party for the king, no one, like Captain Carteret, was influential enough to sway the inhabitants to either side. In consequence, as their religion was at that time the Presbyterian, they naturally inclined to the parliament, which was warmly supported in England by the Presbyterians; and, moreover, the arbitrary government of Sir Thomas Leighton[1] may have been remembered to the preju-

(1) "Sir Thomas Leighton,—governor of the isle of Guernsey, well versed in matters of state, as well as the army,—sent into France afterwards, in 1591, of special trust, to advise

dice of royalty. Besides, most of the parochial clergy were French Calvinists, who had sought an asylum in the island from the cruel persecutions of their own sovereign, and who doubtless inculcated republican principles. Added to these influences, was the more frequent intercourse with England and other countries,[1] as the commerce and navigation of Guernsey were then as superior to those of Jersey as the commerce and navigation of Jersey are now superior to those of Guernsey. In this last view we are borne out by Heylin, who visited these islands only twelve or thirteen years before the civil war, and who wrote very favorably of the inhabitants of Guernsey, notwithstanding that he was an Anglican divine, and that they were decided Presbyterians.

The king appears to have been well aware of the Presbyterian feeling in Guernsey, as, in a letter dated at Oxford, 9th of December, 1642, he said: "The great distractions and calamities which this our kingdom of England now suffers by the falsehood and disloyalty of some factious and ambitious spirits, who have dispersed untruths of our person and government, make me anxious to prevent the like in other parts of my dominions; and, understanding that this ill spirit, now brought upon our kingdom, begins to be hearkened to in our island of Guernsey, and chiefly upon a false report supposed to have been raised by one Monsieur des Granges, (Peter de Beauvoir,[2]) whom we have known under a better character; and hearing also that our present governor, the earl of Danby, is put out of charge, and the Lord Viscount Scudamore installed into that office, in consequence of which many of our subjects there begin to cast off their subjection and obedience, not only to him and his deputies, who are our royal lieutenants, but even to the law of the island. This information has moved us to write our letters, and direct them jointly to you, both our governor and deputy, and our bailiff and jurats, strictly requiring you, that you make known

the earl of Essex in his action there,—and author of 'Les Loix, Coustumes, et Usages de l'isle de Guernesey, différentes du Coustumier de Normandie, d'antienneté observées en la dite isle,' a fair copy whereof, in eight sheets folio, is in the Harleian Library."—*Note in the Life of Sir Walter Raleigh, vol.* 1, *p.* 92.

(1) The unfortunate earl of Strafford, who was executed in 1641, writing from Dublin, in 1639, to Lady Clare, his mother-in-law, and speaking of his two daughters, says: "Nan, I think, speaks French prettily .... The other also speaks it, but her maid being of Guernsey, the accent is not good."

(2) The name of this ancient Guernsey family, second to none in wealth and station, became extinct in 1810, on the death of Osmond de Beauvoir, Esq., when his large property was inherited by distant relatives. Another member of this family, the Rev. Peter de Beauvoir, of Downham Hall, Essex, whose ancestor, from Guernsey, appears to have settled in England in the seventeenth century, died in 1821, leaving real and personal property worth nearly three quarters of a million sterling; and being without a single heir male of his own name, this immense sum went to a friend or very distant relative, who took the name of De Beauvoir, and was afterwards created a baronet,

to our loyal subjects in that island, that, as we ever have had most especial care to preserve the Protestant profession of the Christian religion, with your ancient government, among you, your liberties, persons, and properties, as settled by the laws and customs of your island, so shall we ever preserve them from all innovations or alterations whatsoever, whereby you may enjoy the blessings of tranquillity under us, as heretofore under our predecessors." But, notwithstanding this explicit assurance of the falling monarch, that he would effect no change in the existing religion of the islanders, they knew that he was thus tolerant only from necessity, and they therefore felt the same distrust of him as did the people of England, a vast majority of whom considered his notions of prerogative to be so high and uncompromising, that they could place no faith in his protestations.—The liberty of conscience is the first element of liberty, and we conceive that any resistance to the slightest violation of that liberty is not only justifiable, but obligatory and meritorious.

The Presbyterian discipline, as we have stated, was introduced into Guernsey in the reign of queen Elizabeth, and the affection for it, in the time of Charles, will appear from the fact that when the military chaplain, who accompanied the reinforcements sent with Lord Danby, in 1629, applied to De La Place, then all-powerful among the parochial clergy, for leave to perform divine service in his church, De La Place assented only on the express condition that neither the Liturgy should be read, nor the communion administered. In consequence of these reservations, says Doctor Heylin, when any one wished to receive the sacrament, he was ferried over to Castle Cornet, where the ceremony was performed in the great hall. During the rebellion and the protectorate of Cromwell, Presbyterianism remained in full vigour in Guernsey; but after the restoration of Charles II., the act of conformity was enforced, and the office of dean revived. But these changes were not effected without much opposition, as the following extract from Le Roy's diary proves: "September 24, 1662.—There arrived in this island a company of 100 soldiers, with a major, captain, and officers, in consequence of some opposition to the act of uniformity, to which the clergy would not conform, and they resigned their benefices, viz. Mr. Le Marchant, at the Vale and St. Sampson; Mr. Perchard, at St. Pierre-du-Bois; Mr. Morehead, at St. Saviour; Mr. de la Marche, at the Câtel; and Mr. Herivell, at the Forest and Torteval. Mr. Peter de

Jersey, having left the town, was established by the dean at St. Andrew's, and Mr. Picot sent to Alderney, minister as before." The Guernseymen were too weak to stand by their religion as did the Scotch at the same time; and reluctantly and gradually they were induced to adopt the service and discipline of the Church of England, though, as recently as 1755, the dean was obliged to have recourse to the civil power to enforce the reading of the Litany; and to this day the surplice is not used in some of the parish churches.—We have travelled somewhat out of our subject to prove that the bias against Charles and for the parliament emanated rather from a religious than a political feeling, although the Norman institutions of the island are essentially democratic and republican, and generate feelings of independence, which quickly resent the slightest attempt at oppression.

It appears by a missive from Sir Peter Osborne to the inhabitants of Guernsey, dated Castle Cornet, December 10, 1644, that during the civil war many Anabaptists, Brownists, and other sectaries, came over to Guernsey "in troops to settle their residence" in the island; and he warned the inhabitants that "though you should drive them hence, as I understand you intend, besides the infection they will leave behind, you may be most assured they will speedily return like crows to your corn." We learn from Edwardes' Gangræna, part 3, 1646, that "there is one Collier, a great sectarie in the west of England, a mechanical fellow, a great dipper, who goes about Surrey and other counties preaching and dipping. He makes baptizing the children of the faithful not only to be vain, but evil and sinful; yea, the commission of baptizing children to come from the devil, or Anti-Christ, or both. . . . . As concerning that Collier whom you speak of in your book, I could give you a large relation, as how he was banished out of Guernsey (he and many more of his followers whom he had seduced) for their heresies and turbulent behaviour." That these sectarian preachers gained many converts in Guernsey is confirmed by Doctor Lightfoot, who, speaking of an assembly of divines at Westminster, in 1644, says :

"August 8.—Mr. Palmer reported a business sent us by my lord admiral, concerning a preacher in the isle of Guernsey, against which there were articles exhibited :

"1.—That he did abjure the church discipline there established.

"2.—Saying it was worse than s——y.

"3.—He refuseth to administer the sacrament of the Lord's Supper, and Baptism, &c.

"4.—That in 1655 there shall be a perfect reformation, and men shall do miracles, &c.

"The preacher himself, one Mr. Thomas Picot, is sent hither prisoner by my lord admiral.

"September 17.—The first thing done to-day was, that the deputy of the colloquy of Guernsey came in, and brought a petition against Picot, the Anabaptist preacher, mentioned before.

"September 19.—There was also mention of Picot, the Anabaptist; and a message was also sent that he might be stopped, and not go for Guernsey, as he was about." [1]

We believe that the Mr. Thomas Picot, just mentioned, was the Mr. Picot who, in 1662, was "sent to Alderney, minister as before." If so, he had probably become an Anglican.

When the civil war commenced, Sir Peter Osborne, knight, was deputy governor of Guernsey, having been so appointed above twenty years before by his wife's brother, the earl of Danby, who was still the governor. Sir Peter resided at Castle Cornet, where he is stated to have kept himself much aloof from the islanders, because, probably, he disliked their religious and political opinions; and his place of residence, inconvenient at all times for any social intercourse between him and the gentry, must have increased the estrangement. In 1642, about ninety of the inhabitants, many of whom so after warmly embraced the cause of the parliament, transmitted to that body numerous articles of complaint, in French, against Sir Peter Osborne, most of which bear the impress of the animosity which already existed between the two parties; the more so as, in a declaration made some years afterwards to Cromwell, the lieutenant-governor is said to have possessed great influence in the island; and in his letter to the earl of Warwick, dated June 22, 1644, it will be seen that he ascribes these complaints to a few mutinous spirits, and states that the people generally were in his favor. The complainants alleged that Guernsey, being a frontier, required a governor expert in military affairs, which Sir Peter was not; that Castle Cornet being a very important place, and enlarged in bastions with artillery, more than six-fold since the time that only fourteen soldiers were ordained for its garrison in time of peace, Sir Peter had not augmented the number of soldiers; that there was a great collection of arms in the

---

[1] Lightfoot's Works, vol. xiii. 8vo., 1824.

castle, sufficient, it was said, for 1,500 men, besides almost eighty pieces of cannon, with what design was not known, as there were only twelve or fourteen soldiers; that Sir Peter had employed the king's grants for fortifying the castle very uselessly, and, in place of erecting dwellings for the soldiers, he had made promenades and *maisons de plaisance*, so that there was not accommodation even for fourteen soldiers; and that he so hated the inhabitants generally, two or three excepted, that he had come several voyages (we suppose from England) without quitting the castle or entering the island, which, if he did enter, it was by lanes and bye-places.

About the same time, several of the persons who had signed the complaints against Sir Peter Osborne, addressed others to him against John de Quetteville, bailiff or chief magistrate of the island, who was accused of having used "most scandalous and opprobrious language against the high court of parliament," in these words:

1.—That now it was held up but by 'prentices.

2.—That they should be curried.

3.—That it was strange such fellows should undertake to rule.

4.—And to show the venom of his spleen against the Commonwealth, he said the wars of Ireland would last these twenty years.

5.—That he hath accused the parliament to take five pounds for every petition that they received, which money the said de Quetteville saith that they employ in a collation.

6.—That they are but two or three left in the parliament, and that it should be presently dissolved.

De Quetteville was moreover charged with violating his oath and taking bribes, an usurper; that he was a man of an obscene and wicked life; and as articles were to be exhibited to the parliament against him — as he held his office of bailiff, *durante bene placito*, during the governor's pleasure — Sir Peter was requested to suspend him, until the parliament might have leisure to vindicate its own honor. Sir Peter doubtless declined to comply with this request, as it probably emanated from that spirit of faction which, under the guise of principle and truth, too often lends itself to calumny and falsehood. The two principal authorities were royalists, and whether guilty or not, it was expedient to effect their removal. Mr. de Quetteville, being subsequently convicted of malignancy to the parliament, was ordered to be seized and sent to

England ; and he appears to have been long imprisoned in
Hurst Castle, so often seen by the islanders on their passages
to or from Southampton.   Here also Charles I. was confined
for three weeks in December, 1648 ; and "Hurst Castle is
now," says Eliot Warburton in his Memoirs of Prince Rupert,
"a gloomy ruin of what was once a gloomier fortress."
"Every thing here was dismal, the apartments, the air, and
the fort.   The stony walk was but a few paces broad, yet in
length two miles : the uninterrupted view of the opposite Isle
of Wight, and the ships of all dimensions daily under sail,
formed the solitary amusement of the king."—*Disraeli.*
When Charles was told that he was to be removed from
Carisbrooke Castle, he said : "To what place?"   "To the
castle."—The castle is no castle.   I am prepared for any
castle ; but tell me the name."   "Hurst Castle."—"Indeed !
you could not have named a worse ! "

Sir Peter Osborne does not appear to have come into open
collision with the civil authorities of Guernsey until some
months after the king had drawn the sword in England, as
both he and they evidently watched the course of events
there, and hesitated at striking the first blow.   Sir Peter
seems to have lived in a state of blockade and seclusion in
the castle towards the close of the year 1642 ; but it is not
until the beginning of 1643 that we discover any evidence of
a decided rupture between him and the jurats.   On the 2d
of February of that year,[1] three of the latter were informed
by one of the constables of St. Peter-Port, that Captain
(afterwards Sir George) Carteret was then in the castle with
Sir Peter Osborne, having arrived at noon from the west of
England with arms and ammunitions of war, which he intended to employ against the parliament, and that it was
believed he was going to France for a further supply.   When
the bailiff, de Quetteville, was told of the circumstance, he
treated it with much lukewarmness, simply observing, it is
said, that if application were made to him for an order to
arrest Carteret, he would grant it.   This answer greatly displeased the three magistrates, who thereupon ordered the
sheriff to repair to Castle Cornet, and to command Sir Peter
Osborne, in their name, to deliver up the person of Carteret,

(1) The civil and legal year in this century commenced on the 25th of March, and the
historical year on the 1st of January, as now ; so that, according to the former, this was
the 2d of February, 1642; but we shall throughout adopt the latter.   Berry and Duncan,
in their Histories of Guernsey, use both styles indiscriminately, which is a source of
much discrepancy and confusion ; for instance, Berry dates the execution of Charles I.
on the 30th of January, 1648 ; Duncan, on the 30th of January, 1649, and yet both are
correct.   Again, by the new style then in use in some parts of Europe, Charles was
beheaded on the 9th of February, 1649.

which demand was of course refused. On the 11th of March, 1643, the court assembled, there being present, John de Quetteville, jun., bailiff; John Bonamy, James Guille, Peter de Beauvoir, Josias Le Marchant, (du Houmet,) Thomas Carey, Michael de Sausmarez, John Brehaut, and John Carey, jurats.

The bailiff stated that he had convened them, in consequence of the receipt of an order from the lords of the parliament of England, tending to the good of his majesty's service, the interests of the parliament, and the conservation of the island; which order he was commanded to communicate to Sir Peter Osborne, knight, the lieutenant-governor, to the court, and to the States of the island : that he had already forwarded it to Sir Peter Osborne, but had had no satisfactory answer. On this point he requested the advice of the court. After the matter had been duly discussed, the sheriff was ordered to wait on the lieutenant-governor, and to desire him, in the name of the court, to have the States convened on the following Wednesday, to take the parliamentary order into consideration.

On the return of the sheriff, he reported that he had been to the castle to deliver the message of the court; that at the great gate he had met the portier and three soldiers, whom he desired to make known to his excellency the purport of his errand. The portier soon came back, and said that he did not believe that he (the sheriff) had been sent by the bailiff and jurats, no more than he had been on the former occasion, when he pretended to be authorized, and coined a falsehood. On this the sheriff shewed the portier his written instructions, and desired him again to announce his presence to his excellency. The portier demanded that they should be read to him, which the sheriff refused, having no such authority. The portier then went a second time, and, on his return, asked in what place, and before what jurats, the sheriff received his instructions. He answered, at the court house, and before all the jurats. On this the portier said, that if the court desired to make any communication to him, they must send one of their own members.

The same month, 22d March, the government of the bailiwick of Guernsey, including Alderney and Sark, was provisionally vested by the parliament in the twelve jurats of the Royal Court, as commissioners, of whom Peter de Beauvoir, des Granges, was appointed president; and they received instructions at the same time for their guidance, of which the following was the first article: "You shall seize upon the person of Sir Peter Osborne, knight, deputy-governor of the island of Guernsey, and upon the castle now in his custodie; and you shall send him in safe custodie to the parliament, to answere such offenses, contempts, and other misdemeanors, as shall be objected against him."

But this order was more easily given than executed, for when the jurats attempted to negociate with Sir Peter, he would listen to no terms of accommodation, and threatened to batter down the town, firing several cannon over and into it, to the great terror of the inhabitants, many of whom at once forsook their houses, and retired into the country. In a letter to the parliamentary committee in London, the commissioners explained the impossibility of complying with their instructions, observing that Sir Peter Osborne kept himself strong in the castle, daily adding to its fortifications; that he would not look at any order issued by the parliament, and they concluded thus: "We cannot expect any more messages from Sir Peter, who obstructs all shipping from entering into, or sailing out of, the harbour, even the fishing boats. Nor will he allow strangers to go to sea; and if this blockade continues, it will be the utter undoing of the inhabitants of this island." And yet this blockade continued nearly nine years, to the great prejudice and loss of the islanders, from which it may be inferred that the parliament refrained from seriously bombarding the castle, lest they should injure it, and vainly hoped that, by cutting off all supplies, they would starve the gallant little garrison into a surrender.

The siege of Castle Cornet commenced on or about the 4th of March, 1643, but throughout that year the islanders were left nearly defenceless, and without ships to protect their trade from the cannon of the castle, which received its scanty supplies from Cornwall, Jersey, and St. Malo. In consequence, it would appear that the Guernseymen began to falter in their allegiance to the parliament, as on the 2d of June we find the earl of Warwick, high admiral of England, thus reproaching them:

"Gentlemen,—I am something amazed, after so long a patience and such good evidences given of your affection for the maintenance of so just a cause;—I say, I am amazed you grow remiss and seem to neglect and draw back, as if it were an indifferent or dangerous thing to defend yourselves, your liberties, and your properties, and, what is of greater consequence, your religion and the purity thereof, against traitors,

papists, atheists, and the like, who have laboured, and daily
do labour, to enthral our liberties and religion, and to bring
us into slavery to themselves, and to the devil, by the darkness of errors and pernicious heresies wherewith they obfus-
cate the Christian air we live in. If this be the main design
with you, what a shame, what a reproach will it be for you
and your posterity, after having begun so well and shewed
the way to Jersey; and having suffered longer than they with
loss of your houses, and such boldness as has made you odious
to your enemies, if you now yield to those enemies, after so
many protestations and humble petitions made to the high
and honourable court of parliament; and after receiving such
favourable orders, provisions, supplies of all sorts, and expenses from them and this kingdom; will you now make
yourselves ridiculous to your enemies, and be guilty of so
foul an apostacy? Consider what I have done for you. Do
you think to subsist against the authority of parliament and
the power of this kingdom? Certainly, if you attempt this,
you will repent too late : but I hope better things from you.
I advise and exhort you, therefore, to unite yourselves one
with the other, and with my lieutenants in all your councils
and endeavours, and judge by what I have already done,
what I will continue to do, if God permits it, and when the
time of the year is favourable, unless you be wanting to yourselves. And so praying God to increase and strengthen your
valour and resolution, as may be for his glory and your good,
with my kind salutations to you all, I rest your very assured
friend."

This cutting letter produced the desired effect, and Guernsey stood firm to the parliament; but soon after, in October,
the islanders complained to Lord Warwick of their calamitous
state, and informed him that the castle had within a few days
received supplies from France and England ; a large shallop
having come from France, and two ships from England, one
of them commanded by Captain Bowden, who had by treachery obtained possession of the persons of three of the parliamentary commissioners, viz. the jurats Peter de Beauvoir,
Peter Carey, and James de Havilland. Bowden, then holding a parliamentary commission, had quitted the island fifteen
days before for Dartmouth. There he was induced by Prince
Maurice to attach himself to the king's party, and he bound
himself by an oath to return to Guernsey and seize the lieutenant-governor, Russell, and the parliamentary commissioners,
by a stratagem. Bowden doubtless relied on the lukewarm-

ness of many in St. Peter-Port towards the parliament, and on the general affection of the country people for the king. Anchoring to the south of the castle, he sent his boat on shore at Fermain Bay, with a letter to Russell and the commissioners, requesting them to come on board, as he was too ill to land, to consult with him on matters of great importance. On receipt of this letter, the lieutenant-governor sent a Captain Sippins[1] on board the George, of Dover,[2] (Bowden's ship,) to receive information from England, and to request Bowden to capture a vessel which had arrived from Weymouth, laden with stores for the castle, and which was then anchored near Brehon, out of the reach of the land batteries. Sippins was detained on board the George, and Bowden sent his boat again to Fermain Bay, with the same coxswain and crew, and with a second letter to the same purport as the first, adding, that he would capture the king's vessel off Brehon without difficulty. De Beauvoir, Carey, and de Havilland, happened to be dining with the lieutenant-governor; and, after consulting together, they agreed to go off to Bowden's vessel, which they did from Fermain Bay, in a boat belonging to the island. They were received with open arms by Bowden, who conducted them into his cabin, where they found two other naval commanders, Jones and Simpson, in the king's service. The three officers, who appear to have been originally merchant captains, strongly urged the jurats to co-operate with them, first by offers of advantage, and next by threats of punishment; but they remained true to their duty, and notwithstanding were treated with every courtesy and respect.

Bowden next determined to steer for Jersey, in the hope of entrapping the parliamentary authorities there by the same stratagem; but the lieutenant-governor of Guernsey had previously dispatched a boat to put them on their guard, and the George returned to Guernsey, anchoring under the cannon of Castle Cornet. Sir Peter Osborne insisted on the three prisoners being delivered into his hands, as their detention in the castle would facilitate the reduction of the island. Against this Bowden and Simpson strongly remonstrated, for the prisoners had promised them fifty jacobuses if they

(1) Captain Sippins appears to have joined Bowden in his design, as, according to Whitelock's Memorials, the former was condemned to death in October, 1644, by a parliamentary court martial, "for endeavouring to betray Guernsey;" but he was reprieved at the desire of Major-General Skippon, and ultimately pardoned.

(2) In the narrative in Duncan's History, this vessel is called the Bramble, which Bowden had probably previously commanded, and had exchanged for the George, at Dartmouth.

would land them at Dartmouth. Sir Peter, however, was determined; and on the following day sent his boat for the prisoners, who, between nine and ten at night, were brought to the eastern side of the castle, and compelled to ascend a ladder thirty-two feet high to reach the ramparts, where they were received by the porter, attended by forty armed men, and ten to twelve who were unarmed, among them the sons of Sir Peter Osborne, his chaplain, and Mr. Amias Andros, a Guernseyman, adhering to the king. They were then conveyed to an apartment in the underground dungeons, the lowest but one in the fortress, and for bedding were given three old pillows and three filthy coverlids. Indeed, their treatment appears to have been unnecessarily rigorous, and they complained particularly of their diet, which was, however, perhaps as good as that of the garrison. The rain water they drank was saturated with lime, owing to a cannon ball, fired from one of the land batteries, having knocked part of the wall into the cistern. But the second night after their incarceration, the porter left them twenty bundles of cotton to sleep upon; and a few days subsequently, Captain Darell, lieutenant to Sir Peter Osborne, and who was connected with the island, his wife being a De Beauvoir, lent them comfortable bedding and covering. Having resolved to attempt their escape, the three prisoners, on the 23d of November, commenced cutting a hole through the floor with their knives,[1] to enable them to obtain some old cotton match which was in the dungeon beneath; and on the 30th, after much labour, they succeeded in drawing up some with a tenter hook, which they luckily found in their room. This cotton they twisted into three ropes, one to descend from the window to the base of the dungeon, another to be used in dropping down the first wall, and the third to serve for their descent down the last wall. At length, on Sunday, the 3d of December, 1643, after a close confinement of forty-three days, they succeeded in effecting their escape, by dropping into the dungeon beneath, the door of which they opened by bending the cramp iron of the lock; and, descending the first and second walls of the castle, they ran along the western beach without being challenged. It was low water, and when they reached the passage to the town, a sentry saw them, and instantly gave the alarm, crying out: "Fire! fire! the prisoners are escaping." The cannon appear at first to have missed fire, but were at length discharged, some with

(1) The knife used by Mr. P. Carey on this occasion is still preserved by his descendants.

balls, others with grape shot, which fell around the fugitives without striking them. Having reached the steps of the south pier, they were recognized, and the news being carried to the church at the close of afternoon prayers, the whole congregation rushed out to congratulate them on their happy deliverance. A full narrative of their imprisonment has been preserved, which causes us the more to regret that another as copious of the defence of Castle Cornet was not written by one of the gallant cavaliers engaged in it, and treasured with similar religious care by his descendants. That narrative was written by Mr. Peter Carey, and we give the following extract, as it may serve to trace the place of imprisonment :

" From thence," (the ramparts which they ascended,) " we were taken into the hall, where Sir Peter saw us to his content, viewing us with Captain Darell from the balcony which looks into the hall. After this, we were lodged in one of. the deepest dungeons, under the lower ditch ; a place so subterranean and humid, that our hair became wet ; and from thence we were unable to see light, but through the keyhole. The next day, which was Thursday, at two o'clock in the afternoon, a great quantity of old wet match, which was in the chamber above, was removed into that which we occupied. That being done, we were all three placed in it. [the upper chamber.] In our new apartment, we had only a small window to look through, which had a north-east aspect."

The following order was evidently directed against the parliamentarians in Guernsey :

" Translation of the order of the queen regent of France,[1] prohibiting the traffic of the isles, without their governors' passes.

" It is ordained unto all captains and governors of the maritime towns of Picardy, Normandy, and Britany, to the lieutenants and other officers of the admiralty, unto whom it shall appertain, not to permit any of the inhabitants of the isles of Jersey and Guernsey, or otherwise called Gergé and Grencezé, to. transport any victuals or any other provisions and merchandizes out of this kingdom, unless they have a pass from Sir Philip Carteret and Sir Peter Osborne, governors of the said isles, his majesty commanding to the said captains and governors of the maritime towns to cause the said ordinance to be carefully executed. At Paris, the 20th of May, 1643."

The Earl of Warwick to the inhabitants of Guernsey.

" Gentlemen,—I received a letter from you lately, by which I do understand your good will and affection toward me, for which

(1) Anne of Austria, mother of Louis XIV.—*Pseudo Mastix*, p. 66.

Q

I heartily thank you, and take very kindly from you, and shall be ready at all times to endeavour to deserve your kind expressions therein.

"I have been informed that Captain George Carteret hath procured an order from the State of France, that none of the inhabitants of your island, nor that of Jersey, should have any trade or commerce in any part of France without they had Sir Peter Osborne or Sir Philip Carteret's hands to licence them thereunto, which licence hath made me the more careful to permit this corn and wool, being one hundred and four score quarters of wheat and rye, and forty todds of wool, to be transported unto you. I have granted some other warrants to others to do the like for your island and Jersey. I shall desire you, gentlemen, that this my favour may not any way be misused, by suffering either of the said governors, or any that do adhere unto them, to have any share of this corn or wool.

"The guns for battery, which you sent for, are in readiness, as I am informed, and I believe would have been with you long ere this, if it had not been for the contrary winds that have blown so long that way; and in expecting of them, and the gentlemen that come with them, I have forborne writing to you all this time.

"I am sorry to hear that Sir Peter Osborne is so resolutely bent against you; I doubt not but you and the rest of the good people there will make such resistance against him as may return to your praise and honor, for that you fight in the defence of God's cause, which is your religion and the liberty of your country.

"I desire to hear from you as often as you can, and in particular how you have disposed of all the corn and other necessaries which I have of late permitted to be brought to your island. And that you will let me understand wherein I may do you, or any of the inhabitants there, any favour or courtesy, which I shall be very ready as

"Your assured loving friend,

"On board the Prince Royal, at   "WARWICK.
  St. Helen's Point, June 27, 1643.

"To my very loving friends Mr. Le Grange, (de Beauvoir,) Mr. Havilland, Mr. Marchant, and the rest of the gentlemen and inhabitants of the island of Guernsey."

On the 16th of September, 1643, Sir Peter Osborne was summoned by the parliamentarian lieutenant-governor, Russell, and in his reply he said: "For the surrender of this castle without his majesty's pleasure, signified under his royal signature, or by the Right Honorable the Earl of Danby,— these islands being no ways subordinate to other jurisdiction, but to his majesty alone, as part of his most ancient patrimony enjoyed by those princes, his glorious predecessors, before that, by claim or conquest, they came to have interest in the crown of England,—no summons, by virtue of what power soever, hath command here, nor can make me deliver it up to any but to him by whom I am trusted and to whom I am sworn, that have never yet made oath but only to the king. And God, I hope, whose great name I have sworn by, will never so much forsake me but I shall keep that resolution (by yourself misnamed obstinacy) to maintain unto my sovereign that faith inviolate unto my last."—This reply is as remarkable for its truth and felicity as for its loyalty, the Anglo-Norman Islands being only subject to the sovereigns of England, as dukes of Normandy; and the people considering themselves rather as the conquerors than the conquered.

At this time—and in the year 1680, as appears by a sketch of the town and harbour of St. Peter-Port, discovered in the British Museum, in 1851,—only the south pier is depicted, with very little quay, and the houses were built principally on the sea side, to which they were confined, with the exception of the eastern part of Fountain street, and perhaps of Berthelot street: in consequence, nearly the whole of the town was exposed to the cannon of Castle Cornet, and in a series of resolutions passed by the parliament, in November, 1647, we find: "And whereas divers of the inhabitants have sustained great loss by Sir Peter Osborne's beating down their houses with shot from the castle, and have been at great charges in making fortifications against the said castle;" it was ordered that they be reimbursed out of the surplus of the island revenue. We doubt if the inhabitants of St. Peter-Port then numbered 3,000, as the entire population of Guernsey was about 8,000 souls. In the year 1615, there were only 347 houses in St. Peter-Port, and 1,008 houses in the country parishes, total 1,355 houses, which, at an average of five and a half persons per house, would give a population of 7,342 souls. Even as late as the year 1727, the population of the island was only 10,500, and of the town scarcely 4,500 souls. In 1745, the town was still confined to the sea side and its immediate vicinity, as in an engraved sketch of St. Peter-Port, taken in that year from Castle Cornet, by an engineer officer, afterwards General Bastide, there is scarcely a house to be seen to the westward of the present Cornet street, High street, Pollet, and Glatney; Fountain street not being visible from the castle.

In August, 1643, twenty-three "Articles for the Garrison in His Majesty's Castle Cornet" were issued by Sir Peter Osborne, of which the eight first were as follow :

"1.—Imprimis, that no soldier do reveal the secrets of the house or conceal any thing that may tend to the disservice of the king and prejudice of the castle, or may concern the safety and honour of the governor, upon pain to be shot to death.

"2.—Item, that none be found absent from the place of watch appointed to them, until they be relieved by order, or drawn off by command. And that all men, at a time of alarm, shall repair to the place appointed them to that end; neither that any be found sleeping upon their watch, upon pain of death.

"3.—Item, that none shall be found to put off their clothes in the night, so long as the water shall be passable on foot between the castle and the town, upon pain of severe punishment, at the governor's discretion.

"4.—Item, that all soldiers keep their arms clean and serviceable, having their "bandellers" [1] always filled with powder and bullets, and match ready, upon pain of imprisonment.

"5.—Item, that any soldier, by day or night, who shall discover any people either to come in boats at high water, or otherwise at low water, by the sight of fire, or by hearing them so coming, shall presently cry aloud Arm, Arm, Arm, and discharge their muskets withall, although undiscerned by them, upon pain of death.

"6.—Item, that no swearing, cursing, or any evil words tending to discord or quarrel, be so much as heard amongst the soldiers in the house, upon pain of paying to the poor man's box two pence at the first fault, and imprisonment, at the governor's discretion, if he persist.

"7.—Item, that none draw blood one of another, or strike within the house, upon pain of the loss of his or their right hand.

"8.—Item, that whosoever shall presume to make offer to strike his officer, shall lose his hand ; and whosoever shall strike his officer, shall be shot to death." [2]

In the king's letter, from Oxford, dated December 9, 1642, Viscount Scudamore is named as having been appointed governor of Guernsey by the parliament, in place of the earl of Danby, a royalist ; but Lord Scudamore does not appear to have exercised his appointment, and in June of the following year the government of both Jersey and Guernsey was

---

(1) Bandoleers—in French *bandoulières*—small wooden cases, each containing a charge of powder for a musket.

(2) It was only in 1718 that a clause in the mutiny bill enabled courts martial to punish mutiny and desertion with death, such crimes having been previously only cognizable as capital offences by the civil magistrate. But Macaulay states that when war was actually raging in the kingdom, a mutineer or deserter might be tried by a military tribunal, and executed by the provost-martial. No standing army existed in England before the civil war.

conferred on the earl of Warwick, who nominated Robert
Russell as his lieutenant in Guernsey, and Leonard Lydcott
as his lieutenant in Jersey. Lord Warwick himself at the
same time received a long string of parliamentary instructions
for his guidance, and was ordered to take care that the Protestant religion was maintained in the islands; to seize the
persons of Sir George Carteret and Sir Peter Osborne, with
their adherents, sending them in safe custody to England;
and strictly to prevent the islanders from assisting the rebels
in the county of Cornwall, or from holding any intercourse
with them. But, as we have already intimated, Lord Warwick
had not a sufficient force to comply with these instructions.

Soon after his arrival in Guernsey, in 1643, Russell levied
taxes upon the inhabitants for the public charges, and thereby
caused great discontent. But Russell was resolute, and sent
a company of soldiers into the parish of St. Saviour[1] to enforce
the collection, when two of the parishioners were killed and
one was wounded. Upon this the islanders rose in arms, and
compelled Russell to promise that he would in future be
guided in his proceedings by the States and Royal Court—
he also apologized for the occurrence at St. Saviour's, and
declared that he had ordered the soldiers not to fire unless
they were attacked. Sir Peter Osborne endeavoured to take
advantage of this outbreak; and, according to Mr. Peter
Carey, would in all probability have obtained possession of
the island, had not his letters providentially been intercepted
before they were circulated among the inhabitants. Jeremie,
in his unfinished history of Guernsey, mentions that the two
guns, used by the people in their insurrection against Russell,
were buried by them in the street opposite to his residence,
near the top of Fountain street: this seems improbable, as
cannon were then very scarce, and much wanted; but it is
certain that two guns were taken up on the spot mentioned
not many years since, and embedded in the front wall of a
house adjoining, where they may still be seen.

On the 9th of August, 1643, the Royal Court passed an
ordinance to the following effect: "Considering the extreme
necessity we stand in for means of defence against the invasion of our enemies, strict prohibition is given this day to all
the inhabitants in no way to leave the island, on the penalty
of having their goods seized and applied to the public use in
the manner the authorities may deem fit, excepting the deal-

(1) Jeremie (afterwards Sir John) states that the soldiers were sent to St. Saviour's to
enforce an order against Mr. Leonard Blondel; and he adds, that Mr. James Guille, of
St. George, commanded the islanders when they rose against Russell.

ers in stockings, who are in the habit of going to Paris for the conducting of their business in this place, such dealers having the liberty of leaving, but no others." Thus it is evident that the parliamentary islanders were very apprehensive of a royalist invasion, and moreover that the chief, if not the sole, trade of Guernsey consisted in the knitting and exportation of woollen frocks and stockings.

About the month of September, 1643, Sir Peter Osborne deputed Amias Andros, seigneur of Sausmarez, already mentioned, to Prince Maurice, then in the west of England, to represent the distressed state of Castle Cornet, and to urge the necessity of men and supplies being sent for its defence. Mr. Andros was also instructed to recommend to his highness that not less than 500 men should be sent for the reduction of Guernsey, and to secure it from a second revolt. He was also to ascertain " what account" the royalists in England made of the island " for a retreat in extremity, and press the likelihood of it." And although it was very proper to offer a general pardon, yet Sir Peter conceived " it meet for the king's honour not to be without limitations, and exceptions of some principal authors of these troubles, for the terror and example of future times." Accordingly, Mr. Andros was to deliver the names of those " that are to be excepted out of the pardon, to be brought to their trial. That is to say, all the commissioners ; Bonamy, the jurat ; John Bonamy, his son ; L'Espine, that was constable ; Picot, the minister ;[1] La Place, governor of Sark ; Girard, of the Câtel parish ; and John Le Febvre and Colas Guille, of St. Martin's."

When the Guernseymen, in March, 1643, declared openly for the parliament, and commenced the siege of Castle Cornet, their example was quickly followed in Jersey, where the people were at first either lukewarm for the king, or tamely permitted a minority of native parliamentarians to rule them. Leonard Lydcott, Lord Warwick's lieutenant, arrived in that island on the 29th of August following, duly empowered to exercise the functions of his office. Although Mont Orgueil and Elizabeth Castles were still vigorously defended for the king, Lydcott had been informed that the majority of the Jerseymen were secretly attached to the interests of the parliament, and he looked forward to a speedy termination of the contest. But he found the feelings of the people so generally in favor of Charles, that the arrival of Captain Carteret from St. Malo, on the 19th of November, with two

(1) Evidently the Anabaptist minister, already mentioned.

or three small vessels, was the signal for the precipitate departure, on the 21st, of Major Lydcott, Michael Lemprière, and a few others, for England, while many of less note escaped as they best could, in boats to Guernsey. From this critical period to the end of the war—no less than eight years—Carteret retained Jersey in its allegiance to the king. The Jerseymen, who had not eluded punishment by flight, felt the full weight of Carteret's vengeance, for he imprisoned all those who had been most active in favor of the parliament; and as soon as the commissioners appointed by Charles arrived in the island, he imposed upon them heavy fines, while the property of the fugitives was confiscated and sold. Little anticipating this sudden change of affairs, the parliament had previously given to Jersey and Guernsey each six pieces of artillery, viz. two demi-cannons and four culverins, all of brass, with fifty barrels of gunpowder and a proportionate supply of cannon balls, &c.; also 300 muskets, and drums, wheelbarrows, shovels, and spades; the whole taken from the Tower of London.

While Captain Carteret was at St. Malo, he caused two pataches[1] to be built there to carry supplies to the castles of Jersey and Guernsey. One of these pataches, being laden with provisions for Castle Cornet, was treacherously delivered by the crew, composed of three Englishmen, to the parliamentary authorities in Guernsey; and "thus," observes Chevalier, "was Captain Carteret ill served and betrayed at the commencement."

CHAPTER XIII.

CHARLES I.—1625 to 1649. (Continued.)

On the 7th of February, 1644, the earl of Marlborough[2] anchored near Castle Cornet, with four royalist ships of war, mounting each from thirty-four to sixteen guns, when Sir Peter Osborne and he agreed to summon Guernsey; but the islanders threatened to fire upon the boat which conveyed the letter. The earl, "seeing the obduracy of the people," fired

(1) Patache, a cutter, a pinnace, an armed tender.
(2) "The earl of Marlborough, who was general of the artillery."—*Clarendon.*

a broadside into the town, as a parting salute, and proceeded on with his vessels to St. Catherine's bay, in Jersey, where Captain Carteret and he determined on preparing a force to attack Guernsey; but, in consequence of long continued bad weather, and the lukewarmness of the Jerseymen, the enter-. prize was relinquished. The two commanders then went together to St. Malo, and the squadron was laden there with provisions and warlike stores for the king's use in England. On his arrival in Guernsey, the earl addressed the following letter to Sir Peter Osborne:

The Earl of Marleburgh to Sir Peter Osborne. [o]

"Sir,—I am sorry to hear of your distress by Captain Andrewes, (Andros,) and wish it were as much in my power as my will to relieve you. I am come out with much ado and with ordinary preparation, and was fain to give extraordinary promises to my men to come hither; other way had I none, they going out upon shares without any wages, and therefore grumbling at every minute's stay. I promised them some supply from you, of such things as I wanted, namely, powder and swords. The truth is, I extremely want both, having but twenty-four barrels for thirty guns: if your store be reasonable of both, I hope you will spare some of either. If you can, it will encourage my men to stay somewhat the longer, and secure my riding here the better from the parliament ships,[1] which, with the first wind, I believe, will seek me out.

"I have sent this afternoon to Colonel Carteret, at Jersey, to see what he can do towards the getting of men, and expect an answer to-morrow.

"I have sent you as much as my boats can well stow, and mean to-morrow to send you what else I can spare without the overthrow of my voyage; but I hope it may prove enough till more come. If Colonel Carteret can do nothing, I could wish Captain Andrewes might be despeeded for the court for the gaining of a peremptory order for the sending over some men.

"Sir, I beseech you to believe me one that will be ready to serve you to my uttermost; and if I shall not answer your long expectation of mine arrival, impute it not to any unwillingness in me, but to the necessity which does enforce me to comply with those men that, as long as I have occasion to use them, must be humoured beyond reason in many things.

"We had a dispute to-day concerning summoning the island— the difference was that Captain Andrewes propounded the exemption of some particulars out of the pardon: my commission goes

(1) "March, 1644.—The parliament ships chased the earl of Marlborough; but he, though two to one, did not think fit to fight with them."—*Whitelock's Memorials.*

for all. But, I beseech your mind in writing by this bearer, and let me know in what farther service you will please to command,

"Your humble servant,

"The Road, this Monday night." "MARLEBURGH.

When the siege of Castle Cornet had endured about a year, Russell and his captains, on the 22d of February, 1644, communicated to Sir Peter Osborne [1] an ordinance of the parliament, that whosoever should declare for it before the 1st of March ensuing, should have their lands, goods, &c., which were sequestered, wholly restored to them, otherwise they should be sold for the parliament's use. They further offered him liberty safely to depart with all his officers and soldiers, and all things appertaining to him or to them, for England or elsewhere, adding: "This denied, believe us you will never obtain the like." The gallant cavalier returned an unqualified defiance to this proposal, in the following letter:

Sir Peter Osborne to the Parliamentary Officers in Guernsey. [o]

"Gentlemen,—Far be from me that mean condition to forfeit my reputation to save an estate that, were it much more than it is not, would be of too light consideration to come in balance with my fidelity, and in a cause so honorable, where there is no shame in becoming poor, or hazard in meeting death. Example is not always a safe rule; precedents must be clear of all exceptions. The reasons I gave in my former answer for my resolution, which I must still hold, will acquit me of being seduced. Whosoever hath the confidence to do it, I can make no such declaration. For I have weighed my grounds and know them true, and shall let you know that nothing else, by the grace of God, can work change in me. When I fall so low as to desire a treaty, it shall be in your power to refuse me what you please; but, in the mean time, I entreat you to consider against whom you serve and for whom—against your lawful and gracious king, and for these islanders, faithless and unthankful. Let those who lead you, mislead you not still, and make you return without merit and too late, which I wish you may seasonably prevent, promising you my best assistance to make your peace for you all to your most advantage, as your true-hearted countryman and your loving friend. "P. O.

"Castle Cornet, February 23, 1643-[4.]"

The estate was that of Chicksands priory, in Bedfordshire, which had belonged to his family since the year 1576; and although Sir Peter wrote to the king, in October following,

(1) "Sir Peter Osborne and Sir Thomas Fanshawe for deserting the parliament, whereof they were members, were discharged of their offices, which were conferred upon others."—*Whitelock's Memorials.*

that it was sequestered ; yet it is gratifying to know that it is still in the possession of his lineal descendant, Sir George Osborn,[1] the sixth baronet.　Sir Peter Osborne also firmly, but civilly, rejected the advances of Lord Warwick, who, with many arguments and promises, endeavoured in this year to prevail upon him to surrender the castle.　It appears by a certificate of the royal court that, in March, 1644, a house in St. Peter-Port was in ruins, and "damnified " to the extent of £230 sterling, " by the shooting and battering which Sir Peter Osborne, knight, has, for a long continuance of time, made against it with his ordnance from the castle." This house belonged chiefly to Mr. Peter Carey, one of the jurats who had escaped from the castle, and who was very active in the parliamentary cause.

In the early years of the war, though the parliamentarians were by far the stronger party in Guernsey, yet the royalists were formidable, and plotted several secret conspiracies.　One of these was detected by the imprudence of an individual, who, when intoxicated, disclosed the designs of Sir Peter Osborne, and revealed the names of his principal partizans, the ringleaders of whom were seized and sent to England. In February, 1644, we find Mr. Peter Carey, in a letter to the earl of Warwick, begging that some vessels might be sent to quell " a mutiny on the part of the common people against the lieutenant-governor and those well affected towards the parliament, which mutiny still continued, and, unless speedily repressed, threatened to terminate in very serious consequences." This mutiny was soon after quelled ; but our impression is, that, although a great majority of the upper classes and townspeople were parliamentarians, the peasantry generally were attached to the king, and hence arose the unseemly treatment which the latter experienced at the hands of the soldiery, by whom they complained to Cromwell " they had been kept under like slaves, affronted, threatened, beaten."　In this impression we are confirmed by Sir Peter Osborne's " missive," in 1644, already quoted, in which he said, that " forasmuch as divers seditious persons, inhabitants of the town of St. Peter-Port, stirred up with ambition and covetousness, have sought, by troubling the peace and quiet of the inhabitants of this island of Guernsey, to make themselves great," &c., " whose wicked proceedings the generality of the country, as I am well assured, have in detesta-

(1) It does not appear why Sir Peter Osborne's descendants dropped the final e, which was formerly considered as a mark of aristocracy, and Sir Peter always used it.

tion." The family of de Sausmarez, whose ancient fief at St. Martin's had passed by marriage into the hands of Amias Andros, was probably for the king, as its name is not mixed up in any of the occurrences in Guernsey at this period, and some of its members are said to have contributed towards the necessities of Charles II., when he visited Jersey. The seigneur of the Fief *le Comte* at that time, Peter Priaulx,[1] was also a royalist; and James Le Marchant, jurat, is stated by a descendant to have remained in Guernsey that he might promote the royal cause, which he did so openly, that proceedings were instituted against him by order of the long parliament, and it was with difficulty that he effected a precipitate retreat into Normandy.

In May, 1644, Captain Carteret and his relative, the seigneur of St. Ouen, resolved on trying to surprise the island of Sark, then in possession of the Guernseymen, who, during a greater part of the war, maintained it with a garrison of a captain and thirty soldiers. The Carterets were the more anxious to succeed, because the revenues of Sark chiefly belonged to one of them, Monsieur de St. Ouen, and they accordingly equipped four shallops, which left Jersey well armed and manned; Captain Lane having two of the shallops with the chief command, and Captain Chamberlain the other two. The weather not being favorable, the two commanders lost sight of each other on the passage, and did not arrive together, or at the appointed rendezvous. Captain Lane, who had the best boats and seventy-two men, found himself near the land, and, on being hailed by a sentinel on shore, answered that he came from Guernsey; but the guard, which consisted of only three men, fired two muskets, and then took to flight, while Lane, supposing that Captain Chamberlain had gone back, stood off and returned to Jersey.

In the mean time, Chamberlain had reached another part of Sark, and landing with his men, they seized and disarmed first the guard, and next the captain in his bed, neither making any resistance, as they were surprised. During the same night, they also made prisoners of nearly all the men on the island, and possessed themselves of the cannon, powder, &c., expecting that Captain Lane would arrive in the morning to their support. But when daylight came without any succour, the courage of Captain Chamberlain and his men fell as that of the Sark people rose, on the latter ascertaining the small

(1) The Fief *le Comte* remained in the Priaulx family from 1630 to 1732, and in the latter year it came into the possession of the Le Marchants, as related in Chapter III.

number of their assailants, who were only thirty-two men,
and that there were no vessels near to assist them.   The
men being still prisoners, the women set fire to the beacon,
as a signal to Guernsey; but as the light was not seen, the
Sarkese fired two or three cannon, when the Guernseymen,
supposing that something wrong had occurred, dispatched
promptly an armed force, by which Chamberlain and his men
were captured without resistance, and brought with their two
boats to Guernsey. This easy capture and recapture of Sark,
the account of which we have condensed from Chevalier, does
not accord with Sir Walter Raleigh's opinion of its strength,.
as narrated *ante :* the island is doubtless, however, naturally
almost inaccessible. We suspect that Chamberlain did not
get possession of Little Sark, where probably the beacon and
cannon were fired; and it is singular that he did not escape
in his boats when he saw the Guernseymen coming. One
would almost infer from this that " he had caught a Tartar "
instead of a Sarkman, and that the latter would not let him
go. Captain Chamberlain, on his arrival in Guernsey, was
strictly confined in irons, and Sir George Carteret afterwards
tried hard to exchange him for other prisoners, especially for
an English captain imprisoned in Castle Cornet; but the
Guernseymen would on no account release him, inasmuch as
he was a brave man, and was well acquainted with their
island, having been reared among them. He escaped once,
and was going to Castle Cornet when he was recaptured,
and chained in a cell in the town. At length, after a close
confinement of nearly two years and a quarter, a boat came
from Cherbourg expressly to aid in his escape; and, with the
assistance of the Norman crew, he made a hole in the wall
and filed off his fetters when he got to the boat, and was taken
to Cherbourg.[1]

The 4th of July, two Guernsey pataches arrived in the
neigbourhood of Jersey, one carrying five cannon and the
other only one : they captured five boats, of which four were
coming from Chausey with vraic; these four they took to
Guernsey, and released the other.

Sir Peter Osborne to King Charles I. [o]

" May it please your most sacred majesty.

" I should not assume the boldness to offer this into your royal

---

[1] " November 24, 1653.—Letters that the French picharoons do much mischief on the
coast near Jersey: that Captain Chamberlain, an old pyrate, sent a letter to Colonel
Hean, (Haines,) governor of Jersey, that if the Jerseymen would not contribute towards
his maintenance, he swore by the heavens that he would throw as many of them as he
did meet with into the bottom of the sea."—*Whitelock's Memorials.*

hands, had I well known unto whom else to address myself. For this long siege hath kept me, if not wholly ignorant, at least in much uncertainty of English affairs, and who, under your majesty, have the managing of business now. I therefore most humbly desire this presumption may by your majesty be thus graciously excused; the extremities, which I forsee we may shortly be reduced unto, pressing me to give the advertisement in time, lest peradventure the remedy may come too late. For unless we can be furnished with a speedy and complete supply, during this season that makes the road unsafe for ships to lie upon us, hereafter, when they are like to return, it will grow very difficult, if not impossible, to relieve this castle. Whilst I had the ability and credit to subsist, I strove upon my own strength against all necessities, the best I could. But now, unable longer to struggle with them, become too many for me, I am forced to crave assistance that I may not fail your majesty's expectation for want of succour, which I shall never do for want of truth. Of the importance of this place there will need no other argument than the pursuit of those who, with such expense and diligence, seek to be masters of it. In whose resistance how much I have already endured these twenty months, I willingly am silent in, lest I might seem to complain myself of that which I esteem my honour, and value as a happiness, if, by any sufferings of mine, I may have done your majesty the least service. For my estate in England, it remains either sequestered or disposed away from me; which I mention with no other end but only to make it appear in what need I stand of further help, having nothing left to serve your majesty with, but with my life, which likewise upon all occasions I shall, by the grace of God, be most ready to lay down, to approve myself to the last,

" Your majesty's most humble
and most loyal subject,

" From your majesty's fort,   .   " PETER OSBORNE.
Castle Cornet, October 3, 1644."

Sir Peter Osborne—writes Chevalier in 1644—who had taken refuge in Castle Cornet, seeing that his victuals were consuming, sent his wife to St. Malo to forward him provisions from thence. In this way, much of his money was spent, and he wrote on the subject to the king, who caused supplies to be sent to him, and also requested Captain Carteret to take care that the place was not neglected, his majesty engaging to repay him. In consequence, Captain Carteret sent from time to time a boat with provisions, as they were required. He sent his galley also to carry provisions, and to convoy the other boats that went with her. She went twice, and the second time had a warm engagement with the

Guerseymen, who attempted to intercept her, because a soldier had escaped from the castle into Guernsey, where he
gave information that the garrison was in great want of
provisions, and that, unless some quickly arrived, it must
necessarily surrender.   A strong force was in consequence
placed round the castle, so that the boats dared not approach
it.   Upon this, Captain Carteret sent his galley the second
time, under Captain Bowden, to carry provisions and to
convoy two other boats similarly laden.   Three days before
they left Jersey, it was known in Guernsey that these boats
were coming, and the Guernseymen surrounded the castle
with shallops and boats, to prevent its receiving the expected
supplies.   The galley and one of the boats left Jersey as the
night was setting in, and the other boat some time after.   As
the galley came near the castle, she was perceived by a
patache, which fired a gun as a signal, and she and all her
companions gave chase.   The galley was surrounded on
all sides, and a patache came within pistol shot: from her
Captain Bowden received a musket ball, which cut the *ban-
dier* attached to his shoulder.   Being thus pressed, he ordered
the helmsman to keep away, so as to bring his gun to bear on
the patache ; the gun was loaded with grape shot, and it was
discharged across a shallop, when great cries were heard from
the enemy, who at once saved themselves, and did not again
come to the attack.   There were thirty-six men, gallant and
well armed, in the galley, and they plied their assailants so
well with musketry, that the latter dared not approach too
near ; and in spite of the Guernseymen, they reached the
castle safe and sound, without one killed or wounded.   The
boat also arrived two hours after, having encountered or seen
nothing.   Nevertheless, the two vessels were not out of danger, as the Guernseymen fired upon them from three batteries
on shore, and there was only one little creek at the back of
the castle, where the guns could not reach them, and into
which the two vessels were taken.   The galley, after her
escape, and while near the castle, received a shot which did
some damage, but without injuring any person on board: in
the combat she received shots through her sails.

The second boat, which left Jersey after the galley, could
not arrive that night, the tide failing her ; she was pursued
by a patache, and compelled to run for the coast of Normandy, where she remained two or three days on account of
contrary winds.   The people in the castle thought she was
taken, and were astonished one night to hear the men call to

them, they having experienced no obstacle on their passage, excepting from a shallop at the back of the castle, and which the boat passed before she was perceived. On the shallop's crew seeing her, they weighed anchor and pursued, but it was too late.

The lieutenant, Russell, finding that the castle was victualled, and that there was no remedy, withdrew most of the vessels which blockaded the castle, and even some paliamentary ships went to England, for they were at great charges in Guernsey, thinking to starve the garrison. Two parliamentary ships and some frigates had passed the summer in protecting the island, and in the endeavour to prevent supplies being conveyed into the castle. But all in vain—the Guernsey people were extremely harassed, (*fatigué*) their lieutenant, Russell, having made them great promises, and said that in a short time the castle must surrender if no supplies reached it: the better to encourage them, he promised them a sum of money if they captured the galley, and prevented the conveyance of provisions to the garrison. In this fond hope they had spent a great deal of money in providing vessels and men, the least of the latter having eight sols a night. If they had succeeded, the garrison would have been in imminent danger, as they were at their last biscuit when the galley and boats arrived. However, the castle was victualled towards the end of August, and as winter and bad weather were then approaching, the beleaguering vessels could no longer remain in safety. In consequence, all through the following winter, boats went with the supplies to the castle, and returned as freely, the only vessel which remained at anchor on the bank having at last gone to England and left the passage free.

A.D. 1645.—In February, an armed patache, with thirteen men belonging to Guernsey, was surprised and taken by two boats sent with soldiers for the purpose from Castle Cornet. This patache anchored constantly at night near the castle, with the design of capturing the boats which brought it provisions from Jersey; and being seen one evening at anchor under Herm, the soldiers went in search of her. When the boy, who alone was keeping watch, perceived them, he called the captain, and he came on deck armed; but it was too late, as the boats were close alongside. The captain, Joseph, who was an Englishman, and two of his men, fought bravely, wounding two or three of their assailants; but the captain being badly wounded in the arm by a pistol shot, the patache was captured and sent to Jersey.

On the night of the 3d of May, a boat left Jersey, laden with provisions for Castle Cornet, and was becalmed all that night and the next morning, when, being seen from Guernsey, she was captured by a patache sent for the purpose, and brought into that island. The Guernseymen thereupon made great rejoicings, and fired the guns of the town, batteries, and vessels, merely for the capture of a small boat of six tons and five men, without any means of defence. This was their first exploit, and their first prize of the boats which carried provisions to Castle Cornet.

The 10th of May, Captain Carteret sent his galley with provisions for Castle Cornet, fearing to send boats, on account of the one which had been captured, as just related. The galley was well manned and armed, because there were two frigates at Guernsey, sent by the parliament, and three shallops, all to prevent supplies being conveyed into Castle Cornet. As soon as the galley appeared, these vessels got under sail, and pursued her as a pack of dogs pursue a hare. The shallops came first, thinking to take the galley, and both sides fought bravely, but neither could the shallops take the galley nor prevent her reaching the castle, where she discharged her provisions in safety. She received three or four shots in her sails, and Captain Bowden was slightly burnt in the face by the bursting of a swivel; but there were none killed or wounded. When she was near the castle, a cannon shot from the shore cut one of her oars in two, upon which Sir Peter Osborne fired seven cannon shot into the town. The next night, the galley left the castle for Jersey, and was pursued by the frigates, which could do nothing, as the galley both rowed and sailed, and went twice as fast as they. Sir P. Osborne prepared ten cannon to fire upon the town, in case the inhabitants fired upon the galley as she left the castle.

In the years 1644 and 1645, Sir Peter Osborne complained of the conduct of Colonel Carteret,[1] who at first refused to send him any, or at least sufficient, supplies from Jersey for the use of Castle Cornet, without some assurance and bond for the payment; and these complaints seem to have been the better founded, because the colonel had already commenced those privateering expeditions against the parliamentary merchant shipping, by which he became individually so much enriched; thus we learn from Chevalier's Chronicle

(1) The naval captain became a militia colonel during the civil war.

· that, in one cruise, in 1644, Captain Bowden, who had acted so traitorous a part in Guernsey, brought him some 5,000 livres from the sale of his prizes. This backwardness on the part of Colonel Carteret was, however, flatly denied by the king's three commissioners in Jersey, and Chevalier certainly does not confirm it; but they probably were not aware of a bond being sought from Sir Peter Osborne, who, on the other hand, did not perhaps sufficiently bear in mind that the colonel had not a very large insular revenue wherewith to maintain his own garrisons; that the boats with provisions ran great risk of being captured; and, above all, that Jersey did not then produce food enough for its own inhabitants, as during the civil war it was occasionally in a state of famine. Thus it is likely that the altercations were not without faults on both sides; for if Colonel Carteret were avaricious and calculating, Sir Peter was rendered, by his difficulties and the constant wants of his soldiers, somewhat exacting and querulous. A bitter feud was the result, as will be shewn by the next two letters.

Colonel Carteret to Sir Richard Browne. [o]

" Havinge lately received and sent away an express to courtt, with letters I then received from my Lord Jermin, adresed unto the Lord Digby, for hasteninge of such orders and directions from his majestie as are requisitt for the preservation of this place in the king's obedience, I hope your honor will pardon me if I now presume to represent unto you the just apprehension I have of the loss of the castle of Guernzey, which hath hythertoe bene preserved, (through God's blessinge upon my indeavors,) as may be collected by the probabillities heare insueinge.

"Whilste my lady Osborne remained at St. Mallo, she would never be ruled in what concerned the releife of that castle, which made her undertakings in that behalfe to prosper accordingly, they miscarryinge for the most parte. And when she left St. Mallowes to goe to the Par: by whome she is since restoored to her fformer livelyhood, it was not without suspicion that she went to harken to overture for the delivery of the castle into ther hands, sundry messengers havinge past toe and fro betweene her and Sir Peter aboute that time.

" Since which noethinge I have done for the succor of that place hath bine aceptable unto him, one while findinge fault with the provisions I send thethier, though the choyce of all I could gett; another while refusinge those very things for which I was spoken to in his name, as beere, pease, &c.; and sometimes againe seekinge to tye me to imposibillities with fearefull threats, he breakes up all the vessells I send thethier, and keepes my men to

R

serve him against there wills in steed of his owne, which he turnes upon my hand after much suffring, without money or cloathes: he conceales all his designes and intentions from me, and gives out when he sends any body one way that they are to goe another; wittness his eldest sonne who, being thought to be at Paris, is now discovered to be in England, where if he succeed noe better in his designe then he did the last time. (*sic.*) And now very lately that a small boate laden by him with provisions went at noune day directly to a parliament shipp on purpose to be, as it was, taken. A kinswoman of Sir Peter's (Mrs. Davers[1]) came hither from him three dayes agone; I was at the watter side when she landed, to send a boate with provisions for the castle of Guernzey, which she was not willinge should be let goe, (though the wind and tyde served,) till she had spoken with Capt. Darell: she brought me nether letter nor message from Sir Peter, nor tould me any part of her minde, ether for stay heare or departure hence, which made me send soune after to Capt. Darell, desireinge him the wind was faire, that the shallop she came in might be returned that night with some of the provisions I have heare in readines for that castle, which she had noe souner notice of but she imbarqed her selfe secretly therein for St. Mallo, notwithstandinge there was another vessell bound for that place at the same time, wherein she might have bine well acomidated. I have since heard that she intends thence to take passage for London. I thought it my duety to remonstrate to your honor how necessarrye it is for his majesti's service, that a provisionall order or commission be speedily direct to Captain Nathaniel Darell, lieutenant-governor of Guernzey, or to Mr. Andrewes,[2] native of the isle, (who hath bine in the castle ever since the rebellion,) athorisinge them to use all possible meanes for the continuance of that place, which is of excedinge great importance, in regard of the strength and amunition in it, and the situation of it, in his majesti's obedience. Or els for avoydinge of umbrage, which I alsoe submit to your lord's best judgment, that the said order be conditionall in case it should please God to take away the said Sir Peter, that then Captain Darell should be intrusted with that place, and Mr. Andrewes, if the said Captain Darell should deceass, and nether of them to leave the castle, but upon very urgent occassions: whensoever you shall be pleased to honor me with your commands, the spedier conveance will be by the way of Paris.[3]

"To Sir Richard Browne.
          "Jersey, ffeb. 4th, 1645."

(1) The name of Danvers appears then to have been sometimes spelt Davers.

(2) Amias Andros, seigneur of Sausmarez Manor, St. Martin's, Guernsey.

(3) When Mr. Peter Carey was deputed to proceed to London, in 1645, the bailiff and jurats, in their instructions to him, said: "Being in London, pray write to us by way of France, and all other opportunities."

A copy of this letter was sent to Sir Peter Osborne, probably without the knowledge or sanction of its author, and the following is his indignant and triumphant refutation of the cruel charges and inuendos brought against a gallant man, whose lengthened trials and sufferings ought, one would think, to have shielded him from such imputations; although it is due to Sir George Carteret to add that his suspicions may have been aroused by the circumstance of Lady Osborne being a sister of Sir John Danvers, a very influential parliamentarian.

Sir Peter Osborne to (apparently) Sir Richard Browne. [o]

At my wive's coming to St. Malo, she was wholy guided by Sir G. Carteret, whome she reposed much confidence in, and so desired to oblige, that she receaved him and his whole family into her house, till by reason of her losses sustayned, and the indirect dealing she found, she was forced to seeke other assistance; being in great danger to have been soone exhausted, and disabled to give us the succour which yet she still got the meanes to do. For when her mony was spent, and plate sold, she made no difficultie among strangers to ingage her self in a great debt for the reliefe of this castle, till her credit at last fayled. In these straights and our great extremity, she had made a shift to send us to Jersey a seasonable releife, where, committed to Sir George's trust, it lay two months, wasted and untransferred, whilst we were starving, brought from little to less, and in conclusion for bread to foure biscuits a man for a weeke; the rest of our provisions growing no less scant. That where as our number was purted into three devisions, we coulde alowe those only at night a little porrage, that were then to have the watch, the other two devisions going without any thing, supperless to bed. Nor could my son Charles, sent thether of purpose to hasten away those her provisions, (none other expected of Sir George,) procure them to be sent before his returne to St. Malo, desirous to have comforted his mother with that good newes. So that, oppressed with trouble and greife, she fell into a desperate sicknes, that her self, and all those about her, feared her life. Of the condition that we were now in, the parliament had from our enemies continuall advertisement, and imployde vessell after vessell, with all the shalupes the islanders could set forth, to ly day and night upon us; and they conceaving it a good tyme agayn to summon me, I receaved a letter to that purpose from the Earle of Warwicke in very fayre termes, to which I lykewise made a civill answere; but such as was agreeable with my allegeance to his majestie, and that left him hopeles of working any change in me. I have both the letters to produce when tyme serves. In the middst of these distractions and miseries, my wife sick, without monye, frends, and hope, was driven to embarke her self for England in a ship of Holland, so far from recovery that she scarce felt the amendment of two dayes. Nor could that, her compelled departure, give suspicion of her going to harken to overtures for the surrender of the castle, which she with so much carefulnes, and expense to the uttermost of her meanes and credit, had so long preserved, and who had one of her sonns then at Bristoll in his majestie's service, and at her going away furnished an other[1] whome she also sent to the king: her eldest being left with me to runn the hassard of my fortunes, lyke to be ill enough. And though I doubt not but this will appeare sufficient to wash off these maliciously invented slanders, my holding of this castle ever synce, now ten months more, with much sufferings and extremity, and without all taynt of disloyaltie, that must needes in this tyme have broken out, will shewe the clearness of my innocence, and the impudence of his untruthes.

"Synce her going, Sir George hath from tyme to tyme deluded us with promises, and hassarded us with delayes, that I have beene constrayned to send boate upon boate, till left at last with out any to send upon what urgent necessity so ever, so that we wanted men to performe the duty of our watches. And when at length he thought good to supply us with something, it was allwayse with a scarce hand, nothing answerable to our wantes, and the charge of our men that lay there, and who could not be dispatched, that the reckonings he makes in his bills ariseth to a strange proportion in extraordinaries to his majestie's great charge; and yet this his castle unsupplyed, we having for this twelve month, and above, never been able to allow our souldiers more than one biscuit a day, and a little porrage for theyre supper; and have beene forced for necessity to use the stuff sent us to make candles, and to dress our boates, to frye the poore John,[2] limpits, and herbes we eate in the best mess, though we concealed it from them, and made no complaint, and lived thus about three weekes. The provisions, though ill conditioned, carry the prices of the best, yet have I not returned back any thing he sent, how faultie so ever. In so much that, secure of that, he hath not forborne to put againe upon us the sortes we have found fault with, to vent and issue out to us, what he could not else tell how to dispose of. Nether Captain Darell nor any of myne admitted to see the choosing, putting up, number or weight, of what he sent, he still saying 'cross me not,' 'let me alone,' and much displeased if any sought to looke into it.

"His next charge is, that with fearfull threates I seeke to tye

(1) In a marginal note, and in a different hand, is the following: "This sonn hath synce beene killed in this service." His christian name was Charles.

(2) "Poor John," hake dried and salted, a corruption of *pauvre gens*, the French term for this fish.—(*Malone.*) When Jersey surrendered to Blake, sixty thousand weight of "Poor John" were among the stores of Elizabeth Castle.

him to impossibilityes. I knowe not what may appeare fearfull to his apprehension. If he can make proofe of these menaces by my letters, I shall be much ashamed of my folly. Nor do I seeke impossibilityes, credibly informed that many in Jersey have contributed greate sumes for this place by expres name, though theyre service and merit be concealed, and the monye converted to other uses.[1]

"For the breaking up of all the vessells he sends, he knowes very well, from the report and viewe of his owne people, that I never brake up any, but such as his and our enimies shot, and foule wether made utterly unserviceable. But if it had been so as he would have had it understood, as done of purpose, our extreme want of firing would have excused me, and cast the blame upon him, that was continually informed of it, and yet nether sent us coale, having plenty, nor that which was our owne, which he kept a twelve moneth, while we were forced to pull downe all that was combustible about our houses, to burne our timber, which I now much want, and at last, which I was exceedingly troubled to be reduced to do, to burne our carriages for our ordnance that were good and serviceable, and our tables and our dores, &c.

"Whereas he sayth I turn my soldiers upon him with out monye or cloathes. I part with none willingly, but onely such as, with our hard diet being sick, would have perished heere. And I hope it will be held reasonable that I should ridd myself of the sick for our owne safety and theyre preservation. And lykewise, that all places under his majestie's obedience should be open to receave and releive such as have undergone so much, of whose miserable sufferings I need no witness, having the testimony of my accuser, though he sayth it to make me seeme the more uncharitable to send them without monye and cloathes, that have nether to give them, and he well knowes it.

"The rest of his charges are so frivolous that I conceave them unworthy the replying to, as namely, that in so great necessity I should be consenting to the yeelding up of a good shalupe to our enimies (and no small boate as is pretended) laden with provisions that we stood in neede of, and were hardly gotten for us by my sonne, together with the loss of a surgeon that had already receaved a good part of his wages, and whome I much solicited for, to quit me of one that I had then in mistrust, loosing with all divers provisions bespoken for my owne particular and health, which I can not looke to have procured for me agayne. A subtilty that my greate wantes, emptie purse, and distance from frends, was not lyke to permit to come into my imagination,

---

(1) In a letter dated Jersey, 6th June, 1645, Thomas Wright, who was one of the defenders of Castle Cornet, informed Sir Peter Osborne that a private collection of upwards of £300 had been made in Jersey for Castle Cornet, but that Sir George Carteret said the money was given for the relief of his castles.

much less to suffer me to put in execution that curious invention. As lykewise, that my sonn, charged to be guilty of all this, is not sent to Paris as was thought, and where he might be safe, but by Sir George's industry discovered to be in England, the same whome I now send with this my answere.

"I come now to the last charge, being againe brought to the uttermost, not above a fortnight's bread left, and dispayring of supply from Sir George, I was driven to seeke all shifts to help my self, and therefore sent Mrs. Davers, my wives kinswoman, (that hath had her part in all our miseries,) to St. Malo, with my apparell and some trunks of linnen left in her custody, to make tryall what she could instantly get in provisions for us upon that pawne or sale; which busines she so well despatched that in sixe days she came back to Jersey, in theyre viewe chased by a pyrate, and narrowly escaping by running with great danger among the rocks. Yet, at her comming away the next day, she could not obtayne of Sir George one seaman of his (for she requested no more) the better to man her boate, in case she met with the same man of warr or any other, whereof those parts were then full. The hassard of the loss of our provisions and the best shalupe I had, and which then brought me the greatest supply that I ever receaved in such a boate, nothing at all moving him, nor the danger and entreaty of a gentlewoman, nor the aspersions cast upon her (convinced of untruthe by her returne) working any remorce in him by way of compensation, to have afforded her that small courtesye.

"In conclusion, touching the advice he gives for the prevention of my supposed disloyaltie, so certayne in his apprehension, that one of those courses must instantly be taken. If his majestie can be brought to have my truth in jealously, after so long proofe of it, I silently, with all obedience, submit to his royall pleasure, though most loath, I must confes, to have such a marke of his disfavour and diffidence stampt upon me, as may in sorrowe close up those dayes which, in these long and many sufferings, I had the comfort and hope should have found a joyfull end in his service.

"Castle Cornet, June the 18th, 1645."

The two preceding letters are literal transcripts of the copy, with the exception that the abbreviated words, customary at that period, are mostly given at length, for the greater convenience of the unpractised reader in old writing. To the simple and touching appeal of Sir Peter Osborne, it is due to him to add here, in further refutation of these unmerited suspicions against his honor and fidelity, that on the 31st of December, 1645, Lord Warwick again wrote to him from London, exhorting the injured cavalier to deliver up the castle, and assuring him that, if he would submit to the parliament, he should have all his estate and exchequer place restored. Moreover, his letters to Amias Andros, which are given in the "Chronicles of Castle Cornet," and which were written in all the confidence of friendship, without a suspicion of the charges which Sir George Carteret a few months subsequently brought against him, assuredly afford no proof that the author was plotting with his wife for the surrender of the castle, although the difficulty he experienced in obtaining provisions and fuel, the latter especially,—the king being unable to assist him on account of his own necessities,—and the constant straits to which he was reduced, would almost have excused his going over to the parliament. Prince Charles appears to have been so convinced of his innocence, that he wrote to Sir George Carteret from Liscard, on the 21st of July, 1645—we are particular throughout in giving dates, as they are the landmarks of history[1]—and commanded him to send supplies to Sir Peter Osborne, that were intended for Castle Cornet, immediately away, and to give him all other assistance.

The following copy of a letter was found among the papers of Sir Peter Osborne; it is not addressed, but, from the context, it was evidently intended for Sir George Carteret, and dispatched before any knowledge of the complaints which the latter had made against him to Sir Richard Browne. We give the exact orthography of the copy :

"Sr—The feare you have least the king's service heere may suffer by delayes, is a consideration so noble, that I am now most glad to see you take it into your thoughts; it being a mischeeffe and disease we have beene long, long sick of, and miserably have languished under. But for the better advancement of his ma-tis (majesty's) service, I wish yt, (that) to have made this supplye more compleate, you had not omitted in some proportion the most necessarye, which is biscuit; for, with that and water, we could yet make a shift to live : not to intertayne our lyves for any self respects, but onely in this important place to serve the king with them, which els, the greate and tedious sufferings in all manner of extremityes that we have, these two yeares and above, endured, would long agoe have made us weary of, and willing to have changed for a quiet grave. Whether it be our fortunes to be kept in a still consuming state, or to be preserved and saved, we shall soone fynde by the course taken for us hereafter, and in the meane tyme will not fayle with patience and fidelity to performe our dutyes.

"May ye 11, 1645.   "Your hble. servant.

(1) In consulting Clarendon and later historians, we have experienced great difficulty in ascertaining the periods of the occurrences which they narrate.

"I heare you have taken a vessell fraught with good Newcastle coale, whereof we stand in great want, and desire we may be furnished out of that, and not from the remaynder of your former prise, good for little or nothing.

"I referr the reward of these men to yo-self, (yourself,) who best know how to please them: and having no experience, am loath to make ignorantly bargaynes for the king."

We learn by a letter from Mr. Peter Carey, dated June 2, 1645, "that there are eight or ten ships and pataches, which do not move out of the road, being appointed for the conservation of the isle."

In September, 1645, the ship Hollandia, of Flushing, of 400 tons, and carrying thirty soldiers, (? seamen,) anchored in Guernsey roadstead, windbound from St. Malo. The master declared on oath, before the lieutenant-governor, that he had been informed at St. Malo, that the royalist fleet, with partly French soldiers on board, was to attack the island, which, when reduced, would afford shelter to the king's vessels; and that, as it was midway between the coasts of England and Britany, the royal cruisers could avail themselves of every opportunity to put to sea, and capture the parliamentary ships, having a safe retreat in case of pursuit. This intelligence created great consternation among the authorities, who immediately deputed Mr. Peter Carey, the gentleman already named as having escaped from Castle Cornet, to proceed to London for assistance to repel the meditated attack, and to urge the necessity of a squadron being sent to Guernsey. Mr. Carey sailed with a contrary wind on board a galley, commanded by Captain Williams, and arrived at Portsmouth on September 19th: quickly mounting on horseback, the usual mode of travelling in those days, he reached London late in the evening of the 20th. There, Lord Warwick presented him and his credentials to the committee of parliament, which resolved to reappoint his lordship governor of Guernsey and Jersey for another year, and gave Mr. Carey a letter to the vice-admiral, desiring him to furnish the vessels prayed for, to the extent of his ability. They further empowered Mr. Carey to require two hundred muskets for the use of the island. Lord Warwick also gave him a letter to the vice-admiral, in which, after mentioning that the house of peers had ordered that a convenient number of ships should be sent for the defence of Guernsey, he said, "to which I shall only add my particular desire that, from time to time, as there shall be occasion, you will be careful of that island, the preservation of it in the parliament's power being of much importance. For this end, you will spare as many vessels as you can conveniently, until the danger lately represented be over, for which end I also hope to obtain an order for land soldiers to be sent from hence." Mr. Carey, who displayed great activity and zeal in the important trust confided to him, left the metropolis on the 2d of October, by water, for Gravesend. Landing there, he instantly started for Canterbury, where he slept that night. Early on the following morning, he reached Dover Castle, where the vice-admiral was residing, and to whom he presented his letters. After a conference of two hours, that officer granted him seven vessels, which number Mr. Carey declared to be indispensable; and, at once embarking on board the Nicodemus, she sailed for Portsmouth to procure a pilot, which port she reached on the 4th of October. The squadron set sail that evening, and arrived in Guernsey on the following day. With the exception of the Nicodemus, the squadron remained until the plan of the royalist marine was rendered abortive, and the danger had passed away; but it is surprising that, if the crews were not strong enough to attack Castle Cornet, they did not succeed in intercepting every supply for the garrison, as, according to Chevalier, (*post*,) the vessels remained at anchor on the bank part of the winter. In the instructions given to Mr. Peter Carey for his guidance in the mission just mentioned, was the following:

"3.—That the parliament will order what shall be done of the prisoners, who are detained in the belfrey,[1] either to be sent over, or released upon caution. Many of them have not been the chief actors in the late commotions,[2] as you may represent, but are silly fellows, who have great families."

In the following letter, Sir Peter Osborne gives a simple but touching description of the disinterested sufferings and losses which he and his family had sustained in the royal cause, and he very justly complains of the underhand treatment which he had experienced in Jersey, where his soldiers appear to have been instigated to bring frivolous accusations against him:

Sir Peter Osborne to the King's Commissioners, in Jersey. [o]

"Noble gentlemen and my honorable friends,—I present you with my most humble thanks for what you have already so

(1) The belfrey was a building in the churchyard of St. Peter-Port, commonly called "Le Cimetière des Sœurs."

(2) We are not quite sure whether the date of Mr. Peter Carey's letter, February, 1644, was not that of the civil year, in which case the mutiny mentioned *ante* in this chapter occurred in 1645.

carefully done, and what you have been pleased to oblige yourselves unto for the time hereafter.   But I beseech you withal to
consider whether our state can abide long delays, that it may not
languish under promises; your solicitation of the lieutenant-
governor [1] is principally needful, this place depending immediately upon his hand and will, who hath it in his power to expose
us to hazard, whereby, if misfortune befall us, some blame may
peradventure happen to reflect upon those that may not be faulty
neither.

" Whereas you have been let to understand that we are furnished with arms more than our present use requires: the truth
is, that our store is no more than enough, having no smith able
to mend those out of order by casualty and negligence of soldiers,
nor stocks to supply when any are broken.   I beseech you therefore, to excuse me if I dare not part with any, after so much
waste, and whilst we remain in the same dangers, though most
desirous to gratify you therein.   I could spare you a few corse-
lets,[2] if they may do you service.   But our pikes are too heavy,
useful upon a wall only, and we may have employment for them
ourselves.

" And now, I pray, give me leave, for his majesty's service to
add a few lines, briefly to complain myself without your offence.
The power and extent of your commission, understood amiss by
my company, hath produced dangerous effects, and heartened
them in much disobedience, possessed with an opinion that you
have authority to command and dispose of this place and of me
as you please.   By your letter, you seem to assume no such
thing, but to disclaim it rather.   I therefore entreat you to
declare yourselves in that particular to my soldiers there, that
unawares you be not made authors of the mischief that may
chance unhappily to come upon it.

" Disorders in some of them are grown so high, that guilt
being never void of fear, they have framed articles against me,
addressed, as I hear, to Sir George and to you, seeking their
security in the change of their commander, which, as I am likewise informed, are both received and sent for England.   My
case is most hard, after such trials and proofs of my truth without
all exception, that soldiers and mean persons should be heard
against me, their governor, of whom should be always presumed
the best, and my accusers at least with sharpness rebuked, if not
punished.   It is not possible, in so long and hard extremities of a
three years' siege to keep men without discontents, that have
neither clothes, nor pay, nor meat,—drinking water, with but one
meal a day, I wanting the means to give them better allowance,
and to make our provisions last the longer to hold out this place.

(1) Sir George Carteret.
(2) Corselet, a light armour for the fore part of the body.

What they have endured I could not remedy, and have myself suffered the same as well as they, and beyond the example of any, during these troubles, which I may the rather presume to say that I speak it of miseries, and to justify my actions only, and not to boast. But I have the innocence that gives me peace and assurance to despise these calumnies, having my confidence placed in God and the king, whom I have truly served, without consideration of the ruin of myself, my wife, my children, and my house; of whose princely goodness I nothing doubt, nor he (I hope) of my integrity. Put upon the necessity of his majesty's service to write you this, let it not, I beseech you, incense nor bring me into displeasure with you, or diminish your care of the safe transportation of our relief, nor retard your dispatch. The specious pretences of my accusers, to continue in their duty to the king, are not to be believed, disproved with their demeanour toward me, by his majesty's authority, in command over them. For my desires, be pleased to permit that I refer you to Captain Darell, who hath order to wait on you with my important requests; and accept, I pray, the tender of my humble service, most respectfully presented by

"Your most humble servant,

"Castle Cornet, Oct. 30, 1645."   "P. O.

This being the season, says Chevalier, in which Captain Carteret was accustomed to victual Castle Cornet, he did his best to supply it, and sent three boats laden with provisions, which left together. The smallest arrived safely, another was driven away to the coast of Normandy, and the third returned to Jersey on account of contrary winds, and because her provisions were wet. Afterwards, boats were prevented for a long time going to the castle by contrary winds, and in the meanwhile there arrived at Guernsey seven parliamentary frigates, which anchored on the bank near the castle, and remained there part of the winter, coming occasionally near Jersey, and convoying the vessels which traded between England and St. Malo; they were also intended to protect Guernsey, and to prevent Castle Cornet being victualled.

On the 22d of December, Captain Carteret sent two boats laden with provisions for Castle Cornet, which left on Monday evening, and arrived safely the same night: having discharged their provisions, they started before daylight to return to Jersey, and arrived the following day, bringing with them Monsieur de Saumares (Andros) and one of the castle gunners, who came to see their wives, who were in Jersey. Two days before the departure of these boats, Captain Carteret had sent another boat, of the burden of nine or ten tons, laden with supplies for the said castle, viz. coal, cider, wine, bread, pork, pease, turkeys and other poultry, codfish, mutton, and the meat of a fat ox, which Captain Carteret sent to Sir Peter and the garrison, for their Christmas. When this boat was near the castle, her crew perceived seven or eight vessels at anchor also near it, and supposing them to be parliamentary vessels, they were seized with fright and returned to Jersey; but these vessels were Dutch, homeward-bound, which had there anchored to await a fair wind. The boat, however, arrived safely at the castle on the 3d of January, and discharged her lading in open day, before the castle gate. Sir Peter walked outside near those who were unloading the coal, and a great many persons were on the pier of Guernsey observing them, but they did or said nothing.

CHAPTER XIV.

CHARLES I.—1625 to 1649. (Continued.)

A.D. 1646.—On the 15th of January, writes Chevalier, Sir Peter Osborne's chaplain arrived in Jersey, to inform Captain Carteret that he had received a summons from the earl of Warwick, whose messenger was a Jerseyman, by name Charles Marret, one of those whom the commissioners had adjudged to death because he was king's receiver under Major Lydcott, and also for having been in arms against the king's party in Jersey. Having arrived in Guernsey to accomplish his mission, Marret went half way to the castle in a little boat bearing a white flag, when Sir Peter sent his boat to meet her, and the messenger delivered his letters. He had brought two bottles of wine with him, one Spanish, the other claret, to give to those who came to fetch his letters, which they drank to the health of the king and the parliament, and that of each other. The bottles being empty, the castle men went back to fill them with the same kind of wine, to shew that they had also Spanish wine and claret, and they returned to drink to the health of each other as before, while Sir Peter read his letters. After he had read and considered them, the messenger was informed that he would shortly send his answer. Sir Peter then assembled the entire garrison, officers and soldiers,

and informed them that he was summoned to surrender the
castle, and to deliver the keys to Lieut.-Governor Russell ;
that he was asked to go to London, where he would be
received by the parliament and replaced in possession of his
estate in England ; and that the said officers and soldiers
were to receive their pay, past and present, with other similar
advantages promised in the letters, to induce the garrison to
render the place. After having read these letters and deli-
berated together, Sir Peter inquired of his lieutenant, captains
and soldiers, if they were still determined to stand by him
and support him in holding the castle for the king : the
greater part answered that they were so resolved, and to shed
their last blood for that purpose. Some of the soldiers, who
were tired of so long a detention, without being able to move
out, would have willingly consented to the surrender, seeing
that they were promised their pay ; but the greater part were
resolved, with Sir Peter, not to yield either to gifts or to
promises. Sir Peter sent a copy of his letter to Captain Carteret, requesting him in all haste to victual the castle for a
year, and to send him some fresh soldiers, as also two of his
gunners, who were then in Jersey to see their wives. Captain
Carteret dispatched promptly boat after boat, with supplies
and fresh men, who left on the 25th of January. In one of
the boats, which left eight or nine days after, Monsieur de
Saumares, (Andros,) of Guernsey, returned to Castle Cornet,
for he adhered strongly to the king ; he was in Jersey when
Sir Peter was summoned. The boats all arrived safely, and
returned on the 8th of February. And on the 12th, Captain
Carteret sent two more boats with provisions from St. John's,
which went and came back in safety. Sir Peter Osborne
wrote to Milord Warwick, and sent his letter by the same
messenger, who was in Guernsey awaiting it.

On the 25th of February, Captain Carteret sent a boat of
five tons burden with supplies to Castle Cornet. The Guernseymen did not prevent the boats from thus going and returning, and there was only a small parliamentary frigate of six
guns for the protection of their island. The preceding summer they had repaired their houses, which Sir Peter had
previously battered and injured with cannon shot, and which
they were now again inhabiting. The fear of being cannonaded from the castle prevented their offering any obstruc-
tion to the provision boats, and having only a small frigate of
six guns to defend them, they were humbled during the last
two or three months of the winter.

On the 19th of March, Sir George Carteret sent a boat
with provisions to Castle Cornet; she was only of the burden
of three tons, and was six weeks on passage, on account of
contrary winds. She arrived one Thursday, during the night,
when the provisions were discharged. The next morning,
the Guernseymen, seeing this boat, with another which had
also come with provisions, before the castle gate, fired cannon
both on them and on the castle; and the boats, being pierced,
were compelled to retire to the back of the castle, out of the
fire of the battery; but they were able to return to Jersey at
the end of two days. The whole of Friday, the 20th of
March, the land batteries did not cease firing on the boats
and castle, and the interior of the latter was greatly damaged,
the roofs of the houses and part of the ramparts being injured,
and chimnies knocked down; but the garrison had none
killed or wounded. The Guernseymen did this previously to
attempting the castle by assault, for they published through
the town that the inhabitants of the houses within reach of
the castle should leave them and retire to Fountain street,
which was out of the reach of the cannon. All the winter
they had allowed the boats with provisions to discharge before
the castle gate, without hindrance; and whether they had
orders from the parliament of England to act thus, or whether they had been reprimanded for allowing the castle to be
victualled or otherwise, it was not known.

To return to Sir Peter Osborne, who was in the castle and
heard the balls whistle past his ears. When he saw that the
Guernseymen were not content with firing on the boats, but
that they attacked him also, he allowed them to go on for a
little time, and then, as if awaking suddenly, he paid them off
in their own coin with several discharges of cannon on the
town, in which there were balls of 36 lb. each. These discharges did great damage to the inhabitants, by the injuries
which their houses sustained, the more so as the preceding
summer they had repaired the damages which Sir Peter had
done them at the beginning of the troubles, by firing above a
thousand cannon shot upon the town. This time the castle
fired seventy-eight cannon shot upon the town, as was reported by the Jersey boats' crews then in Guernsey. And
the land batteries then fired double that number on the castle
and on the boats.

Sir Thomas Fanshawe to Sir Peter Osborne. [o]

"Sir,—I am commanded by the prince to come to this place,
and by the help of Sir George Carteret to convey unto you such

provisions as might for the present be gotten. I came by the way of St. Malo, where I fortunately met with Mrs. Danvers, who told me what you had most need of in the castle, which I have provided, (being six months' victuals,) by the hands of such as have been your agents upon the like occasion heretofore. I am likewise commanded personally to attend you with a letter from his highness, a copy of which I have sent you; but finding the passage to be at the worst, this time of moonshine and so dead a calm, I have deferred my journey till a darker time; but that no time might be lost because the year grows high, I have thought fit with the soonest to give you an account of what I have to say. His highness, that your good service and his majesty's affairs might not be neglected, has sent me hither to look after fit supplies of all kinds, which you shall stand in need of, and that shall be in his power to give you, upon my solicitation on your behalf, which I shall very much rejoice to do. But with all, he endeavours the speedy reducing of Guernsey. Now, I am to ask you from him what you can advise towards the effecting of this. I am likewise, upon his highness' commands, to tell you what discourse I have had with Sir George Carteret concerning the same, who propounds two ways, either by a considerable force of ships and men, if he can get them, to invade the island, or else to come with a lesser number and surprise the town, where he believes to be the persons of the best and most men of quality in that island, upon which he conceives the whole island will yield. To accomplish either of which he must enter by the castle, and if there be occasion, upon any blow received, he may secure the remainder of his forces there, without which, he says, he cannot possibly undertake the work. It is true there is this open objection against it, that such forces as shall so come in will be able to master the castle if they be so disposed, so as you shall not be assured to give that account of your command and trust which his majesty hath imposed in you. Against this I can say no more, but that if his highness shall command (notwithstanding this objection) any of these proceedings, it may be you may think fit to allow it as a discharge of that obligation. I do clearly and candidly deal with you. I do not know of any such resolution in the prince to do this; but do believe it is possible this may prove to be the case. Sir George Carteret does seriously and solemnly profess (and I have reason to believe him) that he will cordially join with you in all things which shall be most for the advance of his majesty's service in that island; and, sir, upon so long an understanding of you as I have had, I can assure myself of all that can be done by you towards that end. Sir, I shall desire your particular answer to this letter, with any thing more which shall best conduce to the taking of Guernsey, and that you would inform me how and when I may be likely to have the best passage to

wait upon you, being to return, if it please you, speedily back
again. Sir, I am extremely sensible of the great suffering which
you have had. I have sent word from St. Malo to his highness,
how you were lately summoned from my lord of Warwick, and
your answer to it, which I know will be welcome to him. Having no more to trouble you with at this time, I rest, sir,

"Your very affectionate friend to serve you.
"THOS. FANSHAWE.

"Jersey, 25th [? March] 1646.

"Sir, I have sent you a letter from your eldest son, whom I
left well at Falmouth.

"Sir,—Captain Darell being very desirous to go to you, I
have desired [him] to stay for the speedy conveyance of those
provisions which are coming from St. Malo to you; when that is
done, he will be with you, or sooner, if you will command him
away."

On the 2d of April, as we learn from Chevalier, Sir Thomas
Fanshawe left Jersey in the night for Castle Cornet, in a
shallop commanded by Captain Bowden, being sent by the
Prince of Wales to reconcile the differences between Sir Peter
Osborne and Sir George Carteret. Sir Thomas was a knight
of the Bath, bearing the red ribbon, and he had a brother
who was secretary to the Prince of Wales.

On their arrival at the castle, they found the garrison in a
state of mutiny, and Sir Peter shut up in his house with two
pieces of cannon pointed against the door, to prevent his
leaving the house, and the porter of the castle a prisoner.
The cause was, that Sir Peter had struck the gunner and
others with the flat of his sword; and notwithstanding that
the skin was not cut, they were greatly irritated, as they
would not submit to correction, saying that they all suffered
for the same cause and in the same quarrel. Sir Thomas
was much astonished, and reproved them prudently, shewing
them mildly that they were guilty of a great fault, seeing the
importance of the fortress which they held for the king, and
which might have been lost, had they been attacked while
thus divided. He thus brought them to reason, and re-united
them in concord, telling them in an amiable and familiar
manner that he was sent by the prince to thank them for
their good and faithful service to the king. Sir Thomas remained six days at the castle, and he promised Sir Peter that
provisions should be sent to him, as also wine for himself and
his friends, as their only beverage was water. After many
conferences, Sir Peter told Sir Thomas that he was resolved
to keep the castle for his majesty with his last breath, and all

the garrison said the same. Sir Thomas, seeing this resolution, begged of them to live in amity with each other; he then took his leave of Sir Peter and of every one individually, and returned safely to Jersey, having, both in going and returning, passed close to the parliament ships, which were at anchor near the castle, the crews of which either did not, or pretended not to, see the shallop.

Early in 1646, Sir Ralph (created Lord) Hopton, while commanding the king's army in the west, was driven into Cornwall, when the consternation of the royalists was such that, in March, the Prince of Wales passed from Pendennis castle, near Falmouth, with his council, including Sir Edward Hyde and Lord Colepepper, to the isles of Scilly; but, not being considered safe there, he embarked on the 16th of April for Jersey, where he landed on the following day with his suite.[1] The prince had not quite completed his sixteenth year, and was therefore the more easily influenced by Sir George Carteret, who seems again to have urged the removal of Sir Peter Osborne from his government, as Sir Peter arrived in Jersey on the 29th of May, having transferred his command to Sir Baldwin Wake, and bid a final adieu to the castle, in which he had been besieged about three years and a quarter, and after having been the resident lieutenant-governor and governor of Guernsey twenty-five years. It must have been, however, some consolation to this devoted royalist, under his present ill-treatment, to remember, that, fifteen months before, he had received a letter from king Charles, dated Oxford, January 23, 1645, in which that sovereign, under his own sign manual, graciously acknowledged his "eminent deservings;" and, moreover, that Sir Edward Hyde, afterwards Lord Clarendon, had written to him from Pendennis castle, on February 13, 1646, that they had the castle much at heart, and were thoroughly satisfied with his services. He was indeed the inspiration and the mainstay of this protracted defence, and, having set the example, it was followed by his successors. On the 16th of June, 1646, prince Charles also signed a document on parchment, declaring that he approved of his conduct, both in defending Castle Cornet and in resigning his government to accommodate the king's affairs; in other words, to gratify Sir George Carteret, who in Jersey was too powerful and too useful to be denied any favor. The prince, moreover, promised to reward him

(1) Including Lord Hopton, who, after disbanding his troops in pursuance of a capitulation, joined the Prince of Wales in Scilly, and accompanied him to Jersey.

S

at a convenient season ; but, as he died before the restoration, the only recompense awarded to his family for his distinguished services appears to have been the grant of a baronetcy to his son. His intercourse in Jersey with Sir George Carteret could not have been agreeable to either ; and after a residence of about ten weeks in that island, he retired to St. Malo, where he was residing three years later, (1649,) still exerting himself in the royal cause. At the close of that year, we lose all trace or mention of Sir Peter Osborne, as the transient remembrance and ungrateful requital of his services—the separation from his wife and children—and his daily increasing necessities appear to have combined to induce him to proceed to England, to enter into some composition for the remainder of his estate. In parting with this noble cavalier, we feel as if taking leave of an old friend, and cannot but regret that he did not survive to enjoy in his own person the fruits of his loyalty, always supposing they had been such as would have consoled him for his constancy and sufferings. It is very singular that no mention is made of him by Lord Clarendon in his history. That in public life he was an able man, is proved by his correspondence. We have no means of ascertaining his private character, but his grateful and generous feeling is well exemplified in the following letter to the wife of his friend, Amias Andros :

"Good Mrs. Samares,—Your welcome letter is come safely to my hands, whereby I understand your happie arrival into these parts, escaped from the ill usage of your enemies. The comfort you have given me by the short account you have made of my wife and poore family, I humbly thank you for, of whose state I have remayned long doubtful. That great God, who keepeth us both, is able with his blessing to make a little enough. Amongst your kindred in Jersey, I can not doubt but you will find assistance and courtesey. Yet least your virtuous constancie and goodness for her and me (for which I hold myself much obliged) may do you prejudice, I beseech you favour me so much to accept of this inclosed, which I present unto you with my best respects and thankfullness. But [sic] you finde my estimation there so little valewed, that it proves to you of no use, complaine of the change of my fortune and not my good will. Forbeare, I pray, to looke for an answere to the l [latter] part of your letter, and have the patience not to expect your husband yet.

"Your most humble servant,

"Castle Cornet, Oct. 30, 1645.   "PET. OSBORNE.

"Prizing every courtesie of yours, and assured of the true hart it comes from, I am verry sorry that I have not the glass you mention.

"To my worthy friend,
"Mrs. Elizabeth Andrewes,[1] Samares, at Jersey."

Sir Peter Osborne was born in the year 1585, so that he was about thirty-five when he first came to Guernsey, and fully fifty-seven when the siege of Castle Cornet commenced: he was a person of good family and influence, and holding the office of treasurer's remembrancer of the exchequer, as also possessing a landed estate in England, it seems strange to us that he should have accepted a post which involved a frequent, if not a constant, residence in Castle Cornet, certainly not a desirable abode, on many accounts, to a man of interest and fortune. But Sir Peter appears, by Warburton, to have obtained, 19 James I., (1621-2,) the reversion of the governorship of Guernsey, in the event of the death of his brother-in-law, the Earl of Danby,[2] who died in 1643, and consequently he succeeded him in that appointment, as, in his commission in 1646 to Sir Baldwin Wake, knight, he styles himself "governor of his majesty's island of Guernsey." His grandfather, Peter Osborne, Esq., (born 1521, died 1592,) was also treasurer's remembrancer of the exchequer as well as keeper of the privy purse, in the reign of Edward VI. This Mr. Osborne was a man of great understanding, active and zealous for the reformation, and was imprisoned in the reign of Mary. In that of Elizabeth, he was in much esteem with Lord Burleigh, and was one of the high commissioners for ecclesiastical affairs. He married twice, and by his first wife, Miss Blyth, had twenty-two children. He purchased Chicksands priory, the present seat of the family, of which the most remote ancestor authenticated was Peter Osborne, of Burleigh, in Essex, who died in 1442. Sir Peter, who was son of Sir John Osborne, knight, married Dorothy, daughter of Sir John Danvers, of Dantzey, county of Wilts, (by Elizabeth, daughter and coheir of John Nevil, Lord Latimer, by his wife, Lady Lucy, second daughter of Henry Somerset, Earl of Worcester.) Dorothy, Lady Osborne, was sister to Henry Danvers, Earl of Danby, privy councillor to

---

(1) Mrs. Andros was Elizabeth Stone, sister of Sir Robert Stone, knight, cupbearer to the queen of Bohemia, and captain of a troop of horse in Holland. Amias Andros, her husband, was related to the Carterets, his mother being a daughter of Amias de Carteret, seigneur of Trinity Manor, Jersey, and bailiff of Guernsey.

(2) This Earl of Danby left no issue male, and Macaulay, in his History of England, third edition, vol. i., page 234, speaking of the reign of Charles II., says: "The chief direction of affairs was now entrusted to Sir Thomas Osborne, a Yorkshire baronet, who had in the House of Commons shewn eminent talents for business and debate. Osborne became lord treasurer, and was soon created Earl of Danby."

Charles I. and knight of the Garter. The earl, in 1632, gave the botanic garden at Oxford, which lies on the east end of the city, and opposite to Magdalen College, having purchased five acres of land of that college, and enclosed them with a wall. He also settled an annual revenue for the maintenance of the garden, which he furnished with a great variety of plants and herbs, chiefly for the use of the medical students. Sir Peter Osborne had nine children, among whom John, first baronet, created 1660-1, and Dorothy, married to the renowned Sir William Temple. He died in 1653, less than two years after the surrender of the castle, aged about sixty-eight, and was buried in Campton church, county of Bedford. We cannot tell how he acquired the grant of knighthood, which in his day might be purchased with money at a reasonable rate, it having been from very early times a source of revenue to the sovereign. Among the forty councillors of state in the first year of the Commonwealth, 1649, one of whom was "Lieut.-General Oliver Cromwell," we find the name of Sir John Danvers,[1] knight, already mentioned, who probably assisted his brother-in-law, Sir Peter Osborne, to recover his estate of Chicksands priory, which was founded about A.D. 1150, by Pain de Beauchamp. Of this priory it appears that the two quadrangles and cloisters are yet entire, and have been converted into a modern mansion.

As the name of Sir George Carteret[2] occurs so often in this narrative, in connection with that of Sir Peter Osborne, a somewhat copious notice of him will not be misplaced here. Little certain is known of his early life. He was the nephew and son-in-law of the elder Sir Philip Carteret, lieutenant-governor and bailiff of Jersey, to whom he was appointed successor by the king, on the 3d of October, 1643. Captain Carteret (observes Falle in his History of Jersey, quoting from Lord Clarendon) was comptroller of his majesty's navy, and a man of great eminency and reputation in naval command. He stood so well, in the opinion even of the parliament, for true honor, courage, and abilities, that when they committed the fleet to the Earl of Warwick in opposition to the king, the two houses had cast their eyes upon him for vice-admiral. But he knew better what became him than to

---

(1) "For his affection and adhering to the parliament," Sir John Danvers was deprived of the estate of his brother, the Earl of Danby, by the will of the latter.

(2) The original name was de Carteret. Sir George, we believe, was the first who dropped the "de."

accept of an employment from them, unless the king had judged it expedient for his service. Unhappily, his majesty did not judge it such, nor would consent that one of his servants should so far countenance their undutiful proceedings as to be any ways concerned with them, which the noble historian laments as a most fatal error. For, to use his own words, " if Captain Carteret had been suffered to have taken that charge, his interest and reputation in the navy was [were] so great, and his diligence and dexterity in command so eminent, that, it is generally believed, he would, against whatsoever the Earl of Warwick could have done, have preserved a major part of the fleet in their duty to the king." Durell, in his Notes on Falle's History,[1] throws doubts on this statement, believing that, in 1642, Captain Carteret was only about twenty-three years of age, when he could scarcely have acquired that high professional distinction which would have induced the parliament to offer him the second command, with the rank of vice-admiral. The reverend annotator, therefore, conceives that the high character thus given to Captain Carteret was rather what he justly deserved at a later period of his life, than the consequence of any thing he had yet done when the troubles commenced. But, as he was then already comptroller of the navy, we think that he must have been several years older, and especially as Durell himself mentions that Carteret died at an advanced age, when, according to his own belief, he could only have been sixty-two or three. In Baker's Cæsarea, it is stated that at his death Sir George Carteret was nearly eighty years of age.

During the eight or nine months, in 1643, that the parliament was in possession of Jersey, with the exception of Mont Orgueil and Elizabeth Castles, Captain Carteret resided at St. Malo, where he was employed by the king to sell the prizes captured from the parliamentarians, with the proceeds of which he supplied the castles in Jersey with provisions, and the royalists in the west of England with ammunition.

Colonel Carteret, as he was then styled, was created a baronet in May, 1645, and he undoubtedly was an extraordinary man, who rose during the civil war to the highest eminence. He possessed much energy of character, and a mind capable of forming and executing great designs; for there is something chivalrous, nay, almost romantic, in a gallant commander posting himself on a small island, and

(1) The Rev. Philip Falle's History of Jersey, with Notes and Illustrations, by the Rev. Edward Durell, M.A.   Jersey, 1837. — We consider Mr. Durell's annotations far more valuable than the history.

there boldly upholding the falling cause of his sovereigns, always faithful to them under every reverse of fortune, and inflicting great mischief on their enemies. This he did for above eight years, and it at length required the presence of Blake, the first naval officer of that age, with a large land force, to compel him to surrender. And when obliged to capitulate, he managed matters with so much address, and obtained such favorable terms, that one might almost suppose he had himself dictated the articles to the conquerors. Thus far his character was that of a hero and a statesman; but historical truth compels us to reverse the portrait, and we do so with regret, as it is always an ungracious task to expose the failings of eminent men. His own countryman, who therefore cannot be suspected of any national bias, the Rev. Edward Durell, M.A., rector of St. Saviour, Jersey, in his interesting and valuable notes already mentioned, two or three incorrect ones excepted, animadverts with much severity on some reprehensible traits in the character of Carteret, who, he observes, used unduly his high office as a means of aggrandizing and enriching himself and his family. His loyalty, he justly states, was not that of an Aristides, as, by his preying on English commerce, he carried off about £60,000, a very large sum at that period, and part of which ought, we think, freely to have been devoted to the relief of Castle Cornet, as surely he was not carrying on war with the parliamentarians on his own private account. After making every allowance for the exasperation of civil discord, Durell says that there was something particularly vindictive in his nature; and certainly his treatment of Sir Peter Osborne, now come to light, is a further confirmation of this blot on his character. Durell, who however speaks highly of his merits as a commander, adds, that "his rapacity, his avarice, his despotism, and his cruelty, have escaped general reprobation, by having been officiously withheld from the press, and the knowledge of posterity." Moreover, the deposition of Captain Darell, given in the "Chronicles of Castle Cornet," is very discreditable to him, as he refused to return, agreeably to his promise, an acknowledgment or bond of Sir Peter Osborne for supplies furnished to Castle Cornet, and which had been entrusted to him for perusal only. He retired to France after the reduction of Jersey, where he never permanently resided afterwards, and at the restoration he was re-appointed comptroller of the navy. In the first parliament after that event, Sir George was chosen member for Portsmouth; but in

October, 1669, he was expelled the house, for issuing money, as treasurer of the navy, without legal warrant; in 1673, he was appointed one of the lords of the admiralty; and in 1676, one of the commissioners of the board of trade. He was a proprietary governor of a province in North America, and gave to it its present name of New Jersey. He died in England in 1681, at an advanced age. A few months after his death, his grandson, Sir George Carteret, who had succeeded him in the baronetcy, was created Lord Carteret;[1] and his male posterity, after running a distinguished course among the English nobility, became extinct in the person of Robert, Earl Granville, in 1776. Like Sir Peter Osborne, Sir George Carteret also lost a son, Sir Philip Carteret, in battle; he was the father of the first Lord Carteret, and fell in the same ship and engagement against the Dutch, in 1672, in which his father-in-law, the Earl of Sandwich, was slain.

Amias Andros, having actively participated, and been very confidentially employed, in the defence of Castle Cornet, is also well entitled to a brief biographical notice. His ancestor, whose original name appears to have been Andrews, corrupted in French to Andros, was from Northamptonshire, and became connected with Guernsey by being lieutenant to the governor, Sir Peter Mewtis, and by marrying, in 1543, Judith de Sausmarez, who brought the fief or manor of Sausmarez, at St. Martin's, into the Andros family. His descendant, Amias, was marshal of the ceremonies to Charles I., in 1632;. and in August, 1645, many of the garrison of Castle Cornet, probably induced thereto by their sufferings, and it would seem with the ungenerous concurrence of Sir George Carteret, sought to get him appointed as their commander. Mr. Andros was nominated bailiff of Guernsey, in 1651, but he only entered into that office in 1661, after the restoration. He was father of Sir Edmund Andros, who was knighted in 1681, and was governor of New York and New England before the revolution of 1688, and after that event governor of Virginia and Maryland.[2] Amias Andros, seigneur of Sausmarez, keeper

(1) The eldest son of the first peer was the celebrated Lord Carteret, afterwards Earl Granville. He went ambassador to Sweden in 1719, and was twice secretary of state, as well as twice viceroy of Ireland. He was an agreeable companion, and a great encourager of learned men. He died in 1763.

(2) Sir Edmund Andros, in his government of New York and New England before the revolution, incurred the dislike of the colonists, and is represented as "a man who disgraced superior talents by the unprincipled zeal and activity with which he rendered them subservient to the arbitrary designs of a tyrant!"—"His friend and colleague, Randolph, boasted that, in New England, Andros was as arbitrary as the Grand Turk."

of the castle of Jerbourg, and hereditary cupbearer to the king, in Guernsey, (the two last mere honorary offices,) as also major-general of the militia—a rank never given before or since in the island—died in 1674, aged sixty-four years, and was interred in the parish church of St. Martin, in which a monument exists to his memory and that of his wife, who is therein stated to have shared in the troubles and exile to which her husband was exposed for many years. Two of Amias' brothers, military officers, were slain,[1] one in the service of the king of Bohemia, son-in-law of James I. of England, and the other in 1644, during the civil war.

Chevalier writes, April 17, 1646 : "The Prince of Wales arrived in Jersey [from Scilly] this day, (Friday,) in a frigate of about 160 tons burden, and mounting 24 guns, accompanied by two smaller vessels, one of six and the other of four guns. The frigate was named 'The Black Proud Eagle,' and commanded by Captain Wake. On their passage, only three small vessels were seen near Guernsey, steering towards the coast of Britany. The prince, his six ministers, noblemen and persons of quality, and guards, with their several attendants, numbered about three hundred. No salute was fired either by the frigate or the castle, and no flags were hoisted, excepting that the frigate had the royal ensign on her bowsprit, as fortune having been adverse to the new comers, it was thought that their visit was not one for rejoicing." The prince left Jersey on the 25th June, after a sojourn there of sixty-nine days : he embarked in Captain Bowden's frigate, and landed in Normandy the same evening. On the 12th of May, two of the prince's frigates left Jersey to convoy to Castle Cornet, a vessel of above fifty tons burden which was laden with provisions, and carried also Sir Baldwin Wake, whom the prince had knighted in Elizabeth Castle, and appointed as Sir Peter Osborne's lieutenant, so as to relieve Sir Peter, and bring him to Jersey to recruit himself after so long a captivity, he having been besieged in the castle nearly four years. Sir George and he did not agree, which was the reason why Sir Baldwin was sent in his place. But when the frigates and vessel came near Guernsey, they were chased back by the parliamentary fri-

But, "after the British revolution, Andros conducted himself irreproachably as governor of Virginia." He died in London, in 1715, at a very advanced age.—See *Grahame's History of the United States of North America*, vols. i. ii. from which the above extracts are taken.

(1) Their uncle, Lieutenant John Andros, was mortally wounded at La Rochelle in 1624, and died fifteen days afterwards.

gates pursuing them nearly to Elizabeth Castle. The vessel, after landing her provisions and some men to reinforce the garrison, was to be broken up to serve as fire-wood. On the 14th of May, the prince and his council judged it expedient to send four frigates to convoy this vessel and two boats with provisions, viz., the frigate of 24 guns, which had conveyed him to Jersey, Milord Digby's frigate of 12 guns, and the two Dunkirk frigates, one of 25 and the other of 24 guns, which Milord Colepepper had brought to Jersey. Sir Baldwin Wake was captain of the prince's frigate, with Captain Bowden [1] under him, for the passage to Guernsey. They left on Thursday, towards sunset, and were some four hundred men in these four frigates, all resolved to carry the provisions to Castle Cornet, or not to return. They sailed all night, but in the morning the wind calmed, and a fog arose, which prevented their seeing very far. Nevertheless, in passing near Sark, they were perceived: and two guns were fired from Herm, as a signal to a large ship of 800 tons and 40 guns, which protected Guernsey. Her guns were of brass, and the greater part double culverins. [2] The Guernseymen had a shallop between Sark and the castle, the crew of which, seeing the frigates, fired a gun to prepare the parliamentary -ship and the batteries on shore. The ship, which was at anchor on the bank, got under sail, but, owing to the fog, she could discover nothing, and knew not which way to steer. The Jersey frigates, notwithstanding, brought the vessel and two boats to Castle Cornet about sunrise, the people on shore not perceiving them until they were near the castle, when the land batteries fired upon them, which the castle returned, each side doing their best. The large ship, hearing the cannonade, approached the castle, and the frigates gave her each a broadside, which she returned, killing five or six of their men, besides wounding many. She then pursued them to near Sark, but finding that they outsailed her, she returned to her anchorage on the bank. It was not known whether she sustained any loss. As the frigates were coming to Jersey, the crews saw the castle and the town firing upon each other; the former, with its new governor, firing above a hundred cannon shot, which the latter fully returned.

(1) Captain Bowden appears to have been employed on every occasion of difficulty in supplying the castle, and he must have been a bold man, as, had he been captured, he would probably have been hanged as a traitor.

(2) This reminds us of the line in the old sea song on the battle of "La Hogue," in 1692, than which song later poets have perhaps produced nothing finer:

"Let fly a culverin, the signal for the line."

The prince sent some pistoles by Sir Baldwin Wake for the soldiers, who had received no payment for a long time, so that the meanest had two pistoles and a half. This encouraged them greatly, a pistole being ten francs.

On the 5th of June, the great ship of 800 tons and 40 guns, and two little frigates, came from Guernsey to the coast of Jersey ; and, as they doubled the Corbière, the two Dunkirk frigates were leaving the roadstead of St. Aubin on their return home, the Prince having dismissed them. While they were saluting Elizabeth Castle, the three vessels appeared before it, coming down under full sail, when the two Dunkirk frigates went along the rocks of St. Clement and La Roque, and anchored under Mont Orgueil castle. The parliamentary frigates did not pursue them, but remained above two hours before Elizabeth Castle, knowing well that the prince was there, and making their bravadoes in his sight. After capturing three fishing boats and despoiling the crews, they returned to Guernsey.

In the beginning of August, Sir Baldwin Wake discovered an English soldier, who thought to escape from Castle Cornet, and carry away a boat laden with provisions. He was informed against by a prisoner, to whom he had said, as a secret, that he would open his prison door, and that a boat was coming with provisions from Jersey, into which they would throw themselves, and go to Guernsey. The governor gave the prisoner his liberty, and imprisoned the traitor, who was put to the torture. In the end he confessed such a design, upon which Sir Baldwin consulted his council, by whom he was condemned to be shot, so as to cause a fear and terror among the rest of the garrison. Three musketeers were chosen to execute the sentence, viz., an Englishman, a Jerseyman, and a Guernseyman, who fired upon him at the distance of about a perch, and he was killed outright.

On the 2d of December, there arrived in Jersey a boat laden with about twelve tons of provisions, which Sir Peter Osborne had sent from St. Malo to Sir George, to be forwarded to Castle Cornet, viz. bread, beef, pork, pease, codfish, rice, three hogsheads of gruel, and two hogsheads of wine. Sir Peter sent also in this boat the aged porter of the castle, who had quitted it with him, and always remained with him : he sent also with the porter one of his men, named Mr. Ray, and the two were to go to the castle with the provisions, and to bring thence the effects of Sir Peter to St. Malo. Sir George did his utmost to forward the provisions and the two passengers at once ; but the Bretons, who had brought them, would not take them on to the castle, fearing the cannonades. Sir George was therefore obliged to insure their boat against accidents. They went on the 8th of December, and arrived safely, but they did not discharge their cargo before the gate, because the castle people told them that a boat, which had arrived three days before them, had been fired upon while unloading before the gate. They went in a creek at the back of the castle, just wide enough to receive their boat, and discharged there. But on leaving in a clear moonlight, they were perceived from the shore, and three cannon shot were fired at them without doing any damage : they returned safe and sound to Jersey on the 12th of December.

This boat brought the effects of Sir Peter and the porter, and carried them to Sir Peter at St. Malo, viz. beds, linen, table furniture, stoves, chandeliers, and trunks, some of which were so heavy that it required six men to carry each of them on board the boat. The said porter was old, being nearly eighty years of age. They remained together at St. Malo, waiting patiently the issue of affairs. Sir Peter had sent his wife to England before he left Castle Cornet, she having remained some time at St. Malo, and from thence taken passage to England, where she was well received, for she was of a high origin, (car elle était sortie de grande parenté,) and Sir Peter also, both being of noble and ancient families. She was enabled afterwards to assist her husband, his estate being sequestered by the parliament, because he was on the king's side, and kept the castle well and faithfully.

Sir George Carteret had sent to Castle Cornet, a boat of six or seven tons burden laden with provisions, which left three days before the Breton boat freighted by Sir Peter. This (Jersey) boat arrived during the night : the next morning, the Guernseymen,—seeing her lying between the castle and the town, and within reach of their battery,—wishing to give a proof of their prowess and skill, discharged a volley of cannon at the boat, which they repeated as if on an enemy's squadron of vessels of war. The boat received ten or twelve cannon balls, which pierced her through and through ; but there was no one on board. She was hauled up very high near the castle gate, which was the reason why they fired upon her. After this day she was not fired upon, and in the night her crew repaired her, and came to Jersey.

Sir Baldwin repaid the Guernseymen with interest, pointing and discharging forty pieces of cannon on the town, after the

departure of the boat.   There were at this time three parliamentary vessels at anchor on the bank, which vessels did not
prevent the boats with provisions passing to and fro, as they
were lately arrived.   If the Guernseymen had allowed the
boats to go and come freely and peaceably, the town would
not have been fired upon; but they commenced, and Sir
Baldwin finished.   And what gave the castle people more
courage was that they were victualled for a long time, and
were reinforced by fresh men who had come from the castle
of Pendennis,[1] so that the garrison amounted to ninety men.
The day that the Guernseymen fired on the boat, they fired
also on the castle, together above 120 cannon shot, so that
they damaged the houses and roofs, but killed or wounded
none.   When they had done, Sir Baldwin Wake gave them
a parting volley, reserving himself for another time; and on
the following Sunday he cannonaded them so rapidly and
furiously that the report was easily heard in Jersey, and the
smoke seen.   The Guernseymen returned the same, both
sides doing their best.   Before Sir Baldwin was governor of
the castle, Sir Peter had acted a different part towards the
town, firing on it night and day, and causing it great havoc:
the Guernseymen did the same on the castle, which was
greatly damaged.

A.D. 1647.—Colonel Russell wrote, January 26, to Sir B.
Wake at Castle Cornet, to inform him that by certain intelligence lately received from England, he was assured that the
Scottish army had returned home, and that the king was
confined at Holmely House, near Northampton.   In consequence, he recommended him to treat, as many had done,
rather than continue a prey to certain ruin.   In reply the
next day, Sir Baldwin said, " that being bound by the laws
of God, and my sworn allegiance to my sovereign lord and
master the king, and my duty to his royal highness, engageth
me to let you know that no misfortune whatsoever shall make
me fail or alter in my resolution in preserving this place."
While Castle Cornet was thus steadily maintained for the
king, the island became a prey to intestine discord and party
feuds; and the bitter hostility of the two rival factions presented a miniature resemblance of the hatred which existed
between the cavaliers and the round-heads in England.   One
party, apparently the king's, was supported by a majority of

(1) After the surrender of Pendennis Castle, near Falmouth, thirty-nine of the garrison
came to Jersey.

the jurats and other members of the States ; the other consisted of Peter de Beauvoir, the bailiff ; Peter Carey, then the
sheriff ; (both prisoners together at Castle Cornet in 1643,)
and the douzaine of St. Peter-Port. The first open attempt
against the bailiff's authority was made in March, 1647, when
Mr. de Quetteville, who had been imprisoned by the parliament in Hurst Castle, laid claim to that office by virtue of a
commission which he held from Charles I., dated as far back
as 1631, and disputed the legality of the appointment of
De Beauvoir by the Earl of Warwick. This bold step can
only be accounted for by the lukewarmness or weakness of
Russell, or by the confidence of the native royalists in their
strength. The Court, having previously named John Carey
as judge delegate, to preside during the differences between
the two bailiffs, ordered De Beauvoir to deliver up the official
seals, and upon his refusal each party carried its complaints
to England. De la Marche went to London, pretending
to be a deputy sent by the States to obtain the remodelling
of the existing provisional commission, so as to include a
majority of his friends. Gosselin, then the friend of De
Beauvoir and Carey, was also in the capital to watch the
movements and circumvent the designs of his competitor,
who attempted to prevail on parliament to order several
Guernseymen to appear personally at Westminster, there to
give evidence ; and, as few could have borne that expense,
he hoped by this manœuvre to suppress a portion of the testimony that militated against his own views. The Royal Court,
alarmed at these proceedings, promulgated a declaration to
the effect, that the inhabitants were exempt from personal
attendance out of the bailiwick, citing several orders in council passed in the reign of Elizabeth and her successors, to wit,
of the 21st of June, 1565, the 9th of October, 1580, the 9th
of June, 1605, and the 27th of June, 1627 ; and they then
specially appointed Mr. Peter Carey, their attorney, to defend
the rights and privileges of the island before parliament.
This active parliamentarian[1] soon arrived in London and presented a statement to the council, in which he enlarged on
the important services already rendered by the provisional
commissioners in Guernsey and the losses they had sustained,
and concluded with praying that they be retained in office.
Notwithstanding the critical state of the nation, and the vital
importance of the affairs then under discussion in both houses

(1) Had Mr. Carey thought himself connected with royalty, he doubtless would have
espoused the cause of the king, as did Lucius Cary, Lord Falkland.

of parliament, the deputies were, it would appear, heard often at great length, and with much attention. Gosselin, in a letter of the 20th of May, and others of a subsequent date, mentions several interviews with the speaker of the House of Commons, and adds, that long debates had taken place on matters relating to the island. Carey was, to a certain extent, successful in the object of his mission.

On the 3d of November, 1647, the lords and commons assembled in parliament passed a series of resolutions for the regulating and well ordering of the affairs of Guernsey, Alderney, and Sark, in consequence " of the great sufferings of the well affected inhabitants of the town and island of Guernsey, and the adjacent isles of Alderney and Sark, for their adherence to the parliament, against the open and avowed enemies thereof." At the same time four members of the House of Commons, viz. Edmund Ludlow, John Weaver, John Birch, and John Harrington, Esqs., or any two or more of them, were constituted commissioners, and authorized to hear and examine the complaints and griev- ances of the said inhabitants. The first of these commission- ers, Edmund Ludlow, was the celebrated republican, and one of the members of the high court of justice which condemned Charles I. to the scaffold. On the death of Ireton, he held the command of the army in Ireland, but was deprived of it for opposing the usurpation of Cromwell. He died in exile at Vevay, in Switzerland; and his Memoirs, which are curious and accurate, were printed after his decease. We know not whether he was one of the commissioners who came over to Guernsey.

When the commissioners reached the island, Henry de la Marche exhibited articles of complaint against Colonel Rus- sell; and Peter Carey was called upon to declare whether the complaints were true or false. Mr. Carey stated that Russell had seized part of the property of individuals named by De la Marche, without consulting the provisional commissioners, the jurats; that he had received the whole revenue of the island, and applied but very little of it to the public service; that he levied taxes on the inhabitants contrary to law, which had caused the insurrection of the year 1643, and induced some to favour the views of Sir Peter Osborne; that he had seized prizes brought into the island, and disposed of them according to his pleasure; that the soldiers on guard at his residence were paid by the inhabitants; that he had refused to pay for services he had agreed upon, in consequence of

which those appointed to watch Castle Cornet had neglected
their duty; that he had refused his passport to those who
wished to proceed to London, and there lodge their complaints; and that he had only made one attempt on the
castle, and that most unsuccessfully.

These serious charges being fully substantiated, Russell
was recalled, and the powers of his successor were controlled
by the presence of, it seems, four parliamentary commissioners.
That successor was Colonel Alban Coxe; but Russell returned again about a twelvemonth afterwards, and was reinstated in his former office. The spirit of faction, however,
continued, and the commanding influence of De Beauvoir
and Carey appears to have excited the enmity of De la
Marche, Gosselin, and Dobrée; so that a long series of recri-
minations and impeachments arose between them and other
individuals. Carey was first impeached, but he proved his
innocence. Joshua Gosselin, just mentioned, a jurat, next
proposed seventeen articles of impeachment against Mr. de
Beauvoir, who was a bosom friend of Mr. Carey;[1] and as
the charges were much more serious, they were carried before
the council of state. De Beauvoir was accused of causing
several persons to be imprisoned for refusing to pay a tax of
£660 sterling, illegally levied; of adjudging debts to be paid
by some of the inhabitants to the governor, (Russell,) and of
sequestrating their estates, which the governor applied to his
own use; of counselling the said Russell to seize divers of the
inhabitants, and compelling them to ransom their estates by
sums of money which were delivered up to the governor; of
causing the dismissal of Mr. de Quetteville, bailiff, that he
might succeed to that office; of not administering justice
impartially; of abusing parliament in petitioning for the
office of bailiff, and not mentioning that he was suspended,
and that the former bailiff, then living, claimed the office;
and of compelling "the poor people of the isle to lose their
time in law suits, by making unusual speeches, uttered to
please his own vanity, and not for the despatch of business, or
the good of the people, who often lost whole days on matters
which ought to be terminated on the first hearing."

In reply to this impeachment, De Beauvoir sent a detailed
justification to the council of state, answering each charge
separately. He observed that the articles were signed by

(1) Mr. Carey left behind him an interesting but unconnected account in MS. of the
proceedings in Guernsey during the civil war, a copy of which we have consulted; but
some allowance should certainly be made for his recital of the part he took in the transac
tions of this eventful period, especially as that account was evidently written for his
justification and that of his party.

Mr. Gosselin only, and that, with respect to the delay in law suits, he despatched as many as three hundred cases in one day, which, he quaintly added, was as much as could well be done! In answer to a charge of being a railer, and public calumniator in open court, abusing every court day some one of the people, magistrates and parochial officers, and tolerating the same conduct in his relations and friends, he stated, "that knowing drunkenness to be the capital sin of Guernsey, whenever he had occasion to address the people, he represented to them what a foul and beastly thing it was to see the officers of justice drunk." Whether he alluded to the jurats, or to the court or parochial officers, does not appear; but, although such an accusation is very discreditable, great allowance must be made for the assertions of a judge standing on his defence, especially as his replies, in some cases, partake more of recrimination than of refutation, and as he seems to us to have been a man of an imperious and intriguing character, and not always mindful of the truth.

Among the reasons given by De Beauvoir why his accuser (Gosselin) had rendered himself unworthy of holding any magisterial office, was this: "Because he is an avowed enemy of the government of England, having declared that he wished to see a king on the throne." This charge, which might have been of essential service to Gosselin some years afterwards, he then resented as an atrocious calumny, and quoted instances of his inviolable fidelity to the Commonwealth. How he managed at the restoration to acquit himself of this short-sighted line of defence does not appear, but he doubtless easily changed sides, and then became as staunch a royalist as he had before endeavoured to prove himself a zealous republican.

Whether in consequence of another complaint to the commissioners, or from the late impeachment, Mr. de Beauvoir was deprived of his appointment as bailiff, and the jurat Bonamy was named judge delegate. But this arrangement was of short duration, for, in 1653, the twelve jurats were directed to fulfil the duties of bailiff in rotation; and by the same order, five of the jurats, viz. James Guille, John Blondell, John Brehaut, Thomas Carey, and Peter Brehaut, were discharged "by reason of their great age and infirmity of body;" and the States were "required to proceed to the election of five other fit persons in their stead." In February, 1655, however, Peter de Beauvoir was re-established a third time as bailiff, and so continued until the restoration.

About the period of these impeachments, another singular proceeding took place, which arose from a complaint made by Mr. Bonamy against James Le Marchant, the jurat, already mentioned. A petition being presented to parliament by the former, in which he stated that he had been insulted in the discharge of his duty by the latter, and that he could attribute this conduct to no other cause than his own zeal in favour of the Commonwealth, his case was referred to the States, with an order to institute an instant inquiry into its truth. That body therefore met, and Le Marchant, who was in heart a royalist, finding that he could no longer evade the decision of the members, fled from the island.

It is an extraordinary circumstance, which proves in some measure the strength of the friends of the old government, that although the bishops were, in England, deprived of their right of sitting in the house of peers; although the episcopal form of church government was abolished, and the clergy prevented from interfering in lay assemblies, they still continued members of the States of this island. An attempt was indeed made to remove them, but it proved abortive.

We return again to Chevalier's Chronicle for a few occurrences in this year. (1647.)

On the night of the last day of March, Sir George sent a boat to Castle Cornet with letters and supplies for Sir Baldwin Wake, none having gone since the 29th of January. The boat belonged to St. Malo, and was of the burden of from two to three tons. She returned to Jersey during the night of the 6th of April, and reported that the land batteries and the castle no longer fired on each other, that they had not interchanged shots for some time, and that even their provisions had been discharged before the gate of the castle, without interruption from the batteries; that there were only two or three ships of the parliament on the bank, and several English vessels at anchor, which were waiting for convoy, and which these ships were to escort to England.

May 7.—On this day, two boats (one of seven and the other of six tons,) which had gone on the 29th of April with provisions to Castle Cornet, returned with a fine clear moon. They did not attempt to discharge before the gate of the castle, as they feared being seen and cannonaded from Guernsey. They went therefore behind the castle in two little creeks, and discharged their provisions as formerly. The next day, the Guernseymen having perceived them in the creeks, seeing only their masts, because their hulls were screened by the

T

rocks, nevertheless fired two cannon shots from the land batteries, one of which passed between the mast and the rigging of one of the vessels, and the other between the two masts, without doing any damage. These boats were well tossed in the creeks by bad weather and contrary winds. While they were awaiting a fair wind, a large ship of 500 tons and mounting 40 guns arrived on the bank, and sent her boat to the castle for a pilot for St. Malo; but there being none there, the crew went on to the pier of Guernsey, where they obtained a pilot. In returning to their ship, they passed by the castle, and brought as a present to Sir Baldwin Wake a quarter of veal and one of mutton from Guernsey. They mounted by a ladder to the top of the walls, because the castle entrance was blocked up; but the Guernsey pilot remained outside. The Flemings offered their services to Sir Baldwin, and told him that he had only to speak if he wanted any thing from on board their vessel; on which Sir Baldwin thanked them, when they took their leave and departed.

August 23.—This day Sir George sent a small boat to Castle Cornet, laden with provisions and necessary refreshments; she arrived happily, and landed at the said castle some barrels of biscuit, beer, pease, pork, &c., and returned to Jersey at the end of two days, not having been molested by those on shore or at sea, notwithstanding there were two parliamentary frigates anchored on the bank.

To the townsmen the unparalleled defence of Castle Cornet must have been attended with much excitement and no little peril, as the marks made by shot, from the guns of the castle, on the walls of the ancient church [1] of St. Peter-Port, appear to have been still visible during the last century; and it is said that a gentleman, who was walking in front of the old court-house, at the *Plaiderie*, was killed by a cannon ball, his fate being the more cruel because he was a zealous royalist. At that eventful period, the eastern side of the Pollet was not built, and there were no houses between the court-house and the castle, so that the former was exposed to the shot of the latter. Tradition states that the court-house was constantly fired at, and this is confirmed by the fact that about thirty years since, while workmen were employed in removing an old hedge on the estate of the Côtils—then the property of the late John E. Tupper, Esq., and now of his son, which

(1) Consecrated August 1, 1312. — "Inquisitio de certis libertatib, pro eccl'ia Sancti Petri in Insulâ Gernesey." An. 45. Edw. III. (A.D. 1371.)—*Calendarium Inquis' post mortem.*

hedge adjoined the southern side of "the New Ground," or
public walks—some twenty cannon balls, one we believe of
18 lb., and many of which we have seen, were dug out of the
earth into which they had evidently penetrated when fired
by the garrison at the court-house, which stood in a direct
line between the Côtils (anglicé, Cliffs or Hills) and the castle.
Castle Carey now stands on part of this estate, and cannon
balls have been within a few years occasionally discovered on
breaking up the grounds of the Côtils.

In 1849, we were fortunate in obtaining a copy of an old engraving of Castle Cornet, as it existed in 1672, or a few years
after the siege—a copy which very few in the island, like
ourselves, had ever heard of or seen. This engraving appears to have been taken from a painting in the possession of
the Earl of Winchilsea, whose ancestor, the seventh earl,
married the sister and heir of William, the last Viscount
Hatton, and thus became possessed of the painting. On a
comparison with the present fortifications, it will be found
that, in the lapse of nearly two centuries, the castle has
undergone surprisingly little change, and that its main features have been preserved. But, unfortunately, a very fine
and lofty keep, or *donjon*,[1] which stood on the highest part,
where the signal post and flag staff now stand, and added
considerably to the commanding effect and beauty of the
fortress, has disappeared, having fallen when the southern
part of the castle was destroyed by the explosion of the powder magazine, in December, 1672, as will be related in the
sequel. The "gayabe," or watchman, stood all day on this
donjon, and when he saw any ship coming near the island, he
struck two strokes on a large bell; when a boat came towards
the castle, only one stroke. The keep was sometimes styled
the tower, and it was the citadel wherein, in former times, the
besieged made their last efforts of defence. "Camden's
Britannia," edited by Bishop Gibson, second edition, 1722,
says of Castle Cornet : "It made a better figure before its
upper walls and buildings, which were very high and noble,
with a lofty tower seen above all the rest and carrying the
standard, were blown up by lightning. As to its strength, it
remains the same in the main, the powder having had little
or no effect on the ramparts and batteries, which lay lower."
—Also : "For therein resides, for the most part, the governour of the island, with a garrison, who on no account will
suffer either French, or women, to come into it." The pre-

(1) "Donjon Turricula, partie la plus haute, la plus forte d'un château, faite en tour."

sent generation is more gallant, and ladies will not find the
gates of the castle barred against them.

Alderney.—By a commission dated November 3, 1643,
Colonel Russell appointed Peter Le Febvre, seigneur de
l'Epine, as his lieutenant in Alderney, and instructed him to
take especial care not only "that God be duly served, and
that the Gospel be regularly preached," but "that all Papists
and Roman Catholics be expelled, and that no one who has
manifested the slightest leaning towards their superstition be
suffered to remain in the island." This is another proof of
the conjunction of outward form and intolerance so common
in that age; and if the example were given by the church of
Rome, it was too often followed by her opponents, even when
there was no political necessity. Russell himself appears to
have been a weak fanatic, as when the Guernseymen rose in
arms, in 1644, against his illegal taxation, they stipulated that
the Brownists, by whom he was guided and surrounded,
should be sent off in a vessel about to sail for England.

CHAPTER XV.

CHARLES I.—1625 to 1649. (Continued.)

IT will be assisting the reader to narrate in brief the events
of the civil war, from the battle of Edge Hill, in 1642, to the
execution of the king. The campaign of 1643 was one of
chequered fortune on both sides, although the royal arms
were successful in the west—in the middle of this year, the
parliament resolved to call the Scotch covenanters to their
aid, and the following winter they marched into England,
12,000 strong. In 1644, the battle of Marston-Moor, in
which about 25,000 men were engaged on each side, was
ruinous to the king's cause, as was in a less degree the second
battle of Newbury, although here victory and defeat were
nearly balanced. A treaty was entered into at Uxbridge;
but as the parliament insisted upon the abolition of episcopacy, to which Charles would not consent, hostilities were

renewed. The battle of Naseby,[1] on the 14th of June, 1645, decided the civil war against the king, who displayed great courage on this occasion, but lost his artillery, baggage, and cabinet. He fled first to Leicester, pursued by Fairfaix; thence into Wales; and on the 29th of August arrived at Oxford, then one of the strongest places in the kingdom; but, on the approach of Fairfax and Cromwell, he threw himself, in May, 1646, under the protection of the Scotch, who disgraced themselves by delivering him to the parliament, on the 30th of January, 1647. The ill-fated monarch was kept in close confinement at Holmby House, in Northamptonshire, until a detachment of the army forcibly conveyed him away to the head quarters, and thence to Hampton Court, where he was treated with some respect, as the parliament and the army were at variance, the former being chiefly Presbyterians, and the latter Independents. The king effected his escape from Hampton Court in November, 1647, with an intent to quit the kingdom; but he was taken and detained in the Isle of Wight. Here another negociation was opened, but it failed; and the army and parliament concurring to bring him to trial, he was condemned, in January, 1649, to suffer as a traitor. Only three days were allowed him to prepare for death; and on the scaffold, before his palace at Whitehall, he evinced much fortitude, piety, and resignation. In his domestic life, Charles was a fond husband and father, but its extreme purity is considered doubtful or exaggerated; his public character has been very differently estimated, but if its distinctive traits were, as many have thought, and still think, despotism and duplicity, much allowance should be made for the arbitrary times in which he lived —when, by sovereigns and courtiers, monarchy was believed of divine right—and for the manifold defects of a kingly education. This belief is well exemplified in the answer of Charles, when the death of Lord Northampton was commended to his sympathy: "Is it not enough that he has died for his king?" Selfish and unfeeling as this answer will now appear, it must not be judged by the present standard.

1648.—On the 10th of January, Sir Baldwin Wake informed Sir Peter Osborne, who was still at St. Malo, that

(1) "But, after his defeat at Naseby, his affairs were, in a military sense, so irretrievable, that in prolonging the war with as much obstinacy as the broken state of his party would allow, he displayed a good deal of that indifference to the sufferings of the kingdom and of his own adherents, which has been sometimes imputed to him."—*Hallam.* Mr. Hallam next proceeds to state that as the sea was yet open to him, Charles should have sought an asylum in France, or, still better, in Holland.

Castle Cornet had lately met with great misfortunes in the loss of boats and provisions: and although Sir George Carteret seemed very careful of the garrison, and of himself especially, their condition was " very mean, having neither butter nor oil with fish or pudding, bread ten weeks, flesh a month, fish and wheat answerable to our flesh, coal in very good proportion." In April, the queen and the prince sent, from St. Germain en Laie, through Lord Jermyn, to Sir Peter Osborne, a bill of exchange of 300 pistoles, (3,000 francs,) for the relief of Castle Cornet, to be employed as Sir Baldwin Wake should desire. In August, we find the last named officer in England, whither he had gone apparently for the purpose of obtaining men for the reduction of Guernsey, and supplies for Castle Cornet: he writes that Lord Ormonde had offered men out of Ireland, and that the prince had allowed him £800 sterling in the richest sort of indigo for the maintenance of the garrison until March following; the indigo, which was " a staple commodity," he was endeavouring to sell at Newhaven, in Sussex, but, being only able to obtain half its worth, he preferred keeping it.

While the Presbyterians were uppermost in England, the naval affairs went on smoothly. The Earl of Warwick was entirely devoted to them, as were all the officers appointed by him; and every summer a strong squadron was fitted out, by which the trade of the nation was tolerably protected. But, in 1648, when the Independents came to prevail, it was resolved to remove the Earl of Warwick from his command, notwithstanding the services he had rendered; and his removal was so displeasing to the seamen, that in the summer of that year, those on board the parliamentary fleet lying in the Downs declared for the king, and, after setting Colonel Rainsborough, the new admiral, and such officers as adhered to him, on shore, they sailed over to Holland, where the Prince of Wales then was. The prince, taking the command, sailed soon after with nineteen vessels, of which seven or eight were English, from Helvoetsluys for the coast of England, where he took many rich prizes; but, being foiled in his other attempts there, he returned late in August to Holland, whither he was followed with a superior fleet by the Earl of Warwick, who had been reinstated, and who induced the English seamen to serve again under the parliament. Sir Baldwin Wake recommended the prince to proceed to Guernsey with his ships, as did Sir Peter Osborne early in September from St. Malo, but his advice arrived too late: Had the prince come to Guernsey, in place of returning to Holland, the island would doubtless have immediately surrendered; and thus, having possession of its pier and roadstead, he would have been enabled very seriously to annoy the parliamentary trade and the southern coasts of England.

As it was foreign to this history to introduce more of Sir Peter Osborne's correspondence than we have done, it may not be amiss to recapitulate briefly a few of the most striking facts which the letters contain.

Of Charles I. it is stated, that he requested Sir Peter to hold out to the last, observing to his son : " I cannot name particulars, but I assure you I shall reward this good service of your father ; " and only fifteen months before his execution, when Sir Peter, through his son, solicited his majesty's commands, the unfortunate monarch replied : " I can give no commands, for now I am commanded ; but when I shall be in any condition to employ his loyal affections, he shall know that he is a person I have a very particular regard to : commend me to him, and tell him I am beholding to him." When a proposition was made to the king to convey Guernsey to France for a sum of money, he declined it, as he did another to permit the French to reduce the island for him ; doubtless because he thought that they would never willingly restore it. In October, 1647, when Charles said that he was commanded, and felt himself at the mercy of his opponents, the royalists appear by the above mentioned correspondence to have placed their chief dependance on his fortitude, and his constancy to his principles and friends, which even then were considered so immoveable that the very mention of his name seems to have caused an awe in the two houses of parliament. It was the knowledge of these qualities which doubtless led the parliamentary chiefs to believe that no faith could be placed on the slightest concession of the resolute but infatuated monarch, and that the liberties of England, as well as their personal safety, could only be secured by his death.

That there were occasional murmurings and discontents among the soldiers in Castle Cornet was not surprising, when we learn that, after a three years' siege, they were without clothes, or pay, or meat ; drinking water, with but one meal a day ; not having received " one penie of pay these three years." In one letter, we find " the escape of a soldier run from us to the enemy ; " in another, that a combination, to escape to the enemy with a boat and provisions, had been discovered, " and the author of it, as he well deserved, had

been shot to death ;" and in a third, that by the bursting of
a piece of ordnance, the gunner and his mate had been killed,
" necessary men that must needs be supplied."—" We have
not any kind of medicine in the castle," wrote Sir Baldwin
Wake, and the garrison surgeon at that time was a Frenchman, whose professional skill may be fairly estimated by his
salary of only ten pence a day! even although that sum
represented a far higher value than at present.

Of Sir Baldwin Wake,[1] beyond the mention made of him
in these pages, we have been able to ascertain but little, the
present baronet of that surname being unable to supply us
with any information on the subject; but as it appears by
Debrett's Baronetage, edition 1840, that the third son of
Sir Baldwin Wake, of Clevedon, county of Somerset, created
a baronet on the 5th of December, 1621, was also named
Baldwin, this son may have been the worthy successor of
Sir Peter Osborne, the more particularly as his eldest brother,
the second baronet, raised a troop of horse for Charles I.[2]
Lord Clarendon speaks of him once in the following terms,
when the Prince of Wales was debating, early in 1646, on his
removal from Pendennis Castle, near Falmouth, to Scilly :
" In the end, having advised Baldwin Wake to cause the
frigate belonging to Hasdunck, and the other ships, to be
ready upon an hour's warning," &c. ; and he seems to have
been both a naval and military officer, a common practice in
that age. His answer (ante) to Colonel Russell's letter, urg-
ing him to surrender the castle, in January, 1647, is very
honorable to him. He appears also to have been generally
upon bad terms with Sir George Carteret, notwithstanding
that, in January, 1648, he wrote that Sir George was very
careful of him. Early in September, 1648, Sir Baldwin was
in England, but he must have resumed his charge the same
month, as there is a letter from him, dated " Castle Cornet,
to Prince Rupert, September 14, announcing his safe arrival
in this important place ; dispatches an officer to give Prince
Rupert information concerning it."[3] His stay did not pro-

(1) R. commisit Thome Wake de Lyddell custodiam Insula. R. de Guerneseye Jereseye
Serk & Aureneye & alia. Insula. eisdem Insulis adjacencium hend' & regend' &c. usq
festum Sci Michis reddo quingentas libr. Ita qd, &c. Edw. III.—*Abbreviatio Rotulorum
Originalium.*
    Baldwinus Wake, Edw. I., Anno 10, (A.D. 1282,) is mentioned in the *Calendarium Inquis'
post Mortem* as possessing about 155 manors, &c., in different English counties.

(2) Among the knights who attended Charles II. to Jersey, in September, 1649, and
arrived with him the same day, we find in Chevalier's Chronicle the name of Sir E. Wake.

(3) Warburton's Memoirs of Prince Rupert, vol. i. page 534.—In this volume we also
find the following abstract, " Legge, Colonel, Castle Cornet, to Prince Rupert, January 15,
[1648 or 9,] after his long imprisonment is allowed to remain within twenty miles ; whenever he gets a pass, will be ready to go into any place wherever Prince Rupert can
employ him." We have endeavoured in vain to procure a copy of Colonel Legge's letter.

bably extend beyond the following spring; if so long, as Chevalier relates that he went to seek the prince, who gave him money, and that he never returned, his subsequent fate being unknown. His command could not, therefore, have exceeded three years, and for some months the castle was evidently left in charge of another officer. His successor was Colonel Burgess, and during this singular siege the period of each command was about as follows, viz.

Sir Peter Osborne, March 3, 1643, to May 28, 1646......3 years 3 months.		
Sir Baldwin Wake, May 29, 1646, to May, 1649......3 ,, 0 ,,		
Unknown, about May, 1649, to Oct. 26, 1649......0 ,, 5 ,,		
Colonel Burgess, Oct. 26, 1649, to Dec. 19, 1651......2 ,, 2 ,,		

Total ....8 years 10 months.

1649, February 22.—On this day, says Chevalier, there arrived in Jersey a frigate of the parliament, named the Heart, signifying in French Le Cœur; she was considered the second fastest sailing vessel in England, and it was she that had taken a small frigate belonging to Sir George Carteret. The Heart mounted ten guns. After the death of the king, part of the crew, seeing how the parliamentarians had laid their sanguinary hands on the person of their sovereign, resolved to go over to the Prince of Wales, holding the parliament in horror; and they only awaited a favorable moment to effect their purpose. One day, when they were at anchor in the Downs, the captain and some of the crew went ashore, and did not return that night. The royalist party at once availed themselves of this opportunity, and sent those on shore in the ship's boat who would not join them, having seized them while asleep. They then immediately set sail for Jersey, with a fine north-east wind. The frigate's crew consisted of seventy or eighty men, of whom only twenty-two had secretly resolved to take her to that island. The master was named Collin, and him they made their captain; among them was the surgeon and the boatswain. Being arrived then opposite Elizabeth Castle, and not knowing the entrance to the roadstead of St. Aubin, they fired a gun as a signal for a pilot, having no boat on board to come on shore for one. The people of the castle seeing them tack, perceived that they were strangers, but no one would venture on board, fearing that she was a parliament ship designing to entrap them, and perhaps to carry them away. At all hazards, however, Sir George sent a little boat to them with three men of the castle,

who were joyfully received on board, and allowed to take the
frigate to the roadstead. In entering, she saluted the fort
with nine guns, which the castle returned with five. Having
anchored, the master (now the captain) proceeded to the castle
with two or three of the principal officers, and, on leaving,
the ship saluted them with three guns. Sir George received.
them with a hearty welcome, when they recounted their
doings, and said that they had come voluntarily to serve the
Prince of Wales, not approving of the manner in which
affairs were conducted in England. They offered their services to Sir George, as well as the charge of the frigate, and
he at once appointed the said Collin as her commander. Men
were immediately sent on board to prepare the ship, so that
she might proceed to Guernsey to endeavour to capture the
frigate which had taken the vraicking boats at the Pierres de
Lecq, and before the adhesion of this frigate to the prince,
now called by his loyal subjects Charles II., was known.
On the same day, Sir George also sent on board Captain
Skinner and Captain Bowden with above fifty men, so that
with her own crew the frigate had nearly eighty men, and,
at about seven o'clock in the evening, they set sail on the
very day of their arrival in Jersey. All that night they kept
on a wind, so as to get to windward of Guernsey, and in the
morning came round, as if arriving from England. Having
reached the bank, they saluted the town as they were accustomed to do when they had been to convoy vessels to or from
St. Malo, and the townspeople knew her at once to be the
Heart. There was a frigate at anchor near Fermain, under
the guns of the land batteries, which was the one they were
in search of. Her crew, observing the Heart salute the
town, weighed anchor, that they might learn the news from
England. The Heart, while pretending to furl her sails, kept
drifting with the view of drawing the other frigate beyond the
reach of the land batteries, which having accomplished, and
being now within musket shot, she hailed and fired a gun,
followed by a shower of musketry. On this the Guernsey
frigate made all sail towards the land; but it was too late,
the Heart calling to her crew to strike, and firing incessantly
upon them with small shot. They called out: " We are on
your side;" "We are from Guernsey;" "We are for the
parliament." And the others answered: "We are for Charles
II.;" "Strike for Charles II." The Guernseymen continued
making for the land, but the Heart had drawn them so far
that they could not escape her; and seeing that they would

not strike, she ran her bowsprit into their rigging, by which manœuvre the head of their mainmast was broken and the mast dismantled. At the same instant the Heart's crew jumped on board, and became masters of the little frigate, which had only thirteen men, the captain, (Effard,) who was a Jerseyman, and the remainder being on shore. Many musket shots were fired at the prize; but, although several bullets lodged in her sides, she had none killed or wounded. Her thirteen men were sent below, while the captors repaired the sails to take her to Jersey; of the prisoners, ten were Guernseymen and three Jerseymen. This frigate was one of those which the parliament had given to Guernsey to cruise against the Jerseymen, and prevent their conveying supplies to Castle Cornet. She had four guns, and was well armed with muskets, carbines, pistols, swords, &c., and was victualled for six weeks for the twenty-two men who composed her crew. She was the second of the three frigates given by the parliament to Guernsey. The largest was commanded by Captain Bonamy, of Guernsey, and the smallest by Captain Lemprière, of Jersey. Bonamy was in England with his frigate, and that of Lemprière was in St. Sampson's harbour; otherwise the latter would also have been captured and brought to Jersey, the more as no suspicion was entertained of the Heart. The two Jersey captains (Effard and Lemprière) had sided with the parliamentarians at the commencement of the troubles in Jersey, and had fled from the island with the rest. When the commissioners came here, they condemned them to death in their absence, and ever afterwards they did their worst to the Jersey people, avenging themselves on those who were not to blame. The prize was called the Scout. Of the three Jerseymen on board, Sir George sent two to the old castle, (Mont Orgueil,) and the third entered the Heart to go cruising. Part of the Guernseymen also entered in the frigates, and the others were sent to France, Sir George giving each " a piece of eight " to assist them in returning home.—To return to the Guernsey frigate. She was taken at about ten in the morning, in sight of the garrison of Castle Cornet, who, being ignorant of the cause, were greatly surprised to see a parliament frigate capture a Guernsey one on the same side, the more as they recognized the Heart, which they had often seen at anchor on the bank near the castle. But when they observed both vessels steering for Jersey, they suspected that there had been some stratagem. The two vessels arrived in Jersey at four o'clock the same day, and saluted the castle, the Heart with nine guns returned by five, and the Scout with three guns returned by one. The former anchored in the Great Road, and the prize was taken under St. Janne, which is the harbour of Elizabeth Castle; she was quite new, having been built the preceding year, well equipped, and ready to sail to prowl about Jersey and Chaussey, and to cruise for the vessels which traded with St. Malo; but she was prevented. Thus Captain Effard lost his frigate, his commission, his clothes, and his honour, for being so negligent in remaining so long ashore. As to his men, when captured, they were as poorly clad as one could see, and had not a *sous* in their purse; but otherwise they were powerful, robust, and determined men, refusing to surrender and strike their sails, until compelled by force.

March 2.—Sir George sent the Heart frigate to cruise with a crew of about eighty men, English and Jerseymen, on Friday evening, the 2d of March; and the next evening she returned to Jersey with two prizes, viz. a Guernsey vessel of thirty tons burthen, laden with Bordeaux wine and earthen-ware, and an English vessel of sixty tons burthen, bound from St. Malo, with a ballast of oysters in the shell for London, where she belonged. These oysters, as well as the cargo of the Guernsey vessel, were landed at Elizabeth Castle.

The Prince of Wales to Sir George Carteret, Bart.

Charles P.—Trusty and well-beloved, we greet you well. We having some time since conferred the command of his majesty's fleet upon our right dear and right entirely beloved cousin, Prince Rupert, he hath, by his great industry and endeavour, brought the same in a condition to be ready to set sail with the first opportunity, and hath instructions from us to put in at Jersey, and to endeavour the reduction of Guernsey, if he shall have means to attempt the same with probability of success. We entreat you, therefore, not only to give him your best advice in that particular, but all the assistance you may, in case he shall think fit to make any attempt upon the said island of Guernsey.

Given under our hand and seal, the 11th day of January, [1649,] in the twenty-fourth year of the reign of the king our royal father.

To our trusty and well-beloved Sir George Carteret, bart., lieutenant-governor of the island of Jersey.[1]

Prince Rupert sailed from Helvoetsluys on the 21st of January, 1649, with a squadron of eight ships, very weakly manned, and passing through the straits of Dover with a

(1) From Warburton's Memoirs of Prince Rupert, vol. iii., page 261.

strong north-east wind, quickly arrived at the rendezvous, Kinsale, in Ireland, where the prince first heard of the king's death on the 30th of January. Part of the squadron was dispatched to relieve the Scilly Islands, but Prince Rupert never came to Jersey; and after being blockaded nearly all the summer in Kinsale, he set sail early the following winter for Portugal, proceeding thence to the Mediterranean.

Whitelock, in his Memorials, July, 1649, says: " Letters that 500 Irish were landed at Jersey, designed (as was imagined) to second the plot for surprising Weymouth, Portland, and other garrisons." Among them doubtless Guernsey.

Charles II. was at the Hague when his father was executed; but the Dutch, fearing the Commonwealth of England, were soon anxious for his departure. Whither to go he knew not, but at length he proceeded to St. Germain. Here he expected to hear daily of the taking of Dublin, which was in possession of the parliament, and was besieged by the Marquis of Ormonde. Being finally disappointed, Charles resolved on spending the winter in Jersey, because, says Lord Clarendon, " as the king had received no kind civility from France since his last coming, so it was notorious enough that his absence was impatiently desired by that court, though he had not been in any degree chargeable to them." Charles, hoping to receive in Jersey better news from Ireland, to enable him to proceed thither, sent to his brother-in-law, the Prince of Orange, " that he would cause two ships of war to ride in the rode before St. Maloes," to be at his disposal. " These ships did wait his pleasure there accordingly." But, on hearing of Cromwell's successes in Ireland, the king dismissed these two Dutch ships. Falle, after mentioning that Charles in his perplexity determined on coming to Jersey, adds, without giving the day, month, or year: " It was in autumn that his majesty came to us, and he staid with us till the spring following. As he found us the same dutiful people, so we him the same easy, humane, affable prince; which perhaps needed not be mentioned, it being the known character that distinguished him all his life. None were denied access to him, neither did he disdain invitations and entertainments from our little gentry, whom of himself he would sometimes honour with a visit at their habitations, as he rode about the island; with all parts of which he grew so well acquainted, that (having some skill in the mathematicks) he drew a map of it with his own hand, intending no doubt to keep the same in remembrance of a

place where he had enjoyed more peace and quiet than
hitherto any where else within or without his dominions. The
map at present is, I know not how, got into the Heer Van
Aldershelm's Cabinet of Curiosities at Leipsic, in Saxony,
where it is shewn to travellers.[1]   At his first being here, he
had given order for the construction of a fort, to be in the
nature of an outwork to Elizabeth Castle, which finding now
perfected, he would have it called by his own name, Charles'
Fort. It has been since incorporated with the castle, by
enclosing with walls and ramparts a long slip of ground which
parted them."

On Monday, 17th of September, 1649, writes Chevalier,
Charles II., king of England, arrived happily in Jersey for
the second time,[2] having come the first time on the 17th of
April, 1646.   He was in Holland when the fatal blow was
inflicted on his father, and then came to join his mother, the
queen, in France.   The two Dutch ships, which had brought
Sir George Carteret from St. Malo, were held in readiness in
the roadstead to go for the king, but were detained by contrary winds, and there only went for his majesty the privateer
of Captain Sedlethon, a new vessel of Captain Barnet, and a
Fleming, who had come to Jersey to get a commission to
cruise against the parliament ships.   These three vessels,
mounting but three guns each, were accompanied by sixteen
or eighteen boats.   Captain Bowden had had the honour of
carrying the prince from Jersey to France, and he now had
the honour of bringing him, as king, from France to Jersey.
Captain Bowden commanded a barge of eighteen oars and
two swivels, well armed also with muskets, carbines, pistols,
and swords, which had been built for the prince when he first
visited Jersey, and she was sent to convey the king on board
Captain Sedlethon's privateer, which was intended for his
reception.   The king, with his brother, the Duke of York,
and a few noblemen, embarked on board the barge at Cou-
tainville, a place on the coast of Normandy, about two leagues
from Coutances; and as the sea was smooth and the wind
favorable, his majesty preferred crossing [3] in the barge, which
was of only four tons burthen, and was escorted by the three
vessels. The royal party arrived happily at four o'clock in the
afternoon, when his majesty was saluted by the two Dutch ships.
in the roads with twenty-seven guns from one, and twenty-

(1) Dr. Brown's Travels, p. 172.

(2) Charles II. at this time was only nineteen years of age.

(3) The distance across was about twenty-seven English statute miles.

two guns from the other; and the three vessels which had escorted the king fired three guns each. When his majesty entered Elizabeth Castle, it saluted him with twenty-one guns and a volley of musketry, and Fort Charles fired three guns. The king, his brother, and some of the lords remained at the castle. When the evening came, bonfires were lighted all over Jersey on the heights within sight of the castle; and soon after the cannon were fired by all the twelve parishes, as also volleys of musketry, and the bells were rung everywhere until midnight, the whole in great rejoicing, to celebrate the arrival of our sovereign lord the king, Charles II., among us in this his island of Jersey, and who possesses only this poor island, Scilly, and the Isle of Man. Guernsey, on the contrary, has rejected her king, his ordinances and commands, having turned to the stronger side, according to human appearances; while Jersey has obeyed the voice which says: "Fear God, honour the king." In Guernsey, there is only the castle which holds for the king, the which is separated from the land, and the Guernseymen have done their best to prevent its being victualled, thinking by famine to reduce it for the parliament.

September 18.—The day after the arrival of the king, the boats, which had brought his attendants and baggage, returned to fetch the horses and carriages: there were 120 horses, three coaches, and two waggons. On this day also there came two parliamentary frigates, sent from Guernsey, where the salutes for the king's arrival had been heard; these frigates came almost within gun shot of Elizabeth Castle to spy and discover what vessels there were in Jersey.

September 19.—The day following, which was Wednesday, the two frigates returned, with four other frigates and two large ships, before the castle, to shew themselves, so that the king, the Duke of York, and the lords in attendance, might see the bravadoes which they made. They were ships which had arrived in Guernsey on the Monday that the king arrived in Jersey, and had been sent from England to protect Guernsey, because they feared that the king would send forces to reduce it. Shortly before these ships came tacking in front of the castle, the boats arrived there with the coaches, and Captain Sedlethon, who was the convoy, came behind, ranging along the land close to the rocks; the frigates fired some guns at him, which he returned, both without effect, as they were not within cannon shot. They anchored at night under St. Ouen's, and returned the next day to renew their bravadoes before the castle ; nevertheless, they could do nothing against the vessels which had escorted the king.

It is surprising that Falle, in his History of Jersey, the first edition of which was published only forty-five years after the second arrival of Charles in that island, did not enter more into detail relative to his sojourn there, as such details could then have been easily obtained. Happily, the omission has been in some measure supplied by Chevalier, a most minute and industrious chronicler. Charles is said to have left a gold stick and a gold spur with the family of De Carteret, to be used whenever any member of the royal family visited Jersey : he left also a brace of holsters, a horse cloth, a pair of gloves, and a table cover, at the house of Mr. Elias Dumaresq. The last of his name, who held these relics, was an old lady, who died in the summer of 1840.

" The king, with the Duke of York, about the beginning of September, repaired to the isle of Jersey. After he had ' settled' the affairs of that island, he had an eye upon reducing the island of Guernsey, which was then under the parliament's power ; but Castle Cornet, the chiefest fort thereof, was under his authority. A very gracious declaration, after several insinuations, was sent into the island ; but it proved ineffectual, for Russell, the governor for the English Commonwealth, had got 500 fresh men into it."— *Baker's Chronicle.*

By a commission from " Thomas Lord Fairfax, lord general of all the land forces under the pay of the parliament in England, Wales, and in the islands of Guernsey and Jersey, and in the town of Berwick," dated October 22, 1649, Colonel Alban Coxe[1] was appointed governor of Guernsey " in the absence of the present governor, Colonel Russell," and was required " to make his present repair to the said island." In another commission of the same date from Lord Fairfax, Colonel Coxe was authorized " from time to time, so often as occasion shall require, to call courts martial of commission officers under his command, (yourself being president,) and according to the laws and ordinances of war, to proceed to sentence and execution against such as shall offend against the said laws and ordinances, provided that if the sentence of the court shall extend to the taking away of limb or life, that in such case you suspend the execution until you have transmitted the proceedings of the court sealed up to the judge advocate of the army, and my pleasure known therein."

(1) These and the following particulars relative to this officer are extracted from his papers and letters in the British Museum.

October.—At this time it pleased the king, with the advice of his council, to give Milord Percy the government of Castle Cornet, to take care of it and to aid Sir George, so that nothing might be wanting for its supply. Milord Percy sent, with the king's authority, a lieutenant-governor, whom before going the king knighted; he was called Lieutenant-Colonel Burgess,[1] and he left in the night on the 25th of October, in a new shallop, which was well laden with provisions, and arrived the same night. She was very welcome, and the garrison and crew rejoiced together, drinking healths and firing several cannon. The shallop returned to Jersey on the night of Saturday the 28th, bringing from the castle six men ill with scurvy; they had their legs, and even their faces, swollen for want of fresh victuals and good beverage. The said castle was neglected through the hatred which existed between Sir George and Sir Baldwin Wake, who had previously been the governor, and had gone to seek the prince, who gave him money; but Sir Baldwin never returned, and it is not known what became of him, whether he was drowned or otherwise.—*Chevalier.*

John Bradshawe, President of the Council of State, to Colonel Alban Coxe.

" By several informations, we are satisfied of the great necessity that the forces[2] under your command, appointed for Guernsey, should with all expedition be transported thither. We therefore desire you to make your present repair to Weymouth,[3] to hasten their embarking; and for what remains to be done for your victual here, or any other provision, we desire you to leave the care thereof to some other here, by whom it may be dispatched and sent about by sea to meet you there, for we would not have you lose so much time as to attend yourself about it.

" Signed in the name and by order of the council of state appointed by authority of parliament.

" J. BRADSHAWE, President.

" Whitehall, November 10, 1649."

From the same to the same.

" By late letters received from Guernsey, we see how necessary it is that all possible expedition should be used for the transportation of those men into Guernsey which are appointed thither under your command. The treasurers have been spoken with, who inform me they have furnished the money. We there-

(1) Colonel Burgess was the officer who surrendered the castle, in December, 1651.

(2) These forces consisted of five companies, each of one hundred privates, exclusive of officers and non-commissioned officers.

(3) Weymouth appears to have been then considered, as it is still, the best port of communication between England and these islands.

v

fore desire you to lose no time, but forthwith apply yourself to Colonel Popham,[1] and upon conference with him for your better dispatch, to repair to the place where the shipping is ready for you, and transport yourself and men without any further delay.

"Whitehall, November 12, 1649."

Colonel Alban Coxe to President Bradshawe.

"My Lord,—I suppose it may be imputed to my slowness that I yet remain here, and therefore am bold to give your honor this short attempt, that I may continue my reputation with your lordship and that thrice honorable council whom you represent.

"My Lord,—Our provisions and other necessaries have been long a ship board; nothing to do, if the wind come fair, but get aboard ourselves; and it was Saturday last, about twelve at noon, before the ship I was enforced to hire here (which carries our provisions and one company) could get out of the harbour into the road; the wind then coming fair, I presently sent order to march on Sunday morning, by five of the clock. The companies were here and ready to embark; but the weather being foul and the wind contrary, I was enforced to remand them back to their quarters. I shall be diligent in the performance of the States' weighty service, and endeavour at all times to improve myself, my lord, &c.

"Melcomb Regis, December 18, 1649."

"*Enacted in the States,* [*of Guernsey,*] *the 4th of January,* 1649. [1650.]

"The Colonel Cox, Esq., governor of the island of Guernsey, having represented to the States (convened for the hearing of his commission) that it was needful that lodging and accomodation should be presently provided for five companies of soldiers, sent by the parliament in this island,[2] and desiring that three of them should quarter in the town and places adjacent, one in St. Martin's and places near it, the rest in the Castel, St. Sampson, and the Vale; it hath been ordained and resolved, that the quartering of the said soldiers shall be made according to the desire of the said governor, without prejudice to the "wright" (*sic*) of the said parishes for the time to come; and because that the parishes of St. Saviour, St. Peter, Torteval, Forest, and St. Andrew, are for the first time freed of the said lodging, it is ordered that the constables of the said parishes shall presently furnish as many beds, with their appurtenances, as they are bound, according to

(1) After the execution of the king, one of the earliest acts of the council of state was the removal of the Earl of Warwick from the post of high admiral, and the appointment of Blake, Dean, and Popham, to command the fleet.

(2) "1650, January 10.—The ship which carried the souldiers unto Guernsey, returned to the general rendezvous of the ships at Stokes Bay." — "January 15. Letters that the forces landed in Guernsey wanted accommodations of beds, &c., and were fain to lye in a church ever since they were landed." — "That two frigates of the prince prepared from Jersey to attempt Guernsey, hearing of the parliament's souldiers there, were presently diverted."—*Whitelock's Memorials.*

the rates and proportion of the number of soldiers that they should have lodged, according [to] the list delivered them this day for the purpose, which beds they shall bring in town to-morrow at noon, part of them to serve in the town for the surplus of their number, and the rest for the parishes above named ; for the performance of which the said constables are commanded not to fail in the time above said, as they shall answer to their peril to the said governor.

"It hath been ordained this day that the English shilling, being worth twelve pence sterling, shall go in this island for twelve sols tournois in payment and receipt, and other species of English money to (*sic*) proportion ; being prohibited and defended to all inhabitants and strangers to refuse it to the said price upon pain to answer the infraction of the said ordinance, which shall be published, that none should pretend cause of ignorance."

Colonel Roger Burgess to Colonel Alban Coxe.

"Sir,—As concerning the castle, [Cornet,] I am here entrusted by his majesty to keep it to whom of right it belongs, and for whom I will keep it against all power whatsoever that shall oppose it. This is my absolute resolution, so that you may surcease from any further message of this nature.

"I rest your servant,
"January the 9th, 1649." [1650.]   "ROGER BURGESS.

Colonel Russell, writing to the council of state, in pursuance of its orders of November 10, 1649, requiring him to give an account of the state of Guernsey, said, that in July, 1643, he took upon him the government of the island, and found the people ready for any impression ; but, since the king's death, he had "been as a lambe amongst wolves at the mercy of the islanders," some he won over, others he awed, but many of late had been seduced by a few factious spirits, which, for the securing of Guernsey, had made him importunate for soldiers. He adds, that the revenue and casual profits had been employed in the service of the parliament, and found all deficient ; and yet he wanted not accusers, as if he had enriched himself by the island, whereas indeed it had impoverished him : that since the coming of the commissioners the remedy had been in effect worse than the disease, as the revenue was immediately suspended, and two of them, viz. Mr. Wall and Mr. Frith, had acted with and for the mutineers, who had assembled the States without orders from him or the court, released persons imprisoned by him, attempted to seize packets, &c. "The chief managers of that faction here are not above seven, viz. Mr. Bonamy, Mr. J.

Carey, Mr. Gosselin, Dobrée, Andrew Monamy, Mr. de la
Place, and Mr. Charles de la Marche; the rest are venal
instruments, as Henry de la Marche and Mr. Haviland:
this I shall assert upon my life and honour, that had not I im-
portuned, and the parliament speedily sent, forces, the island,
through the divisions, had been possessed by the enemy." . . .
" The chief actors in the last meeting were Mr. Bonamy and
Mr. Gosselin, whom I had sent up had my power equalled
my authority, and Colonel Coxe affirmed his authority did
not look backwards.   I shall conclude all in a word—for
near seven years' service they have rewarded me with disobedience and ingratitude ; and now they contend not what
power they obey, but that they may enjoy universal liberty."

Russell, who by his own shewing was in the wrong, as
otherwise the two commissioners and Colonel Coxe would
have supported him, concluded his statement as follows :

" My opinion I humbly present :
" 1. That the forces intended for the ' straights' [1] should first
  attempt Jersey, that being of most consequence in relation to England and France.   It may done *obiter* or in
  the way and suddenly, the islanders being more terrified
  by a good fleet than a great army.
" 2. Guernsey castle will hardly be taken till then.
" 3. Should Rupert's ships escape and leave their men in
  Jersey, the place would be invincible.
" 4. And my humble desire is, that the said chief mutineers
  may be sent for to answer their misdemeanours before
  your honours."

When, in 1644, the islanders rose in arms against Russell,
as mentioned in Chapter XII., he engaged by a written agreement, dated November 22 of that year, that as it was reported
he had sent to England for troops, he declared and protested
that he had not done, or would not do, so.   He appears to
have been as incapable as he was mercenary and faithless.

December 15.—On Friday night, the 14th and 15th of
December, the king and his council dispatched in great haste
a boat laden with provisions for Castle Cornet, having learnt
that the last boat sent by them had been wrecked and broken
to pieces against the rocks near the said castle ; but the crew
and a part of the provisions were saved, as were the remains
of the shallop, which was of the burthen of seven tons ; and
all saved was taken to the castle.   With the remains of this

----

(1) This apparently alludes to the fleet under Blake and Popham, which was sent to the
Mediterranean in pursuit of Prince Rupert.

shallop and other timber, a boat of four tons burthen was constructed, with which some of the garrison went twice during the night to the little island of Herm, the only resident on which was a farmer, with his wife and children, who tended the cattle which the Guernseymen sent there to fatten. The first trip, they killed some cows, which were cut up in quarters and carried on board the boat, and then taken to Castle Cornet. The second trip, they brought away three or four head of horned cattle, so that in the two trips they took nine head of oxen, cows, and young beasts. The farmer had orders from the Guernseymen to make them a signal with fire, if he were molested by any one; but the men in the boat made him promise not to make the signal until they had reached the castle the second time, or otherwise they would return and carry him to Jersey, as they had done once before. This he promised to do, and only made the signal when he thought they had arrived at the castle. The Guernseymen, seeing the signal, went over to Herm with their *pataches*, but too late. The said boat came to Jersey with the hides of the cattle and the dog of the farmer; the crew had left Jersey with their shallop, which was quite new, on the 26th of November, and they returned to Jersey on the night between the 14th and 15th of December, which was the same night that the last boat left Jersey for Castle Cornet; but they did not perceive each other. The last boat arrived safely, and discharged her provisions without being incommoded by any one; she returned on the 19th instant. These two boats, being at anchor in the haven of Elizabeth Castle, were both knocked to pieces by bad weather during the night of the 23d of December.[1] — *Chevalier.*

"December, 1649.—Letters from Guernsey complaining of the want of ships for securing that island, and relating the French news."—*Whitelock's Memorials.*

From two documents which have very recently come to light, it would appear that the islanders attributed the continued resistance of Castle Cornet, in some measure, to an absence of zeal or capacity in the parliamentary officers in Guernsey, as about the year 1650, Captains Bonamy, De Havilland, and Guille, with fourteen lieutenants and sergeants of the different militia companies, which were not then em-

---

(1) At this period there was no harbour at St. Hélier, and, according to Chevalier, the Jersey shipping, employed in the Newfoundland trade, wintered in his time at St. Malo, for want of a safe harbour in that island. Mr. Dumaresq, who wrote in 1685, says: "There is a small pier unfinished under the castle walls, (Elizabeth's,) at the east end, by a sally port, where the castle boats are usually kept, and where greater vessels may be safe, but the entrance is narrow and dangerous, though good enough for boats."

bodied into regiments, signed a memorial or remonstrance to
Major Harrison, the acting lieut.-governor, setting forth that
they had certain information of the feebleness of the garrison
of Castle Cornet, as much from the few soldiers therein as
from their sickness, and want of food, ammunition, and lodging, in consequence of which they were reduced to despair,
and rendered incapable of standing an assault ; that the remonstrants, moreover, had ascertained, by the way of France,
that great preparations were making in Jersey to relieve the
castle with men, provisions, ammunition, and vessels of war.
The remonstrants, therefore, with the consent of a sufficient
number of the inhabitants, who volunteered to effect the
reduction of the castle, requested permission to make the
assault, and to be furnished with the ladders which had been
sent for that purpose from England ; in which case they
bound themselves to storm the castle in a few days, to the
end that the troubles and inconveniences, which the inhabitants had so long sustained, might cease, and that their zeal
and affection to the parliament might be manifested.   This
assault, we believe, is that mentioned in the second document
before us, from which we make the following extracts : "That
the storming of Castle Cornet was undertaken the first week
of April last, to the loss of the liberties, lives, and health of
many soldiers, which for certain had avoided so great an evil,
had they had as careful, vigilant, and understanding commanders as they were obedient and courageous soldiers." . . . .
"The truth is, that Castle Cornet was in great distress, and
unable to abide a storm, by reason of the paucity, weakness,
and manifold discouragement of the soldiers therein.   This is
true, by the relation of divers men from the said castle informing the same things at several times, as they were taken
in boats upon the sea, or as they escaped and rendered to the
island, and besides, by the very confession of the castle men,
at and after the time of the storm.   But the opportunity was
neglected for many weeks, which sore vexed the inhabitants,
who saw the parliament's service and their own deliverance
neglected ; wherefore, with real intentions and in great numbers, they offered and prepared themselves to subdue their
long, cruel, and very insensible enemy ; whereupon the commanders over soldiers were ashamed, and resolved to venture
upon the castle, yet in such a manner that they suffered boats
to depart the island, whereby the Jerseymen had intelligence
of their design and preparations, and therefore sent relief to
the said castle three or four days before the said storm.   And

besides, the said commanders shortened and weakened the parliament's ladders that they were unfit for service."—The document proceeds to state that the attack was made at night and at an improper time of tide, so that, by the desertion of the boatmen who ferried the assailants over, the latter were unable to return after the attack had failed.   It next denies an assertion, which might prevent further attempts, that the castle, with three score men, could keep out three thousand, "it being ordinary for those that are beaten to extol and magnify their enemy, that their disgrace may seem the less." "And, in truth, Castle Cornet is strong but little, and is commanded by the island, and the houses therein may be beaten down to the ground, and breaches made in the wall. And some sides and parts of the castle are without flankers and considerable strength.   Besides, if it be not accessible by land, many boats may pass soldiers with equal, if not with better, speed."   And, evidently in allusion to the military authorities, the document concluded thus : "God and the parliament send better men into Guernsey than those which hitherto have had the managing of affairs therein."

We can nowhere discover what was the numerical strength of the garrison of Castle Cornet while it was defended by Sir Peter Osborne ; but, judging from implication and from the difficulty which he experienced in obtaining provisions, we doubt if it ever exceeded three score, or at most four score, men at arms, of all ranks.   Under Sir Baldwin Wake, in December, 1646, the garrison, according to Chevalier, amounted to ninety men, while we learn from Le Roy that the number was reduced to fifty-five men, when the castle surrendered five years afterwards.   The islet, even with its probably additional tanks, appears now incapable of supplying more than one hundred men with water, a want of which is so much to be dreaded by a beleaguered garrison, as indeed it was by Sir Baldwin Wake in the summer of 1646.   In the following instructions as to the best means of reducing Guernsey, it will be seen that Sir Peter states that the castle was then rendered incapable of lodging more than three score soldiers, or of holding provisions for as many men as would be thought requisite by a *coup de main* to surprise the town. These instructions are without date, but they appear to have been written in March or April, 1646, and to have been addressed either to Lord Colepepper or to Lord Jermyn, in Paris, as we gather from Mr. John Osborne's letter to his father, dated St. Malo, March $\frac{18}{28}$ of that year.

[o]

"The number of men required for the reducing of this island, and to secure it reduced, can be no fewer than eight hundred men, furnished with able officers, expert pylots, and good land guides; no considerable partie lyke to appeare for the king; if any do, it wil be feare that brings them in, rather than love. Let not this number be thought too greate, since the busines is not with the islanders alone, but backt with the parliament of Engl., that will not loose theire footing they have gotten heere.

"The best place for landing is, in my opinion, the shore under the windmill of the Vale, somewhat to the right hand of the hougue called Boulevert La Pere. It lyes between the towne and the castle of the Vale. But it is a shore full of rocks, and will not admit ships to come neere, insomuch that all must be done with shalupes. For the guard of this place, there is onely one peice that lyes upon it to impeach a landing.

"The tyme can not be prescribed, but must be referred to honest and good pylots, if such may be found; the wyndes, and especially the tydes, that runne strongly heere, being in that matter of cheife consideration.

"But the event of this attempt being uncertayne, least all be hassarded at once, the principall thing requisite to be first done is to have this castle well and plentifully supplied in all kindes for a twelvemonth, and to put in threscore men for the increase of the guarison, and to give opportunity for the releife and refreshing of those that have languished under the miseries of so long a seige; that so this important fort may be sure to be kept safe for his majesti till an other essay, in case the first attempt fayle.

"That a considerable and sufficient sum be made over hether for the payment of the souldiers that have not receaved one penie of pay these three yeares, of which they growe now dispayrefull, and to encourage the fresh men that shall be put in, as lyke wise to hyre boates, and reward such as bring provisions, and for other services.

"Now, in answer to your lordship's further demands, I conceave that, from the castle may be given but small assistance to the reducing of the island, it chiefly serving to command the rode and the entrance into the peire, and made now uncapable to lodge more than threscore souldiers, or to hold provisions for the sustentation of so many men as may be thought meete by saly to surprise the towne, the lowe water not allowing more for the attempt and the retreate than two hours, and not alwayse so much.

"The ships necessary for this business may be estimated best by the number of the men they shall be appoynted to transport, and the ships there enemies may have here to encounter them, or may be lyke to increase upon the alarme given in England.

"The action would [? should] be wholly committed to English, both for commanders and souldiers. The islanders never lyke to submit to the French,[1] it being also dangerous to do it by that nation that pretend a clayme, and therefore to be suspected they will not yeild up there conquest, but keepe what they get. And the naturall animosity betweene the islanders of Guernsey and Jersey is so well knowne, that I believe it would make those, that might els yeild, more obstinate to resist to the uttermost any of Jersey that shall endeavour to reduce them, 'for I knowe 'one[2] who hath suffered for the king's cause, and whose hart is 'his, hath solemnly protested that his hart is so agaynst those of 'Jersey, that, if they should attempt it, he would returne into 'Guernesey to joyne and dy with his countrimen in theyre re- 'sistance.'[3]

"At one and the same tyme (for it must be then about high water) some ship, under the command of a resolute and good seaman, would [should] be designed to run directly within the peere, (exposed to the hassard to come of [off] as she can,) that may amaze and distract those of the towne, and give the more liberty to the landing of the men under the wyndmill of the Vale. In lyke manner, another ship, under a brave and expert commander, to be appoynted at the same instant to runne into the harbour at the castle of the Vale, which, being altogether put in execution, with the blessing of God, will carry the business.

"Lastly, that consideration be had of provision and victuall for the souldiers to be kept in garrison to master the islanders, and for the resistance of such forces the parliament will certainly send, for in respect the island is not able of itself to feed so many mouths that will be then put upon them to nourish besydes inhabitants.

Endorsed : "My father's directions how to reduce the island."

The animosity between the sister islands, referred to in these instructions, although certainly any thing but natural, doubtless existed, and at this time must have been increased by political differences. That animosity has happily long since disappeared, because, in consequence of a more frequent intercourse, the islanders are better known to each other, although perhaps there always was, and is still, a spirit of rivalry between them. As Guernsey has outlived her commercial superiority, partly because, as Mr. Inglis expresses

(1) Captain Marryat, in the "King's Own," says: "But, Debriseau, are you not a native of Guernsey, which is part of the British dominions?"—"Bah! it's all one, mon ami; we islanders are like the bat in the fable, beast or bird, as it suits us,—we belong to either country; for my part, I have a strong natural affection for *both*." Sir Peter Osborne, it seems, thought otherwise, and assuredly this little sally at the national indifference of the Anglo-Norman Islanders is more humorous than just.

(2) Mr. Amias Andros was probably the individual alluded to.

(3) The passage in inverted commas is crossed out in the rough draft of these instructions, and was evidently omitted in the fair copy.

it, "there is less work and more play than in Jersey ; less of
the business of life and more of its elegancies ;" and to this
remark we regret to add, that the former island rivals many
Roman Catholic countries in the number of its holidays and
idle processions ; while Jersey, since the peace of 1815, has,
much to her credit, taken a very decided start of Guernsey[1]
in navigation and trade, enterprise and prosperity, notwithstanding she is more embayed, has a less secure roadstead, and
possesses fewer natural capabilities for the contruction of a
pier,—art thus triumphing over nature ; and as it is only since
the plying of steamers, and the presence of a far greater
number of British residents, that Jersey is becoming more
English than Guernsey[2]—it may not, therefore, be thought
invidious to conclude that the reason why the Guernseymen
of the civil war would have fought against the Jerseymen
with greater obstinacy, was, that they considered them as
more French than themselves, and as less advanced in comfort and civilization.   In this conclusion we are borne out by
Heylin, already quoted, as also by the late Mr. Chenevix, an
acute observer, who resided in these islands during the years
1814-15, and who, in his Essay upon National Character, observed : "Among the islands depending upon England, the
character of none are more worthy of notice than those of
Jersey and Guernsey.   The former is more warm and fertile,
and slants towards the south ; the latter is poorer, and its grand
declivity fronts the north.   Jersey is more vain — Guernsey
more proud.   Both retain traces of their former French connection, particularly among the lower orders, but Jersey by
much the most : both have acquired many characteristics of
their modern British dependence, but Guernsey more than
Jersey.—Jersey is the France, Guernsey the England, of
these islands ; and few countries unite so much affluence and
prosperity to so large a stock of morals and simplicity as the
latter."   And Dicey, who wrote in 1751, says : "The people
[of Guernsey and Jersey] in their original language alike
also ; but in their customs and manners, the inhabitants of
Guernsey come nearer the fashions of the English."   Speak-

(1) The author of this history endeavoured, in 1837, to explain the causes of this change
in the fourth volume of the Guernsey and Jersey Magazine, under the head of "Commerce
of Guernsey." In 1851, he paid a short visit to Jersey, and was astonished at the immense
improvements which had been made in the environs of St. Hélier since the year 1840.
The present rising generation will scarcely believe that in 1830, when he first visited Jersey,
St. Peter-Port was a far gayer and a more bustling and commercial town than St. Hélier,
part of the Newfoundland trade being then carried on from St. Aubin.

(2) We, however, greatly question whether becoming more English be desirable for
either island, as English manners and habits have generated, and will continue to generate, an English scale of expenditure, quite incompatible with their equal laws of inheritance.

ing of Guernsey, in 1834, Inglis said : " In fact, the people of all ranks are more English." As the members of an ancient but decayed family love to look back on the importance and respectability of their ancestors, so Guernseymen may perhaps be excused if they still cling to the by-gone better days of their forefathers.

1650.—On Saturday, the 2d of February, the boat which the king had sent on Thursday with provisions for Castle Cornet, returned safely to Jersey, bringing Colonel Burgess, who came to speak to his majesty and to receive his commands. In leaving Guernsey, they were pursued and attacked by a *patache*, sent on their track by the Guernseymen ; this *patache* had a small cannon and two swivels, with some twenty men on board, and that of Jersey had only eleven men, who defended themselves valiantly, fighting for three hours *en braves*, and by good fortune had none killed or wounded ; they did not know whether the Guernseymen had any or not. However, by their courage they escaped the clutches of these rebels to their king.—*Chevalier*.

On Wednesday, the 13th of February, the king of England, Charles II., left Jersey, between nine and ten in the morning. for France, on his way to Holland, according to his promise to the Scotch commissioners, who had arrived in Jersey on the 6th of December last. The king embarked in his barge from Elizabeth Castle, to go on board Captain Amy's frigate, which awaited him in the roads. The Duke of York and Sir George Carteret attended the king to the frigate ; and when she was ready to get under sail, the duke took leave of his brother, the king, upon which they embraced each other tenderly three times, with tears in their eyes. The duke and Sir George returned to the castle, the frigate having got under weigh for France, with a fresh south-west wind, but no salute was fired either from the castle or the frigate. The king arrived happily on the coast of Normandy at three o'clock ; he had sojourned in Jersey four months and twenty-six days, which made one hundred and forty-nine days, having left on the one hundred and fiftieth day of his arrival. The king, at his departure, appointed the Duke of York governor of Jersey, and Sir George his lieutenant ; my Lord Jermyn having ceded the government to the duke by an agreement between the king and himself. The king also gave to the duke the government of Castle Cornet and of the island of Guernsey, when it should please God to place him on the throne.—*Chevalier*.

The preceding mention of Lord Jermyn's name induces
us to notice a charge of treachery which has been brought
against him by Berry.—This nobleman is accused of lending
himself to a design of the French, in 1646, to take possession
of both Jersey and Guernsey by means of 2,000 men, to be
sent from France for the ostensible purpose of reducing the
latter island for the king of England ; and, as a reward for
his perfidy, Lord Jermyn was to receive a dukedom and
200,000 pistoles.   To counteract his reported intrigues for
this object, an association was entered into in Jersey by Lord
Capel, Sir Edward Hyde, Sir Ralph Hopton, and Sir George
Carteret, the articles of which are given in the Clarendon
State Papers, II., 279.   Whitelock also mentions that there
was an intention of selling these islands to France, and Mr.
John Osborne, writing from Rouen, about October, 1646, to
his father, Sir Peter, said : " It is secretly whispered here,
but it is publicly talked of in Paris, that both the islands are
to be delivered to the French, and my Lord Jermyn is to be
made duke and peer of France.   This intelligence I have
from a very good friend of yours and mine when I was in Sr.
(sic.) Now Dunkirk is taken, if they should have the islands,
they would be masters of the whole Channel from east to west,
and there would be nothing wanting for an invasion, which
they already promise themselves.   These considerations do
enforce me to make a step to Paris, being I am so nigh ; not
that I will discover any knowledge of it, but only to inform
myself of the truth, which is so probable that I am only
troubled to seek out a remedy."   It is very probable that
Lord Jermyn may have proposed to reduce Guernsey by
means of French troops; but all reasonable proof of a traitorous motive on his part appears to us to be wanting : moreover, it may well be doubted that the French government,
notwithstanding its great anxiety to seize on these islands,
would have ever promised him so enormous a sum, at that
day, as two millions of francs, especially when it is remembered that the act of treachery could not be accomplished
without a war with England, which Cardinal Mazarin was
not disposed to undertake at that time.   In any case, Lord
Jermyn may have been only the passive instrument of the
queen of England,[1] as Lord Clarendon insinuates that a criminal intimacy existed between them, and of which there is
now no doubt.   Although Lord Jermyn's character is drawn
by Clarendon with no friendly hand, yet he certainly was

(1) Princess Henrietta Maria of France, daughter of the renowned Henry IV., and wife
of Charles I., whose evil genius she was in many respects.

more instrumental in the preservation of Castle Cornet than any of Charles' courtiers, and it was to him that Sir Peter Osborne, while at St. Malo, looked chiefly for funds for that purpose. Lord Jermyn was afterwards Earl of St. Albans.

CHAPTER XVI.

CHARLES I.—1625 to 1649. (Concluded.)

THE execution of the misguided and unfortunate Charles,[1] on the 30th of January, 1649, was a great political error, as was proved, only eleven years after, by the Restoration; his close imprisonment or his continual exile would have tended far more than his death, which made him a martyr, to perpetuate the Commonwealth; and the dreadful lesson was lost even on his two sons and successors, who merited his fate far more than himself. On the decease of the king, no serious impression had been made on Castle Cornet, although Russell had been removed, partly for his single unsuccessful attack upon it. Thus Mr. Peter Carey said: " The deponent knows but one attempt the said lieutenant-governor made against the castle, which had a very bad success; during which attempt the said lieutenant told the deponent he stood at a rock called " La Vermière, which is between the island and the castle." It was, however, subsequently assailed at least once or twice; and in an assault about May, 1650, the parliamentarian Major Harrison's " resolute and gallant party" were taken prisoners by the garrison of the castle.[2] On this subject, Dicey, whose descriptions, it must be admitted, are sometimes exaggerated and marvellous, says :

"Castle Cornet, it must be observed, is an invincible place, situated upon an inaccessible rock, having little or no avenues to it. In the time of the grand rebellion, it held out a tedious long siege, yet was never taken, although assaulted with the utmost vigour two several times, by Oliver's forces, when the soldiers in it were most of them sick with the scurvy ; but, after all attempts

(1) Hallam, speaking of the escape of Charles from Hampton Court, says, that "he might probably, with due precautions, have reached France or Jersey." But he was unfortunately persuaded to go to the Isle of Wight.

(2) "May 31, 1650.—Letters from Guernsey that Major Harrison had besieged the castle, and made 150 shots at it."—*Whitelock's Memorials*

to have taken it proved ineffectual, and in which great numbers were slain, the gallant cavaliers who defended this impregnable fortress withstood the enemy with the bravest intrepidity, and underwent many hardships, until their provisions were wholly spent; when they were forced to surrender upon honorable terms; not before they had obtained the sum of £1,500 sterling, to secure themselves, when marched out, from farther distress by Cromwell's party.

" This castle stands before the town and harbour, east by south, and commands all the road and avenues in that part of the island, where the channel is very narrow and dangerous. In this castle the governors usually made their residence, and received the respects of all captains, commanders, and masters of ships, before they went into the island."

In England, the royal cause was irretrievably undone towards the close of 1645 : in September of that year, Bristol, a very important place, was somewhat discreditably rendered by Prince Rupert, and in a few months after, every stronghold had also submitted to the parliament, with very few exceptions, the last being Oxford, which capitulated on the 24th of June, 1646, after two months' siege; yet Castle Cornet adhered unflinchingly to Charles, notwithstanding these contagious examples and defections, and amid sufferings which might well have excused an honorable capitulation. That such a capitulation would have been fully justified appears by an order from the king, dated Newcastle, June 18, 1646, to such garrisons as still held out for him in England, in which order he requested the several loyal governors " to make their compositions upon the best terms they may; for the truth is, I cannot relieve them." We know not whether Sir Baldwin Wake, who three weeks previously had succeeded Sir Peter Osborne in the command of Castle Cornet, ever saw this royal order; but certain it is, that he did not take advantage of it, and the siege was continued for three years longer, until the execution of Charles, when it will naturally be supposed that so astounding an event would have been followed by the immediate surrender of the castle, or at least towards the close of the same year, when there were about eight hundred republican soldiers in Guernsey; but the little garrison still resolutely persisted in its hopeless defence, and the parliament found sufficient employment in bringing the refractory Scotch and Irish to obedience : it was not, therefore, until nearly three years after that execution, when the fortunes of Charles II. had been effectually over-

thrown at the battle of Worcester,[1] September 3, 1651, that a
fleet, under the celebrated Blake, conveying a strong land
force, was dispatched to effect the reduction both of Jersey
and Castle Cornet.[2] Blake had, in the previous month of
June, subdued the Scilly Isles, which were held by Sir John
Granville for Charles II., and the privateers of which, like
those of Jersey,[3] inflicted much loss upon English commerce.
Castle Cornet capitulated on Monday, the 15th of December,
the same day on which Elizabeth Castle, in Jersey, was evacuated ; and thus Castle Cornet had the honour of being the
last spot, not only in the Anglo-Norman Islands, but in all
the British European dominions, which surrendered to the
parliamentarians, as the garrison, consisting of about fifty-five
men, stipulated to hold it until Friday, the 19th of December.
That day must indeed have been one of general rejoicing in
St. Peter-Port, as even the royalists in heart doubtless breathed more freely at the thought that they had at last got rid of
such disagreeable neighbours, although to the inhabitants of
either party it must have been an affecting sight to witness
the emaciated and ill-clad garrison emerging from that strong-
hold, which they had so long and so faithfully defended, and
wending their way across the rugged passage which at low
water separates the fortress from the town. And, surely,
none could behold this little band of gallant men lay down
their arms without a thrill of respect and sympathy. The
articles of capitulation, dated December 15, were highly favorable to the besieged, whose gallant resistance had indeed well
merited the consideration of their enemies. The first article
was an agreement for the suspension of hostilities and the
delivery of the castle four days later to Colonel John Bingham ; the officers and soldiers of either party keeping in the
mean time their respective guards and quarters. The second
is curious, as denoting the mode of military surrender at that
period : " That Colonel Roger Burgess, governor of the said
castle, with all the officers and soldiers appertaining to the

---

(1) After the battle of Worcester, a reward of £1,000 was offered for the apprehension
of Charles, who was thus described : " For the better discovery of him, you may take
notice of him to be a tall man, about two yards high, his haire a deepe browne, more to
black, and hath been (as we heare) cut off since the destruction of his army at Worcester,
so as now it is not very long."

(2) " 1651, November 24.—Letters that the enemy in Castle Cornet, in Guernsey, were
besieged, and very high ; but the inhabitants of Guernsey island were generally the
parliament's friends."—" December 29. Letters that Cornet Castle in Guernsey island was
surrendered to the parliament upon articles."—*Whitelock's Memorials.*

(3) " March 30, 1648.—Letters from St. Malloe, in France, advising that a pyrate about
Jersey had made prize of a vessel of the parliament's, going for Ireland with cloath and
apparel for 6,000 soldiers." — " Order for a letter to the parliament's agent in France to
desire the king to seize the pyrate, and restore the ship."—*Whitelock's Memorials.*

said garrison, shall have liberty to march forth with their
arms, and all their wearing apparel of whatsoever kind, drums
beating, ensigns displayed, BULLET IN MOUTH, and match
lighted AT BOTH ENDS, into the island of Guernsey, there to
lay down all their arms, except their swords, and those they
shall be permitted to wear, enjoy, and take away ; and the
said governor, and the commissioners to this treaty, shall each
be allowed one case of pistols." [1]　The third and fourth articles provided that Colonel Burgess, with his officers and soldiers, should be supplied with the necessary provisions, according to their respective ranks, for the full space of twenty days,
whether on shore or on ship board, without any charge ; that
such as desired to repair to England, Jersey, or France, should
be transported thither with safe convoys and with all convenient speed, no oaths or engagements being imposed upon
any of them for three months from the day of their arrival in
England or Jersey ; and that all or any of them should be at
liberty to sell their estates within three months, and withdraw
themselves, " with their goods and families, out of any of the
parliament's quarters." The fifth and sixth articles stipulated
for an act of indemnity for Colonel Burgess and his garrison,
for any acts committed by them by sea or land against the
Commonwealth of England from the year 1640, and that they
should be at liberty to repair to their several estates and
counties, and there abide if they pleased without any restraint,
all sequestrations against any of their estates being " forthwith declared void, without any composition whatever." The
eighth article was as follows : " That Colonel John Bingham
shall well and truly pay, or cause to be paid, to Colonel Roger
Burgess, or his assigns, the just and entire sum of £1,500
current English money, on Thursday, the 18th of this December, at or in the house of Mrs. Carey, widow, (that being the
appointed place of meeting,) and that in consideration of the
great civility showed by the said Colonel Burgess and his
garrison to Major Harrison's resolute and gallant party, that
became prisoners in the assault thereof." The ensign, Thomas
Cromwell, mentioned in the tenth article, was probably a relative of the Protector.

　Thus Castle Cornet was maintained for king Charles and
his son, by the endurance and heroism of its garrison, during
the long period of nearly NINE years, or the whole of the civil

(1) At the surrender of Bâton Rouge, in West Florida, to the Spaniards, in September,
1779, the British troops claimed to march out "with drums beating, matches lighted
AT BOTH ENDS, colours flying, &c. ; but the BULLET IN MOUTH had then apparently ceased
to be considered an honorable compliment by the vanquished.

war—a defence which, with the fabulous exception of ancient Troy, we believe to be unparalleled, and which now appears almost incredible. It is true that the modern art of attacking fortified places was then in its infancy, and that the island possessed few or no heavy battering cannon; but when it is considered that this isolated and diminutive fortress stands on a barren rock, to which there is only access at noon and midnight for a few days in every month, and that it is almost, if not quite, within hail of St. Peter-Port, one cannot but admire the inviolable constancy and resolution of Sir Peter Osborne, his successors, and their companions in arms, who, for the space (we love to repeat it) of NINE weary years, maintained this solitary place of exile, shut out as it were from the world, cheered by little or no intercourse with their friends or relatives, without prospect of relief, almost abandoned by the sovereign for whom they suffered in his extremity, and subjected to every possible trial and privation!! Surely, these devoted soldiers had achieved for themselves and their country a name and fame which ought not to have exposed them to the wilful ignorance or culpable neglect of contemporary historians. Lord Clarendon, above all, shares in this reproach, because he must have been cognizant of the noble defence we have narrated; and yet we will not do him the injustice to suppose that, in his unpardonable silence, he was influenced by the sinister reports of Sir George Carteret, with whom, while in Jersey, he was in daily and most friendly intercourse, and whose gallant resistance to the parliament he has related at some length. Hume, as we have shewn in a foot note, states that the Countess of Derby, in her defence of the Isle of Man, "retained the glory of being the last person in the three kingdoms, and in all their dependent dominions,[1] who submitted to the victorious Commonwealth:" this he evidently did to gratify the noble family of Stanley; but we learn from "Whitelock's Memorials"[2] that that island was surrendered about the 1st of November, or nearly seven weeks before Castle Cornet. We have no wish to detract from the merits of the courageous countess, whose husband was executed for his loyalty, in 1651; but we cannot, with any regard to truth, permit the Isle of Man to claim an honor which belongs

(1) Hume is here also incorrect, as Barbadoes, the Leeward Islands, and Virginia, surrendered to the parliament several weeks after the Isle of Man.

(2) "1651, November 9.—Letters that the whole Isle of Man, with all the forts and castles in it, were surrendered to the parliament's forces."—"November 10. Letters of the particulars of the taking of the Isle of Man, the summons sent to the Countess of Derby, and her soldiers deserting of her, and the articles of rendition of it to the parliament, without a shot or blow struck. That they had there great store of arms, and ammunition, and ordnance."—*Whitelock's Memorials*, folio edition. London, 1682.

W

unquestionably to Castle Cornet; and even had it been otherwise, we hold that there was much more glory in the defence
of a small sea-girt fortress under the circumstances we have
described. By this surrender, Guernsey was at length relieved from the calamities to which it had been subjected
during the civil war. The occupation of Castle Cornet by
the royalists had kept St. Peter-Port in a continued state of
siege, above ten thousand cannon shot having, it is said, been
fired into the town; while the Jersey privateers preyed upon
the external commerce of the islanders. What little shipping
trade there was, was chiefly carried on at St. Sampson's harbour, although some of the Norman boats ventured to the
Piette. Even as late as the 16th of May, 1650, we find the
jurats writing to Bailiff de Beauvoir, who was then in London,
as follows: "We also entreat you to procure us some good
vessels of war to protect our roadstead, for Jersey is full of
frigates, (? privateers,) and the trade of the island will be
entirely destroyed if we have not this protection, and then
we shall be in the abyss of misery.[1] Not a few of the townspeople, exposed to the guns of the castle, were forced to
remove into the country, which, from the existing troubles
and the exactions of an unpaid and licentious soldiery, became
nearly uncultivated. Indeed, the poverty of all classes was
finally so great, that the States, or insular parliament, by an
unanimous decision, were under the necessity of enacting that
no debts of any kind should be sued for, except arrears of
house and ground rents, and this for a whole year. At this
distance of time, it appears inconceivable that the castle could
be supplied, if the parliamentarians had exercised ordinary
vigilance, as it now seems that two or three rowing gallies,
well manned and armed, could easily have captured the boats
coming in "the dark moons" from Jersey with provisions.
And the bad weather, which would have kept these gallies in
port, would have equally prevented the boats from crossing
over. But war in that age lacked the science and the vigour
of the present, partly because the belligerents were mere
novices in the more modern art of providing the necessary
funds for it, at the expense of posterity.

(1) Extracts from Whitelock's Memorials, 1651:—February 21. Letters that several
merchantmen have been taken on the western coast by the Jersey pyrates.—February 26.
Letters that two Dutchmen, laded with salt, came to an anchor within half a league of
Dartmouth castle: that presently after two Jersey pyrates came up with them, cut their
cables, and carried them away: that the castle shot at them, but could not reach them.—
March 1. Letters of Jersey pyrates very bold upon the western coast.—March 6. Letters
of several ships taken by the pyrates of Jersey.—March 15. Of the want of fregats upon
the western seas to keep in the pyrates of Jersey.—March 17. Of the Jersey pyrates
taking several merchant ships, and none of the parliament fregats to help them.—March 19.
Letters of pyracies committed by those of Jersey.

English historians give all the credit to Blake[1] for effecting the reduction not only of Scilly and Jersey, but of Castle Cornet; and although he or some of his officers may have appeared before the castle, we can discover no evidence to that effect, or still less that his ships attacked it. Jersey having surrendered, it is clear that Castle Cornet was become untenable; and the garrison, with immediate starvation staring them in the face, had no other alternative than to capitulate: this however they did, not with Blake or his captains, but with the parliamentary lieutenant-governor of Guernsey, who probably never would have agreed to pay the little garrison so large a sum in those days as £1,500, had the castle been threatened by a strong naval force.

A passing mention has been made of the surrender of Elizabeth Castle, and as it is a sister fortress of Castle Cornet, although larger, being situate about three quarters of a mile from the main land, and accessible also on foot at low water, a brief description of it, and the details of its reduction by the parliamentary forces, may not be unacceptable.

Until the erection of Fort Regent, which took its name while George IV. was regent, Elizabeth Castle was, as Mont Orgueil[2] had previously been, the principal fortress of Jersey. The islet on which it is built is about a mile in circuit. The castle was first designed in 1551, in the reign of Edward VI., and, to defray part of its cost, all the bells in the island, reserving only one to each church, were ordered to be taken down and sold! In 1586 and the years following, the upper ward, which properly is queen Elizabeth's castle, was erected, every householder in the island contributing four days' work towards it. The lower ward is the castle of king Charles I. begun 1626: Charles' Fort was added during the civil war. Sir Edward Hyde, afterwards Lord Clarendon, resided twenty-six months in Elizabeth Castle, occupying a small house, (says Durell,) that stood in the lower ward, adjoining the chapel, both which buildings have long since disappeared. But Chevalier states that he built a handsome house of three stories in the castle. One of these houses long retained the name of *La Maison du Chancelier*, and in it he compiled a

(1) "Blake sailed from Scilly with the fleet to Jersey, where he arrived in the month of October, and reduced it by the end of the year; as he did likewise Cornet Castle, which was the only place that held out for the king in Guernsey; and thus secured the sovereignty of the sea, in this part of the world, for the parliament."—*Campbell*.

(2) The first mention that we can discover of this castle is as follows: "A.D. 1372. An. 46 Edw. III. Rex dilectis sibi Edmundo Rose, constabulario castri nostri de Gurry in Insulâ de Jereseye," &c.—Edmund Rose resided in Guernsey. The earliest mention of Castle Cornet under that name is in the Extent of Edw. III., An. 5, A.D. 1331.

part of that work which was formerly pronounced the noblest history in the English language, although we conceive it to be written too much in the spirit of party, and wonder that it does not even mention such an eminent parliamentarian as Colonel Hutchinson.   Moreover, as we have adduced one proof of its erroneous narration relative to Guernsey, so many instances of its inaccuracy, perhaps excusable enough in so voluminous a work, may be seen in Lord Ashburnham's Vindication of his ancestor, the faithful attendant of Charles I.[1] Clarendon unquestionably drew, with a masterly hand, the characters of those who acted a leading part in the stirring but troublous times of the great rebellion, and yet few will now approve of his concluding delineation of Cromwell : " In a word, as he was guilty of many crimes against which damnation is denounced, and for which hell fire is prepared, so he had some good qualities, which have caused the memory of some men in all ages to be celebrated ; and he will be looked upon by posterity as a brave, wicked man." Such was the Protector as pourtrayed by Clarendon ; but, assuredly, the dark shades of the picture have not been confirmed by posterity ; and, happily, recent and more impartial historians, untrammelled by contemporary animosities or prejudices, have done justice to the superior mind and vigorous administration of Cromwell.   And when Clarendon thus anathematized the character of the man who made England feared to the uttermost boundaries of Europe, he must have known that Charles II., in 1654, offered £500 a year, and knighthood, to any one who would destroy Cromwell by "pistol, sword, or poison, or otherwise," as appears in a proclamation given by Thurloe ; and the exiled monarch was only stopped in this guilty and cowardly course by the declaration of his intended victim, that if any attempt to assassinate him should fail, he would make an exterminating war of it, and destroy the whole of the royal family, as he had instruments to execute his purpose whenever he required them.   And the dread of this retaliation, with so unprincipled an opponent, was a better security to the Protector than his guards.   In the travels of Sir Philip Skippon, knighted by Charles II. at Whitehall, in 1674, and son of the well known parliamentary major-general, it is related that the secretary of the republic of Switzerland constantly took off his hat whenever the name of

(1) Mr. Forster, in his admirable Life of John Pym, exposes the "falsehoods, carelessness, disingenuousness, and meanness," of Clarendon in his history.   Brodie, Hallam, Macintosh, &c., are also very severe on the noble historian, who seceded from the popular to the king's party.

Oliver Cromwell was mentioned, and this several years after his death, holding his memory in the greatest veneration, as the patron and protector of the reformed religion, calling him, "Olivarius beatæ memoriæ." [1] No such mark of respect was ever. paid to the memory of Charles II. or to that of Clarendon's own son-in-law, James II.—But, to return from this digression :

On the 20th of October, 1651, about four score sails, which were but part of the fleet under Blake, appeared in sight of Jersey, and on the same day came to an anchor in St. Ouen's bay, which is quite open to the prevailing westerly winds, and therefore very dangerous to vessels riding there. But the sea was unusually smooth at that advanced season, which was considered an unfavorable omen by the islanders, who were further depressed by a report that the king was a captive at the mercy of his enemies ; so that it required all· the authority of Sir George Carteret to prevent many from laying down their arms. On the 21st and 22d of October, the fleet got under weigh and made a feint of landing troops at different points, that they might thereby distract and tire the militia ; and on the night of the 22d, Major-General Haines succeeded in landing a strong body of his men, after having experienced a vigorous resistance. The next day he was in possession of the open country, and the fort of St. Aubin yielded almost as soon as summoned, its example being followed by Mont Orgueil, on the 27th of October. The fleet had a most narrow escape, as on the 23d a furious storm from the west arose ; and had not the landing of the troops enabled the vessels to obtain shelter, the greater part would probably have perished, as did a large ship, which was dashed to pieces against the rocks, and not one of the three hundred men on board was saved.

Elizabeth Castle, to which Sir George Carteret retired, was resolutely defended : the garrison consisted of 340 men, and was supplied with provisions for eight months. After a peremptory summons from the parliamentary commander, and such an answer from Sir George as became him, cannon were pointed against the castle. The artillery could not be brought nearer than St. Hélier's hill, a distance of about three quarters of a mile, and all the injury done in many days, from the continual fire of twelve 36-pounders, amounted to only

(1) "All the reformed churches scattered over Roman Catholic kingdoms acknowledged Cromwell as their guardian. The Huguenots of Languedoc, the shepherds who, in the hamlets of the Alps, professed a Protestantism older than that of Augsburg, were secured from oppression by the mere terror of that great name."—*Macaulay.*

the beating down of some parapets, which were soon replaced with turf. It was now far in November, and intelligence arrived that the king, after escaping from the battle of Worcester, had succeeded in reaching Fescamp, in Normandy, on the 22d of October, the very day that the landing in Jersey was effected. At length the parliamentarians drew up on the hill two large mortars, from which they fired shells of thirteen inches in diameter and two inches thick into the castle; and one, breaking through two strong vaults, set the powder on fire, destroyed the provisions, and killed outright forty soldiers of the garrison, besides armorers, carpenters, and other workmen. Sir George sent his chaplain, the Rev. Mr. Durell, afterwards dean of Windsor, to France, to inform the king of this misfortune; and his majesty, in answer, desired Sir George to act according to his own discretion, advising him rather to accept honorable terms of capitulation than to protract a defence which must ultimately prove unavailing. As the castle was still tenable, no breach having been made, and no appearance of an assault, Sir George concealed the king's message, and the siege continued. But, as the number of the garrison daily lessened by death and desertion, and as there was no possibility of procuring recruits or supplies, he called a council of officers, and laid the king's letter before them. They determined to yield to necessity, and the castle was given up on the 15th of December, after enduring a siege of about seven weeks. Sir George Carteret's usual good fortune did not desert him on this occasion, as he obtained a very advantageous capitulation, by the first article of which he was granted a full indemnity for his previous conduct, was even exempted from paying any composition for his property like many other royalists, and was confirmed in the quiet enjoyment of all his possessions. He was moreover permitted to go to and from France without any hindrance; and one of the vessels moored near the castle was placed at his disposal for his own passage. The besiegers must have considered the castle to be almost impregnable, or they would scarcely have granted such favorable terms to an adversary who had so little claim to their indulgence. Sir George went to Paris to give the king an account of his gallant defence, and remained with his family in France, "under many mortifications," (relates Lord Clarendon, but which we doubt,) "by the power and prosecution of Cromwell, till his majesty's happy restoration."

We have lingered long in the narration of those interesting

events of which the Channel Islands were the scene during the civil war, because those events have been not only imperfectly, but, what is worse, unfairly described. If Jerseymen exult in the part taken by the majority of their ancestors during that great struggle, the people of Guernsey need not be the less proud that their forefathers ranged themselves on the side of civil and religious liberty. In Jersey, the conduct of the leading parliamentarians—Lemprière, Dumaresq, and Herault—contrasts most favorably with that of Sir George Carteret, their principal opponent; and he who studies the history of that momentous period without partiality or prejudice, will find his best sympathies enlisted in the cause of constitutional freedom—will feel no little contempt for those who, in humble imitation of the ass kicking at the dead lion, could treat with indignity the mouldering remains of such men as Blake, Ireton, and Cromwell.[1]

CHAPTER XVII.

THE COMMONWEALTH.—1649 to 1660.

ON the advent of Cromwell to supreme power, a declaration was drawn up and presented to him, explaining the wretched condition of Guernsey. This declaration commenced by exhibiting the great poverty of the inhabitants, only one twentieth part having any substance, and of these only two or three persons had £200 per annum, not ten £100 per annum, and not thirty £50 per annum. Mr. P. de Beauvoir, des Granges, is spoken of as "a man of strange temper and disposition, who, from his aspiring desire to be bailiff of the island, and ever since he was ousted by council on complaint of articles, has left no stone unturned to reinstate himself in the said office." The island is described as then containing a population of about 8,000 souls, and among the most interesting matter at the present day is the following :

"The land is subject to manifold dues, not elsewhere levied in such a manner ; but, in such a miserable place as Guernsey, all

(1) "Cromwell was no more ; and those who had fled before him were forced to content themselves with the miserable satisfaction of digging up, hanging, quartering, and burning the remains of the greatest prince that has ever ruled England."—*Macaulay.*

ploughed land pays tithe, and also a most grievous custom, called campart. This campart is the twelfth of every sheaf of the field, to which the generality of the island is subject. Campart is of two sorts: some belong to the state, and produce, one year with the other, £91 sterling. Others are the property of individuals, and amount, one year with the other, to one hundred and seventy livres ten sous tournois.

"The ground is let at a very high and dear rate. An acre of Guernsey measure being but about one third of the English acre, yields commonly of yearly rent three bushels per acre.[1]

"Poverty compels the inhabitants to sell their lands, and of all the price their inheritance is sold at, as many times thirteen as there are numbered, so much is pretended to be the right of the governor. Hence it comes to pass that there is an universal discouragement from ploughing and improving the island, two thirds being covered with fern and furze; and those who do cultivate the land act from sheer necessity, and not from the hope of profit, as there are deducted from the increase of the fields, chief rents, homages, services, tithes, and campart, which amount to one sixth of the value, and on some estates to one fifth. Rent must also be added to the expense of vraicking, dunging, ploughing, weeding the ground, reaping and thrashing the corn. It generally happens that every other year the husbandman is behind hand, and holds not his principal; and in a bad year, every one is a loser. Hence it arises that the island is commonly in great distress, and the countryman in a mean condition, more especially in a bad year, when he has not sufficient corn to pay his rent and supply himself with food. Such are the constant causes of poverty within, to which may be added the exactions of the governor.

"Since the year 1642, a mass of evils, like a flood, have overflowed the island and all that was left good in the condition thereof. The inhabitants, for declaring themselves in favour of the parliament, and remaining faithful to it, have lost their ships, their traffic, and their trading; their harbour and port have been closed and shut up by the rebellion and revolt of Sir Peter Osborne, in the castle called Cornet. The inhabitants, during the heat and danger of the war, were in continual fears, services, and watchings, commonly twice a week, sometimes thrice; they had frequent alarms from Jersey, from Castle Cornet, from Normandy, from Britany, and from the king's ships; they were always in arms, as in a garrison, a frontier place remote from England; they constructed fortifications and several other works for their defence, and were at their own charges for reducing and keeping Sark. They have paid for the maintenance of frigates to prevent relief being given to the castle, for beds, candles,

(1) In 1652, wheat rents were affixed at seven livres, or ten shillings the quarter of four bushels, and thus land was let at seven shillings and six pence per vergée. Two vergées and a half are as nearly as possible equal to one English acre.

fire for the soldiers, and divers other disbursements, amounting to above thirty thousand pounds. But what grieved the island most, being an evil undeserved, was the filling it with soldiers, though for seven years before, by the mercy of God, and the faithful endeavours of some active inhabitants, they had preserved themselves and the island in obedience to the parliament; and when the king was put to death, and his party and interests were brought low in England, there was no reason to fear for the inhabitants, who were then kept under like slaves, affronted, threatened, beaten; their orchards robbed, their trees cut down, and their sheep stolen. The parliament promised that the soldiers should be no charge to the inhabitants, yet they took no notice that the island was almost undone and could not bear the burden. In England, soldiers pay for their bedding, fire, and candle, or else are quartered at inns and alehouses; but the soldiers extorted this entertainment from us. In this particular the island has paid, in five years, above seven thousand two hundred pounds.[1]

"Touching the fidelity of the inhabitants. The fidelity, inviolable affection, and adherence to the crown and state of England from the conquest, appear from the acknowledgment, approbation, esteem, and special commendation of several kings, queens, and of the late parliament, which have been communicated from time to time to the inhabitants of Guernsey, as it appears by the records of Edward II., Richard II., and Henry IV.

"Parliament, on the 23d of March, 1643, did commend the faithfulness of the inhabitants, and did heartily thank them for the same; and, as a token of the confidence they reposed in the fidelity and manhood of the said inhabitants, they committed the government of Guernsey and the management of affairs to twelve of the inhabitants. And indeed all the inhabitants have been most loyal and obedient in all their services, to their great expense and to the great dangers and perils of their persons, for the crown and state of England. King Edward III., in the fifteenth year of his reign, praises them for their constancy and magnanimity in preserving the island, and acknowledges their great losses and perils of body. They suffered and overcame many evils in the reign of Richard II. The strong castle of Mont Orgueil, in Jersey, was taken by the French; Guernseymen recovered it, whereof several princes make honourable mention.

"The island of Sark has been twice lost: the Guernseymen recovered it, and during the civil wars have for a long time kept a garrison there at their own expense. Castle Cornet has revolted thrice, by the perfidy of the captains and governors. Sir Peter

[1] In May, 1650, the jurats urged Bailiff de Beauvoir, who was then in London, to represent to the lords of parliament the necessities and poverty of Guernsey, and to beseech them "to provide pay and provisions for their soldiers, and also, if they judge proper, to remove some of them, as their expenses are too heavy, and, with the blessing of Providence, the island may maintain its independence as well with a portion of them as with all of them."

Osborne was the last, who, with thousands of great shot, battered the houses of St. Peter-Port about the ears of the inhabitants ; but, notwithstanding all the mischief he did, neither his promises nor threats could move the inhabitants from their affection and loyalty. On the two former occasions, the inhabitants recovered the said castle.

"They also humbly crave the renewal and increase of some of their privileges, viz. for wool and calves' skins. Also, as the licenses are given, not only for the use of the bailiff and jurats, but also for the inhabitants, they humbly crave to have the disposal of them.

"Castle Cornet, as it is at this day, and as it has been for many years, commanded by a governor and lieutenant-governor, and other officers, with private soldiers, provisions, ammunitions of war, building of platforms, walls, works, and dwellings, with such repairs as the governors have from time to time thought convenient for themselves, or for the place, will be found to have cost annually three thousand pounds sterling to this state. It cannot be presumed that this state should undergo so great a charge in maintaining the said castle, if it were not represented as useful and serviceable, either for repelling a foreign enemy, or retaining the islanders in their duty : in both which cases it is humbly conceived the said castle is altogether useless, and that we shall endeavour to make appear by reason and experience.

" As to matter of defence against invasion, it should be remembered that there are several places in the island, distant from the said castle some three, some four, some five miles, so that no cannon from thence could hinder an enemy from landing at pleasure : then the said castle is surrounded by the sea, except one hour, or thereabouts, in a fortnight's time, so that the soldiers from within the castle cannot sally out into the island by land, nor by boats, there being no shelter for them about the castle, and they would be at the mercy of such guns as might be planted upon the harbour and places adjacent.

" And it has been observed during the late troubles, that ships did securely ride in the roadstead out of command of the castle, from which many thousands of shot were cast away without annoying them ; neither did it hinder the soldiers and others from coming into the island.

" As to the curbing the inhabitants of the island, if there were cause, it may be considered that the islanders are a great deal too numerous to be mastered by the ordinary guard of the castle in open field ; and all that can be done by the guns from the castle can but batter some houses in the town ; an island of this extent not being likely to be awed by a castle remote from it, as has been proved by the experience of nine years.

" It may be further observed, that the islanders have never

deserted the English interest, as may more at large appear by the different charters granted by the several kings and queens of England from time to time, and by their constant fidelity to the state and to your highness. Besides, there is no likelihood that an island, consisting wholly of Protestants, and enjoying very large privileges, should turn towards any of the neighbouring princes, whose subjects are so vassalized in their consciences and estates. Again, their political interests fasten them to England, without the commerce whereof they can have no leather or wool for their manufactures.

" It has likewise been observed that, during nine years of the late wars, the said castle having revolted, (although the governor had great influence and exerted it to the utmost,) yet he was not able to seduce the islanders, nor face them in the field ; but, on the contrary, the inhabitants besieged the castle, and would in all probability have reduced it in a month's time, if they had been furnished with such mortar pieces and grenades as were used for the reduction of Elizabeth Castle, in Jersey, a stronger place than this, and twice the distance from the land ; and yet it was reduced in less than six weeks.

" It may be further considered, that if an invasion of the island were attempted, it is very likely that not only the governor and the soldiers would retire into the castle, but most of the principal islanders would crowd into it with them, and strive to save the best of their goods there, to the discouragement of the rest and the loss of the whole ; whereas, were this castle reduced to a block house, and some of the expenditure of war, and some of the public revenue employed to fortify the island, the castle would be as serviceable as it is now, and the island much the stronger.

" These things being so, it remains to be unfolded how the said castle came to be of that consideration with our late princes, it being anciently no better than a block house. First : Queen Elizabeth was persuaded by one Chamberlayne, captain there, to enlarge it with a platform : next, one Leighton found a necessity for girding it with a stone wall ; after him, the Lord Carew, and then the Earl of Danby, (whose deputy was Sir Peter Osborne,) not being content with the revenues of the island, have, from time to time, made it their business, through friends at court, (under pretext of augmenting or repairing the works for the safety of the island and the honour of the nation,) to draw great sums of money out of the exchequer, as would be manifest if the records were searched, and that for the enriching themselves, as is clear by the testimony of many persons yet living, who remember that the said governors have constantly made the poor inhabitants bestow their labour on the said works for little or nothing."

This appears to have been the age of complaints against the different insular functionaries, both civil and military :

we have already noticed those against Sir Peter Osborne and
Bailiff De Quetteville, who were royalists; and we now extract the following from a " Copy of some Articles written
by Nathaniel Whit, Receiver of Guernsey, against Colonel
John Bingham," the parliamentarian officer to whom Castle
Cornet was surrendered in 1651. These charges do not appear to have been attended to, as Colonel Bingham was
governor of Guernsey until 1660 :

" That the said Colonel John Bingham hath often cheated the
state by false musters, making one muster in five or six months,
and yet sending up rolls (to the commissary of the musters) of
monthly musters, as if they had been constant musters taken
according to the practice of the army; also by mustering men
absent in England, Ireland, and elsewhere, upon particular occasions, and that for five or six months together; there being no
real muster made here from the latter end of November, 1651, to
the 8th of March following, nor from that time till July following, 1652, and from July, 1652, to the beginning of December
following.

" That the said Colonel Bingham hath converted to his own
use six months' additional pay, at 3s. 6d. per diem, allowed by
the establishment to the eldest captain in the said garrison, that is
to say, from the 23d August, 1652, to the 7th February following.

" That the said Colonel Bingham, about the 22d of March,
1652, carried with him to England four brass guns, and converted
them to his own use.

" That the said Colonel Bingham, about the 18th of March,
1652, sold six iron guns to an inhabitant of the said island, and
gave him a pass under his own hand to transport the same for
St. Malo.

" That the said colonel hath mustered and taken constant pay
for one Mr. Thomas, chaplain or minister to the said garrison,
who hath been absent thence ever since the month of June, 1652,
until 1653, and hath all that time served in the town of Wareham,
in Dorsetshire; and no cause made known unto the said garrison,
unless it be that the said colonel and minister divide the pay
betwixt them."

If Mr. Whit can be believed, the colonel was guilty of
several other malpractices, such as converting the revenue of
the island to his own use; seizing the cargo of a Dutch ship
wrecked on Guernsey, " to the value of £400, or thereabouts,"
on which cargo he would neither pay salvage to the poor
people, nor make restitution, " as is said ;" appropriating to
himself from Castle Cornet, after its surrender, several articles
which belonged either to the state or to some of the inhabit-

ants; and, lastly, carrying away with him on his departure "about twenty-three or twenty-four slabs of unwrought tin, which he had taken out of the Adventure frigate, of Plymouth, pretending confiscation, for that the same had payd no duties in England, part whereof belonged to one Mr. John Mervin, an English merchant;" although it appeared by a certificate from the Court of Exchequer that the said tin had been regularly cleared.—The last charge was as follows:

"That the said Colonel Bingham, about the 22d of March, 165$\frac{2}{3}$, before his departure for England, left with his ensigne a dormant letter, to be exhibited in court and presented by the said ensigne to the lieutenant-bayliff and the rest of the jurats a month after his departure, whereby he ordered that all legall proceedings in courte against some particular persons, as well resident in the island as absent, should be stopt, to the great breach and violation of the lawes and customs of the said island and the great dissatisfaction of the peaceable people thereof; thinking by his interest in parliament, the greatness of his friends and allies, so to overawe such as were under him, that he should never be called to an accompt either for this or any thing contained in the precedent articles."

However selfish and parricidal Cromwell may have been in procuring the downfall of the Commonwealth, in April, 1653, and in causing himself to be declared Protector, his usurpation of unlimited power has this excuse, that his domestic government possessed many merits, and that his foreign policy was worthy of England and of his own commanding genius. Berry wrote as if, during the civil war, Guernsey sided with the king; and, copying Falle, speaks, in his ponderous history, of the calamities and sufferings of these islands "under the usurpation," which he says "were now governed by the most arbitrary tyrants and fanatics; the established religion was trampled under foot; the soldiery (a frantic herd of sectaries of all sorts) at free quarters, without check or control, committing every sort of outrage, turning the churches into guard-houses and stables; property of all kinds in a state of sequestration, compositions for estates exacted, and every kind of oppression licensed without restraint." As regards Guernsey and its dependant islands under the protectorate, these assertions are ridiculously untrue, especially as relates to the established religion of the inhabitants, which was only "trampled under foot" after the Restoration; and the Rev. Edward Durell, in his Notes on Falle, (No. 59,) states that "Cromwell's conduct towards the inhabitants [of

Jersey] seems to have been particularly lenient." He adds, that Sir George Carteret, after Major Lydcott's departure from Jersey, in 1643, " did not treat his adversaries with the same moderation, the chief of whom were driven into exile, and their property confiscated, while those who remained were subjected to heavy fines and long imprisonments." Indeed, we believe that no man's character was ever more cruelly maligned and misrepresented than that of Cromwell ; and that these islands were not oppressed during his administration, will appear by the following extracts from Burton's Diary :

" October 6 and 7, 1654, were wholly spent upon the distribution of the number of members to serve in future parliaments. We agreed with the instrument in the whole number of four hundred, Jersey and Guernsey being left out, because not governed by our laws, but by municipal laws of their own, and we differed but little in the particular distributions.

" January 8, 1656.—Resolved, that the islands of Guernsey, Jersey, and Wight, be left out of the bill for excise. Mr. Bond and Mr. Downing said : ' These isles are poor, and were never charged in any time, not so much as with customs. All kings and queens are careful of the poor people.' "

The Protector, who is said to have felt deeply the loss of his constant and sincere friend the Earl of Warwick, so often mentioned in these pages, died on the 3d of September, 1658, which day was the anniversary of his great victories of Dunbar and Worcester. " Cromwell had the virtues and affections of private and domestic life. As a son, husband, father, friend, his heart was full of tenderness, generosity, and faith ;"[1] and surely these excellent qualities should extenuate in some degree the failings of his political career. Soon after his death, at which period the garrison of Guernsey consisted of only one company of foot, the islanders transmitted to his son and successor, Richard, a petition, in which, after supplicating the confirmation of their privileges, they begged of his highness to extend to them (of course on payment) the same allowance of wool from England as had been granted by his father to the inhabitants of Jersey, because the population of Guernsey had so much increased that more than 6,000 persons earned their living by making worsted stockings and other woollen articles. In consequence, 1,000 tods of wool were the least quantity required, which quantity, equally divided, was only 4½ lb. each in a year. That the population had much in-

(1) History of England, continued from Sir James Macintosh.

creased is very improbable, and the petitioners had evidently forgotten that four or five years before, it had been represented to Cromwell as amounting to about 8,000 souls, which makes the statement of the number of persons employed in the woollen manufacture utterly incredible.

Castle Cornet possesses other attractions besides those of a purely military character, as the antiquarian may wander over it with profit, and its summit presents, on a clear day, a variety of prospects such as few can behold without pleasure and admiration; for on the west is seen the pier and hilly town of St. Peter-Port, with queen Victoria's tower and the eastern coast of Guernsey; on the north, the roadstead, Vale Castle, and Belgrave bay, with Alderney and the Casket rocks and light-houses in the distance; on the east, the islands of Sark, Herm, and Jethou, and the coasts of Normandy; and on the south, Fort George, Doyle's pillar, and the island of Jersey, with frequently a little flotilla trawling for flat fish on the bank, or catching mackerel.—In the castle the governors long resided and held their miniature courts, possessing as they did almost sovereign sway over the seven inhabited islands and islets of the bailiwick. And among the by-gone inmates of this sea-girt fortress, whether as guests or state prisoners, are some whose names are still remembered—the chaplains Cartwright and Bradshaw, Burton, General Lambert, and Lucy St. John, the wife of Sir Allan Apsley, and the mother of Mr. Hutchinson, who wrote the well known memoirs of her husband, Colonel Hutchinson. A condensed notice of each will satisfy curiosity.

Thomas Cartwright, an eminent puritan divine, was born in Hertfordshire, in 1535, and educated at St. John's College, Cambridge, where he obtained a fellowship, which he afterwards exchanged for one of Trinity. In 1567, he proceeded B. D. and became a popular preacher. His opinions were adverse to the hierarchy, and he was complained of by Archbishop Grindal, in consequence of which he was hindered of his doctor's degree, and deprived of his fellowship; he then went abroad, and was chosen minister to the English merchants at Antwerp, and afterwards at Middleburg. On his return to England, he endeavoured to subvert the ecclesiastic order, and to establish the Genevan discipline. He also wrote several pieces on that side, which were answered by Doctor Whitgift. Cartwright was imprisoned, but obtained his liberty through Lord Burleigh and the Earl of Leicester, the latter of whom appointed him master of his hospitals at Warwick, where he died in 1603, aged sixty-eight. He wrote a Harmony of the Gospels in Latin, printed at Amsterdam in 1647; a Commentary on the Proverbs, and other works. To these details from the *Biog. Brit.* we are enabled to add, that Cartwright was late in life chaplain of Castle Cornet, and that he was in Guernsey in the years 1591, 5, 7, 9, and in 1601. He evidently possessed great influence in the island, as the people were decided Presbyterians; and at a synod of the ministers and elders of all the islands, assembled at St. Peter-Port, in 1597, Cartwright and Snape affixed their signatures next after the governors of Jersey and Guernsey, and before the other ministers. That courtly historian, Falle,[1] speaking of "a faction" in England which had imbibed the Geneva discipline, says: "Nothing could please that party more than to hear of what was done in these islands. It raised their hopes, and made them more insolent. As with people embarked in the same cause, they must needs now open a correspondence with us. To that end, Cartwright and Snape, two fierce incendiaries, and noted leaders among them, were dispatched hither, whom the governors entertained with great kindness, making the first chaplain of Cornet Castle, and the other of Mont Orgueil, to each of which posts a competent salary was annexed. In what year precisely they came, and how long they staid, I cannot say." To have spoken of Cartwright as a fierce incendiary reflects no credit on Falle, who in ability seems to have been much his inferior, as Cartwright greatly distinguished himself in the disputations held at Cambridge, on the visit of queen Elizabeth, in 1564; and in 1570, his reputation caused him to be appointed the Lady Margaret's professor of divinity. Such was his popularity, that on his preaching at St. Mary's, it was necessary to take out the windows. Moreover, he was sincere, disinterested, and charitable; and it is acknowledged that he was treated with great severity.[2]

Bradshaw, a puritan instructor, was recommended by Cartwright to Sir Thomas Leighton, with whom he was abiding

(1) Falle was born in Jersey in 1655, and educated at Exeter College, Oxford. He presented his valuable collection of books to that island, and died unmarried, at Shenley, when nearly ninety years of age.

(2) "The ostensible founder of this new school [Puritanism] was Thomas Cartwright, the Lady Margaret's professor of divinity at Cambridge. He began, about 1570, to inculcate the unlawfulness of any form of church government, except what the apostles had instituted, namely, the Presbyterian. A deserved reputation for virtue, learning, and acuteness, an ardent zeal, an inflexible self-confidence, a vigorous, rude, and arrogant style, marked him as the formidable leader of a religious faction. In 1572, he published his celebrated Admonition to Parliament, calling on that assembly to reform the various abuses subsisting in the church."—*Hallam.*

at Castle Cornet, as tutor to his children. "Thither Bradshaw addressed himself, and, through God's goodness, arriving safe there, was with all kinde and courteous entertainment by them received. And indeed such was Mr. Bradshaw's demeanour, wheresoever he came, that he left behind him a grateful memory—not unlike therein to musk or civet. The which (sweet scent) continued after his departure thence, not among the French ministers alone in that island, but also among such of the old garrison soldiers, on whom Master Cartwright's ministry had had some efficacious and gracious work, who—as Sir Peter Osborne, who had afterwards the government of that place, hath been known to relate—would be oft talking of one Master Bradshaw that had lived some time there, and speak with much affection of him."—*Clarke's Lives.*

Henry Burton, another celebrated puritan divine, was born at Birdsal, in Yorkshire, in 1579, and, like Cartwright, educated at St. John's College, Cambridge, but took his degree of B. D. at Oxford. He was afterwards clerk of the closet to prince Henry and to prince Charles, of which appointment he was deprived for a libel against the bishops. After this he obtained the rectory of St. Matthew, Friday Street, in London; but, for some seditious and schismatical libels, he, Bastwick, a physician, and Prynne, a lawyer, were prosecuted in the Star Chamber, in 1637, and sentenced to a fine of £5,000, the loss of their ears, the pillory, branding on the cheeks, and close imprisonment for life![1] Garrard, writing to Lord Wentworth, said: "Some few days after the end of the term, in the palace yard, two pillories were erected, and there the sentence of the Star Chamber against Burton, Bastwick, and Prynne, was executed: they stood two hours in the pillory; Burton by himself, being degraded in the high commission court three days before; the place was full of people, who cried and howled terribly, especially when Burton was cropt."! Burton was confined in Castle Cornet; Bastwick, in Scilly; and Prynne, at Mont Orgueil, in Jersey. These barbarities did not end here, as Lilburne and Wharton were condemned, the former to a fine of £500; the latter to the same fine, clipping, and the pillory, for printing and pub-

(1) "Henry Burton, formerly chaplain to the king, when Prince of Wales. He thought proper to assail the prelates of the church—of whose characters he must have been pretty well informed—as 'blind watchmen, dumb dogs, ravening wolves, anti-Christian mushrooms, robbers of souls, limbs of the beast, and the factors for anti-Christ;' and as may naturally be supposed, the whole hierarchy, with Laud at their head, assisted each other in hunting him down, and in worrying him when he was down."—*The Court and Times of Charles I.*

x

lishing one of Burton's libels! Sir Peter Osborne does not
appear to have been very strict in his treatment of Burton,
who by his sentence was to be debarred of the use of pen,
ink, and paper; and yet he found means, while in the castle,
to write an answer to "Bishop Laud's Relation of his Conference with Fisher." He likewise wrote there some other
controversial pieces, but could not get them printed. And
yet the Rev. John de la Marche, the rector of St. Andrew's,
Guernsey, at this period, relates that from the chamber in
Castle Cornet, in which Burton "was buried alive," the sun
or moon could not be seen on any day of the year; that the
partition of the chamber was of earth; and that it was the
same in which he himself had been kept prisoner in 1633.
After an imprisonment of about three years, the three victims
of the Star Chamber, Burton, Bastwick, and Prynne, were
recalled by the parliament, in 1640; and, on landing in England, were not only received with acclamations, but attended
by crowds to London, which city they entered in triumph,
with rosemary and bays in their hats, and their way in many
places strewed with flowers. Previously to the departure of
Burton from Guernsey, he was entertained by the island
clergy, who warmly sympathized with him. He was restored
to his living, and died in 1648.

John Lambert was descended from an ancient family in
Yorkshire, in which county he was born in 1619; and in 1639
he married Frances, daughter of his neighbour, Sir W. Lister,
then in her seventeenth year, and said to have been a most
elegant and accomplished woman. Lambert was in the law at
the commencement of the civil war, during which he greatly
distinguished himself. After Cromwell's death, such was the
influence of Lambert, that Charles was recommended by some
to secure his services by the offer of marrying his daughter;
but no actual overtures appear to have been made on either
side.[1] At the Restoration, he was tried and condemned, but
was pardoned, and exiled to Guernsey.[2] Mrs. Hutchinson,

(1) Lord Hatton, an old royalist, suggested this proposition in the following terms:
"The race is a *very good gentleman's family*, and kings have condescended to marry subjects. The lady is pretty, of an extraordinary sweetness of disposition, and very virtuously
and ingenuously disposed; the father is a person, set aside his unhappy engagement, of
very great parts and noble inclinations.—Clarendon State Papers, 592. Yet, after all, Miss
Lambert was hardly more a mis-alliance than Hortense Mancini, whom Charles had asked
for in vain."—*Hallam.*

(2) "November 17, 1661.—Arrived at Castle Cornet, John Lambert, general of the sectarian rebels in England, enemy of the king, and prisoner for life."—*Le Roy.* Peter Le
Roy, who, in previous entries in his diary, had spoken with all due respect of Oliver
Cromwell, and "Son Altesse Monsieur Richard, fils du susdit Ollivier," now abused the
parliamentarians, having doubtless, like many of his superiors, easily changed sides when
royalty became in the ascendant. Peter appears then to have been as general a Christian
name in Guernsey as Philip is now in Jersey.

in her Memoirs, speaking of the imprisonment of her husband and other parliamentarians, in the Tower, in 1663, says: "Warrants were signed for carrying away most of the prisoners; some to Tangier and to other barbarous and distant places: among the rest, Colonel Hutchinson was designed to the Isle of Man." At that time, the Anglo-Norman Islands were doubtless thought quite as "barbarous and distant" as the Isle of Man, and it was probably on that account that General Lambert was banished to Guernsey. Hume says that "General Lambert survived his condemnation nearly thirty years, and that he lived contented in Guernsey, forgetting all his past schemes of greatness, and entirely forgotten by the nation. He died a Roman Catholic." But English historians are all at fault in stating that Lambert ended his days in Guernsey, as, after being confined there five or six years, he was removed, in 1667, to the fortified island of St. Nicholas, at the entrance of Plymouth, where he died in 1683, aged about sixty-four, after a total confinement of above twenty years! He is said to have been the first person who introduced the Guernsey lily into England, and, during his residence in Guernsey, to have amused himself with cultivating flowers, and copying them with his pencil—an art which he had acquired from Baptist Gaspar. By a royal warrant, dated Whitehall, February 17, 1662, Mrs. Lambert, with her three children and three maid servants, was permitted to come to and remain in Guernsey with her husband, "under the same confinement he himself is, untill our further pleasure be known;" and by another warrant, dated November 18, 1662, and addressed to Lord Hatton, the governor, "Collonell Lambert" was allowed to reside on the island as long as his comportment was worthy thereof, evidently in place of being confined in Castle Cornet, as he had previously been.

Mrs. Hutchinson, in her husband's memoirs, states that her mother, Lucy St. John, before her marriage, accompanied her brother's wife, Lady St. John, who was a daughter of Sir Thomas Leighton, to Guernsey. There Lucy St. John "went into the towne, and boarded in a French minister's house, to learn the language, that minister having beene, by the persecution in France, driven to seeke his shelter there. Contracting a deare friendship with this holy man and his wife, she was instructed in their Geneva discipline, which she liked so much better than our more superstitious service, that she would have been contented to have lived there, had not a powerful passion (attachment) drawn her back." (to England.)

Mrs. Hutchinson adds, that her mother was not kindly treated by her uncle, with whom she resided after her return from Guernsey, "whereupon she left his house with a resolution to withdraw herself into the island, where the good minister was, and there to weare out her life in the service of God." But while deliberating, she was induced by Sir Allan Apsley to marry him. These French Calvinist clergymen, whom Falle doubtless considered as incendiaries, certainly appear to have possessed great influence with their fair hearers.

Until the year 1811, Castle Cornet served as the common gaol or prison of the island, offenders being condemned by the Royal Court to imprisonment there, often *en basse fosse*, i.e. in an underground dungeon, which was exceedingly damp and unwholesome, and may yet be seen. The following ordinance of that body, which does not appear to have been the more lenient for its sour puritanism, will perhaps induce the reader to think that the punishment often exceeded the offence: "4 Oct. 1602. Seeing the incontinence which is daily committed by many young men, who, before marriage, get their betrothed with child, to the great dishonour of the glory of God, scandal of the church, and infamy of the parties, it is ordered by justice, that any young men so offending shall be constituted prisoners at Castle Cornet, *en basse fosse*, for fifteen days on bread and water."—But the prison was difficult of access in bad weather, and its inconvenience was complained of as early as 1607. In March, 1552, some Roman Catholic priests were confined in Castle Cornet, as appears by a metrical 'complainte' written by them whilst in prison, in which they lament the destruction of the images, sacred vessels, and vestments, and the hardships to which they were exposed by the persecutions of the rectors, then in possession of their benefices. A corrupt copy of this poem is preserved in the Register of St. Saviour's church, under the date of 1638. Their offence was probably non-conformity to the Anglican Service Book, which Edward VI. had ordered to be used in the Channel Islands; though, in the same order, he very strangely allowed the islands to remain under the jurisdiction of the Bishop of Coutances. During the revolutionary war, it was customary for the inhabitants— all of whom between the ages of sixteen and sixty were enrolled in the militia—to be taught military exercise on the Sunday. Several of the Wesleyans, deeming this practice a desecration of the sabbath, refused to conform to it, and were, in consequence, repeatedly fined and imprisoned. One of them was incarcerated during four months at Castle Cornet, in a miserable cell which was part of the time exposed to the wind, there being no glass frame to the windows, and where some of his companions in captivity were common felons! Mr. Warburton, a herald and celebrated antiquary in the reign of Charles II., wrote, in 1682, a treatise on the history, laws, and customs of Guernsey ; and, relative to the prison and gaoler, he said : " The portier of Castle Cornet is the keeper of all prisoners whatever, whether for debt, or criminals. He has been always appointed by the governor, but gives security to the bailiff and jurats for the safe keeping of such prisoners as are by them committed to his custody. The Extent of Edw. III. says : ' Dominus rex habet unum janitorem castri, qui percipit per diem XII fortæ monetæ.' But his salary is now as the governor thinks fit to allow him ; besides which, he receives a customary duty of some small quantity of wine, salt, and earthen pots out of all ships unloading any of these commodities in the island. His fee, at the entrance of a prisoner for debt, is 2d. ; for keeping him, 2d. per diem ; and likewise 2d. per diem for his bread and drink, if the portier provide it for him.[1] If a prisoner for debt has liberty to go into the town, he is to pay the portier 4d. per diem, and allow the diet of a man to attend him ; if he goes beyond the town, 8d. per diem, with the diet of a man to attend him as a keeper. If such a prisoner has not wherewithal to pay the portier's fees, the person at whose suit he is imprisoned is obliged to pay them. There have been anciently several places in the island where prisoners have been kept ; but it is now time out of mind, that there has been no other prison than such rooms in Castle Cornet as the governor has thought fit to assign for the portier's use.—The executioner is provided by the governor, and has no certain salary,[2] but receives only what the governor thinks fit to allow him."

(1) The allowance of a prisoner for subsistence is now (1854) 9d. per diem : this more than quadruple increase is not owing to the proportionally increased value of wheat, as from the year 1677 to 1686, inclusive, the current price of wheat was affixed at 7 livres, or 10s. per Guernsey quarter, equal to £1. 5s. per Winchester quarter ; and in 1850, wheat was affixed in the same manner at 10 livres 8 sols, or 14s. 6d. per Guernsey quarter.

(2) The executioner has now 15s. a week, besides 2s. 6d. lodging money, and certain fees when his services are required, which happily is but seldom. This appointment is almost a sinecure, and it ought to be abolished.

CHAPTER XVIII.

CHARLES II.—1660 to 1685.

THE islanders had suffered so much from the exactions of the parliamentarian soldiers who were sent to it towards the close of the civil war, not during the protectorate, that they joyfully proclaimed Charles II. at the Restoration, May 29, 1660, although probably with many misgivings as to the treatment they would experience at his hands, for having sided with the Commonwealth. They also sent a deputation to congratulate his majesty on his accession, and expressed every contrition for their past conduct! The deputies, elected by the States, were Sir Henry De Vic, Bart., Amias Andros, of Sausmarez, bailiff of Guernsey, Captain Darell, and William De Beauvoir; and upon their petition setting forth that the inhabitants acknowledged their great guilt, for which they implored his majesty's pardon, a full and effectual pardon was ordered to pass the great seal, in which it was stated, that Sir Henry De Vic, knight and baronet; Mr. Amias Andros, as above; Edmund Andros, his son; Charles Andros, brother of the said Amias; and Nathaniel Darell,[1] also as above; "had, to their great honour, during the late rebellion, continued inviolably faithful to his majesty, and consequently had no need to be included in this general pardon." Henry De Vic, a native of Guernsey, was employed by Charles I. in treating with the celebrated Duke de Rohan and the French Protestants for the relief of La Rochelle.[2] De Vic, who married a daughter of Sir Philip Carteret, Bart., of Jersey, and probably owed his rise to the interest of his father-in-law, was subsequently " Resident for king Charles I. nearly twenty years in Brussels, afterwards Chancellor of the most noble order of the Garter." He shared in the exile of Charles II., and was by him created a baronet in 1649, by letters patent, dated at St. Germain, in France, September 3; but the title has long been extinct, as for many years has been in Guernsey the name of this ancient family, one of which was bailiff, or chief magistrate of the island, in the year 1596.

(1) This evidently was not Captain Darell, Sir P. Osborne's lieutenant, but his son, afterwards lieutenant-governor of Guernsey.

(2) Continuation of Sir James Mackintosh's History of England.

We have expressed our conviction that the people of Guernsey boldly sided against Charles I. more from a religious than a disloyal feeling, for they had previously, as they have since, been remarkable for their attachment and adherence to the sovereigns of England, as Dukes of Normandy ; and it has been shewn that, though adhering to the parliament, many were royalists, while others repented themselves of the transfer of their allegiance. It must, however, be borne in mind, that the Genevese church was then much imbued with republicanism. But, judging by the conduct of the unprincipled Charles and of his priest-ridden brother James, it would seem that the Guernseymen had properly appreciated the character of the Stuarts, who were, for a long series of years, as remarkable for their misfortunes as for their total disregard of the lessons of adversity.

After the troubles, commissioners were appointed by the king to draw up a report for settling the affairs of Guernsey and the other islands within its bailiwick : they were, Sir George Carteret, vice-chamberlain, and the gallant defender of Jersey ; Sir Hugh Pollard, governor of Guernsey ; Mr. John Ashburnham, of the bed chamber ; and Colonel Ashburnham, cofferer of his majesty's household. "In consequence of their report," says Duncan, "the privy council issued an order, of which the following is the substance : His majesty left the privy council to decide whether he should renew the charters of the island ; he appointed certain gentlemen to the office of jurats ; ordered the ancient pier dues to be continued, and required the governor to draw up an account of all recent appropriation of those funds ; ratified the judicial proceedings of the island ; commanded the erasure of all deeds on the registry recorded against the government of his present majesty or his predecessor ; directed that a new Extent, or rental of his majesty's revenue, should be drawn up by the bailiff and jurats ; ordered those who had seized and sold his majesty's goods to be proceeded against ; commanded the oath of allegiance and supremacy to be administered throughout the bailiwick, with the same formalities as in England ; empowered the bailiff or his lieutenant to pass all contracts for the sale of land, in the same manner as was practised before the wars, and granted a free pardon to all who had supported the rebellion. In reference to Alderney, the king consented that a brief, passed in the eighteenth year of the reign of James I., should be renewed for constructing a fort in that island ; and he further directed, that until the fort was complete, six soldiers and one serjeant from each of the garrisons of Jersey and Guernsey should be sent to Alderney by the respective governors of those islands.

"The provisions of this order clearly shew that the king retained little or no resentment against the islanders for having sided with the parliament and the protector, and that he was disposed to grant a generous amnesty for the past. But the dismissal of certain jurats, and the appointment of others, without the form of an election, was highly unconstitutional. When the governor, Lord Hatton, however, dismissed subsequently two of the jurats who had incurred his displeasure, his majesty ordered that ' all elections of jurats should for the future be made according to the charter and ancient custom of the island.' The court, anxious to prove itself deserving of the royal favour, faithfully enforced the commands of his majesty; and on May 15, 1661, the names of Oliver and Richard Cromwell were erased from the public registry : the court further ordered that all contracts, passed during the usurpation under the seal of the island, should be deemed null and void, and directed that all such contracts should be renewed within a year, counting from Michaelmas day next ensuing, under the penalty of their being considered invalid and illegal."

We have already mentioned the losses which the civil war inflicted on the island, and no stronger proof can be given of the poverty and distress to which it was reduced, than the circumstance that, shortly after the Restoration, the States of Guernsey resolved to present a petition to Charles, praying that Guernsey might be united to England, and that acts of parliament might from that period have the force of law here. This short-sighted proposition was favourably received by the council, whose answer, which was registered on the insular records in October, 1663, was to the effect that parliament would take the matter into consideration as soon as the importance of the affair, and the multiplicity of other business, would allow them to do so.

In giving the few following extracts from a copious diary or journal kept by Peter Le Roy, in French, it is necessary to add, that he was born in Guernsey about the year 1600; that he was schoolmaster of the Câtel, and next of St. Martin's parish ; and that he was sworn greffier or registrar of the feudal court of Sausmarez, St. Martin's, October 10, 1657. Some of his notices are very characteristic and amusing :

"December 19, 1651.—The garrison of Castle Cornet, amounting to about fifty-five men, surrendered with composition, and marched out of the said castle with their commander; the said castle having held and resisted against the island for the space of eight years and nine months, or thereabout, during which time there were more than 30,000 cannon shots[1] fired on the town.

"January 18, 1657.—There were three lords (seigneurs) of England sent prisoners to Castle Cornet.[2]

"February 28, 1659-60.—Major Henry Wanseye replaced Colonel Bingham as governor; and the next day the royal court, the clergy, and the town douzaine, went to wait upon him at Castle Cornet. On the 19th of March, the States of the island met in the town church, when the said governor presented his commission.

"May 31, 1660.—Charles II. proclaimed in Guernsey, in presence of Captain Sharp, the lieutenant-governor; Mr. Peter Carey, lieutenant-bailiff; the jurats, clergy, &c., with ringing of bells; half companies of the most expert of the militia under arms, *feu du joie*, and great rejoicings. The proclamation was read by Abraham Carey, the prevost, in six places, viz. before the Plaiderie, at the Grand Carrefour, before Berthelot Street, before the cage, at the church door, and on the pier.

"February 6, 1663-4.—Mr. Darell, the lieutenant-governor, caused Mr. John de Quetteville, lieutenant-bailiff, in consequence of some difference between them, to be removed from his seat of justice; and the Wednesday following, the said lieutenant-governor sent him to prison at Castle Cornet,[3] after which Mr. John Brehaut was made judge delegate, and Mr. Peter Carey his assistant.

"February 17, 1663-4.—My Lord Hatton arrived in this island, as 'grand gouverneur,' with his brother and two of his sons. As soon as Lord Hatton landed at Castle Cornet, he liberated Mr. de Quetteville from prison, and the Monday following all the justices were ordered to appear before the said governor at the castle, where were constituted prisoners Mr. Peter Carey and Mr. William de Beauvoir, du Houmet, and Mr. James de Havilland, and the greffier (registrar) suspended. After being kept in prison eight or nine days, they were liberated under bail, remaining suspended until the case was decided."[4]

(1) This appears to be an exaggeration.

(2) These were doubtless either some of the republican leaders hostile to Cromwell, or royalists; as, in the autumn of 1656, among the former, Vane was imprisoned in Carisbrook castle, Rich in Windsor, and Harrison in Pendennis castle. Among the latter, Lord Willoughby, of Parham, John Ashburnham, and others, were committed to the Tower.

(3) For this stretch of power, Captain Darell, jun., was displaced by Charles II. from his office of lieutenant-governor; and Mr. William De Beauvoir was ordered to pay £15, and Mr. Peter Carey £5, to Mr. de Quetteville.—(Vide Duncan's History, p. 109.)

(4) This entry is ambiguous, and it is doubtful whether Mr. de Havilland and the greffier were committed to prison, or only suspended from their offices.

Captain Waterhouse, Lieut.-Governor of Guernsey, to A. Andros, Esq.

[Extracts.]—" Yours by Sir Philip Carteret and others I have received. Seeing a frigate lying under Sark in a storm, the next morning I sent Loiner in his shallop to see what they were : it proved to be the governor of Jersey, with Sir Philip. I have done him right as unto his possession of Sark, where his brother now is. I have sent a brace of bucks, one unto the governor, the other unto Sir Philip Carteret. This day I had the States assembled to recall Du Houmet's [W. de Beauvoir] commission by them. Gosselin presented a letter from Du Houmet to him as judge delegate, which made me produce yours in the assembly, and Mr. Havilland read so much as concerned Du Houmet's actings. Mr. Havilland and Mr. Quetteville, and Mr. John Sausmarez, and Mr. James Marchant, read theirs. The result of all was, that a letter of thanks should be written unto Sir George de Carteret, for his great favors unto this people, and one other unto Sir Henry De Vic, yourself, and Mr. Darell, giving you power to act in their behalf; and a tax speedily to be laid, whereby to supply you with dust : in the mean time some of the jurats, the ministers, and others, have lent about sixty pounds sterling, which will be immediately returned unto you.

" Castle Cornet, August 25, 1660."

Major Walters to Lord Hatton.

[Extracts.]—" Since my last, I have found some trouble about one Marchant, once a minister in this island. Mr. Dean[1] was pleased to communicate the conditions of the man to me, and his sense of them, upon which I conveyed him to the castle, where, with such reasons as were given, the lieutenant-governor[2] resolved to keep him prisoner; at which he, exclaiming with open mouth, protested boldly for one night; and the next day petitioned the jurats for justice, pretending he was imprisoned by a court martial. This day, the jurats take this business into debate : what the result will be, or how Mr. Darell will carry himself, I know not. But, whatever they do, I believe here is matter against him, and such as, if proved, will call him to London, there to answer with the hazard of his neck. Yesterday, Mr. Dean, Mr. d'Anville,[3] and the lieutenant-bailly,[4] acquainted me with ill things of him, which, if they prove, your lordship shall be acquainted with. But this man's apprehension is not sufficient: Bonamy and Monamy, Eleazar Marchant, Peter Careye, James Marchant, and Havilland, must be made exemplary, or no quiet will ever be established here. They are so confident of your not coming, that they conclude all is their own. All those who are honest are in very great apprehension, and wish infinitely for your presence.

" Guernsey, July 18, 1663."

(1) John de Sausmarez, rector of St. Martin's, and afterwards canon of Windsor.
(2) Captain Darell.   (3) Charles Andros.   (4) John de Quetteville.

The minister alluded to in the preceding letter was the Rev. Thomas Le Marchant, a sturdy Presbyterian, and a talented author, of whom we have already spoken with much regard, because we respect the scruples, even if mistaken, of a clergyman who, rather than violate his conscience, resigns his benefice, and perhaps gives up his bread.   This excellent man, after taking his degrees at Cambridge, passed some years at the academy at Caen, where he enjoyed the friendship of the learned Bochart and Huet, who corresponded with him on his return to Guernsey.   In the king's warrant, dated Whitehall, September 30, 1667, it is ordered that "whereas Thomas Le Marchant hath been a long time prisoner in the Tower," on his entering into recognizance of £1,000, "that he shall not at any time presume to go to the island of Guernsey, unless he hath special license from his majesty so to do, and shall behave himself for the future as a dutiful and loyal subject," &c., "the said Thomas Le Marchant be, and he is hereby, discharged from his imprisonment."

In a letter, in French, dated Guernsey, August 8, 1662, the dean informed Amias Andros, bailiff, then at Westminster, that on that day Mr. Le Marchant had resigned to him his parishes, (St. Sampson's and the Vale,) rather than be examined relative to the accusations which were brought against him, and that he had given security to the lieutenant-governor of 1,000 *escus* for his good conduct in future.   The dean adds, that the jurats had so well taken the thing in hand, that no one in the island dared say a word against episcopal government, all the upper classes being Episcopalians, and only the common people being otherwise.   Writing to Amias Andros in Guernsey, dean de Sausmarez, under date of Westminster, March 9, 1664, says: "Thomas Le Marchant will soon have that which he has long merited, and his boastings (*vanteries*) will no longer have their course."   And on May 13, 1665, the dean says: "Thomas Le Marchant is in the Tower, and will continue there until 'le prophète du creux Robilliard soit accompli.'"—Mr. Le Marchant married Olympe Roland, by whom he had three sons, of whom Eleazar was afterwards bailiff of Guernsey, and one daughter, wife of Peter Priaulx, *seigneur du Comte*, and subsequently of *four* other husbands.

From the copy of a Letter, in the handwriting of Amias Andros.

"Tuesday, the 1st November, (1664,) my Lord Hatton made his solemn entry in his government in great pomp and magnifi-

cence. He came from the castle [Cornet] in a barge purposely
made for that object, and had for his guard twenty-four soldiers
with halberds, who marched before him; twenty others who had
carbines, who came after in blue 'casaques;' and twenty-six
gentlemen marched before him bareheaded in the midst of the
halberdiers; and before him marched his secretary, who had on
both sides of him two footmen, who carried two patents, the one
for the government, the other for his instructions; and in this
equipage they marched to his palace and throne; and behind him
at a distance marched his two sons and his brother; Mr. Clement,
the marchant; next came the justice, pell-mell with the soldiers
without taking notice of them. Being come to the church gate,
he was harangued by Mr. Janon, accompanied by several ministers. Being come to his palace, he went up by an ascent on the
right hand, and the justice by another on the left, where in the
midst was a chair of state, raised one foot above that of the bailly,
and above his chair, "a state," under which was also his son on his
right hand. And after he had caused his patent and instructions
to be read in Latin and French, he caused one douzenier for each
parish, together with two constables and two treasurers for each,
to be sworn. And of all these, there will not be found twenty-six
conformists but are of the most violent against the ecclesiastical
government, and the same against monarchy. After that he
displayed a book, which contained about two quires of paper, in
the which was written what he had to say to the people; and
being fallen upon the justice, [the jurats,] defamed them, by all
ways and means imaginable, to the people, calling them factious,
rebels who made factions against the king; and moreover made
cabals to deliver the island to foreign princes; that they were
thieves, who robbed the king and held the poor people at 'lands;'
that it was to the poor people he would do good, and many words
to that purpose; and that all those who had appeared against
their governors had been ruined, and that they should take care
not to fall into the like faults.

"After he had insisted upon these things above an hour, he
began to draw out of their graves those that have been dead near
two hundred years, to declaim against them in this public assembly, and 'caus'd' all the acts of court, which he had intelligence
were in the rolls one hundred years since, to the disgrace of baillys
and jurats; but the night intervening, he retired, remitting the
rest to another time. And the most of the inhabitants of the
island were in 'armes' from six in the morning till six in the
afternoon, and were ranked in order, from his landing place to
his palace, as he causes it to be called. The Friday, 11th November, he summoned Ch. A. [Charles Andros] and his counsel to
be in the castle at two in the afternoon, to hear his report betwixt
him and P. Priaulx, for the Fief le Conte, and, being come in the

hall, caused the report to be read before above sixty persons; and after, he began to give to the king's procureur, or attorney, the most bitter injuries that can be thought on, and next fell upon Ch. A., calling him foul-mouth, infamous cabalist against the king, traitor, and that he ought to throw himself at the king's feet to demand him pardon; to which he answered:

"That it was not in the power of any man to impose upon him any stain of disloyalty against his king, having served him faithfully, and often exposed his life for his service; that in case he could prove the least disloyalty against him, that he would cause him to be punished by the severest extremity the laws would allow; that, for his part, he would not plead the act of oblivion [1] for any fault that he had committed against his sovereign; that he had rather lose his life than his honor. Many other injuries he received, too long to be here recited. And those present at all this were Tho. Marchant; I. de Quetteville; Mathew Herivel; Will. Marchant; Natha. White; Peter Priaulx, Marchant's son-in-law; Elear. Marchant, brother to Thomas; and many others who were sent for to be present at this . . . . . .

"I make you judge of the state wherein we are reduced: our honor and reputation being taken from us by the dirt and filth thrown upon us, by calumnies and unjustifiable injuries; our ancestors drawn from their graves, and brought upon the stage; our judges and magistrates being rendered infamous in the ears of the common people; our jurisdiction abject and despised, and almost in a downfal; our liberties enslaved; our laws broken; our privileges lost; our lives and goods exposed to the mercy of some persons;—this is the sad condition we are reduced into. Pray endeavour by all means to bring a remedy to all those evils with which we are at present infolded, and to employ all your friends, and the interest you have for the good of your country, and advise a course to be taken in it. I think it would be seasonable to endeavour with the soonest to have an order from his majesty to cause four or five persons to be called over to give an ample relation of all passages here, who may without fear inform of truth of things; and if that may be obtained, pray delay not to give us notice of it by the way of France, and by all the most expeditious ways. If that may not be obtained, endeavour to find some other expedient to have us come, for it will be impossible for us to come out of the island without his majesty's own order. The merchants cannot go after their trading" . . . . . .

[From the context, it is evident that this letter was addressed by Mr. Amias Andros to Sir Henry De Vic, Bart., who appears to have been consulted on all the public affairs of the island, relating to which we have before us five letters of his, three in French and two in English. Writing from Windsor, June 16, 1670, to the bailiff and jurats of Guernsey, Sir Henry says: "Au

(1) In that Act it was declared that Mr. Charles Andros had been inviolably faithful to the king.—See *ante*.

reste comme je suis dans un aage trop advancé pour une vie de cour, et a cet effet je me suis retiré en ce lieu pour y estre plus a repos et a mon aise, j'ay peur pour l'affection que j'ay a notre pauvre pays de pouvoir aux occasions qui se pourroient rencontre en mon absence qu'il n'y fust faute de moy, et comme je ne cognoisse qui soit plus capable a tous esgards d'y supplier, j'ay prié le Major Andros de vouloir que je le feisses mon député, pour en mon absence y pouvoir paretre et agir.   Cela ne m'empescher [a] pas pourtant de faire un tour en cour, quand l'affaire sera d'importance, et que ma santé le pourra permettre," &c.]

Although the inhabitants of Guernsey had opposed the arbitrary government of Charles I., the reign of his son— thanks evidently to the influence of Sir George Carteret, Sir H. De Vic, and Amias Andros—was auspicious to the island, as he not only confirmed its privileges generally, but, in 1668, granted it a charter, in which were recited the various concessions of his predecessors.   Moreover, many complaints having been made against Lord Hatton, the governor, who, among other charges, was accused of having sold to the French some brass guns,[1] which he had taken from Castle Cornet, he was recalled by the king, in February, 1665, in consequence of this violation of his duty, and also of his arbitrary interference with judicial authority;[2] and Colonel Jonathan Atkins was appointed to command during the absence of that nobleman, whose son Christopher, Lord Hatton, had the reversion of the post.   The provisional governor was strictly charged to maintain the privileges of the islanders.   In 1666, Guernsey was placed in a posture of defence, the French having then some design on the islands, and which design was frustrated by the secret communication of the lady of Marshal Turenne, as related in Chapter XI.   It was at this time that the captain of the isles of Chausey (Vaucour) was detected in Guernsey when tampering with some of the inhabitants, whom he suspected of disaffection, and particularly with General Lambert, already mentioned.   But the general, it seems, preferred any government to a French one, and therefore having made a free discovery, Vaucour was apprehended, and, as a convicted spy, suffered death.   It may have been this discovery which procured for Lambert the favor of his removal to England.

(1) We know not whether Lord Clarendon, who died in exile at Rouen, in 1678, alludes to this accusation, when speaking of Sir Christopher (afterwards Lord) Hatton in his history, he says: "Sir Christopher Hatton, a person of great reputation at that time, which in a few years he found a way to diminish."

(2) Colonel Atkins, writing to Amias Andros, in April, 1667, says: "But to make our disturbance the greater, which doeth not a little amaze the people, my Lord Hatton has sent to his small correspondents that he is recovered, and will soon pursue his businesse, and doubts not very shortly to return hither, which makes the people in a very unsettled condition, they fearing it more than the coming of the ffrench."

Colonel Atkins to Amias Andros, Esq.

[Extracts.]—"The other day a ship laden with goods from St. Malo to a very considerable value, a great part thereof coarse canvass and some money therein, came here upon the accompt of Mr. Carey, and others his associates. An Irishman came master of her, who it seems had bought some pistols and carbines to make some profit thereof." [Colonel Atkins having been informed by two merchants of a rival association that there were arms on board for conveyance to Ireland, caused the vessel to be unloaded, when 'only six case of pistols and seven carbines' were found.] "I trouble you with this relation, to let you see that our jealousies one of another still remain. But I do not find the price of stockings is at all advanced by these [merchants] more than the other, nor that they keep their word with me, and lay out but very little money to buy them, but rather drive another kind of trade with woollen cloth and other commodities. But I am glad to be content with any thing that portends subsistence, for I do every day more and more see the necessities of the people increase, so that if we cannot continue this little trade, and procure leave to import our commodities into England, you may well judge the consequence there, and how miserable we shall soon be.

"I find they are very suspicious in England we grow very rich, and the emulation is great against us upon that accompt. It were well if we found it so, but I am sure I do not; but most men now-a-days are so apt to prefer their own interests to the king's, that they think we do the same, which I am sure we have not done; but I need not declare this to one that knows it.

"We are very busy in making preparations for our summer's trial: we are getting up our works forth at Fermain and "Mer Peroin," have our stores of biscuit in every parish of the island ready: some ammunition and arms would much encourage us, which we hope your solicitations will obtain.

"P.S.—Commend me to Mun:[1] tell him they are fitting out the privateer as fast as they can.[2] I encourage it all I may, but some others seem concerned that it will take as they suppose from them. I should not care if there were ten more. I am for ruining the enemy, let us fare as we can.

"Castle Cornet, February 23, 1666." [7]

From the same to the same.

[Extracts.]—"I was a little surprised when by yours of the 16th February, which came to my hands the 3d instant, as also by one from your son from Portsmouth, I was advertised of his

(1) Edmund, afterwards Sir Edmund Andros.

(2) The fitting out of this privateer now seems a violation of the privilege of neutrality, unless she were intended to cruize solely against the Dutch.

so sudden departure for the Barbadoes expedition . . . . . . But
since he must go, I am glad he goes in so honorable a place as
major.[1] Ever since I received your letters, which I sent presently to your lady, I have been shut up in the castle by such
stormy weather, and such cold winds, and so much snow, as the
most concludes hath never been seen here before ; and I believe
the French will find they have made a little too much haste with
their fleet, for that part which is out from Brest hath had this
whole week such weather as will make them fit to go in again,
for they cannot avoid to be extremely tattered and disabled. . . . .
At last, Colonel " Kingsbey," the agent for the prizes, is arrived,
for such is his title in the letter written to us from the lords commissioners.   I doubt the time is much spent of getting prizes this
year, and I believe the employment will hardly answer his nor
their expectations, notwithstanding the great benefits imputed to
us, which I am sure is yet in embryo.   But I hope they will be
so just as to pay us for what we have done, and those officers that
have acted with us for them.

"Castle Cornet, March $_{5}^{8}$, 166$_{7}^{6}$.
"To his honored friend, Amice Andros, Esq., his majesty's bailiff
of his island of Guernsey, at his lodging over against the
White Nag in James' Street, Covent Garden, London."

From the same to the same.

" CASTLE CORNET, March 25, 1667.

" Sir,—Tis so latelie that I writt to you, that I shall not have
much now to say to you; but I cannot omitt to relate how bravelie
the men of St. Martyn's have behaved themselves at sea.   They
have brought in a prize of sixty tun, a flie boate belonging to
Amsterdam, that is laden with wine, ptum,[2] figs and rosin, and
is without dispute cleere prize.   They likewise encounterd with
another at sea, of nyne or ten guns, with their two guns, of which
they were fayne to borrow one of mee; but receivd so much
damage in their hull, sayles, and rigging, and having ffive of their
twenty-ffive men hurt, they were forcd to leave her; but man-
fully after this tooke the same they brought in, which had likewise two guns.   I have given you this relation that you may see
your countrymen will fight.   I beseech you present my service
to Mr. Deane, [Sausmarez,] Mr. de Haviland, and Mr. Martin,
and desyre them they will this tyme accept this letter as to them
all.   Your good lady is well, and so are the rest of your relations,
and all theirs.   Forget mee not to all our friends, nor with which
assurance   I am, Sir, your very affec. freind and serv.

"J. ATKINS."

(1) There is a letter from Colonel Atkins, dated Castle Cornet, January 26, 1666, [! 1667,]
addressed " To my much esteemed friend, Ensign Andros," so that his advancement
had been very rapid.

(2) *P'tum*, the true native American, and Guernsey and Jersey, word for French PETUN,
toubac or tobacco.

From the same to the same.

"Castle Cornet, Nov. 18, 1667.

"Sir,—It is a rare thing now to heare from England, and tis as hard a matter to send thither, for St. Malo's is the place they all send to, and now they have no need of us, they give us a goe-by: wee are verry desyrous to heare how things goe in England, of which we are very ignorant. Wee heare of your disagreements, for which we are very sorry; and your attempts uppon great ones doeth somewhat startle us; for since wee have peace, wee pray now for unitie;—wee conserve it still amongst our selves, and if some unexpected change doe not alter us, wee are well inough. Your lady is well and all yours; but your brother Danville hath beene very ill, but recovers againe. I am glad you have assurance of Muns [Edmund Andros] being well. Wee have had such stormie weather as never man see; our merchants have receivd some damage thereby, but the Jersie men much more. Tis very long since wee receivd any letters from England. Heere are two vessells come from Hampton, bound for Jersie, who say that Fiott put out from the Isle of Wight three days before them, with whom I heare my letters are: wee hope they are put into some port of the west. Present mee to all our freinds. My humble service to Sir George Carterett and Sir Henry De Vic. Without alteration, I am, Sir,

"Your freind and servant,

"J. Atkins.

"For his honored freind, Amias Andros, Esq.
bayliffe of his majesti's island of Guernzey."

Sir Henry De Vic, Bart., to Major Edmund Andros.

"I did write unto you upon Thursday last what was my sense touching the election of a jurat, since which time I hear that my Lord Hatton hath written unto my Lord Arlington, and no doubt hath represented the passages in the late election with the disadvantage that may be, in order that either he may be made umpire and have the casting voice, or else that he may obtain his former design of having his friend, Mr. William Marchant, to be made a jurat.[1] I confess that by that I have understood and seen that the said election hath been but too tumultuous, and that tumult hath proceeded from the insolent behaviour of de Grange [Mr. de Beauvoir] his party, which was so great as I wonder less how your father should be mistaken in one voice, which to remedy, the expedient I did propound in my last I think may suffice, and if it be not approved, methinks this other may be taken; that

(1) Mr. William Le Marchant was elected a jurat in 1671. We observe that, in the seventeenth century, gentlemen of the first families were much more anxious to obtain a seat on the bench than they are now, because the magisterial duties were then comparatively very light.

Y

Mr. Dean and Mr. Havilland, one of the jurats, who are here, and are both of them electors, may be admitted to give their voices as if they were present there. I pray you acquaint my Lord of Arlington with this letter, to prevent those inconveniences that might otherwise arise . . . . . .

"For Major Andros, at the Earle of Craven,
    his house in Drury Lane.

"Windsor, this 12th August, 1671."

On the death of the first Lord Hatton, in 1670, his son, Lord Hatton, succeeded him as governor of Guernsey. He was far from following in his father's footsteps, as he steadily promoted the prosperity of the island, and watched over its interests; but, after a residence of two years, an awful calamity befell him and his family, by which he lost his mother and his wife. On the 29th of December, 1672, the magazine of the castle was exploded, as we shall narrate in the words of Dicey, who, it will be seen, relates some very extraordinary escapes, which savour rather of the marvellous:

"On Sunday night, about twelve o'clock, the day abovementioned, the magazine of this castle was blown up, with the powder in it, by thunder and lightening. The night was very stormy and tempestuous, and the wind blew hard at south-west, to which aspect the door of the magazine exactly fronted; and the thunder bolt, or clap, which accompanied this dreadful calamity, was heard to come circleing (or, as it were, serpentining) over the platform, from the south-west. In an instant of time, not only the whole magazine was blown up in the air, but also all the houses and lodgings of the castle; particularly some fair and beautiful buildings, that had just before been erected at great expence, under the care and direction of the Right Honourable the Lord Viscount Hatton, their then governor, who was at the same time within the buildings of the castle; all which buildings [1] were, with many others, reduced to a confused heap of stones, and several persons buried in the ruins.

"In the upper part of the castle, at a place called the New Buildings, was killed by this accident the Right Hon. the Lady Dowager Hatton, by the fall of the ceiling of her chamber, which fell in four pieces, one of them upon her breast, and killed her on the spot.

"The Right Honourable the Lady Hatton, wife to the governor, and daughter to the Right Honourable the Earl of Thanet, was likewise destroyed in the following manner: her ladyship, being greatly terrified at the thunder and lightening, insisted

(1) These buildings appear, by the engraving before mentioned, to have been erected on the southern summit of the islet, and adjoined the keep, or tower.

(before the magazine blew up) upon being removed from the chamber she was in to the nursery, where, having caused her woman to come also to be with her, in order to have joined in prayer, in a few minutes after that noble lady and her woman fell a sacrifice, by one corner of the nursery room falling in upon them, and were the next morning both found dead.

"In the same room was also killed a dry nurse, who was found dead, having my lord's second daughter fast in her arms, holding a small silver cup in her hands which she usually played with, which was all rimpled and bruised; yet the young lady did not receive the least hurt. This nurse had likewise one of her hands fixed upon the cradle, in which lay my lord's youngest daughter, and the cradle almost filled with rubbish; yet the child received no sort of prejudice. Besides these, one Ensign Covert; Mr. William Prole, the Lord Hatton's steward; and a considerable number of other persons, were all destroyed by the same accident.

"Having given this account of those who perished, I shall briefly mention some of those also who escaped, and were most miraculously preserved in this extraordinary and uncommon disaster.

"First, the Right Honourable the Lord Viscount Hatton, their governor, who at that time had his appartment in a very neat convenient house, which his lordship had built him, about two years before this affair happened. This house stood north by east from the magazine, and very near it. His lordship, at the time it blew up, was fast in sleep, and was actually, by the explosion, carried away in his bed upon the battlements of a wall, which was battered by the sea, between rugged precipices, just adjoining to his house, and was not awaked but by a shower of hail that fell upon his face, and made him sensible where he was: this, no doubt, must appear very extraordinary, but is averred to be fact. A most miraculous preservation indeed, in as much as that the house wherein his lordship was so taken away was razed to the very ground, nothing of it being left standing but the door case. From those battlements on the wall, his lordship was conveyed by two blacks (who among other servants attended him) to the guard-room of the castle, under the deepest affliction, to know whether his lady had escaped, or what was become of her, offering a thousand pounds to whomsoever should bring her alive to him; but no news could be learned of her ladyship's fate until it was clear day, when she was found crushed to death, in the manner before related.

"Under his lordship's appartments was a chamber belonging to the lieutenant of his company of foot, who, by the violence of the shock, was carried out of his room, part of which fell in, and he was tumbled in a very extraordinary manner into an entry on the ground floor, but received no manner of hurt.

"At the upper buildings of the castle were several appartments, and people in them all, particularly the Lord Hatton's two sisters; (one of whom I imagine to have been the late Countess of Nottingham,) the ensign of my lord's company, and his wife; with several other persons. Upon my lord's two sisters fell, or rather glanced, a beam, both ends of which happened to be between them in such a manner, that although they were both together before it fell in, yet they could not afterwards get at each other, but were pulled out of their room through a hole, made on purpose in a partition wall, and neither of them received any sensible hurt, nor did any others in those apartments receive any harm, notwithstanding several of the rooms fell in, wherein many of them at that time were fast in sleep; and some of the floors were in heaps of rubbish about them, as they lay in their beds."[1]

We have been favored with a copy of the original manuscript, from which Dicey compiled the preceding narrative, and, according to an endorsement on the manuscript, evidently in his own handwriting, it appears that he was indebted for the details to Mr. Dobrée, "a very ingenious worthy gentleman, a native of Guernsey, and a considerable merchant of London." Dicey has omitted the following occurrence, which is given in the manuscript: a Sergeant Cotton was blown in his bed over a high wall, and within a few inches of the mouth of a well; when he recovered consciousness, he knew not where he was; but as several ammunition beds were burning about him, he got out of his bed, and endeavoured to pass through the sally port. Being unable to do so, he proceeded to the south point, where he was discovered by the sentinel, who challenged him to stand. But as the sergeant continued to approach, the sentinel thought that he was a ghost, "nevertheless, standing upon his punctilios, made ghost to speak, who, knowing him by his voice, settled his spirits, and so the sergeant did bid him to come to help, at which sayings the centinell was much surprised, having heard nothing of the blow, for the wind carried it away from him."—Dicey states that a considerable number of persons were destroyed by the explosion, but the manuscript mentions that only seven were killed, besides several others hurt or wounded. This number is confirmed by the register of burials in the parish of St. Peter-Port, which register gives their

(1) "Il arriva en ce temps-là un accident au château de Gernsey dans la Manche, où le tonnerre étant tombé dans le magasin, mit le feu à 200 tonneaux de poudre, qui firent sauter le château, sans que le commandant, qui était couché alors, eut d'autre mal que d'avoir été enlevé en l'air par la violence de la poudre. On dit aussi que l'on trouva sous les ruines un enfant vivant, pendu à la mamelle de sa mère, qui était morte et écrasée."— *Histoire Universelle*, Leyden, 1763.—The quantity of powder named is doubtless greatly magnified.

names and other particulars in French, and, translated literally in English, is as follows :

"'Madame' Elizabeth de Montagu, widow of the late Lord
Hatton, governor of this island, having been killed in the ruins
and rubbish of the 'donjon' of Castle Cornet, which was struck
with a clap of thunder, and blown up by the gunpowder therein,
on Monday, the 30th of December, 1672, about one o'clock in
the morning, having been embalmed, her bowels were deposited
in the church on Tuesday, the 31st of the said month.

"'Madame' Cecile de Tufton, wife of my Lord Hatton, having
been killed by the same accident, and being embalmed, her bowels
were deposited in the church with those of her mother-in-law, on
the said 31st of December.

"Mr. William Prole, steward of my Lord Hatton, having been
crushed in the same ruins, was interred in the church, 31st December, 1672.

"Miss Eleanor Plott, having been crushed in the same manner,
was interred in the church the same day, 31st December, 1672.

"Mrs. Catherine Willis, Lady Hatton's nurse, having been also
crushed in the same ruins, was interred in the church the same day.

"Judith Pointing, having died of the same accident, was interred in the church the said day, 31st December, 1672.

"Mr. Richard Covert, ensign in the company of Captain
William Sheldon, lieutenant-governor, having been also crushed
in the same ruins, was interred in the church the first day of the
year, Wednesday, 167?."

This dreadful catastrophe filled the inhabitants of Guernsey
with grief and consternation, for Lord Hatton, by his paternal
government, was already much endeared to them, as were his
wife and mother, "on account of their eminent piety, sanctity, and good example." The royal court, "considering
the greatness of the loss as a proof that the wrath of God was
extremely excited against the inhabitants, in consequence of
their iniquities! and that it was their duty to humble themselves before him, to implore his pity, and to supplicate him
to stay his judgments," appointed Wednesday, the 15th of
January, as a day of fast and humiliation, when all the inhabitants were expressly commanded to assemble in their several
parish churches. The court also issued an order, forbidding
all persons to purchase timber or any other article from the
castle. The king immediately sent over some engineers to
repair the damages, and put the fortress in a state of security ;
on which the royal court, at the request of the governor,
ordered the constables to send thirty men daily to the castle
to grub up the foundations, affixing a penalty of fifteen sols

per day on those who refused to comply. From this period, Castle Cornet ceased to be the residence of the governors; and in winter, it must certainly have been a very lonely and inconvenient one, although the necessary buildings had been erected for their accommodation. But while the governors resided at Castle Cornet, they were enabled to diversify the scenes of their lonely residence by an occasional excursion to Herm, to shoot deer, pheasants, or rabbits; or to fish at the Grande Mare; or to shoot over the Clos du Valle, Guernsey containing a great many hares at that period, and long afterwards. In those days the intercourse with England was very rare and uncertain,' as may be inferred from one of Colonel Atkins' letters, just given; and we find him also writing, in April, 1667, to Mr. Amias Andros, then at Westminster, as follows: "Notwithstanding that the winde hath been so long at north-east, that we have almost forgot what other winds were used to blow, yet have we [not] heard from you nor received any newes from England, but by some letters which Captain Ffox hath got about Brooke's prize."—North-east winds are now as prevalent in April as they were then, and even nearly fifty years later the communication with England was as slow, as intelligence of the death of queen Anne, on the 2d of August, 1714, was first received in Guernsey six days afterwards by a vessel from St. Malo. Now, the evening mails from London, unless prevented by strong adverse winds, regularly reach Guernsey by steamers from Southampton three times a week, by eight or nine o'clock the next morning, which would have been considered a miracle by our ancestors, who, when they went to London, a century and a half ago, which they did rarely, are said to have made their wills, lest they should never return. The human mind is apt to dwell on the past, as affording more real happiness than the present, and to consider this as a degenerate age; but surely the existing certainty and rapidity of communication by sea and land do not confirm the impression. There was, however, formerly we believe less anxiety and less covetousness, at least in Guernsey, because there was more domestic economy. To how many may not now be applied Cicero's reproach to Catiline: "Alieni appetens, sui profusus."

By an order in council, dated June 11, 1670, the privilege of the States to elect a sheriff was confirmed, it having been

(1) We find that a letter written by Sir Peter Osborne, in London, to Mr. Thomas Andros, in Guernsey, dated May 28, 1621, only reached the latter on the 21st of June following; and that another letter from Mr. Amias Andros, bailiff, dated Guernsey, December 26, 1664, containing complaints against the first Lord Hatton, only reached the secretary of state, Henry Bennet, on the 2d of February following.

proved that they had enjoyed this right from immemorial custom.　In 1678, Guernsey was again threatened by the French, and some troops were sent over for its protection, with an order, dated February 2 in that year, and addressed to the bailiff and jurats, to provide quarters for the troops, and prevent any discord among them ; and also to take care that they daily pay for their quarters—a proof of the king's good feelings towards the inhabitants, for it is the first example on record concerning the payment of soldiers.　In this reign, Castle Cornet was placed under the control of the ordnance, to which department it has since remained attached, being by it repaired or enlarged, and provided with stores and ammunition.　This change was a great relief to the islanders, who were previously subjected to many charges and duties on its account ; and the former governors were accused of making the poor inhabitants bestow their labour on the castle for little or nothing. ·

Speaking of the Habeas Corpus Act, which was passed into a statute in 1679—a statute which, although eminently remedial, introduced no new principle or conferred no new right upon the subject—Hallam says : " The court of king's bench had already been accustomed to send out their writ of habeas corpus into all places of peculiar and privileged jurisdiction, where this ordinary process does not run, and even to the island of Jersey, beyond the strict limits of the kingdom of England ; and this power, which might admit of some question, is sanctioned by a declaratory clause of the present statute.　Another section enacts, that ' no subject of this realm that now is, or hereafter shall be, an inhabitant or resiant of this kingdom of England, &c., shall be sent prisoner into Scotland, Ireland, Jersey, Guernsey, Tangier, or into ports, garrisons, islands, or places beyond the seas, which are, or at any time hereafter shall be, within or without the dominions of his majesty, his heirs or successors,' under penalties of the heaviest nature short of death which the law then knew, and an incapacity of receiving the king's pardon.''　And, in a foot note, Hallam adds : " The court of king's bench directed a habeas corpus to the governor of Jersey to bring up the body of Overton, a well known officer of the Commonwealth, who had been confined there several yeais.—*Siderfin's Reports*, 386.　This was in 1668, after the fall of Clarendon, when a less despotic system was introduced."　In implying that the Habeas Corpus Act was extended to these islands at or before that period, Hallam was mistaken ; and Overton was clearly a state prisoner sent from England, and placed in the sole custody of the governor of Jersey : had it been otherwise, and the writ of the court of the king's bench been directed to the royal courts of Jersey and Guernsey, it certainly would have been disregarded, being a violation of the privileges of the islanders, as will be shewn in the sequel.

Falle, in the introduction of his History of Jersey, thus describes the value of these islands : " For these islands are to be considered as a frontier or advanced guard towards an ennemy's country. And such places do always, in the very nature of them, suppose and infer a charge for forteresses and garrisons. Should the French, by the conquest of these islands, (which God forbid,) extend themselves into the Channel, they would repine at no expence laid out upon them. And then England might possibly, in few years, see another Dunkirk rising out of the sea." And to this passage he adds the following note : " Let this that follows serve for a proof of what the French might do here if they were masters. Towards the end of the reign of king Charles II., some able engeneers, with the Lord Dartmouth, were sent to take a more perfect view of these islands ; and on that side of Guernezey which lies to the north-west, and looks into the Channel, they found and pitched upon a place excellently fitted by nature for the construction of a mole and bason, wherein a fleet of capital ships might lye.[1] A draught was made of the port, and an estimate brought in of the charge. But the work remained without execution by reason of the bad state of the exchequer at that time ; and the king lived not to resume the same when his affairs were in a better condition. Such a place as this in the Channel, to be a station for large men of war, the French would purchase at any rate, having, in all their coast from Dunkirk to Brest, none but *havres de marée*, i.e. tide harbours, wanting a sufficient depth of water for such great ships.—(From the Memoirs of the Sr. de Samarez.")

JAMES II.—1685 to 1689.

This bigoted sovereign was not long in attempting to subject Guernsey to his religious opinions. Roman Catholic soldiers were quartered in the island, and a governor of the same persuasion was appointed : mass was performed, and the design of supplanting Protestantism was apparent. Such a scheme was very odious to the inhabitants, and they gladly

(1) Grand Havre, or Great Harbour, near the Vale church.

·seized the first opportunity of defeating it. On the other hand, James appears to have been solicitous to define and secure the judicial prerogative of the royal court, for in June, 1687, he ordered a letter to be written to Charles Macarty, Esq., described as captain of a company in the Earl of Litch-field's regiment, and commander-in-chief in Guernsey. The letter cautions Macarty, who from his name was probably an Irish Roman Catholic, "that the articles of war do not in any manner empower a court martial or military officer to punish any offenders, except such as are in his majesty's pay as soldiers, nor take cognizance of any inhabitant of Guernsey for injuring a soldier, further than to cause him to be pro-ceeded against by the law of the place, the articles of war in Guernsey authorizing only the trial and punishment of offences or quarrels that happen between soldier and soldier, and not between a soldier and an inhabitant, which offences are to be judged by the civil magistrate only."

During the quiet which followed the Restoration, the manufacture of stockings, &c., in the islands increased, and James, on petition, granted annually 4,000 tods of wool for Jersey, 2,000 for Guernsey, 400 for Alderney, and 200 for Sark, all to be shipped from the port of Southampton. He also appointed William Steevens to reside in Guernsey to sign and seal certificates of the landing of commodities, and perform the same duties as had been introduced into Jersey by an order in council, dated the 17th of December, 1679.

WILLIAM AND MARY.—1689 to 1702.

At the time of the Revolution, the Guernseymen were, as they now are, eminently Protestant, this feeling having doubt-less been strengthened by the dreadful punishment inflicted on the three poor innocent women and the infant, as related in the reign of Mary. Thus it is, happily, that intolerance and cruelty usually defeat themselves, and serve only to con-firm the victims of religious persecution in their opinions.

On being informed of the landing of the Prince of Orange at Torbay, in November, 1688, the civil authorities of Guern-sey, without waiting the issue of his enterprise, concerted measures with the senior Protestant officer of the garrison to secure the island to his cause ; to disarm the Catholics, who formed a considerable part of the soldiery ; and to confine the lieutenant-governor, whose political principles were doubt-ful. They fixed on the day when the officer, with whom they had concerted the plot, was to command in rotation; and on that day the chief captain of the town militia, accompanied by most of his corps, seized upon and disarmed the Catholic officers and soldiers in St. Peter-Port, notice thereof being immediately given to the commander at the castle, by a signal previously arranged. He then quickly drew out the garrison, which being assembled on the parade, the Protestants, with their muskets loaded with ball, marched out of the ranks; and facing about, presented their pieces at their comrades, compelling them to lay down their arms. This incident is noticed by Campbell and other authors, who are of opinion that from it arose the king's unwillingness to rely any further upon his navy, in which he had previously placed much confidence, the seamen having gained the principal credit on this occasion, although in truth it was entirely due to the Protestant spirit of part of the military and of the inhabitants. And considering the cruel and vindictive character of James II., it must be admitted that this was a very bold undertaking, as it would assuredly have proved of serious consequence to its promoters and to the island, had that bloodthirsty monarch continued on the throne.

Two or three years after the accession of William and Mary, an invasion of these islands was much apprehended; and the Earl of Peterborough, uncle of the celebrated commander of that title, was sent with troops for their protection. In 1692, Guernsey was twice visited by large British squadrons, as on the 14th of April, Rear-Admiral Carter, who, a few weeks after, was killed at the battle of La Hogue,[1] was ordered to sail with twenty-four ships to the islands of Jersey and Guernsey, "and there taking pilots, to proceed to the coast of France, near St. Mallo, and cruise forty-eight hours; longer than which time it was not thought convenient that he should stay, unless he found an opportunity of doing service. From thence he was to sail to 'Cape de Hague,' and to stand as near in to Havre-de-Grâce as the safety of the ships would permit; and if no service could be done there, to return forthwith to Spithead, if he judged it not for the security of the islands to continue longer on the French coast, in which case he was to send the earliest advice he could of his intentions."[2] On the 3d of July, Admiral Russell, with the same English

(1) If the battle was named after the Cape, as is probable, it was correctly La Hague; if after the roadstead of La Hogue St. Vast, where thirteen French ships were burnt, its English name is correct.

(2) Burchett's Transactions at Sea, from 1688 to 1697. London, 1703.

and Dutch fleet with which, on the 19th of May, he had fought the battle of La Hogue, almost in sight of Guernsey, arrived in the roadstead of that island, "where he was constrained to anchor, for the weather being thick, the pilots would not venture over to St. Mallo ; nor was there a little reason to suspect their judgment ; but that which gave the admiral the greatest uneasiness was the account he received from two captains, who had long used the trade, that there was not good ground for more than forty ships to ride : so that he called a council of war, to consider whether it might be most proper for the whole fleet to go over, or to send a detachment to view the place ; and they came to the following resolution, viz. that part of the fleet should proceed off of St. Mallo, and bring an account whether the whole, or what numbers thereof, might ride there. Accordingly, Vice-Admiral Rooke was sent with a squadron, in conjunction with Vice-Admiral Callemberg, who commanded the Dutch detachment." [1] The remainder of the fleet must soon after have left Guernsey, as it was forced by bad weather into Torbay, "where the admiral did impatiently expect the return of Sir George Rooke." [1] On the 13th of July, the latter officer, who in 1704 took Gibraltar, returned from St. Malo, and made a report in five articles, of which the first was as follows : "The ground is flat and even from Guernsey to Cape Farrel, [Fréhel,] shoaling a fathom or two every two or three miles, all the way over to the Cape. The ground is generally very rough, and in some places rocky, especially near St. Cymbre." [1] [Césambre.] The liability of the Anglo-Norman Islands to attack at this time will be better understood by remembering that France, under Louis XIV., was then by far the strongest European power by land, and that during the long reign of that monarch, (1643 to 1715,) prior to the battle of La Hogue, she had at sea no superior. That naval victory would probably otherwise have afforded little subject for exultation, seeing that the combined English and Dutch fleets amounted to ninety-nine ships of the line, while the French had only sixty-three, some of which were detached before the engagement. And notwithstanding this enormous disparity of force, the French admiral, whose fleet was several leagues to windward, did not hesitate to bear down on his opponents, probably however in the belief that the English

(1) Burchett's Transactions.—In this work we find the *Jersey* and *Guernsey*, ships of war. These names, with that of the *Alderney* subsequently, have long disappeared from the Navy List ; but surely they would be more appropriate than the *Arrogant*, *Growler*, or *Jasper*.

admiral, who was a secret adherent of James, would either pass over to his old master, or offer no effectual resistance.[1]

"The fear of invasion was not removed till 1692. In that memorable year, John Tupper, Esq., of Guernsey, at some personal expense and risk of capture, passed either through, or in sight of, the French fleet, and promptly conveyed to Admiral Russell, who commanded the combined English and Dutch fleets, lying at St. Helen's, intelligence that the French admiral, Tourville, was in the Channel. As a reward for this patriotic service, Mr. Tupper was presented by William and Mary with a massive gold chain and medal, which are now in possession of his heir male; and his descendants are permitted to bear them as an honourable augmentation to their arms and crest. The famous naval battle of La Hogue was the result of Mr. Tupper's information— a battle which annihilated the French marine, and relieved Guernsey from all immediate alarm of hostile aggression."— *Duncan.* The tradition in the family, relative to this medal and chain[2] is, that the aforesaid John Tupper, being in London after the battle, was sent for by a king's messenger, and on reaching the secretary of state's office, he was told that the king had expressed a wish to see him, to thank him in person for the good service he had rendered his majesty, and that the king had given orders that the medal and chain should be presented to him.

The military preparations required to repel the expected invasion were accompanied by grievances to the inhabitants of Guernsey, who complained to the king, August 8, 1689, "that they were compelled to raise a general tax to provide quarters for such officers and soldiers as cannot be lodged in public houses, and among them, for divers inhabitants who have enlisted as soldiers, and have habitations of their own; also that they were much oppressed by the soldiers not paying their landlords for the arrears due for their diet, the constables not being called upon, as has been the custom, to see the accounts adjusted and cleared between the landlords and

---

(1) "Russell, though compelled to win the battle of La Hogue against his will, took care to render his splendid victory as little advantageous as possible."—*Hallam.*

(2) Similar medals in silver, without the chains, are supposed to have been bestowed on the captains in the fleet, as five are known to be still in existence in England. The obverse bears the effigies of William and Mary, and the reverse represents a ship of the line engaging the French admiral, Tourville, in the "Royal Sun," with other ships in the distance, under the singular legend of "Nox Nulla Secuta Est;" and on the exergue, "Pugn. Nav. Int. Ang. et Fr. 21 Maii, 1692."—See *Hunter's Orders of Knighthood.*

In February, 1854, queen Victoria presented to Captain Gaspard Le Marchant Tupper, Royal Artillery, and a lineal descendant of the aforesaid John Tupper, an engraving of herself, handsomely framed, "as a token of her majesty's appreciation of his attention in executing two drawings for her majesty," by request, of views of the camp at Chobham.

soldiers at the removal of quarters." This complaint was referred to Viscount Hatton, the governor, and the privy council afterwards granted such redress as the case required.

About the year 1699, a battalion of six companies of the royal regiment of fusileers having arrived in the island, three companies were quartered at Castle Cornet, and the other three in the town, the latter chiefly in private dwellings, there not being room in the public houses to receive them, in consequence of which the inhabitants incurred a weekly expense of £4 for their quarters. The States presented a petition to the king on the subject, and his majesty being informed that the barracks in the castle could nearly hold the four companies ordered to remain in the island, commanded that they should be lodged in the barracks, with the exception of twenty-four men who were to be distributed among the public houses, until new barracks were built. Three soldiers of this regiment were convicted of coining and uttering false French half-crowns, and one of them suffered death, the other two being pardoned by an order in council of 21st December, 1699.

The whole of this reign was auspicious to Guernsey, as although at its commencement the islands were deprived of their ancient charter of neutrality, yet the privilege appears to have been so little valued that its loss did not draw forth a single murmur or remonstrance from the inhabitants, who doubtless considered the withdrawal as amply compensated by the faculty of fitting out privateers and making war on the commercial marine of France. So great was their success, that 1,500 prizes are said to have been made by Jersey and Guernsey during the reigns of William and Anne. This number may seem exaggerated, but the prizes were, doubtless, chiefly small French coasters; and we are confirmed in this opinion by a commission, now before us, granted by George, prince of Denmark, lord high admiral, and bearing date the 11th of June, 1702, to Captain Edward Browne, of the ship " called the Two Brothers, of the burthen of about *four* tons, to set forth in warlike manner the said ship called the Two Brothers, under his own command, and therewith, by force of arms, to apprehend, seize, and take the ships, vessels, and goods, belonging to France or Spain," &c. This *mighty* privateer we presume to have belonged to Jersey, and no doubt, with many others of the same description, was sent forth to wage war on the enemy's coasting trade. Whatever may now be thought of the morality of this mode of warfare, certain it is that at that time, and for above a century later, the islanders of all ranks pursued it, on the breaking out of a war, with the greatest avidity, so as to make or enrich many a family. Privateering was at its height during the French revolutionary wars commencing in 1793, and especially when Spain was drawn into the contest against England, the rich argosies from Mexico and Peru offering a temptation which many could not resist. It was the number of privateers at this period which caused Edmund Burke to observe, that these islands alone might rank among the naval powers of Europe; and whatever may have been the motive, they unquestionably contributed their full share to that naval pre-eminence which is the chief dowry of Great Britain.—To return to William. A few months before his death, the people of Guernsey, in an address, dated November 8, 1701, testified their great obligations to him, and expressed their inviolable fidelity to his government. The vaunted privilege of neutrality was already forgotten; and William, having prevented the introduction of popery into the island, where it was held in the greatest horror, was undoubtedly much beloved by the inhabitants.

At the close of the seventeenth century, it is evident that the people of these islands were just beginning to emerge from that state of indigence which had long been the heritage of their ancestors. Thus Lord Carew, in 1616, spoke of Guernsey as being very poor; and after the civil war, the inhabitants complained, apparently with truth, of great distress and penury; two thirds of the island, they said, being covered with fern and furze. It was only, as we have just shewn, in the reign of William III. that privateering brought wealth and commerce to the islands. That wealth was the commencement of a great social change, as, anterior to its introduction, the highest classes, with very few exceptions, could only provide for their children by callings, such as now would be thought to degrade their more aristocratic descendants. Commissions in the army and navy, and employment abroad, were then unobtainable; the parochial clergy were held in so little estimation that the livings were usually filled by Frenchmen; the fees of the advocates were trifling; medical practitioners there were none; and thus in the best families the young men had no other resource than one to cultivate the small patrimonial estate, another to enter into some local retail business, and a third to command one of the few vessels belonging to the island. This was the natural result of the very limited extent of Guernsey and of its equal laws of inheritance, as certain it is that a landed gentry, in the English sense of the term, cannot long exist where estates are divided at every generation. In consequence, the Anglo-Norman, however well born, who fondly pictures to himself his ancestors of the seventeenth, or even of a great part of the eighteenth, century, as living in the same ease and independence as the fundholder of the nineteenth, will be egregiously mistaken; but the comparison is equally applicable to those English families which are descended from the younger sons of the cavaliers who fought at Naseby, or witnessed the Restoration [1] How poor the islands were in the early part of the seventeenth century will appear by the following letter [2] from Mr. (afterwards Sir) Henry De Vic, before mentioned :

Henry De Vic, Esq., to Lord Conway.

"St. Martin, [Isle of Rhé,] Aug. 7, 1627.

"I know your lordship is not unmindful of our poor islands, notwithstanding, I will make bold to recommend them to your lordship's accustomed care. I know the lords are sensible of their present condition, but not answerable to their present misery, which these troubles between us and France have so augmented by the interruption of their small trade, that I protest to God, I know not which way they can avoid their utter ruin, unless some means be used from England to prevent it by some relief. All the money they had heretofore in the islands came out of France, from their traffic of stockings, which being now cut off, unless some way be found out that may set the poor people on work as that did, I see not how they can live. For it must be by manufacture that they shall subsist, the islands affording no commodities of their own to vend abroad, and having no shipping to transport foreign commodities from one kingdom to the other. If the governor be permitted to bring over money into England, as he usually doth for his annual rents there, I do not think there will be any money at all left in the island. If I speak more sensibly of this than I ought, your lordship will excuse it upon the affection that I owe, and which I will bear as long as I live, unto my country. One thing more I have to recommend unto your lordship, and that is, Sir Philip Carteret's business, on whose side you shall find, upon examination, more justice than hitherto hath been conceived of his cause.[3] As for myself, your lordship

---

(1) It is indeed certain that the progress of wealth and civilization has been quite as great in England, since the Restoration, as in these islands, and probably more so in Scotland and Ireland. Macaulay's History of England furnishes many proofs of these changes

(2) From Lord Hardwicke's State Papers, vol. ii., p. 44.

(3) What his cause was we are unable to discover, but Sir P. Carteret was very despotic if a tithe of the charges, brought against him by the Jerseymen, in 1643, were correct.— See Falle's History of Jersey, with Durell's Notes, pp. 311, 314.

will be pleased to think upon me, when occasion serves, as one that will always be your lordship's most humble and most devoted servant.   "HEN. DE VIC."[1]

The following are some of the ordinances of the royal court during the seventeenth century :

"September, 1605.—It is ordered that artisans and labourers shall take per day as follows, and shall not take more, under penalty of 60 sols tournois fine, half to the king and half to the informer.

"Ship carpenters, 9 deniers sterling, if maintained by their masters, (aux despens des maîtres,) and 18 deniers if not so maintained.

"Common carpenters, 5 deniers, and 10 deniers, as above.

"Stone cutters and master masons, 5 deniers, and 10 deniers, as above.

"Common masons, 4 deniers, and 8 deniers, as above.

"Roofers of slate, 5 deniers, and 10 deniers, as above.

"Roofers of straw, 4 deniers, and 8 deniers, as above.

"Gardeners, the best, 4 deniers, and 8 deniers, as above.

"Labourers, common, 3 deniers, and 6 deniers, as above.

"The said artisans and labourers shall be subject, from September to March, to commence their work before sunrise and to continue it until dark ; and from March to September, to commence their work at five o'clock, a.m., and to continue it until seven o'clock, p.m., under the penalty before named.

"April, 1611.—The pound, weight of Guernsey, to contain eighteen ounces, weight of Rouen ; and all articles sold by weight to be sold by the weight of Rouen.

"October, 1615.—All tavern keepers to inform the lieutenant-governor of the name and quality of the strangers lodging with them, in twenty-four hours after their arrival, under penalty of being imprisoned twenty-four hours in a dungeon (en basse fosse) for the first time, and for the second the same penalty, and not allowed to keep a tavern ; and this on account of the great troubles of which there is an appearance in France.

"April, 1618.—Interest reduced from 10 to 8 per cent. per annum, and in October, 1623, from 8 to 6 per cent.

"October, 1625.—Mr. John de Quetteville (jurat) undertakes to bring into the island, in the month of March next, a paviour to pave the streets of the town, with whom he is to agree according

(1) Henry De Vic was sent by Charles I. to Bordeaux, in 1696, to order the English merchants trading there to return forthwith, and to send home all their ships. In 1662, he became comptroller of the Duke of York's household, with a salary of £400 a year. He died in 1672, leaving two children, viz. Charles, who married his cousin, Rachel Briard, and Margaret, wife of John, Baron Frecheville. Sir Charles died young in Guernsey, when the baronetcy became extinct. In a painted window at the church of Stavely, in Derbyshire, there was, and probably still is, an escutcheon containing two coats impaled : 1, Frecheville ; 2, De Vic, or, three galtraps and chief sab.

to the price usually given in England, exclusive of his passage from and back.

"May, 1661.—It having pleased the sacred majesty of our sovereign 'sire' the king, by advice of his very honorable privy council, to command that the names of Oliver and Richard Cromwell, and other tyrants and usurpers, inserted in the public registries of this island, be erased and cancelled,—the court, in rendering humble obedience to the said commandment, has ordered and orders that the names of the said tyrants and usurpers be erased, &c. &c.

"January, 1684.—All foreigners to leave the island in six weeks, and no strangers to reside without permission of the governor. The clergy ordered not to marry a native to a stranger or a stranger to a native, without informing the governor, as prescribed by the ordinances of the royal commissioners."

CHAPTER XIX.

THE narrative has now reached the commencement of the eighteenth century, and as our object in undertaking this work was chiefly to supply the many deficiencies of preceding historians, in regard to the early annals of Guernsey and to the civil war, we care not to relate all the local events, often of little present or future interest, which occurred from the accession of Anne to that of Victoria, especially as during that long period the island was exempt from hostile attack. It therefore only remains to us to select, from a mass of materials, the most striking or memorable incidents from the year 1700, and to describe them as concisely as possible.

ANNE.—1702. GEORGE I.—1714.

The reigns of Anne and George I. require little other notice than that, under the former sovereign, impressment of sailors, *not actually inhabitants of the islands,* was enforced in Jersey and Guernsey, in 1707; and that the latter, in 1717, confirmed the ancient right of the islanders to import freely their produce and manufactures into England : surplus produce there was probably none, and the manufactures consisted of woollen stockings or frocks. Although the royal court

z

directed the sheriff and constables to seize all stranger sailors, and empowered them to break open the doors of any house in which they suspected they were secreted ; yet the inhabitants, much to their credit, threw every obstacle in the way of impressment — a practice which, we conceive, can only be justified in cases of early prospective or actual invasion.

Edmund Andros had succeeded his father Amias as bailiff in 1674, with power to nominate a lieutenant during his long non-residence : he was also a colonel of dragoons, and after his return from his successive North American governments, he was constituted lieutenant-governor of Guernsey by Queen Anne, who dispensed with his executing the office of bailiff, and accepted Eleazar Le Marchant as lieutenant-bailiff; the said Le Marchant being empowered to execute the office of bailiff, and, in case of absence or illness, to appoint a deputy, as long as Sir Edmund remained lieutenant-governor. Against this monopoly of power, James de Beauvoir and eight of the jurats protested, but in vain, the queen being recommended by the lords of council to dismiss their petition, and to confirm the authority of Eleazar Le Marchant.

GEORGE II.—1727 to 1760.

The douzaine of St. Peter-Port having, in May, 1727, petitioned council against two acts of the royal court, dated in 1717 and 1720, by which the standard weights had been altered, and represented that the weights were a branch of the royal prerogative, his majesty in council declared the said acts null and void, and fixed the standard of weights to consist of eighteen ounces to the pound, as it remains at this day. —In 1731, another order in council, relative to certain dues for the support of Greenwich Hospital, was sent to Guernsey and Jersey for registry, and it contained a clause of great constitutional importance, as it enacted that, " for the *future*, whenever any act shall be passed in the parliament of Great Britain relating to the said islands of Guernsey and Jersey, printed copies of such acts shall be transmitted by the board of his majesty's privy council, as soon as conveniently may be, to the royal courts of the said islands, signifying to them, at the same time, his majesty's pleasure to register and publish the said acts, and cause the same to be carried into execution."—In 1735, it was decided by another order in council that real estate in England was not taxable in Guernsey for poor rates.

In May, 1737, the little islands of Herm, Jethou, and

Lihou, with the pond of the Grande Mare, near Vazon Bay, now marshy ground, which pond contained the wonderful carp described by Heylin, were leased out to individuals on fee farm rents, for terms of sixty-one years, renewable every twenty-one years, at a fine certain of three years reserved rent. By the order in council which authorized these leases, the governor, Major-General Sutton, was instructed to "insert a saving clause of the right of the inhabitants of Guernsey, and also of Sark, to go upon the coasts of the small islands to fish and also to cut vraic, and to fetch from thence stones for building and other uses, in the same manner they have hitherto done." And the lords of the committee further reported to his majesty, "that as to the oyster bank mentioned in the governor's memorial, it does not appear to them that the same was a part of your majesty's demesne," and in consequence the governor was not empowered to grant any lease thereof. This oyster bank was doubtless that now existing to the south-east of Castle Cornet, on what is called the Great Bank. In the year 1837, a premium was offered for oysters from this bank, with the view of affording employment to the fishermen in winter, and upwards of 60,000 were dredged from it; but, owing to the depth of water, it was found that the oysters would not bear competition with those from France, and the fishery was discontinued. The Great Bank, which is two miles long by about half a mile broad, is the resort of turbots, brilles, soles, &c.; and on it the parliamentary vessels usually anchored during the civil war, out of the reach of the guns of Castle Cornet.

The islet of Herm was long kept as a game preserve for the governors,[1] who had also the exclusive right of shooting in the Close of the Vale. (Clos du Valle.) Thus, on the 8th of September, 1716, we find the royal court authorizing the king's receiver, Mr. Peter Martin, to hold an inquest for the purpose of discovering the persons who had killed stags, roebucks, and pheasants, on the island of Herm, and also who had been sporting in the Clos du Valle, contrary to the ordinance. We have often heard from an old gentleman, now deceased, who remembered when the two last deer on Herm were killed, about the year 1773, that the stags were in the habit of swimming from thence to the Vale, a distance of rather less than two miles at low water, to feed, and then returning; always taking the proper tide each way.

On the 3d of October, 1744, a large fleet, under the com-

(1) See Lord Carew's Instructions to Bailiff de Carteret, in Chapter IX.

mand of Sir John Balchen, returning from Gibraltar to England, was dispersed by a violent storm, and several ships
suffered considerably. Sir J. Balchen's flag ship, the Victory,
of 110 guns, was separated from the rest of the fleet on the
4th, after which she was never seen or heard of more. It is
generally supposed that she struck upon the Caskets, as
repeated signals of distress were heard by the inhabitants of
Alderney; but it blew so violently that it was impossible to
give her any assistance. Thus perished the finest first-rate
man of war in the world, one of the best admirals in the
British service, eleven hundred sailors, and a considerable
number of volunteers, many of whom were of families of
distinction.[1]

In 1755 commenced the war with France, known in English history as the seven years' war. Early in the following
year the French made great preparations for the invasion of
Guernsey and Jersey, collecting troops at Granville and St.
Malo for that purpose, and reinforcements were sent from
England to these islands. In June, 1756, the command of a
squadron of ships, to be employed in their protection, was
conferred on Captain, afterwards Lord, Howe, who received
instructions to take possession of Chausey and its islands, on
which an Irish brigade in the service of France was stationed;
to harass the enemy by every possible means; and to destroy
the coasting trade between the northern and western provinces. The squadron consisted of six frigates and two
sloops, together with four transports for the conveyance of
troops; and such was the expedition with which the armament was prepared, that on the 13th of July, Howe proceeded
from Jersey for Chausey with four companies of General
Blockland's regiment, and one company of invalids from
Guernsey. The French commandant, when summoned to
surrender, at once gave up the place, on being permitted to
retire with military honours to Granville; and Howe, finding
that it would require time and expense to put the works in
a proper state of defence, as also at least 500 troops for their
garrison, determined to destroy them, which was effectually
and speedily done. And having ascertained that the French,
in consequence of the blow thus opportunely struck, had
abandoned their designs on the Anglo-Norman Islands, and
withdrawn their troops towards Brest and other distant ports,
he left a part of his squadron to annoy the coasting trade,
and returned to Plymouth towards the end of the year.

(1) Campbell's Lives of the Admirals.

As in the year 1628 the French threatened to retaliate the descent of the English on the Isle of Rhé by an invasion of the Channel Islands, so in 1758 they also threatened them in retaliation of the unsuccessful attempt, made under Sir John Mordaunt, to destroy the docks, arsenal, and shipping, at Rochefort during the preceding year. But Mr. Pitt, then prime minister, resolved that England should be the attacking, rather than the attacked, party. With this view, and in the hope of inducing the French government to withdraw a portion of its forces from the continental war, two fleets sailed on the 1st of June, 1758,—one of seventeen sail of the line and several frigates, under Lord Anson, from Spithead, to blockade Brest, where a considerable naval armament was in a forward state of preparation—the other consisting of the Essex, of 64 guns, four ships of 50, three frigates of 36, three of 32, and three of 28 guns, besides eleven sloops, bombs, and fire ships, thirty store ships, cutters, and tenders, and one hundred sail of transports, from St. Helen's, the whole under the command of Commodore Howe, who hoisted his broad pendant in the Essex. In this fleet were embarked three regiments of guards and other infantry, amounting to fifteen battalions, 400 artillery, 540 light horse, together about 13,000 fighting men, sixty pieces of cannon and fifty mortars, commanded by the Duke of Marlborough.

Lord Anson stood away west, while Commodore Howe steered athwart the Channel, with the wind at south-east. Notwithstanding the season of the year, the night proved so tempestuous that one of the store ships rolled away her masts. The following morning, they made Cape La Hague, and that night anchored in the race of Alderney. On the 3d, about noon, one of the transports struck upon a rock, near Sark, and was lost; but the troops on board were saved. On the 4th, Commodore Howe anchored within three leagues of St. Malo. Next morning, before break of day, he weighed and stood into the bay of Cancalle, so called from a village of that name, near which ten companies of grenadiers landed the same evening with little opposition, although there were in the village seven companies of foot and three troops of horse, who retired to St. Malo. The entire disembarkation was completed on the 6th; and on the 7th, at dawn, the army proceeded towards St. Malo in two columns, and after a march of six miles encamped about a mile from the town. The same night, at low water, the piquets made their way, close under the walls, to the harbour, where they found a 50-gun ship, two 36-gun frigates, upwards of twenty privateers, and seventy or eighty merchant ships, to which they set fire with combustibles provided for that purpose; and the magazines of pitch, tar, and other naval stores, shared the same fate. A dreadful scene of conflagration ensued, as the flames raged the whole night, without the least attempt from the garrison to extinguish them, or to molest the English. Preparations were now made for laying siege to the town; and in the meanwhile a battalion of guards marched to Dol, about twelve miles up the country, where they remained one night, and returned next day. A party of light horse penetrated a few miles further, and fell in with the French videttes, two of whom they took and brought prisoners to Cancalle. But the duke, having received advice of a large force of the enemy collected to cut off his retreat, and being informed that the siege would occupy a month, he returned with the army on the 10th to Cancalle, where the troops were re-embarked. The fleet sailed from Cancalle on the 16th, and was driven back by contrary winds. On the 22d, the ships sailed again, and next day passed Jersey and Guernsey, the design being to attack Cherbourg or Havre; but the weather prevented every attempt made to land near either port, and the whole fleet arrived at St. Helen's on the 1st of July, just one month after their departure from that anchorage.

On the return of this expedition, so unproductive of any advantage either to the nation or the persons employed in it, part of the troops were sent to Germany with the Duke of Marlborough, who was pretty well sickened with his late cruize, as were the other officers of rank. The remainder of the army, under Lieut.-General Bligh, an officer nearly worn out with age, of no talents, but of unquestionable bravery, embarked again on board of Howe's fleet, which sailed from St. Helen's on the 1st of August, and anchored in the bay of Cherbourg on the 6th. Next morning the ships weighed, and brought up in the bay of Marais, two leagues west of the town, where a more secure landing could be effected. On the 7th, at two, p.m., the grenadiers and guards landed under cover of an incessant fire from the fleet, and were opposed by nearly 3,000 men posted behind the sand banks. The enemy was attacked with such vigour that they quickly fled in great confusion and with considerable loss, leaving behind them two brass cannon, while of the English about twenty men only were killed or wounded. The remainder of the infantry being disembarked, the troops marched to the village of Erville, and there pitched their tents for the night. On reconnoitring the nearest fort, called Querqueville, the following morning, it was found deserted, so that the light horse were now landed without interruption, and the army proceeded in two columns towards Cherbourg, which they entered on the 8th, without firing or receiving a single shot, the town and all the forts being abandoned by the French troops. The inhabitants, relying on a promise of protection, remained in the town, and received their hostile visitors with hospitality, but, to the disgrace of British discipline, their confidence was abused, as no proper means were taken to restrain the licentiousness of the soldiery, until the complaints of the sufferers reminded the general of this part of his duty.

The English proceeded to demolish the basins, and two piers forming the entrance into the harbour, which had been constructed by Louis XV. at a vast expense ; the batteries, forts, and magazines of the port, as well as those along the coast, were also destroyed. While the engineers were thus employed, the light horse were sent to scour the country, and to reconnoitre a French camp at Valognes, four or five leagues from Cherbourg. The demolition being completed, the army, on the 16th of August, marched to Fort Galet, and there embarked without molestation. Twenty-seven ships were burnt in the harbour ; one hundred and seventy-three pieces of iron ordnance and three mortars were rendered useless ; and twenty-two brass cannon were sent to England, when they were exhibited for some time in Hyde Park, and drawn through the city in triumphal procession.

As General Bligh was instructed " to carry a warm alarm along the coast of France, from the easternmost point of Normandy, as far westward as Morlaix inclusive," he considered that Granville ought to be the second object of attack ; but as 10,000 of the enemy had assembled in Normandy, the design on that town was abandoned. Morlaix would next have been attempted, had not advices been received from England that a strong force was prepared at Brest to oppose any descent on that part of the coast. The general and commodore, therefore, thought that they should best fulfil the king's instructions by landing the troops in the bay of St. Lunaire, rather more than one league west of St. Malo, and marching them against that town. The fleet accordingly left Cherbourg on the 18th of August, but, owing to contrary winds, it was the 3d of September before it reached St. Lunaire. Next day the troops landed without opposition, and encamped on an eminence. Four days were spent in deliberations on the feasibility of an attack upon St. Malo, and it was finally determined to be impracticable. Three hundred grenadiers were in the meantime detached to destroy the shipping in the harbour of St. Briac, which was done ; but instead of finding 150 vessels, as reported, the number proved not to exceed fifteen. The boisterous state of the weather having rendered it dangerous for the fleet to remain in St. Lunaire bay, it was resolved that the troops should march overland to the bay of St. Cas, about three leagues to the westward of St. Malo, and that the ships should proceed thither to receive them. The troops had to make a detour to reach the village of Gildau, where the river they must necessarily pass was fordable at low water, and they marched so leisurely that they were nearly four days reaching the place of embarkation. In fact, the general intended to remain at Martignon on the way, so as to create all the alarm he could, and compel the enemy to call off troops from Germany, had he not there learnt from some deserters that the French were encamped within two leagues of him in great force, and that they meant to give the English battle the next morning. It afterwards appeared that they amounted to upwards of 10,000 men, under the command of the Duc d'Aguillon. Nevertheless, General Bligh continued so totally unapprehensive, that he ordered the usual drums, preparatory to a march, to beat the next morning at three o'clock. The drums beat accordingly, and the army marched in a single column towards St. Cas, which is about a league from Martignon. If the troops had marched in two columns, they would have reached the beach in half the time. The French followed, but did not attempt to molest the embarkation until they saw they might successfully attack the rear guard of 1,400 grenadiers, who alone remained on the beach. They then brought their field pieces to bear, and a shocking carnage ensued, as, when the English retreated to their boats, they were insufficient to receive even half the number on shore, so that about seven hundred men were either killed, drowned, or taken prisoners : among the slain were Major-General Drury, Lieut.-Colonel Wilkinson, and Sir John Armitage, a volunteer. As the boats approached the shore, many of the seamen were killed or wounded, and the rowers, hesitating to proceed, lay upon their oars. Howe, observing this, and perceiving the cause of their backwardness, jumped into his barge, rowed into the midst of the fire of shot and shells, and, standing upright in his boat, waved to the seamen to follow him : his example so animated their drooping spirits, that no one now thought of shrinking, but all strove to pick up the poor soldiers, who were swimming or wading into the sea. This disaster was attributed to the want of military knowledge and experience in the English general, as he foolishly gave ear to those about him, who talked of marching through France with a single company of British grenadiers. He was the only sufferer on the return of the expedition, although he had effected much more than his predecessor, the Duke of Marlborough. The cold reception he met with, and an intimation that he would not be received by the king, determined this unfortunate but high-minded veteran to resign a commission which he could not retain with honour. —We have dwelt the longer on these occurrences, because they are rendered locally interesting by the vicinity of the scenes of action to these islands, which, it need scarcely be added, remained unmolested during the reign of George II.[1]

In May, 1756, the lieutenant-governor, Sir John Mylne,[2] Bart., detained a Swedish vessel laden with iron, &c., and bound to St. Malo, which had put into the roadstead for a pilot; whereupon the master sent a summons in his own name to the lieutenant-governor, requiring him to appear the same day before the royal court, that he might see him, the said master, protest against all damages arising from his detention, such being then the usual way of summoning in the island, so that the protest might be recorded. The matter was communicated in such a manner to council, that their lordships reported " that the conduct of the court cannot but be looked upon as unwarrantable and derogatory to his majesty's royal authority, vested in the commanding officer of the island, as likewise a contemptuous proceeding against his majesty's command." The court, moreover, was informed of his majesty's dissatisfaction at its proceedings, and was commanded not to presume to act in the like manner for the future, but that in all cases where it might have any doubt with regard to the conduct of the commanding officer, it was to send over a representation of the fact, that his majesty might signify his pleasure thereupon.—We have before us the rough draft of a letter in answer from the court to the lords of council, from which we make the following extracts ; but we know not whether the letter, which commenced by expressing the

(1) Barrow's Life of Howe.—Campbell's Lives of the Admirals.
(2) Sir John Mylne was captain of an independent company of invalids in Guernsey, in 1783.

amazement of the court, and concluded by praying for inquiry and redress, was transmitted, or attended to :

"What will your lordships think when we openly declare and solemnly affirm, that in this accusation presented to your honourable board, there is not one single word of truth, nor even the least shadow of grounds to colour the same ; so far from it, that Sir John, a day or two after he had made the said arrest, consulting about and desiring the advice and concurrence of this court on several proposals, among others he mentioned the abovesaid arrest which he had made, to which the court made answer : ' That it was a thing which did wholly and solely belong to his province, that this court had nothing to do with it, and that he might act therein as he thought most fit.'

" If Sir John can make out any more than what we have thus informed your lordships, we may indeed be at a loss how to answer it ; but we are well satisfied he cannot. In all this, my lords, this court has been meerly passive, as it is allways in cases of like nature, barely attesting or recording that a protest has been made, without any adjudication whatsoever, being the ordinary style of this court, constantly practised ever since our first records.

" And now, my lords, if the premises are entire truth,—if this court did never summon Sir John Mylne,—if this court had never threatened him with any costs or damages whatsoever, if he did not release the ship, as we do solemnly affirm it to be true,—how shocking must it be to your lordships that any one should presume to impose on your lordships such monstrous untruths, which have brought on us those heavy censures and sensible reflections contained in your lordships' letter above mentioned, to which, we humbly beg leave to say, we have given no room for."

During the middle of the eighteenth century, although the population of Guernsey was scarcely 11,000 souls,[1] the means of subsistence, or at least of employment, seem to have been inadequate to the maintenance of the inhabitants, so that emigration was resorted to at that early period : thus, about the year 1752, this advertisement appeared in Boston, N.A. : "To be sold, Guernsey boys and girls, for a term of time, on board the sloop Two Brothers," — evidently to pay their passage across the Atlantic. At that time, the children of the lower orders in Guernsey were wont to say that if they were disobedient, their parents would send them to Boston.

(1) "13 Fév. 1727.—Habitants trouvés se monter en nombre à 10,500, dont la ville en faisait 4,500, de sorte qu'allouant un denerel de grain la semaine à chacun pour sa subsistence, il nous faut annuellement 21,000 quartiers de bled."—Extracted from the Greffe.

Alderney.—During the civil war, the island was subject to the lieutenant-governor of Guernsey ; but, after the Restoration, Charles II. granted it, with all its profits, to Edward de Carteret, James de Carteret, and Clement de Constein, gentlemen, who at once made over their grant to Sir George Carteret, and from that period Alderney became a government independent of that of Guernsey. In 1683, the title to the island was disposed of for a certain consideration by the trustees of Sir George Carteret, deceased, to Sir Edmund Andros and dame Mary, his wife, to whom and to their heirs Charles II. regranted it for ninety-nine years, from April 28, 1683, under a reserved rent of thirteen shillings per annum. Sir Edmund, dying in 1713 without issue, bequeathed the island to his nephew, George Andros, who also died the same year ; and his rights devolved on his infant daughter, Anne : she died in 1721, when her aunt, Anne Andros, wife of John Le Mesurier, succeeded her, and thus brought the government into the family of Le Mesurier, in which it remained above a century. In 1763, the grant was renewed to another John Le Mesurier for a second term of ninety-nine years ; and from that period the governor resided usually on the island. In 1825, the last hereditary governor of Alderney, Major-General Le Mesurier, surrendered his patent to the crown for a valuable consideration, and the island has since formed part of the government of Guernsey, as it generally did in ancient times.

CHAPTER XX.

GEORGE III.—1760 to 1820.

DURING this reign, which was the longest in English history, these islands emerged from a state of comparative poverty and seclusion to one of prosperity and importance, however evanescent; because, as regards Guernsey, the causes which produced such beneficial effects have chiefly passed away. It was only, however, after 1824, when a steamer from Southampton and another from Portsmouth first commenced plying weekly, that strangers can be said to have visited these islands in summer, or made them their permanent residence,

very few coming over before that time, unless on business, or
as belonging to the garrison and squadron. In this chapter,
we shall shew accurately what the condition of Guernsey was
about the year 1775, when it would seem that the spirit of
improvement began to develope itself, owing to the addition
made to the garrison, and the increased intercourse with
strangers during the first American war. Little, however,
was done to embellish the town, or to facilitate the communication with the country, until the commencement of the
present or nineteenth century.

About the year 1768, of the eight rectors in the ten parishes
of Guernsey, one was an Englishman, Dean Crespin, of French
extraction, six were Frenchmen, and one was a Swiss, so little
inducement had the natives to accept church preferment in
the island at that period. A Guernseyman, the Rev. Joshua
Le Marchant, fellow of Pembroke College, Oxford, was soon
after appointed rector of St. Peter-Port. At present, the
eight rectors are natives of Guernsey.

In 1775, the town of St. Peter-Port extended northerly
to the Long Store, southerly to the lower half of Hauteville,
and westerly from Fountain street to Country Mansell, including the Bordage and Mill street. Pedvin street was not
built, and the present market place was a garden. Berthelot
street existed almost as it is now, but Smith street was complete only on the north side, the south reaching only to the
pump;[1] and from thence to the upper part of Berthelot street
and New Town, the land was in fields and gardens. Indeed,
a gentleman, lately living, remembered shooting a woodcock
where the gaol now stands. The houses in Park street,
Mount Durant, Mount Row, New Town, Canichers, Paris
street, &c. &c., with very few exceptions, have been erected
since. The principal streets were paved, but there were neither public lamps, nor sewers, nor flagged footpaths. The
lower part of Fountain street was so narrow, and the houses
on each side projected so much at every story, that the inmates could almost shake hands across. High street was
nearly as narrow and unsightly. The parish church was the
only place of worship in St. Peter-Port, and there was neither
a dissenter nor a chapel in town or country.

From Lord De Saumarez's house, at the top of Smith

---

(1) The proprietor of the field from the pump upwards offered about this time to throw
back the hedge for a mere trifle, so as to widen Smith street considerably, but "the
wisdom of our ancestors" refused the offer, and hence the narrowness of this principal
outlet of the town.

street, to the church of St. Mary de Castro, there were only eight houses bordering on the road. St. James's street and Candie road were miserable lanes, only wide enough for a cart, and without footpaths ; the Grange road was equally narrow, but it had a wide footpath. The house on the Grange road, a little above and facing Doyle road, was built by Mr. William Brock for his summer residence only, his winter one being in High street, about half a mile distant ; and when Mr. Henry Brock built Belmont, he was told that the roof would be blown away by the westerly gales, and that he might as well erect his house on Rock Douvre. St. Peter-Port possessed some large houses, but throughout the island the generality were small and mean, with low and dark rooms, and to obtain shelter they were buried as much as possible. The furniture, even in the best, was poor and deficient, and many a gentleman's parlour was uncarpeted, having only a sanded floor.[1]

The present site of Fort George and its outskirts contained some of the finest corn fields in the island. Government house was then situated at the top of Smith street, as at this moment ; but two or three years previously, it was that now called the haunted house at the Tour de Beauregard, between Cornet street and the Bordage. The garrison consisted of four companies of invalids, who were quartered at Castle Cornet, as there were no barracks ; but many of the soldiers were permitted to live in town, and serve as porters. One entire and two half regiments of foot, as also two more companies of invalids or veterans, were soon after added to protect the island during the American revolutionary war.

The royal court held its sittings in a mean detached building at the Plaiderie, now used as a store, and the public records were kept in the private house of the greffier, while two cells at Castle Cornet constituted the public prison, both for debtors and criminals ; but an insolvent debtor, or bankrupt, was a *rara avis* in those days. The meat and vegetable markets were held on Saturday only, in High street, from the church to the corner of Berthelot street ; and fish was sold in the afternoon, as it was chiefly caught by the town fishermen, very little being brought in from the country

---

[1] The author well remembers, about the year 1804, a gentleman of an ancient Guernsey family residing in his own house in High street, St. Peter-Port, in which house he usually sat in a small front parlour, with a sanded floor and little furniture ; and yet he was a jurat, and the second richest man in the island, if not the first. Three of his sons became general officers,—one a jurat, another the dean of Guernsey, and another receiver-general, while one of his daughters was the wife of a distinguished major-general, who was slain in the Peninsula, and the mother of a baronet.

parishes. The New Ground existed as a public promenade, having been purchased by the parish in 1764; but, having already described the state of Candie road, we need scarcely add that the avenue from the town to the New Ground was most wretched. There was only one master in Elizabeth College, which was held in the house now occupied by the vice-principal, but lately much enlarged. A theatre was fitted up in a store near the hospital, and a small company of actors came over every three or four years to perform in it.

The shipping of the island consisted of one ship, three or four brigs, and a few sloops and cutters. The square-rigged vessels (none of which were copper-fastened or sheathed) were usually employed in bringing tobacco and staves from Virginia, rum from the island of Santa Cruz, and brandy and wine from Cette and Salou. Wines were occasionally received to be stored for account of English merchants, and re-shipped when required. There were no pipe carts, and pipes of wine and spirits were conveyed singly on sledges, or slides, drawn by two oxen and four horses. Hogsheads were occasionally slung to poles and carried by porters. Bills on London or Paris were seldom seen, as the trade was very limited, and the incomes of the gentry were chiefly derived from their "rentes." The money in circulation was English and French gold, but principally guineas and six livre pieces; and local bank notes did not exist. There were three or four small breweries and a few insignificant manufactories of rope, tobacco, and candles, but no iron foundries, distilleries, &c.; and many articles, now made here, were imported from Southampton and Bristol. Soap came chiefly from Marseilles. The town parish was assessed at 47,360 quarters, paid by 399 individuals, averaging 118 quarters each. The island possessed neither a newspaper,[1] nor a printing press,[2] nor a single hot or greenhouse, and the inhabitants did not appear to be very partial to physic, as there were only three medical practitioners, and not a druggist.

The fish caught round, and the fruit grown in, the island, were consumed by the inhabitants at a cheap rate, because there were no steamers to carry either away.—The steamers have certainly enhanced the expense of living in Guernsey.

(1) The first newspaper, a small quarto sheet, printed in the island, was in French, and appeared in 1789; the first, in English, was published in 1803.

(2) In the Harleian MSS. there is a letter from Mr. Walsingham to the Lord Burleigh, dated at Vernon, in France, May 25, 1571, in which he "desires that a Book of Common Prayer, translated into French, (of which he has seen some printed in Guernsey,) may be sent to him to shew to monsieur." We think that Walsingham was in error as to the place of printing.

There was no government packet, or post-office, and the communication with the metropolis was carried on by the small Southampton traders, which crossed very irregularly. During the American war, some of the London newspapers were sent to Brixham, to be forwarded by the cutters from thence, as these vessels could reach the islands with a south-westerly wind, which was directly adverse from the Needles. A retired shipmaster, who was nearly fifty years in the South-ampton trade, mentions that, about the year 1788, when he first commenced, a cutter, which then made eight voyages to and fro in a year, was considered to have been actively em-ployed; but that he himself, long afterwards, made twenty-nine voyages, or fifty-eight passages, in the same period in a smart cutter. He adds, that one of the traders between Jersey and Southampton only made four voyages a year, her sails being always unbent at Southampton.

The principal families resided chiefly in High street, with a few in Cornet and Smith streets, and the Pollet: they usually dined at one, took tea at four or five, and supped substantially on meat or fish at eight or nine o'clock. These early hours extended, in some measure, even to company; and, notwithstanding, the inhabitants maintained a constant social intercourse, as the money which is now spent in general entertainments, few and far between, and in carriage hire, was then devoted to more frequent, genuine, and rational hospitality. It must be added, however, that the convivial meetings of the gentlemen, who had few amusements or intel-lectual resources, were often stained by hard drinking. The public assemblies were held weekly in a large room at the bottom of the Pollet; and the ladies were not the less happy, or the less lovely, because they walked to parties in hoods and pattens: indeed, it was not until after the peace of 1815 that hack carriages were introduced.

The language of all classes in their own families was, with few exceptions, either French or Guernsey French, chiefly the latter; but the upper classes could speak English, as they were generally educated in England, where these islands were then as little known as the Orkneys are now.

The roads throughout the island were only wide enough for a cart, but the greater part had a narrow high footpath, and when two carts met, one had to go into a field, or in a recess called *gensage*, to allow the other to pass: the roads were, moreover, extremely rough, and often flooded in winter. Those who resided in the distant parishes, and remember the diffi-

culties of communication with the town, might now parody
the well known distich of the highlands of Scotland :

> Had you seen these roads, ere a credit to our soil,
> You would hold up your hands, and bless General Doyle.

In consequence, the inhabitants of the country had so little
intercourse with each other, or with the town, that their
parishes could be discovered by their different accents.   It
must be confessed, however, that the lanes formed a most
agreeable shady walk for pedestrians in summer, as the high
hedges on either side were planted with trees, and covered
with wild primroses, violets, and harebells.   Carriages were
almost useless, as excursions were made on foot or on horseback, and the few which existed were gigs, substantially constructed without springs.   It was about this time that Lieut.-
Governor Irving introduced the first four-wheel close carriage,
with a pair of horses, seen in the island.

Thus, in 1775, Guernsey was comparatively unimproved,
badly cultivated, and without easy means of communication,
either externally or internally.   We have said that parties
met at an early hour, and even as late as the year 1796, at a
ball and supper given by the gentlemen of the island, at the
assembly rooms in St. Peter-Port, to Major-General Small
and the officers of the garrison, on the 18th of January, to
celebrate the queen's birth-day, "the company" was requested
"to assemble at six o'clock."—The late king, William IV.,
while Prince William Henry, visited Guernsey twice, the
first time as a midshipman in the Hebe frigate, and the second
in command of the Pegasus, of 28 guns.   On the latter occasion a ball, apparently without a supper, to prepare which
there probably was not time, was given to him by the Guernsey gentlemen, on the 7th of June, 1786, the entire cost for
nearly two hundred persons present being only £36. 4s. 8d.,
or 14s. 6d. per head for the fifty gentlemen who subscribed,
as we learn by a copy of the account :[1] twenty-five years
later, balls and suppers given to the naval and military officers cost about £500 ! so great was the sad change effected
in a few years by a large garrison and squadron, and a greater
intercourse with strangers.[2]

(1) The items were : tea-and coffee, £4. 18s.; fourteen pounds of wax candles, £2. 16s.;
lemons and sugar for punch and negus, 19s. 3d. ; twelve packs cards, 9s.; two pair gloves
for his royal highness, 3s.; one set of fish for quadrille, lost, 9s. 6d.; wine, &c., £7. 11s. 6d.;
confectionery, £9. 3s. 9d.; music, £4. 13s.; breakage, 18s. 6d.; corkage on six dozen and
nine bottles of wine, at 3d., £1. 0s. 3d.; rooms and attendance, £3. 3s.; total, £36..4s. 8d.

(2) The natural consequence of this senseless extravagance has been that the interchange of public parties, then annual, between the garrison and the inhabitants, has
ceased for some years.

In reviewing the state of Guernsey nearly eighty years ago, we must not forget that both England and France, the pioneers of European civilization, were then very far behind what they now are in roads, buildings, equipages, literary gratifications, and the other comforts and elegancies of life. The steam engine has since given an impetus to every species of improvement, which might otherwise have lain dormant for another century.—One of our informants remembered, when he was at school at Southampton, in 1775, that the stage coaches, of which there were only two, set out from thence for London at four o'clock, a.m., and only reached their destination at nine o'clock, p.m. Even more than thirty years afterwards, the coaches were thirteen or fourteen hours performing the same distance. Now, the journey is performed in less than three hours by rail!—Speaking of the mode of living in the capital of Scotland, in 1745, Chambers' Edinburgh Journal of March 1, 1845, says: "The accommodations possessed by families of good figure were generally limited to three or four rooms, not more than one of which would be unfurnished with a bed. Of the middle ranks, most lived in bed-rooms. Arrangements now deemed indispensable for cleanliness and delicacy were unknown."

In 1775, there arose between the bailiff, William Le Marchant, and ten of the jurats,[1] serious differences, which were referred by both parties to the privy council, of which the printed report fills no less than 257 pages. The bailiff—who is still remembered as a magistrate of great ability,[2] but of imperious and violent temper—having, of his sole authority, and without the knowledge of the jurats, ordered the greffier, Joshua Gosselin, not to register the contracts passed before the courts of St. Michael and Le Comte, his injunction was complied with; and thus a custom, established for nearly two hundred years, was suppressed. In February, an appeal was brought before the royal court by a tenant of the Fief le

(1) John Guille, of St. George, John de la Mare, Charles Andros, Thomas Dobrée, Richard de Beauvoir, Nicholas Dobrée, Nicholas Reserson, Peter de Jersey, Elisha Tupper, and John Carey.

The author will perhaps be excused for quoting, in memory of his grandfather, the following extract of a letter, dated February 24, 1775, to ten of the jurats, from the bailiff, who had recently met with some reverses of fortune: "Vous deviez cependant, si je dois la censer de vous, décider autrement de la droiture de ma conduite, puisque vous n'ignorez pas, que si j'étois pour être influé dans les devoirs de ma charge, j'en ai, en cette occasion, tous les motifs, par la considération de votre confédération puissante, des coups que j'ai reçu de la fortune, qui abatient ordinairement l'esprit et le cœur, et plus encore des services éminens que j'ai, dans ces malheureuses conjonctures, reçu de quelques-uns de vous, nommément de M. Tupper, à qui moi et ma famille auront une obligation éternelle."

(2) While a jurat, Mr. Le Marchant published a clever work, intituled "The Rights and Immunities of Guernsey."

Comte, when the bailiff declared that he was fully resolved
not to permit that or any other cause of the same nature,
which had been first tried by the said two feudal courts, to
be decided by the royal court, as those feudal jurisdictions
exercised an undue authority, vexatious to the inhabitants
and repugnant to law.   Although this might have been true,
the jurats present naturally remonstrated at their not being
consulted ; and, as if to widen the breach, the bailiff told them
in a letter, " that on any action being introduced before the
court, which he thinks contrary to law, dishonest, or derogatory to the king's authority, he has the sole right of rejecting
it." This difference produced other contentions, which were
the more unfortunate because the government was at that
time occupied with matters of momentous importance—the
commencement of the American war of independence.   The
bailiff, persisting in his determination, ten[1] of the jurats absented themselves from the court, a measure which nothing
could justify, and particularly as they had not yet received an
answer to their appeal to his majesty in council.   In consequence, the bailiff and jurats were ordered, by an order in
council of March 10, 1775, to resume their duties in the
manner they had been accustomed before the differences
arose, without prejudice to their rights, " until the matter of
the said differences shall have been heard, and his majesty's
determination thereupon be signified." This order was obeyed
accordingly ; but the bailiff would not give way, and the
jurats wrote on the subject to the lieutenant-governor, Irving,
who declined interfering.   Soon afterwards, October 7, the
dissentient jurats solicited of his majesty to accept of their
resignation, that there might be no longer any interruption of
justice, and on the 17th of May, 1776, their prayer was
granted ; but the electors evidently siding with them, re-
elected the whole, as appears by an order in council, dated
July 12, 1776, requiring them to be sworn in ; the bailiff
having refused to declare them duly elected.   But four of
these re-elected jurats, viz. T. Dobrée, R. de Beauvoir, N.
Dobrée, and J. Carey, refusing to serve again, and imploring
his majesty to order the States to proceed to a new election,
such election was so ordered.   The new jurats were, John
Carey, Thomas Dobrée, James Hubert, and Peter Falla.

By another order in council, also dated July 12, 1776,
Lieut.-Governor Irving was directed, with the assistance of

(1) The two remaining jurats were Laurence Flott and Daniel De Lisle, the seniors on
the bench, and both elected in 1742.

any two persons he might think proper, to examine into the
ancient usages and customs of the island as regarded the
disputes subsisting between the bailiff, royal court, and greffier.
The lieutenant-governor having taken Peter de Jersey, jun.,
and John Carey, jun. Esqs., to his assistance; and they having
examined the several witnesses on each side, and made their
reports to council, their lordships decided that the bailiff had
no right to refuse to register, or to order the greffier not to
register, any of the contracts which came from the feudal
courts of the island, or to take upon himself to admit or
reject causes which came from the said courts, without the
concurrence of the jurats. By the same order in council,
dated December 11, 1776, it was further ruled :

"That the royal court hath the right to make ordinances to
regulate the exportation and importation of provisions; but that
the permission to sell provisions brought by foreigners into the
island is to be given by the bailiff, and if· he refuses to give such
permission, the reason of such refusal may be examined by the
royal court, and the bailiff's refusal be controlled thereby.

"And, lastly, that the bailiff hath no right to give permission
to strollers, musicians, or other persons, to make publick exhibitions in the island, without the concurrence of the jurats, but that
such permission ought to be given by the royal court."

During the American revolutionary war, two attempts
were made by the French on Jersey, and happily both
proved unsuccessful. The first was in 1779, when on the 1st
of May the prince or count of Nassau, with nearly 3,000
men and about fifty flat-bottomed boats, convoyed by five
frigates and some armed cutters, appeared in sight of the
island early in the morning, and attempted a debarkation in
St. Ouen's bay. But the enemy was so vigorously received
by one wing of the 78th regiment and the militia, that after a
most feeble attack, and an equally spiritless attempt to land
in St. Brelade's bay, they relinquished the enterprise, with
very little loss on either side.

The vessel, which was immediately dispatched to England
with the intelligence, fell in with Admiral Arbuthnot, who
was bound to New York with a squadron of ships of war,
and an immense convoy of about four hundred sail, with
reinforcements, stores, &c., for Sir Henry Clinton. He at
once ordered the convoy to wait for him at Torbay, while he
proceeded with the squadron to the relief of Jersey, where
he however arrived too late, as the French had retired; and
their ships intended to cover the landing, were soon after-

wards destroyed in the bay of Cancalle, in Britany, by Sir James Wallace, with a 50-gun ship, two frigates, and two brigs.

In the attack just described, the Baron de Rullecourt was second in command, and another invasion being planned, to be under the orders of that officer, who was of a bold and fiery temper, about 2,000 troops were collected at Granville, with a sufficient number of transports, and some privateers for their protection : the rewards of his success were to be the rank of general, the order of St. Louis, and the government of Jersey. On Christmas night, 1780, a fire was discovered blazing between Rozel and La Coupe, in Jersey : it continued burning for about eight minutes, when it was answered by another on the coast of Normandy. These preconcerted signals were made at a time when no British ships of war were on the station, so that the island had at least one traitor within, as well as national enemies without.

Notwithstanding the tempestuous weather which then prevailed, Rullecourt's impatience was so great that he embarked the troops, and put to sea. The consequence was the dispersion of his fleet of small vessels in a storm, by which ten of them, with fully half the troops, were driven back to France, and never rejoined him ; while he, totally ignorant of their fate, sought shelter with the remainder among the islands of Chausey, which lie between Normandy and Jersey. Profiting by the first fair weather, he set sail again on the 5th of January, 1781, and, with the aid of a traitorous Jerseyman, who had formerly lived at La Roque, and was an experienced pilot, reached Jersey with barely 1,000 men, at eleven o'clock, p.m. His vessels were driven by the current to Le Banc du Violet, at the south-east corner of the island, some three miles from St. Hélier ; and although this was not the spot intended for the debarkation, the troops were ordered to land : about 600 got on shore, two of the vessels being wrecked with the gunners and musicians, most of whom perished, and the remainder kept on board the other vessels by the tide. No alarm was given ; and as the blame for this gross negligence has generally been imputed to Lieut.-Governor Corbet, we think it but common justice to him to give the following extracts from his defence at the court martial :

"The ' chef de garde' was intoxicated, and neglected to fix his centinel on the battery, which in situation so perfectly commands the shore, that no such noise as the landing of troops, even at a much greater distance than where the French landed, could escape the ear of any man who was awake."— " He sent no tide patroles, which my general orders strictly enjoined, and which the immediately preceding reports of the performance of that duty led me to be assured were uniformly obeyed. He quitted his guard himself before the day, and suffered his men to follow his example, in disobedience to the standing orders, which direct the night guards not to quit their posts till relieved an hour after it is light."—"By this neglect of an inferior officer of militia, the landing was secretly effected, and the market place of St. Hélier's filled with the enemy's soldiers soon after the day began to dawn, without the least alarm from any quarter."—"No judgment or diligence in those who command can avert the consequence of such gross negligence and disobedience in those who are to obey."

A surprise arising from negligence[1] was indeed the only chance of the invaders, as there were about 1,900 British regulars and probably an equal number of militia on the island, so that in fact the attacked, when collected together, were certainly six to one to their assailants! We estimate the force of the regulars as follows :

Wing of 78th, Highlanders.............350 men.
„   of 83d Regiment...............350 „
95th Regiment.......................700 „
Six Independent Companies...........400 „
One Company of Artillery.......... ..100 „

1900 men.[2]

Rullecourt, leaving about 100 men in the boats and in the adjoining redoubt of Grouville, so as to secure a retreat in the event of a reverse, proceeded to St. Hélier with the rest of his troops, avoiding the shore, that he might not be discovered at any of the guard-houses ; and having reached the market place, the sentinel there was killed, and the guard surprised : one man, however, escaped and ran to the general hospital, in which was quartered the wing of the 78th. The lieutenant-governor was in bed when first informed of the enemy's presence, and he was quickly taken prisoner, although he appears to have had time to escape, as he dispatched two messengers to give the alarm to the regulars, who were quartered in different parts of the island.

(1) In the Guernsey and Jersey Magazine for June, 1837, is a long account of the "French attacks on Jersey in 1779 and 1781," under the signature of "An Old Jersey Militiaman," who candidly says : "A small party of militia, who guarded a redoubt at this place, thought themselves so secure, and were so shamefully remiss in their duty, as to be seized asleep by the enemy, who were thus for several hours upon the island without the slightest alarm being given."

(2) The garrison in Guernsey at this time consisted of a wing each of the 78th and 83d regiments, (a singular arrangement,) 96th regiment, six independent companies, and one company of artillery.

At break of day, the inhabitants were astonished to find the market place filled with French soldiers; and well they might, as not even a gun had been fired. Major Corbet was conducted to the court house, and informed by Rullecourt that resistance was useless, as he had landed 4,000 men ; that the British troops near La Roque were prisoners; and that he had two battalions in the vicinity of the town. Rullecourt, then producing articles of capitulation, required Major Corbet to sign them, and said that, in default of instant compliance, he had orders to burn the town, with the shipping, and put the inhabitants to the sword. The lieutenant-governor at first refused, in consequence of his being a prisoner ; but at last, to avert the threatened destruction, he and the fort major, Hogge, signed the capitulation; the king's solicitor-general, Durell, the constable of St. Hélier, La Cloche, and other Jerseymen, firmly and nobly refusing to do so.

Rullecourt now conceived himself to be master of the island, as at his bidding Corbet sent orders to the English troops not to move from their respective barracks, and afterwards to those on the heights to bring their arms to the court house. Corbet also ordered Captain Aylward, the commandant at Elizabeth castle, to surrender that fortress; but his orders were happily disobeyed ; and at length the chief part of the regulars and the militia, having assembled near the town, advanced under Major Pierson, of the 95th, the next in command. Separating into two divisions, the British pressed forwards towards the market place, where the action was soon decided ; for Rullecourt being mortally wounded, the next senior officer, seeing the hopelessness of resistance with such a disparity of numbers, requested Major Corbet to resume his authority, and to accept of the surrender of the French as prisoners of war. But this success was unfortunately damped by the fall of Major Pierson, who was shot dead in the market place. This was the first essay in arms of this young officer, who was only twenty-four years of age : he was interred within the parochial church of St. Hélier, in which a monument was erected to his memory at the cost of the island, in grateful recognition of his services. The next in command to Major Pierson was Captain Campbell, of the 83d ; and thus, with so large a force of regulars, there was only one regimental field officer. The remains of Rullecourt were buried in the churchyard of St. Hélier, and the prisoners were in a few days sent to Plymouth.

During the engagement in the town, the redoubt at Grouville, which mounted four guns, was gallantly retaken by part of the grenadiers of the 83d regiment, with fixed bayonets, and without firing a shot. Thus the whole of the French engaged were either killed or taken prisoners; but it is due to Rullecourt to add that, once on shore, he appears to have conducted his desperate enterprise with great skill and resolution: his death and that of his youthful opponent remind us of the fall of Montcalm and Wolfe. Major Corbet was tried by a court martial, held at the Horse Guards, in May, 1781, when "the court, having duly considered and weighed the evidence given in support of the charge against the prisoner, Lieut.-Governor Moses Corbet, with that produced by him in his defence, are of opinion that he, the said Moses Corbet, is guilty of the whole charge exhibited against him; and doth adjudge that he be therefore superseded in his command of lieutenant-governor of the island of Jersey." But he is said to have received a pension; and this lenient sentence proves that he was not guilty of treachery, as has often been, and is still, asserted. His faults were in signing the capitulation while a prisoner, and in sending orders to the troops afterwards: for signing that capitulation, Fort-Major Hogge is said to have died of grief two years later.

The casualties on both sides were as follows:

British, at La Roque, or the redoubt of Grouville.—Regulars: killed 7, wounded 8. In St. Hélier: regulars killed, 1 officer and 4 rank and file; wounded, 1 sergeant and 27 rank and file. Militia: killed, 4 rank and file; wounded, 3 officers and 26 rank and file. Total, regulars, killed 12, wounded 36; militia, killed 4, wounded 29. Grand total, killed 16, wounded 65. The casualties among the officers were: 95th regiment, Major Pierson killed; east regiment of militia, Lieutenants Godfray and Aubin, and Ensign Poignand, wounded. Mr. Thomas Lemprière, aide-de-camp, and Mr. Amias Lemprière, merchant, were also wounded.

French, at La Roque: killed, officer 1; rank and file, 20; wounded, officer 1; total, 22; so that no quarter appears to have been shewn there. In St. Hélier: rank and file, killed, 57; wounded, 73; total, 130. Grand total, killed, 78; wounded, 74; together 152, exclusive of 417 prisoners; the entire French loss on the island being 569 men.

Thus this very insignificant French force was only rendered formidable by its landing and march to St. Hélier being effected during the darkness of a long winter's night, and the uncertainty which prevailed in regard to its numbers:

had that force appeared by day-light, we are satisfied that the
Jersey militia alone would have defeated it; otherwise it certainly would be useless to embody any militia in these islands;
and, therefore, we hold that there was no subject either for
boasting or exultation in the failure of this fool-hardy and
ill-concerted invasion.

A cutter from Jersey brought to Guernsey the startling
intelligence that the French were in possession of the former
island, and that the latter might also be attacked on the following day. An officer of the Guernsey militia wrote in his
journal: "January 6, 1781.—News that Jersey is attacked
by the French, who have actually landed; great alarm here;
the militia under arms all night."—Lieut.-Governor Irving
instantly adopted the necessary measures for the defence of
Guernsey, and proclaimed martial law. The night was passed
in a state of feverish excitement; but the next day, another
vessel arrived with the glad tidings that the invading force
had been defeated: then cheer succeeded cheer, the bands
played merrily, the bells were rung, martial law terminated,
and both the regulars and militia were dismissed.

The first attack on Jersey in 1779 probably suggested the
erection of additional fortifications in Guernsey, as Fort
George dates its commencement in 1780. The promontory
of Jerbourg, so strong by nature, would have been the best
site, had it not been too distant from the town, Castle Cornet,
and the roadstead.

The governor of Cherbourg, about the period of the attempted conquest of Jersey, in 1779 or 1781, wrote of the
Anglo-Norman islands as follows:

[Translation from the French.]

"These two islands [i.e. Guernsey and Jersey] are the despair
of France at the breaking out of each war, through their remarkably active privateers, which always commence by capturing a
great number of vessels, and destroying all communication and
commerce between the channel ports, before France can adopt
any precautionary measures to protect her coasting marine by
vessels of war. The habit of encountering the dangers of the
sea renders the natives very brave; they have well disciplined
regiments of militia, excellent marksmen, and who alone are
almost capable of repulsing any enemy who might descend on
their shores. Animated by a true sense of their own interest,
their attachment to the English government is devotedly loyal.
Good neighbours during peace, closely united by the contraband
trade, which enriches them, with the inhabitants of the neighbouring coasts of Normandy and Britany, they become formida-

ble enemies when war is declared, or rather, they are always in a state of warfare, now against the custom-house officers of the two kingdoms, now against the French commercial marine. A population of this character greatly enhances the natural strength of these islands."

It has been shewn in Chapter IX. that an order in council, dated June 9, 1605, gave authority to the governor of Guernsey to imprison persons for twenty-four hours at his discretion ; and the following is an instance of the exercise of that authority. In December, 1783, Mr. Thomas Knight, a merchant of Bristol, arrived in the roadstead in a vessel belonging to himself, the Rainbow, John Roach master : the vessel carried a pendant, and it seems that the orders of Lieut.-Colonel Basset, the commander-in-chief, to take it down, were disregarded. In consequence, Mr. Knight, while transacting his business in the town of St. Peter-Port, was arrested by an officer and soldier, whereupon he demanded to be carried before the bailiff, and his request was complied with. The bailiff, William Le Marchant, being informed of the cause of the arrest, told the officer that he knew of no authority in the commander-in-chief to issue such orders, much less to enforce them by seizing and imprisoning any British subject on such a pretence. The officer replied that he would communicate the bailiff's opinion to Lieut.-Colonel Basset, and ordered the soldier to take Mr. Knight as a prisoner to the guard-house, upon which Knight claimed in vain the protection of the bailiff; and from the guard-house in the town he was removed to Castle Cornet.

The bailiff having assembled the court, that body sent the crown officers to represent to the colonel that the said arrest and imprisonment were subversive of the rights of the subject and of the privileges of the island, in order to induce him to set Mr. Knight at liberty. The colonel answered, "that any person who disobeyed his orders, he had a right to imprison for twenty-four hours; that he had confined Mr. Knight for having hoisted his pendant, contrary to his (the commander-in-chief's) orders ; and that he considered this affair as a private dispute between him and Mr. Knight : " the crown officers having informed him "that the court did not consider it as a private affair, but an infringement on the rights of the subject, and a violation of the rights and privileges of the inhabitants of this island," Colonel Basset replied, "that he did not mean to infringe the rights of the people, but that he was authorized to act as he had done, and would support or enforce his authority, and that the court might complain of him if they pleased."

On receiving these answers, the court decided : first, that from time immemorial vessels in the roadstead had been per-mitted to carry a pendant when no king's vessel was present, and therefore that the commander-in-chief exercised a vexa-tious right, unknown to his predecessors ; secondly, that the pretension of the commander-in-chief that he had the right to imprison for twenty-four hours any person who disobeyed his orders was illusory, (illusoire,) such right never having been exercised within the memory of man by any of his predecessors, excepting in very grave cases, and for which they were answerable ; and, thirdly, that as regarded the reparation claimed by Mr. Knight, the court, considering that Colonel Basset was not amenable to it for the present, would certify the claim, so that it might be referred to the wisdom and justice of the sovereign. The court further re-solved to represent the entire matter to his majesty in council, which was done on the 13th of December ; and on April 20, 1784, their petition was transmitted to Lieut.-Colonel Basset, who was required forthwith to return his answer thereunto in writing. That answer appears to have been satisfactory, the matter dropping there ; and as the *Algerine* order in council has never been repealed, it is clear that any individual in Guernsey is still liable to be imprisoned for twenty-four hours, at the discretion of the lieutenant-governor, although he would be a bold officer who would now exercise such an authority, the existence of which at this day is a disgrace to constitutional government.

On the 24th of March, 1783, the inhabitants of Guernsey were startled by a very daring mutiny at Fort George, in the 104th regiment, consisting entirely of Irish, and number-ing there about six hundred men, for they were not joined by the grenadier company, which was quartered at Vale castle, under Captain Fenwick. The mutineers had been quartered during the winter in the citadel, and though con-stantly troublesome to the country people, they had been kept in tolerable discipline until a few discharged men of the 83d regiment arrived from Portsmouth, and related the impunity with which they, and the soldiery in England gene-rally, had set the laws at defiance. The men of the 104th were thus prompted to insist with their officers that the gates should not be shut, that they should have liberty to go where they pleased, and, it being peace-time, that they should do no more duty. Lieut.-Governor Irving appeased the outbreak by imprudently granting these demands, and quiet was preserved for a few days; but, on the 24th, while the officers were seated in the mess-room after dinner, they were alarmed by the whistling of musket balls among them, which came through the door and windows. To avoid the shots, they were obliged to creep on their hands and knees, and were some time in this situation, until the sergeant-major advised their running off, which they did, the gates being fortunately open, and, though fired at, they all escaped unscathed, excepting two, who concealed themselves in a coal-hole. This attack was known in the town about eight o'clock, p.m., and at first it was feared that the 18th regiment, or Royal Irish, would join the mutineers, or at least refuse to act against them; but, to its honor, the 18th turned out to a man, while the militia artillery and infantry of the town immediately assembled to assist in suppressing the revolt. The three country regiments were ordered to patrol their own districts, and to hold themselves in readiness to join the main body.

At near midnight, Lieut.-Governor Irving proceeded against the mutineers with the 18th regiment, under Major Mawbey, a company of regular artillery, the militia artillery, and the town regiment, the last under Colonel George Lefebvre. On arriving near Fort George, without beat of drum, the 18th regiment, with the town grenadiers and light company, four pieces of artillery, and two howitzers, lined the front under cover of a low hedge, at about one hundred yards distance: four of the battalion companies of the town regiment guarded the avenues on one side, and the other four were in reserve. A summons being sent into the fort, a parley ensued; but the mutineers declared that they would on no account lay down their arms, and several straggling shots were fired. Messages continued till about four o'clock the next morning, when the lieutenant-governor, being on the field admonishing some of the deputies, a fire was opened upon him and part of the line, which was returned. Soon after, the four militia companies in reserve were ordered to the right, to occupy a commanding position, when the mutineers, seeing themselves surrounded, and hearing that the whole force of the island was marching against them, quitted the fort, and piled their arms, probably under the assurance of pardon, as no example appears to have been made.[1] On the 7th of September, at a

(1) My father was a young subaltern officer in the grenadiers of the town regiment of militia on this occasion, and I have often heard him relate the part taken by that regiment against the mutineers, and how readily the men marched up to Fort George.—F. B. T.

convocation of the States, the thanks of that body were presented to all who were engaged in suppressing the mutiny, and one hundred guineas were voted to be distributed among the men of the Royal Irish, and of the regular artillery.

Although the Reformation was introduced into these islands by Henry VIII., it does not appear to have been *legally* established in Jersey until the year 1548, or the second of Edward VI., and such was probably the case in Guernsey. Two years later, April 15, 1550, Edward confirmed the authority of the Roman Catholic bishop of Coutances over the Protestant islanders! In 1565, the Anglican was superseded by the Calvinist discipline; and in turn, about a century later in Guernsey, the Church of England prevailed, and Presbyterianism was forcibly suppressed by Charles II., who lived and died a Roman Catholic! The affection of the people of Guernsey for Calvinism gradually died away, so that Dicey, in 1750, said: " Dissenters they have none." A great change has since taken place, as now (1854) nearly half the population are dissenters. The first who established themselves in Guernsey were the quakers or friends, their society being formed in the island in 1782, by Claude Gray, who had been a Roman Catholic! The Methodists made their appearance in these islands in 1783, and in 1786 Dr. Adam Clarke was sent over to them by John Wesley, as a preacher: he was subjected at first, both in Jersey and Guernsey, to the most violent personal indignities, which more than once endangered his life; and his reception was very discreditable to the islanders, who had forgotten that their grandfathers had professed a different religion to themselves. In 1787, Mr. Wesley himself, then in his eighty-fifth year, visited " the French islands," as he or his biographer called them; and the following extract from the Life of this eminent and excellent man, descriptive of his voyage and sojourn,[1] is interesting :

" On Monday, August 6, 1787, Mr. Wesley, with Dr. Coke and Mr. Bradford, set off from the Manchester Conference to visit the French islands. On the 11th, they sailed from Southampton, but contrary winds and stormy weather obliged them to

(1) An anecdote, in connection with the visit of Mr. Wesley to Guernsey, may be worth recording. Mr. Wesley waited on Mr. Le Marchant, as rector of the town parish, and was courteously received. Another rector, not a native, who happened to be present, and who felt probably not very kindly disposed towards the visitor, said somewhat abruptly, as Mr. Wesley was approaching, " Who is this fellow ?" " Fellow of Lincoln" (the college at Oxford, in which Mr. Wesley had actually held a fellowship,) was the rector's ready reply. To this instance of good-natured tact Mr. Wesley was fond of alluding. The little-minded country rector has long since been forgotten, but the name and memory of John Wesley will live as long as the world endures.

fly for refuge, first into the port of Yarmouth in the Isle of Wight, and afterwards into that of Swanage. On the 14th, they expected to reach the isle of Guernsey in the afternoon; but the wind turning contrary, and blowing hard, they were obliged to sail for Alderney. But they were very near being shipwrecked in the bay. Being in the midst of rocks, with the sea rippling all around them, the wind having totally failed. Had they continued in this situation many minutes longer, the vessel must have struck on one or other of the rocks. So they went to prayer, and the wind sprung up instantly, and brought them about sunset to the port of Alderney.

"At eight the next morning, Mr. Wesley preached on the beach, near the place where he lodged ; and, before his hymn was ended, had a tolerable congregation. Soon after he had concluded, the governor of the island waited upon him with very great courtesy ; after which he, with his company, sailed for Guernsey.

"On his arrival, he went into the country, to the house of Mr. De Jersey, a gentleman of fortune,[1] whose whole family have been converted to God. At five the following morning, he preached in a large room of Mr. De Jersey's to a very serious congregation ; and, in the evening, to a crowded audience in the preaching house in the town of St. Peter. On the 18th, he and Dr. Coke dined with the governor, who studied to shew them every mark of civility. On the 20th, he sailed for the isle of Jersey. Mr. Brackenbury received him on his arrival, and in his house he frequently preached to exceeding serious congregations. 'Even the gentry,' observes Mr. Wesley, speaking of his visit to this island, 'heard with deep attention. What little things does God use to advance his own glory! Probably,' continues he, 'many of these flock together, because I have lived so many years! And, perhaps, even this may be the means of their living for ever!'—In the country, he preached in English, Mr. Brackenbury interpreting sentence by sentence ; and even in this inconvenient way of speaking, God owned his word. Being detained a considerable time by contrary winds, the assembly room was offered him, in which he preached to very large congregations, and to the profit of many.

"On the 29th, the wind still continuing to blow from the English coast, he returned to the isle of Guernsey, where the winds, or rather a kind Providence, detained him till the 6th of September. Hardly a gentleman or lady in the town of St. Peter omitted a single opportunity of attending his ministry. So universal and steady an attendance of the rich and the gay, he never before experienced. During this visit, he was favoured with singular powers of elocution ; and delivered a series of discourses,

(1) Mr. Henry De Jersey, of Mon Plaisir, was an *agent de cour*, or law agent, and a substantial farmer, rated in 1787 at 200 quarters, which represented a capital of £4,000.

peculiarly suited to his hearers. On the 6th, a ship sailed for Mount's Bay, in Cornwall; and, the wind not permitting him to sail for Southampton, he took his passage in it, and on the next day landed at Penzance.

"There is now a surplus of native preachers in the French islands, several of whom have visited France, and have formed societies there; so that there is a prospect of the work of God spreading in that large and populous kingdom." [1]

In 1792, when Austria and Prussia declared war against France, a rumour prevailed that Guernsey would fit out privateers to capture French vessels. In consequence, the merchants of the island drew up a circular letter, which they addressed to the merchants of the maritime towns of France, and of which the following is a copy. It received sixty-two signatures, and did credit to the character of its authors:

"Gentlemen,—The merchants of the island of Guernsey, having taken into their consideration the calumnious rumours now in circulation, which declare that they are about to avail themselves of the favourable opportunity now presented of enriching themselves at the expense of France, by arming privateers under the colours of her enemies:

"Considering that the number of vessels suited for such a purpose at their disposal, the known activity of the inhabitants in the late war, and the advantageous locality of the island, seem to justify such a suspicion, if it were not formally disavowed:

"Considering, moreover, that an armament against France would be as criminal at this day, (as it might compromise the mother country,) as it was formerly lawful, and a proof of their attachment to the mother country, when involved in war:

"The merchants have resolved to repel so odious a calumny by a formal declaration of their sentiments: they renounce every prospect of advantage and all interested considerations, which might be easily but infamously acquired by any attack on the commerce of their neighbours. They solemnly bind themselves not to engage, directly or indirectly, in any hostile armament against France, so long as she is at peace with England.—Dated Guernsey, 2d of May, 1792."

During the winter of 1793-4, an expedition, consisting of several frigates, the requisite number of transports, and eight regiments of infantry, under Lord Moira, arrived in the roadstead, where they took on board another regiment of infantry, forming part of the garrison. These troops were intended to make a descent on the coast of France, in support of the royalists; but, owing either to the boisterous season of the

(1) Life of the Rev. John Wesley, A.M., by the Rev. H. Moore. London, 1824.

year, or to some other cause, they returned soon after to England, without accomplishing their original object.[1]

On the 7th of June, 1794, a British squadron, consisting of the 36-gun frigate Crescent, the 32-gun frigate Druid, and the 24-gun frigate Eurydice, with two or three armed luggers and cutters, the whole under Captain Sir James Saumarez, of the Crescent, sailed from Plymouth for Guernsey and Jersey, with orders to ascertain, if possible, the enemy's force in Cancalle bay and St. Malo. The next morning, at dawn of day, the British ships, when about twelve leagues to the N.N.W. of Guernsey,[2] and with a fresh N.E. breeze, fell in with a French squadron, composed of two cut down 74s, or rasées, each mounting 54 guns, two 36-gun frigates, and one 14-gun brig. On discovering the decided superiority of the enemy, who had 100 guns and 3,556 pounds in weight of metal more than the three English ships, Sir James ordered the Eurydice, which was a dull sailer, to proceed to Guernsey, then in sight, while the Crescent and Druid, following under easy sail, engaged and kept at bay the French squadron. When the action commenced, the English small craft returned to Plymouth. At eight o'clock, a.m., the Eurydice being so far in shore as to run no risk of capture, the other two British frigates made all sail for the Hanois; but the French headmost ship gained so fast upon them, that Sir James tacked in the Crescent, so as to save the Druid, and stood along the enemy's line. The French commodore now made sure of capturing the Crescent; but Sir James, having an experienced Guernsey pilot on board, John Breton by name, ordered him to steer the ship through a narrow passage between the rocks, which had never before been attempted by a king's ship; and, defying his pursuers to follow him, he reached the roadstead in safety, to their no small surprise and vexation. While passing through the passage, Sir James inquired of the pilot if he were sure of the marks, and was answered: "I am quite sure, sir, for there is your house, and there is mine."

Major-General Small, the lieutenant-governor, who with the garrison and inhabitants had witnessed this masterly escape, issued a general order, highly laudatory of the promptitude and skill displayed by the officers and men of the three

(1) The oyster banks to the southward and eastward of Castle Cornet were so broken up by the anchors of the transports, which drove upon them, in a northerly gale, that they were soon after dredged for a short time.

(2) Duncan, following James in his Naval History, erroneously says that the British fell in with the French squadron "off the island of Jersey."

ships, particularly of the Crescent, whose captain, it was added, was a native of the island, in sight of which he had evinced
so much presence of mind and nautical experience.

During the horrors of the French revolution, a vast number of royalists fled from their own country to escape the
deadly persecutions which threatened them, and not a few
found an asylum in these islands, where they were received
with hospitality and kindness, which several gratefully returned, when in their power, after the restoration of the
Bourbons, in 1814.   Many were men of noble family.

Sunday Drilling of the Militia.—From the Life of Wilberforce.

" It was the natural consequence of his public character that
those who were in any difficulty, especially if it was connected
with religion, applied at once to him as the redresser of their
wrongs.   The Sunday drilling, which had just been introduced
into the Channel Islands, was most offensive to the religious principles of the Wesleyan Methodists; and their refusal to conform
to the appointment of the local government subjected them, in
many instances, to fine and imprisonment.   They appealed to
Mr. Wilberforce, and, whilst still at Broomfield, he had seen
Mr. Dundas upon the subject, and procured the promise of his
interference in their cause.   He now heard from Dr. Coke, that
not only were these oppressive measures still maintained, but that,
on the 18th of October, [1798,] at the States meeting of the isle
of Jersey, it was determined to proceed to banishment against
those who refused to perform this military duty.   To appeal
against this bill he moved hastily to London; and having reached
Broomfield on the 10th of November, 'went on the 13th to town
on the methodist business,' but found that 'neither Pitt nor
Dundas were come.'   Within a few days, he convinced Mr.
Dundas of the injustice of such a needless violation of the rights
of conscience; and after some delay succeeded in getting 'the
Jersey methodists' cause decided in their favour—'banishment
bill assent refused.'"

Towards the close of the year 1799, two divisions of Russian troops, which had been engaged, in conjunction with the
English, under Sir Ralph Abercrombie and the Duke of
York, in the ill-fated expedition to Holland, undertaken by
the British and Russian governments for the re-establishment
of the Prince of Orange, were landed in Guernsey and Jersey; the introduction of foreign troops into England being
prohibited by the Bill of Rights.   The entire force was under
the command of General Viemenil,—a Frenchman, who, on

the restoration of the Bourbons, was created a field-marshal,—and consisted of about 10,000 men, of whom 6,000 were quartered in Guernsey, on Delancey Heights, part in the barracks already erected there, and the remainder in temporary wooden buildings. A disease, contracted by exposure to the marshy grounds of Holland, and still lingering among them when they arrived here, carried off some hundreds, who were buried in a small enclosure at the foot of the hill on which stands Vale castle, where their graves are still to be seen. Their conduct towards the inhabitants was at first peaceable and orderly, although they were excessively fond of ardent spirits; and, having plenty of money, they indulged in them freely, swallowing immense quantities in a raw state at one draught. But previously to their embarkation, one of the soldiers was committed for a rape, of which the evidence was, however, insufficient to convict him; and in June, 1800, while the transports were in the roads to convey them to Russia, another, who was stealing vegetables on a farm which had frequently been plundered by them before, was fired at and wounded by the proprietor. This so exasperated the whole division, that fears were entertained of their revenging themselves on the inhabitants generally; and as the British garrison was very small, it required all the tact and conciliation of the lieutenant-governor, Sir Hew Dalrymple, of Cintra memory, to prevent an outbreak. The influence of their general, Sedmoratzky, was also exerted to the same purpose, and the troops embarked; but the guns at Castle Cornet were kept shotted to prevent their relanding.[1]

The Duke of Gloucester, brother of George III., being on an aquatic excursion, landed in Guernsey in 1765, and was hospitably entertained by Mr. Matthew Saumarez,[2] father of the first Lord de Saumarez, at his large house, near the Plaiderie. The duke's son, bearing the same title, also visited the island in September, 1817, in the Tigris frigate, from Weymouth, and remained a few days, being received with every mark of loyalty. At either period, the visit of the sovereign was as little anticipated as that of a steam vessel.

(1) The anniversary of the Emperor Paul's birth occurring whilst they were here, they celebrated it with great pomp, the officers giving a grand ball in honour of the day, to which the principal inhabitants and the English officers in the garrison were invited. The ball was given at the assembly rooms, which were splendidly and fantastically decorated, whilst the market place, and the avenues to it, were, as if by magic, transformed into a beautiful parterre, the walks of which were thickly strewed with fine sand: the whole, being brilliantly illuminated at night, had a very imposing and pleasing appearance.

(2) Mr. Saumarez, and several other passengers, were drowned in March, 1778, on their passage from Guernsey to Weymouth; the vessel having been upset in a squall near Portland, and only one boy saved.

2B

CHAPTER XXI.

GEORGE III.—1760 to 1820. (Concluded.)

In the year 1800, Mr. Stiles was sent over to Guernsey by the British government, in the capacity of commissioner, with a view to the suppression of the illicit trade, which was then very extensively carried on from Guernsey and Alderney with England and Ireland, and had been more or less so for about a century. On the 15th of December, the royal court replied to several interrogatories submitted to that body by Mr. Stiles, and the answers are so descriptive of the state of the island at that time that we give them entire :

" *First Question.*—What is supposed to be the number of inhabitants of this island, exclusive of strangers ?

" *Answer.*—Upon an exact census, the number in each parish is found to be :

St. Peter-Port	8,450	Vale	842
St. Mary De Castro	1,453	St. Andrew	675
St. Martin	1,132	St. Sampson	652
St. Pierre-du-Bois	1,130	Forest	552
St. Saviour	933	Torteval	336

Total population, 16,155, exclusive of sailors in his majesty's service, privateers, and merchant vessels; also of strangers not permanently settled, who may amount to 2,000 or 3,000.

" *Second Question.*—What number does the militia consist of, and at what age are they required to bear arms, and what duty do they perform ?

" *Answer.*—The militia consists, according to the last estimate, of 3,158 men, and 455 lads[1] from fourteen to sixteen years of age, which is the age at which they begin to be trained ; and the duty performed by the militia is to keep watch at different posts round the island, and to be ready to attend with their arms and accoutrements at any rendezvous assigned to them by the commander-in-chief and their officers, to be disciplined and reviewed, and on any signal of alarm.

" *Third Question.*—What foreign trade is in general carried on to, and from, the island, and how has the war affected it?

" *Answer.*—The foreign trade carried on by the inhabitants is in the importation of wines, brandy, and fruits from France, Spain, Portugal, Madeira, and Italy ; rum from the West Indies ; tobacco and grain from America ; and fish from Newfoundland.

(1) These numbers are either an error in the copy or a gross exaggeration.

The exportation is in such brandies and wines to America, Quebec, and the West Indies; large quantities of these liquors are intended to be exported to Great Britain and Ireland; the tobacco is destined for Hamburg, Embden, and the Baltic, exclusive of what is sold to smugglers. We subjoin the exact particulars of such trade. Many brandies are exported to Madeira and America. At the first place they are bartered for wines, which are carried to the West India Islands, and again bartered for rum and other produce, which is sometimes carried to Quebec in exchange for provisions to be carried to Newfoundland, and there bartered for fish, which is shipped to Portugal and the Mediterranean, whither we also export cargoes of pilchards from Cornwall, for account of the inhabitants who have large concerns in that fishery; the brandies carried to America are bartered for corn, rice, and staves, and brought hither. Several assorted cargoes, and especially prize wines, are annually exported direct to the West India Islands, where they have entry, and some to those islands which only admit those goods from England, where they are accordingly first landed, and also to Quebec, and there they are bartered for wheat and flour, which are imported into this island, or for provisions which are carried to Newfoundland, and there bartered for fish for the above named markets, or these islands.

" But a great part of our trade consists in the deposit of goods brought hither, to be regularly re-imported into Great Britain and Ireland, from France, Spain, and Portugal; this occupies our warehouses, built at great expense, and gives bread to coopers and labourers, and freight to many of our own and British vessels in the legal transportation of such goods to all parts of the United Kingdom; and the freights paid here for the goods are a considerable source of circulation and benefit to the island, as it is calculated that above one quarter part of the amount of such freight is paid in the island in wages to the crews, and in provisions, repairs, and necessaries for the vessels, and otherwise laid out here in the purchase of different articles, most of which are of British manufacture. We also beg leave to observe, that many of the tobaccos brought hither are purchased by such masters of neutral ships, as adventures, when bound to their own country, besides what is bought here by the crews. And, in the year before the war, the quantity of manufactured tobacco brought hither by the French amounted to above £150,000, which they smuggled back into Normandy and Britany. In this manufacture, many indigent boys and girls are employed.

" The whole of this deposit trade facilitates the operations of the fair trader in the United Kingdom, as the merchants order their goods by parcels as they want them, and for such ports as may be most advantageous. But Hamburg has, during the whole year, carried away about one half of the deposit trade of

brandies designed to be re-imported into Great Britain, and which
might be limited to this island instead of throwing the profit to
foreigners, and indeed to the advantage of the mother country,
as it would keep considerable sums at home, favour the rate of
exchange with the continent, and not leave British property exposed to the chance of events, and to sequestration and confiscation in foreign ports.   The quantity of goods, however, exported
from this island must, in a great measure, be known to you, and
it must be very considerable, as the three undersigned have alone
shipped, since the 1st of October, 3,325 pipes, and 983 hogsheads
of brandy and wine, and the war has generally increased the
several branches of trade.

"*Fourth and Fifth Questions.*—What number of privateers
have been fitted out this war, and what is the number at present?
What number of persons have been generally employed in such
privateers?

"*Answer.*—There have been thirty-five fitted out this war,
carrying 250 guns and 1,716 men, and there are at present twelve
privateers, carrying 148 guns and 670 men; but had the salvage
been one half, there would have been double that number, for the
French having had little or no trade this war, the only encouragement has been the chance of recaptures, and of prizes from the
Spaniards; and the value of our captures, which last war exceeded £900,000, has not been probably much less this war,
without, however, enriching the inhabitants in the same proportion, because a great part of the value consists in recaptures, and
the expense of privateers is more considerable.   We have also,
since your departure, been particularly indebted to our privateers
for sending in three prizes with 500 tons of Spanish wheat, which
has preserved us, we really believe, from a state of scarcity,
which, without that supply, would have bordered upon famine.

"*Sixth Question.*—What manufactures are carried on in the
island?

"*Answer.*—The knitting of stockings, waistcoats, &c., for
which 2,000 tods of wool are allowed to be exported from England; and some English persons have lately erected a glass house,
intended chiefly for the blowing of bottles, and where the fire is
also applied to the making of salt.   Another manufactory for
salt has been set up and substituted for our ancient salt pans,
since when other ancient and very extensive salt pans have been
· converted into arable fields, and been sown this year for the first
time with corn.   There are also several manufactories of tobacco
for the consumption of the island, part of which is also sold to the
masters and crews of neutral vessels, as well as to the smugglers.

" We cannot conclude without observing, that if ten to twelve
thousand guineas are every week carried by smugglers to the
continent, of which there is no doubt, it is so far from being the

case here, that money is, and has been so scarce for a long time, that government has paid a premium of $2\frac{1}{2}$ and $3\frac{1}{2}$ per cent. for cash to pay the garrison. The merchants and tradesmen do the same.

(Signed)   "ROBERT PORRET LE MARCHANT, Bailiff.

"DANIEL DE LISLE BROCK.

"WILLIAM LE MARCHANT."

The illicit trade was not effectually suppressed until the year 1805, when the "act for the better prevention of smuggling" was extended to these islands by the British legislature. Previous to its suppression, this trade was carried on in cutters and luggers of from 80 to 130 tons register, built at Hastings, Mevagissey, Polperro, and other English ports, and the greater part were owned in England, as the inhabitants confined themselves chiefly to the sale of goods to the smugglers; and, on the outbreak of a war, either purchased these vessels, or fitted out their own as privateers, for which they were admirably adapted. The smuggling crews were almost entirely English, well acquainted with their own and the Irish coast, and almost every man of whom was the *beau-ideal* of a British sailor : active, daring, and prodigal of their dangerous gains, they forgot, in the pleasures of the day, the risks of the morrow, the favourite season for their vocation being the winter. As the simplicity and morality of the islanders at and after that stirring period were remarkable, it will naturally excite surprise how either could exist in, or in the neighbourhood of, a sea port which was long frequented by the crews of smugglers and privateers; and yet it is an undoubted fact that both existed in a higher degree than at this moment. We can only account for the apparent anomaly by attributing the cause to the greater prevalence of the French language among the lower classes, which prevented their having much social intercourse with the stranger seamen. It should also be remembered that the mass of the inhabitants, especially those living in the country, had no participation or interest whatever in the illicit trade.

On the renewal of hostilities between Great Britain and France, in 1803, Lieutenant-General Sir John Doyle was appointed to the then responsible situation of lieutenant-governor of Guernsey. He at once proceeded, with a zeal which nothing could check, to place the island in a complete state of defence. Breastworks were raised round the coast, batteries were erected in every bay, the citadel of Fort George was strengthened, and the insular militia was brought to a state of discipline and perfection which it had never yet attained. A tract of land containing about 300 English acres, known as the Braye du Valle, which was overflowed by the sea at high water, was recovered in 1803 from its dominion, at the expense of government; and although at first, to all appearance, little better than a bed of sand, yet when publicly disposed of by order of the crown, it produced no less than £5,000; and by draining and judicious husbandry, corn now grows, cattle graze, and many farm houses stand, where, at the commencement of this century, rolled the billows of the Atlantic. This, however, was not the only benefit conferred on the island during the long administration of this excellent officer and good man, whose memory is justly dear to the islanders. At his intercession, the money obtained from the sale of the Braye du Valle was devoted by government to the formation of new roads, one of the greatest boons ever conferred on Guernsey—a measure which encountered the most ignorant opposition, especially from those most benefitted, (the country people,) and was only carried by a rare combination of tact and perseverance in the character of Sir John Doyle. These new roads were commenced in 1810, and the two first constructed were, one from St. Peter-Port to Vazon, by the Rohais, La Houguette, &c.; and the other from the town to Le Rée, by St. Martin's, the Forest, Plaisance, &c. The length of these two roads was about eleven miles, and the estimated cost was £8,773. By an order in council, dated August 15, 1810, Sir John Doyle was authorized to draw bills on the treasury for a sum not exceeding £5,000, to be applied to the completion of the new military roads leading to Vazon and Le Rée.

In the spring of 1803, it was apprehended that Napoleon Bonaparte had a design on these islands, in consequence of the great preparations making at St. Malo; and Rear-Admiral Sir James Saumarez, Bart. and K.B., was appointed to the command of the naval station, of which Guernsey was the rendezvous, on account of its roadstead: the squadron consisted of six frigates and six brigs and cutters, which were chiefly employed in blockading the French coast between Havre de Grace and Ushant, and especially in watching Cherbourg, Granville, and St. Malo. In July, the *Minerve*, 46-gun frigate, Captain Jahleel Brenton, one of the squadron stationed off Cherbourg, got aground in a fog within reach of the batteries, and after a protracted resistance, during which eleven men were killed and sixteen wounded, was compelled to surrender. A considerable flotilla of gun vessels having assembled at Granville, Sir James Saumarez proceeded thither in September, in the Cerberus, 32, with the Charwell, 18, Captain Philip Dumaresq; Kite, 18, Captain Philip Pipon; (both captains, natives of Jersey;) the Sulphur and Terror, bombs, and the Eling and Carteret, cutters. On the 14th and 15th, the town and port were bombarded for several hours with shells, the fire of the ships being returned by the batteries on the heights and the gun vessels at the entrance of the pier. The enemy's flotilla is said to have been much damaged; but, although Sir James, before commencing the bombardment, humanely sent a flag of truce to announce it to the commandant, with a request that he would remove the women and children, yet the inoffensive inhabitants appear to have been the principal sufferers, if not in life, at least in property. Such is generally the case, and assuredly this mode of warfare is abhorrent both to religion and humanity. The flotilla at Granville was intended for Boulogne; and, being delayed in going to the latter port until late in the year, owing it is said to the damage received in the bombardment, many are stated to have been lost in a storm in and near the Race of Alderney.—In December, the Shannon was wrecked in a gale, under the batteries of Cape La Hague, and the Grappler was lost at Chausey, the crews of both vessels, which belonged to the squadron, being made prisoners.

The successes of the French revolutionary armies on the continent, together with the threats of an invasion of England itself, excited apprehension in the minds of the British government for the safety of the Anglo-Norman Islands, and their garrisons were gradually augmented until about the year 1805, when that for Guernsey was definitively fixed at 4,000 infantry, and one company of artillery. For their accommodation, barracks were successively erected at Amherst, near the New Ground, Delancey Heights, Lancresse Common, Le Rée, Richmond, Grand Rocque, and Jerbourg. Martello towers were also built to protect the principal landing places, and remain now as monuments of the ignorance of the art of military engineering at that day, the wide part of the loop-holes being outside instead of in, so as to give every possible facility to the enemy to throw in his shots.

In 1809, the Duke of Brunswick Oels, son of the ill-fated Duke of Brunswick, who was mortally wounded at the battle of Jena, in 1806, arrived in Guernsey with part of his corps of "Sable Yagers," their chief having been abandoned by

Austria, when she succumbed to Napoleon, and compelled to escape from the continent. Their uniform was black, in memory of his father's death, to revenge whose misfortunes and ill-treatment was the determined purpose of the son, so that the lace of the cavalry, and that of the officers of the infantry, was disposed like the ribs of a skeleton, and the chakoes of both cavalry and infantry bore on the front a death's head, with the cross bones underneath. These troops were stationed at Delancey barracks, and the duke himself resided here some time. He is known to have repeatedly remarked, that he never had met with a people who appeared so happy and contented as those of Guernsey; and it is stated that, shortly before the battle of Waterloo, where he gallantly fell, he intimated his intention of revisiting the island.

Cromlech at l'Ancresse.—In the year 1811, a large cromlech was accidentally discovered, completely buried by the drift sand, on an eminence near the beach at l'Ancresse, in Guernsey: it is 45 feet in length by 15 feet in width, and nearly 8 feet in height within the area at the western end, whence it gradually contracts on each side and at the top, towards the eastern end. This space is covered by five larger and two smaller blocks of granite, which are not in contact: the western block is computed to weigh about thirty tons, it being nearly 17 feet long, $10\frac{1}{2}$ wide, and $4\frac{1}{2}$ thick; and it was probably placed there by means of rollers. The second block is 16 feet long, the third smaller, and so they gradually diminish to the seventh. This fine cromlech was left filled and most imperfectly explored until the year 1837, when, after considerable labour, it was cleared of sand, and its primæval contents exposed, at the expense and through the antiquarian zeal of F. C. Lukis, Esq., before mentioned. On the floor were then found two layers consisting of human bones, urns of coarse red and black clay, stone and clay amulets and beads, bone pins, &c., the layers, like those of cists, being separated by flat fragments of granite: the lower stratum was laid on a rude pavement on the natural soil. The remains were deposited in a singular manner: the unburnt bones occupied either end of the floor, the middle third being allotted to those which had been submitted to the action of fire; not a vestige of charcoal was to be detected with them. The bones of individual skeletons were heaped together confusedly, and each heap surrounded by a small ring of round flat pebbles; the urns, which were of remarkably rude shape and material, being near or within the rings. Some heaps consisted, as it were, of parents' and children's ashes mingled together, for within the same ring of pebbles were the bones of persons of all ages : an unusual quantity of bones of very young children were found. The lower stratum only contained the burnt bones, among which likewise a few tusks of the boar, perhaps worn as trophies of the chase, and consigned to the fire with the hunter's dead body. Four flat discs, from six to twelve inches in diameter and one in thickness, and formed of the same ware as the urns, were also found, and doubtless served as lids to some of the urns, which had broad flat edges : as these lids are furnished with central handles, it may be inferred that the urns were replenished from time to time, the cromlech being a hollow vault or cata-comb. In no instance was the urn used to contain the ashes of the dead, and it was doubtless filled with liquid or food at the time of sepulture : about 150 urns were removed from this cromlech — some were quite entire, and of those broken many have been restored. As time and ages elapsed, and, possibly, as all memory of the departed became lost, their remains were removed to make room for others ; those so removed were placed in the intervals between the props, and were lost to sight ; but further space being again required, many cart loads of limpet shells, and a little yellow clay, were strewn upon the original deposit ; and flat stones, as already said, were placed over all to form a new floor.[1]

During the reign of George III., two natives of the baili-wick, Peter Perchard and Paul Le Mesurier, were lord mayors of London, and the latter was also member of parlia-ment for Southwark.—Another native, Peter Carey Tupper, British consul for Valencia and member of the supreme junta of that kingdom before he was twenty-four years of age,[2] highly distinguished himself during the war in Spain, from 1808 to 1814, and is honorably mentioned in Napier's history and in the Duke of Wellington's despatches.[3]—It is also cre-ditable to the military character of the little island of Guern-sey, that of the five British generals killed in action in 1812, two, whose names follow in the obituary of the Annual Army

(1) "Observations on the Celtic Megaliths, by F. C. Lukis, M. D.," ARCHÆOLOGIA, vol. xxxv., accompanied by sketches of the exterior and interior of this great cromlech.

(2) Born in June, 1784, and died at Madrid in 1825, aged forty.

(3) We have perused a volume in MS. of Mr. Tupper's despatches to the different British authorities in England and Spain, descriptive of the war on the eastern coast of the Penin-sula : a selection of these despatches would well repay publication, as many are very interesting.—Marshal Suchet, in his *Mémoires*, makes mention of Mr. Tupper's exertions.

List for 1813, were Major-General Le Marchant, 6th dragoon
guards, at the battle of Salamanca, and Major-General Sir
Isaac Brock, K.B., 49th foot, in America.[1]   And yet, anterior to the year 1775, very few of the natives entered either
the army or the navy, probably from want of interest, and
subsequently also from finding sufficient occupation at home;
thus the first Guernseymen who attained the rank of general
and admiral respectively were John Tupper, created a major-
general October 12, 1793, and the late Lord de Saumarez,
created a rear-admiral of the blue January 1, 1801.—Peter
Paul Dobrée, another native of Guernsey, succeeded Dr.
Monk, late bishop of Gloucester, as regius professor of Greek
at Cambridge, in 1823 : an office which, he used to mention
with pride, had been held by another native, the learned Dr.
Duport.   While on this subject, we may add that a Guernseyman, the Rev. Dr. J. A. Jeremie, was appointed regius
professor of divinity at Cambridge in 1850.   The island had
previously given a professor to the university of Oxford,
Dr. William de Beauvoir, of Pembroke College, who was
elected professor of medicine in 1729, and died the year following.   In his funeral sermon, the preacher observed that,
" like the beautiful lily of his native island, he had flourished
among them but one year."

In 1813, the bailiff, Mr. (afterwards Sir Peter) de Havilland, presented a petition to the Prince Regent in council,
praying that he and the crown law officers of Guernsey might
be allowed the same salaries as those, holding similar appointments in Jersey, had received since the year 1797, the constitutions, laws, and usages of the two islands being the same.
In support of this claim, Mr. de Havilland stated, among
other allegations, that the salary of the bailiff in 1331 was
thirty livres tournois, while that of the governor was two
hundred livres tournois, both per annum : that the said salary
of thirty livres was recorded in 1439, and that it had ever
since continued at the same amount.   This petition was accordingly granted, the salaries being for the bailiff £300, the
procureur £100, the comptroller £50, and the greffier £40
per annum, to commence on the 1st of January, 1814, and to
be paid out of the crown revenues of the island.   In September, 1813, the royal court assembled to consider the order
in council, and the jurats unanimously resolved to petition

(1) The other officers were Major-Generals Bowes, Craufurd, and McKinnon, who all
fell in Spain.

against that part of it which gave a salary of £300 a year to
the bailiff; but their petition was rejected, and very properly,
although the bailiff, being removeable at pleasure, is perhaps
not sufficiently independent of the crown. In Jersey, the
fees of the bailiff are so much higher and more numerous,
that the appointment is said to produce £800 per annum,
while in Guernsey it is now scarcely worth £400 a year; and,
with the very onerous duties attached to the office, which
requires much talent and labour, and a competent knowledge
of at least two languages, (French and English,) there is no
judicial functionary in the British dominions who is so under-
paid as the bailiff of Guernsey.[1] The salary of the procureur,
or attorney-general, has since been raised to £200, there being
now no comptroller, and that of the greffier to £60 per annum.

A principle of the highest constitutional importance was
decided by the privy council, in 1813, in consequence of the
royal court having attempted to levy taxes on the parishioners
of St. Peter-Port without their consent. On the 1st of
November, 1810, that body, which has contrived to concentrate within itself nearly all the insular government — being
ever omniscient, (?) and, like Aaron's rod, ever omnivorous —
passed an ordinance, by which great alterations, at the estimated cost of about £1,500, were to be effected in Cornet
street, and the constables were ordered to advance the necessary sums, to be afterwards repaid to the parish, wholly or in
part, by lotteries. In March ensuing, a parish meeting was
held to consider the ordinance, when the constables were
expressly enjoined not to advance the parochial funds for
any work whatever, without the previous consent of the
parishioners; and the constables and douzeniers were moreover authorized to defend the parish rights, in the event of
coercive measures being adopted by the royal court, which
did not now attempt to enforce its ordinance; it was suffered
to lie dormant, but was not rescinded.

In August and September, 1811, the royal court endeavoured to compass its object by indirect means, as it ordered
the constables to advance the necessary sums for paving the
Truchot and for work in Pedvin street. Another parish
meeting was convened, when the decision of that in March
was confirmed; and as both constables obeyed their consti-

---

[1] The present bailiff, Mr. P. Stafford Carey, is the first English barrister who has
held the appointment, having been previously recorder of Dartmouth and judge of the
borough court of Wells; so that his object in seeking it must have been not emolument, but
a desire to be the chief magistrate of an island in which his ancestors had been settled, and
filled the chief offices for many centuries.

tuents, they were charged with disobedience by the royal court, which arbitrarily imprisoned them in the public gaol !

The whole question was then submitted to council, and its decision was in favor of the parishioners, it being clearly shewn that although the court could order *repairs* to be made, it could not originate any *new* work, and that it was not empowered to levy money on the inhabitants, by States or parochial tax, without their consent. The following extract from the order in council, dated August 28, 1580, was adduced as decisive of the point : " Whereas they (the inhabitants) complain that there is a greater tax laid upon them by the bailiff and jurats for the tenth of their calves, pullets and lambs, than in former times it has been accustomed ; it is ordered that the said taxations, laid upon the inhabitants in lieu of tithes, shall be propounded to the GENERALITY, as in like cases has been accustomed, and after the same being by them allowed, her majesty shall be moved to yield confirmation."

In the year 1813, the sea, which had in early times swallowed up large tracts of land, threatened, from the defective state of the coast defences, to overflow the low lands on the western side of the island ; and the sum required to avert the danger was estimated at above £10,000, which the country parishes, subject to this charge, were unable to raise. The finances of the States were also in a very depressed condition, as, with a debt of £19,137, and an annual charge for interest and ordinary expenses of £2,390, the entire revenue, arising from the harbour dues, publicans' licenses, &c., was only £3,000 a year, thus leaving only £610 for unforeseen outlays and improvements. It must moreover be remembered, that antecedently to the new roads first undertaken by Sir John Doyle, in 1810, very little had been done in the way of improvement ; the island being, as we have shewn, comparatively in a state of nature. Under these disadvantages it was resolved to introduce indirect taxation, and on a petition from the States, that body was authorized by an order in council, bearing date July 23, 1814, to raise one shilling per gallon on all spirituous liquors consumed in the island for the term of five years. It is only to be regretted that this impost had not been levied fifty years earlier, as, with the large garrison and squadron, it would have produced in that period some £300,000, a sum which, if properly expended, while felt by no one, would have effected incalculable good. The average receipts of the impôt during the first five years — 1815 to

1819, inclusive—were only £2,278 a year, owing probably to the quantity in store in 1814 not being correctly given; as, since 1820, the amount received has frequently exceeded £6,000 a year. In 1850, it was £5,861. 11s. 7d. In December, 1851, the dues for the construction of the new piers were first levied, chiefly as follows, viz. six pence per gallon on wine, six pence per ton on shipping, and one shilling per ton on goods, coals, &c.

In the spring of 1814, the war between England and France ceased—a war which, with one short intermission, had continued since 1793, or for eighteen years; but the peace only dates from 1815, when the crowning victory of Waterloo sent Napoleon a captive to St. Helena. The people of Guernsey had been so long strangers to repose that they hailed its return with unbounded joy, as we well remember, little foreseeing that the artificial prosperity, which the war had engendered, would cease, and be the ruin of many who had calculated on its continuance. Although provisions were enormously dear; flour varying from £5 to £7. 10s. the sack of 2½ English cwt. nett; meat being at 1s. to 1s. 3d., and butter at 2s. 3d. to 2s. 9d. the pound,[1] and other articles in proportion, yet war prices were accompanied by more than corresponding profits. The farmer was eminently prosperous, and the mechanic and labourer obtained constant and remunerating employment. The merchants were generally successful; and, as their capital increased, became more confident and enterprising. A large local trade was created by the supply of the garrison, which usually consisted of about four thousand men, with two general officers and a numerous staff, and of the squadron, composed occasionally of some twenty pendants, under a rear-admiral, who resided in St. Peter-Port, and had his flag flying in the roadstead. Even Alderney was governed by a general officer, and garrisoned by a whole regiment. The upper ranks in Guernsey exercised a liberal but simple hospitality, and maintained a constant social intercourse with the officers of either service. The assembly rooms, opened twice a week, were crowded, and the theatre was every winter often filled almost to suffocation. In many of the streets were nightly heard sounds of music and dancing issuing forth from the various public houses, and the labour of the working classes was sweetened by these and similar enjoyments. Indeed, the welfare was

(1) These prices were, moreover, nearly 18 per cent. higher than at present, because there was a premium of about 5 per cent. on cash instead of one on bills on London, varying of late years from 3½ to 5 per cent.

general, and there was little local want or poverty to repress this exhilarating state of existence. The sudden change caused by the peace will be described in Chapter XXIII.

In March, 1818, Captain N. Dobrée, R.N., a very fine young man, and nephew of the late Admiral Lord de Saumarez, was drowned, with three other natives of the Câtel parish, in gallantly attempting to save the crew of a foreign vessel, wrecked on the rocks in front of Cobo bay.

Having already said that in 1775 no government packet came to Guernsey, we cannot better close the reign of George III. than by shewing at a rapid glance the mode of communication with England during his time, and four years afterwards. The first packet established by government between England and these islands was in 1778 : she was a cutter, which, soon after the war broke out with France, was removed from the station between Dover and Calais, and plied as often as practicable from Southampton ; but when peace took place in 1783, she returned to her former station. Antecedently and subsequently, letters for the islands were addressed to the care of agents at Southampton, who paid the postage, and forwarded them by the traders—small sloops of some fifty tons, and for the sailing of which from Southampton passengers were often detained there a week or more, especially during strong contrary winds. And even while the packet ran, the letters were sent by her in the same manner through the agents, as neither Jersey nor Guernsey had a regular post-office. During the two wars with France, commencing in 1778 and 1793, the Southampton traders frequently came under convoy ; and the dilatoriness and uncertainty of the intercourse, both for correspondence and passengers, will be apparent from the circumstance that a gentleman, not long deceased, was nearly three months on his passage from Southampton to Guernsey, in the summer of 1793. The trader in which he embarked reached Cowes in a few hours, and the next day was joined by the convoy from Portsmouth. They weighed anchor and sailed several times, but never got beyond Yarmouth, being baffled by contrary winds and calms. At length a fair wind came, and they reached Guernsey, to the great relief of the passengers. In 1794, two post-office packets, both cutters of about eighty tons, commenced running weekly from Weymouth to Guernsey and Jersey : they sailed alternately on the Saturday evening, and, with a fair wind, reached Guernsey the next morning. In 1811, a third cutter was added, and from that time until 1827 the packets plied twice a week, leaving Weymouth on the Wednesday and Saturday evenings. They were frequently from thirty-six to forty-eight hours reaching Guernsey, sometimes twenty-four hours from Guernsey to Jersey, and in winter the reception of two or three mails by the same packet was no uncommon occurrence. The Chesterfield, packet, on her passage from Weymouth, was captured by a French privateer, about the year 1811, and carried into Cherbourg, with some of her crew and passengers killed and wounded. The cutter, Sir Francis Freeling, is supposed to have foundered in a violent gale, in September, 1826, on her passage from Weymouth, to Guernsey.—The author of this history was very glad to get back to Weymouth, in Christmas week, 1810, on his return from school, after being out fifty-four hours, and drenched in his berth, the packet having shipped a sea off the Caskets, which filled her cabin, swept her decks, and carried away her two boats, bulwarks, &c. Had the packet been a steamer, she would have arrived in Jersey several hours before the terrific gale commenced

During the greater part of the war with France, from 1803 to 1814, the communication between Southampton and Guernsey was maintained chiefly by three cutters of about eighty tons each, which had no fixed days for sailing, but crossed as often as their cargoes and the winds permitted. These cutters ran the whole war without loss or capture, excepting one, the Brilliant, which was taken by an American privateer and dispatched for Cherbourg; but the prize master, mistaking Alderney for the French coast, gave charge of the helm to a seaman of the Brilliant, who wisely kept up the deception, and steered the cutter into the harbour of Alderney, where she was immediately recaptured. A passenger never embarked in these traders without a bottle or two of wine and a basket of provisions, as the passage frequently extended to two days and nights, and often longer, sometimes to five and six days : he was considered fortunate if he were not more than thirty hours at sea.

GEORGE IV.—1820 to 1830.

In 1820, a petition was presented to the bailiff, Sir Peter de Havilland, requesting the States to impose dues on all French vessels arriving in Guernsey, equal to those paid by English vessels in France. That magistrate refused to submit this request to the States; and in 1824 the application was renewed, the bailiff then being Daniel De Lisle Brock. The petitioners represented that antecedently, in time of peace, the trade between the island and the neighbouring coasts of France was carried on by Guernsey vessels, but then it was the reverse, French vessels reaping all the advantage of the traffic; that some years before, the States of Jersey, with the sanction of the king in council, had adopted the law proposed; and further, that parliament had passed an act, authorizing the levy of duties on all foreign vessels arriving in Great Britain and Ireland, proportioned to those which English vessels paid in such foreign countries. It appeared that in France English vessels paid 3s. 6d. per ton. Mr. Brock, in his answer, strongly advised the petitioners to abandon their object, but promised to submit their petition to the States, should they persist in it. He shewed the folly of instituting any comparison between a large country like France and a small island like Guernsey, whose prosperity was dependant on free trade. He said that, far from following the example recommended, he hoped that the island never would know prohibitory duties and fiscal restrictions; and he humorously added, in allusion to a remark that Guernsey ought to follow the example of all civilized countries, that it reminded him of the traveller, who, seeing a man hanging on a gallows, congratulated himself on having reached a civilized country. He explained that the proposed duties would prevent vessels from coming to the island to land or dispose of part of their cargoes, and that the ruin of the *entrepôt* trade would be the consequence. These arguments, however, produced no effect on the country douzaines: they persisted in their demands, which were, in fact, an indirect attempt to exclude French provisions; and on their petition being submitted to the States, it was very properly negatived. The good policy of this rejection will be apparent from the fact, that the French vessels, which carried on the trade for a few years after the peace, have long since been driven out of it by Guernsey vessels, the weekly supplies from St. Malo being now received by two Guernsey cutters, to which the French people themselves give a preference; and, moreover, that English statesmen, with a truer idea of the advantages of free trade, have removed many of the clogs on foreign commerce and shipping in England.

In November, 1825, the Greek brig of war Cimoni, on her

return from England to Greece, was wrecked on Alderney, whence the crew was conveyed to Guernsey. The nature of their reception will be seen by the following letter from Captain Miaulis, son of the celebrated Greek admiral of that name, to the Greek deputies in London :

[Translated from the Greek.]

" Gentlemen,—Being on the point of quitting England, I consider myself obliged by duty to express the sincere gratitude I, my officers, and crew, entertain towards the inhabitants of Guernsey in general, and particularly towards the lieutenant-governor, Sir John Colborne,[1] and the family of Mr. Tupper,[2] resident in that island, for their most generous and benevolent conduct towards us.

" If any thing can possibly alleviate the misfortunes of those who are shipwrecked on a foreign coast, far from their native country, unacquainted with the language of the people among whom chance has thrown them, it is the meeting with men of liberality and humanity. Such, we thank Heaven, has been our lot ; and we can assure the inhabitants of Guernsey that, whilst we live, their conduct will remain indelibly engraven on our hearts.

" You will oblige me and my officers by giving publicity to this letter. Treatment like that we met with should not remain unrecorded.   " Yours, &c.

" DEMETRIUS ANDREAS MIAULIS."

The following paragraph also appeared in a Portsmouth newspaper of the 31st of December, 1825 :

" This morning, sailed the Aurora, for Hydra, having on board forty of the crew of the Greek brig of war Cimoni, lately wrecked on the isle of Alderney, from whence they were taken to Guernsey, where they received the greatest kindness and attention from the lieutenant-governor, Sir John Colborne, and the inhabitants, who, in addition to having provided them with food, clothing, and lodging, whilst on the island, raised for them a most liberal subscription, and gave £5 to each of the crew on their leaving Guernsey. We are requested to state that, for the kindness they have received from the governor and inhabitants of Guernsey, they feel the deepest gratitude, and beg to return their most grateful thanks. It is perhaps impossible to express the high sense they entertain of the kindness they experienced better than

(1) The present Lieut.-General Lord Seaton, G.C.B., &c. Sir John, who was highly esteemed and respected in Guernsey, relinquished its government for that of Upper Canada, the most western harbour of which province he named PORT SARNIA, in honour of this island.

(2) A few months later, Lieutenant E. W. Tupper, of the Sybille frigate, and a member of this family, was mortally wounded on Sunday, June 18, 1826, in action with Greek pirates, near the island of Candia, the Sybille having forty-four officers and men killed and wounded in her boats on that occasion.

2c

in their own words, which were: 'The people of Guernsey behaved to us like angels, not like men.'"

Sir John Doyle revisited Guernsey in 1826, and was received by the inhabitants with warm demonstrations of attachment and regard. A public dinner was given to him; and
he had the pleasing opportunity of seeing the monumental
column at Jerbourg, which had been erected during his absence, by the States of the island, in grateful remembrance of
his administration. He died in 1834, aged seventy-eight.

WILLIAM IV.—1830 to 1837.

In 1832, one of the most ancient and vital privileges of the
Anglo-Norman Islanders—that of being tried solely in their
own local courts, and not impleaded out of the islands—was
placed in peril, by an attempt being made to extend the
Habeas Corpus Act to them; and the attempt naturally caused
great apprehension. On the 1st of June in that year, a petition was presented to the House of Commons by the parish of
St. Pancras, in Middlesex, setting forth at great length that
John Capes—a beadle of the said parish, having proceeded to
Guernsey with James Streep, his wife, and two children, and
William Locker, all paupers chargeable to the said parish—
was detained in the island because he refused to take back
the said paupers, whereupon the petitioners presented a memorial to the privy council stating the detention; "and it
appearing that the only remedy they had was by a formal
appeal, which would be attended with considerable delay and
expense, they applied to the lord chief justice of England for
a writ of Habeas Corpus to bring before him the said John
Capes, which his lordship was pleased to grant." In March,
the writ was accordingly served on the deputy-sheriff, by
whom Capes was detained; but, as he made no return thereto,
the lord chief justice issued a warrant for his apprehension,
which warrant was executed in May by one of his lordship's
tipstaffs, who was himself taken into custody for a short time,
and not permitted to bring the said deputy-sheriff from the
island. In consequence, the petitioners prayed the assistance
of the house for procuring the return of Capes, and for rendering the Habeas Corpus Act efficient.

The said James Streep and William Locker appear to have
been born in Guernsey, while their fathers were serving as
soldiers in the island during the war; and the parishes of
St. Peter-Port and the Vale, which were thus sought to be
charged with their maintenance, refused to receive them on

the plea that they had not acquired a legal settlement; the insular law being that the children of strangers, although born in the island, acquire no settlement unless they reside in it until they are of age.—Indeed, when we state that upwards of 50,000 British troops were successively quartered in Guernsey alone from 1793 to 1814, it must be evident that the maintenance of their necessitous offspring, who chanced to be born in the island, would be attended with ruinous consequences to the inhabitants; and as well might Gibraltar or Malta be similarly charged.

The lord chief justice having doubtless represented the *contempt* or denial of his authority to government, the royal court was directed by an order in council, dated June 11, 1832, to register an act passed in the fifty-sixth year of George III., viz. "An act for more effectually securing the liberty of the subject." A similar order was sent at the same time to Jersey, when the royal courts of both islands resolved to suspend such registry until the result of their representations on the subject was known; and at a meeting of the States of Guernsey convened for the occasion, the bailiff and king's procureur were deputed to proceed to London to make such representations; the bailiff and king's advocate of Jersey also proceeding thence for the same purpose.

Capes, the beadle, having, in March, given a pledge that he would not leave the island, remained at large in Guernsey until the early part of August; but, as he withdrew that pledge, and refused to give bail that the paupers should not become chargeable therein, he was committed to gaol, where however he remained only four days, from the 3d to the 7th of August.—Two days after his release, and before it was known in London, Mr. Hume, M.P. for Middlesex, who had presented the petition from St. Pancras, again brought forward the detention of Capes before the House of Commons; and, having expressed an intention of moving an address to the king for his liberation, he was informed by the hon. George Lamb, the under secretary of state for the home department, "that the authorities from Guernsey were then in London, and that they had written to the island for the man's discharge," when the matter dropped. Mr. Lamb, wishing to prevent a further discussion on the subject, as well as, doubtless, perceiving the injustice that was attempted to be inflicted on these islands, not only in compelling them to maintain paupers who had acquired no legal settlement, but in depriving them of their very dearest privilege—thus enforcing one wrong by another more cruel — had previously recommended, in a private interview with Mr. Brock, bailiff of Guernsey, that Capes should be immediately released and permitted to leave the island. The beadle embarked for England accordingly, accompanied, however, by the paupers he had brought with him in December; but their maintenance, during a sojourn of about eight months on the island, was not exacted. Although it will be seen from this statement that the question was got rid of by a species of compromise, and was not finally determined: yet the islands undoubtedly gained their point, as they neither became charged with the paupers, nor acknowledged the dependance of their courts on those of Westminster, nor registered the Habeas Corpus Act when directed to do so by an express order in council.

In a letter to the president of council, the deputies from the islands, when returning home, stated that one of the clauses in the Act of Habeas Corpus "would not apply to prisoners about to be tried in Jersey and Guernsey, where no assizes are proclaimed, and no judge of assize is sent, so that under the other provisions of the act a prisoner might immediately before his trial, nay, during the trial itself, obtain a writ, and thus impede the course of justice. Such a measure would, no doubt, be often had recourse to, when all other chances of avoiding punishment failed; and the criminal jurisdiction of the royal courts would be nugatory."

In October, 1832, Guernsey was visited by a short but very malignant attack of Asiatic cholera, which excited much consternation, and carried off, in a fortnight, about 100 persons, chiefly in the town of St. Peter-Port, and among the lower classes. A noble subscription of £1,558 1s. 5d. was raised by the inhabitants, and other individuals connected with Guernsey, for the relief of the indigent families of the victims. In Jersey, this dreadful epidemic appeared upwards of two months before it visited Guernsey, the first case occurring on the 6th of August, and it there raged about ten weeks, during which period it attacked 787 persons, and proved fatal to 341. The neighbouring islands of Alderney, Sark, Herm, and Jethou, happily escaped the pestilence.[1] The preceding sum was distributed as follows, strangers as well as natives, who died in Guernsey of the cholera, partaking in the benefit:

(1) In the summer of 1849, cholera again appeared in three of these islands, and the deaths thereby were about as follows: Jersey, 306; Guernsey, 80; and Alderney, 10.— In Guernsey, £758. 18s. 7d. were raised for the families of the victims.

Twenty-three widows, so made by the cholera, £10 each...£230	0	0
Sixty-four orphans, under 16 years of age, invested in the Savings' Bank for their benefit, £10 each......... } 640	0	0
Fifteen orphans, above 16 years of age, £5 each............ 75	0	0
Relief to casual sufferers.......................................455	4	6
Balance invested in Guernsey States' securities, at 3 ℔ cent. per annum interest.............ᴛ..................... } 157	16	11

£1,558 1 5

"In giving this statement," says Duncan, "it is proper to add, that the prominent features in the Guernsey character are a warm spirit of charity; strict frugality, occasionally bordering on parsimony; and extreme punctuality of payment." And in speaking of the case of Streep and Locker, the same author observes: "The parochial authorities of Guernsey, in common justice we are bound to state the fact, do, from pure motives of benevolence and humanity, voluntarily take on themselves the maintenance of many widows and children of Irish and other paupers, who die in the island, such widows and children having no legal or accessible place of settlement." Mr. Duncan, be it remembered, was an Englishman, who resided in Guernsey for a few years; and if the inhabitants are charitable at home, they are certainly quite as liberal for objects abroad.—In the year 1815, they, at that time, almost entirely native, and not exceeding 20,000 souls, raised above £1,500 for the gallant men who fell at Waterloo. In 1822, the same inhabitants subscribed about £700 for the relief of the Irish, "while," according to Chambers' Edinburgh Journal, April 18, 1840, "the land proprietors of one of the Irish counties, where the distress was experienced, could only raise £100." In 1831, upwards of £600 were again collected in Guernsey for the same purpose, and the following remarks appeared in an Irish newspaper, the Ballina Impartial, on the subject: "While with due gratitude we acknowledge the contributions transmitted from England, through the central committee, we feel ourselves especially bound to notice the transcendent liberality of the people of Guernsey. That island, though not exceeding thirty miles in circumference, has, in proportion to its extent, done more on behalf of the famishing poor of Mayo, than any other place from which relief has been furnished." In 1845, nearly £400 were subscribed in Guernsey, for the sufferers by the fire at Quebec; and, in 1846, £45 were collected in one congregation for the sufferers by the fire at St. John's, Newfoundland. During the famine in Ireland, of 1846-7, caused by the potatoe blight, Guernsey nobly stood forward with a subscription of nearly £3,000, besides a quantity of old clothing, for the relief of the starving-people there.—It moreover appears from a list given in Duncan's History, pages 367-9, that above £4,000 were annually raised in the island, in 1840, for religious and philanthropic institutions.

The system of parochial taxation which obtains in Guernsey is peculiar to the island, as all property, whether personal or real, in or out of the bailiwick, is assessed for local wants, with the sole exception of real estate in England and Jersey, as contributing there to the maintenance of the poor. In 1833, several of the wealthy parishioners of St. Peter-Port sought to overthrow this system, in an appeal to council, in the celebrated case of Carré William Tupper, esq., and others, *versus* the constables of the said town. The case may be briefly summed up thus : the appellants contended that an ordinance passed by the royal court in April, 1821, by which the annual tax had been raised, was illegal and inoperative, as not having been sanctioned by council ; and, moreover, that there was no law in Guernsey authorizing the assessment of British and foreign funds for parochial wants. The respondents answered, that the judgment of the royal court of the 23d February, 1833, by which the appellants had been sentenced to pay their proportion of the tax, was conformable to the ancient laws and customs of the bailiwick ; and also, even supposing that the present mode of rating required modification, which they denied, the law could not be altered by the royal court in its judicial capacity ; but that such change or modification must be obtained by application to the legislative authorities of the island ; and, in the event of redress being denied, by an appeal to council.—Part of this argument, however, was a mockery, seeing that the same body, which had passed the ordinance in 1821 in its legislative capacity, had decided on it judicially in 1833. Suffice it to add, that the lords of the privy council decided against the appellants, whose expenses amounted to nearly £2,000, including £600 paid by them for the costs of the parish, which were taxed at that sum, and yet the parish was a loser by nearly £200 ! Thus the long established system of taxation was happily confirmed, as all property, whether real or personal, should contribute to the maintenance of the poor ; but we conceive that the cost of the lamps, pavements, and tun-nels in St. Peter-Port, should be paid by a house rate, especially as many proprietors of houses, who reside out of the parish, are exempted from a burthen which so much enhances the value of their property.

The memorable corn questions of the year 1821 and 1835 now claim our attention. In 1821, an act of parliament was passed at the instigation of the landed interest, which prohibited the importation of foreign corn into the Channel Islands whenever its entry for consumption was prohibited in the United Kingdom; and the royal court of Guernsey was compelled, after much demur and a long delay, to register this act, the consequences of which would have proved fatal to the prosperity of the island, and caused its depopulation to a great extent, had not the obnoxious clause been repealed the following year through the exertions of Mr. Brock, the bailiff, and Mr. James Carey, jurat, who were deputed by the states to represent them on this vital question.

In 1834, it was generally asserted by the agriculturists in the west of England, that the privilege of importing corn, the growth of the Anglo-Norman Islands, into the United Kingdom, *free of duty*, had been abused; and Mr. Weston, the collector of the customs at Weymouth, was sent over to investigate the charge; but, on inquiry, he could not substantiate it. By some mistake in including all the corn, native and foreign, exported from Guernsey, not only to England, but to other countries, although the foreign wheat sent to England was cleared in Guernsey, and paid duty in England as such, the commissioners of customs stated in a report to the board of trade, that " it would appear that the quantity of wheat annually exported from Guernsey to the United Kingdom has exceeded the quantity grown in the island by upwards of 2,000 quarters." In consequence of this singularly erroneous statement, Mr. Baring, the president of the board of trade, brought a bill into parliament, in 1835, to deprive the islands of this, their ancient privilege; and deputies were named by both States to proceed to London to advocate its continuance, the one for Guernsey being Mr. Brock, the bailiff, and the two for Jersey, Colonel Le Couteur, and Mr. Le Breton, the attorney-general. Owing to their remonstrances, a select committee of the house of commons was appointed to inquire into the matter, before whom it was triumphantly proved that Guernsey, in place of exporting 2,000 quarters more than she grew, had only exported, of her own growth, 539 quarters out of 4,595 quarters annually grown! The bill was therefore withdrawn; but it was thought at the time, by many in these islands, that as the privilege excited the jealousy of the landed interest in England, and as it was of so little value to the inhabitants, its voluntary relinquishment would have been the better policy, the original intention of the grant being clearly perverted the moment that the consumption exceeded the production, and that foreign corn was required to replace the native wheat exported. The committee, already alluded to, published a very long report, dated the 17th of June, 1836, from which we extract the concluding paragraph :

"Upon a careful consideration of the whole subject, your committee see no reason to believe that the privilege possessed by the Channel Islands, of freely importing their produce into this country, has been made use of to any material extent, as a means of introducing foreign corn ; and they feel bound to add, that it is strenuously denied by the deputies from the islands, that it has thus been abused even in the smallest degree, and that their assertion has not been opposed by any direct proof; and your committee are therefore of opinion, that it would not be expedient to abrogate or infringe those privileges which are now enjoyed by the inhabitants of these islands, and which were conferred upon them in consideration of the signal services which, at various periods of our history, they have rendered to the crown and people of this country."

The abolition of the corn laws by Sir Robert Peel in 1846 has since set the question at rest, for as long as corn and other agricultural produce are admitted into England duty free, or nearly so, the privilege, which the islands still enjoy of importing their products into that kingdom free of duty, becomes of none effect.

CHAPTER XXII.

VICTORIA.—1837.

IN April, 1842, Major-General William Napier, C.B., the celebrated historian of the Peninsular War, was appointed lieutenant-governor of Guernsey ; and as the inhabitants felt proud at having an officer of his distinguished literary reputation placed over them, they received him with more than usual cordiality, deference, and respect. We may add here that Mrs. Napier,[1] who was a niece of the celebrated Charles James Fox, was from first to last an especial favorite, honored and esteemed by the upper classes for her talents and social virtues, and endeared to the poor by her charities. For about a year, matters went on smoothly, although it was quickly seen that the new lieutenant-governor possessed great vivacity of temper, which was ascribed to the continual suffering caused by very severe wounds and hard service : he spoke in public, as he wrote, well and fluently ; extolled the appearance and discipline of the militia ; and praised the mode of administering the laws and institutions of the island. But in the summer of 1843, differences unhappily arose between him and the royal court, which continued and kept the inhabitants for above four years in a state of feverish excitement and discontent. These differences occurred too recently to be described with historical impartiality ; but as this work would be incomplete without some account of their origin and progress, we shall narrate the leading facts as dispassionately and accurately as we can.

In June, 1843, General Napier—having been informed that a Frenchman of bad character, named Du Rocher, was then residing in Guernsey—directed one of the constables to arrest him, in order that he might be expelled from the island, the charge against him being not only that he had committed bigamy in Jersey, but that he had written, we believe, threatening letters to his victim there from Guernsey. Du Rocher, hearing that the police was in search of him, obtained an asylum under the roof of Mr. Orchard, an English resident, in whose family he was French preceptor, and there remained concealed. Le Conte, another Frenchman, an occasional gardener and servant of Mr. Orchard, was employed by his master to execute commissions for Du Rocher ; and the police, ascertaining this, questioned him, when he returned evasive but respectful answers. Du Rocher left the island in August ; and the lieutenant-governor caused Le Conte to be imprisoned, on the plea of his having " annoyed the constable in the execution of his duty," his sole offence being that he had refused to betray a fellow-countryman and his master's secrets. On being released the next morning, the constable, by order of his excellency, informed

(1) Mrs. (now Lady) Napier is the daughter of the Hon. General Fox, and the granddaughter of the first Lord Holland. She has inherited the appearance and the talents of her race.

Le Conte that he must leave the island, a few days being allowed him to settle his affairs, and he obeyed quietly, making no appeal to the civil power; while the constable, who chanced to be a militia inspector in receipt of government pay, did not, as is customary, report the case to the bailiff and the crown officers. Mr. Orchard was more culpable than Le Conte; but, being an Englishman, he was not molested.

This expulsion, becoming known through the local press, created much ferment, and was warmly condemned as harsh and cruel. The royal court—having ascertained from the constable that he had acted under the orders of the lieutenant-governor, and conceiving that both had exceeded their authority—sought a friendly and constitutional conference with his excellency on the subject. When, accordingly, the magistrates attended by appointment at his private residence, they were received with studied formality: on reaching the house, a sergeant's guard saluted them, and, on being ushered in between the sentries on each side of the entrance, they were shewn into a room which was vacant. After a short time, the folding doors of the adjoining room were thrown open, and the lieutenant-governor was discovered in his full uniform, and seated, with a small table near him, on which was his military hat; in the back ground were the fort-major, and the constable as militia inspector, both in uniform; the government secretary; and the guests of the house, Mr. Roebuck, M.P. for Bath, and Mr. Popham, who certainly had no business there; at a respectful distance in the rear were the procureur and comptroller, who had preceded the court by half an hour. All, with the exception of the lieutenant-governor, were standing, and the room was without a seat, save that occupied by him! The bailiff, on entering, went forward towards his excellency, who rose to receive him; and the rest of the court, following the bailiff, made their obeisance to the lieutenant-governor, he and all remaining standing. On the bailiff adverting to the subject of the interview, the lieutenant-governor interrupted him by saying that he would only communicate with the court through the bailiff, and would not allow the jurats to take part in the conference. Some demur being expressed at this, the bailiff was told that he and his colleagues had better return to the courthouse; and after they had considered the matter, another interview might take place. The bailiff then proposed that they should retire for a few minutes into another room to consult in private; and there the magistrates unanimously decided to reject the lieutenant-governor's terms, as contrary to all precedent. So unusual and offensive a reception only served to widen the breach between the lieutenant-governor and the royal court; while the native inhabitants, almost to a man, took part with the latter, conceiving that the insult thus offered to the highest civil authority was a general one.

Next came the case of Fossey. On new year's evening, 1844, a party of nine soldiers of the 48th dépôt casually met on the highway, and most violently assaulted, an Englishman, named Clark, as also his wife. The injuries sustained by Clark were such that his medical attendant at first declared upon oath before the royal court that he could not answer for his life, which however in a few days he pronounced out of danger. Fossey was the only culprit who could be identified; and on Saturday, January 20, he was condemned to *two* months' imprisonment, whereof the first and last fortnight solitary and on bread and water. The next day, without making the slightest inquiry of the bailiff or the law officers of the crown, General Napier wrote to Sir James Graham, the home secretary of state; and the result was a free pardon from the queen, " in consideration of some circumstances humbly represented unto us." On receipt of this pardon, in place of having it first verified and recorded by the royal court, as customary, Major-General Napier proceeded, accompanied by his staff, to the gaol on the 15th of February, and demanded the instant liberation of Fossey. The gaoler hesitating to comply without consulting his superior, the sheriff, the lieutenant-governor threatened to effect the release by military force, and for that purpose dispatched an officer to Fort George for troops, whereupon the gaoler submitted and liberated the convict. Not satisfied, however, with this submission, Major-General Napier prosecuted the gaoler before the royal court for disrespect of her majesty's warrant, when the gaoler was unanimously acquitted.

These two acts of Major-General Napier drew forth two petitions from the royal court to the sovereign in council, which were supported by a humble memorial of the inhabitants. The court prayed that in any conference with the lieutenant-governor the jurats should, as heretofore, take part; that any alien domiciled in Guernsey, not being a dangerous person, and charged only with a private offence, should not be liable to be deported without trial; and that Major-General Napier should be directed to regulate his future government of the island conformably to its laws, cus-

toms, and chartered rights; as also that he should not exercise
martial jurisdiction contrary to the usual course of justice,
except in time of war, or for the prevention of some imminent
danger. But the wide-world reputation of Major-General
Napier as an author was such, and his interest with the government was so great, that it was quickly seen that a small
and powerless community like that of Guernsey had undertaken an almost hopeless task in endeavouring to prove that
he had been wanting in common judgment and discretion;
for throughout these and the subsequent differences Sir James
Graham identified himself with the lieutenant-governor, and
now insisted that the complaints against one of his subordi-
nates should in the first instance be made through him as
secretary of state for the home department, and not to the
privy council. Lord Wharncliffe, the president of that body,
however, over-ruled this pretension, and agreed to receive
the petitions and memorial, thereby acknowledging the ancient rights of the islanders to lay their grievances directly
before council. But by some official contrivance, Major-
General Napier, who was the party accused, was taken out
of the cause, and the crown substituted in his place, which
proceeding rendered it very difficult, if not impossible, for the
lords of council to enter into the real merits of the points in
dispute; moreover, during the whole of the hearing of the
cause, which lasted five days, Sir James Graham found time
to be present, and that he influenced the judgment there was
little doubt. By that judgment, January 13, 1845, their
lordships ruled that the lieutenant-governor had the right of
deporting aliens without the consent of the royal court, but
that the jurats were entitled to take part in any conference.
As regards the case of Fossey, it was decided that the gaoler
ought to have discharged the prisoner on the production of
the royal pardon; but that as the gaoler was not the servant
of the lieutenant-governor, the latter " was not warranted in
enforcing obedience to the writ by the threat of military or
other force." This judgment, to obtain which the island was
saddled with heavy expenses, gave very limited satisfaction:
in our opinion, it was of little consequence whether the jurats
could speak in a conference or whether the queen's pardon
required to be verified by the royal court, but it signified
much that an unoffending alien should not be lightly deported, in time of profound peace, at the whim or caprice of any
one man, albeit the lieutenant-governor of Guernsey—an
appointment held in the last century by officers of humble

rank and pretensions ; and we should sadly belie our liberal principles, we should indeed repudiate our ardent love of general liberty, if we did not warmly and indignantly protest against the decision of council on this memorable occasion. That decision was a worthy pendant of the vile one which, in the reign of James I , authorized the governor to imprison for twenty-four hours without accountability, "it not being then thought meet that he should be restrained to commit any islander to prison upon such cause as he (the governor) should think to have justly deserved imprisonment"!

The statement in answer to the two petitions from Guernsey was signed by J. A. Roebuck and H. Waddington, but the conclusion bears unmistakeable evidence of its being written by the author of the Peninsular War—it is as follows :

"Thus, when the lieutenant-governor receives the bailiff and jurats in form, he treats not so much his sovereign with respect as them with disrespect.

"But when he does not class the royal court with *all others*, and does not thereupon require it do what its sovereign commands him, by his name of office, to do *forthwith*, he still treats them with disrespect.

"If he refuse the aid of soldiers to the civil authorities, when they ought not to require it,[1] he gives way to riot, and *inflicts the violence of unrestrained mobs on the inhabitants.*

"But when unaided, and obstructed by a civil functionary bound to obey him, he talks of requiring the aid of soldiers, *he recurs to martial law.*

"When he legally executes a legal and royal warrant, as directed thereby, he *alters and abolishes existing legal forms.*

"But when he has recourse to law, he *is far from acknowledging the irregularity of his conduct, and perseveres in wrong.* And when, as legally required, he *forthwith* sets free a pardoned prisoner, he infringes the privileges and liberties of the island.

"From this latter charge the character and habits of the lieutenant-governor will defend, if the law did not justify, him ; for he, with others, has endured much in war, that the liberties of all might not be overwhelmed ; and now he is endeavouring to liberate the numerous English inhabitants, and those, he hopes not few, natives of Guernsey, who do not view the acts or expressions of the royal court without concern, from the miserable servitude of vague and undefined law. Nor have the pursuits of the lieutenant-governor, in time of peace, rendered him insensible to the early history of a warlike people, nor uninterested in, and un-

(1) Previous to General Napier's arrival, the constables occasionally required and received the aid of the garrison in securing offenders ; but he issued an order, by which the troops were not to be so employed without his express sanction.

mindful of, the claims of their descendants, over whom his sovereign has placed him.

"But if there were no associations in history, nor connection between the English and Norman races, the lieutenant-governor would not require any other motive for performing his duty than that such was his duty. For this reason, in defence, not in disregard of liberty, he has asserted his rights as the representative of the sovereign of Guernsey, while he has denied what he thought were undue claims of the royal court, and he has thereby subjected himself to (he trusts, a temporary) misunderstanding, and to the hasty and passing condemnation of some whose good word, in favour of these his legitimate exercises of authority, will not be refused, when reflection shall have had its opportunity, and the decision of her majesty in council shall have settled the questions in dispute."

Major-General Napier was not a man to retrace his steps or to make the slightest concession, and it soon became evident that there could be no peace or cordiality between him and the civil authorities. But, nothing worthy of mention occurred until Monday, May 20, 1844, when her majesty's steam frigate Dee arrived early from Portsmouth, bringing a queen's messenger, who immediately landed and delivered his despatches to the lieutenant-governor. A few hours later another steam frigate, bearing the awful name of Blazer, also anchored in the roadstead, her decks being crowded with troops; and the next morning her majesty's brig Nautilus arrived with more troops, as did the Atalanta steamer on Wednesday; the entire number consisting of about 600 men of the dépôts of the 23d, 42d, 97th, and 2d battalion rifle brigade, from Parkhurst barracks, in the Isle of Wight. Never shall we forget the amazement of the inhabitants at this large accession of force; some supposing that England had suddenly declared war against France, and others that the troops were to guard Daniel O'Connell, who was to be incarcerated in Castle Cornet, as Burton and General Lambert had been; but it afterwards transpired that they had been hurriedly dispatched to quell an insurrection of the islanders against the lieutenant-governor, and moreover that a wing of the 49th regiment at Winchester had received orders to hold itself in readiness for the same purpose!! General Napier publicly denied all previous knowledge of the coming of these troops; but certain it is that his representations, although they may have been misunderstood, were the cause of their being sent.—On the 15th of May, a young gentleman of the Câtel parish died, and on the 20th, just as the funeral was about to leave the house, a *post mortem* examination of the corpse took place, either by order or at the request of the lieutenant-governor, who it seems had received private information that the deceased had been poisoned, lest he should divulge a conspiracy which had been formed to assassinate Major-General Napier; but the result proved that he died from natural causes. In consequence of this information, the militia was prevented from assembling as usual to celebrate the queen's birth-day on the 24th of May, lest a chance bullet or ramrod might do the work of the conspirators; and yet the lieutenant-governor rode or walked about unattended, and had no guard at his private residence.—Soon afterwards three country gentlemen, two of them officers of the militia, were placed on their trial before the royal court, by orders of Sir James Graham, for a participation in the alleged conspiracy, when, after a searching investigation, they were fully acquitted, Major-General Napier, it was asserted, having previously attempted to stifle all inquiry into this vile accusation. In the mean time, the "army of occupation," as we called it, left the island after the stay of about a month; and never was an expedition dispatched from any country on a more ridiculous errand, the authorities in England, and we believe the lieutenant-governor himself, being heartily ashamed of it. Indeed, we may safely assert that the militia of Guernsey, with whom General Napier was at first highly popular, would rather have formed a rampart of their dead bodies for the security of his person than entered into any design against his life.

Next came the grand demonstration of the islanders, which was held on Tuesday, July 2, on the New Ground, and at which from 12 to 13,000 persons assembled to vote certain resolutions, of which the first was as follows:

"1. That imputations having been recently thrown upon the loyalty of the inhabitants of this island, an humble and dutiful address be presented to her most gracious majesty, expressive of the sorrow which has thereby been occasioned to the said inhabitants, and assuring her majesty of their devoted and unaltered loyalty to her majesty's person and government."

This and the other resolutions were carried by acclamation, and during the proceedings, which occupied about two hours, not only were some excellent speeches delivered by both natives and strangers, but there was in the vast assemblage an intensity of feeling and a spirit of devotion which proved beyond all doubt that the people of Guernsey were sincerely

attached to the British crown; while the triumphal arches,
festoons, flags, and various mottos and devices, also testified
to their unswerving loyalty. The meeting was presided over
by the venerable General Sir Thomas Saumarez, and the
address, signed by 5,684 adult males, was taken to London
by himself; but as there was no prospect of an early levee,
it was presented to the queen through Sir James Graham,
who declared that he was not aware of any imputation of
disloyalty having been cast upon the inhabitants *generally!*
In August, " the suspension of the militia parades and reviews, which had taken place in pursuance of an order emanating directly from her majesty," was removed, having lasted
about three months; and the several regiments, by command
of the secretary of state, assembled on the 12th, at Fort
George, to fire a *feu de joie* for the birth of an infant prince.
In September, the States of Guernsey voted an address to
the queen, for the purpose of vindicating the inhabitants from
the imputations of disloyalty and sedition which had been
cast upon them; and, in acknowledging its receipt, Sir James
Graham directed his secretary to say, that " he had never
failed to entertain the strongest and most confident reliance
in the general loyalty and good feeling of the people of
Guernsey." If so, why were 600 men sent over a few months
previously?—the garrison and the militia would surely have
been able to put down a few seditious spirits, had there been
any, which we confidently deny.

Such was to Guernsey the eventful year of 1844; and
although it was evident that there could be no peace as long
as Major-General Napier remained in the island, yet his
government was continued for three years longer! It would
be tedious to describe all the heart-burnings during that time;
and therefore, passing over the lieutenant-governor's quarrels
with three of the jurats as personal to themselves, and other
minor acts, we shall only mention the dismissal of Captain
Guerin, of the 1st or east regiment of militia, in December,
1845, on the plea that it was not expedient for the public
service that he should continue to hold a commission. When
that officer asked for the reasons of his dismissal, which reduced him to the ranks, they were refused him; and his
appeal to Sir James Graham to the same effect was made in
vain! Sir James, however, issued an order that no officer in
the militia in any of these islands should be dismissed in future
" without the express sanction of the secretary of state;" thus
significantly condemning the dismissal just mentioned. This

order was kept secret in Guernsey until May, 1848, when it was published by Major-General Bell. In a case in Upper Canada, almost parallel to that of Captain Guerin, in 1836, shortly before the outbreak there, an officer of the militia was dismissed by Sir Francis Head, whereupon that officer made an appeal to Lord Glenelg, the colonial secretary of state, and Sir Francis was commanded to reinstate him; his lordship at the same time observing, "that every consideration must yield to the irresistible claims of justice;" whereas Sir James Graham in effect declared that every consideration must yield to the claims of favouritism! And yet the Canadian officer was supposed to be disloyal, and had told Sir Francis Head, after his dismissal, that his statements were "altogether untrue;" but, on the other hand, Canada was strong, and Guernsey was weak and defenceless. Two lieutenant-colonels and five captains of the Guernsey militia, prefering to carry a musket to holding their rank under so degrading and precarious a tenure, resigned their commissions when they found that all redress was denied to Captain Guerin: one of these officers was Lieut.-Colonel Henry Tupper, who had lost two brothers, four uncles, and three first cousins, by the bullet, and two brothers in the wave; total, *eleven* near relatives prematurely cut off, and many of them in the public service. Whether on account of these claims we know not, Lieut.-Colonel Tupper was not made to serve as a private as long as Major-General Napier remained in the island, on the plea that the uniforms in store were too small for him, but after his departure one was quickly found; and when Major-General Bell first reviewed all the militia on the New Ground, *private* Henry Tupper was the right hand grenadier of the 1st or east regiment; in other words, *le premier grenadier*, not of France, but of Guernsey. We mention this exemption from service for about two years in justice to General Napier, conceiving it to be honourable to him, especially as Mr. Tupper was his warm opponent. Suffice it to add, that one of the first acts of his successor, we believe at the request of Sir George Grey, was to reinstate with the same rank Captain Guerin and the seven officers who had resigned — a second tacit condemnation of the dismissal of Captain Guerin.

At length, in June, 1846, Lord John Russell succeeded Sir Robert Peel as premier; and in this change of ministry Sir James Graham was replaced by Sir George Grey, whose grandfather, the first Earl Grey, was governor of Guernsey from 1797 to 1807. It soon appeared that General Napier

2D

had lost his influence at the Home Office; but he remained
in the island until the close of the following year, when
it is understood that his written and oral communications
became so offensive to Sir George Grey, that the latter insisted on his removal with the Duke of Wellington, then
commander-in-chief.   He was accordingly succeeded, early
in 1848, by Major-General Bell; but many of his opponents
in Guernsey were not sorry to learn that his removal had
been softened by the colonelcy of the 27th regiment and a
knight commandership of the Bath—distinctions which his
undying history and gallant services unquestionably merited.
When General Napier first arrived in Guernsey, it was our
hope that, as he was a liberal reformer, he would suggest and
promote the necessary changes in the feudal and worn-out
institutions of the island, and, above all, that he would seek
to give the people their just influence in the States, or insular
parliament, seeing that the royal court and clergy are all
powerful in that assembly, and the people powerless.[1] This,
indeed, would have been a work as worthy of his genius as
the expulsion of Le Conte and the dismissal of Captain Guerin
were beneath it; the one would have made all lovers of
constitutional freedom in the island his friends, as the other
made them his uncompromising adversaries. It is painful[2] to
write thus of the government of an officer whose peninsular
history has afforded us so much enjoyment, whose colloquial
powers we have listened to with pleasure, and, above all, whose
"fighting" family has done the state so much service; but to
have said less than we have would have been a pusillanimous
evasion of our duty as an historian.

In September, 1844, Mr. F. C. Lukis—in examining the
remarkable cromlech of Du Tus or Du Hus,[3] situate near
Paradis, in the Vale parish, Guernsey—discovered, on opening
one of the compartments, two skeletons "in a vertical kneeling posture," placed "side by side, but in opposite directions."
"The teeth and jaws were well preserved, and denoted an
adult rather than an old age."   "The skeletons appeared to
be about the same size, and were those of men."   Mr. Lukis
adds : "The perfectly regular position of a person kneeling
on a floor in an upright posture, with the arms following the

(1) The States of Deliberation are thus composed : royal court, 14; rectors, 8; deputies
of the douzaines, 15; total, 37.

(2) The more so, as when Mr. Brock, the bailiff, died, General Napier evinced, in a
manner as creditable to his feelings as it was gratifying to the family of the deceased, an
anxious desire to pay every respect to his memory.

(3) See Archæological Journal for April, 1845.

direction of the column, pelvis, and thigh bones, and gradually surrounded by the earth, in like manner as may be conceived would be done were persons buried alive, will give an exact representation of this singular discovery."

Visit of Queen Victoria, in 1846.—On Sunday evening, August 23, at about six o'clock, a squadron of four steamers, one of them bearing the royal standard, was descried from St. Peter-Port off Jerbourg point, and soon after these vessels cast anchor in the roadstead. The squadron, which had left Plymouth in the morning, consisted of the royal yacht Victoria and Albert, with her tender the Fairy, and the Black Eagle and Garland. On board the first, commanded by Captain Lord Adolphus Fitzclarence, were her majesty, Prince Albert, her consort, and the young Prince of Wales and Princess Royal. A royal salute was quickly fired from Fort George, and the news of the queen's arrival spread with the rapidity of lightning, penetrating even into the churches and chapels, then filled with their respective congregations. The heights and piers were soon crowded with spectators; and at dusk the houses in sight of the royal yacht were illuminated. In the mean time the lieutenant-governor, Major-General Napier, went on board the Victoria and Albert, when her majesty's commands were conveyed to him through Lord Alfred Paget. On his return to the pier, shortly before nine o'clock, he announced to the assembled crowds that the queen, desirous of seeing her subjects in Guernsey, and of giving them an opportunity of seeing her, would land at nine o'clock the next morning, proceed in her carriage to take a cursory view of the island, and re-embark at eleven. This announcement was received with enthusiastic cheers; and many retired only to spend the night in hurried preparations for the morrow; the militia officers especially being engaged in warning their men. Indeed, few allowed themselves their usual rest; and in the country every man, woman, and child, who was able to move, was on foot at daybreak; while the town was alive at a very early hour with persons busily at work in decorating the streets and houses with flags, crowns, garlands, mottos, &c. The vessels in the harbour and roadstead were dressed in their gayest attire, as were the signal staffs at Castle Cornet and Fort George.

At half-past seven, a.m., the royal court met and prepared an address of congratulation and homage, which was presented to her majesty on landing, it being previously intimated that as none of her ministers were on board, the queen would not answer the address until after her return to England.

The five militia regiments assembled under arms at Choisi at six o'clock, not a single man, who was able to attend, being absent. The dépôt of the 27th regiment was stationed at the south slip, where the royal standard was erected, and furnished the guard of honor; and next to them were the militia, who continued the line through High and Smith streets, and up the Grange road, the troops together amounting to about 2,500 men. But the most interesting part of the preparations was an assemblage of some seventy young ladies, belonging to the principal families, who, mostly arrayed in white and carrying in their hands baskets of flowers, were stationed close to the landing place, and presented a group of great beauty and attraction.

The queen and the prince embarked in the royal barge a few minutes before nine, under a salute from Fort George, and were accompanied by Lord A. Fitzclarence, steering; Lord Alfred Paget; the Viscountess Jocelyn; Hon. Miss Napier; Sir James Clarke, her majesty's physician; and G. E. Anson, Esq., Prince Albert's secretary. The day was every thing that could be desired, fine and clear, so that the sea and land views were seen to advantage; and as the barge was pulled towards the pier, some thirty pleasure boats under sail followed her, the wind being easterly: this and the landing[1] were the most striking parts of the spectacle. Her majesty was received by the authorities, and as she stepped on shore the young ladies before mentioned commenced singing the national anthem, accompanied by the band of the 27th dépôt. The queen, leaning on Prince Albert's arm, walked on carpeting to her carriage, the young ladies strewing flowers at her feet, and she was followed by her attendants and the authorities.

As the royal barge approached and entered the pier, the queen was greeted with loud demonstrations of joy and gratitude: the guns at Fort George were still firing, the church bells were ringing, the several bands were playing the national anthem, and thousands of voices were sending forth hurrahs of delight, her majesty and the prince cordially acknowledging by bows and smiles these marks of enthusiasm and welcome. Never before had so inspiring a scene been witnessed in Guernsey, and never before was a sovereign received with warmer proofs of affection. But had there been more time,

(1) A handsome stone, with an inscription, now commemorates the spot where the queen landed.

the salutes should have been given from Castle Cornet, as all salutes were during the last war, when the sound boomed over the waters and was heard throughout the town. The seemingly stifled report of some small cannon at Fort George ill accorded with the vociferous but respectful acclamations of the islanders; and the truly exciting scene of the royal landing and embarkation would have been rendered still more imposing—and yet most imposing it was—had the fair queen of these isles been saluted from the fortress which recalls so many deeds of gallantry, and is pregnant with so many historical associations.

The queen and prince, with Lady Jocelyn and Miss Napier, having entered the first royal carriage, a barouche drawn by four horses, and the attendants in another royal carriage, the royal party proceeded round the south side of the town church up High street, Smith street, the Grange road, Petite Marche, (now Queen's road,) down what is now Prince Albert's road, and up Colborne road to Fort George, being every where greeted with loud cheers. The royal *cortège* then continued through the fort, passed Sausmarez manor and St. Martin's church, the Ville au Roi, Mount Row, and the Grange, back to the south pier, at the steps of which, near the light-house, the queen entered the royal barge at about half-past ten, the fall of the tide preventing her embarking where she had landed. Both piers and Glatney esplanade were lined by the 27th dépôt and the militia, and as the barge was pulled off, the guns of Fort George again saluted, the bands struck up " God save the Queen," and the assembled multitudes, gentle and simple, expressed their feelings in loud and continued cheers, which were recognized by her majesty in a manner which seemed to declare that she believed and appreciated their sincerity. The royal squadron left the roadstead soon after eleven, a.m.; and, passing through the Swinge, Alderney at the same time greeting the queen with a salute, arrived at Cowes the same evening before nine o'clock. The royal children did not land; but while the queen was on shore, the Prince of Wales fished and hooked a whiting, the first tenant of the deep he had ever caught.

On entering High street, the queen and prince appeared agreeably struck with the profuse display of decorations there, and with the numberless happy faces which were beaming welcome on them from the houses. On approaching Fort George, the prince seemed delighted with the beauty of the surrounding scenery, and he inquired the names of the islands in sight. When the coast of Normandy and Cape La Hague were pointed out to him, he spoke to the queen, who appeared equally delighted at seeing the cape from which a great naval battle takes its name. Although Edward IV. and William IV. came to Guernsey before they ascended the throne, we believe that Queen Victoria is the first reigning sovereign of England who ever landed on the island, King John's visit being, as we have shewn, more than doubtful. The royal presence was so unexpected, that no preparations were made for it, and consequently the demonstrations of joy, of devotion, and of loyalty, were spontaneous and imperfect, but there was a hearty good will among all, an evidence of gratification which could not be mistaken; and if her majesty's reception was less costly and ceremonious than that of Jersey, ten days later, its deficiencies were more than compensated by its cordiality. The people of Guernsey felt doubly grateful to the queen for appearing among them at a time when, in consequence of differences with the lieutenant-governor, imputations had been cast upon their loyalty; and the wounded feelings of the islanders, from 600 armed men being suddenly sent over in 1844 to dragoon them into submission, were soothed from the moment her majesty landed.[1]

It was considered very significant that, when Major-General Napier went on board the yacht on Sunday evening, he was not received by the queen, whereas in Jersey her majesty on arrival received Colonels Dixon and Le Breton, as the representatives of the lieutenant-governor, Major-General Sir Edward Gibbs, who from wounds and infirmities was incapable of going off in person. It was probably Sir George Grey, who suggested to the queen that her presence in Guernsey would test the charges of sedition and disloyalty which had been so cruelly brought against its inhabitants.

In the afternoon, the following order was issued:

" The lieutenant-governor, Major-General Napier, is happy to be able to communicate to the royal artillery, to her majesty's 27th regiment, to the royal Guernsey militia, and to the inhabitants generally, that her majesty, at the moment of re-embarkation, personally expressed to the lieutenant-governor her pleasure at the reception she had met with, and her entire satisfaction with the arrangements made.

(1) " Our sovereign came with healing in her hand. The rays of kindness shed from the royal presence, have dissipated all the clouds that lowered on our land. The insult of *the six hundred soldiers* is effaced; the tales of conspiracy and disaffection, got up by miserable slanderers, are sent back with contumely to the bosom of their authors; truth, so long and so sedulously concealed, has been brought to light by the sovereign herself; and Guernsey once more stands erect in the presence of its queen, rejoicing in the recognition of its fidelity, and smiling with scorn on its baffled enemies."—*Guernsey Star*, Sept. 2, 1846. The editor of the *Star* and author of this extract is an English gentleman.

"These are nearly her majesty's words, and the lieutenant-governor feels that it would be presumptuous to add any thing beyond his congratulations upon such a distinguished honour.

"Havilland Hall, August 24, 1846."

On Monday, the 31st of August, the inhabitants of Guernsey were assembled on the New Ground, in virtue of an invitation to that effect issued by the lieutenant-governor, when his excellency read to them the following letter:

"Whitehall, August 28, 1846.

"Sir,—I have the honour to inform you that I have received the queen's most gracious commands to take the earliest opportunity of expressing to you, as lieutenant-governor of Guernsey, her sense of the affectionate loyalty with which her majesty was received upon the occasion of her late visit to that island. The feelings of attachment and devotion to her majesty's person and government, so conspicuously exhibited upon that occasion by the inhabitants of Guernsey, have been, I am commanded to assure you, peculiarly gratifying to her majesty; and I am to request that you will, as lieutenant-governor of the island, make known these her majesty's sentiments to her faithful subjects there.

"I beg to offer you my congratulations upon your having witnessed the loyal demonstrations which have called forth this gracious expression of her majesty's sentiments, and imposed upon you a duty which, upon every account, must be gratifying to your feelings.   "I have the honour to be, sir,

"Your obedient servant,

"Major-General Napier, &c. &c."   "G. GREY.

The inhabitants of Guernsey being naturally desirous of commemorating her majesty's visit, as just narrated, a subscription was set on foot for that purpose; and on the 9th of December, 1846, a meeting of the subscribers was held in St. Peter-Port, when it being reported that the contributions amounted to nearly £1,200, it was unanimously resolved to erect a tower on the spot occupied by the New Ground mill, the site having been gratuitously offered by the heirs of the late Peter Mourant, Esq. The Victoria Tower has since been erected, at a cost of above £2,000.—The following letters best continue the subject, and are well worthy of being preserved:

"Government House, Guernsey, May 27, 1848.

"Sir,—I cannot deny myself the pleasure of acquainting you with certain proceedings which took place here this day, being that fixed for the celebration of her majesty's birth-day.

"The corner stone of a very handsome tower, to be erected in commemoration of the queen's most welcome visit to Guernsey in the year 1846, and to be called the Victoria Tower, was laid by me in presence of the bailiff, and all the island authorities, militia, and a very large proportion of the island population.

" I cannot in adequate terms describe the spirit of loyalty and good feeling which appeared to pervade the whole assemblage, nor do I believe that within the wide range of her majesty's dominions there exists a more loyal and well-disposed people.

" New colours were afterwards presented by me, in her majesty's name, to the four infantry regiments of the royal Guernsey militia, and were received with every demonstration of gratitude and attachment to her crown and person.

" I do not venture to expect that any notification of these proceedings should be laid before the queen ; but there is so great and striking a difference between the mere passing of a loyal address by a corporate or other small body of men, and the spontaneous, enthusiastic expression of the same feeling by many assembled thousands, that I cannot but hope the events of this day will indirectly, if not otherwise, be brought within her majesty's knowledge.

" To you, sir, as well as to myself, they possess a real interest which will, I trust, render it unnecessary for me to offer any apology for having thus addressed you on the occasion.

" I have the honour to be, &c.

(Signed) " John Bell, Lieut.-Governor.

"The Right Hon. Sir G. Grey, Bart., &c. &c."

" Whitehall, May 31, 1848.

" Sir,—I have had the honour of laying before the queen your letter of the 27th instant, conveying to me the gratifying account of the proceedings which took place in Guernsey on the occasion of the celebration of her majesty's birth-day.

" I am commanded to express to you her majesty's deep sense of this new proof of the loyalty and attachment of her faithful and excellent people of Guernsey ;[1] and I am to state that it will afford her majesty great satisfaction to be able, on some future occasion, again to visit the island.

" I have the honour to be, sir,

" Your obedient servant,

" George Grey.

" Major-General Bell, &c. &c., Guernsey."

In September, 1846, two royal commissioners, T. F. Ellis and T. Bros, Esqs., barristers at law, arrived in Guernsey from Jersey, having been appointed by the queen to inquire

(1) We have the best reasons for believing that these were the queen's own words to the secretary of state, when her majesty directed him to acknowledge the communication of Major-General Bell.

into the criminal laws of the Channel Islands. Their report, minutes of evidence, records, &c., relating to the bailiwick, occupy no less than 390 folio pages; so that it is utterly impossible for us to give even a digest of the same, which however is the less material as very few of their recommendations have as yet been carried out, or seem at present likely to be. The following extracts from the report are interesting:

"The criminal law of Guernsey is derived from sources similar to those pointed out in our first report, as the origin of the criminal law in Jersey; namely, first, the customary law; secondly, the charters; thirdly, the orders of the sovereign in council; fourthly, the ordinances of the local legislature; fifthly, certain statutes of the realm.

"The royal court claim and have exercised, from the beginning of the fifteenth century, the right of acting as a legislative body at certain courts, called Chefs Plaids. The royal court consists of the bailiff and twelve jurats. The Chefs Plaids are held three times in the year: on the first Monday after the 15th January; the first Monday after Easter week; and the first Monday after the 29th of September. The bailiff and at least seven jurats, with the procureur and contrôle de la reine, constitute these courts. The governor, also, has the right to be present; the crown vassals attend to do homage; and one of the constables of each parish is also bound to appear, by virtue of an ordinance of the Chefs Plaids made in the early part of the present century. The law is, in fact, always proposed by the law officers of the crown. The enacting power rests with the bailiff and jurats alone, after hearing the conclusions of the law officers; if the votes be equally balanced, the bailiff has a casting vote, besides his original vote. But the constables have the right of making observations in favour or disapproval of any proposition submitted to the court. Private individuals also, whose interests are likely to be affected by the proposed law, may be heard in person or by counsel against it. The governor possesses no veto; but, in the event of any provision affecting his rights or duties, it is usual to submit it to him for his approval prior to its being proposed; and, although his consent is not necessary to its enactment, it would probably, in the absence of such consent, be disallowed by the privy council on his complaint. The laws so passed are called Ordonnances. They take effect by the mere power of the royal court without the intervention or approbation of the lords of your majesty's privy council, or the assent of your majesty's governor in the island, or the concurrence of the general body of the people.

"The origin of a power so extensive is not clearly ascertained, nor the limits within which it can be lawfully exercised accurately defined. We were referred to an article contained in an order in council, of the date of 1568, as the earliest recognition of this right by the crown.

"The jurats, in an answer transmitted to the privy council on the 10th of January, 1737, thus define the powers of the royal court: 'We never pretended to be invested with the power and authority of making laws, and it is what neither we nor our predecessors before us ever assumed ; but we beg to acquaint your lordships that this court has always, as well by the nature of our constitution as by virtue of sundry charters from the crown, and other express orders in council, deemed itself authorized and empowered to make regulations, and set down such rules and methods as were necessary for enforcing and putting in due execution the laws of the island.' The practice, however, has greatly exceeded these limits.

"It has already been stated that all laws, exceeding the limit within which the ordinances of the royal court are confined, require the confirmation of your majesty in council. This extends to laws passed by the States of the island, as distinguished from ordinances of the royal court in Chefs Plaids.

"The history of the States is involved in much obscurity. It is probable that they originally were constituted on the model of the Trois Etats in Normandy ; the bailiff and jurats corresponding with the noblesse ; the rectors of the parishes answering to the clergy ; and the douzaines, an elected body in each parish, representing the Tiers Etat.

"We have described at length the legislative functions of the court, sitting in Chefs Plaids. Powers so extensive and undefined appear to us inconsistent with the legislative powers exercised over the bailiwick by your majesty in council, and irreconcileable with any thing like popular principles.

"According to the theory of the Guernsey constitution, the jurats may on one day, sitting in a court of Chefs Plaids, make an ordonnance without the consent of your majesty, against the will of the functionary representing the crown in the island, and without consulting the body of the States ; and, on the next, sitting as a court of justice, may proceed to put their own construction on it and to execute the law of their own making, without their decision, in any matter of criminal law, being capable of review by any superior authority. It would be consistent with the due exercise of the legislative power that the States should frame laws for the island, subject to your majesty's concurrence. But it is contrary to the ordinary exercise of your majesty's high prerogative that the legislative power, which in Guernsey resides in the crown, should be delegated to one of the three estates of the island so as to render that body capable of enacting laws without your majesty's concurrence. This power of the royal court in Guernsey could have had no legal origin except from a grant by the sovereign. It seems to us doubtful whether it must not, from its nature, be referred to usurpation. But, at any rate, we submit to your majesty that it would more properly be confided to the whole body of the States, and that it ought not to be permitted to rest in the royal court.[1]

" In suggesting the changes which we think expedient, it is our desire not to interfere unnecessarily with existing institutions which long habit has rendered congenial to the inhabitants, and which their want of intercourse with other countries causes them to value, in our opinion, above their real worth. We are anxious not to offend even the prejudices of a people who are devotedly attached to your majesty's person and government, who are for the most part satisfied with the existing state of things, and who do not feel the force of many of the objections which strike us as of the greatest moment. The island does not as yet present the same party struggle which exists in Jersey. The population of Guernsey is much smaller, the influx of strangers less, the course of life more stagnant,[2] the intelligence of the people less active, and their influence on the local government of the island less direct. These causes present a reason for non-interference which does not exist in the former case, and induce us to suggest a remedy less complete, than that which we have suggested in our first report. We think, however, that certain alterations are imperatively required.

" In the constitution of Guernsey, the political power resides almost exclusively in the same individuals who are entrusted with the administration of justice. The bailiff and jurats possess the legislative, and, to a great extent, the executive power, as well as the judicial; so that it becomes impossible to propose any change in the constitution of the royal court, which shall not involve a considerable alteration of the political institutions of the island. We are thus compelled to propose changes which extend beyond a reform of the criminal law of Guernsey, and yet are necessarily suggested by the consideration of the constitution of the tribunals entrusted with its administration.

" We recommend that legislation by the court in Chefs Plaids should be entirely abolished. We suggest that the enactment of local laws, for the future, should be confided to the States of Deliberation with the assent of the lieutenant-governor, as the representative of your majesty.

" The court in Alderney consists of a president, called the

---

(1) We entirely concur in this suggestion of the royal commissioners, especially if the States were made more popular.

(2) This stagnation is, we conceive, in some measure owing to the little direct influence which the people exercise in the initiating and enacting of the insular laws : thus the new harbour works, now at last in the course of erection, were not undertaken when they were most called for and most required, and when their cost would have been much less felt than at present, because the commercial classes, who offered to be taxed for them, had no voice in the matter.

jndge, and six jurats, two crown officers, called, as in Guernsey, the procureur and contrôle, the greffier and the prévôt.

"The judge receives his appointment from your majesty.[1] The six jurats are elected for life by the rate-payers of the island: if, from infirmity, they desire to resign, they apply to the States of Alderney, who transmit the application to the royal court of Guernsey, which decides upon it. The procureur, contrôle, and greffier, also receive their appointments from the crown. The prévôt is an officer named by the States of the island: he formerly held office for a year only; but, within the last four or five years, the Alderney court of Chefs Plaids have passed an ordonnance making the office perpetual. The prévôté consists of twelve persons; these serve for twelve years, if they live so long; but, in case of death, the place is filled up. The twelve hold, in rotation, the office of deputy prévôt for one year.

"There are also two constables and two deputy constables, chosen by the court. They are annual officers, the two who have been chosen as deputy constables for one year, becoming constables for the year following.

"The procureur has an annual salary of £40. The contrôle has no salary; and that office at present is not filled up, the procureur being the only advocate in the island.

"The jurisdiction of the court of Alderney, in matters of a criminal nature, is confined to a preliminary investigation into the fact of crime. It may examine, and, if satisfied that the charge is without foundation, may dismiss the complaint; but it possesses no power of trial or punishment. When an offence is committed in Alderney, the party charged is apprehended by the constable, and brought before the judge and at least two jurats. The witnesses are examined, and the interrogatoire of the prisoner taken by the court. The examinations are then reduced to writing; and, if the court is of opinion that there is sufficient evidence to put the prisoner on his trial, an act of court is made referring the matter to the royal court in Guernsey. This mode of proceeding is provided by an order in council of the 21st of June, 1585, which directs that the jurats of Alderney 'shall refer criminal causes to the royal court, as was always the custom.' The prisoner is committed to the custody of the prévôt of Alderney, whose duty it is to convey him to Guernsey.

"The court of Alderney also has the power of making local ordonnances, in the nature of police regulations, and for the repair and maintenance of the highways, obedience being enforced by a fine. The ordonnances must be made either at a court of Chefs Plaids or at a meeting of the States. These are constituted of the same members; but the States meet whenever there is occa-

(1) The judge has a salary of £150 a year, which is certainly insufficient, now that Alderney, from its naval station and fortifications, has become of so much importance.

sion; the Chefs Plaids only twice in the year, on the first Monday after Michaelmas and the first Monday after the 15th of January. The body consists of the judge, the six jurats, the crown officers, and the douzaine, which last is a body of twelve, elected by the rate-payers of the island for life, or until they obtain permission, for infirmity, to be discharged. The governor also has the right of being present; and, when he cannot attend in person, he deputes some one who takes the oaths as lieutenant-governor for the occasion.

"The constables in Alderney are mere officers of police, and have no place in the court sitting in Chefs Plaids, nor in the States.

"The judge, and at least two jurats and seven douzeniers, with one of the crown officers, must be present to constitute the court. The enacting power resides with the jurats alone, the bailiff, in case of an equality of numbers, giving a casting vote. The crown officers and the members of the douzaine are, however, both consulted. The course is, upon a measure being proposed, for the judge, first, to ask the opinions of the crown officers. After they have been heard, the opinion of the douzaine is asked through the president, who is the senior member; after which the jurats decide on the proposition, which thereupon becomes law, and is binding on the inhabitants of Alderney.

"An appeal against its enactment lies to the royal court in Guernsey, which has power to annul an ordonnance of the court of Alderney. It is however contended, in Alderney, that the Guernsey court has no power to make an ordonnance binding on the inhabitants of Alderney, and that no one can be summoned before it for the breach of an ordonnance made by the court in Alderney, the jurisdiction of the Guernsey court in such case being only appellate.

"Besides the making of ordonnances, the taxes for the relief of the poor are raised, and the value of the wheat rents for the year are fixed, at the court of Chefs Plaids.

"At present, the court at Sark consists of the seneschal or his deputy, who is the judge of the court; the prévôt, who acts in the threefold character of procureur, serjeant, and prévôt; and the greffier. These officers are all appointed by the lord, and sworn in before the royal court in Guernsey.

"The seneschal of Sark has complete jurisdiction in the case of petty offences, having the power of punishing by way of fine to the amount of three livres tournois, and by imprisonment to the extent of three times twenty-four hours. In all cases which require a severer punishment, he is bound to send the case before the royal court in Guernsey.

"The island is divided into forty tenements held of the lord, which, by letters patent of the 9th of James I., were made incapable of partition. The holders of the forty tenements, with the lord, the seneschal, the prévôt, and the greffier, now constitute the court of Chefs Plaids in Sark. The lord must be present in person, or by some one authorized to appear for him. The seneschal or his deputy presides. No one has a vote at the Chefs Plaids who is not a tenant.

"Ordonnances are passed there for roads, and rates are imposed for the maintenance of the poor and other purposes of local taxation and police. After the project has been discussed and adopted by the votes of the majority of the tenants, the seneschal requests the assent of the lord to its enactment. If it is given, the ordonnance is registered, and has immediately the force of law. If, on the contrary, the lord withholds his consent, no registration takes place; but the majority of the tenants may appeal to the royal court of Guernsey, who claim the right of compelling the registration of the ordonnance, and thus giving it the force of law. There seems reason for doubting whether this power resides in the royal court, as it is denied that the royal court, sitting in Chefs Plaids, can make an ordonnance to bind the inhabitants of Sark. It is, however, not disputed that it possesses the power of reviewing ordonnances made by the court of Sark, and annulling those which are contrary to a known superior law.

"The Chefs Plaids also appoint two police officers, namely, a constable and a vingtenier. Each office is held for a year, the vingtenier of one year becoming the constable of the year following."

Two Earthquakes in Guernsey.—On Friday, December 22, 1843, at 3 h. 53 m. p.m., a loud rumbling noise was heard in every part of the island, accompanied by one or two shocks, which lasted about four seconds. Persons out of doors felt the earth heave under them, in some cases so violently as to compel them to lay hold of the nearest object for support. The banks and hedges appeared to be in motion, and in the houses the furniture was rocked. Buildings were distinctly seen to heave and shake, as well as the pier walls of St. Peter-Port and the massive quay of St. Sampson's harbour. The vane of the town church was violently agitated, and the bell struck twice. The inhabitants, unaccustomed as they are to such convulsions of nature, did not at first attribute the shock to its real cause. No damage was done beyond the fall of a few tiles, bricks, &c. The shock was felt precisely at the same time in Jersey and Sark; and the sea was during the greater part of the day in an unsettled state, although the weather was then, and had been for some days, quite calm. The crews of two vessels, which were beating about the roads, distinctly felt the shock, as did some persons, in a fishing boat at anchor, about half a mile to the southward of the island.

On Friday, April 1, 1853, at 10h. 30m. p. m., a strong shock was also felt throughout the island; to some the effects being like a violent gust of wind, and to others like the rolling of a heavy carriage, or the distant detonation of electricity. Many who were in bed, but awake, felt an upheaving, and heard the rattling of the furniture; while others asleep were awoke by the concussion, and, springing up, rushed alarmed out of their rooms. The height of the barometer was 29.40, and rising at the time; the night fine and starry: and there was no previous indication of the forthcoming phenomenon. The shock was felt at about the same time at Jersey, South-ampton, Portsmouth, Coutances, Caen, Rennes, Nantes, &c.

Having in Chapter XX. described the state of Guernsey about the year 1775, we must not conclude the general his-tory of the island without a brief notice of its aspect and condition in 1854, whereby will be seen at a glance the won-derful changes which have occurred in the short space of eighty years—changes evidently greater than in several pre-ceding centuries—so altered are the habits and manners of the natives of all ranks. Now, the usual dinner hour of the upper classes is from four to five o'clock, and for company an hour or two later; while they go to balls at nine or ten o'clock, hours at which their great grandfathers returned from them. Excellent roads intersect the island in all direc-tions; and private and hack carriages and pair, or with one horse, are very common; even the country people coming to market on Saturdays in their one-horse chaise. The com-munication with England and France by steamers is so easy and certain, that the inhabitants think much less of a trip to London or Paris, or on the Loire and Rhine, than they did formerly of a passage to Southampton or St. Malo: thus many go annually to Vichy, in the south of France, and to the baths in Germany, for the benefit of their waters. A passenger who leaves Guernsey at nine o'clock, a. m., reaches London, viâ Southampton, at ten o'clock the same evening.

Among the modern public buildings in St. Peter-Port are the court-house; gaol; meat, fish, and vegetable markets; the college; the churches of Trinity, St. James, and St. John's; Bethel chapel; Victoria tower; and the militia arsenal. The hospital has also been considerably enlarged. The assembly rooms were built by private subscription in

1782. The old town, although from the solidity and durability of the houses not susceptible of much change, has been greatly improved within the present century, and a few of the streets have flagged footpaths.   In the island, there are some five and twenty dissenting chapels ; so that sectarians lack not.—There are three newspapers ; two in English and one (Gazette) in French ; (the Star published three times and the Comet twice a week ;) many printing presses ; and several booksellers, who sell English publications at a lower price than in London.—In 1775, there was not a single hot or green-house ; ˙ now there are some hundred graperies and conservatories.—The islanders are kept alive by the presence of nine physicians, fifteen surgeons, three dentists, and eleven druggists ! And yet there was formerly so little inducement for medical men to practise in Guernsey, that, on the 12th of October, 1632, the States granted " to Mr. Samuel de la Place, minister of the church, and exercising the profession of medicine in this island, the annual sum of twelve quarters of wheat, as a pension, to be paid by all the parishes according to the accustomed rates ; " and, for above a century subsequently, the few resident practitioners were chiefly Frenchmen of low origin and very doubtful professional ability.   In the early part of the present century, scarcely a medical man kept either horse or vehicle ; and when a countryman required his attendance, which was rarely, he brought his own nag for the use of " Monsieur le Docteur."

High street and Fountain street have been widened : the houses in the former have been converted into shops, and the descendants of those who once occupied them have removed to " the west end," or into the country.   The town of St. Peter-Port has more than doubled in extent and population, and the streets, shops, and many private dwellings, are lighted with gas ; but unfortunately there are now some 150 houses untenanted and to be let, because since free trade has been ˙wisely adopted in England, the strangers, who lived. in Guernsey for the sake of cheapness, have returned home : it was about the year 1825 that they commenced coming over as residents, and about 1850 that the majority left the island. But many are still induced to come over and remain for the mildness of the climate, especially during the winter months.

In contemplating some of these changes, we cannot but regret that the early habits and the economy of former years have not been more preserved, as late hours and costly entertainments, few and far between, have destroyed sociability.

Large houses, several servants, and costly furniture, are ill adapted to our limited area, depressed commerce, and equal laws of inheritance;[1] and it is painful to think that many old families will struggle in vain to preserve a respectable station. The islanders have, in their style of living, copied too much from England; but a *soireé à la Française* would become them more than champagne dinners and suppers, which often partake quite as much of ostentation as of hospitality. Very gloomy anticipations are generally entertained as regards the future prosperity of the island; and, casting aside the trammels of custom and bad example, it were wise to return to the more rational visiting of the last century. There has, however, been a great change for the better in the disappearance of inebriety; and any individual guilty of excess at parties, would now be scouted from all genteel society. Happily, intellectual have in a great measure replaced sensual enjoyments; and he who loves to dwell on "the wisdom of our ancestors" should remember that on most points we possess all their wisdom, with much more experience; for we live in an age unparalleled in the great advances which have been made in every branch of human enterprise and science.

From the MS. of a Guernsey jurat, now deceased, written in 1839 or 1840, we extract the following:

"A few alterations in things within my recollection, that is, within sixty years, or since 1780, when I was twelve years old, and first went to school in England.

"*Dress for Men.*—Powder was universally worn, with a tail or a club, which I found most troublesome. Cocked hats, except for boys, who sometimes wore round. Buckles, which by kicking made my shins very sore. Short breeches with knee buckles, often leather with top boots. No Wellington trousers or boots; no morning frock coats; although the body coats were much longer than the present ones, and waistcoats were much longer than they are now made. No black or coloured cravats.

"*Dress for Women.*—Powder universal, commonly of the reddish cast, with high head dresses. (The powder tax of Pitt did more for the beauty and the ornament of women than all the mantua-makers and hair-dressers in the world.) Hoops in common use, when dressed out. Long waists, and uncovered bosoms and arms. High heels to the shoes, which made the women shocking walkers. More silk than cotton dresses. Chintzes common."

"*Shipping.*—The merchant ships are much larger and finer

(1) One of the follies of the times is a needlessly expensive funeral, by which a family is often put to inconvenience. In North America, the relatives and friends usually attend without being supplied with hat-bands and gloves.

2E

now than at that period, and they were then never coppered. The king's ships are perhaps even more improved, and the sailing of both has kept pace with these improvements; but there was a class of vessels which, when a boy, were my admiration, and I could never cease gazing upon them—I mean the cutters and luggers,—the Resolution, cutter privateer, with many others: the Alarm, lugger, was also a beauty; and the smugglers, with their athletic crews, who looked and lived like gentlemen. How many happy hours they have made me pass, by merely looking at them. That hardy race is gone by, and is, it would seem, extinct; for even the present luggers and cutters [1] are no more to be compared to them than the old ships of war to the present ones.—Smuggling, with all its faults, had its advantages too, as it created and kept up a bold and active race of seamen.

"*Improvements.*—The great improvements in my time are the recent ones of steam-boats, railroads, gas, and so many in the comforts of life, produced by the instrument of steam, that it is impossible to enumerate them. Small windows, low roofs, and small apartments were the chief evils of dwelling houses; but they had one convienence which I now always miss—fixed seats to the windows. In furniture, no sofas, and most uncomfortable chairs with straight backs. No silver forks, knives bad, small spoons, and very small tea cups, though more frequently of real China than are now to be found. Bread, shocking in the island. The white wines drank were Mountain and Lisbon; good Port; little good Claret, and no Champagne. No hot-house fruits, or evergreens; but beautiful flowers in abundance,—I think more so than at present; and fruit, I should say, was also more abundant—peaches, nectarines, golden pippins, and codlins: the two last are nearly extinct.

"*Society.*—There was much more conviviality than at present. As a proof of this, the number of clubs, especially of the ladies. Cards were more in fashion, and the hours of meeting conduced more to society. We dined at one, and I believe that two or three was the dinner hour for company. The New Ground and the Pier, of a Sunday, were much more brilliant than they are now, notwithstanding our mighty improvements. Our public walks are so deserted that one would often be tempted to believe there was no one left in the island. The many clubs then in the country for gentlemen are another proof of the difference of the times. I believe our ancestors were happier and wiser than ourselves, notwithstanding our boastings and the march of intellect which we so modestly assume."

(1) In 1840 there were no luggers, and the writer appears to have forgotten the modern cutter yachts, which are very handsome vessels.

CHAPTER XXIII.

COMMERCIAL AND STATISTICAL.

NOTWITHSTANDING that Guernsey possesses the only natural harbour, (St. Sampson's,) and the best roadstead in these islands, her commerce and navigation appear to have been extremely limited up to the close of the sixteenth century, because neither one nor the other could long exist to any extent without the necessary facilities, such as piers, quays, slips, &c. ; and the pier of St. Peter-Port was only commenced about the year 1580. Anterior to that period, the chief occupation of the inhabitants was farming and fishing, and they led an almost patriarchal life : the island produced sufficient food for their own consumption, while the conger and mackerel fishery, in early times a staple branch of commerce, and, after its decline, the knitting of woollen stockings, frocks, &c., enabled them to supply their few external wants.

We cannot reconcile the statements of Henry De Vic and Heylin, relative to the shipping of Guernsey early in the seventeenth century. The former, in August, 1627, wrote as follows : " For it must be by manufacture that they shall subsist, the islands affording no commodities of their own to vend abroad, and having no shipping to transport foreign commodities from one kingdom to the other."—On the other hand, Heylin, who visited the islands in March, 1629, says, with " the conveniency of the peer, which is also warranted with six peece of good cannon from the town, it is no marvell if the people betake themselves so much unto the trade of merchandize. Nor do they traffic only in small boats between St. Malo and the islands, as those of Jarsey, but are masters of good stout barks, and venture into all these neerer ports of Christendom." This is a palpable contradiction as regards Guernsey ; but as De Vic, who was a Guernseyman, was soliciting some favor for the islands from the English government, his object was perhaps to prove them more indigent than they really were. After mentioning that the poorer sort were " exceeding cunning" in the manufacture of wool, which was the principal export, Heylin, as will be seen in Chapter X., expatiates on the benefits to the island of the

privilege of neutrality. On this last point, he evidently copies
Camden, as they both restrict the privilege to Guernsey only,
whereas it certainly extended to Jersey. We cannot discover,
however, that the privilege was attended with much benefit
to the commerce of Guernsey ; and although maintained by
the royal court and respected by the sovereign in council, it
appears to have been very dependent on the caprice or cupi-
dity of the governors—especially of Sir Thomas Leighton—as
is proved by several acts of the royal court and orders of the
lords of the council, from 1586 to 1667. Thus, we learn by
a decision of the royal commissioners, in 1607, "that in
November, 1594, George Paulet, then lieutenant here, by
order from Sir Thomas Leighton, did arrest a ship of St. Malo,
coming from Newfoundland, laden with fish and train oil,
supposing the same to belong to her majesty's enemies, which
ship was afterwards, by the bailiff and jurats, ordered to be
released ; and yet, notwithstanding, the said lieutenant would
not release the said ship and goods, until Robert Bowlin
entered into bond in the sum of 500 crowns, with condition to
procure a discharge for the said ship and goods from the lords
of the council within four months. Whereupon the inhabitants, finding the arrest of the said ship to be prejudicial to
their ancient privileges and liberties, employed Andrew Harris, jurat, to procure a discharge as well of the said ship as of
the said bond, which discharge was granted by the lords,
bearing date April 30, 1595."—Returning to the privilege
of neutrality, it must be remembered that in those days there
were numerous free ports in Europe, which taking no share
in the wars, possessed all its advantages ; for instance, the
towns and cities of the celebrated Hanseatic league, and the
free and commercial states of Italy. Falle mentions that during the greatest heat of the war about La Rochelle and the
isle of Rhé, (1627,) the hosiers of Paris and Rouen had free
access to these islands, and carried off many bales of stockings, as those of Coutances continued to do, down to the reign
of Charles II. And yet during the civil war[1] and after the
Restoration, the islanders had already commenced privateering, which they continued with so much success, as before
related, after the revolution of 1688.

In 1680, the description, name, and burthen in tons, of the
vessels belonging to Guernsey were as follow : [2]

(1) Mr. Peter Carey deposed that Colonel Russell, the parliamentary lieutenant-governor
of Guernsey, had given commissions to sea captains; that he seized on the prizes brought
into the island, and disposed of them according to his pleasure.

(2) The list before us gives also the names of the owners and masters; of the latter, a
few appear to have been of the best families.

"'Pinke' Society, 120; 'barke' Providence, 70; pinke John, 50; ketch St. Peter, 40; total, 280 tons, or 70 tons average: these four vessels English built, and then at Newfoundland.

"Pinke Palm Tree, 100; pinke —, 80; pinke Robert, 60; barke Elizabeth, 30; ketch Mary, 25; double shallop David, 8; and hoy Success, 8; total, 311 tons, or about 44 tons average, and these seven vessels also English built.

"Barke Hopewell, 30; barke Peter, 30; barke William, 20; barke —, 18; barke Adventure, 15; and barke William, 10; total, 123 tons, or 20½ tons average: these six vessels, and also 'a ship called the Charles,' of which the tonnage is not given, French built."

Grand total, exclusive of the Charles: seventeen vessels of the united burthen of 714 tons, or 42 tons each, average, the whole probably not carrying more than one modern ship of 500 tons.

Previous to the cessation of the privilege of neutrality by William III. in his order in council of August 8, 1689, the internal trade of Guernsey, was confined to the import and knitting of wool, while the external consisted of a very small share in the Newfoundland fishery, and the employment of a few vessels to and from the neighbouring ports of England and France. At this time, about 6,000 pair of stockings average are calculated to have been made weekly in Jersey, half at least of the population there depending upon the manufacture; and allowing half that number for Guernsey, or 150,000 pair per annum, at one pound of wool for three pair, 2,000 tods of wool were required yearly for the stocking manufacture in the latter island alone. Living frugally on their small estates, or on their "rentes," or engaged in some retail business in St. Peter-Port, the upper ranks had little inducement to enter into extraneous commerce, for which their habits unfitted them. These "rentes," being usually paid in kind, it happened subsequently in good harvests that the large holder knew not how to dispose of the wheat, and he occasionally sent it to Spain, as was the case about the year 1750, when Mr. Carey, of the Vrangue, agreed with those who owed him wheat "rentes" to exchange them for money "rentes" at seven livres, or ten shillings per quarter. These "rentes" in 1811 and 1812 would have been otherwise payable at twenty-eight livres, or £2 per quarter.

The commerce of Guernsey, in any way worthy of the name, dates its origin from the reign of William and Mary, when the English merchants came over to purchase the

French goods captured by the privateers, and particularly
brandies, which met with a ready sale. When peace was
restored, new ideas of trade gradually developed themselves
among the inhabitants, who had now acquired some capital. The funding system, perfected by William III., gained
ground in England, and that money, which the government
acquired easily, was spent unsparingly. As a natural consequence, the duties were increased to meet an increased
national expenditure, and at every increase the temptation to
evade these duties became stronger. The English smuggler
resorted to Guernsey for his cargoes of spirits, tobacco, tea,
and other highly taxed commodities, for which he found a
ready and profitable sale on his own coast; and it cannot be
a matter of surprise if the inhabitants were induced to import
and keep in store the goods constantly in demand. Another
lucrative branch of trade also arose from the entrepôt, or
deposit, of wines, spirits, and other foreign goods destined for
legal entry into Great Britain and Ireland; because, as the
duties, which often far exceeded the original cost of the goods,
were exacted on importation, the merchant was compelled to
have recourse to some secure deposit, whence he could receive
his goods as he sold or required them. Wines, particularly,
as they improve with age and care, were sent hither for that
purpose. Thus Guernsey was to the British merchants what
the bonding warehouses now are; and immense vaults and
stores were in consequence constructed, which, being durably
built with stone, will long remain as sad monuments of gone-
by prosperity.

With these advantages the trade of the island slowly but
progressively increased; but, until the commencement of the
first American war, in 1775, it appears to have been confined
chiefly to importing and selling spirits, &c., to the English
smugglers, and to receiving goods in deposit, as the insular
shipping then consisted of only four or five square-rigged
vessels, and a few sloops and cutters. From this time, however, it began to augment rapidly, owing to a combination of
favourable circumstances in quick succession, and which in a
few years raised the commercial prosperity of Guernsey to
the highest pitch—far higher than she will probably ever
attain again. To defray the enormous expenditure of the
wars commencing in 1775 and 1793, new and higher duties
were levied by the British government; and as the temptation
to smuggling increased, so this island became a larger depository of goods than ever. Many privateers were also fitted

out, and proved very successful. Moreover, the disturbed state of France, during the revolution, naturally induced the exportation of goods from that country to a place of security; and wines, brandies, &c., were brought over to Guernsey in such quantities, that the vaults and warehouses, numerous and capacious as they are, were totally inadequate to their lodgment, so that some cargoes were stored in fields, under temporary coverings. A single merchant received, for account of one firm in London, 2,491 hogsheads and 17 cases of Claret and Hermitage, by American vessels from Bordeaux, in 1795. About the same time the pier of St. Peter-Port was frequently crammed to the very mouth, and there were some twenty or thirty vessels in the roadstead waiting to enter.

Although this island was greatly benefitted by the illicit trade, yet it was far less injurious to the United Kingdom, than if carried on from the continent, whither the smuggler would otherwise have resorted for his supplies, and paid for them in specie. Many a cargo of brandy, then imported into Guernsey, was purchased with one of British pilchards or codfish; and, above all, the smuggling vessels, with their daring crews, were, on the breaking out of each war, converted into privateers; and while they enriched the islands, as well as England, proved a serious annoyance to the enemy. These palliating circumstances, and a knowledge that smuggling from the continent could not be prevented unless by strictly guarding the British coast, probably induced the government to pause in suppressing the traffic from these islands, as its attention was frequently drawn to the subject. " In 1709, an order in council was obtained by the island, which repealed former orders procured, ex-parte, by the commissioners of customs, tending to establish their officers in this island. In 1717, an authentic act of the States of Guernsey, dated 6th March, proves that the lords of the treasury, wishing to establish custom-house officers in the island, judged it necessary to obtain the consent of the States, which were then moved to take the proposal into consideration, and unanimously rejected it. In 1720 and 1722, other attempts were made by the commissioners of customs; a deputy was sent over by the island, and again prevailed in council. In 1767, an order in council did, for a short time, impose restrictions on the trade of the island," [1] as did another in 1771; but, on a representation of their inutility and inexpediency, the Government was soon induced to allow them

(1) Appendix to the Rights and Immunities of Guernsey, 1805.

to remain dormant; although in 1767, the registrar's office, or custom-house, was established in Guernsey with the following appointments and salaries:

A registrar..£60	
A waiter and searcher...............................£40	
Two boatmen, and to keep a boat................£50	
	£150

And in Jersey:

A registrar..£60	
Two waiters and searchers, each £40............£80	
Two boatmen, and to keep a boat................£50	
	£190

In Chapter XXI., the suppression of the illicit trade in 1805 was briefly noticed.—By the act of parliament for the purpose in that year, and by another passed in 1807, such regulations and restrictions were enforced as, without touching on the legal commerce of the islanders, attained the desired object. Every opposition was, naturally, at first offered to these enactments—the late Bailiff Brock, then a jurat, was sent to London as a deputy of the States, to protest against them—and it was urged that they were not only subversive of our most sacred rights and charters, repeatedly confirmed by different sovereigns since the conquest, but that they were impolitic and inexpedient. But the moment it was perceived in the island that the government was determined to effect the suppression, the merchants resolved to discountenance the traffic; and the royal court completed by its ordinances what the acts of parliament, sent over with and confirmed by orders in council, had begun. These acts and orders were framed with as much regard as possible to the privileges of the island; their provisions extended only to goods and ships at sea, or afloat; they altered nothing on shore; the civil jurisdiction, police, and laws of the island, remained intact. The chief feature of the new acts was, that they extended the laws for the suppression of smuggling generally to the distance of one hundred leagues from the United Kingdom, instead of a few leagues from the coast, as before; and thus brought the Anglo-Norman Islands, with respect to all goods afloat, within the operation of those laws.

At the same epoch, another measure conspired to deprive Guernsey of both the particular branches of trade which she had so long enjoyed. We have said that the acts of 1805 and 1807 effectually suppressed the illicit traffic; and, by the introduction of the bonding system, the island ceased, in a great measure, to be the depository of goods for legal importation into the United Kingdom. But, although nearly the whole continent of Europe was closed to British commerce by the French decrees and English orders in council, yet the presence of a large garrison and naval squadron, both of which required extensive supplies, rendered these commercial deprivations comparatively innocuous to all classes at the time. Fortunately also, the Peninsula was soon after driven into a war against France, and its ports, as well as those of its immense colonial possessions, were opened to British enterprize, when our merchants were not slow in availing themselves of the advantage. Many of their vessels were most profitably employed, from 1808 to 1815, in carrying codfish from Newfoundland to Spain, where, owing to the destruction and waste of the armies, it rose from fifteen shillings, its usual peace price, to sixty shillings nett per cwt. From Spain, these vessels usually took a cargo of wine, brandy, &c., to Rio de Janeiro, or the River Plate, returning home with sugar, coffee, and hides; and so lucrative was this traffic occasionally, that upwards of £9,000 were cleared by a brig of about 150 tons burthen, in one of the circuitous voyages we have described. We must add, however, that she ran without insurance and without convoy,—an immense saving, when it is considered that the risk from American privateers was so great as to raise premiums to 15 and 20 per cent. for a voyage across the Atlantic, without convoy. The Guernsey vessels, sailing well, usually ran without convoy, and very few were captured; but when insured, the high premiums were a great drawback to their profits, as few of the voyages in those days were unprofitable.

The island was also greatly benefitted during the last three or four years of the war, by what was termed the license trade, Napoleon then relaxing his anti-commercial decrees, and permitting various goods to be exported from, and imported into, France, in vessels under a neutral flag. His chief motive was to obtain Peruvian bark and other drugs, of which his armies were in great need; and although the British government refused at first to allow of their exportation, yet they willingly sanctioned the traffic in many other goods, and at last removed their prohibition as to drugs. Guernsey was the principal mart of this licensed interchange of commodities between two nations, which had been for nearly twenty years waging war against each other, "almost

to the knife ;" and although the traffic was carried on amid
many restrictions, risks, and difficulties, constantly varying
as the caprice, or jealousies, or wants of either power prompted, yet it was very lucrative; and it was of essential service in
introducing corn into the island, which at the time was much
wanted, the Baltic ports being closed against it.

On the proclamation of a general peace, in 1815, a new era
may be said to have arisen in the commerce of Guernsey, as
the successive artificial supports, which had given it existence
about the year 1700, and afterwards sustained it for upwards
of a century, were then suddenly withdrawn. During the
previous forty years, with two short intermissions, Great
Britain had been engaged in wars such as the world before
never saw, such as the mind of man in anticipation could
have scarcely conceived, and such as, for the credit of humanity, it is devoutly to be hoped, will never be seen again.
But, as we have shewn, these expensive wars were highly
beneficial to the Channel Islands, and enriched Guernsey in
particular, although not entirely to her permanent advantage,
as we shall attempt to prove in the sequel. This was indeed
a heart-stirring period, a time of high excitement, as the tide
of wealth was constantly on the flow ; and all classes, with
perhaps the exception of those who lived on limited incomes
in the funds, partook of the joyous influence.

The return of peace, however, at once changed the scene,
and at first affected so deeply the interests of all classes, dependent on trade for a subsistence, that many gloomy fore-
bodings were entertained for the future, not only as to the
commercial, but as to the general prospects of the island.
The immediate removal of the garrison, excepting one regiment, and of the whole squadron, excepting a solitary cutter,
deprived numbers of employment. The failure of the corn
harvest throughout Europe, in the years 1816 and 1817, increased the distress of the lower orders, and associations were
formed for their relief. Many, aided by previous savings or
charitable assistance, were compelled, for three or four years
successively, to emigrate to the United States of America in
island vessels fitted up expressly for their accommodation;
and, settling as much as possible together, they have since
named their circuit of abode " Guernsey County," which is in
the State of Ohio. Stores and vaults, which, during the war
had been constantly filled, now became almost worthless ;
many who had purchased houses and other buildings in the
town at a high rate, in wheat rents, were unable to pay them

in consequence of the scarcity of corn, and were ruined;[1] the insular shipping, consisting of fast sailing vessels of comparatively small burthen, lost much of its value; and several large capitalists retired from business, preferring to invest their properties in public securities, especially the French funds, which then yielded an annual interest of about 8 per cent. Fortunately, the foreign trade sustained no serious check during this period, and the island vessels continued to be advantageously employed, meeting for three or four years with but little opposition from the commercial marine of the continent, which had been, in a great measure, destroyed during the war, and could not be immediately replaced. And happily the depression, which all sudden unfavorable transitions will create, yielded by degrees to time and to more encouraging circumstances. The accumulated earnings of former prosperity remained, and it was gradually seen that sufficient employment could be found for the labouring classes, as the island was susceptible of numerous improvements, which, in the natural desire of taking fortune at the flood, had been delayed or overlooked. Shipbuilding was introduced; the stone trade increased; numberless dwelling houses were erected in the town parish, for the accommodation of natives and resident strangers; large sums were expended in public works; and, above all, a great reduction took place in the price of corn and other provisions. The facilities of steam navigation soon after caused an influx of visitors during the summer season, and the money spent by them here was, and is still, of essential benefit to the trading classes. Thus, if on the one hand the commercial prosperity of Guernsey sustained a serious check on the cessation of the illicit trade and of the war, it must be admitted, on the other, that, since the peace of 1815, the general appearance of the island has altered vastly for the better, and those who remember it before that time, as we do, must be struck with the change. The country is every where dotted with new substantial cottages; its narrow and almost impassable lanes have been converted into excellent roads; the land is better cultivated, and has greatly enhanced in value; and the breed of cattle, horses especially, is much improved.

(1) We would earnestly caution others to take warning from their fate, and not to purchase any building payable chiefly in wheat rents, as the day may return when they will be fixed at 40s. the quarter, instead of 15s. to 17s. 6d., as of late years. A paternal legislature would interdict all sales of buildings on such terms, in the same manner as it renders all gambling transactions illegal. The system applicable to land is good, but defective and often cruel in regard to buildings. To make the rent of a house dependent on the price of wheat, tends in many cases to deprive the proprietor of the means of purchasing bread for his family during a scarcity of corn. For instance, wheat rents were affixed in 1852 at 17s., and in 1853 at 27s., per quarter.

The shipping of Guernsey engaged in the foreign trade, which was chiefly limited to Havannah, Brazil, and the River Plate, was as follows :

In 1818.........26 vessels.........4320 tons.........or 166 tons average.
   1823.........35   ,, ...5748 ,, ...,, 164   ,,
   1833.........35   ,, ...6236 ,, ...,, 180   ,,
   1834.........37   ,, ...6631 ,, ...,, 180   ,,
   1837.... 24   ,, ...4832 ,, ...,, 201   ,,

Up to 1833, these vessels were usually laden on account of the owners, who merely gave orders and paid commissions on both the outward and homeward cargoes, excepting when the former consisted of potatoes and bricks, the only export from the island : this was clearly a forced trade, which became a losing one as soon as the continental merchants embarked in it, and sold their own imports of coffee, sugar, &c., thus saving the heaviest commission, "pickings," &c. The carrying of codfish terminated with the peace of 1815, and from about 1834, when there were serious losses by the sudden fall of colonials, many of the Guernsey vessels were employed on freight, for which however they were ill adapted, as being of little burthen from their size and sharpness : indeed, they were always much too small for profit. Up to 1835, the island vessels were constantly engaged in carrying wine, brandy, &c., from the Mediterranean to the Brazils and the River Plate ; but this trade gradually declined, and has now entirely ceased. The race of speculative merchants, such as carried on business in Guernsey during, and several years after, the war, may be said to have become extinct about the year 1845, a large commercial establishment at Rio de Janeiro, the partners in which held two-ninths of the shipping engaged in the foreign trade in 1836, having been abandoned in 1842. Fortunately, several small capitalists in Guernsey, about 1835, turned their attention to freights in the supply of London with fruit from the Azores, Spain, Lisbon, &c., and built many fast schooners in the island for that purpose. They also availed themselves of another resource in the coal and stone trade, the former of which, during the days of insular prosperity, appears to have been overlooked. Previous to 1815, there were only two colliers belonging to Guernsey ; but the number gradually increased, and the island is now almost entirely supplied with coal by its own shipping. Another advantage has moreover arisen of late years from three or four London houses sending their wines to the islands to be stored and bottled, and reshipped when fit for use, as they save thereby the heavy advance and interest of the duties :

this trade reminds one of the entrepôt of the last century, and not only gives considerable employment to many, but renders the stores in St. Peter-Port of more value.

We have mentioned elsewhere that the commerce and shipping of Guernsey were formerly as superior to those of Jersey as the commerce and shipping of Jersey are now superior to those of Guernsey; and as the change must appear singular to those unacquainted with the cause, we shall endeavour to explain it; although it is certainly natural that Jersey, being the larger and more populous island, should take the lead. But that is no reason why Guernsey has at present scarcely a vessel engaged in the carrying or freight trade of Brazil, the River Plate, and Havannah. Nature has, however, given one advantage to Guernsey over Jersey, in its better roadstead and nearer proximity to England, in consequence of which numberless yachts from Cowes, Plymouth, &c., visit the former island every summer, and there, taking in their supplies of wines, spirits, groceries, tobacco, &c., greatly benefit the dealers in those articles, as also the hotel and livery stable keepers, pilots, &c.

In saying that the wealth acquired, during the wars between 1775 and 1815, was not altogether permanently advantageous to Guernsey, we meant that it was unfavorable to the exercise of patient industry, and that it engendered habits incompatible with the successful prosecution of peaceful and legitimate commerce. While the merchants of Guernsey were engaged in importing tobacco from Virginia, and spirits from various countries, for the supply of the illicit trade, those of Jersey were employed in establishing fisheries in North America; one trade, as we have shewn, suddenly passed away, but the other will probably continue as long as Great Britain possesses the supremacy of the seas. The former entailed a higher rate of wages and a more expensive mode of living; the latter was originally established, and is still continued, by the greater cheapness of labour and the less cost of production. This advantage extends its beneficial influence to every other commercial undertaking; and, in consequence, Jersey not only possesses her grand staple, the North American cod-fishery, but the oyster fishery on the French coast, and the Honduras and African trades; and, above all, she is largely engaged in shipbuilding, not only for native account, but for Liverpool. In none of these sources of employment can Guernsey be said to participate in any way, and she certainly will be excluded from them all, until her mechanics and tradesmen labour on the same terms as those in the sister island. Thus Liverpool has recently lost much of its shipbuilding, and even of the repairs of vessels, because the carpenters there refused to work under much higher wages than were paid in other English ports.

In Jersey, those engaged in building, navigating, and supplying ships, are satisfied with a smaller profit than evidently obtains in Guernsey, and they reap the benefit by larger sales and more constant employment. The wages of carpenters and seamen generally are fully 10 per cent. less in Jersey than in Guernsey, and a vessel can be built and equipped for about £2 sterling per ton less in the former than in the latter island. In consequence, between the years 1832 and 1835, several vessels for the foreign trade were built in Jersey for Guernsey owners. And, after what we have stated, the following amounts of tonnage, in five different periods, can be no matter of surprise :

JERSEY.

In 1807.........	76 vessels......	6655 tons......	736 men......	88 tons average.
1817.........	79 ,,	...... 8167 ,,	...... 587 ,,	......103 ,,
1827.........182 ,,	......16583 ,,	......1658 ,,	...... 91 ,,
1836.........232 ,,	......20864 ,,	......2048 ,,	...... 90 ,,
1853.......363 ,,	......33273 ,,	......2892 ,,	...... 92 ,,

GUERNSEY.

In 1807.........114 vessels......10450 tons......	940 men......	91 tons average.
1817......... 64 ,,	...... 6825 ,,	...... 390 ,,	......106 ,,
1827......... 75 ,,	...... 7879 ,,	...... 580 ,,	......105 ,,
1836......... 86 ,,	...... 9486 ,,	...... 668 ,,	......110 ,,
1853.........135 ,,	......16207 ,,	......1048 ,,	......120 ,,

The reason of the Jersey average tonnages being less is, that many of the vessels are small cutters engaged in the oyster fishery. A great number of the Guernsey vessels are employed in the stone and coal trades, which accounts for the large increase in tonnage ; but these vessels are of inferior value, many being old, and none coppered. They, however, equally require shelter, and the increased tonnage is another argument in favor of the new pier works in Guernsey, which have now many opponents, chiefly among the upper classes, who forget that to stand still, while our neighbours are going ahead, is to retrograde, and to check all enterprize and industry.

In Jersey, in June, 1854, there were nineteen vessels on the stocks, admeasuring together 5,853 tons, or 303 tons average. Among them were two ships building for Liverpool account, one of 2,200 tons, and the other of 1,050 tons !

(1) In June, 1854, Jersey possessed 366 vessels, admeasuring 34,979 tons.

the remaining vessels were for Jersey. The builder of the said two large ships had three other vessels on the stocks, admeasuring together 900 tons; so that one builder alone, Mr. F. Charles Clarke, had five vessels, admeasuring 4,150 tons, or 830 tons average !

In Guernsey, in June, 1854, there were only four vessels on the stocks, admeasuring together 1,050 tons, or 262 tons average. If the pier works now in progress provide good building yards, with the necessary facilities for landing heavy timber, and, above all, if the Guernsey shipwrights be wise enough to work at the same rate as those in Jersey, ship-building may gradually increase, when Guernsey possesses a more sheltered pier with deeper water, as she will ere long, besides a better roadstead,[1] than Jersey. Indeed, the pier of St. Hélier, perfect as it is as a piece of workmanship, is very badly situated, being open to the south-west and the billows of the Atlantic, and liable to fill with sand from having a sandy bay in front. The people of Jersey deserved a better site for a pier, because they have done every thing in their power to foster their trade and navigation.

Shipbuilding in Guernsey may be said to have commenced in 1815, as previously to that period only four or five small cutters or luggers had been built in the island, and even large vessels were often sent to England for repair. Nothing but a forced trade and large profits could have overcome such disadvantages. From January 1, 1815, to October 1, 1837, the recapitulation of decked vessels built and launched in Guernsey was as follow :

	Ships.	Tons.	Brigs.	Tons.	Schooners.	Tons.	Cutters.	Tons.
To Dec. 31, 1827	4	915	26	4821	3	283	31	1021
From Jan. 1, 1828	3	766	6	1176	19	1788	7	302
	7	1681	32	5997	22	2071	38	1323

making a total of ninety-nine vessels, admeasuring 11,072 tons, or 112 tons each average. The nineteen schooners were chiefly built from 1835, for the English fruit trade.

Stone trade commenced about the year 1760, when large pebbles only for paving were shipped from Grand Harbour and La Perelle Bay for England ; and seven or eight years after, English stone cutters came over to prepare the regular paving stones. For many years the trade was very limited, but it began increasing soon after the peace of 1815, and it

(1) On the 27th of July, 1839, there were fifty or fifty-one French vessels, chiefly chasse-marées, in the roads and pier, taking shelter during westerly gales, and it is well known that no French crew puts in without purchasing British woollens, tobacco, rum, &c. In-deed, the coasters often call here expressly for that purpose.

received a considerable addition a few years after, when spalls or unbroken stone for macadamizing were first required. The trade is almost exclusively carried on from St. Sampson's harbour, between which and St. Peter-Port an omnibus was first established in 1837.—The late Bishop Watson, in his Chemical Essays, made a comparison of the weight of Guernsey paving stone and Aberdeen granite, and the difference of greater weight in favor of the former was above 19 lbs. in the cubic foot.   In 1819, the duty was rescinded in England on stone from these islands, and vessels laden solely with it were, by the Act of 6th of Geo. IV., exempted from the obligation of taking pilots.   In 1854, the price per ton for spalls or unbroken stone was 2s. 4d., and for road metal or small broken stone 4s. 9d., both on board ; and the average freight to London for some years has been about 7s. 6d. per ton.   In 1830, the shipment was about 30,000 tons, and in 1853 it had risen to 113,321 tons, requiring, at 200 tons each, about 550 vessels, nearly all of which unload in the Thames.

Manufactures.—The principal articles now manufactured are flour, biscuit, cordage, soap and candles, bricks, and tobacco and snuff.   There are three or four breweries, and there were also about as many distilleries for the extracting of spirits from potatoes for the English market ; but the distillation appears to have been unprofitable.   The first manufactory of Roman cement was established in 1819, and the first iron foundry, of which there are now two, in 1828. Previously to this period, all cast-iron goods were imported from England.   Gas was first introduced in 1830, the manufactory at the Amballes being completed in that year.   During the last war, much of the flour consumed in the island was imported from Southampton, as, although there were many wind and water mills, wheat could not be got from the continent.   These mills being found inconvenient and uncertain, the first steam engine for the grinding of wheat was erected in 1833, and there are now four steam mills of from twelve to eighteen horse power each, one of the establishments combining both steam and water power.   A few years since, the manufacture of flour from foreign corn, both for home consumption and export, became a valuable source of local employment, although the millers complained that in the British colonies no favor was shewn to flour manufactured in these islands over that manufactured in Hamburg, Copenhagen, &c., the same duty being levied on both.   Free trade has apparently put a stop to the export of flour.

Potatoes.—For several years the export from Guernsey was considerable, as will be seen by the following returns to the 10th of October in each year:

1833-4............	92,296 bushels.	1836-7............	227,303 bushels.
1834-5............	51,480 „	1837-8............	237,170 „
1835-6............	95,954 „	1838-9............	267,733 „
	1839-40............	376,160 bushels!!	

But, after 1840, the export gradually diminished, and almost ceased with the potatoe blight in 1846. In 1853, the import exceeded the export.

In Chapter XXI. we described the mode of intercourse with England during the long reign of George III., since which time steamers have almost entirely superseded sailing vessels both for the mails and passengers, although at first their introduction was stoutly opposed by the mariners and pilots of the old school, who asserted that no steamer could make way against a strong contrary wind and tide, or live in such seas and weather as she must necessarily encounter in crossing the Channel. The first steam vessel ever seen in Guernsey was the Medina, of about 100 tons, which arrived from Southampton on the 10th June, 1823, after a passage of fifteen hours; and, as will be easily imagined, the pier and the various eminences were crowded, so as to have a view of her as she came in. A second steamer, the Royal George, of 387 tons, reached the island on the 6th of September, in the same year, with Sir John Milley Doyle, on his way to Spain.

In 1824, two steamers of about sixty horse power, the Ariadne and Lord Beresford, commenced running weekly for the summer, the former from Southampton and the latter from Portsmouth, at a main cabin fare of a guinea and a half. The Ariadne left Southampton, on her first trip, at six o'clock, a.m., on the 8th of June, arriving in Guernsey at seven o'clock, p.m., or in thirteen hours, and in Jersey at eleven o'clock the same evening. With this single exception, the Southampton steamers left that port at six and seven o'clock, p.m., for years, so as to approach the islands on the following morning. In 1825, the Lord Beresford ran also from Southampton, and eight or nine years after both she and the Ariadne were replaced by the Lady de Saumarez and the Atalanta, vessels of greater size, power, and speed, which in 1840 ran each twice a week during the summer, at a reduced fare of a guinea. In 1835, a winter communication with

2F

Southampton was, for the first time, maintained once a week
by one of these steamers.

In 1826, the Sir Francis Drake, which still runs, (1854,)
commenced plying between Plymouth and the islands during
the summer months. Another steamer also plied from Tor-
quay in summer, for three or four years, up to 1852.

In 1827, a few years after the introduction of mail steamers
on the Holyhead, Liverpool, and other stations, the three
Weymouth sailing packets were replaced by two steamers, a
third being added in 1828. They plied as before, twice a
week, leaving on the Wednesday and Saturday evenings.
The steamers from Weymouth were discontinued in April,
1845, and replaced by contract steamers from Southampton,
from whence the first regular mail reached Guernsey on Sunday morning, the 27th, and continued three times weekly,
instead of twice as previously. As these contract steamers
left Southampton at seven o'clock, p.m., they usually arrived
in Guernsey at four and five o'clock, a.m., or in the dark in
winter. This being found both inconvenient and dangerous,
and causing a delay of twenty-four hours in the receipt of the
London mail, the steamers have, since June 30, 1848, left
Southampton at midnight with the London mail of the same
evening, occasionally performing the passage to Guernsey in
seven hours and a quarter! Previous to the last named
period, the mail steamers arrived in, and returned from, these
islands on the Sunday, thus causing a very unnecessary desecration of the Sabbath; but, on the petition of the inhabitants,
the days of arrival were changed from Sundays, Wednesdays,
and Fridays, to Tuesdays, Thursdays, and Saturdays, the
packets returning on Mondays, Wednesdays, and Fridays.

It would be tedious to pursue the subject further, by giving
a detail of the various steamers which have plied between
Guernsey and Brighton, Shoreham, or London, and have been
withdrawn; but in summer a steamer usually runs between
Jersey, Guernsey, and London. Since about the year 1848,
a small steamer has plied between Alderney and Guernsey:
when the communication between the two islands depended
on sailing vessels, an interval of a month in winter often occurred before a passenger could proceed from one to the other.

———

The tenure of real estate in the Channel Islands is peculiar
to them, it partaking of the double nature of mortgage and
freehold: thus, A, preferring to sell his land to cultivating it

himself, *gives it to rent*, as the term is, to *B*, who usually pays
as much as he conveniently can in money, and for the remainder of the purchase binds himself to pay annually a
certain number of quarters of wheat. The money payment
is a security to *A* that *B* shall faithfully farm the land, and
pay the wheat rents regularly ; if *B* fall in arrear, then *A*, by
a process called *saisie*, may eject him permanently, and *B*
forfeits the money he paid on entering into possession. These
remarks apply to the heirs of *A* and *B* in perpetuity. As
soon as the contract is passed, *A* ceases to be the proprietor
of the land, which belongs solely to *B*, as long as he pays
the rents due upon it. These rents can be paid or exacted in
kind ;[1] but, as a money payment is often preferred by both
parties, the average price per quarter, during the current year,
is affixed by the court of Chief Pleas, at Easter, and thus
the value of wheat in Europe may be correctly ascertained
for several centuries. " Experience has proved," says Duncan, " that under this tenure, a spirit of industry and economy
is generated, producing content, ease, and even wealth, from
estates which, in other countries, would hardly be thought
capable of affording sustenance to their occupants." Owing
to this tenure, the land in Guernsey, altogether amounting to
about 15,500 English acres, is greatly subdivided, twenty
such acres, equal to fifty Guernsey vergees, being considered
a large estate ; and although corn, cattle, poultry, &c., are
admitted duty free, the occupying proprietor, whose land
would let at £4 sterling the English acre, usually prospers,
and is enabled to pay the wheat rents due on his little farm.
But if the island were partitioned into thirty farms of 500
acres each, the result would quickly be a vast diminution in
the produce and the ruin of the tenants, if they paid the
above mentioned rent. And what is worse, numberless small
proprietors, now happy and contented in conscious independence, must either emigrate or become servile and discontented daily labourers.[2] The law of primogeniture, we need
scarcely add, prevails to a very limited extent,[3] although it

(1) In November, 1809, the royal court decided that rents were payable in wheat, the
growth of the island, which was a physical impossibility, Guernsey not then producing a
tithe of the rents due; but happily this decision was overruled by king in council, who
ordered that rents might be paid in foreign wheat.—See *Duncan*, p. 473.

(2) Macaulay, in his admirable history, states that more than a seventh of the population of England, in the seventeenth century, derived their subsistence from little freehold
estates. He speaks highly of these small landholders, and observes that those who cultivated their own fields and enjoyed a modest competence, " then formed a much more
important part of the nation than at present."

(3) By the law of 1840, the eldest son, out of certain boundaries in the town of St. Peter-
Port, gets from fourteen to twenty-two perches of land, or on the average about one-fifth
of an English acre; and, as he has the choice, he naturally selects the spot on which the
house and offices stand.

would doubtless be better if the eldest son were entitled to the whole estate, when not exceeding eight or ten English acres, as soon as his brothers and sisters became of age, and on payment of the widow's dower. The system of landed tenure which obtains has been recommended for Ireland, where the population amounts to scarcely three hundred souls to a square mile, and yet the peasantry are miserable and disaffected, while the islanders are happy and loyal, and sincerely attached to the British government. Agrarian outrage and murder are unknown; and sure we are that the introduction of a similar system of tenure in Ireland, with some modification, would do more for its well-being and pacification than all the measures of coercion which have been, or can be, framed for the repression of outbreak and crime in that unhappy country. The landlords are as much the victims of the present system as their wretched tenants; because, having no visitable neighbours, nö society within many miles, they are necessarily absentee, and seek that recreation abroad which they cannot find at home. If land were divided among the children, until the estate was reduced to fifty or a hundred acres, and then to be always the inheritance of the eldest son, there would be a resident proprietary, and the persons interested in the preservation of order would be increased ten, or perhaps twentyfold. Guernsey affords a living proof that the evils of Ireland are not irremediable,—that the poor need not be annually passed through a fiery furnace; but, unless the laws of entail and primogeniture be repealed, or greatly modified, in the latter country, there can be no permanency in her regeneration. If in Guernsey there be no powerful or wealthy landed aristocracy,—if, in fact, there be, in the English sense of the word, no aristocracy at all, most of the upper ranks deriving their wealth from, or being still connected with, commerce,—there is, what the philanthropist will value much more highly, an absence among the natives of that squalid want and misery which unhappily still exist in so many parts of Great Britain and Ireland, and which, we conceive, may in some measure be traced to class legislation.

Wheat rents, when not paid in kind, are affixed in livres tournois, fourteen of which are equal to £1 sterling; so that one livre of twenty sols is worth 1s. 5¼d. How great the variations have been in the value of wheat, the following decennial table will shew, in Guernsey quarters of four bushels, two and a half such quarters being about equal to the English imperial quarter:

Liv. Sols.		Liv. Sols.		Liv. Sols.
1610............... 4	0	1700. 8	0	1790...............12	0
1620............... 4	0	1710. 8	0	1800...............28	0
1630............... 6	0	1720. 6	10	1810...............24	2
1640............... 6	10	1730. 6	0	1820...............12	12
1650............... 6	10	1740. 7	10	1830...............16	16
1660............... 9	0	1750. 7	0	1840...............13	6
1670............... 7	0	1760. 8	0	1850...............10	3
1680............... 7	0	1770. 10	0		
1690............... 5	10	1780. 11	0		

In the years 1811 and 1812, rents were affixed at 28 livres, or £2 sterling. But in 1834 and 1835, they were as low as 8 livres 15 sols, or 12s. 6d., (or about £1. 10s. per English quarter,) being the lowest rate since 1769, in which year they were at 8 livres tournois.

The gradual accumulation of wealth in the town and parish of St. Peter-Port will be seen by the following details :

"The first tax list existing in the constables' office is dated in 1715, the constables and donzeniers of the parish of St. Peter-Port, duly authorized by the chief pleas, having, on the 8th of March, proceeded to raise 500 livres tournois (£35. 14s. 3d. sterling,) to purchase powder, matches, and other ammunitions of war, required for the magazine of the said parish. The inhabitants were then assessed at 16,531 quarters, on which $7\frac{1}{2}$ deniers (about one half-penny) per quarter were levied. The highest rates were those of Thomas Le Marchant, Peter Etienne, (Stephens,) and John De Sausmarez, bailiff, assessed at 500 quarters each,—a large property in those days, and the lowest rate was five quarters. This tax list is signed by John Bouillon and Daniel Painsec,[1] constables, Richard de Jersey, Nicholas Carey, John Mauger, Abraham Monamy, James De Havilland, John Dobrée, A. Le Messurier, Nicholas Dobrée, Joshua Gosselin, John Tupper,[2] Thomas Gosselin, Henry De Jersey, James Perchard, and John Bowden, douzeniers.

"The next tax list also bears date in 1715, the inhabitants, on the 21st of March, having been duly assessed for 700 livres tournois, to pursue the cause against Mr. William Le Marchant, relative to l'Hyvreuse, before king in council.

"The third tax list is dated in 1720, when 1,000 livres tournois were levied for the repair of the guard-house at Fermain, the rent of the guard-house at Belgrève, the purchase of powder, and other parochial wants. The inhabitants were this year assessed at 17,648 quarters, Thomas Le Marchant, sen., paying on 600 quarters, the highest rate.

(1) A singular conjunction of names, both now extinct, as well as that of Monamy.

(2) The individual to whom the gold medal was presented by William and Mary, as related at page 346.

"The fourth tax list is dated in 1724, the constables and douzeniers having, on the 14th of December, proceeded to raise 4,000 livres tournois (£285. 14s. 3d.) for the relief of the poor. The inhabitants were now assessed at 23,200 quarters, and the rate was 3 sous 6 deniers (three pence sterling) per quarter. The highest amounts were : Nicholas Dobrée, Thomas Le Marchant, and Peter Carey (de la Brasserie,) rated at 600 quarters each. This is not stated as being the first tax raised for the poor; but, having made reference to the account books in the hospital, we find that it was so, as will appear by the following extract from the account current of the collectors for that year, viz. ' Pour la première taxe levée sur les habitants de la dite paroisse, le 14 de Décembre, 1724, pour la subsistence des dits pauvres.' The oldest account of the collectors, now existing in the hospital, is dated in 1634, when, and previously to 1724, the poor were relieved by rents and money bequeathed for that purpose by charitable individuals, contributions at the communion table and church door, and fines exacted by the royal court. They appear also to have been relieved as the *pauvres honteux* now are, as the hospital was not built till 1742.[1]

"From 1724, the inhabitants of St. Peter-Port appear, by the books in the constables' office, to have been annually assessed as at present, with occasional intermissions, for the various parochial wants; and we now proceed to give details of the assessments, every ten years, commencing with 1730.

"In 1730, the inhabitants raised 4,000 livres tournois on 20,878 quarters, charged at 3 sous 10 deniers per quarter, and payable in four instalments. The highest amount paid was by Peter Stephens and son, rated at 600 quarters.

"In 1740, the assessment for the poor was also 4,000 livres tournois on 21,894 quarters, at 3 sous 6 deniers per quarter. The highest tax was that of Thomas Le Marchant, rated at 600 quarters—the lowest tax was five quarters.

"Of 1750 there is no record; but in 1751 we find that 4,000 livres tournois, payable in two instalments, were again raised for the poor, ' in the hospital,' on 25,278 quarters, at 3 sous 2 deniers each. Thomas Le Marchant was taxed at 800 quarters, the highest rate, and the lowest was still five quarters.

"In 1760, two taxes were raised, viz. 4,000 livres tournois for the soldiers' quarters, cleaning muskets and bayonets, a new pump, &c., and 5,000 livres tournois for the hospital, both on 33,312 quarters, rated at 2 sous 6 deniers for the former, and 3 sous for the latter. This is the first year in which we observe any taxes of four figures; James and John Le Ray being rated at 1,200 quarters, and William Brock and his sons at 1,000 quar-

(1) The individuals who had charge of the poor were styled "Diacres" until 1663, since which period they have borne the title of "Collecteurs des Pauvres."

ters. Of single individuals, the highest assessments were Thomas Le Marchant and James Le Marchant, rated at 700 quarters each. No inhabitant was rated this year under 10 quarters, as is the case at present.

"In 1770, the inhabitants were assessed 6,000 livres tournois for the poor, on 44,155 quarters, at 2 sous 9 deniers per quarter, and payable in two instalments. The entries of four figures this year, in one line, are as follow, viz. John Carey, and widow John Le Ray, 1,600 quarters; William Brock, sen., 1,350 quarters; heirs of William Brock, jun., 1,300 quarters; widow and son of Peter Stephens, 1,260 quarters; John Brock, jun., 1,100 quarters; and Thomas Carey and children, 1,000 quarters.

"In 1780, three assessments were made, viz. 1st of March, 10,000 livres tournois, on 61,930 quarters, at 3 sous 3 deniers each, for parochial debts and other public expenses; and 1st of December, 8,000 livres tournois, on 61,925 quarters, at 2 sous 9 deniers each, for the same purpose; and 6,000 livres tournois for the poor, also on 61,925 quarters, at 2 sous each, together 24,000 livres tournois, (£1,714 5s. 8d. sterling,) and the rate 8 sous (nearly seven pence) per quarter. The individuals highest rated on the 1st of December, were John Carey, 1,950 quarters; Elisha Tupper, 1,850 quarters; Nicholas Maingy, sen., 1,650 quarters; heirs of John Brock, 1,420 quarters; Peter Mourant, 1,400 quarters; and Richard De Beauvoir, 1,020 quarters.—In the tax of the 1st of March, this year, £30 a year interest in the English funds were estimated at 40 quarters, and £1,000 capital, at 50 quarters, as at this moment, being the first notice of the kind in the tax books.

"In 1790, the assessment was 7,000 livres tournois on 77,100 quarters, at 2 sous each, for the hospital. There were seven individuals rated at four figures, of whom two at 2,000 quarters and above, viz., Elisha Tupper, at 2,300 quarters, and John Carey, son of John, at 2,030 quarters.

"In 1800, two taxes were levied, both on the 22d of May, viz. 10,000 livres tournois on 94,455 quarters, at 2 sous 2 deniers each, for poor strangers, pumps, lamps, rents due, &c., and 14,000 livres tournois, on 94,455 quarters, at 3 sous each, for the poor, and repairs of hospital, together 24,000 livres tournois, or nearly 4½d. per quarter. This year we find fourteen persons rated at four figures, of whom only one at 2,000 quarters or above, viz. Elisha Tupper, rated at 2,450 quarters.

"In 1810, five taxes were raised, viz. on the 28th of June, two sums of £800 sterling each, on 98,955 quarters, at 4d. each, for the hospital and constables; 5th of October, £1,901. 3s. 1d. sterling, on 101,395 quarters, at 4½d. each, towards the high roads to Vason and Rocquaine; and 28th of December, £1,600 for the constables, and £1,200 for the hospital, on 96,075 quar-

ters, 7d. each, making together, this year, £6,301. 3s. 1d. sterling,
and the rates 15½d. per quarter.—There were twelve rated at
four figures, of whom two of 2,000 quarters, or above, viz. Sir
James Saumarez, 2,800 quarters, and James Carey, 2,000 quarters.   It was in 1804 and 1805 that the calculations were first
made in sterling, and that those in livres tournois were discontinued.

" In 1820, three taxes were also raised, the whole on 137,760
quarters, viz. £1,600 sterling, for pumps, lamps, &c., and
£1,600 for the hospital, both at 2¾d. per quarter, and £600 for
the *pauvres honteux*, or external poor, at 1½d. per quarter, together £3,800, collected at 6¾d. per quarter.—Twenty-six persons
were now rated at four figures, of whom seven at 2,000 quarters
or above, viz. Sir James Saumarez, 5,000 quarters; John
Allaire, 4,900 quarters; Thomas Priaulx, 4,500 quarters; Carteret Priaulx, 4,200 quarters; Peter Stephens, 2,500 quarters;
Anthony Priaulx, 2,150 quarters, and widow and children of
Daniel Tupper, 2,050 quarters.—On the 10th of February, this
year, the royal court decided that the taxes should be raised, for
the present, on income as heretofore, and not on capital, as
sought by some of the parishioners, who urged the injustice of
their income, and not their capital, in the French and other
foreign funds, being taxed, those funds being then considerably
under par, and yielding 7 to 8 per cent. on the capital invested.
But, by an entry in 1824, we find that the system was then
changed, and capital became, as it now is, the basis of parochial
taxation, property of any kind, worth £1,000, being assessed at
50 quarters.   Although this system is analogous to that established in 1780, as already cited, yet it bears hard on those whose
income is derived from the English funds,—for instance, this
year (1854) the 3 per cent. consols were assessed at 88, and an
individual possessing £1,000 consols was charged for 44 quarters,
although the net interest is only £28. 5s., income tax deducted.
It is, however, manifestly impossible to establish any system of
taxation which will not press unequally on some individuals, and
we think the present mode as equitable as will ever be attained,
while the property of the parishioners is invested in so many
channels quite unknown to our ancestors.

" It may be well here to observe, that the immense increase of
38,805 quarters between 1810 and 1820, was owing, first, to a
number of American prizes captured in 1811-12, one being a ship
from Calcutta worth about £60,000; and, secondly, in a great
measure, to the fortunate investments of many of the parishioners
in the French funds, after the peace of 1814, large sums having
been transferred from the English funds and other sources into
the French 5 per cents. under 60 and 70, by which means the
incomes of many were increased by at least one-third, and a

proportionate increase in the number of quarters naturally followed, income and not capital being then, as we have already observed, the rule of taxation.

"In 1830, three taxes were raised simultaneously on 150,805 quarters, viz., £1,400, at 2⅜d. per quarter, for the hospital; £700, at 1⅛d., for the *pauvres honteux;* and £1,500, at 2⅝d. for other parochial purposes; together £3,600, or 6½d. per quarter. In this year, we find twenty-one individuals possessing incomes of 1,000 quarters and above, of whom five were assessed at 2,000 quarters and above, viz. John Allaire, 5,500 quarters; Thomas Priaulx, 4,200 quarters; John Carey, son of John, 2,120 quarters; Hilary Rougier, 2,075 quarters, and Joseph Collings, 2,000 quarters.

"In 1840, the following taxes were raised on 152,930 quarters, representing a capital of £3,058,600 sterling, viz. £1,400 for lamps, pumps, poor strangers, &c.; £1,800 for the hospital; £1,100 for the external poor, or hospital out-pensioners; and £150 for the parish church, together £4,450 sterling, collected by a tax of 7½d. per quarter, from 825 rate-payers, whose property thus averaged £3,700 capital, or about £185 annual income. It is well to mention now, that the douzaine, to avoid fractions, and to allow for the deduction of individuals over-taxed, usually fix the rate a little higher than the amount actually required. In this year, we find twenty-one individuals of four figures, of whom seven of 2,000 quarters and above, viz. John Allaire, 7,000 quarters; Thomas Priaulx, 3,200 quarters; Mary Le Marchant, 2,450 quarters; John Carey, (queen's receiver,) 2,350 quarters; Sir William Collings, 2,310 quarters; Hilary Rougier, 2,300 quarters; and John Collings, 2,000 quarters.   In 1838, the property of the parish was rated higher than it had ever been; viz. 156,350 quarters, on which £5,537. 7s. 11d. were raised at 8½d. per quarter.   The decrease in 1840 was chiefly owing to a serious depreciation in the value of the shares of the ' Bank of the United States,' at Philadelphia, in which many of the rate-payers were interested, to the extent, it appears, of about £150,000 original cost, and of which nearly the whole was ultimately lost, one gentleman losing £33,000.

"In 1850, the town parish was assessed for £7,413. 16s., at 12½d. per quarter on 142,345 quarters only, the falling off arising from the French revolution of 1848, and the consequent depreciation of all the European funds.   In 1850, nineteen individuals were taxed at four figures, of whom five at 2,000 quarters and above, viz. Mrs. May, 5,845 quarters; Mrs. Thomas Collings, 5,400 quarters; (both born Allaire;) John Le Marchant, 2,760 quarters; Hilary Rougier, 2,700 quarters; and Sir William Collings, 2,550 quarters.

"In 1853, the parish of St. Peter-Port was assessed for

£7,709. 16s. 3d., at 1s. 1d. on 142,335 quarters; and the nine country parishes were rated together at 63,640 quarters, viz. St. Sampson's, 4,241; Vale, 6,258; Câtel, 14,717; St. Saviour's, 6,463; St. Peter-in-the-Wood, 7,642; Torteval, 1,495; Forest, 3,330; St. Martin's, 12,853; and St. Andrew's, 6,671. Thus, in 1853, the entire property of the ten parishes of Guernsey, both real and personal, was valued at 205,975 quarters, or, at £20 per quarter, £4,119,500 sterling.

"It has already been shewn that in the space of one hundred and twenty-five years, (1715 to 1840,) the wealth of the town parish augmented nearly tenfold, the annual average being 1,091 quarters; although, considering the difference in the value of money and the mode of living, it is certain that 500 quarters income in 1715 were fully equal to 1,500 quarters in 1840. In 1715, and for many years subsequently, a considerable part of the property of the higher ranks, which was taxed, consisted in 'rentes foncières,' or perpetual mortgages on the insular estates and houses; now, it is chiefly invested in public securities, and partially in shipping, trade, houses, and furniture. Since 1838, there has been a downward tendency in the total amount of the rateable parish property, and it is of course very difficult to predict its future rule; but with the present paucity of resident strangers, the depression of insular commerce and navigation, and the more expensive habits and wants of the existing generation, it is too probable that the decrease will continue. On the other hand, as long as the British, French, and other governments, keep faith with their creditors, no serious diminution is to be apprehended, unless indeed the division by degrees of the large fortunes, lately and still existing, have that tendency. Should, however, any sudden general check arise in the payment of interest, either from national bankruptcy or the resolve of the people to repudiate its large debts contracted by their ancestors, often for unholy purposes, the result, in the parish of St. Peter-Port, would be attended with effects too disastrous to dwell upon or contemplate.—The recent discoveries of gold in Australia and California happily render the chance of repudiation more improbable.

"For the information of strangers, it may be well to add, that a quarter of rent is estimated at £20 capital, or £1 annual income: this has always been a general rule, but the income has occasionally varied, as now, with the price of the funds. A livre tournois is divided into 20 sous of 12 deniers each, and is worth 1s. 5½d., 14 livres tournois being equal to £1. sterling."

ISLAND OF SARK.

In the Harleian Miscellany, vol. iii., there is a "perfect description of the isle of Serke, appertaining to the British crown, and never before publicly discoursed of," in a letter dated April 1, O.S. 1673, "from a gentleman now inhabiting there, to his friend and kinsman in London." He begins by stating that "the Anne, of Bristol, touching here [probably Guernsey] homewards bound, brought safe those commodities I gave you the trouble to send me;" and, in describing the topography of "Serke," says: "Yet nature, as if she had here stored up some extraordinary treasure, seems to have been very solicitous to render it impregnable; being on every side surrounded with vast rocks and mighty clifts, whose craggy tops, braving the clouds with their stupendous height, bid defiance to all that shall dream of forcing an entrance. Two only ascents or passages there are into it: the first, where all goods and commodities are received, called La Soguien, where, for a large space through a solid rock, there is a cart-way cut by art down to the sea, with two strong gates for its defence, (wherein most of the storage for navigation, as masts, sails, anchors, &c., belonging to the island, are kept,) and two pieces of ordnance above, always ready to prevent any surprise; the other is La Frikerée, where only passengers can land, climbing up a rock by certain steps, or stairs cut therein, to a vast height, and somewhat dangerously; nor is it possible there for above one person to come up at once."

He next narrates the singular manner of its capture from the French, and, speaking of the elements, says that the air was so pure that it was not rare to meet with a hearty old man of four score, "although I know not one physician in the island, and perhaps we live the longer for their absence."—"Our water, I confess, is sometimes not very ready, and yet we have no less than six very fine springs generally running."

"Our earth or soil is for the most part hot and sandy, yet fruitful enough to afford all necessaries to its inhabitants; excellent for bearing all kind of roots, as parsnips, carrots, turnips, &c., and very well stored with fruit trees, for the most part planted of late, furnishing us with cyder. Fern we have of most sorts, but not in any extraordinary quantity; our pasture is but short, yet exceeding sweet, and therefore we have rare mutton, but no great plenty of beef, and cows only enough to supply us with milk and butter; for our cheese we have generally from England.

"Our firing is for the most part furzes, and sometimes turf; for we have but little wood, and no timber at all growing throughout the whole island; so that we are forced either to make shift with old apple tree for our houses, or furnish ourselves as well as we can with deal.

"For belly-timber, our three staple commodities are fish, fowl, and rabbits: of the first, a little industry will purchase us a hundred sorts, particularly a large fish we call a *crack*-fish, which we split, and, nailing it to our walls, dry it in the sun for part of our winter provision; as also a large shell-fish, taken plentifully at low tides, called an *ormond*,[1] that sticks to the rocks, whence we beat them off with a fossil or iron hook: it is much bigger than an oyster, and like that good, either fresh or pickled, but infinitely more pleasant to the gusto, so that an epicure would think his palate in paradise if he might but always gormondize on such delicious ambrosia. (to borrow Aretine's phrase, upon his eating a lamprey.)

"For fowl, your city cannot be better furnished with woodcocks or widgeons, besides the abundance of duck, mallard, teal, and other wild fowl, with clift pigeons, with which, at some seasons, almost the whole island is covered.

(1) Ormer (*haliotis tuberculata*). The ormer, when cooked, somewhat resembles a veal cutlet: in Guernsey, an immense number are brought to market in February, March, and April, or are sent to Jersey.

"Of conies, we have everywhere exceeding plenty, and yet, lest we should want, nature has provided us a particular warren, placing at a small distance in the sea an island[1] of about half a mile every way over, which is inhabited by nothing else, whither we commonly go a-ferreting, and have thence such abundance, that it has been confidently told me some families here have made fifteen or twenty pounds a year only of their skins. If all this rich fare will not content you, we have a most excellent pottage made of milk, bacon, coleworts, mackerel, and gooseberries, boiled together all to pieces, which our mode is to eat, not with the ceremony of a spoon, but the more courtly way of a great piece of bread furiously plying between your mouth and the kettle.

"But, lest you should think we mind too much our bellies, take next a survey of our political government. First, for our defence, we have a captain, with about forty soldiers, who continually keep guard, and are maintained by contribution of the inhabitants; then we have a court of judicature held every Tuesday, where an honest fisherman we call the judge; another, at present his son, that is entitled Monsieur Le Provost, a person that has the gift of writing, and learning enough to read the obligation of a bond, serving as clerk or recorder, with five other sage burghers that are justices, or some of them, meet, and without any tedious formalities, intricate demurrers, special verdicts, wire-drawn arguments, chargeable injunctions, multiplied motions, or endless writs of error, briskly determine all causes *secundùm æquum et bonum*, (according to their mother-wit and grave discretions,) except in criminals where life is concerned, in which case the offenders are immediately sent away for trial and punishment to Guernsey."

The writer next mentions that the islanders are of the reformed discipline, and have an Huguenot minister, who "hath lately begun to teach grammar to the children, with writing and arithmetic, erecting a school for that purpose." Speaking of the mode of dress, he says: "Each man religiously preserving his vast blue trunk-breeches, and a coat almost like a Dutch fro's vest, or one of your watermen's liveries. Nor are the women behind hand with them in their hospital gowns of the same colour, wooden sandals, white stockings, and red petticoats, so mean they are scarce worth taking up. Both sexes, on festivals, wear large ruffs, and the women, instead of hats or hoods, truss up their hair, the more genteel sort in a kind of cabbage net; those of meaner fortunes in a piece of linen; perhaps an old dish-clout turned out of service, or the fag-end of a table cloth, that has escaped the persecution of washing ever since the Reformation.

"Let me conclude with a word or two of our trade, which, I confess, is not very great to the Levant or either of the Indies; Bristol, and some other of your western ports, being the furthest places of our traffic; for the grand and almost only manufacture of our island being knitting, which our people perform with a wonderful dexterity, both for stockings, gloves, caps, and waistcoats, men, women and children, being brought up to it; so that you may commonly see thirty or forty of them assembled in a barn, which you would take for a conventicle of your sweet singers of Israel; for, though all ply their knitting devoutly, yet at the same time they tune their pipes, and torture some old songs, with more distracted notes than a country quire does one of Hopkins' psalms. These commodities, when finished, we vend into England at the places aforesaid, having several small vessels for that purpose, and thence in return furnish ourselves with necessaries.

"All this, though you read it not till Michaelmas, was told you at Serke, this first of April, O.S. 1673."

[Doubtless the trade of Sark was carried on through Guernsey. The writer says that he went to Sark from Southampton; and he adds, that he will drink his London kinsman's "health in a black jack of French wine, which, paying no custom, we have here as plentifully cheap as in France itself."]

(1) Brechou, or Isle des Marchands.

CHAPTER XXIV.

MILITIA OF GUERNSEY, &c.

THAT a defensive force or militia existed in the Anglo-Norman Islands from very early times, has been shewn by a mandate of Edward III., dated in 1337, ordering an armed array of the inhabitants; and in Guernsey it was chiefly this array which encountered Sir Owen of Wales, when he invaded the island in 1372. Exposed as all the islands were, from their frontier and isolated position, to constant attacks, it is evident that the natives could only preserve their connection with England, after the loss of Normandy in 1204, by some sort of military organization, which provided for the compulsory service of every man able to bear arms; and this obligation was the more necessary, because, for several centuries, there were no permanent English garrisons, excepting perhaps the retinue of the governors. Indeed, it has ever been one of the indispensable conditions of national existence that every man should be prepared to defend his country against hostile invasion. Accordingly, there was in every parish in Guernsey, not possessing a common, a small strip of land for the exercise of archery, which land is still called " Les Buttes,"[1] anglicé The Butts, or the spot on which the target was placed —a practice doubtless derived from the Normans, who at the Conquest excelled in the use of the bow, which had been much neglected, if not totally discontinued, in England during the Saxon era; and to the arrows of the invaders the victory of Hastings is generally attributed. In England, after the Conquest, all who held lands by knight's service were bound to attend the king in war, within or without the realm, mounted and armed, during forty days, beyond which period they could be retained only by their own consent and at the king's expense, their vassals being also compelled to accompany them. Independently, however, of these tenures, Edward I. and Edward II. made arbitrary levies of other persons of sufficient estate, which levies, being unconstitutional, were abolished by Edward III. on the petition of his first parliament; and thenceforth he and his successors, in

[1] " Butte, petite élévation pour placer le but où l'on tire en blanc."—*French Dictionary.*

their wars with France, recruited their forces by contracts with men of rank and influence, who procured voluntary enlistments through means of very high pay. By the statutes of Henry II. and Edward I., every man was bound to furnish himself with arms and equipments according to the value of his lands and goods, and such was the law in these islands; but that the arms were not very costly, may be inferred from the report of the royal commissioners, Conway and Bird, who reviewed the Jersey militia in 1617, and said: "The armes specified are exceedingly defective; those called by the generall names of bills, but many bare staves, with noe iron at all, no cuirasses, not twelve pikes, few muskets." This description applied equally to the Guernsey militia, as Heylin, speaking of it in 1629, wrote: "Their trained band consists of only 1,200, and those, God knows, but poorly weaponed."

The first ordinance extant relating to the Guernsey militia is dated April 5, 1546,[1] and commands all the male inhabitants, on their allegiance, to obey their captains, who are also commanded to see in their respective parishes that the haquebuts,[2] bows, and bundles or quivers of arrows, (*haquebuttes, ars, et trousses,*) are in order; that the bulwarks (*boulvars*) are constructed; and that the munitions are always ready, as they shall answer. And all those who are ordered by their captains to provide arms shall obey.—The next ordinance is dated May 15, 1549, and enacts that the bailiff shall have the survey and charge of all the town parish, and shall cause bulwarks to be erected wherever they are required: he was also empowered to send, without any process, for the goods of any man neglecting to work at the said bulwarks, after being duly warned, and cause them to be sold by the market crier, (*au cry du marchy,*) to pay the person employed at the work in his stead. The bailiff was also encharged to inspect every man's "hacquebutte," and to furnish one, with its appurtenances, to such as had none, fining each defaulter four sols "et denier" per day. And to the captains in the other parishes was granted the same authority as to the bailiff.

During the stay in Guernsey of the royal commissioners, Gardner and Hussey, in 1607, the inhabitants complained "that great sums of money have been levied upon the isle for armour, namely, to buy rondaches and muskets, whereof Mr. Peter Carey was factor, and received the money, but

---

(1) In 1543, long bows, cross bows, and all other weapons, were by law exempted from arrest for debt in Guernsey.

(2) "Haquebut, a sort of gun, called also a harquebuse."—*Bailey's Dictionary.*

hath hitherto given none account." Mr. Carey, then lieutenant-governor, answered that, " touching the armour," he was
appointed, in 1585, by Sir T. Leighton, to whom he had rendered an account, and was "not bound to yield the same
unto the complainants." He, however, did so to the commissioners, who were quite satisfied ; but those who paid the
money, and certainly had a right to see the account, obtained
no redress. The inhabitants of St. Peter-Port complained
that the governor had taken upon himself to dispose of the
rents belonging to the maintenance of their parish church,
" to pay gunners at such stipend as he would himself;" and,
relating to the payment of gunners, the commissioners ordained "that the bailiff and jurats shall be judges thereof."—
The inhabitants of the "Valle" prayed that the parishes of
St. Peter-Port, St. Sampson, Câtel, and St. Martin, should
" contribute with them towards the maintenance of their artillery, as they are bound thereunto;" and " Mr. Lieutenant
(Carey) being desired by us to declare his knowledge thereof,
saith that the parishes of St. Peter-Port, St. Sampson, St.
Martin, and the Castle, do maintain a *sacre* of their own
within the parish of the Valle, and in a place called Lancresse ;
and that the other piece of ordnance, which particularly
belongeth to the parish of the Valle, ought to be maintained
by themselves and none other:" the commissioners in consequence decided accordingly.— The inhabitants of St. Peter-
du-Bois having solicited the commissioners " to be mediators
for them to his highness for the supply of some pieces of
artillery, that they do want by reason of the dangers of their
sea coast," the commissioners answered that they had "taken
the opinion of the Lieutenant (Carey) touching the desired
artillery, who assureth us that there is already more artillery
in the isle than the inhabitants are well able to maintain, and
therefore see no cause why we should at this time yield unto
their desire therein."

Returns of the militia of Guernsey, reviewed by Sir Peter
Osborne, 27th of August, 1621 : St. Peter-Port, 312 ; St.
Sampson, 57 ; the Vale, 114 ; Câtel, 120 ; St. Saviour, 130 ;
St. Peter-du-Bois, 120 ; Torteval, 45 ; St. Martin, 136 ;
St. Andrew, 63 ; Forest, 60 ; total, 1,157.

The following instructions for the Guernsey militia were
found among Sir Peter Osborne's papers, without date, but
probably written between the years 1625 and 1630 :

" Orders to be observed by the captaynes and severall companies.

"That upon alarme they come to the severall places appoynted for, theyre rendez-vous, as namely, for the towne, &c.

"That upon sight of any fleete, horses with saddles be sent to the towne from each parish.

"That the constables, with the vinetaniers, attend the captayne, or, in his absence, his lieutenant, or any other officer appoynted by the captayne, to receave the word, upon setting of the generall watches.

"That the watch be duly survayde by the captayne, or some other officer by his appoyntment.

"That every man be commanded to have no less than one pound of powder and bullets, answerable of his own store and provision.

"That Mr. Bayliff and the Jurates visit the powder to be sold in towne, and to seaze upon that which is ill and unserviceable.

"That every parish have a close cart, covered also with a tarpaulin, to transport theyre powder and math drye, and that they have besyde a body barrell.

"That the powder and lead in towne be distributed to the severall parishes that can make just clayme to it.

"That the ordnance in all places throughout the island be sufficiently mounted, and namely, those at Lancresse, the Pezari, and Rocquaine, and viewed by the captaynes.

"That there be good draught ropes and takling for all the ordnance, to remove them upon occasion.

"That such as are to attend the ordnance carry spades and pickaxes, to cleare the way, if occasion be.

"That the persons lyable to bring horses for the ordnance attend that service, and come also with horse and cartes.

"That all the brest workes throughout the island be generally and speedily repayred and made up, and especially the fortifications at Fermayne.

"That theyre be sufficient store of drumes, and those serviceable and fitt ; that provision be also made of heades, cords, and hoopes.

"That all captaynes and lieutenants carry partizans,[1] and every sergeant a halbert.

"That the beacons be made ready, and fired upon all occasion of alarme.

"That every one repayre speedily with his armes to the place of rendez-vous, upon the alarme given, and presume not to depart from his cullers with out his captayne's order and leave.

"That every man watch in his turne, or finde one to watch for him, and that none be exempt, except the captaynes only."

(1) The partizan was a light pike, with an axe affixed near the head, and used either for striking or thrusting.

The following are extracts from the diary of Peter Le Roy:

" September 16, 1656.—A general muster, held at the *Grand' Mielles*[1] by the 'Honorable' Colonel Bingham, our chief governor, and with him the 'noble' Colonel Squire, both members of parliament, when there were:

" Two companies of the Town ...... 340 men.
 From St. Sampson's .... 60 ,,
  ,, the Vale. .... 140 ,,
  ,, the Càtel .... 160 ,,
  ,, St. Saviour's .... 160 ,,
  ,, St. Pierre-du-Bois .... 140 ,,
  ,, Torteval. .... 48 ,,
  ,, the Forest . ... 100 ,,
  ,, St. Martin's. .... 180 ,,
  ,, St. Andrew's. .... 90 ,,

" Thus the number of men who there appeared carrying arms and keeping rank and file, amounted to 1,418,[2] without counting the captains and other officers, the old men and others exempted from carrying arms, the absent and the sick, and a great number of young men who had not yet been obliged to carry arms.

" June 29, 1664.—At a general muster of the militia, before Lord Hatton, there were eleven companies, consisting of 1,324 soldiers carrying arms, exclusive of officers and all those who assisted at the cannon, others without arms, and the aged men who were exempted."

Captain Waterhouse, Lieut.-Governor, to Mr. John Le Gros.

" Sir,—Lieutenant Richard Winne, haveing urgent oocations to goe into England, I desire that in his absense you will take care of the militia of the island of Sarke, and keep the said isle for his highnes the Lord Protector of England. Not else at present, but that I am your affectionat frind,

" CHARLES WATERHOUSE.

" Castle Cornet, April 14, 1659.
 " ffor his respected frind, Mr. John Le Gross,
  Judge of Sarke Isle, These."

Lieut.-Governor Darell to Captain William Le Marchant.

" You are hereby to take notice that when the right honorable the Lord Hatton, our governor, shal bee upon our coast, I shall give you warning thereof, by fyring three peices of ordnance from the castle, and that you order the bells to bee runge, and that your

(1) A large common in the Càtel parish, about half a mile to the N.N.E. of Cobo Bay, much enclosed since the diary was written.

(2) According to the usual calculation that one-seventh of the inhabitants are fit to bear arms, this number would give a population of fully 9,926 souls, and St. Peter-Port probably contained about 3,000 souls.

ordnance bee fyred after the castle shall have answered the frigot's salutacon, and likewise that you observe the same order when that my lord shal bee welcomed into the castle, which shal bee made knowne unto you by the shooting of the ordnance; and at night that bonfires bee made in your parish.

"You are likewise to have a care that all the armes in your company bee fixt.

"NATHANIELL DARELL, Lieut.-Governor.

[February, 1664.]

"Endorsed: 'ffor my cousen, Captaine William Marchant, captaine of the fforest.'"

Lord Hatton to the Captain of the Parish of St. Andrew.

"Capitaine de la paroisse de St. André.

"(LS.)—Il vous est expressement enjoint que vous ayés à comparer devant moy, Mercredi, le 29e du courant, à neuf heures du matin, ès Grands Mieles, avec touts les officiers et soldats de vostre compagnie, fournis des armes et amunition suffisant. Et que fassés trainer les canons de vostre paroisse à la mesme place à faire moustres generales avec les autres compagnies de ceste isle. Et entretemps vous ferés par vous et les officiers de vostre susdite compagnie une reveue des armes de chasque soldat de vostre compagnie, afin qu'ils soient fixes et en bon ordre; et auparavant le jour appointé pour les moustres generales, il vous est enjoint d'assembler les officiers et soldats de vostre susdite compagnie, afin de les exercer et instruire en l'art militaire, et qu'ayés à m'advertir du jour que tiendres cette moustre particulière. ffinalement, auparavant le dit jour des moustres generales, vous estes enjoint de m'apporter une liste des noms et qualités de chascun des officiers et soldats de vostre dite compagnie, et de l'amunition, canons, et d'autres nécessaires de milice appartenants à vostre paroisse, et pareillement que m'envoyés au plustot que pourrés les canoniers de vostre paroisse: à quoy n'y ait faute en aucun article. Donné au Chasteau Cornett, le 14e de Juin, 1664.

"CHR. HATTON."

Towards the close of the seventeenth century, the militia was divided into thirteen companies; and, according to Mr. Dumaresq, of Jersey, who wrote in 1685, the whole formed in one body commanded by the governor, or his lieutenant. In 1680, by an apparently official return, the captains and strength of the thirteen companies were: St. Peter-Port, four companies, Captains Daniel de Beauvoir, William Le Marchant, John Martin, and Samuel Dobrée, 521 men; St. Sampson's company, Captain Abraham Carey, 103 men; Valle company, Captain John Boullion, 119 men; St. Mar-

tin's company, Captain John Andros, 198 men ; Câtel company, Captain Charles Andros, 182 men ; St. Andrew's
company, Captain Isaac Carey, 105 men ; the Forest company, Captain John Bonamy, 120 men ; Torteval company,
Captain Nicholas Le Huray, 169 men ; St. Peter-du-Bois
company, Captain Thomas De Lisle, 183 men ; and St.
Saviour's company, Captain George Andros, 202 men ; grand
total, 1,902 men : but this number, in a population of less
than 10,000 souls, is now incredible. These companies appear to have been embodied into three regiments early in the
eighteenth century, when the title of colonel was first established, although in Jersey it was introduced about the year
1620, or a century earlier.—Amias Andros, bailiff, who died
in 1674, was major-general of the Guernsey militia.   The
first mention that we find of the three regiments, with colonels and lieutenant-colonels, is in an ordinance of the Chief
Pleas, in 1730 ; and by a commission granted by Lieut.-Gover-
nor Dollon, dated St. Peter-Port, September 20, 1727, Thomas
Le Marchant, Jun., was appointed " captain of one company
of militia of the parish of the Câtel, in the regiment of the
Honorable Colonell William Le Marchant, Sen. Esq."

Lieut.-Governor Giles Spicer having intimated to the
royal court, in March, 1719, that, in conformity with an order
from the secretary of war, he had sent to Plymouth the soldiers who were in garrison in the island, so that Castle Cornet
was left defenceless, the court authorized him to appoint daily
such a number of the militia as he deemed necessary for the
guard of the castle, and of the harbour of St. Peter-Port.
At this time, Great Britain was in close alliance with France,
and at war with Spain, which government dispatched, in
February, 1719, a strong force from Cadiz under the Duke
of Ormond, with the design of landing in the west of England ; but the expedition was dispersed near Cape Finisterre,
a few days after its departure, and rendered abortive. Ormond
was an adherent of the Pretender, who had many partisans
among the English, as well as among the Scotch and Irish.

Application having been made to government, in 1740, for
twenty-five field pieces, muskets, barracks, &c., the lords
justices decided that no cannon should be sent, because " so
lately as the year 1732, all the guns belonging to the garrison
in Guernsey, which were defective, were exchanged, and
thirteen iron ordnance, with stores proper for them, were sent
thither." They, however, empowered the lieutenant-governor

to arm the inhabitants, on any emergency, with the 500 muskets lodged in Castle Cornet, " taking particular care that they be returned safe, when the occasion for issuing them cease." The barracks in Castle Cornet, being in a ruinous condition, were ordered to be put into as good repair as they were capable of, " for the accommodation of the two companies in that castle." But, although muskets were refused in 1740, 1000, with bayonets, &c., were sent, in 1744, from England for the militia ; evidently for the poorer classes only.

STATE OF THE THREE REGIMENTS OF MILITIA AT GUERNSEY, ACCORDING TO A GENERAL REVIEW MADE THE 25th OF JUNE, 1750.

Colonels.	Captains.	Lieutenants.	Ensigns.	Serjeants.	Drummers.	Soldiers.	King's Muskets.	Bayonets and Belts.	Cartouch Boxes.	Balls.	Flints.
Elisha Le Marchant, Esq. ...	7	4	4	20	2	600	350	350	350	2100	3500
William Le Marchant, Esq...	6	6	6	17	6	550	325	325	325	1950	3250
Charles Andros, Esq.	7	5	6	21	7	650	325	325	325	1950	2250
TOTAL..................	20	15	16	58	15	1800	1000	1000	1000	6000	9000

Thomas Le Marchant, Major ; John Andros, Major ; John Brock, Captain and Acting Major.

ESTABLISHMENT OF GUERNSEY.   Per Diem.

Lieutenant-Governor £0 10 0
Chaplain. 0 6 8
First master gunner 0 2 0
Four other gunners, at 1s. each.................... .... 0 4 0
Allowance for fire and candle, at the rate of £40 per annum.40 0 0

In 1755, the governor visited Guernsey, and Sir John Mylne, Bart., the lieut.-governor, on the 6th of June, directed Colonel William Le Marchant to send "his part of the six field pieces (which the king gave to the island) on the 15th instant, in perfect good order, for to salute my Lord De la Warr upon his arrival." The island had not been visited by its governor since the time of the second Lord Hatton, and Lord De la Warr was the last who visited it.

Sir John Mylne to Colonel William Le Marchant, of l'Hyvreuse.

" Guernsey, July 4, 1755.

" My Lord De la Warr finding by the present establishment of the militia in Guernsey that a regiment does consist of six or seven companies only, which makes them too numerous to be duly disciplined and commanded by the officers, his lordship has therefore thought fit to order that every one of the three regiments of militia shall consist of ten companys for the future; and that the three majors, with Captain [de] Havilland, do meet to take the speediest and most proper methodes to accomplish the same forthwith, by ordering all the captains of the three regiments to give in to the majors the ' vingtenier's' list of their companys immediately. His lordship has likewise ordered the St. Sampson's company of the town regiment to be joined to the Câtel regiment. These orders to be communicated to all concerned, and put in execution without loss of time."

Appended to the preceding letter is the following general militia order, signed by Sir John Mylne :

" It is my Lord De la Warr's orders that there shall be but two stand of colours to each regiment, and these are to belong to the colonels' and lieutenant-colonels' companys, the field officers being each of them to have companys.

" The names of proper persons for to be captains, lieutenants, and ensigns to the additional companys, to be given in to the majors this day, remembering allwise his lordship's intention to have captains of the best familys.

" The captains to give a list to the majors immediately of the men that was ordered some time ago to be draughted out of the militia for gunners to forts, &c., because of them two companys of artillery are to be formed : one captain, two lieutenants, four sergeants, four corporals, two drummers, and seventy privates each company, to be the establishment. The majors must likewise have the names of proper persons to be officers to these two companys."

In pursuance of Lord De la Warr's orders, the officers reported that " we have, in obedience to your lordship's order and Sir John Mylne's directions, reduced the companys, and completed ten to each regiment, exclusive of two companys for the artillery, draughted out from the whole."—A document without date, but evidently written soon after this change, mentions that his majesty had granted " yearly, during the war, fifteen barrels of powder to the indigent in the thirty companies of the island, to be expended in reviews and on field days."

The following remarks are extracted from a manuscript, neither signed nor dated, but evidently written about 1755:

" The present great confusion and disorders in the militia of Guernsey proceed from the great irregularities committed by Lieut.-Governor Spicer.

" 1. He created a captain-lieutenant to every company, which occasioned many broils and disputes between those new officers and the ancient lieutenants, for their posts when regimented.

" 2. He created the captains of batteries, whom for the most part were people, some that had a disgust for their captains or other officers; some by laziness, to have but little or nothing to do; and others by pride, imagining not to be subordinate in that new post to any officer, but to the governor alone.

" 3. He also formed a regiment of artillery officers, and gave them those high titles of honorable colonel, &c., of artillery, and this to many persons of the lowest extraction and meanest character.

" Many other ridiculous commissions were granted by that governor to accumulate guineas, which he extorted from those and all other officers for their commissions.

" Lieut.-Governor Dollon, who succeeded him, did the good office to break the captain-lieutenants; but as to the rest, made things rather worse, for he not only raised the price of commissions, but also obliged the officers to pay for the renewing of them, which he took advantage to do twice in about nine months time.   I have myself three commissions of captain drawn out within the space of fifteen months: the first from Mr. Spicer, dated June 16, 1726; the second from Mr. Dollon, at his first coming in the island, dated December 1, 1726; and the third from the same lieutenant-governor, at his majesty's accession to the throne, dated September 20, 1727, for all which I was obliged to pay as for new commissions.

" The same lieutenant-governor raised a troop of horse, or rather a troop of men, whom upon any emergency were the seven-eighth part of them reduced to run the country to borrow, or hire for the day, very mean and pitiful horses; and as that pretended company were seldom said to be in a condition to make a proper appearance, they were by that means often exempt from any duty, which was the principal view; and that occasioned a jealousy and discouragement to the infantry, which I am afraid will not only be the case if continued, but will also draw so many officers and persons fit for those posts, as to render it impracticable to fill up the vacancies in the infantry, and by that means screen several gentlemen from doing their duty.

" Lieut.-Governor Graham, who was the next, continued every thing much upon the same footing; but he committed a great irregularity in favor of Mr. John Brock, who was a lieutenant in one of the country regiments, [the company of Torteval,] by giving him the commission of captain in the town regiment, and this over the heads of the lieutenants belonging to it, who, without offending Mr. Brock, were at least as well qualified as himself for that post, and which gave them so much discouragement that they all laid down their commissions, and from which time there has been no lieutenants in that regiment.

"Lieut.-Governor Strahan, though he had all the commissions renewed, shewed himself more generous than his three predecessors, by extorting nothing from them, as they had all done; and though he would not take upon himself to break officers created before his time, he made however the captains of batteries subordinate to the officers of militia, and in the last war issued out an order that, in case of any attack, the officers of artillery should obey the commanding officer of infantry contiguous to them, which was very necessary, as those gentlemen before pretended to be independent."

[Next follows a narrative of certain disputes relative to the lieutenant-colonelcy of the town regiment, which is now of no interest.]

"February 21, 1756.—[Extracts.]—Whereas the commander-in-chief of this island hath received a letter from Lieut.-Governor Strahan, that a declaration of war by the French is expected every moment in London,[1] the island of Guernsey is therefore desired to be upon its guard.

"As a watch will become more necessary in the night time than in the day, it is the commandant's orders that a corporal and four privates of the militia do parade at the several watch-houses at five o'clock, p.m., and to come off at seven o'clock, a.m., till the 1st of April ensuing, viz. at Jerbourg, Sommeilleuse, the Vale, and the Roque du Guet, at the Câtel. . . . .

"The whole militia to hold themselves ready to turn out at a moment's warning, according to former orders.

"Places of rendezvous for the country regiments, viz. the company of Torteval and those of St. Peter's, at the Câtel church-yard; the Forest and St. Andrew's, at St. Martin's church-yard, and the rest at their respective church-yards; and the town regiment, at their captains' quarters.

"That all the men of the militia, who are incapable to provide themselves with arms and ammunition, be acquainted immediately where the store-houses of their respective companies are kept, that they may repair to them in case of an alarm, to be supplied with them, and join their companies.

"The visiting rounds (surguet) of the several watches to be performed by the subaltern officers of the militia and the troop of horse, each at their turn, beginning with the troop, two in com-

(1) Great Britain declared war May 18, and France June 9, 1756.

pany, that is, four in all every night: they are to begin any time betwixt ten at night, and end an hour before daybreak, which rounds are always to have the parole; and so is the commanding officer of each watch.

"In case of an alarm, the commanding officer of the watch is immediately to light the beacon, and to dispatch one of the watch to the commander-in-chief, and another of said watch to the nearest commissioned officer of the militia, who is ordered to see the bells set a ringing, and a cannon fired; and this is to be done in every parish.

"That the sergeants of the horse and foot do regulate amongst themselves to see the watches set.

"February 28.—The officers that oversee the bulwarks, to report every man that neglects his duty.

[Here follows a distribution of the watches, viz. seven companies each for Jerbourg, the Vale, the Câtel, and the Sommeilleuse, and two companies for Pleinmont ; total, thirty companies.]

"As the troop is quartered all over the island, they are to do the above duty with the company nearest to them, with the subalterns of the companies.

"The bulwarks belonging to the town and Vale are forthwith to be completed ; the town to begin on Monday next, and at the Vale Wednesday next. The captains of artillery are to call for a list, as the companies are now divided between the sergeants and corporals, of the houses where the men are quartered, and the batteries round the island to be equally divided amongst the companies ; a sergeant or corporal appointed to command each battery, and they to take out their men every Sunday to their respective batteries to learn the exercise of the great guns: those of the town to learn upon the pier, Fort Mansell, and Hougue-à-la-Père. The three guns nearest to the pier heads to be always kept loaded with powder only, for a signal of alarm.

"March 3.—The majors to see that the covered waggons of each parish are repaired. . . . . The whole militia to provide themselves with bayonets, fitted to their firelocks.

(Signed)   "JOHN MYLNE."

Sir John Mylne having represented to the royal court that the watch, at night, at "l'Angle, au Clos du Valle" was extremely neglected, because the men of the town regiment did not attend there, notwithstanding his orders, that body issued an ordinance, dated August 19, 1758, that every person who was bound to attend, and did not do so in person or by substitute, should pay 14 sols tournois for each default, which fine was to be expended by the captain in getting the duty properly performed, and in the purchase of fuel, candles, &c., for the men employed at " l'Angle."

About the same time, the officers of the town regiment drew up a long remonstrance in French, addressed to the royal court, complaining of the great hardship of themselves and their men being compelled to mount guard and go the rounds (*faire guet et surguet*) at l'Angle, in the north extremity of the Vale parish, to reach which guard they often ran the risk of being drowned in passing the Braye, from not knowing the roads and tides : they urged, moreover, that as the company of the Vale consisted of sixty or seventy men, which was double the number of several of the companies of the town, and that as the regiment of the Câtel had been augmented, and that of the town diminished of the company of St. Sampson's, the regiment of the Câtel ought to perform the duty at l'Angle, the more so as the watch commenced at sunset, the working man lost a day's wages by being obliged to leave town at three o'clock, p.m., and not returning until ten o'clock, a.m., on the following day. It does not appear how the matter was arranged, but the complaint was certainly well founded.

By a "state of the field train," &c., in the several parishes of Guernsey, dated March, 1758, we find that the brass ordnance consisted of eighteen pieces, viz. one 6-pounder at St. Martin's ; twelve 3-pounders, of which six on the pier ; one 2½-pounder ; one 1½-pounder ; and three 1¼-pounders.

During the summer of 1780 or 1781, three French privateers, two brigs and one cutter, with 200 soldiers on board, were despatched from Cherbourg by the famous General Dumourier, to take the island of Alderney. Under the cover of the night, the privateers came to an anchor within musket shot of the guard-house of the Château à l'Etoc, where they were perceived about two o'clock in the morning, it being at that time moonlight. There being very little wind, the French were attempting to land in Corblet's bay. The militia guard was only composed of four men, namely, John Ozard, Peter Gaudion, William Harris, and another, who, perceiving the object of the invaders, immediately opened a fire upon them, which was so well directed as to kill several of the Frenchmen on board the privateers. There was, at that moment, in Alderney roads, a large English privateer, mounting 18 guns, commanded by Captain Chandler, who, upon hearing the report of the guns from the battery, instantly beat to arms. The weather being very calm, and every thing quiet, the alarm was heard by those on board the French vessels, and, supposing that the whole militia were under arms, as soon as daylight appeared the privateers weighed anchor, and directed their course towards Cherbourg.   In the meantime, Captain Chandler got under sail, and pursued the enemy.   Having come up with them, he gave them several broadsides, but they succeeded in reaching their port of destination, and Chandler directed his course to Jersey.   Thus, by the courage of four men, the enemy was prevented from landing, and ultimately forced to retire without effecting their purpose.

By a deliberation of the parishioners of St. Peter-Port, in 1733, captains of militia were exempted from serving as "collecteurs des pauvres;" and, in 1761, one of the reasons given for the purchase of the New Ground was, that the town militia was obliged to go to the " Grand' Mielles," in the Câtel parish, to exercise.

In 1780, the regiment of field artillery, the service in which corps had previously been confined to the batteries, was formed by Colonel Nicholas Dobrée, and the west regiment of infantry by Colonel Peter De Lisle, when the Guernsey militia became divided into four regiments of infantry and one of artillery, as now; the parish of St. Peter-Port furnishing the 1st or east regiment, facings white, and the regiment of artillery;   the Vale, St. Sampson's, and the Câtel, the 2d or north regiment, facings green;   St. Martin's, St. Andrew's, and the Forest, the 3d or south regiment, facings blue ; and St. Saviour's, St. Peter-in-the-Wood, and Torteval, the 4th or west regiment, facings black. Until about the year 1835, the three country regiments were usually called by their facings.

In the year 1780, the royal court passed the following ordinance for the compulsory equipment of the militia :

" On the representation of the lieutenant-governor, the Honorable Paulus Æmilius Irving, that it would prove a certain and considerable advantage for the defence of the island against invasion, if the local militia were furnished with a red coat and white stockings, when under arms, inasmuch as that would identify the said militia in the eyes of the enemy with the soldiers of the line, which would inspire greater terror into the enemy, however efficient the militia may be, and because many persons are already so furnished ; the court, having heard the opinions of the crown lawyers, and desiring to concur in every thing which may contribute to the defence of the island, has ordered that all persons who have the means shall furnish themselves with a suitable red coat, and the ornamental facings and collars of their regiments, and white stockings, under the penalty of ten livres tournois ; and, as to the poor, they are to be furnished by their respective parishes, the whole within this day and the 1st of May next, after which day every militiaman is prohibited from appearing under arms unless dressed in a red coat, as stated above, and white stockings, when ordered by their commanding officer, under the penalty of three livres tournois. The said ten livres tournois to be applied thus, eighteen sous to his majesty, and the surplus to the parish of the delinquent; and the three livres tournois to be applied thus, eighteen sous to his majesty, and the surplus to the company of the delinquent; and the poor are bound to take care of the clothes and stockings furnished them by their parish, and return them, from time to time, as may be required, to such officer as may be appointed by their parish, without permission to use them, except under arms, under pain of punishment. And the artillery regiment is also ordered to furnish themselves with the uniform worn by artillery regiments, and not to appear unless so dressed, for artillery exercise when called upon by their commanding officer, under the same penalties as stated above."

Against this ordinance deputies from all the parishes, excepting the Vale, St. Peter-in-the-Wood, and St. Peter-Port, remonstrated, and represented that the generality of the inhabitants of the country parishes only possessed a very trifling property, and especially those in Torteval, who were only taxed for the most part at three, five, or ten quarters of wheat rent; that the charges, to which they had been subject " during the present course of hostilities, had been excessive, since the country paid two-thirds of the taxes for the public works, according to the established rates; and that they were obliged to serve as watch or patrol, and to go under arms twice a week, which occupied a great portion of their time. The following is one of the numerous paragraphs in the remonstrance of the deputies:

" We beg the court to observe, that the militia of this island is totally different from the militia of England, they being paid by the sovereign, clothed by the government, and subjected to military discipline; whereas the militia of this island are volunteers, being simply a citizen militia, which receives no pay, which recognizes no power but the civil power, but who, after the example of their forefathers, are ready to fight against every enemy who may assail their persons or properties."

The royal court having refused to repeal their ordinance, a petition against it was presented to his majesty in council, December 15, 1780, signed by the deputies of the whole of the ten parishes of Guernsey, and several other inhabitants. On the 17th of May, 1781, the lords of council took this petition into consideration, and ordered a copy thereof to be transmitted to the royal court, who were required to return their answer forthwith in writing, and to forbear levying the fines imposed by their ordinance, until the question, whether the court had power to enact it, should be determined. Here the matter dropped, in consequence of the government, in 1782, sending over clothing and accoutrements from England;[1] and this practice has ever since been continued, the officers only finding their own equipments. But every man in the bailiwick, from the age of sixteen to sixty, is not only legally bound to provide himself with the necessary arms and accoutrements; but to turn out whenever ordered; to mount guard at night in war time, in his turn; to repair the bulwarks, a duty not now exacted; to keep the garrison, when troops of the line are absent; and, in short, to perform every military service for insular defence.

During the last war, about the year 1807, three natives of the Forest, fishermen, were impressed by a ship of war, while fishing near that parish. They belonged to the south regiment of militia, then commanded by Colonel Harry Dobrée, who claimed them from Sir Edmund Nagle, the rear-admiral on the station. He refused to release them, and the matter was referred by Sir John Doyle to the secretary of state, when an order was transmitted from the admiralty for their immediate release, Sir John having claimed them as part of the force under his command, and strongly urged the necessity of the militia being protected from impressment.

In 1799, on the recommendation of Sir Hew Dalrymple, the lieutenant-governor, an inspecting field officer of militia was appointed from the line, Lieut.-Colonel Sir Thomas Saumarez being the first; but in 1818, after the peace, the office was abolished. In 1810, an assistant-inspector was appointed to each regiment of militia, with 4s. per day, and forage for a horse: they were militia officers, and their duty was to attend the drill of the recruits, take care of the arms and clothing, and to go the rounds by night. Soon after the peace of 1815, two inspectors only were retained; and in 1830 the establishment was further reduced to one deputy inspector, with 3s. a day and forage. In 1843, the deputy inspectorship was

(1) Extract from G. O. for the Militia, Head Quarters, April 11, 1782.—" His majesty having been graciously pleased to make a present of clothing and accoutrements to the militia of this island, it is to be issued to them immediately; and the commanding officers of regiments and companies are to see them served properly. And the lieutenant-governor recommends it to the men to have them fitted, and hereby directs that they are not to be worn but when ordered. And he hopes they will be kept clean and in good order.—Signed, P. Æ. Irving.—Peter de Jersey, aide-de-camp."

abolished, and one chief assistant-inspector, with 3s. a day, and £25 a year for forage; five assistant-inspectors, with 2s. a day, and £25 a year for forage; and five drill sergeants, with 1s. a day, were appointed. In 1853, the sixteen light 6-pounders of the artillery, which had been in use about thirty years, were exchanged for twelve 9-pounders and four 24-pound howitzers, with which they practised for the first time in September of the same year, at l'Ancresse, before Lord Raglan, master-general of the ordnance; Sir James Graham, first lord of the admiralty; and several officers of rank.

In 1831, the militia of the Anglo-Norman isles was made *royal*, with the distinctions thereof, by William IV.; when Lord Melbourne, December 30, 1830, wrote: "The 6th January next will be the fiftieth anniversary or jubilee of Monsieur De Rullecourt's defeat, and of the capture of himself and his whole force, after he had made good his landing, and taken possession of the town of St. Hélier; and his majesty is desirous that that day should be the day fixed for making his intentions known to the militia of the islands." In consequence, the facings were made blue at the next issue of clothing. William IV. also first appointed a Jersey and Guernsey militia aide-de-camp to the sovereign, Colonel John Guille, of St. George, being named by a commission, dated September 14, 1830, "aide-de-camp for the service of our militia in Guernsey." Colonel Guille resigned the appointment in 1843, when he was made bailiff; and he was succeeded by Colonel James Priaulx.

The militia of Guernsey now (1854) consists of five regiments, viz. artillery, of four companies; infantry, 1st or east, of nine companies, including two of rifles; 2d or north, 3d or south, and 4th or west, each of eight companies, including one of rifles; total available strength, in the event of a war, nearly 3,000 men. The artillery is horsed by the States, and free of expense to government.—In a G. M. O. of June 30, 1854, it was announced that it "has been determined by authority, that whenever vacancies happen in the royal Guernsey militia, lieutenant-colonels commandant shall be substituted for full colonels;" and, by the same order, an assistant-inspector was appointed, for the first time, for Alderney; in which island all the militia are, in future, to be employed in the batteries.

BIOGRAPHICAL NOTICES.

SIR EDMUND ANDROS, KNIGHT,

Was born in London, in 1637, his father, Amias Andros, being then marshall of the ceremonies to Charles I. From a boy, he was brought up in the royal family; and, in its exile, commenced his career of arms in Holland, under Prince Henry of Nassau. Upon the Restoration, in 1660, he was made gentleman in ordinary to Elizabeth Stuart, queen of Bohemia. In 1667, he was major in the regiment sent to Barbadoes; and in 1672 Major Andros was commander of the forces in that island. In the latter year, the palatine and proprietors of the province of Carolina, by patent in which allusion is made to his merits and services, conferred on him and his heirs the title and dignity of Landgrave, with four baronies, containing 48,000 acres of land, at a quit rent of one penny an acre. In 1674, on the death of his father, he succeeded to the office of bailiff of Guernsey, the reversion of which had been granted to him by the king. The same year, he was commissioned to receive New York and its dependencies from the Dutch, pursuant to the treaty of peace, when he was constituted governor of that province; and on his return from thence, in 1681, he was knighted by Charles II. In 1683, Sir Edmund Andros was sworn gentleman of the privy chamber to the king, and the same year the isle of Alderney was granted to him, as already mentioned. In 1685, he was colonel of Princess Anne of Denmark's regiment of horse, and the following year James II. appointed him governor, &c., of Massachusetts, New Hampshire, Maine, New Plymouth, &c., and soon afterwards of Rhode Island and of Connecticut, thus comprehending the whole of New England; and subsequently New York and New Jersey were also added to his jurisdiction. After the revolution, William III. preferred him to the governorship of Virginia, and his majesty honoured him by adjoining to it, at the same time, that of Maryland. In 1704, under queen Anne, he was extraordinarily distinguished by having the lieutenant-governorship of Guernsey conferred upon him, whilst he also continued bailiff, as before related. Sir Edmund was married thrice, but left no issue, and died at Westminster, in 1713, aged seventy-five.

MAJOR-GENERAL SIR ISAAC BROCK, K.B.

Mr. William Brock, who died in 1776, had three sons and one daughter, viz. William, married to Judith De Beauvoir; John, married to Elizabeth De Lisle, daughter of the then lieutenant-bailiff; Henry, married to Susan Saumarez, sister of the late Admiral Lord De Saumarez; and Mary, wife of John Le Marchant, Esq.

The said John Brock and Elizabeth De Lisle had a family of ten sons and four daughters; and Isaac, the eighth son, was born in Guernsey, October 6, 1769. He entered the army, by purchase, in the 8th regiment, in 1785; and although he was an ensign five years, he became lieutenant-colonel, commanding the 49th regiment, in 1797, having purchased the intermediate steps with great rapidity. During the campaign in Holland, in 1799, he distinguished himself at the head of his regiment, which, in the battle of Berghen, on the 2d of October, had two officers killed and five wounded. It was a very cold day, and Colonel Brock's life was in all probability preserved by his wearing over his stock a handkerchief, which was perforated by a bullet, but which prevented its entering his neck. He was second in command of the land forces at the memorable attack of Copenhagen by Lord Nelson, in 1801, in which he was to have led the 49th in storming the principal of the Treckroner batteries, in conjunction with 500 seamen under Captain Fremantle ; but the obstinate defence of the Danes rendered the attempt impracticable, and Lieut.-Colonel Brock continued on board the Ganges, of 74 guns, one of the ships engaged. His next younger brother, Savery, served under him in the 49th, and had his hat torn from his head by a cannon or grape shot, while in the act of pointing one of the guns of the Ganges. In the following year, Lieut.-Colonel Brock proceeded to Canada with his favorite 49th, and there remained, with only one intermission, (when he returned on leave to Europe,) until the period of his death. In 1803, while in command at York, (now Toronto,) he was suddenly informed that two or three companies of the 49th at Fort George, under the junior lieutenant-colonel, with whom they were discontented, had formed a conspiracy to imprison their officers while they marched to Queenston, seven miles distant, and there crossed over by the ferry to the state of New York. Lieut.-Colonel Brock instantly proceeded to Fort George, and suppressed the conspiracy in a manner which justified the remark that truth is often stranger than fiction ; four of the ringleaders being afterwards shot at Quebec. In 1806-7, Colonel Brock commanded the troops in the Canadas for above a year, until the arrival of the governor-general, Sir James Craig. In 1811, he obtained his promotion as a major-general, when the Duke of York at length consented, in consequence of his repeated applications, to gratify his wishes for more active employment in Europe, and Sir George Prevost was authorized to replace him by another officer ; but when the permission reached Canada, a war with the United States of America was evidently near at hand, and Major-General Brock, with such a prospect, was retained, both by honour and in-clination, in the country ; the more so as Sir George wrote to him that he valued his services highly, and that he hoped he would not be deprived of his assistance at that critical period of affairs.

At the commencement of the second American war, in June, 1812, Major-General Brock was administering the civil as well as the military government of Upper Canada, and he could scarcely collect 1,500 troops for its immediate defence. But he quickly received voluntary offers of service from the militia, most easily embodied, while the Indian warriors, in considerable numbers, soon after joined him at Amherstburg. The American government, previously to its declaration of war, had detached to the Michigan territory an army of about 2,500 men, under Brigadier-General Hull, an old revolutionary officer of high reputation, who, said the president, in his message to congress, " pos-sessing discretionary authority to act offensively, passed into Upper Canada, with a prospect of easy and victorious progress." Having reached the Cana-dian village of Sandwich, Hull issued, on the 12th of July, an ably written proclamation to the provincials, in which he said : " Had I any doubt of eventual success, I might ask your assistance ; but I do not. I come prepared for every contingency. I have a force which will look down all opposition, and that force is but the vanguard of a much greater." Brock was at Fort George watching the enemy on the Niagara, when he heard of Hull's invasion ; and, after issuing a proclamation to defeat the object of that circulated by the American general, he returned to York to meet the provincial legislature, which, on account of the war, he had called together for an extra session.[1] The session was short, and on the 5th of August, Brock again left York for Fort George, and for Long Point, on Lake Erie. On the 8th, he embarked at the latter place, with 40 rank and file of the 41st regiment, and 260 of the militia forces, in open boats, which reached Amherstburg on the evening of the 12th. Hull, after wasting nearly a month in preparations for the siege of

(1) James' Military Occurrences of the late war between Great Britain and the United States of America. London, 1818.

Fort Amherstburg, retraced his steps precipitately to Fort Détroit, whither he returned on the 8th of August. Brock immediately determined, with his very inferior and motley force, on following the enemy into his own territory, and on attempting, by a sudden and resolute attack, the annihilation of his army in that quarter. With this view the troops were marched to Sandwich, where a few guns were placed in battery, from which a fire was opened against Fort Détroit, on the 15th of August, on which day Brock sent across a flag of truce, with a summons, demanding the immediate surrender of the garrison ; but Hull replied that he was prepared to meet any force which might be at the disposal of the British general. Nothing daunted, and contrary to the opinion of the next in command, Brock issued orders to cross the strait or river, which is here about three-fourths of a mile in width, on the following morning, in the hope of inducing the enemy to meet his little force in the field. Accordingly, on the 16th of August, 330 regulars, with 400 militia, and about 600 Indians, together 1,330 men, were embarked, with five pieces of light artillery, in boats and canoes of every description, and soon effected a landing without opposition. Contrary to Brock's expectation, the Americans abandoned a favourable position, and retreated into the fort on the advance of the British. Ascertaining that the enemy had taken little precaution on the land side, Brock resolved on attempting to carry the fort by assault. While the various columns were forming for that purpose, a flag of truce was unexpectedly seen issuing from the fort, and soon afterwards the British troops marched in, Hull having assented to a capitulation, by which the Michigan territory, Fort Détroit, with thirty-three pieces of cannon, the Adams, vessel of war, and about 2,500 troops, were surrendered to the British arms. The success that attended this first enterprize, in which the militia had been engaged, produced an electrical effect throughout the two provinces. It inspired the timid, fixed the wavering, and awed the disaffected, of which last there were a few. It also induced the six nations of Indians, who had hitherto kept aloof, to take an active part in our favor. Te-cum-seh, the celebrated Indian chief, who was slain in 1813, headed a party of his warriors on this occasion. Previously to crossing, Brock asked him what sort of country he should have to pass through in case of his proceeding further. Te-cum-seh, taking a roll of elm bark, presently etched upon it, with his scalping knife, a plan of the country, with its hills, woods, rivers, morasses, and roads, which was perfectly intelligible. Pleased with this unexpected talent and with the gallantry of Te-cum-seh, the British general, after his entry into Détroit, publicly took off his sash and placed it round the body of the chief, who received the honor with evident gratification. But being seen the next day without his sash, General Brock, thinking that something had displeased the Indian, sent his interpreter for an explanation. The latter soon returned, and stated that Te-cum-seh, not wishing to wear such a mark of distinction, when an older, and, as he said, an abler warrior than himself was present, had transferred the sash to a Wyandot chief! Leaving a small force in Détroit, Brock hastened to the Niagara, a command he had relinquished for the purpose of undertaking an achievement which his energy and decision crowned with such unqualified success. His services on this occasion were, on the 10th of October, rewarded with the order of the Bath, which was then confined to one degree of knighthood only, but he lived not long enough to learn that he had obtained so gratifying a distinction, the knowledge of which would perhaps have cheered him under the mortification of being subsequently restricted to defensive operations.

In transmitting his despatches to the governor-general, Brock expressed his intention of proceeding immediately to the attack of the naval arsenal at Sackett's harbour, on Lake Ontario. Had its destruction been accomplished, of which there was then little doubt, the Americans would not so easily have built and equipped the fleet, which the following year gave them the ascendancy on that lake. But, unhappily, Sir George Prevost disapproved of the enterprize, and commanded Brock to remain on the Niagara frontier. The latter felt the disappointment most acutely, and subsequent events too truly proved that, had he been permitted to pursue that course which his zeal and foresight dictated, his valuable life might have been spared, and a very different series of incidents in that war have claimed the attention of the historian.

The Americans, burning to wipe away the stain of the capture of Détroit, and apparently determined to penetrate into Upper Canada at any risk, concentrated with those views an army of about 6,000 men, partly militia, under Major-General Van Renssalaer. To oppose this force, Brock had under his command only 1,500 men, including militia and Indians, but so dispersed between Fort Erie and Fort George (thirty-four miles apart) that only a small number was quickly available at any one point. A considerable number of the enemy crossed over from Lewistown, before daybreak, on the 13th of October, and gained possession of the shore near Queenston. Having arisen before daylight, according to his usual custom, and hearing the report of cannon and musketry, Brock galloped eagerly from Fort George to the scene of action, distant seven miles, after directing Major-General Sheaffe to bring up the troops as soon as they could be assembled. On his reaching Queenston, he found the flank companies only of the 49th, with a few of the militia, warmly engaged. Soon after, observing the Americans to waver, he ordered a charge, which he personally accompanied; but as they gave way, the result was not decisive. Retiring to the heights, the enemy opened a heavy fire of musketry, and, "conspicuous from his dress, his stature, and the enthusiasm with which he animated his little band, the British commander was singled out by the American riflemen;" and about an hour after his arrival the fatal bullet entered his left breast, and passed through his right side. He lived only long enough to utter this dying exhortation: "My fall must not be noticed, or prevent my brave companions from advancing to victory." But his provincial aide-de-camp, Lieut.-Colonel M'Donell, having soon after fallen, and Captains Dennis and Williams, commanding the flank companies, being severely wounded, the handful of British was compelled to retire.

In the afternoon, the British troops having assembled from various points, and now equal in number, quickly compelled the enemy to surrender, upwards of 900 men being made prisoners. So beloved was Brock by the 49th, that his death is said to have cost the invaders many a life on that day, which otherwise had been spared. After lying in state at the government house, the deceased was interred with every military honor, in a cavalier bastion, at Fort George; and as soon as the funeral solemnities were ended on the British side, the Americans, by a previous intimation from their general, fired a compliment of minute guns on theirs!!! In person, Sir Isaac Brock was tall, erect, and well proportioned, his countenance was fine and benevolent, and his manners were frank and engaging.—One of his brothers, Ferdinand, a lieutenant of the 60th regiment, was slain in the defence of Bâton Rouge, on the Mississippi, in the first American war; and another, John, a lieutenant-colonel, was killed in 1802, in a duel at the Cape of Good Hope, in consequence of his having, as steward of a public ball, very properly resisted the introduction, by his antagonist, who was a captain in the army, of a female of disreputable character. Another brother was the bailiff, or chief magistrate of Guernsey; and the tenth and youngest brother, Irving, who died at Bath in 1838, was "the accomplished translator of Bernier's Travels in India."

"His royal highness the Prince Regent," observed Earl Bathurst, in a despatch to Sir George Prevost, "is fully aware of the severe loss which his majesty's service has experienced in the death of Major-General Sir Isaac Brock. This would have been sufficient to have clouded a victory of much greater importance. His majesty has lost in him, not only an able and meritorious officer, but one who, in the exercise of his functions of provisional lieutenant-governor of the province, displayed qualities admirably adapted to

2H

awe the disloyal, to reconcile the wavering, and to animate the great mass of the inhabitants against successive attempts of the enemy to invade the province, in the last of which he unhappily fell, too prodigal of that life of which his eminent services had taught us to understand the value."

The American president, Madison, alluding to the battle of Queenston, in his annual message to congress, said: "Our loss has been considerable, and is deeply to be lamented. That of the enemy, less ascertained, will be the more felt, as it includes, amongst the killed, the commanding general, who was also the governor of the province."

A national monument was raised to the memory of Sir Isaac Brock in St. Paul's;[1] and a lofty column having been erected on Queenston Heights by the provincial legislature to the hero of Upper Canada, as he is still termed in that country, his remains, and those of his gallant aide-de-camp, Lieut.-Colonel M'Donell, were removed on the 13th of October, 1824, from Fort George, in solemn military procession, to the monument. One of his regimental companions, Colonel Fitzgibbon, in transmitting a detail of the ceremonies of the day, thus pathetically expressed himself: "Nothing, certainly, could exceed the interest manifested by the people of the province upon the occasion; and numbers from the neighbouring state of New York, by their presence and conduct, proved how highly the Americans revere the memory of our lamented chief. Of the thousands present, not one had cause to feel so deeply as I, and I felt as if alone, although surrounded by the multitude. He had been more than a father to me in that regiment which he ruled like a father, and I alone of his old friends in that regiment was present to embalm with a tear his last honored retreat."

The column, which was 127 feet in height, and 477 feet above the level of the Niagara river, which skirts the Heights, bore the following inscription:

UPPER CANADA
HAS DEDICATED THIS MONUMENT
TO THE MEMORY OF THE LATE
MAJOR-GENERAL SIR ISAAC BROCK, K.B.
PROVISIONAL LIEUTENANT-GOVERNOR AND COMMANDER OF THE FORCES
IN THIS PROVINCE,
WHOSE REMAINS ARE DEPOSITED IN THE VAULT BENEATH.
OPPOSING THE INVADING ENEMY,
HE FELL IN ACTION NEAR THESE HEIGHTS,
ON THE 13th OCTOBER, 1812,
IN THE 43d YEAR OF HIS AGE,
REVERED AND LAMENTED
BY THE PEOPLE WHOM HE GOVERNED,
AND DEPLORED BY THE SOVEREIGN
TO WHOSE SERVICE HIS LIFE HAD BEEN DEVOTED.

On the 17th of April, 1840, an Irishman, who had participated in the recent rebellion, and escaped across the frontier, introduced a quantity of gunpowder into the monument for the fiendish purpose of destroying it; and the explosion caused so much injury as to render the column quite irreparable. The indignation of the Canadians was aroused, and at a vast meeting on Queenston Heights, on the 30th of July following, resolutions were adopted for the

(1) This chief of the branch of the once great tribe of the Hurons visited England some time ago. I afterwards saw him in Quebec, and had a good deal of conversation with him. When asked what had struck him most of all that he had seen in England, he replied, without hesitation, that it was the monument erected in St. Paul's to the memory of General Brock. It seemed to have impressed him with a high idea of the considerate beneficence of his great father, the king of England, that he not only had remembered the exploits and death of his white child, who had fallen beyond the big salt lake, but that he had even deigned to record, on the marble sepulchre, the sorrows of the poor Indian weeping over his chief untimely slain.—*Hon. F. F. De Roos' Travels in North America, in 1826.*

restoration of the monument.[1] The lieutenant-governor, Sir George Arthur, presided at this meeting, which was attended by the principal inhabitants; a detachment of royal artillery, who fired a salute on the occasion; a detachment of dragoon guards; and the 93d regiment. (highlanders.) The gathering, as it was called, was observed in Toronto as a solemn holiday; the public offices were closed and all business was suspended, while thousands flocked from every part of the province to testify their affection for the memory of one who, nearly thirty years before, had fallen in its defence. History, indeed, affords few parallels of such long cherished public attachment! On the termination of the proceedings, 600 persons sat down to dinner in a temporary pavilion erected on the spot where the hero fell, and after the queen's health had been drunk, Chief Justice Robinson rose and said:

"I have now to propose the memory of the late gallant Sir Isaac Brock, of Colonel M'Donell, and of those who fell with them on Queenston Heights. That portion of you, gentlemen, who were inhabitants of Upper Canada while General Brock served in its defence, are at no loss to account for the enthusiastic affection with which his memory is cherished among us. It was not merely on account of his intrepid courage and heroic firmness, neither was it solely because of his brilliant success while he lived, nor because he so nobly laid down his life in our defence; it was, I think, that he united in his person, in a very remarkable degree, some qualities which are peculiarly calculated to attract the confidence and affection of mankind,—there was, in all he said and did, that honesty of purpose which was so justly ascribed to him by a gentleman who proposed one of the resolutions,—there was an inflexible integrity, uncommon energy and decision, which always inspire confidence and respect,—a remarkable union in his whole demeanour of benevolence and firmness,—a peculiarly commanding and soldier-like appearance,—a generous, frank, and manly bearing,—and, above all, an entire devotion to his country. In short, I believe I shall best convey my own impression, when I say it would have required much more courage to refuse to follow General Brock, than to go with him wherever he would lead."

About £5,000 having been subscribed for the purpose, the foundation stone of a splendid new monument on Queenston Heights was laid in great state and before a vast assemblage, October 13, 1853, the remains of Sir Isaac Brock and his aide-de-camp being interred for the third time. The column, which is of the Roman composite order, with its pedestal, is to stand on a platform, and its entire height, including a statue of the hero, is to be 185 feet, there being only one column in Europe higher, either ancient or modern, viz. that in London, erected in commemoration of the great fire of 1666.

Among the numerous other testimonials of the estimation in which Sir Isaac Brock was held, our limited space enables us to give only the following:

"Thus ended in their total discomfiture the second attempt of the Americans to invade Upper Canada. The loss of the British is said to have been about 20 killed, including Indians, and between 50 and 60 wounded. The fall of General Brock, the idol of the army and of the people of Upper Canada, was an irreparable loss, and cast a shade over the glory of this dear-bought victory. He was a native of Guernsey, of an ancient and reputable family, distinguished in the profession of arms. He had served for many years in Canada, and in some of the principal campaigns in Europe. He commanded a detachment of his favorite 49th regiment, on the expedition to Copenhagen with Lord Nelson, where he distinguished himself. He was one of those extraordinary men who seem born to influence mankind, and mark the age in which they live. Conscious of the ascendancy of his genius over those who surrounded him, he blended the mildest of manners with the severity and discipline of a camp; and though his deportment was somewhat grave and imposing, the noble frankness of his character imparted at once confidence and respect to those who had occasion to approach his person. As a soldier, he was brave to a fault, and not less judicious than decisive in his measures. The energy of his character was strongly expressed in his countenance, and in the robust and manly symmetry of his frame. As a civil governor, he was firm, prudent, and equitable. In fine, whether we view him as a man, a statesman, or a soldier, he equally deserves the esteem and respect of his contemporaries and of posterity. The Indians who flocked to his standard were attached to him with almost enthusiastic affection, and the enemy even expressed an involuntary regret at his untimely fall. His prodigality of life benefit the country of his services at the early age of forty-two years. The remains of this gallant officer were, during the funeral service, honored with a discharge of minute guns from the American, as well as the British

(1) A public subscription was soon after opened for this purpose. and the six nations of Indians contributed the (for their diminished numbers and limited means) large sum, of £167.

batteries; and with those of his faithful aide-de-camp, Lieut.-Colonel M'Donell, were interred in the same grave at Fort George, on the 16th of October, amidst the tears of an affectionate soldiery and a grateful people, who will cherish his memory with veneration, and hand to their posterity the imperishable name of BROCK."—*Christie's Historical Memoirs of the War in Canada.* Quebec, 1818.

"General Brock was killed at the battle of Queenston Heights, and the place where he fell was pointed out to me. The Canadians hold the memory of this brave and excellent man in great veneration, but have not yet attempted to testify their respect for his virtues in any way, except by shewing to strangers the spot on which he received his mortal wound. He was more popular and more beloved by the inhabitants of Upper Canada than any man they ever had among them, and with reason; for he possessed, in an eminent degree, those virtues which add lustre to bravery, and those talents that shine alike in the cabinet and in the field. His manners and dispositions were so conciliating as to gain the affection of all whom he commanded, while his innate nobleness and dignity of mind secured him a respect almost amounting to veneration. He is now styled the hero of Upper Canada, and, had he lived, there is no doubt but the war would have terminated very differently from what it did. The Canadian farmers are not over-burthened with sensibility, yet I have seen several of them shed tears when an eulogium was pronounced upon the immortal and generous-minded deliverer of their country."—*Howison's Upper Canada.* London, 1821.

DANIEL DE LISLE BROCK, ESQ.

BAILIFF OF GUERNSEY.

This able magistrate, the third son of John Brock, Esq., was born in Guernsey in 1762, and closed a long and useful career in 1842, aged nearly eighty. In 1785, he went by sea to the Mediterranean, and spent upwards of a year in visiting Spain, Malta, Sicily, Italy, Switzerland, and France. In 1798, he was elected a jurat of the royal court; and the greater part, if not the whole, of the public documents of that body, were from that period written by him. In 1821, on the death of Sir Peter de Havilland, he obtained the high and responsible appointment of bailiff, or chief magistrate, of Guernsey.

Between the years 1804 and 1810, Mr. Brock was deputed by the States and royal court of Guernsey no less than four times, as their representative to government, in matters connected with the trade and privileges of the island, and in these missions he distinguished himself by his luminous papers. In 1821, he was again deputed to London on the corn question, which has been narrated *ante;* and the obnoxious corn law, as regarded these islands, was not only repealed, but several important privileges were conceded to their trade and navigation, especially free intercourse with the British colonies. So highly were his exertions appreciated, that when Mr. Bailiff Brock returned to Guernsey, July 24, 1822, he was received with the greatest enthusiasm; and at a numerous meeting it was decided to present a piece of plate to him, as a testimony of the value attached to his public services. Upwards of £300 were quickly raised for the purpose; and other less valuable, but not less gratifying, testimonials were presented to him. Nor was Jersey less grateful, as a public meeting was also held in the town of St. Hélier, when the thanks of that island and a handsome piece of plate were unanimously voted to him.

In 1832, Mr. Brock was deputed to London with Mr. Charles De Jersey, the king's procureur, to act in conjunction with the bailiff and procureur of Jersey, in opposing the extension of the Habeas Corpus Act to these islands, as also narrated *ante.* The mission was so far successful, that the attempt was not persevered in.

The last occasion, being at least the seventh, on which Mr. Brock went to London as the representative of Guernsey, was in 1835, when these islands were menaced with the deprivation of the privilege of sending their corn to England, duty free. (*Vide ante.*) The remonstrances of the several deputies prevailed; and so highly were Mr. Brock's services on this occasion valued by both islands, that the States of Jersey gave him a piece of plate of the cost of £100, while the States of Guernsey voted that portrait which now adorns the interior of the court-house, and which will afford to succeeding generations the means of contemplating his highly intellectual countenance and venerable form. From this period, until within a few days of his death, Mr. Brock was unremittingly engaged in his public duties.

Mr. Brock left one son, Eugene, a captain in the 20th regiment, who died at Bermuda soon after him, unmarried, and one daughter, since deceased, also unmarried. In features and robustness of frame, although not so tall, as well as in vigour of intellect and decision of character, the bailiff strongly resembled his brother, Sir Isaac Brock.

It is a proof of the sagacity and foresight of Mr. Brock, that when new pier works were proposed in his time, he invariably advocated the junction of Castle Cornet with the main land, as now being effected, and that he always refused to support any other plan.

The royal court, having met to appoint a judge delegate to replace *pro tempore* the late bailiff, unanimously requested the family of the deceased to allow him to be buried at the expense of the States of Guernsey, and the funeral was in consequence a public one—an honor never before conferred on any individual in Guernsey. "For though Mr. Brock," said the editor of the Star, "had enriched his country with numerous and inappreciable benefits—though he bequeathed to it an inestimable heritage in his deeds and in his example—he died in honorable and ennobling poverty, resulting from his disinterestedness, his integrity, and his patriotism." The funeral *cortège* consisted of the various civil and military authorities, the clergy, the officers of the 48th dépôt and of the five regiments of militia, the constables and douzeniers of each parish, &c. &c., the whole comprising nearly 500 persons, while the procession was witnessed by about 8,000 persons.

COLONEL SAUMAREZ BROCK, K.H.

Born in Guernsey, September 16, 1785; purchased, in 1803, an ensigncy in the 52d, and, in 1804, became a lieutenant in the 48th, in which regiment he obtained his company, by purchase, March 18, 1805, at the early age of nineteen. In 1807, he exchanged into the 43d, and served with it in the celebrated light division at the battles of Vimiera, Vittoria, Pyrenees, Nivelle, Nive, and Toulouse, besides numerous skirmishes and affairs of outposts, viz. at Vera, passage of the Bidassoa, Tarbes, three days near Arcangues, &c. At Vimiera, August 21, 1808, Captain Brock had his ankle bone very severely shattered by a musket ball which passed completely through, and he was compelled to return to England. For his services in the Peninsula, he received the war medal with six clasps; and some doubt having been expressed by the Board of General Officers of his having been present at Nivelle and the Nive, in consequence of his name appearing as sick at Vera in the monthly returns of the 43d, Major-General W. Napier gave him the following certificate:

"Colonel Saumarez Brock, serving as a captain of the 43d regiment, under my command, was present to my certain knowledge at the battles of the Nivelle and the Nive; and at the former action he was senior captain of two detached companies employed on a very important duty, which was executed with every possible gallantry and success.

"W. NAPIER, Major-General.

"Guernsey, August 24, 1847."

Captain Brock was also present at the sanguinary attack on New Orleans, in January, 1815, and soon after at the surrender of Paris, the 43d arriving from America too late to participate in the battle of Waterloo. He purchased a majority in the 43d, in October, 1815, and was present in 1834, as lieutenant-colonel of the 48th, in the Coorg campaign, in India. After having served in the four quarters of the globe, and combatted the enemy in three, Colonel Brock, who was a nephew of Admiral Lord de Saumarez, and a first cousin of Sir Isaac Brock, died in Guernsey, in April, 1854, a few weeks only before the brevet in June, in which he would have been included as a major-general. He married Catherine, daughter of Thomas De Sausmarez, Esq., but left no issue.

MAJOR-GENERAL THOMAS CAREY, late of H. M.'s 3d GUARDS.

This officer was the sixth son of John Carey, Esq., jurat, who was the father of three general officers, and a member of a very ancient Guernsey family.

In January, 1794, at the age of sixteen, young Carey obtained his first commission in the 3d foot guards, and joined the battalion then serving in Flanders with the army under the Duke of York, sharing in the hardships of the retreat through Holland in the severe winter of 1794-5. Before two years had expired, he was so fortunate as to succeed to a lieutenantcy in the regiment, with the army rank of captain. In 1796, he was appointed major of brigade to the troops serving in Guernsey. In January, 1799, he rejoined his battalion, and soon after embarked with the expedition to Holland. He was at the landing of the army under Sir Ralph Abercromby, near Camperdown, on the 27th of August, and also in the severe action fought on the 10th of September, in defending the position of the Zype, as well as in the successive battles of the 19th of September, and the 2d and 6th of October following. During this period of active service, he was nominated to the adjutancy of his battalion, a situation important in all corps, but more especially so in the guards.

In the year following this appointment of adjutant, when a brigade of guards was formed and detached to Ireland, he was selected to accompany it as a major of brigade, in which capacity he embarked with the expedition to Egypt, and served throughout that campaign, for which he obtained the distinction of a medal. He was present at the first landing of the troops in Aboukir bay, and at the subsequent hard-fought battles of the 13th and 21st of March, on which occasion England had to deplore the loss of one of her best and bravest commanders, in the fall of the gallant Abercromby. He was likewise at the reduction of Alexandria: during this campaign he suffered, in common with many others, from a violent attack of opthalmia, which deprived him of sight for a time, and threatened permanent blindness; but this he happily escaped. On his return to England, in 1802, he resumed the duties of adjutant, until his promotion to a company, with the rank of lieutenant-colonel, in 1803.

With this promotion, a higher sphere of service opened the road to further distinction. He was fixed upon for the responsible staff appointment of assistant adjutant-general to the forces, and, as such, was employed with the army in Hanover, in 1805, as well as with the expedition to the island of Zealand, in the following year, and was present at the siege and surrender of Copenhagen.

He afterwards accompanied Sir Harry Burrard to Portugal in the same capacity, and, joining Sir Arthur Wellesley on the eve of the battle of Vimiera, he shared in that well-contested action, in which he received a slight wound. He continued with the army in its advance into Spain, under Sir John Moore, and was in the retreat so marked by the privations and hardships to which the troops were unavoidably exposed, and which was followed by the battle of Corunna, in 1808. In conveying orders to the troops about to engage, he met their gallant chief on his way to the position in which he was to fight his last battle. On announcing to him that the enemy was advancing, the general replied, with a countenance brightened by the intelligence, " that is just what I have been wishing," and, putting spurs to his horse, galloped to the field rendered for ever memorable by his victory and death.

On the arrival of the army in England, Colonel Carey was posted to the eastern district, as assistant adjutant-general, and thence proceeded with Lord Chatham, as his military secretary, on the expedition to the Scheld, in 1809. He was at the reduction of the island of Walcheren, and at the siege of Flushing; and, on his return home, resumed his duties in the eastern district under his lordship, with whom he enjoyed the most intimate and lasting friendship. Here he continued until promoted to the rank of major-general, in 1814.

In the month following his promotion, the major-general married Caroline, the fourth daughter of Mr. Samuel Smith, of Woodhall Park, Herts, M. P., who died soon after giving birth to a daughter, now the wife of Francis Dickinson, Esq., of Kingweston, Somerset. In 1823, he married, secondly, Mary, the eldest daughter of Mr. William Manning, M.P., by whom he had no issue, but whose unremitting and affectionate attentions soothed and cheered the last sickly and suffering year of his life.

In the course of his career, Major-General Carey was present at three sieges, eight general actions, besides minor affairs, two retreats, and two disembarkations in the face of the enemy. But a severe acute disorder, contracted in the service, and which paralyzed all exertion, rendered employment impossible after the return of peace; and, having displayed every Christian virtue in his retirement, he died May 24, 1825, in his forty-seventh year.

MAJOR-GENERAL SIR OCTAVIUS CAREY, C.B., K.C.H.

Born 1785, was a younger brother of the last named officer, and entered the army in March, 1801, as a cornet in the 3d or king's own dragoons : rising rapidly, he became a captain of infantry in August, 1804, a major in November, 1809, and a lieutenant-colonel in September, 1811.

He was present at the siege of Scylla, in 1809, and served zealously on the eastern coast of Spain, from February, 1812, to the close of the war in 1814. When a major, he was selected to command a free corps of Calabrese, which soon attained efficiency and skill as light troops. Lieut.-Colonel Carey was at the taking of Alcoy, the action of Briar, the battle of Castilla, the siege of Tarragona, and the action at Ordal. At Briar and Castilla, he and his corps achieved great credit by their dexterity and courage; but it was at Ordal that their conduct was most conspicuous. The Calabrese were attached to the light division, which was posted at Ordal in advance, and which was thus furiously attacked at midnight, September 13, 1813, by a very superior French force from Barcelona. After a severe conflict and a heavy loss, the division was compelled to retire from want of support. The Calabrese, having been posted considerably to the left of the position, was separated from the main body, and must have been taken prisoners had not Lieut.-Colonel Carey, with great promptitude and daring, cut his way through the rear of the French column, although with heavy loss, and reached Villa Nova, where he impressed some vessels, on board of which he embarked his weakened corps, and rejoined the army at Tarragona, to the infinite surprise and satisfaction of Lord William Bentinck, who had given them up as lost.

Colonel Carey subsequently commanded the 57th regiment, and was made a major-general in January, 1837 : having been appointed to the command of the Cork district, he died in London, in March, 1844, after a severe and protracted illness, leaving a widow (Harriet Hirzel, daughter of Robert P. Le Marchant, Esq., bailiff,) and thirteen children. He was created a C.B. in 1815, a knight bachelor in 1830, and a K.C.H. in 1835.

Of his sons, who have all entered the military service, two gallantly fell in action, viz. the eldest, Octavius, lieutenant 29th regiment, at the battle of Moodkee, Northern India, December 18, 1845; and the fifth, Hirzel, lieutenant 74th highlanders, in command of a company at Waterkloof, in the Kaffir war, November 6, 1851, on which day Colonel Fordyce, of the 74th, was also killed.

THE REV. PETER PAUL DOBRÉE, M.A.

FELLOW OF TRINITY COLLEGE, AND REGIUS PROFESSOR OF GREEK AT THE UNIVERSITY OF CAMBRIDGE.

This eminent scholar was born in Guernsey, June 26, 1782, of a family which had come from France, upon the massacre of St. Bartholemew, in 1572. He was the son of the Rev. William Dobrée, rector of St. Saviour's parish, in that island, a clergyman eminent for tenderness of conscience, unaffected piety, and earnestness in the cause of religion, qualities which descended to him from his father, Mr. Peter Dobrée, merchant of the city of London, and author of a treatise on the Lord's Supper, a work which has passed through many editions, evincing considerable thought and learning, and written throughout in the pious and affectionate spirit that distinguished the life of the author.

Mr. Dobrée received the early part of his education at Dr. Valpy's school, at Reading, and having been entered as a pensioner at Trinity college, Cambridge, in 1800, he took his degree of B.A., in 1804, as a senior optime. He was subsequently elected a fellow of Trinity college, an honor which he had to contest with very able competitors. The present Bishop of Gloucester, Dr. Monk, the biographer of Bentley, was another of the successful candidates at the election.

He had by this time acquired a name in the university, by his diligent attention to classical criticism. The most eminent residents there became his intimate friends, especially the celebrated Professor Porson, Mr. Blomfield, fellow of Trinity, now Bishop of London, Mr. Kaye, fellow of Christ's, late Bishop of Lincoln, and the late Mr. Kidd, of Trinity, editor of Horace. Their society, and the pursuit of congenial studies, attached him to the university, and he continued to reside in college until 1811, when he accompanied his relation, Mr. Tupper, the consul for Valencia, into Spain. The war was then at its height, and the country presented scenes on every side which might have been expected to alarm a man of his mild disposition and retired habits. They did not, however, prevent his seeking all objects of interest within his reach. He witnessed the dreadful defeat of the Spaniards, under General Blake, in front of Valencia, by Marshal Suchet, in 1811; and but for his promptitude in penetrating the French lines before they were completed, he would have been made a prisoner on the surrender of that city, a few days afterwards. He succeeded in reaching Denia, which was almost deserted by its population, and the best accommodation he could find was in a church, which afforded an asylum to his companions and himself, until the arrival of a ship that took them to Majorca. He subsequently visited Cadiz whilst it was besieged by Marshal Soult, and he used on his return home to display, with some exultation, a fine edition of Plato by Servanus, and the folio Stephani Thesaurus, the spoils of an Andalusian monastery, which he had obtained at a very moderate price from a bookseller who was in constant apprehension of seeing his stock in trade fall into the hands of the French.

On his return from Spain, he entered into holy orders, but did not take a cure. The remainder of his life was passed in his college, with occasional excursions on the continent, chiefly for literary objects, during which he acquired the friendship of many of the most illustrious foreign scholars. Millai, Boissonade, and Coray, at Paris, and Thiersch, at Munich, were among those with whom he lived upon very familiar terms. The best foreign libraries were liberally opened to him, and he collected there a variety of Greek manuscripts. Such was his taste for this pursuit, that he was once on the point of going as far as Venice, merely to collate a manuscript of Athenæus, praised by Schweighauser. The fruits of his labours abroad were diligently considered at home, and he thus collected a store of most valuable criticism. He contributed to the periodicals of the day, and amongst other writings of that description, he had a share in the celebrated article in the Edinburgh Review, by Bishop Blomfield, on Butler's Æschylus, he being indeed "the learned friend" to whom the author acknowledges his obligations at the close of the article. The Classical Journal for September, 1824, likewise contained his "Greek inscriptions from the marbles in the library of Trinity college, Cambridge,"—a small work, afterwards published separately. It was not until 1820 that he gave his name to any of his publications. In that year appeared his "Porsoni Aristophanica,"[1] containing the text of Plutus, with notes on Aristophanes, by

(1) The title of this work is, "Ricardi Porsoni notæ in Aristophanem, quibus Plutum Comœdiam partim ex ejusdem Recensione, partim e Manuscriptis emendatam et variis Lectionibus instructam præmisit, et Collationum Appendicem adjecit P. P. Dobrée, A. M., Collegii SS. Trinitatis Socius, et Græcarum Literarum apud Cantab. Professor Regius."

Porson and himself. This work established his character as a scholar throughout Europe. In 1822, he published his "Lexicon of Photius," from a transcript by Professor Porson. Not long before, a similar work had been edited at Leipsic by Professor Herman, but it is generally regarded as inferior to that of Dobrée. In the following year, he succeeded the present Bishop of Gloucester as regius professor of Greek—an office which, as we have already said, had been held by Dr. Du Port, another native of Guernsey.

He did not long enjoy these honors, for in September, 1825, he was seized with the cholera, which then prevailed at Cambridge, and soon became in imminent danger. Conscious of his approaching dissolution, he shewed no alarm, but having first desired that a fellow - collegian, whom he believed anxious to obtain a living which he had thought of accepting, should be apprized of his state, in order that the other might have the earliest opportunity of obtaining the preferment, he awaited the result of the disease with the calmness of a Christian philosopher. On the 24th of September he expired, and was buried in the chapel of Trinity college, where a monument has since been erected to his memory, with an inscription in Latin, by his friend, the late Bishop of Lincoln.

In 1831, a collection of his remarks on classical writers was published by his successor as regius professor of Greek, Dr. Scholefield, under the title of "Dobræi Adversaria."

The publications of Professor Dobrée convey a very inadequate idea of the extent of his powers. His extreme fastidiousness, and his indifference to fame, caused him to shrink from authorship. Devoted to the acquirement of knowledge, which he cultivated for its own sake, and not for the applause it yields, and possessing at the same time the native modesty of genius, it was only through the importunity of friends that he was induced to send any of his papers to the press. His hours were passed in laborious investigation and patient study—the only means, as he well knew, of arriving at the true reading of the classical authors. All mere ingenuity in correcting and improving the received text, which, unless based upon sound principles of criticism, serves only to mislead while it dazzles, he utterly despised. The path he pursued was a different one. His object was to ascertain what the Greeks had written, not what they might or should have written. It will readily be conceived, therefore, that German critics found no favor with him. Indeed, he was at no pains to conceal his entire disapproval of that school, and spoke of Bohle's Sophocles, and Schulz's Æschylus, especially the latter, in terms of indignant censure. Notwithstanding these opinions, which were well known, he bore a very high reputation in Germany; and Professor Welcker, of Bonn, the first Greek scholar in Europe, spoke of him to a Guernseyman, who happened to pass a short time at the university, in terms of warm admiration. Had he lived to complete his long projected edition of Demosthenes—his magnum opus—he would have left an imperishable monument of his genius, such as must have silenced all detractors. Unhappily he left it incomplete, and its merit can only be imperfectly appreciated from the fragments which have been made public.

It is only just to add, that he was more than a classical scholar. He had read deeply in metaphysics, and was well acquainted with modern literature.

This sketch cannot be concluded without observing, that Professor Dobrée was passionately attached to his native island. He often regretted not having settled on his patrimony at the Grange; and to be a Guernseyman was a sure passport to his kind consideration. He prided himself on speaking the dialect of the island with correctness, and at one time contemplated a work upon it. He had all the simplicity characteristic of the Guernseymen of the last century, and was, in an eminent degree, warm-hearted and honorable.

The professor never married, and his estate and property descended, on his death, to his only sister, the wife of the late Mr. John Carey, king's receiver-general of the island.

SIR JOHN JEREMIE, LATE GOVERNOR OF SIERRA LEONE,

Son of Mr. John Jeremie, a talented advocate of the royal court of Guernsey, was born in 1795. After having completed a course of legal study at Dijon, in France, he was admitted to the Guernsey bar, where his career was marked by uniform and eminent success. His eloquence and abilities having been brought before the notice of the government, he was appointed, in 1824, first president of the royal court of St. Lucia, in the West Indies. In this office, he was called upon to revise and report on the slave laws then preparing for that island. He was thus led to direct his attention to a subject to which the entire energies of his mind were subsequently devoted. The more extensive his inquiries became, the more deeply was he impressed with a conviction of the enormous evils of the existing system ; and, on his return to Europe, he published "Four Essays on Colonial Slavery," pointing out, with admirable clearness, the general features of slave communities, the ameliorations introduced in St. Lucia, and the practical steps to be taken in order to effect the final annihilation of slavery. This tract, which contained the results of personal experience, honestly and fearlessly declared, produced a great sensation on the public mind, and, doubtless, contributed in no unimportant degree to promote that great measure of emancipation which has shed an imperishable lustre on the name of England.

In the year 1832, he was selected for the office of procureur and advocate-general of the island of Mauritius. Our limits will not allow us to enter into the detail of the various and harassing difficulties which he experienced in that disturbed colony. He had to contend against powerful interests, against deep-rooted prejudices, against national antipathies, against fierce and angry passions. Those difficulties he has described in an ample vindication of his conduct, entitled, "Recent Events at Mauritius," published in 1835.

His exertions and sacrifices were justly appreciated and acknowledged. In the year 1836, he was appointed puisne judge of the supreme court of Ceylon, and, at the same time, he was presented by the Anti-Slavery Society with a valuable piece of plate, bearing an inscription which testified, in the most gratifying terms, their sense of his important services.

At no time did he lose sight of the question on which his thoughts had now for many years been ardently fixed. In June, 1840, he published "A Letter to T. Fowell Buxton, Esq., on Negro Emancipation and African Civilization." It consists of important recommendations to the government, with a view to improve the moral condition of Africa—to draw forth her vast, but neglected resources—to introduce order, industry, and contentment, into scenes of unexampled misery and crime, and gradually to effect, by a series of wise and comprehensive measures, the total extirpation of the most awful scourge that ever afflicted mankind. It was from the same anxiety for the amelioration of the negro race—increased, no doubt, by the appalling fact, which had been lately and forcibly urged, that no less than half a million of human beings were then annually reduced to bondage, or destroyed—that, reckless of personal danger, undeterred by the most discouraging circumstances, he accepted, in October, 1840, the high, but ill-fated office, of captain-general and governor of Sierra Leone and its dependencies. On this occasion he received the honor of knighthood. His friends, while they respected and admired his intrepid courage, could not but reflect, with deep emotions of regret and pain, that he had gone to that fearful climate, where youth and strength are no protection against wasting disease and premature death. Their melancholy apprehensions were too soon realized. Four months had scarcely elapsed since his arrival in Africa, before he fell a victim to the fever prevalent at Port Logo, to which his arduous duties had recently called him. He expired on the 23d of April, 1841, at the age of forty-six. His death, afflicting to all the friends of humanity, is peculiarly so to his surviving relatives. Their only consolation is, that he has left behind him an honorable name, as one who, gifted with great talents, devoted those talents to the cause of justice and mercy; and who, in various employments in the four quarters of the globe, laboured with unwearied perseverance and zeal, to spread the blessings of civilization, and to promote the best interests of man.

JOHN MACCULLOCH, M.D., F.R.S., F.L.S., F.G.S., &c. &c. &c.

Dr. John MacCulloch was born in Guernsey, on the 6th of October, 1773. He was descended from an ancient Scottish family, who possessed considerable property in Galloway, but who had suffered much from their attachment to the cause of the covenant, and their opposition to the tyranny of Charles II. He was the third son of Mr. James MacCulloch, a gentleman who was loved and respected by all who knew him, and Elizabeth, daughter of Mr. Thomas De Lisle, of Smith street, one of the jurats of the royal court of Guernsey.

In his childhood, Dr. MacCulloch was thoughtful and fond of being alone. He seldom played with other children, but when the hours of study were over, was in the habit of going into a room which his father, who was a man of scientific and literary attainments, and a good mechanic, allowed him to call his own, and the door of which he contrived to fasten with a large bent needle in such a manner as to prevent his brothers from entering. Here he amused himself by drawing, carving various articles in wood and cocoa-nut shell; and, at a very early period, in attempts to make gunpowder, and, after he had effected that, in manufacturing fireworks. His family was at this time residing in Cornwall, and the first school he was sent to was the grammar school at Plympton. He was afterwards removed to one at Penzance; and thence, in 1787, to the grammar school at Lostwithiel, where he remained three years, and where his talents seem to have been appreciated by the master.

In 1790, he went to prosecute his medical studies at Edinburgh, where he obtained his diploma of physician, at the age of eighteen, being the youngest man who had ever passed the examination, which was then very severe. He subsequently entered the artillery as assistant-surgeon, and on the 5th of April, 1803, accepted the situation of chemist to the board of ordnance. In 1807, he resided at Blackheath, where he practised as a physician.

About the year 1811, he was engaged by government to make various surveys in Scotland. He in consequence gave up his practice, which he never regularly resumed, although he was frequently consulted. The first business on which he was employed in Scotland, was in a search for stones adapted to the use of the government powder mills. The second was an examination of the principal mountains, with a view to the repetition of the experiments which had been made at Schehallien on the density of the earth. The third had for its object the correction of the deviations of the plumb-line on the meridian of the trigonometrical survey. Whilst he was making these surveys, he also employed himself in geological observations, and in collecting materials for a mineralogical map, as well for his own amusement and instruction, as with the hope that they would become useful to the country at some future time. In 1826, he was desired by government to complete the work he had thus begun; and this was the commencement of the last great public work in which he was employed—the mineralogical and geological survey in Scotland, which was continued every summer from 1826 to 1832, when he completed it. During the winters of these ears, he put in order the observations made in the summer, drew sections, prepared the map, &c. This gigantic work, the labour of one individual, has never been surpassed by any undertaking of a similar nature.

While thus actively engaged, Dr. MacCulloch still found time to publish, between the years 1819 and 1831, several works, the result principally of his labours in Scotland. Two are on geology, three on subjects more exclusively connected with the country in which he was labouring. He also published a treatise on the art of making wines, which reached a fourth edition; and, though unable to follow up the practice of his profession, he never lost sight of it, the proofs of which we have in two elaborate works, one on malaria, the other on remittent and intermittent diseases. He contributed many papers to Brewster's Edinburgh Encyclopædia, and Brande's Philosophical Journal. He published many articles in the Transactions of the Geological Society, and wrote frequently in the Edinburgh and Westminster Reviews, and in the London and New Monthly Magazine.

Dr. Mac Culloch's writings contain internal evidence that they must have resulted from deep thought, based on an intimate knowledge of the subjects he treated of. The acquisition of this knowledge was gained by intense study, aided by a wonderfully retentive memory. The variety of his acquirements was not less remarkable than their extent. Allusion has been already made to his knowledge of medicine, geology, mineralogy, chemistry, and trigonometry. He was also well acquainted with theology, astronomy, zoology, botany, physics, and the mechanical arts. He was skilled in architecture. He drew well, and has left an immense number of drawings. He was a good musician, and his musical compositions shew that he was conversant with the theory as well as with the practice of the science. His accomplishments, as they are called, were cultivated at times which many persons pass without employment. His drawings were done while others were employed in walking or riding. His flowers and herbs were examined, dried, and painted before breakfast in the long summer mornings. When he used to practise music, he did so during the twilight hours. In short, no portion of his time was unoccupied. And the magnitude of his labours appears still more remarkable, from the fact that for many years he was, for a longer or shorter period every year, afflicted most severely by the effects of malaria.

In 1830, he completed a work entitled "Proofs and Illustrations of the Attributes of God, from the Facts and Laws of the Physical Universe; being the Foundation of Natural and Revealed Religion." It was intended for publication in the following year; but its appearance was delayed by the announcement of the Bridgewater Treatises. In obedience to his last will, it was published in 1837, in 3 vols. 8vo.

Dr. Mac Culloch was fellow of the Royal, Linnean, and Geological Societies, and at one time vice-president of the last. In 1820, he was appointed physician in ordinary to Prince Leopold of Saxe-Cobourg. For some years, and till his death, he filled the situation of lecturer on chemistry and geology, at the East India Company's establishment, at Addiscombe.

He married, in the summer of 1835, Miss White, whose family at one time resided near Addiscombe. He was with her in Cornwall, on a visit to his old friend, the Rev. John Buller, of St. Just, when the accident occurred which led to his death, on the 21st of August, 1835. He was thrown out of a pony phæton, by which, in addition to other injuries, his right leg was so shattered that amputation became necessary. The firmness and calmness of his mind, and his entire resignation to the will of God, were manifested during the operation. From time to time he asked questions of the surgeons, and even gave them directions. He, however, only survived the operation a few hours. He was buried in the church-yard of Gulval, a village near Penzance, in which his father had resided for some years.

COMMANDER HENRY MAINGAY, R.N.

The family of Mainguy, or Maingy, has been seated in Guernsey from the time of its earliest records. Thus, at the dedication of the Vale church, in 1117, "John Maingy" is said, among other parishioners, to have been present. We have given from Duncan (page 66, *ante*) the copy of an act of the Chief

Pleas, passed in 1204 by the bailiff and eight of the jurats; but in some copies of the said act four other jurats, including "John Maingy," are named, in place of four mentioned in Duncan's copy, the whole collectively making the twelve jurats. Although such an act may have been passed at a later period, and purposely or inadvertently antedated in the transcript, yet the authenticity of all insular documents anterior to the fourteenth century is very questionable. There is a district situate between, and on the confines of, the parishes of the Câtel and the Vale still called "Les Maingys," which anciently took its name from its proprietors. This name was evidently a corruption of that of Mainguy, anciently, and still, existing in Britany: thus, in a MS. of the Extent of Edward III., "Petrus Mainguy" was one of the jury (Inquesta) sworn to value the lands in the parish of St. Sampson. Maingy appears, however, to have been the usual orthography in Guernsey for several centuries, until one branch of the family, by the queen's royal license, in 1840, changed it to Maingay.

Henry Maingay was a midshipman in the Cæsar, 80, the flag ship of Sir James Saumarez, at the attack of the French squadron in 1801, in the roads of Algeziras, and in the subsequent engagement in the Straits of Gibraltar. In the former action, he was stationed at one of the bow ports of the Cæsar, and five men fell at his side. He obtained his first commission in the West Indies, in 1806, and served as senior lieutenant under Captain Prescott, in the Fylla, 20, and Eridanus, 36, from the beginning of 1813 until the cessation of hostilities, in 1815. He was appointed, in 1816, to the Spencer, 76; and in July, 1821, through the interest of Lord Graves, he obtained the highly-prized appointment of first lieutenant to the Royal George, yacht, Captain Sir Charles Paget, under whom he had the honor of accompanying George IV. to Ireland, in consequence of which his promotion to the rank of commander took place in December following. Captain Maingay died in August, 1846, married, but without issue.

MAJOR-GENERAL LE MARCHANT.

The family of Le Marchant has long been settled in Guernsey. There is a tradition that it passed over from Normandy soon after the Conquest. A fine old gateway, with the Le Marchant arms inscribed on it, stood near Cherbourg, until the revolution.—James Le Marchant was a jurat of the royal court, in the reign of king John. In the following reign, Robert Le Marchant acquired an estate at Bursenhall, in the county of Southampton,[1] and others of the name held lands in Somersetshire, Devonshire, and Herefordshire, in the reigns of Edward I. and II. One of them represented the borough of Wells in parliament.[2] Peter Le Marchant was bailiff and lieutenant-governor of the island during a great part of the reign of Edward I., having been the deputy of Otho de Grandison, whose oppressive administration we have already had occasion to notice. He died in 1335, leaving two sons, John and Denis; John succeeded him as bailiff, and died without issue; Denis married Janet de Cheney,[3] and was the progenitor of the various branches of the Le Marchants, which have since flourished in the island. Of the two chief branches, the younger dates its origin in the reign of Henry VI., from Drouet Le Marchant, who was captain of Beauregard, the citadel of St. Peter-Port, under the celebrated Warwick, the lord of the isles. Others of the family appear likewise to have been soldiers, and to have served with credit, as their honorable conduct is referred to in the grant of the coat of arms now borne by their descendants. It is not known that any of them settled out of the island until the period which we are now approaching.

Thomas Le Marchant, of Le Marchant manor, a younger branch of the l'Hyvreuse family, and lieutenant-bailiff of the island in the reign of George

(1) Testa de Nevill, temp. Hen. 3, Edw. 1.   (2) Palgrave's Parliamentary Writs.

(3) This illustrious Norman family appear to have held great domains in the island, up to the reign of Henry IV.—*Vide* pp. 42 and 72-3, *ante.*

II.; married, first, Catherine Mauger, of the same family with the wife of the Protector, Richard Cromwell : by her he had issue two sons, Thomas and John. He married, secondly, Mlle. Hirzel, a French Protestant lady, of the noble family of St. Gratien, near Amiens, in Picardy, and the heiress of Lewis, Count d'Olon,[1] the lieutenant-governor of the island : by her he had no issue. His eldest son, Thomas, the colonel of the west regiment of militia, was perhaps the most accomplished of the Guernsey gentlemen of his day. He passed many years in Italy and Germany, and was eminent for his taste in literature and the fine arts. He commenced a history of Guernsey, or rather, a commentary on Falle's History of Jersey, for which he is said to have collected materials in Normandy ; but the work was never finished. He married Miss Fiott, and died without issue, at an advanced age, at Exeter, in 1816.

John, the second son, was educated at Pembroke college, Oxford, but he left the university without a degree, upon obtaining a cornetcy in the 7th dragoons, with which regiment he served the last three campaigns of the seven years' war, in the army of Prince Ferdinand, of Brunswick. He retired on half-pay upon the peace of Aix-la-Chapelle, when he married Maria Hirzel, of St. Gratien, the eldest daughter of the Count de St. Gratien, a maréchal-de-camp of the Swiss guards, in the service of France, the niece and eventually heiress of his step-mother. He died at Bath, in 1794, leaving issue two sons, of whom the elder,

John Gaspard Le Marchant, entered the army as an ensign in the royals, in 1783. He accompanied his regiment to Gibraltar, where he passed several years without promotion, and, despairing of advancement in the line, he exchanged into the Inniskilling dragoons. The countenance of Lord Heathfield brought him under the notice of the king, and in three years he obtained his troop. In 1793, he joined the army in Flanders, under the Duke of York ; and having distinguished himself in an attack on the French infantry at Cassel, he was appointed brigade-major to the Hon. General Harcourt, with whom he served the campaigns of 1793 and 1794. In the latter year, he purchased a majority in the 16th light dragoons, then commanded by General Harcourt, and returned to England.

In 1795, Major Le Marchant laid before the commander-in-chief a plan for the introduction of a sword exercise throughout the service, which was adopted and is universally allowed to have promoted, in a very high degree, the efficiency of the British cavalry. For this he was appointed, without purchase, lieutenant-colonel of the 7th light dragoons. His next undertaking was the establishment of an institution for the military instruction both of officers and of youths intended for the army ; and after many difficulties, which nothing but his ardour and energetic spirit and perseverance enabled him to surmount, the royal military college was founded by the king's warrant, in 1802, when he was appointed the lieutenant-governor, with a salary and emoluments, amounting, with his regimental pay, to upwards of £2,000 per annum.

This office he filled for nine years with the most distinguished reputation. Two hundred officers were educated for the staff of the army, under his eye, the quartermaster-generals both of Lord Wellington's and Marshal Beresford's army, together with most of their assistants, being amongst them. He also found time to furnish the commander-in-chief with many useful suggestions for the improvement of the army, not the least of which was the formation of the staff corps, a department which proved so useful in the Peninsular war.

In 1811, having attained the rank of major-general, he was removed from the college to the command of a brigade of heavy cavalry, in the Peninsula. He joined the army in the autumn of that year, and in the following January was employed at the siege of Ciudad Rodrigo, where he attended Lord Wellington during the assault. Being afterwards attached to the corps under

(1) He was an ancient French refugee officer, and had attended Lord Galway as aide-de-camp and secretary at the unfortunate battle of Almanza.

Sir Thomas Graham, he gained great distinction by his conduct at Llerena, in Estremadura, on the 19th of April, where, with only three squadrons of the 5th dragoon guards, he overthrew and dispersed two of the finest cavalry regiments in the French service, with the loss of 500 men in killed, wounded, and prisoners.

At the battle of Salamanca, 22d of July, 1812, General Le Marchant's brigade was posted on the right centre of the allies. The communication between the centre and left of the French having been broken, partly by General Thomiere's rash advance, and partly by his defeat, a bold effort was made by a division of French infantry to restore it and save the day. General Le Marchant saw the importance of the movement, and, notwithstanding great disadvantages of ground, as well as disparity of numbers, for he had only 800 horse to oppose more than 5,000 of the enemy's infantry, he at once charged. The result was glorious, the French division being completely routed, more than 1,500 prisoners taken, besides many killed and wounded. The general led the charge himself, and six of the enemy fell by his hand. Unhappily, his zeal carried him unnecessarily forward in the pursuit, and he received a musket wound in the groin, of which he immediately expired, but not until he had witnessed the perfect success of the charge.

This charge is still considered one of the most brilliant made by the British cavalry during the war, and the entire credit of it is due to General Le Marchant, as his brigade was the only portion of the cavalry engaged in it. The Duke of Wellington, in his despatch announcing the victory, said: "In this charge, Major-General Le Marchant was killed at the head of his brigade, and I have to regret the loss of a most able officer."

The general was only forty-seven years of age at the time of his death. Few officers bore a higher character in the service, or could be more deeply or generally regretted. He wrote several works on cavalry tactics, all of which had a great circulation; nor were his attainments confined to his profession, for he was a skilful draughtsman, and possessed a considerable knowledge both of music and architecture. He stood high in the personal esteem of George III., and lived on terms of great intimacy and confidence with Mr. Wyndham, Lord Grenville, and others of the leading statesmen of his time. A monument was erected to his memory, at the public expense, in St. Paul's cathedral, and a pension of £1,200 per annum settled on his family.

The general married, early in life, Mary, daughter of John Carey, Esq., jurat, by whom he had a family of five sons and five daughters; the eldest died in infancy; the second, Carey, is the subject of the next memoir; the third is Sir Denis Le Marchant, Bart., of Chobham Place, Surrey, barrister-at-law, and clerk of the House of Commons, once M.P. for Worcester; the fourth is Colonel Sir John Gaspard Le Marchant, knight, lieutenant-governor of Nova Scotia, who distinguished himself as a brigadier and adjutant-general of the British auxiliary legion in Spain; and the fifth son is Lieut.-Colonel Thomas Le Marchant, of the 5th dragoon guards. Of the daughters, the only one who has married and settled in Guernsey is the youngest, Anna Maria, wife of Daniel Tupper, Esq., formerly in the army, and now receiver-general of the island.

CAPTAIN CAREY LE MARCHANT, 1st FOOT GUARDS.

The career of this gallant young officer was too brief to furnish matter for a lengthened notice, but the early promise which he gave of distinguished merit entitles his name to an honorable place in this work.

He was the eldest surviving son of Major-General Le Marchant, and was born in Guernsey at the house of his maternal grandfather. Having received a classical education at Eton, he was removed to the royal military college, where he obtained the highest testimonial awarded to the students. In 1807, he was gazetted to an ensigncy in the 1st foot guards, and on joining the regiment he received the appointment of aide-de-camp to Lieut.-General Sir Harry Burrard, K.B., commanding the household brigade in the London district.

In 1810, he left England on an excursion to the Mediterranean and Turkey, then almost the only parts of Europe accessible to an English traveller. He made some stay at Constantinople, where he contracted an intimacy with Count Ludolf, an officer in the Austrian imperial guard, son of the Neapolitan ambassador in England, and himself since distinguished as a diplomatist, with whom he visited Athens and the most celebrated remains of antiquity in Greece. He afterwards partook of the hospitality of the well known Lady Esther Stanhope, at her villa, in Asia Minor, and traversed a considerable portion of the Turkish empire in that direction. Passing thence over into Sicily, he devoted several weeks to a diligent examination of the splendid monuments of art still to be found there, and narrowly escaped death from a fever caught in taking sketches in the neighbourhood of Catania. In the summer of 1811, he joined his regiment at the Isle de Leon, where it was employed in the protection of Cadiz, and in the spring of the following year he was, to his great delight, attached to his father's staff as aide-de-camp.

From this time he bore an active part in the principal operations of the army under Lord Wellington in Spain and France, and displayed on several occasions a zeal, courage, and capacity, which called forth the frequent and warm commendations of the generals under whom he served. He fought by his father's side at Salamanca. Having been subsequently appointed aide-de-camp to Lieut.-General the Hon. Sir William Stewart, K.B., commanding the 2d division, he was present at the battle of Vittoria, where it became his duty to conduct a Spanish division to the attack—an office of great personal danger, in which he acquitted himself with his usual courage, and, to the surprise of all, escaped unhurt. In the first of the battles in the Pyrenees, he was with his general, when the latter was severely wounded, and his division nearly cut to pieces. On finding himself unemployed in consequence, he joined Major-General Pringle as aide-de-camp, and in the next engagement had the gratification of sharing in the praise showered on Pringle's brigade for its exertions on that day. Captain Le Marchant was also present at the siege of San Sebastian, and as the war was approaching its close, he was dangerously wounded at the battle of the Nive, 13th December, 1813, in an attempt to rally a regiment which had fallen into confusion. His gallantry—to use the expression of Sir William Stewart, in a letter written at the time—was the admiration of the field,[1] and appears to have attracted the notice of the enemy, as his cloak and saddle were perforated with bullets at the same moment that he himself was struck in two places. Having been carried into St. Jean de Luz, he expired on the 12th day of March, 1814, in the twenty-third year of his age, and was buried in the ramparts of that fortress. Few young men have left a more enviable reputation. His courteous and prepossessing deportment was in unison with the excellence of his heart. Neither the elegance of his person, his accomplishments, nor his success in his profession, could alter the simplicity of his character. He was truly mourned by those with whom he served, and in his own family, in which he had sought to supply a father's place, his loss was irreparable.

COLONEL HAVILLAND LE MESURIER

Was of a family which has been settled in Guernsey as far back as any authentic records can be traced, and the branch to which he belonged possessed for above a century the government and lordship of the island of Alderney. He was the grandson of John Le Mesurier, Esq., to whom the grant was renewed

(1) Sir Rowland, now Lord, Hill, in a despatch to the Marquess of Wellington, dated 16th December, 1813, said : " I was witness to the activity of Captain Le Marchant and Lieutenant Lord Charles Spencer, aides-de camp to the lieutenant-general." (Stewart.)— See *Naval and Military Magazine*, (December, 1827,) vol. 2, p. 532.

in 1763; the son of Havilland Le Mesurier, commissary-general; and the nephew of Paul Le Mesurier, M.P. for Southwark, and Lord Mayor of London.

The subject of this memoir was educated at Salisbury and Winchester, and was destined for commercial pursuits; but as he earnestly entreated his father to be allowed to enter the army, an ensign's commission was obtained for him in the staff corps, in 1801. Having been admitted into the college at High-Wycomb as a lieutenant in 1803, he passed his final examination there with the greatest credit in the summer following, being highly complimented by the Board. In 1807, he accompanied, on the staff of the adjutant-general, the expedition under Sir John Moore to Sweden, and on its return proceeded with it to Portugal in the same capacity. During the campaign, he neglected no means to acquire both the Portuguese and Spanish languages, in which he finally succeeded. At the battle of Lugo, he had some very narrow escapes; and at Corunna, where Sir John Moore fell, he had his horse shot under him. Soon after his return to England, he was appointed one of the officers to be sent out with General Beresford to discipline the Portuguese troops, and in consequence was promoted, in April, 1809, to a majority, which carried the further step of lieutenant-colonel in the Portuguese service. A few months later, he obtained the command of the 14th Portuguese regiment, which was in a wretched state, most of the officers being old and stiff, and had from 200 to 400 men on the sick list; but with the aid of a very intelligent adjutant, who he said had more of the Englishman in him than any Portuguese he had ever met with, the discipline and efficiency of the regiment were gradually restored.

In April, 1811, Lieut.-Colonel Le Mesurier became Portuguese military secretary to Lord Wellington, and arrived at head quarters the day before the battle of Fuente d'Onore, in which, perceiving the 7th Portuguese regiment, which had been ordered to cover General Houston's retreat, without a field officer, he dismounted and assumed the command of the left wing: having taken post on a rocky ground, he maintained it as long as was necessary, losing eight or ten out of eighty men, and having his arm grazed by a musket ball. Being somewhat disappointed with his staff appointment, he solicited leave to return to his regiment, which after a little delay was granted; and in October he was gratified by the receipt of his commission as British lieutenant-colonel. Lord Wellington, moreover, recommended for a commission his younger brother, Henry, who soon after, while ensign in the 48th, lost his right arm at the battle of Salamanca, July, 1812, and is now a much-respected resident of Quebec. In March, 1812, he was selected to command the fortress of Almeida, at a time that Marmont's movements excited much alarm for its safety. On his arrival, no time was lost in repairing the fortifications and disciplining the garrison, which consisted of newly raised militia. But so completely had the place been dismantled, and so insufficient were these raw troops for any serious defence, that, upon Marmont's appearing before it, every one gave it up as lost. Le Mesurier, however, shewed so good a countenance, prevailing upon his men to accompany him in two sallies, and skirmishing with some of the more advanced troops, that the enemy gave him credit for being stronger than he was, and desisted from any attempt upon the fortress. His conduct drew repeated commendations from Lord Wellington and Sir William Beresford, and he was equally beloved by the inhabitants of Almeida and by the troops. Becoming tired of the comparative inaction of a garrison life, his repeated solicitations to return to regimental duty prevailed, and in May he was appointed to the command of the 12th Portuguese regiment. Some time after, he joined the main army in the Pyrennees, and a few days before his death became full colonel. His corps had scarcely entered into action near Pampeluna, July 28, 1813, when a musket ball penetrated his head, and he fell senseless; nor did he afterwards utter a word, although he lived till the 31st. At his death, he was little more than thirty years of age; and it may truly be said of him that he was an officer of uncommon promise, and of superior

2 i

military talents and acquirements.   To these qualities Marshal Beresford bore
testimony, in his general orders of August 11 : "The death of Colonel Havilland Le Mesurier," he said, "will be felt by the service, as well as by all who
enjoyed his acquaintance." In 1809, Colonel Le Mesurier published a translation of La Trille's Art of War, with notes, which has great merit.

Another brother of the colonel, Lieutenant Frederick Le Mesurier, of the
Blenheim, 74, the flag ship of Sir Thomas Troubridge, perished in that ship,
with all on board, when she foundered in the East Indies, in 1807.

LIEUTENANT PETER LE MESURIER,

Second son of the late Mr. Abraham John Le Mesurier, of the Beaucamps,
was, in 1809, appointed to an ensigncy in the 9th foot, then commanded by
Lieut.-Colonel, (the late Lieut.-General Sir John) Cameron, and almost immediately after sailed with the expedition to Corunna, under Sir David Baird.
He was with his regiment in the expedition to Walcheren, and afterwards in
Spain, at the battles of Salamanca and Vittoria, at the siege of Burgos, in both
assaults of San Sebastian, and finally was killed in action at the operations
connected with the passage of the river Nive, on the 10th of December, 1813.

CAPTAIN PHILIP SAUMAREZ, R.N.

Was the follower and friend of Anson and Hawke, and the brother in arms of
Rodney, Keppel, and Saunders. Falling in the hour of victory, at the early
age of thirty-seven, his career was short but brilliant ; and the inscription on
his monument in Westminster Abbey justly records of him that "he was one
of those few whose lives ought rather to be measured by their actions than
their days."

The subject of this brief memoir was born in November, 1710, and at the
age of eleven he was sent to Southampton for his education, as well as to
acquire the English language, which was then but partially spoken in these
islands. In February, 1726, young Saumarez was appointed a volunteer on
board the Weymouth, 50, fitting for the Baltic station, when he was induced,
in deference to the prejudice then existing in England against French origin or
connection, to change the ancient name of "De Sausmarez," (anglicé Salt-
marsh,) borne by his ancestors, to that of Saumarez, which latter name was
also adopted by two of his brothers, the eldest, John, who possessed Sausmarez
Manor, alone retaining the original name, which is preserved by his descendants to this day. In August, 1736, Mr. Saumarez was made a lieutenant
in the West Indies, and soon afterwards returned to England.

In the memorable expedition to the South Seas, under Commodore Anson,
Mr. Saumarez was appointed third lieutenant of the Centurion, November 28,
1739 ; but the squadron, consisting of six ships of war and two victuallers,
only sailed from St. Helen's in September following. Of these vessels the
Centurion alone returned to England with the commodore, anchoring at Spithead on the 15th of June, 1744, after having performed the voyage round the
world, and been absent from England three years and nine months, bringing
with her a freight of £400,000, the produce of her captures, besides destroying
the value of £600,000 more, which the captors were unable to take on board.

In November, 1740, Mr. Saumarez became second, and in February following
first, lieutenant of the Centurion. The various disasters which attended the
squadron have been so graphically described in the narrative of Anson's voyage,
that it is only necessary to add here that on the capture of the Spanish galleon,
June 20, 1743, on her annual voyage from Acapulco to Manilla, Lieutenant
Saumarez was appointed to the command of the prize, with the rank of post
captain. He proceeded in her to China, where she was sold, and in consequence Captain Saumarez rejoined the Centurion, for a passage to England ;
the admiralty on his arrival confirming his promotion.

After serving in the Sandwich, York, and Yarmouth, each for a few months only, in September, 1746, he was appointed to command the Nottingham, of 60 guns and 400 men, which ship formed part of Lord Anson's squadron. On the 11th October following, he captured the French ship Mars, of 64 guns and 425 men, after an action of two hours, seventy-five miles S.W. of Cape Clear. The Nottingham had three men killed and sixteen wounded, and the Mars about twelve killed and forty wounded. In May, 1747, Captain Saumarez shared in the victory of Lord Anson's squadron over the French fleet under Monsieur de la Jonquière, when nine ships of war were captured from the enemy. In September of the same year, Captain Saumarez joined Admiral Hawke; and on the 14th October following, the memorable action with the French squadron took place off Brest. In this hard-fought battle, the French were inferior in force to the English, but had the advantage of the weather gage, and they fought with great bravery, with the exception of the Tonnant, 80, the admiral's ship, and the Intrepide, 74. These two ships, endeavouring to escape, were pursued by the Yarmouth and Nottingham, which engaged them nearly an hour, and would probably have overpowered them, had not Captain Saumarez been killed by a shot from the Tonnant, when the Nottingham, having lost her master spirit, hauled her wind.

Thus prematurely fell Captain Philip Saumarez, than whom no officer in the navy of his rank and time stood higher for ability and gallantry. By his will he left £100 to the poor of St. Peter-Port; and his corpse, being conveyed to Plymouth, was interred in the old church there with all the honors due to his rank and character.—A tablet, with a suitable inscription, was erected in that church to his memory, as was also a monument in Westminster Abbey.

CAPTAIN THOMAS SAUMAREZ, R. N.

A younger brother of Captain Philip Saumarez, also accompanied Anson in his expedition round the world. In November, 1757, while in command of H. M.'s ship Antelope, he captured a large Bayonne privateer, and was employed in convoying the trade between the West Indies and Bristol. In November, 1758, when lying in the Bristol Channel, Captain Saumarez was informed that a French line-of-battle ship had been seen off Lundy Island, whereupon he immediately slipped his cable, and proceeded in quest of her. The next morning, he sighted the enemy's ship, which proved to be the Belle-queux, of 64 guns : the French captain hove up his anchors, and made a shew of fighting ; but, on receiving a few shots, struck his colours, thus surrendering, with a complement of 470 men, to a ship of inferior force, both in numbers and weight of metal. For these and other services rendered to the trade of Bristol, its corporation, by an unanimous vote, presented Captain Saumarez with a gold cup, valued at one hundred guineas, which is an heir loom in the family. He died in 1764, without issue, at his seat near Rickmansworth, Herts.

ADMIRAL LORD DE SAUMAREZ, G.C.B., &c.

The same necessity, want of space, which has compelled us greatly to condense most of these memoirs, must apply equally to our biography of this distinguished officer and excellent man ; and the following narrative is in consequence a mere epitome of the services of one who, by his own gallantry and personal merits, attained the peerage and the highest honors of his profession.

This history furnishes evidence of the great antiquity in Guernsey of the family of De Sausmarez, and thus the name was spelt until the last century, when, as we have shewn, the father and two of the uncles of Lord de Saumarez anglicized it to Saumarez. Their remote ancestor received from Henry, tenth duke of Normandy, (afterwards Henry II. of England,) the fief of Jerbourg, and was appointed hereditary captain, or châtelain, of the castle of that name, situate within the limits of the fief, in the parish of St. Martin.

James Saumarez was born in St. Peter-Port, Guernsey, March 11, 1757, and having early evinced a predilection for the naval service, he commenced his glorious career as a midshipman at thirteen years of age, and spent the next five years on the Mediterranean station, returning home in 1775. Shortly after his arrival in England, he joined the Bristol, 50, Commodore Sir Peter Parker, which ship formed part of a squadron, with a fleet of transports, having on board a large body of troops, destined for an attack on Charlestown. The first object of the expedition was to obtain possession of Sullivan's Island, situate about six miles below the town, and strongly fortified. Accordingly, the squadron began the attack at eight, a.m., June 28, 1778, by a furious cannonade, which continued, with little intermission, until nine o'clock, p. m. Never did British valour shine more conspicuously : the spring on the Bristol's cable being shot away, she lay for some time exposed to a dreadful raking fire, and at one period her quarter deck was entirely cleared of every one, except the commodore. During this severe conflict, Mr. Saumarez had a very narrow escape, as at the moment he was pointing a gun on the lower deck, of which he had the command, a shot from the fort struck the gun, and killed or wounded every man but himself. A few days after the action, he was appointed acting lieutenant of the Bristol, which appointment was confirmed by Lord Howe. From that period to 1779, Lieutenant Saumarez was actively employed in America; and while in command of the Spitfire, galley, he cleared the coast of the enemy's privateers, and drove on shore and destroyed a ship of very superior force to his own.

Having returned to England, Lieutenant Saumarez was appointed to the Victory, and continued in that ship under different flag officers until his removal, as second lieutenant, into the Fortitude, with Vice-Admiral Sir Hyde Parker. In this ship he participated in the battle with the Dutch fleet, under the command of Admiral Zoutman, off the Dogger bank, on the 5th August; 1781. This action was so severe, that it reminds one of those dreadful sea fights between England and Holland, which were witnessed in the preceding century.

In consequence of the bravery which he displayed in this action, Mr. Saumarez, although only second lieutenant, was promoted to the rank of commander ; the first being wounded early in the action, his duty had fallen on him, and shortly afterwards he was appointed to the Tisiphone, a fire ship.

When the squadron arrived at the Nore, George III., ever desirous of bestowing marks of approbation on his brave seamen, honored it with a visit. On this occasion, Captain Saumarez was presented to the king, who immediately asked Sir Hyde Parker : " Is he a relation of the Saumarezs who went round the world with Lord Anson ? "   " Yes, please your majesty," the admiral replied, " he is their nephew, and as brave and as good an officer as either of his uncles!"

After performing some valuable services in the Tisiphone, Captain Saumarez, by rare good fortune, succeeded in the West Indies to the command of the Russell, 74, in February, 1782, and thus attained the rank of post captain before he was twenty-five! Two months later, he distinguished himself in Rodney's action, on the 12th of April, the Russell engaging the Ville de Paris on the quarter for some time, until the Barfleur came up, when the Comte de Grasse struck his colours. The war terminated early in 1783, and Captain Saumarez returned to Guernsey to enjoy the society of his family and friends.

We come now to the commencement of a series of naval triumphs, which will ever live in the records of the British empire. The French revolutionary war broke out in 1793, and early in January Captain Saumarez was appointed to the Crescent,3 6. In this ship he captured, off Cherbourg, in October following, the French 36-gun frigate Réunion, after a close action of two hours fifteen minutes, in which the Crescent had not a single man hurt! The Réunion in tonnage and number of men was superior, but as her main deck guns consisted of French 12s, and those of the Crescent of English 18s, this difference of metal gave the latter ship a decided advantage. The Réunion lost 120 men in killed and wounded ; and it is due to her captain to add, that he did not surrender until after a very gallant resistance, "a measure the more imperative," says James, "as the British 28-gun frigate Circé, which during the greater part of the action had been becalmed about three leagues off, striving her utmost to get up, was now approaching." This capture procured for Captain Saumarez the honor of knighthood, and the merchants of London presented him with a handsome piece of plate.

The next exploit of Sir James Saumarez displayed in a striking light both his nautical skill and his cool intrepidity, which were happily witnessed by the people of Guernsey. We allude to the masterly escape of his squadron in June, 1794, from a very superior French force off the island, but as the details are given *ante*, it is unnecessary to repeat them here.

From the period of Lord Howe's victory of the 1st of June, it was Sir James' ambition to command a ship of the line, because he used to , say : "Though I shall lose the chance of getting rich, I must have a ship fit to take part in such a triumph." Accordingly, on his own application, he was appointed, in March, 1795, to the Orion, 74, and on the 23d June following he participated in Lord Bridport's action, which he may be justly considered to have begun. In January, 1797, the Orion was one of a squadron sent to reinforce Sir John Jervis, off Cape St. Vincent, and which joined him five days before the battle of February 14. The Orion was for above an hour opposed to a three-decker, the Salvador del Mundo, which finally struck to her, when Sir James ordered his first lieutenant (Mr. Luce, of Jersey,) to take possession. The Orion next stood for another three-decker, which, after resisting for some time, also struck her colours, and hoisted an English flag over the Spanish. Here again, however, we must add, that the Spanish fleet, although vastly superior in point of ships and guns, was most wretchedly manned.

From this period to April, 1798, Sir James was employed in the blockade of Cadiz, being nearly the whole time entrusted with the command of the advanced squadron. His ship next formed part of a small squadron sent under Sir Horatio Nelson to watch the armament fitting out at Toulon, and in May this squadron encountered a violent storm in the gulf of Lyons. In June, Nelson was reinforced by eleven sail of the line, and on the 1st of August the French fleet was descried in Aboukir bay, at the mouth of the Nile. The Orion was the third ship which came into action—an action singular, from having been fought by one admiral with one eye and one arm, at night, and at anchor ! In taking up her position, the Orion, by a single broadside, sank the Sérieuse, frigate, which fired at her. In this brilliant victory, Sir James, as senior captain, was second in command : he received a severe contusion on the side from a splinter, which killed Mr. Baird, his clerk, and mortally wounded Mr. Miells, a midshipman, both of whom were standing close to him. On the 15th of August, Sir James sailed from Aboukir, with six sail of the line and the captured ships, and at Gibraltar received orders to leave the prizes at Lisbon, and then to proceed to England, where the Orion was soon after paid off.

In February, 1799, Sir James was appointed a colonel of marines, and to the command of the Cæsar, 84, in which he joined the Channel fleet. During two successive winters, he commanded the in-shore squadron, off the Black Rocks, to watch more closely the enemy's fleet in Brest, an anxious and perilous service fraught with difficulties ; and such was his sleepless vigilance, that not a single vessel entered or left the port of Brest while he remained on the station. On the 1st of January, 1801, he became rear-admiral of the blue, and hoisted his flag on board the Cæsar, still continuing off the Black Rocks.

In June following, Sir James was sent with a squadron to watch the Spanish ships in Cadiz, being previously created a baronet. Soon after his arrival off that port, he was informed that three French liners and a large frigate had taken refuge in the bay of Algeziras, and he immediately proceeded to attack them; but after a very severe conflict, (July 6, 1801,) in which the squadron had to contend against the Spanish formidable batteries, as well as the French ships, he was compelled to retire with the loss of the Hannibal, 74, which had grounded, and to repair to Gibraltar to refit. This untoward event was chiefly owing to the wind falling calm, which prevented the English squadron from taking the position intended, and left the ships exposed to the enemy's fire, while they were unable effectually to return it.

As no doubt existed that the enemy's ships in Cadiz would come to the rescue of their French allies, every effort was made to repair the British ships, and this, by incredible exertions, was effected in six days, with the exception of the Pompée, which was too much disabled. On the 9th of July, a Spanish squadron of five sail of the line and three frigates was seen steering for Algeziras, and the next day this force was increased by another sail of the line, with a French commodore's broad pendant, the whole comprising, with the Hannibal, ten sail of the line and four frigates, while the English squadron amounted to only five sail of the line, a frigate, and a polacca. The admiral determined, if possible, to obstruct the return to Cadiz of the enemy's ships, which on the 12th, at dawn, were seen preparing to sail, while the Cæsar was still refitting. At one o'clock, they were nearly all under way, and two Spanish three-deckers were already off Cabrita Point, as the Cæsar was warping out of the mole. The enthusiasm of the garrison of Gibraltar, which had witnessed the action of the 6th of July, at this exciting moment, will be easily conceived, and the Cæsar sailed out of the bay amidst deafening cheers and acclamations; even the wounded seamen begging to be received on board their ships, that they might share in the approaching encounter.

The Cæsar brought to off Europa Point, with signals for her companions to close around her, and to prepare for battle. The enemy formed his line off Cabrita, about five miles to leeward, waiting for the Hannibal, which was the last ship to leave Algeziras; but at eight o'clock, unable to work out of the bay, she anchored there again. The enemy then bore up through the Straits, and was quickly followed by the British. At 11 h. 5 m. the Superb, 74, Captain Keats, which was not in the action of Algeziras, opened her fire, and very shortly after the two sternmost ships of the enemy, both Spanish three-deckers, were seen on board of each other on fire. A more grand, yet a more pitiable, scene never presented itself: the gale was fresh, the sea running high, and the flames, ascending the rigging with frightful rapidity, soon communicated to the canvass, which instantly became one sheet of fire. The Cæsar was following these doomed ships so closely, that she had scarcely time to clear them by shifting her helm. At 12 h. 30 m., one of the three-deckers blew up with a tremendous explosion, as did the other soon after. The mind sickens at recording this dreadful tragedy; it must therefore suffice to add, that the San Antonio, 74, was captured by the Superb, and that a French line-of-battle ship would probably also have been taken by Captain Hood, in the Venerable, had not his mainmast, which had been wounded at Algeziras, been shot away. Altogether, the enemy lost three sail of the line and about 2,200 men miserably blown into the air, besides those killed in the 74s, and taken prisoners.

The intelligence of this signal, but in our opinion melancholy,[1] success was so unexpected in England, that it created the greatest astonishment, as it could scarcely be believed that the admiral, in so short a space of time, could have refitted his squadron, and sailed again to attack the enemy of more than double his force.[2] The park and tower guns were fired, and there was a general illumination, not only in London, but in several other towns. Sir James was rewarded with the order of the Bath; and when the thanks of parliament were

(1) The more melancholy, because probably at least three-fourths of the crews of the two Spanish three-deckers were impressed men. One only wish is, that those who authorized this man-stealing had been on board instead of their victims.

(2) Sir James' flag lieutenant, afterwards Captain Philip Dumaresq, of Jersey, was made a commander.

voted to him, Earl St. Vincent, Lord Nelson, and the Duke of Clarence, (William IV.) spoke in the highest terms of his achievement; Nelson saying: "The promptness with which he refitted,—the spirit with which he attacked a superior force, after his recent disaster,—and the masterly conduct of the action,—I do not think were ever surpassed."—The thanks and the freedom of the city of London were also voted to Sir James, accompanied by a sword, of the value of one hundred guineas. The inhabitants of the Anglo-Norman Islands, justly appreciating the merit of their gallant countryman, were not tardy in acknowledging the high sense they entertained of his services. The States of Jersey voted him their thanks, and the inhabitants of Guernsey presented him an elegant silver vase, with an appropriate inscription.[1]

Sir James Saumarez, having been reinforced with five sail of the line, resumed the blockade of Cadiz; and on the renewal of peace, he was detached to give up Minorca to the Spanish authorities, after which he proceeded to England and struck his flag, July 27, 1802. Shortly afterwards he was offered the chief command in the Mediterranean, which he declined; and in 1803, a grant of £1,200 per annum was conferred upon him.

On the commencement of hostilities in that year, Sir James was appointed to the naval command in these islands, which he retained until December, 1806, when he was nominated second in command of the Channel fleet under Earl St. Vincent. He was next offered the chief command in the East Indies, which he declined. Soon afterwards, when war with Russia broke out, Sir James was appointed to the command of the fleet destined for the Baltic, which he retained until 1812. His duties were essentially diplomatic, and among the many important services rendered by him on that station, was the releasing from the power of France the Spanish army under General Romana. On leaving Gothenburg, he was presented with a superb sword, (the hilt set with brilliants,) from the king of Sweden; and during the visit of the Emperor of Russia and the king of Prussia to England, Sir James received the personal thanks of those monarchs for the services he had rendered to the common cause of Europe.

In 1819, he became rear-admiral; and in 1821 vice-admiral, of Great Britain. In 1824, he was appointed port-admiral at Plymouth, which command he held three years, and then closed his long, arduous, and brilliant professional career. It was generally thought that the peerage had been unjustly withheld from him at the conclusion of the war in 1814; but on the coronation of William IV., in 1831, Lord Grey, being the premier, handsomely repaired this injustice by recommending Sir James to his majesty for that honor; and on the 12th of September he was created a peer of the United Kingdom, by the title of Baron de Saumarez, of Saumarez, in the island of Guernsey. When his elevation was known in the island, it created the liveliest satisfaction among all classes; and on the arrival of Lord de Saumarez, the States proceeded in a body to his residence to offer him their congratulations. His lordship was shortly after appointed general of marines, (which office was abolished at his death,) when he resigned the appointment of vice-admiral of England; and in 1834 he was elected an elder brother of the Trinity House. In the same year, he received a highly gratifying mark of favor from the king of Sweden, who sent him a full-length portrait of himself, accompanied by a very complimentary letter from that sovereign's minister for foreign affairs.

Towards the end of September, 1836, Lord de Saumarez, then in his eightieth year, felt that his end was approaching, and he met it with the composure and resignation which became his faith in a blessed immortality. He died at his seat, Câtel parish, Guernsey, on the 9th of October; and, during the funeral, minute

(1) The inhabitants of Guernsey to their gallant countryman, Rear-Admiral Sir James Saumarez, Bart., K.B., whose suavity of manners and private virtues have long engaged their esteem and affection, and whose brilliant achievements have not only immortalized his name, but will for ever reflect lustre on his native isle, and add to the glory of the British empire.

guns were fired from Castle Cornet and Fort George; the bells of all the churches were muffled and tolled; nearly all the shops were closed during the day; and the royal court and clergy were present, as were representatives from numberless families in the island, all anxious to pay the last tribute of respect to the memory of one who had lived and died among them, and whose affection for the land of his nativity formed one of the noblest traits in his character.

In appearance, Lord de Saumarez was the very personification of a British admiral: tall, well formed, erect, and commanding, with features denoting the energy of his character and the excellence of his heart; and well do we remember his noble presence, when, in 1818, in full naval uniform he laid the foundation stone of St. James' church, to which he was a generous contributor. We may add, that his charities, which were unlimited, were often dispensed in secret, and known only to himself and the recipients.

Lord de Saumarez married, October 8, 1788, Martha, sole child and heiress of Thomas Le Marchant, Esq., and Mary Dobrée, his wife. His eldest son, the present peer, is in holy orders; and the only other surviving son, who is heir presumptive to the title, is the Hon. John St. Vincent Saumarez, colonel in the army, unattached.

THOMAS DE SAUSMAREZ, ESQ.

Son of the attorney-general of Guernsey, by Martha, daughter of James Le Marchant, Esq., was born October 10, 1756. He received his early education in London, and was originally intended for the army; his relative, Colonel Burrard, having offered to procure him a commission in the guards; but upon the death of his father, in the year 1774, he was induced, at the solicitation of his mother, to change his views from the military to the civil profession, and, at the early age of eighteen, he received his appointment as solicitor-general of Guernsey upon the promotion of Mr. Hirzel Le Marchant to the vacancy which his father's death had occasioned in the office of attorney-general.

On receiving his appointment, Mr. De Sausmarez proceeded to Rouen, and entered as an "étudiant en droit," devoting himself with much assiduity to the study of the Norman law, and regularly attending the courts of judicature in that city, which were then thronged by the most eminent practitioners at the French bar. In 1777, he returned to Guernsey; and, having been sworn into office as solicitor-general, commenced his professional career in that capacity. In 1793, he was appointed attorney-general, and discharged the duties of this office until the year 1830, when, after a period of fifty-three years' service, he resigned his commission, and retired from public life. From his first entering the profession, Mr. De Sausmarez acquired and maintained, to the period of his retirement, an extensive and respectable practice, in the conduct of which he obtained the veneration of the bar, and the confidence of the bench. He was on many occasions deputed by the States and royal court of the island to defend their interests before the privy council in England; and, in addition to the ordinary duties of attorney-general, he discharged for many years the functions of deputy judge-advocate—an office of no small responsibility during the war, when the garrison of the island amounted to several thousand men, and courts martial were of very frequent occurrence.

On the 31st of March, 1837, when in the full enjoyment of his health and faculties, Mr. De Sausmarez was visited by a severe fit of apoplexy, which deprived him of speech, and the following day, surrounded by his family, he expired at his seat, Sausmarez Manor House, at the venerable age of eighty-one.

Mr. De Sausmarez was twice married; first, to Martha, daughter of Isaac Dobrée, Esq.; and, secondly, to Catherine, daughter of Sir Peter De Havilland, bailiff, by both which marriages he left a very numerous issue.

GENERAL SIR THOMAS SAUMAREZ, KNIGHT,

Was a younger brother of Admiral Lord de Saumarez, and in January, 1776, at the age of fifteen, entered the army as a second lieutenant, by purchase, in the 23d, or royal Welsh fusileers. Quickly embarking for North America, where the regiment was, he was present at the capture and surrender of York Island, and the capture of Fort Washington by storm, in December, 1776, when 3,800 men were made prisoners.

In 1777, Lieutenant Saumarez was promoted to a lieutenantcy, and, exclusive of minor affairs, was present in the severe action at Monmouth, in which the company to which he was attached lost its captain, and one-third of the men were killed and wounded. In 1779, at the early age of nineteen, he purchased a company in the fusiliers, and from that period to the surrender of the army under Lord Cornwallis, at York-town, October 19, 1781, he served as a captain in three general actions, several skirmishes, and two sieges, and distinguished himself on several occasions. Captain Saumarez was one of the thirteen captains taken prisoners at York-town, who were ordered by congress, in June, 1782, to draw lots that one might suffer death in retaliation for the execution of an American officer. Sir Charles Asgill was the destined victim, and his life was only ultimately spared through the intervention of the French government and the kind officers of Marie-Antoinette, the unfortunate queen of France.

At the conclusion of the American war, in 1783, Captain Saumarez was released, and was placed on half-pay, in consequence of the reduction of the army. After several fruitless attempts to obtain employment, he joined the 7th, or royal fusiliers, in 1789, and soon after embarked for Gibraltar, when his tact and judgment were so appreciated by his colonel, the Duke of Kent, that he was honored with the appointment of equerry, and afterwards of groom of the chamber to his royal highness.

In 1793, at the commencement of the war against France, Captain Saumarez was placed on the staff in Guernsey; and the year following, being deputed by the States of the island to present a congratulatory address on the marriage of the Prince of Wales, he received the honor of knighthood. In 1799, he was appointed inspector of the Guernsey militia, which situation he filled till June, 1811, when he became a major-general. In 1812, Sir Thomas Saumarez was appointed commandant of the garrison of Halifax, N.S., and in 1813 he was commander-in-chief of New Brunswick. When, in 1814, he was about to return to England, he received a highly complimentary address from the council of that province. Sir Thomas married Henrietta, daughter of William Brock, Esq. He attained the rank of general in 1838, and died in Guernsey, on the 4th of March, 1845, leaving no surviving issue.

COLONEL SIR GEORGE SMITH, KNIGHT,
AIDE-DE-CAMP TO THE KING,

Who was born in Guernsey in 1760, commenced his career, in 1778, as an ensign in the 25th regiment, and shortly afterwards accompanied it to the relief of Gibraltar. In 1793, being then captain, he embarked, in charge of a detachment, on board the fleet under Lord Hood, and was engaged in the principal affairs at Toulon, including the defence of Fort Mulgrave, a most important post, when he received a severe wound through the thigh; and, in acknowledgment of his spirited behaviour, he was nominated to the staff by Colonel Lord Mulgrave. In a sortie against the works of the enemy, he was a second time wounded.

In the year 1794, he was at the landing in Corsica, the taking of St. Fiorenzo, the capture and destruction of the French frigates and gun boats, and, subsequently, the siege and capture of the two principal fortresses, Bastia and Calvi. He raised a regiment of natives, and was employed in several important commands and distinct services.

Shortly after the evacuation of Corsica, he returned to England, when he was appointed assistant adjutant-general in the Yorkshire district, and held this situation until nominated, in 1799, lieutenant-colonel of the 20th regiment, with which he immediately proceeded, with the army under Sir Ralph Abercromby, to Holland. An attack, on the 10th September, made by a vastly superior force, on a post occupied by the British, near Crabbendam, and which had been particularly confided to him, brought him again, in a very prominent manner, to notice. In spite of the repeated and obstinate efforts of the French to carry this position, they were every where repulsed, and, after sustaining a severe loss, were forced to retire. The following extract, from Sir Ralph Abercromby's official despatch, best conveys the impression of this officer's conduct :

"The two battalions of the 20th, posted opposite to Crabbendam and Zuyper Sluys, did credit to the high reputation which that regiment has always borne : Lieutenant-Colonel Smith, of that corps, who had the particular charge of that post, received a severe wound in the leg, which will deprive us for a time of his services.
"Schuyer Brug, September 11, 1799."

In 1800, he was employed, with the 20th, in an expedition under Brigadier-General the Hon. Thomas Maitland, which was destined to attack various posts on the French coast. It was attended with partial success only, and, the main object not being found practicable, it was given up, and the 20th ordered to reinforce the garrison of Minorca.

The expedition to Egypt, in 1801, in which a part of the troops from Minorca was taken to assist, afforded another opportunity to this officer of eminently distinguishing himself. On the 25th August, Major-General Sir Eyre Coote, anxious to push as near as possible to the enemy's works, employed Lieutenant-Colonel Smith, with the 1st battalion 20th regiment, and a detachment of dragoons, to attack and drive in the advanced posts. He commenced operations after dark, by turning the left of the enemy, and, scouring the hills as he advanced, he effectually accomplished his purpose. The gallant performance of this service is thus noticed in the Gazette :

"The cool and spirited conduct of Lieutenant-Colonel Smith, and the corps and detachment under his command, is well deserving of praise : not a man attempted to load, and the whole was effected by the bayonet."

At the close of the Egyptian campaign, Lieutenant-Colonel Smith proceeded with the 20th regiment to Malta, and soon afterwards the reduction that took place left him at liberty to return to England. Whilst preparing for his departure, he received the most flattering proof of the sentiments of his brother officers, in a letter addressed to him by Lieutenant-Colonel Ross, the same officer who afterwards acquired such distinction at Washington, and whose death, in 1814, near Baltimore, was so justly deplored by his country :

"Sir,—I am directed by the officers of the first 20th regiment to state to you that, as to your constant and unremitting exertions, they feel indebted for the honorable employment upon which the first battalion has been engaged, they must ever with pleasure recollect the period during which they were under your command, nor can they, without feeling the utmost regret, find themselves deprived of a commanding officer to whom they owe so much. Anxious to convey to you the strongest assurances of respect and esteem, they request your acceptance of a sword, which, as a soldier, they trust you will receive as the most marked testimony they can offer of the high opinion they entertain of your merit, of the satisfaction you afforded while in command, and of the regret they feel in losing you.
"May you have health to wear it, and, when you draw it in defence of your king and country, may it be the good fortune of the 20th to be under your command.
"Vittoriosa, March 15, 1802."   "ROBERT ROSS.

Such a mark of admiration and esteem, from a whole corps of officers, was highly creditable to the character of Lieutenant-Colonel Smith, and could not fail being extremely gratifying to the feelings of a soldier. The inscription on the sword states it to be a token of regard from the officers, in testimony of their high sense of his meritorious and exemplary conduct, and it bears the dates "10th September, 1799," and "25th August, 1801," and the motto, "Te duce, quid non ?"

He next filled the situation of secretary to Lord Mulgrave, minister for foreign affairs; and, in 1805, was selected by government to proceed upon a confidential mission to Naples and Sicily. Whilst traversing Sicily in the execution of his duty, he was struck by malaria, and under its effects brought to the brink of the grave, receiving a shock to his constitution from which he never recovered. From Sicily he went to join the Archduke Charles in Germany, to whose head quarters he was attached; and, on his return to England, was appointed to the 82d regiment, which he commanded at Copenhagen, in 1807. Lord Cathcart manifested his sense of Lieut.-Colonel Smith's services in his public orders, as well as in his despatch of September 8 to Lord Castlereagh, relative to the operations before that capital, as follows:

"Lieut.-Colonel Smith, with the 82d regiment under his command, held the post at the windmill on the left, which, for the greater part of the time, was the most exposed to the gun boats and sorties of the enemy, and the unremitting exertions of that officer claim particular notice."

On this occasion, the honor of knighthood was conferred upon him. The same year he embarked on a particular service, under the command of Lieut.-General Sir Brent Spencer; but the great change of affairs in Spain caused it to be relinquished, and he came home with the result of some negotiations entered into with the Spanish authorities at Cadiz.

On his arrival, he received an additional testimony of his majesty's own approbation, by being appointed his aide-de-camp. His exertions amidst the constantly recurring attacks of his disease rendered a short repose necessary; he sought it in his native isle, and was in a slow progress of recovery, when, in 1809, he was again called for on a very important occasion, a mission to Cadiz, and one of his majesty's ships, the Hope, was despatched to take him to his destination. His high sense of military duty never admitted an idea of hesitation; he proceeded thither contrary to the advice of his friends, who, from the weak state of his health, anticipated the fatal event which took place on the 15th of February, within a month of his arrival.

Thus died Colonel Sir George Smith, in the forty-ninth year of his age, at a period when, from the distinction he had already attained, the higher destinies of his profession seemed to be awaiting him.

His remains were conveyed on board his majesty's ship Viper with military honors, the troops lining the streets to the water's edge, accompanied by Captain Stewart, of the 82d regiment, his secretary. This faithful friend had determined not to quit the corpse till he had seen it interred at Gibraltar; but it was fated otherwise. The Viper was never heard of after leaving Cadiz, and is supposed to have foundered, consigning all on board to one common grave.

Sir George Smith was in the army above thirty years, in the course of which he had been three times severely wounded; and though his death might not be accounted so glorious as if he had fallen in battle, yet this consideration is due to his memory, that his life was lost equally in the service, and from the most manifest devotedness to the interests of his country.

Sir George, who was the eldest son of Captain Thomas Smith, royal invalids, and Mary de Havilland, his wife, was united to his first cousin Carterette, eldest daughter of Sir Peter de Havilland, bailiff of Guernsey, and left his widow with two daughters, one of whom married Augustus Frederick Dobrée, Esq., and the other Joshua Priaulx, Esq.

MAJOR-GENERAL HAVILLAND SMITH

Was a younger brother of Sir George Smith, and, entering the army at an early age, was a lieutenant of the 25th regiment in 1793. After serving at Toulon, on the continent under the Duke of York, and in Corsica and Elba, he was appointed, in 1800, major of the 27th regiment, having the brevet rank of lieutenant-colonel. He commanded a battalion during the whole of the memorable campaign in Egypt, and was present at the battle of Alexandria, for which he received a medal.

At Maida, in 1806, he was lieutenant-colonel commanding the 27th regiment, and, by his coolness and presence of mind in availing himself of the discipline of his fine corps, contributed materially to the success of that glorious day. Sir John Stuart, in his general order after the battle, said : "The manœuvre of the 27th regiment, in throwing back a wing to receive the enemy's cavalry, was the strongest token of the excellent discipline of that corps." For this victory, Lieut.-Colonel Smith also received a medal.

In 1810, he attained the rank of colonel, and in 1813 that of major-general : he served in the latter rank for a year on the eastern coast of Spain, and was proceeding, with the English troops there, to join the Duke of Wellington when the war terminated.

In 1816, he was appointed senior general officer on the staff of the Ionian Islands, and died the following year at Corfu, unmarried, after a long and painful illness, in his forty-fourth year.

LIEUTENANT CARRÉ TUPPER, R.N.

The common ancestor of the Guernsey family of this name was John Tupper, son of Henry, of Chichester, Sussex, who settled in the island, temp. queen Elizabeth,[1] on marrying in St. Peter-Port, December 10, 1592, Mary, sole child of Peter Le Pelley, by his wife, Collette, only daughter of Hilary Gosselin, bailiff. The said John Tupper died young, leaving two sons and two daughters ; to two of these children, Peter Carey, lieutenant-governor of Guernsey, was guardian, and Robert Tupper, of Chichester, to the other two, as appears by art. 60 of the causes decided by the royal commissioners, in 1607. The elder son, John Tupper, married his cousin, Elizabeth, daughter of Hilary Gosselin, procureur or attorney-general of Guernsey ; and his elder son, also John Tupper, (who married, in 1655, Jane Roland,) was the father of John Tupper, who received the gold medal and chain from William and Mary, as related *ante ;* and the fatality, which of late years has attended the few lineal descendants of the last-named John Tupper, will appear in the following brief summary :

1. Lieutenant Carré Tupper, H.M.S. Victory, only son of Major-General Tupper, slain at the siege of Bastia, on the 24th of April, 1794.

2. William De Vic Tupper, his first cousin, mortally wounded in 1798, in a duel in Guernsey, with an officer in the army, and died the day following.

3. John E. Tupper, aged twenty, perished at sea, in 1812, in the Mediterranean, the vessel in which he was a passenger, from Catalonia to Gibraltar, having never been heard of since.

4. Charles J. Tupper, aged sixteen, a midshipman of H.M.S. Primrose, drowned in 1815, at Spithead, by the upsetting of the boat in which he was accompanying his captain to the ship.

5. Lieutenant E. William Tupper, H.M.S. Sybille, aged twenty-eight, mortally wounded in her boats, Sunday, June 18, 1826, in action with a strong band of Greek pirates, near the island of Candia.

6. Colonel William De Vic Tupper, Chilian service, aged twenty-nine, slain in action near Talca, in Chile, April 17, 1830.

The four last, sons of John E. Tupper and Elizabeth Brock, his wife, and nephews of William De Vic Tupper, already named, and also of Major-General Sir Isaac Brock, K.B., of Lieut.-Colonel John Brock, and of Lieutenant Ferdinand Brock, who all fell by the bullet.

7. Colonel William Le Mesurier Tupper, of the British auxiliary legion in Spain, and a captain in the 23d, or royal Welsh fusiliers, mortally wounded near San Sebastian, May 5, 1836, aged thirty-two.—Colonel Tupper was nephew of W. De Vic Tupper, and first cousin of the four brothers last named.

(1) In May, 1592, queen Elizabeth granted to "William Tupper, gentleman," some lands belonging to the crown, at Seaford, one of the cinque-ports, in Sussex.

By a most extraordinary coincidence, Brock and Frederick, the sixth and seventh sons of the said J. E. Tupper — both passengers in H. M.'s packets from Rio de Janeiro to Falmouth — died at sea on the same day of the same month, (August 15,) and the remains of both were committed to the deep, the former in 1833, aged thirty, and the latter in 1837, aged thirty-three.

John Tupper, third son of Daniel, by his wife, Elizabeth, daughter of Elisha Dobrée, of Beauregard, obtained, in 1747, a commission by purchase in General Churchill's regiment of marines, that corps being then differently constituted to what it is now. He served as a captain at the celebrated defeat of the French fleet in Quiberon bay, by Sir Edward Hawke, in 1759 ; as a major and commandant of a battalion at Bunker's Hill, in 1775,[1] where he was slightly wounded, and where the marines, having greatly distinguished themselves, won the laurel which now encircles their device ; and as a lieutenant-colonel, in Rodney's victory of the 12th of April, 1782, having been especially sent from England to command the marines in the fleet, nearly 4,000 men, in the event of their being landed on any of the enemy's West India Islands. At his decease, in January, 1795, he was a major-general in the army, and commandant-in-chief of the marines.

His only son, Carré, the subject of this memoir, born in 1765, was made a lieutenant in 1782, a few days after he had completed his seventeenth year, and appointed by Sir Peter Parker to the Sandwich, his flag ship at Jamaica.

The peace of ten years, which soon followed, proved a bar to his further advancement, although during this period he was constantly employed in different ships ; and, in 1791, being then a lieutenant of the Culloden, he saved, in a most gallant manner, the life of a seaman who had fallen from the fore yard into the sea, the ship being at the time under sail on her way out with the squadron from Carlisle Bay, Barbadoes.

In the beginning of September, 1793, while serving in the Windsor Castle, 98 guns, Vice-Admiral Cosby, off Toulon, he volunteered to take the command of Fort Pomet, near that city, the garrison of which consisted of 150 seamen and soldiers. This fort was commanded by an adjacent eminence, on which the enemy erected two batteries, one of two 12-pounders, the other of three 8-pounders, with a 12-inch mortar, and from which they kept a heavy fire on Fort Pomet during the day, as well as endeavoured to surprise it during the night. But by his activity and resolution, not pulling off his clothes for many weeks, Lieutenant Tupper frustrated every attack, and the garrison having, with very great labour and fatigue, strengthened the fort, by placing on the walls large casks and nearly fifteen hundred sacks filled with earth, the defence was protracted until the 9th of December following, when it was found necessary to blow it up. For his services on this occasion, Lieutenant Tupper received the repeated approbation and thanks of Lord Mulgrave, and Generals O'Hara and Dundas, successively commandants of Toulon ; and, on his quitting Fort Pomet, Lord Hood immediately appointed him a lieutenant in his own flag ship, the Victory.

On the morning of the evacuation of Toulon, Lieutenant Tupper again volunteered to accompany Sir Sydney Smith in the perilous undertaking of setting fire to the arsenal and French ships of war in the harbour. Lieutenant Tupper having been charged with the destruction of the general magazine, the hemp, pitch, and other store-houses, he was employed the whole day, with his boat's crew of only seven men, in placing the combustibles, expecting that the gates of the yard would be forced open every moment by the enemy, and that they would be all put to death. On the preconcerted signal being made in the evening, Lieutenant Tupper set fire to the different combustibles, (no officer being in the dock yard that night but himself,) but owing to the wind being

(1) Major Tupper succeeded to the command of the marines, of whom there were two battalions at Bunker's Hill, after the fall of the gallant Major Pitcairn, and was honorably mentioned in the general orders of the day.

very light, the destruction, although great, was not so complete as the awful blaze at first gave reason to suppose. Having performed his dangerous task, Lieutenant Tupper proceeded, in his boat, to assist Sir Sydney Smith and Lieutenant R. W. Miller [1] in setting fire to four sail of the line, which had escaped the flames of the Vulcan, fire ship.

From Toulon, the British fleet proceeded to the reduction of the island of Corsica; and in February, 1794, while near the town and formidable batteries of San Fiorenzo, Lord Hood detached the boats under Captain Cooke [2] to endeavour to prevent the destruction, by the French, of two of their frigates at anchor under the batteries. One of the frigates was burnt, but the other, although scuttled, was saved; and as the boats quickly pushed on towards the town, which the enemy were evacuating, Lieutenant Tupper, being the second person who landed, immediately ran to the citadel, and hauled down the French colours, which he afterwards delivered to Lord Hood.

On the 11th of April, Lord Hood entrusted Lieutenant Tupper with his summons of surrender to the commandant of Bastia, and, singularly enough, he who carried the summons was the only British officer who was slain before the place.

On the 24th of April, 1794, Lieutenant Tupper having volunteered to obtain information, if possible, relative to the state of the French garrison of Bastia, he proceeded after dark on this perilous service, and his boat having unfortunately grounded at ten o'clock, p.m., under the walls, he was endeavouring to get her off when she was discovered by a sentinel on shore, who fired at her, and the bullet unhappily striking Lieutenant Tupper in the heart, he instantly expired.

Thus fell, in the pride of manhood, a most zealous and intrepid officer, whose fate was the more lamented because Lord Hood had promised him the first commander's vacancy, for his services at Toulon, which vacancy occurred only two days after his death, and was consequently conferred on the late Vice-Admiral Sir John Gore. And we have heard, but cannot vouch for the fact, that the Admiralty had promoted him for those services, and sent out his commander's commission, before the intelligence of his death was received in England. Had his life been spared a few years longer, he would probably have found an opportunity of distinguishing himself, in a higher rank, in the many glorious engagements which soon after ensued, as did his more fortunate brother lieutenants at Toulon, Edward Cooke, R. W. Miller, and John Gore.

In person, Lieutenant Tupper was tall and uncommonly handsome, being upwards of six feet in height, well proportioned, and of a most pleasing countenance.

PETER CAREY TUPPER, ESQ., BRITISH CONSUL IN SPAIN,

Fourth son of John Tupper, Esq., jurat, is noticed at p 398 ante. In May, 1808, he was named a member of the supreme junta of the kingdom of Valencia, and was most active in organizing a rising of the Spaniards against the French: in the following month, during the dreadful massacre of the French residents in the city, he was exposed to imminent personal danger in his endeavours to save them; many were rescued by him, and among them the consul. (See *Sir John Carr's Travels in Spain*, 4to. London, 1811.) During the siege of Valencia, 1811-12, Mr. Tupper demanded the direction of the chief battery, that of Santa Catalina, from whence the French camp might be much annoyed,

(1) Captain R. W. Miller, commanding the Theseus, 74, was killed in 1799, by the accidental explosion of some shells on board his ship, employed under Sir Sydney Smith, in the defence of Acre. He commanded the Captain, 74, at the battle of St. Vincent, and the Theseus at the battle of the Nile.

(2) Captain Edward Cooke, while commanding the Sybille, frigate, was mortally wounded in 1799, in the capture of the Forte, a French frigate of much superior force, in the bay of Bengal. The late Commander N. Mauger, of Guernsey, was third lieutenant of the Sybille on this occasion, and first took possession of the prize.

and for the space of thirty successive days, he caused the French considerable damage in killed and wounded.

The following is the conclusion of a letter written to him by the duke [then Marquess] of Wellington, and dated Frenada, 25th of February, 1813 :

"I take this opportunity of expressing my sense of the services which you have rendered to the interesting cause in which we are all engaged, in the different situations you have filled on the eastern coast of the Peninsula. I have read your account of transactions there with the utmost interest, and I sincerely wish you success."

In 1816, the king of Spain conferred on Mr. Tupper, his heirs, and descendants, the title of "Baron de Socorro," (Baron of Succour,) at the solicitation of the municipality of the city of Valencia ; but, by the established regulations in England, he was not permitted to accept of this mark of distinction : a pension of £600 a year was, however, settled upon him by the British government in acknowledgment of his services, which we have not space to enumerate, and he was moreover removed to Catalonia as a better consulship.

On the second entrance of the French into Spain, in 1823, he accompanied the British ambassador, Sir William A'Court, to Cadiz ; and, partly owing to his services on this occasion, his youngest brother was selected by Mr. Canning as consul for Caraccas, with a salary of £1,000 a year, when salaried consuls were first sent out in 1823 to South America. The subject of this notice died at Madrid, April 13, 1825 ; married, but without issue, in the prime of life, while employed in that city in the commission for the settlement of the British claims on the Spanish government. During his long residence in Spain, he formed a very valuable collection of paintings and cartoons, part of which were sent to England.[1] The present Martin Farquhar Tupper, M.A., of Christ Church, Oxford, and the talented author of Proverbial Philosophy, &c., is his nephew.

LIEUTENANT E. W. TUPPER, R.N.

This officer, third son of John E. Tupper, Esq., by Elizabeth Brock, his wife, was educated at Harrow, and commenced his naval career in 1810, in the Victory, of 110 guns, under the care and patronage of the late Lord de Saumarez, with whom he continued some time in the Baltic. He served on the American coast during the latter part of the war, in the Asia, 74, and was present at the disastrous attack of New Orleans, in January, 1815, forming one of a party landed from the fleet, to co-operate with the army. On the night of the storm, this party, in conjunction with the 85th light infantry, attacked some fortified works on the right bank of the Mississippi, and were completely successful ; but the failure of the main assault rendered this success unavailing. In the same year, he joined the flag ship of Sir Thomas Fremantle, who, having been an intimate friend of his late uncle, Sir Isaac Brock, kindly assured him of his influence and support ; but, peace taking place before he had attained the requisite age for promotion, all the bright prospects with which he entered the service were blighted. In November, 1817, on his return in the Active, frigate, Captain Philip Carteret, from the Jamaica station, he passed at the naval college at Portsmouth, and was one of four midshipmen complimented as having undergone a superior examination. In 1823, he was appointed to the Revenge, Sir Harry Neale's flag ship, in the Mediterranean, and placed on the admiralty list for advancement. Early in 1826, he was at length promoted into the Seringapatam, frigate ; but Sir John Pechell, under whom he had previously served for a short time, prevailed upon the admiral to transfer him to his own ship, the Sybille, of 48 guns, "a crack frigate," in a high state of discipline, the crew of which was remarkable for its skill in gunnery.

The Sybille was at Alexandria when intelligence arrived there of the plunder

(1) See Penny Magazine, vol. i. p. 350, and vol. ii. p. 77.

of a Maltese vessel, under atrocious circumstances, by a nest of Greek pirates, on the southern coast of Candia. Sir John Pechell set sail immediately in quest of the delinquents. On Sunday, the 18th of June, 1826, at daylight, two misticoes were observed under sail, near Cape Matala, standing towards the frigate; but, on discovering their mistake, they made for the land, and were followed by the Sybille, into a narrow creek formed by a rocky islet, and the mainland of Candia. On this island were posted armed Greeks, the crews of three or four piratical misticoes at anchor in the creek, and, in a desperate attempt to cut out these misticoes, with the boats, Midshipman J. M. Knox and twelve men were killed, and the first lieutenant, Gordon, dangerously; Lieutenant Tupper, mortally; Midshipmen William Edmonstone and Robert Lees, both very severely; and twenty-seven men were wounded, of whom five died in a few days. Two of the misticoes were afterwards sunk, and many of the pirates were killed and wounded by the frigate's guns.

Lieutenant Tupper commanded the launch, and, although severely wounded in three places, he stood up the whole time, and retained the command of her until he returned to the ship. The bullet, which proved fatal, entered his right breast, and was extracted from under the skin over the false ribs. He lingered until the 26th of June, when he breathed his last, in a state of delirium, on board the Sybille, at Malta, where his remains were interred, and a monument was erected to his memory by his captain and messmates.

The surgeon, in a letter to the family in Guernsey, wrote of Lieut. Tupper:

"When I first saw him, he was firm and cool. He asked me to give my opinion without reserve, and, knowing him to be possessed of great fortitude, I told him that the wound in the chest was of a most *dangerous* nature, but not *necessarily* fatal. He had by this time lost a great deal of blood, but the internal hemorrhage, though the most alarming, was slight. He remained so low for three days, that it was expected he would have sunk, though he still continued collected and firm. On the fourth day he rallied, his pulse became more distinct, and he evidently encouraged hopes. Need I say that I felt myself incapable of destroying them,—indeed, I was not altogether without hope myself. The principal danger was from hemorrhage upon the separation of the sloughs, and my fears were fatally verified, for on the 25th, at noon, it commenced and increased internally, until his lungs could no longer perform their functions, and he died at about three o'clock, on the morning of the 26th. During the whole time he was resigned, evincing the greatest strength of mind. . . . . As it was with unfeigned sorrow that I saw a fine and gallant young man fall a victim to such a cause, so it was with admiration that I witnessed his heroic bearing when the excitement was past, and hope itself was almost fled. I have seen many support their firmness amidst danger and death, but it belongs to few to sustain it during protracted suffering, which is indeed a trial often too severe for the bravest, but through which your lamented brother came with a spirit and resignation which reflected lustre upon himself and family, and endeared him to all his shipmates."

●

COLONEL WILLIAM DE VIC TUPPER.

This highly gifted young man was a brother of the subject of the preceding memoir, their father having had ten sons and three daughters. Having received an excellent education in England, partly under a private tutor, and completed it at a college in Paris, every interest the family possessed was anxiously exerted to indulge his wish of entering the British army; but, owing to the great reductions made after the peace of 1815, he was unable to obtain a commission, even by purchase.[1] Thus cruelly disappointed, he spent two or three years in Catalonia; but the profession of arms continuing his ruling passion, he proceeded, in 1821, to Chile, then struggling for her independence. There his appearance and manners, and a perfect knowledge of three languages, (English, French, and Spanish,) soon procured him active military employment. In a necessarily brief notice, it is utterly impossible to detail the services of young

(1) Only five knights of the Bath have been slain in action, viz. Abercromby, Brock, Moore, Nelson, and Picton. Abercromby's family was rewarded; Nelson's two sisters each received £10,000 from government; and those of Picton were pensioned, while a son of Brock's only surviving sister, who had solicited or received nothing, was unable to purchase an ensigncy, and than that son a finer young man never entered the British army.—Of Moore's family we have no information.

Tupper in the land of his unhappy adoption, and it must therefore suffice to say, that he displayed the greatest talent and bravery, first against the Spaniards, and, after their subjugation, in the civil wars which ensued. He was drawn into the latter, when, in 1829, part of the troops, under General Prieto, attempted to subvert the existing authorities, because, as he wrote, he "considered that no free government or orderly state could exist an hour if the military were once allowed to throw the sword into the scale, and decide points of legislation by the force of arms." In a battle fought near the capital, (Santiago,) the rebel troops were defeated, but Prieto gained that by treachery, which he could not effect by the sword; and when Colonel Tupper resigned in disgust, the earnest entreaties of his old commander, General Freire, unfortunately induced him to accept the government of Coquimbo, which step soon after compelled him to resume the command of his regiment. The rival forces, after several partial conflicts, met again at Lircay, near Talca, on the 17th of April, 1830; and Freire, although deficient both in cavalry and artillery, having most unaccountably sought battle in a vast plain, was routed with great slaughter, after an action of several hours. When all was lost, Colonel Tupper escaped from the field with a slight wound; but he was pursued, overtaken, and "sacrificed to the fears of Prieto, who justly considered him the sword and buckler of the irresolute and vacillating Freire." He was pronounced by an English traveller as "the handsomest man he had ever seen in either hemisphere;" and undoubtedly, his tall, athletic, and beautifully proportioned person, his almost Herculean strength, the elegance of his manners, and his impetuous valour in battle, gave the impression rather of a royal knight of chivalry than of a republican soldier.[1] The influence and popularity which in a few short years he acquired in his adopted country, by his own unaided exertions, and under the many disadvantages of being a stranger in a strange land, best prove that his talents were of the first order, and that he was no common character. And, that affection may not be supposed to have dictated this eulogium, the following impartial testimonies of its correctness are appended, in justice to the memory of one whom a combination of cruel circumstances drove to a distant land to shed that blood, and to yield that life, which he had in vain sought to devote to his own country.

An English gentleman, of ancient family, and author of Travels in South America, who knew Colonel Tupper intimately, thus wrote of him:

"He was certainly one of the finest fellows I ever knew,—one of those beings whose meteor-like flame traverses our path, and leaves an imperishable recollection of its brilliancy..... I have often held him up as an example to be followed of scrupulous exactness, and of a probity, I fear, alas! too uncompromising in these corrupt times."

The American *chargé d'affaires* and consul-general in Chile, in a letter to Captain P. P. King, then of H.M.S. Adventure, both strangers to the family, said:

"The heroism displayed by Tupper surpassed the prowess of any individual that I ever heard of in battle; but, poor fellow! he was horribly dealt with after getting away with another officer. A party of cavalry and Indians was sent in pursuit, and they boast that poor Tupper was cut to pieces. They seemed to be more in terror of him, on account of his personal bravery and popularity, than of all the others. Guernsey has cause to be proud of so great a hero,—a hero he truly was, for nature made him one."

And one of the British consuls in Chile wrote:

"I trust you will believe that any member of the family of Colonel Tupper, who may require such services as I am at liberty to offer, will be always esteemed by one who, for many years, has looked upon his gallant and honorable conduct as reflecting lustre upon the English name in these new and distant states."

An anonymous French traveller, who published in a Paris newspaper, Le Semeur, of the 4th of April, 1832, his "Souvenir d'un séjour au Chili," thus expressed himself:

(1) When he left Europe, in 1821, he was generally thought to bear a striking resemblance to his maternal uncle, Sir Isaac Brock, at the same age. In height, he was about six feet two inches, and his figure was a perfect model of strength and symmetry.

2x

"Les Chiliens sont jaloux des étrangers qui prennent du service chez eux, et il est assez naturel qu'ils le soient, quoiqu'on ne puisse nier qu'ils aient de grandes obligations à plusieurs de ceux qui ont fait Chili leur patrie adoptive. Depuis mon retour en Europe, un de ces hommes, digne d'une haute estime, a cessé de vivre. Je veux parler du Colonel Tupper, qui a été fait prisonnier à la tête de son régiment, et qui, après avoir été tenu, pendant une heure, dans l'incertitude sur son sort, fut cruellement mis à mort par les ennemis. Le Colonel Tupper était un homme d'une grande bravoure et d'un esprit éclairé; ses formes étaient athlétiques, et l'expression de sa physionomie pleine de franchise. Il se serait distingué partout où il aurait été employé, et dans quelque situation qu'il eût été placé. N'est-il pas déplorable que de tels hommes en soient réduits à se consacrer à une cause étrangère?"

And in a pamphlet published at Lima, in 1831, by General Freire, in exposition of his conduct during the civil war in Chile, 1829-30, is the following extract, translated from the Spanish :

"It does not enter into my plan to justify the strategic movements which preceded the battle of Lircay. The disproportion between the contending forces was excessive. Neither tactics nor prodigies of valour could avail against this immense disadvantage. The liberals were routed. Would that I could throw a veil, not over a conquest which proves neither courage nor talent in the conqueror, but over the horrid cruelties which succeeded the battle. The most furious savages, the most unprincipled bandits, would have been ashamed to execute the orders which the rebel army received from Prieto, and yet which were executed with mournful fidelity. Tupper—illustrious shade of the bravest of soldiers, of the most estimable of men; shade of a hero to whom Greece and Rome would have erected statues—your dreadful assassination will be avenged. If there be no visible punishment for your murderer, divine vengeance will overtake him. It will demand an account of that infamous sentence pronounced against all strangers, by a man, who at that time was the pupil and the tool of a vagabond stranger,[2] indebted for his elevation and his bread to the generosity of Chile."

CAPTAIN WILLIAM LE MESURIER TUPPER, 23d ROYAL WELSH FUSILIERS,

AND COLONEL IN THE BRITISH LEGION IN SPAIN.

This gallant officer entered the British army by purchase, as a second lieutenant in the 23d, or royal Welsh fusiliers, on the 4th of September, 1823, and on the 1st of August, 1826, obtained an unattached company, also by purchase, being immediately re-appointed to the 23d by paying the difference. Thus, in less than three years, he attained the command of a company in this distinguished corps. He spent the nine succeeding years chiefly with his regiment, in garrison at Gibraltar, accompanying it in the expedition to Portugal in 1827, under Sir William Clinton. Early in 1835, Captain Tupper, whose reckless feats of daring will long be remembered at Gibraltar, returned with the 23d to England ; and soon after an order in council was issued, permitting and encouraging British subjects to enter the service of the young queen of Spain, whose government had been unable to suppress an insurrection in favor of her uncle, Don Carlos, in the northern provinces. Disappointed in his wish of purchasing an unattached majority, as there was no early prospect of his obtaining one in the 23d, and tired of the inactivity of a garrison life, Captain Tupper was unhappily induced, in conjunction with other British officers,[3] to exchange on half-pay, and to accept of promotion in the British auxiliary legion, then raising, to be composed of 10,000 men, and commanded by Lieutenant-Colonel Evans, M.P. for Westminster, with the rank of lieutenant-general. Disinterested almost to a fault, and possessed of an independent private fortune, Captain Tupper could have no other motive in joining the legion than that of seeing service and of acquiring distinction at the head of a regiment.

(1) General Prieto.   (2) Garrido, a Spanish renegade.

(3) Of the ten officers on full pay of the British army (including one of engineers and one of artillery) who joined the legion, the only two killed in Spain were Guernseymen, viz. Colonel Tupper, and Colonel Oliver De Lancey, captain of the 60th or king's rifles, who was mortally wounded at the head of his regiment near San Sebastian, March 15, 1837, and died on the 22d.

Lieut.-Colonel Tupper was at once appointed to command the 6th, or Scotch grenadiers, which regiment was raised in Glasgow, and whence he proceeded, in August, 1835, with the first division of nearly 400 men, in a large steamer to Santander, touching at Falmouth for coals and water. From Santander he was almost immediately detached to Portugalette, a small town at the mouth of the river leading to Bilboa, and which was then threatened by the Carlists. Here he animated his young troops by his conduct and example, exposing himself on every occasion with the utmost fearlessness. Bilboa itself being closely invested by the Carlists, the 6th was one of the regiments which effected its relief, and a few days after distinguished itself by driving the enemy across the bridge near that town. From Bilboa the legion proceeded to join the Spanish army in the interior, the Carlists in force endeavouring in vain to prevent the junction, and spent the winter at Vittoria, where hundreds fell victims to an epidemic fever arising from the greatest privations.

In the spring of 1836, the town of San Sebastian was vigorously blockaded by the Carlists, who had been for some months employed in fortifying the adjoining heights, and the legion was detached to its relief. The health of Brigadier-General Reid,[1] who commanded the light brigade, consisting of the rifles, 3d, and 6th regiments, having suffered from fever, he was succeeded by Colonel Tupper, who left Vittoria for Santander on the 12th of April, in command of the brigade, the other brigades, with General Evans, following on the succeeding days. The light brigade arrived at San Sebastian on the 22d of April, and the British were received there with every demonstration of joy. The following is an extract from a long private letter, published in the Courier of the 9th of May:

"*San Sebastian, April* 29.—Lieut.-Colonel Tupper, of the 6th regiment, from the high state of discipline of his corps, has been promoted to the rank of colonel; he commands, *ad interim*, the light brigade, two thousand strong, composed of the finest and most efficient men in the legion. Much is expected from the *en avant* dashing character of this officer. Before the expiration of a week a blow will be struck. Notwithstanding the strength of the enemy's lines, and the difficult nature of the country, I have no fears as to the result."

Brigadier Reid, however, reached San Sebastian, and resumed the command of the light brigade, before any attempt was made to dislodge the Carlists from their triple line of defences near that town. The greater part of the legion having arrived, General Evans decided to attack at daybreak on the 5th of May, and three brigades marched out in silence during the night for that purpose. To the light brigade was assigned the assault of the enemy's right and centre; the first line was carried, but the second presented such formidable obstacles, and was so obstinately defended, that the legion was there repulsed with great slaughter of officers, and compelled to retreat under shelter, Colonel Tupper having his left shoulder shattered by a bullet. A breach was at length effected in a redoubt to the left, by shells thrown from H.M. steamer Phœnix; and two regiments of the legion having most opportunely arrived during the day from Santander, they were instantly led to the attack of the breach, which they carried, the leading company being commanded by the gallant Captain John Allez, a native of Guernsey, who fell covered with wounds. While this attack on the enemy's left was in progress, Colonel Tupper sprang forward, and headed his regiment in an assault of the entrenchments on the right. Advancing under a heavy fire, he received another wound in the left arm, and a severe contusion in the side, but pushed on, sword in hand, until a bullet pierced his *schako*, and, entering the right temple, lodged in the brain. Another bullet had previously perforated his *schako* near the top. Thus the presentiment, which he had long entertained that he should fall in the first serious affair, was unhappily accomplished, and thus the wish which he had often expressed of dying in battle, was too fatally realized. He appears to have commanded the brigade in the last attack, Brigadier-General Reid

(1) The present Colonel Sir William Reid, K.C.B., Governor of Malta.

having been previously wounded, and his regiment had nine officers and about a hundred men killed and wounded.

When it was known in Guernsey that the British legion had attacked and carried the Carlist lines after a severe loss, the general impression was that Colonel Tupper had fallen, so responsive was the prediction mentioned in the Times,—a prediction emanating from his well known daring and devotion. When the prediction was verified, but one feeling of sympathy and regret was expressed in the island for the gallant victim; and his brother officers of the 23d evinced the same feeling, by going in a body into mourning.

Notwithstanding that the bullet had penetrated half an inch into the brain, and could not be extracted, Colonel Tupper survived eight days, during the greater part of which he was sensible, and spoke of his approaching dissolution with the utmost composure and fortitude. He suffered at first great pain from the contusion in the side, and at last from the wound in the temple, from which a small detached fragment of the bullet was extracted the day previous to his decease.

Colonel Tupper was a tall and very handsome young man, muscular and well proportioned, and on the 1st of May had completed his thirty-second year, although in appearance he was considerably younger.

The favorable opinion entertained of him by his companions in arms will be seen by the following extracts from the London newspapers of the day, the more impartial as the names of the authors were not mentioned, and are quite unknown to the family :

"*San Sebastian, May* 15.—On Friday, Colonel Tupper, who received a musket shot in the head, whilst most gallantly encouraging his regiment, the 6th, (Scotch,) to the attack in the action of the 5th instant, breathed his last. From the nature of the wound, the ball having entered the forehead and come out behind the ear, little, if any, hopes were entertained of his recovery. On his skull being opened after death, a large fragment of the bullet was found imbedded in the brain. Yesterday he was buried with all due military honors, his own regiment preceding the coffin, whilst detachments from all the others followed it. In the procession were General Evans and his staff, and nearly all the officers of the legion; all the civil, military, and naval authorities of the town, and the captains of the British and Spanish war steamers that were in the port, the French consul, &c. Colonel Tupper was a man of the most daring courage, and an excellent officer. Though his loss is deeply regretted, yet his death may be said to have been expected, as almost every one who saw him, and amongst those the Spanish officers at Vittoria, prophesied that he would fall in the first serious affair in which he should be engaged."—*Times,* May 23.

"*Head Quarters, San Sebastian, May* 15, 1836.—The remains of the lamented Colonel Tupper, who expired on the previous day, from the severe wounds he received in the action of the 5th instant, were yesterday consigned to the grave. He was buried on the spot where he received his mortal wound, in front of the formidable redoubt which his gallantry so mainly contributed in carrying.

"The news of his death pealed like a knell upon the ears of the legion; but one feeling appeared to pervade both Spanish and English—a feeling of deep regret, and an amiable desire to pay the last tribute of respect to his remains.

"At twelve o'clock precisely, the procession moved off in the following order :

A firing party of the 6th regiment, commanded by Lieut.-Colonel Ross.
A Spanish Band.
The Horse of the deceased.

Pall Bearers.		Pall Bearers.
Colonel Colquhoun.	THE BODY.	Colonel Godfrey.
Lieut.-Colonel Churchill.		Colonel M. Ross.

Mourners.		Mourners.
Inspectors-General of	Chief Mourner.	Deputy Inspectors-Gen.
Hospitals.	Adjutant-General.	of Hospitals.
Dr. Culloden.	Brigadier-General Le Marchant.	R. Alcock, K.T.S.
Dr. Dicker.		Dr. Wilkinson.

The remainder of the 6th regiment.
A detachment of artillery.
Officers, Spanish and English, in funeral order.
The Lieutenant General,
Accompanied by the Spanish Governor, Members of the Ayuntamiento,
Colonel Wylde, (his Britannic Majesty's Commissioner,) the French Consul,
Captain Henderson, and the Officers of his Majesty's ship Phœnix.

"Nothing could exceed the staid and respectful demeanor of the population of San Sebastian on this mournful occasion. The streets through which the procession moved—

the road, even as far as the spot where he fell—were lined with people, who were anxious to pay the last compliment to the remains of the gallant soldier, who had, in the very noon-tide of manhood, fallen in their defence. When the procession did reach the fatal spot, where fell one of the brightest ornaments of the legion, it would require the pen of a Scott to describe the scene that presented itself. At our feet was the broad expanse of the Atlantic, and the fair white city shining brightly in the morning sun. Above us the dark gloomy Cordillera of the Pyrenees—before us the ruined redoubt, and the grave yawning for its prey, around which stood a group of officers, of every arm, and a confused mass of natives, in every picturesque variety of costume.

"The beautiful church service of the dead was impressively read by Brigadier-General Reid; and as the coffin was slowly lowered into the grave, the varying countenances of all present but too deeply pourtrayed the feelings of grief and regret by which they were agitated.

"Frank, open, and generous, the soul of honor, brave to a fault, the *beau ideal* of a gallant and chivalric soldier, Colonel Tupper had gained the esteem and respect of all who knew him. Irreproachable in his life, glorious in the manner of his death, to him may fairly be applied the beautiful epitaph of Tacitus on Agricola:

"'Tu vero felix Agricola, non tantum claritate vitæ, sed etiam opportunitate mortis.''—*Courier*, May 23.

"*San Sebastian, May 26, 1836.*—The brave Colonel Tupper, who belonged to General Reid's brigade, had a presentiment of the fate that awaited him, and often mentioned to the general that he should be shot before Christmas. General Reid assured him that he should not, *for he would not allow him* to push on, as he seemed resolved to do. The day before the battle, Tupper said to some of his friends, he felt convinced that he should be killed; yet such was his gallantry, that he entreated General Reid to allow him to pass the river *first*, and the general, instead of restraining him, obtained permission for him from the commander-in-chief that the 6th should pass first. Before he received the fatal wound in the head, he had also got a severe one in the arm, which he studiously concealed."—*Courier*, June 1.

EXTRACT FROM GENERAL ORDER.—"*Head Quarters, San Sebastian, May 17, 1836.*—Here also fell, mortally wounded, the rebel chief Segastibelza. On the other hand, it was in this last charge that Colonel Tupper received his wounds. He was leading on his men with that daring ardour which those who knew him can conceive. He met the fate of a brave soldier, and his honored remains now rest beneath the spot ennobled by his fall."

ADDITIONAL.

1796.—Commander Daniel Guerin, of the *Sirène*, 16-gun brig, perished, with his crew, in the Bay of Honduras; day unknown.

1799.—Lieutenant Thomas Falla, 12th regiment, mortally wounded, April 6, at the siege of Seringapatam, aged eighteen years and six months. A cannon ball, weighing 26 lb., is said to have lodged in one of his thighs, and so inflamed it that the surgeon did not discover the ball until his death, six hours after being wounded, when it was extracted, to the surprise of the whole army.

1809.—Captain Rawdon M'Crea, and Ensign La Serre, of the 87th regiment, killed at Talavera, July 28.

1838.—Ensign Walter Carey, 15th regiment, perished in the conflagration of the officers' barracks at Chambly, Canada, October 19.

1839.—Peter Le Pelley, seigneur of the island of Sark, and for many years jurat of the royal court of Guernsey, drowned while crossing from Sark to Guernsey, March 1.

1840.—Lieutenant B. G. Le Mesurier, of H.M.S. Talbot, mortally wounded at the bombardment of Acre, November 3, and died on the following day.

1841.—Captain R. B. M'Crea, 44th regiment, killed at Cabool, November 17.

1842.—Ensign A. D. Potenger, 5th regiment of Bengal native infantry, killed in January, during the ill-fated retreat of the British army from Cabool.

SUPPLEMENTARY.

A WORK, in two volumes octavo, entitled *Charles the Second in the Channel Islands*, by S. Elliott Hoskins, M.D., F.R.S., (London, 1854,) having been published while the last sheets of this history were going through the press, we are enabled to give here such extracts relating to Guernsey as will illustrate the preceding pages :

[To come in at page 278, *ante*.]

Sir Baldwin Wake to Prince Rupert.

"May it please yo' High.—Accordinge unto yo' order, I doe here presente yo' High. with my saufe arryvall in this importante place. I would willingely have waited on yo' High' myselfe, to have given your High' an accounte of y' state of the castle & island, and what I conceive is fitt to be done for the preservinge of the one and the reducinge of the other, but necesiety forceth my staye here ; I have, therefore, sent this officer to informe yo' High. Humbly takinge leave, I am

"Castle Cornet,   "Yo High. most humble and
   y' 14. Sept. 1648.   faithfull servant,

"For his Highnesse   "BALDWIN WAKE.
   Prince Rupert."

[To come in at page 284, *ante*.]

Charles P. to Prince Rupert.

"Right deare and right entirely beloved cousin, we greet you well. We are assured that it is not unknowne to you how much it importeth the king our royall father and us, to preserve and supply Castle Cornett in the isle of Guernsey. We intreate you, therefore, if the ship now taken prove good prize, to send at least five hundred pounds of the proceeds thereof unto our trusty and well-beloved Sir George Carteret, Knight, lieutenant-governor of the island of Jersey, to be employed in provisions, ammunition, and necessaries for the supply of the said Castle Cornett.

"Given under our hand & seale at the Hague, the ₊₊ of January, 1649.

"To our right deare and right entirely
   beloved cousin, Prince Rupert."

[To come in at page 290, *ante*.]

Mr. Trethewey to Mr. William Edgeman.

"Jersey, 12—22 November, 1649.

[Extracts.]—"Silly [Scilly] continues in a flourishing condition: they had four prizes brought in thither within these ten dayes; two of corn, one of coles, & another of sheepskins: you must give us leave to make the most of small matters, for want of greater.

"Garnsey Castle is indifferent well, Coll. Burgess continues lieutenant-governor, and I believe will be relieved again very suddenly. Sir George Carterett is not well pleased that Lord Percy is the governor there,[1] which may happen to hinder the reducing of that island, which otherwise seemed to be feasible."

[To conclude Chapter XV., page 301, *ante*.]

Charles II. to the Marquess of Ormonde.

"Charles R.—Right trusty and entirely beloved cousin and councellor, we greet you well. Having thoroughly weighed the prudent propositions you sent us by Henry Seymour, concerning the reducing of our island of Guernsey, which at present stands out in rebellion against us; we do not only very well approve thereof, but in order thereunto have employed several persons to see if a competent proportion of shipping might have been hired for transporting from Ireland to Guernsey two thousand, or two thousand five hundred, landmen, but find it altogether impossible for us in these parts to procure so much shipping. Wherefore, that so advantageous and important a proposition as this you have made for reducing that island may not come to nothing, we have thought good by these our letters (expressly sent by this bearer) to desire you to use your best industry and endeavours to get (if it be possible) in Ireland a sufficient number of vessels for transporting of the said men into Guernsey: and we engage ourselves that if, by your means and industry, our said island shall be reduced, we will not only confer the government of the same upon you, but also all the confiscations and forfeitures of the inhabitants of that island towards reimbursement and satisfaction of your charge and hazard in reducing thereof. And whereas for your better effecting of that design, it will be necessary for the ships you send with the said forces to put into the road of Jersey, we shall presently give directions to our dearest brother, the Duke of York, (who now resides at Jersey, and will continue there for some months,) to cause all possible assistance to be given to the persons you shall entrust with the execution of that design.

(1) "To us [Dr. Hoskins] it appears probable that Sir George had all along been desirous of obtaining the government of that fortress; a supposition which will go far to account for his conduct to whatever governor was appointed to that command."

And we likewise send him a warrant and an order directed to the present governor in Cornet Castle in our isle of Guernesey, requiring him not only to give such as you shall employ in that service his best assistance in that design, but to deliver into your hands the command and possession of that castle, and to receive such forces as the commander you shall send with them shall direct, in order to the taking of the said island, not doubting but you will vigorously pursue what you have so affectionately proposed, and which may be of so great importance for our service, which must now be put into execution with all secrecy and expedition, lest the shipping of the rebels of England should prevent you. And for the further encouragement of yourself and those who shall assist you in this important enterprize, we do hereby promise that in case you shall reduce our said island of Guernesey, (which will be a work of singular advantage to our service,) we will take effectual order that you shall have sufficient commission and powers from our dear brother, the Duke of York, and to have under your particular command all such ships, frigats, and vessels, as well Irish as others, as shall put themselves under you, or as you shall be able to draw thither unto you, with such liberty and privileges as are due to the admiral of any squadron. We had acquainted this bearer, Lieut.-Colonel Rawlins, (whom we employed about this service,) with several particulars to be by you considered of in the pursuance of this design, and desire you accordingly to give credit to him. Given at our court at Beauvais, March 3-13, in the second year of our reign, 1649-50." [1]

Henry to the Marquess of Ormonde.

" Beauvais, in our way to Breda.
" March 15th, 1650.

" His majesty hath a most just sense of your services, and the daily difficulties you struggle with in that pursuance; and your further endeavours, by the proposition you lately made to him about the reduction of *Guernsey*, which he conceives to be of that consequence in the posture that his affairs are in at present, that, next *London*, it is the place most to be desired, and he hath at that rate laboured to hire shipping for the transporting those men you promised; but his credit is not of that reputation to speed. If it be possible to supply his failing from Ireland, his majesty will give the fines of all the delinquents in the island, (Guernsey,) which my information tells me did amount to £20,000 [2] in Jersey. The commission that Lord Percy had is recalled, and his majesty intends to keep it in his hands till he hear from you, whether it be possible for you to undertake it from thence. Sir E. Nicholas, whose business his majesty com-

(1) Carte's Collection, vol. i., p. 371.   (2) " More likely *livres tournois* than pounds sterling."

mands me to tell you was done at your request, and to whom
you gave me leave to impart this business to, has command from
his majesty to write to you at large, not only about the command
of this place, but of all such ships and frigates as you shall bring
with you, or shall come in to you, as absolutely as P. Rupert has
from the D. of York, who remains still at Jersey.

" I had forgot in my letter to advertize you that the parliament
had landed 500 men at Guernsey." [1]

[In a foot note at page 300, *ante*.]

Our disbelief of the treachery imputed to Lord Jermyn is strengthened by the following
passage in a letter, written from Jersey, in December, 1646, by Sir Edward Hyde to Lord
Cottington : " Ten days since, my Lord Jermyn took notice before much company of the
report of these islands, and said he believed the French had never such a thought ; but if
they had, he hoped his friends had a better opinion of him than to believe that, upon any
grounds or pretences whatsoever, he could be made an instrument in so infamous a piece
of villany."

APPENDIX.

DOCUMENTS RELATING TO GUERNSEY, &c.

Patent Roll — 10 *John, A.D.* 1208.

The king to the keepers of the islands of Guernsey, ... and his other
faithful people of the same islands, greeting.—Know ye, that we have granted
to Guy de Guivilla, that he and his people shall be received in your land to
annoy our enemies of foreign parts. And therefore we command you that,
for this purpose, you receive them. Witness, G. Fitz Peter, at Southampton,
29th day of May, in the tenth year of our reign.

Close Roll — 15 *John*, 1213.

The king to Philip de Albeny, greeting.—We command you that, of the
land which belonged to Baldwin Wac, in the island of Guernsey, you, without
delay, assess twenty librates of land . . . . . to Thomas Danies, which the aforesaid Baldwin bequeathed to the same Thomas for his service, and that you
keep the residue well in your hand. Witness ourself, at Winchester, on the
20th day of July.

Close Roll — 7 *Henry III.*, 1223.

CONCERNING FOCAGE (HEARTHAGE) OF THE ISLANDS OF GUERNSEY, JERSEY,
&c.—The king to Philip de Albeny, greeting.—We command you, that you
cause to be rendered to us, by your own hands or your bailiffs, whom you
shall appoint for this purpose, the focage to us due from the men of the islands
of Guernsey and Jersey, and Sark, and Alderney, and Herme, as it used to be
rendered in the time of king Richard our uncle, and in the time of the lord
king John our father, sparing no one therein, as you love us. Witness, H. de
Burgh, at Windsor, 19th day of October.

(1) Carte's Collection, vol. i., p. 366.

Patent Roll — 8 *Henry III.*, 1223.

CONCERNING THE ISLANDS OF JERSEY AND GUERNSEY, COMMITTED TO G. DE LUCY.—The lord the king hath committed to Geoffrey de Lucy the islands of Jersey and Guernsey, and other islands of the lord the king, which were in the custody of Philip de Albeny, with the castles which are in them, and all their appurtenances, to be kept during the pleasure of the lord the king. And it is commanded to the same Philip that, without delay, he deliver to the same Geoffrey the islands aforesaid, with the castles aforesaid, and all their appurtenances. Witness, the king, at Westminster, on the 21st day of October, in the eighth year of his reign.

Patent — 16 *Edward II.*, 1323.

The king to his faithful and beloved Otho de Grandison, warden of his islands of Guernsey, Jersey, Sark, and Alderney, or his lieutenant, and to all his bailiffs and faithful people in the same islands, to whom, &c., greeting.—Whereas, we, on account of various errors which have occurred in records and proceedings had before William de Bourne and his fellows, our late justices, sent to the parts of the islands aforesaid, have caused the same records and processes to come before us, and by examination of the same, it is found that the same justices had without warrant, adjudged divers manors, lands, and tenements, belonging to us, to divers men seeking them, and the same judgments by consideration of our court, inasmuch as they concerned our disinheritance, were revoked, on which account, by our divers writs, we commanded you the aforesaid Otho, to take again those manors, lands, and tenements aforesaid, into our hands, together with sums of money which by reason of losses had been adjudged to complainants by the same justices. And we are given to understand, that certain of the aforesaid islanders, refusing to obey such our commands, have with an armed force so impeded the servants of you the said Otho, to whom our said commands were by you committed to be executed, that they can in nowise execute our said commands, to our manifest contempt and prejudice. We, being willing to be fully certified in the premises, and further to do what shall seem fit for the preservation of our right, have appointed our beloved and faithful Gerard Dorous, and Robert de Kellesye, to inquire by the oath of good and lawful men of those parts by whom the truth of the matter may be best known, the names of those who have made such resistance, and where, and what resistance, and how and in what manner, and the full truth of such contempts and resistance, and to certify us thereof openly and distinctly. And therefore we command you, that you be obedient and assisting to the said Gerard and Robert in the premises, as they shall make known to you on our behalf. Whereof, &c. Witness, the king, at Newark, on the 2nd day of February.—By the council.

SUNDRY ORDERS IN COUNCIL.

April 20, 1551.

Letters to the lord chancellor for the addressing of a commission of Oyer and Terminer to the lieutenant, bailiff, and jurats of Guernsey, for the punishment of a rebellion attempted in St. Martin's parish there.

July 7, 1558.

A letter to the jurats and inhabitants of the isle of Guernsey to stand upon their guard, and to do all that in them lieth to withstand such attempts as should be offered against that isle, for the better doing whereof they were required to follow such order as should be prescribed unto them by Mr. Chamberlain, their captain, and to be obedient unto him in all things that should tend to the advancement of the queen's majesty's service there.

June 22, 1565.

Order for the inhabitants of Jersey and Guernsey that their suits should be heard in those isles, and not within this realm, and that no appeals should be made but *au roi et son conseil*.

May 24, 1580.

A letter to Sir Thomas Leighton, knight, requiring him, according to a privy seal sent therewith, to send up the bailiff of that isle, and one James Guille, for the answering of a complaint exhibited against them and the rest of the jurats there by Nicholas Carey, of Guernsey; and that before their coming he examine the matter substantially, and advertise the same.

April 13, 1581.

A warrant to . . . . . one of the messengers of her majesty's chamber to make his repair into the isle of Guernsey, and to bring unto their lordships in his company, without delay, Guillaume Beauvoir, bailiff; Nicholas Martin, and Henry Beauvoir, jurats.

They appeared.

[See pages 152, 153, *ante*.]

April 4, 1586.

A letter to Sir Thomas Leighton, knight, governor of the isle of Guernsey.

That whereas there were sundry fines set upon the people of Alderney by him, in respect of their wilful and lewd offence in suffering certain Frenchmen to pursue her majesty's subjects within her protection, without making any good endeavours to resist them . . . . . (two parts being paid) . . . . . their lordships think good to require them (if he should think it reasonable) that the aforesaid third part uncollected might be remitted, and converted to the public defence, &c.

November 6, 1586.

A letter to Sir Thomas Leighton, recommending the merchants unto him to be courteously used, and not to pay any greater customs than in former time, upon like occasions of repair.

January 10, 1587.

Upon hearing of the matters in controversy between Sir Thomas Leighton, knight, captain of the isle of Guernsey, on the one part; and Thomas Wigmore, bailiff; Nicholas Carey, his lieutenant; James Feand, [?] jurat; John Effard, and John De Vicke, of the said isle, on the other part:

Forasmuch as Lewis Savarte had exhibited to the whole bench of jurats of the isle, articles containing reproachful words against their governor, being her majesty's chief officer there, by the animating and procurement of the said bailiff and jurats, proved by Lewis De Vicke, her majesty's procuror, and not reformed by themselves, after their public hearing of the said articles.

And that the bailiff, his lieutenant, and feud, with some other of the jurats, contrary to their oath, set their hands and her majesty's seal to a public information, and gave also certain instructions, in writing, containing divers false and slanderous accusations that their governor, by tyrannous oppressions, violences, and imprisonment, sought the overthrow of the estate of the whole isle, the general inhabitants of the isle not being made privy or acquainted therewith.

And that they imposed a general tax, &c. &c. &c., without the consent of the inhabitants.

And that the said bailiff and jurats had also, since their coming into England, conspired, &c., to slay or mischief the said Lewis De Vicke, &c. &c. &c.

The said Thomas Wigmore should be deprived of his place of bailiff.

Nicholas Carey, his lieutenant, of that office.

And they, together with feud, committed to the Marshalsea during their lordships' pleasure.

And the governor was ordered to choose a new bailiff, who also should place some fit person to be his lieutenant.

And that the offenders should be bound to their good behaviour.

And that Roswell, their instrument, for example's sake, should likewise be committed, and afterward sent to Guernsey, by direction of the captain and governor of the said isle, there to be imprisoned for a certain time, and to be set on the pillory in the market place, with a paper over his head, whose inscription should be, "For treacherously beating and intending to kill the procuror, her majesty's officer, being hired thereunto, for money, by Richard Wigmore and his confederates."

That Thomas Wigmore should recompense the procuror, and the messenger of her majesty's chamber, for his voyage into Guernsey, being sent for them by warrant from their lordships.

That John De Vicke should . . . . . by order of law, his charges for his employment thither about the said matters against the said bailiff, and the jurats that did set him on work, without charging of the inhabitants.

That the court of heritage and debts should be revived, according to the ancient custom.

Nevertheless, that it is not by that order meant that the privileges or customs of the island should be in any wise infringed or violated, but rather more strictly observed and maintained according to their charters, and her majesty's gracious intent and meaning.

And that the cause of the Frenchman, Savarte, is to be ended, as already was ordered by the consent of Sir Thomas Leighton and the said Savarte, by order of law in the court of admiralty, which order, by their lords' commandment, is here entered into the register of council, to the end it may be duly observed and kept. And that, also, upon the request of Sir Thomas Leighton, the duplicate thereof should be delivered to him, that it might be registered amongst the acts of that isle.

December 21, 1589.

A letter to Sir Thomas Leighton, knight, upon information given their lordships that there were divers French gentlemen and merchants of that nation within that isle, under his government, the number whereof being so great that their continuance and abode there would by all likelihood breed great dearth and scarcity of victuals there.

Forasmuch as they pretended that the cause of their abode there was in regard of their conscience and religion, whereof they could shew no better testimony than by serving their king in that time of so great troubles :

Their lordships signified unto him, her majesty's express pleasure was, in those dangerous times, that he should not suffer any strangers thereafter to abide and reside there, otherwise than they should have occasion for trade and intercourse of merchants, or to pass to and fro.

September 6, 1591.

Order for the restitution of two barks, with corn and salt, belonging to the French king's subjects, taken by a galeass of Southampton, and brought into Guernsey, and sold there as lawful prizes.

And because their lordships knew no authority given to the bailiff and jurats of that island to take upon them to judge and determine of causes appertaining to the office of the lord admiral, their lordships thought it meet that he should inform himself from them how it happened that they had taken upon them to intermeddle in the matter of these two barks, and that he should require them, in their lordships' names, to forbear thereafter to proceed in any such cause until they could make appear unto their lordships by what right or privilege they ought to do so.

INDEX.

De Grac, —— 93, 116, 117.

ADDENDA, CORRIGENDA, ET ERRATA.

Page. Line.

16....36, *for* 485, *read* 481.
42....36, *for* clergy, *read* abbots.
48....27, *for* sixty-third, *read* sixtieth.
56....32, *for* villum, *read* villam.
65........ foot note, *for* at, *read* and.
93....29, *for* the twentieth article, *read* one of the articles.
117....19, *after* De Havilland, *add* Henry.
164....21, *for* 1605, *read* 1603.
171........ foot note (2) to be as follows :
    Father of Dr. Daniel Brevint, dean of Lincoln, and probably son of Mr. Cosmo Brevint, minister of Sark. (*See* Digest of Colloquy, *ante.*)
190........ foot note to Sir Thomas Leighton :
    Sir Thomas Leighton was interred in the church of St. Peter-Port, Thursday, February 1, 1609.
204....15, foot note to 1629 : from a MS.
    " The last plague (peste) in this island of Guernsey was in the year 1629. It commenced in the month of July, and lasted more than a year. Another plague had visited the island thirty - nine years before, (*circa* 1590,) which

was then, and is at present, called The Great Plague."
217....13-19, *dele,* it being the Rev. Elias Picot, who was sent to Alderney in 1662.
229....13, *for* Soon after his arrival in Guernsey, in 1643, *read* In 1644, the year after his arrival in Guernsey.
    To the foot note, *add :* It was Mr. James Guille, jurat, of the Rohais, who so commanded. The entire paragraph and foot note should appear at page 237.
254........ foot note, *for* 1715, *read* 1713.
270....39, *for* 1643, *read* 1644.
274....31, By an entry in the register of burials in the parish of St. Peter-Port, we learn that the gentleman, killed by a cannon ball from Castle Cornet, was Peter Priaulx, seigneur of the Fief le Comte, mentioned at page 235. He was interred on Wednesday, May 1, 1650.
394....12, *for* late bishop, *read* the present bishop.

S. Barbet, Printer, Guernsey.